KT-143-576

# Paris Guide

**Penguin Books**

PENGUIN BOOKS

Published by the Penguin Group
Penguin Books Ltd, 27 Wrights Lane, London W8 5TZ, England
Penguin Books USA Inc., 375 Hudson Street, New York, New York 10014, USA
Penguin Books Australia Ltd, Ringwood, Victoria, Australia
Penguin Books Canada Ltd, 10 Alcorn Avenue, Toronto, Ontario, Canada M4V 3B2
Penguin Books (NZ) Ltd, 182-190 Wairau Road, Auckland 10, New Zealand

Penguin Books Ltd, Registered Offices: Harmondsworth, Middlesex, England

First published 1989
First Penguin edition 1990
Second edition 1992
Third edition 1994
Fourth edition 1995
Fifth edition 1997
10 9 8 7 6 5 4 3 2 1

Colour reprographics by Precise Litho, 34-35 Great Sutton Street, London EC1
Mono reprographics, printed and bound by William Clowes Ltd, Beccles, Suffolk NR34 9QE

## Edited and designed by

Time Out Paris
100 rue du Faubourg-St-Antoine
75012 Paris
Tel: + 33 (0)1.44.87.00.45
Fax: + 33 (0)1.44.73.90.60
for
Time Out Magazine Ltd
Universal House
251 Tottenham Court Road
London W1P 0AB
Tel: + 44 (0)171 813 3000
Fax: + 44 (0)171 813 6001
http://www.timeout.co.uk
e-mail: net@timeout.co.uk

### Paris

**Editor** Natasha Edwards
**Production Editor** Lemisse Al-Hafidh
**Art Editor** Richard Joy

**Advertising Manager** Matt Tembe
**Advertising Coordinator** Philippe Thareaut
**Advertising Executive** Emer McEvoy
**Managing Director** Karen Albrecht

### London

**Managing Editor** Peter Fiennes
**Art Director** Warren Beeby
**Art Editor** John Oakey

**Group Advertisement Director** Lesley Gill
**Sales Director** Mark Phillips

**Publisher** Tony Elliott
**Managing Director** Mike Hardwick
**Financial Director** Kevin Ellis
**Marketing Director** Gillian Auld
**Production Manager** Mark Lamond

Features for the fifth edition were written or updated by:
**Essential Information** Lemisse Al-Hafidh, Ian Sparks **Getting Around** Lemisse Al-Hafidh, Jason Whittaker **Accommodation** Jenny Lefcourt **Paris by Season** Natasha Edwards **Sightseeing** Lemisse Al-Hafidh **Parks & Cemeteries** Natasha Edwards **History** Rachel Kaplan **Paris Today** Julian Nundy **Architecture** Natasha Edwards **Paris by Area** Natasha Edwards, Jenny Lefcourt **Restaurants** adapted from *Time Out Eating & Drinking in Paris Guide* **Cafés & Bars** adapted from *Time Out Eating & Drinking in Paris Guide* **Fashion, Specialist Shops** Nadine Frey **Food & Drink** Jenny Alston **Services** Lemisse Al-Hafidh, Lucy Leveugle **Museums** Simon Cropper, Natasha Edwards, Diana Fowle **Art Galleries** Natasha Edwards **Media** Natasha Edwards, Kelly Zinkowski **Cabaret & Comedy** Toby Rose **Clubs** Mark Pendell, Lucia Scazzocchio **Dance** Carol Pratl **Film** Toby Rose **Music: Classical & Opera** Stephen Mudge **Music: Rock, Roots & Jazz** Dylan Gee, Ben Rogan, Peter Snowdon, Ian Sparks **Sport & Fitness** Caspar Leighton **Theatre** Carol Pratl, Annie Sparks **Business** Karen Albrecht **Children** Nadine Frey **Gay & Lesbian** Jason Whittaker **Study** Paul Greatorex, Lucia Scazzocchio **Women's Paris** Rachel Kaplan **Trips out of Town** Natasha Edwards, Diana Fowle, Alexander Lobrano **Survival** Francis Dougherty.

The editors would like to thank the following for help and information: Emma Brockes, Francis Dougherty, Paul Greatorex, Sarah Guy, Suzanne Hallerman, Ruth Jarvis, Anna of Ladies Room, Caspar Leighton, Lucy Leveugle, Chantal Marette, Cathy Phillips, Nick Royle, Mark Sheerin, Deirdre O'Keeffe.

**Photography** by Jean-Louis Aubert, Tom Craig, Laurence Guillot, Crescenzo Mazza, Jon Perugia, Colm Pierce, Lucia Scazzochio, Rosa Tembe, Brenda Turnnidge, Maddelena della Volpe and Francesca Yorke except for: page 252 ARC; page 227 Biscofberger; page 227 M Chassat; pages 220-221 Hughes Dubois; page 299 Marc Dubroca; page 262 Roberto Frankenberg; pages 83, 297 Alain Goustard; page 219 L S Jaulmes; page 231 F Kleinefenn; page 215 Geneviève Lacambre; page 285 Michel Lamoureux; page 264 Thierry le Goues; pages 65-66, 69, 75 Hervé Lewandowski/Musées Nationaux; page 229 J Losy; page 267 Clodie Martin; page 217-218 Karine Maucotel; page 275 Ros Ribas; page 214 RMN; page 276 Marianne Rosenthal; page 90 Philippe Ruault; page 258 Michel Szabo; pages 78, 81, 84 Collection Viollet; page 213 Christophe Walter.

# Contents

# About the Guide

The fifth edition of the *Time Out Paris Guide* has been thoroughly revised and updated by staff and freelance writers resident in Paris. More than just a book for tourists, it is also for frequent visitors or long-term residents. It covers all the major sights and attractions, but also takes you to hundreds of the city's more obscure and eccentric venues, as well as shops, restaurants, cafés, bars and clubs. We hope you'll agree that it's been worth it.

For up-to-the-minute weekly listings and reviews, look out for the *Time Out Paris* section (in English) in the French listings magazine, *Pariscope*. For more on food and drink, the *Time Out Eating & Drinking in Paris Guide* is a foodlover's bible.

## PRACTICAL GUIDE

Above all, we've tried to make this book as useful as possible. Addresses, telephone numbers, transport details, opening times, admission prices and credit card details are all included in our listings. And, as far as possible, we've given details of facilities, services and events.

All the information in the guide was checked and correct when we went to press; but please bear in mind that owners and managers can change their arrangements at any time. It's always a good idea to phone before you set out to check opening times, dates of exhibitions, admission prices and the like. The same applies to information on disabled access; it's wise to phone first to check your needs can be met.

## BOLD

Where we mention important places or events that are also listed elsewhere in the guide, they are usually highlighted in **bold**. This means you can find it in the index and locate the full listing.

## ADDRESSES

Paris is divided into 20 *arrondissements* or districts, which form a tight snail-shell spiral beginning at Notre Dame and finishing at the Porte de Montreuil on the eastern edge of the inner city limits. Paris addresses include the *arrondissement* in the postcode, which begins with the prefix 750. So for example an address in the 1st *arrondissement* would have the postcode 75001, and one in the 20th would be 75020. Always use this form when writing letters. In this Guide we have referred to the *arrondissements* as 1st, 2nd, 3rd, 4th and so on.

## PRICES

The prices listed throughout the guide should be used as guidelines. If prices vary greatly from those we've quoted, ask whether there's a good reason why. If not, go elsewhere. Then, please let us know. We try to give the best and most-up-to date advice, so we always want to hear if you've been badly overcharged.

## CREDIT CARDS

Throughout this guide, the following abbreviations have been used for credit cards: **AmEx** American Express; **DC** Diners' Club; **MC** Mastercard; **V** Visa.

## LET US KNOW

It shold be stressed that the information we give is impartial. No organisation or enterprise has been included in this guide because the owner or manager has advertised in our publications. Their impartiality is one of the reasons why our guides are so successful and well respected. We hope you enjoy the *Time Out Paris Guide* and that it makes your trip a more enjoyable. However, if you disagree with any of our reviews, or have found somewhere you love and think should be included, let us know; your views on places you visited are always welcome. There's a reader's reply card in the book for your comments.

> There is an online version of this guide, as well as weekly events listings for several international cities, at http://www.timeout.co.uk.

# Introduction

We've covered all the major sights, we've also tried to cover some of the lesser ones: places we've chanced upon, places dear to Parisians' hearts or places where they would never dream of going. This is a Paris of some of the most impressive museums in the world, a Paris of grand opera and grander egos, a Paris packed with unusual shops, a Paris of historic monuments and daring modern buildings, yet a Paris that is also a village, an accessible and lived-in city where every *quartier* has its café and its market and where the best way to discover its pulse is by eavesdropping on the conversation at the *zinc*.

Like any great capital, Paris is multi-layered and sometimes a paradox: a place that lives up to myths and then denies them. At times, it is the most ostentatious city imaginable; at others, one of the most private – where historic facades and gardens are hidden behind massive doors, where each apartment building contains an unseen microcosm of society.

Maupassant condemned guides: 'They lie, they know nothing, they understand nothing, they render ugly by emphatic and stupid texts the most beautiful of countries... Yet', he admitted, 'how much one likes, when travelling, to know a little bit in advance about the region where one is going. How happy one is when one finds a book, or some sincere vagabond, ready to confide to you a few of its visions.' We hope to have done that.

It has been suggested that the invention of the guidebook dispensed with the need actually to visit places (oddly, the first modern guidebooks, published in the nineteenth century, were all to Switzerland). We hope not. Rather we hope that this guide will inspire you to a *dégustation*, to taste Paris in all the city's variety, to discover the reality behind the clichés of the Eiffel Tower, and to lose a few preconceptions, to take the risk of discovering the delights of *andouillette*, of French *chanson* or, equally, of *raï*.

Above all, there is one way to discover Paris: walk. That way you will come across places that no guidebook can cover, a city by its noises, smells and the banal details of everyday life that don't spell out tourism but do say Paris. The French have even invented the perfect verb for it, *flâner*, which roughly translates as to loiter in the street – while looking stylish at the same time, of course.

*Natasha Edwards*

Frittered all your francs? Pas de problem. Western Union can get you money in minutes. Phone someone at home who can deposit the money you need at their nearest Western Union office. Then you collect it, in cash, from your nearest Western Union office. We have 65 offices all over Paris. Many are open 7 days a week. For more details call Western Union on (01) 4354 4612 or (01) 4335 6060.

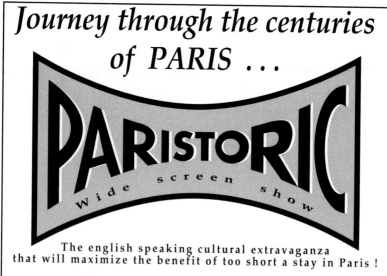

# Essential Information

**When to go, where to change money and the statistics: it's all here in black and white.**

For information on emergencies or staying in Paris on a long-term basis, *see chapter* **Survival**. For transport, *see chapter* **Getting Around**.

## Visas & Customs

European Union nationals do not need a visa to enter France, nor do US, Canadian and New Zealand citizens for stays of up to three months. Nationals of other countries should enquire at the nearest French Consulate before they leave home; if they are travelling to France from one of the countries included in the Schengen agreement (most of the EU, but not Britain, Ireland, Italy or Greece), the visa from that country should be sufficient to enter

France. British citizens on short-term visits can travel with a valid passport. For stays of over three months, *see chapter* **Survival**.

### Customs

There are no limits on the quantities of goods that you can take into France from another EU country for your personal use, provided tax has been paid on them in the country of origin. However, customs still have the right to question visitors. Sporadic checks are also made for drugs. Quantities of tobacco and alcohol accepted as being for personal use are:
• up to 800 cigarettes, 400 small cigars, 200 cigars **or** 1kg of loose tobacco.
• 10 litres of spirits (over 22% alcohol), 90 litres of wine (under 22% alcohol) and 110 litres of beer.
For goods brought from outside the EU:
• 200 cigarettes **or** 100 small cigars **or** 50 cigars **or** 250 grams (8.82 ounces) of loose tobacco
• 1 litre of spirits (over 22% alcohol) and 2 litres of wine and beer (under 22% alcohol)
• 50 grams (1.76 ounces) of perfume
Visitors can also carry up to 50,000F worth of currency without having to declare it. Non-EU residents can reclaim the VAT (*TVA*) paid on some purchases when they leave France, under the *Détaxe* scheme (*see chapter* **Fashion**).

## Insurance

EU nationals can use the French state health service provided they have form E111, available in Britain from post offices, Health Centres and Social Security offices. All other nationals should check whether their country has such an arrangement. The state system will cover you in emergencies,

but the simplest solution for visitors on a short-term stay is to take out private travel insurance before departure. This should also cover you for stolen or lost cash, cameras, and other valuables, as well as medical expenses. For more information on health services, *see chapter* **Survival: Health**.

## Money

The currency in France is the French franc, usually abbreviated to 'F' or sometimes 'FF' after the amount. One franc is made up of 100 centimes, although the smallest coin in circulation is now five centimes. There are coins for five-, ten-, 20- and 50-centimes, one, two and five francs, and the heavier ten- and 20-franc pieces, silver-centred coins with a copper rim. Notes begin with 20F and roughly increase in size according to their value: 50F, 100F, 200F and 500F (new, smaller 200F and 500F notes are now also in circulation). When changing money avoid being given 500F notes, as you may find it difficult to change them elsewhere.

### Bureaux de Change

If you arrive in Paris late at night, you can change money at the Bureaux de Change at Roissy and Orly airports ( 6.30am-11.30pm daily). At the main train stations, the change offices are open daily from 7 or 8am to 7 or 10.30pm (closed Sunday at Gare St-Lazare and Gare d'Austerlitz).

# BANANA CAFÉ

13, RUE DE LA FERRONNERIE - PARIS - LES HALLES

Some banks have cash exchange machines that accept notes of major currencies in good condition. CCF branches have change machines and a bureau de change at: 115-117 av des Champs-Elysées, 8th/01.43.59.04.22; 28 rue de Rivoli, 1st; carrefour de l'Odéon, 6th.

## Banks & Banking Hours

French banks usually open 9am-4.30pm Monday to Friday, and 9am-noon on Saturdays. Some also close at lunchtime (12.30-2.30pm). All are closed on public holidays, and from noon on the previous day (*see below* **Holidays**). Note that not all bank branches in Paris have foreign exchange counters, and commission rates also vary between banks. The state Banque de France usually offers good rates at its branches. Banks readily accept travellers' cheques (you need your passport with you), but may be reluctant to accept personal cheques with the Eurocheque guarantee card, which is not widely used in France.

## Credit Cards & Cash Machines

Major international credit cards are widely used in France, although Visa (the French *Carte Bleue*) is the most readily accepted. Note that French-issued credit cards now have a special security system, with a microchip in each card. The card is slotted into a card reader, and the holder keys in his or her PIN number to authorise the transaction. For non-French cards, ask for your card to be read or imprinted in the conventional way.

Withdrawals in francs can be made from bank and post office automatic cash machines. The specific cards accepted are marked on each machine, and most give instructions in English. Credit card companies charge a fee for cash advances, but exchange rates are often better than bank rates. In case of credit card loss or theft, call the following 24-hour services which have English-speaking staff: **American Express** 01.47.77.72.00; **Diners Club** 01.47.62.75.75; **MasterCard** 01.45.67.84.84; **Visa** 01.42.77.11.90.

### American Express

*11 rue Scribe, 9th (01.47.77.77.07). M° Opéra.* **Open** *All transactions* 9am-7pm Mon-Fri; 9am-5pm Sat. *Bureau de change only* 9am-7pm Mon-Fri; 9am-6.30pm Sat; 10am-6pm Sun; 9am-5pm public holidays.
Bureau de change, poste restante, card replacement, a travellers' cheque refund service and a cash machine for AmEx card holders. Money can also be transferred there from any American Express office anywhere in the world.

### Barclays

*21 rue Lafitte, 9th (01.44.79.79.79). M° Richelieu-Drouot.* **Open** 9am-5.30pm Mon-Fri.
Call the special Expat Service (01.44.79.48.33) for details on direct debits, international transfer of funds, and so on.

### Chequepoint

*150 av des Champs-Elysées, 8th (01.49.53.02.51). M° Charles de Gaulle-Etoile.* **Open** 24 hours daily.

# Number crunching

**58,027,305** Population of France.
**10,000,000** Population of Greater Paris.
**2,000,000** Population Paris *intra-muros*.
**200,000** dogs in Paris, in 165,000 households.
**10 tonnes** of *'merde'* deposited by Parisian dogs each day of the year.
**32 centimes**. The cost to Paris city council of picking up each individual deposit.
**800** Population of monkeys in Paris.
**40kg** bread eaten per person per year in France. This figure has halved in the past 30 years.
**37kg** frozen food eaten per person per year; almost 20 times higher than 30 years ago.
**25 litres** wine drunk per person per year. 30 years ago the figure was almost 100 litres.
**96%** of all French go to restaurants; 41 per cent at least once a month.
**16** Café licences are lost every day in Paris.
**31%** The increase in fast-food restaurants in France over the past 15 years.
**11** bars of soap used each year by an average French family. In England it's 15.

This is the only Paris Chequepoint office open 24 hours. The several other branches in the city are open 9am-9pm, Mon, Sat, and 10am-6pm Sun. No commission is charged.

### Thomas Cook

*52 av des Champs-Elysées, 8th (01.42.89.80.32). M° Franklin D Roosevelt.* **Open** 8.30am-10.30pm Mon-Thur, Sun; 8.30am-11pm Fri, Sat.
Thomas Cook has over 30 offices around Paris, including branches at bd St-Michel, Eiffel Tower and major train stations. They can also issue travellers' cheques.

### Western Union Money Transfer

*Banque Rivaud, 4 rue du Cloître-Notre-Dame, 4th (01.43.54.46.12). M° Cité.* **Open** 9am-5.30pm daily.
Banque Rivaud is the sole agent for Western Union in Paris, with seven branches in the city. Money transfers from abroad should arrive within one hour. Charges are paid by the sender.

## Opening Times & Public Holidays

Standard opening hours for shops are from 9am or 10am to 7pm or 8pm, Monday to Saturday. Some shops also close on Mondays. Shops and businesses often close for lunch for an hour, sometimes more, usually between 12.30pm and 2pm. Many shops are closed for all or part of August.

On *jours fériés* (public holidays) banks, many museums and most shops are shut but the Métro, cinemas and many restaurants keep going. The following holidays are the most fully observed – New Year, May Day, Bastille Day and Christmas.

**New Year's Day** (Jour de l'An) 1 January; **Easter Monday** (Lundi de Pâques); **Fête du Travail** (May Day) 1 May; **VE Day** (Victoire 1945) 8 May; **Ascension Day** (Jour de l'Ascension); **Whit Monday** (Pentecôte); **Bastille Day** (Quatorze Juillet) 14 July; **Feast of the Assumption** (Jour de l'Assomption) 15 August; **All Saints' Day** (Toussaint) 1 November; **Remembrance Day** (L'Armistice 1918) 11 November; **Christmas Day** (Noël) 25 December.

## Smoking

Earnest official health campaigns have made only a slight dent in French lighting-up habits, and in most public places many people still smoke. Under a 1991 law restaurants are obliged to provide a non-smoking area. However, if you ask to be sat in the *non-fumeurs* space you're likely to end up at the worst table in the house, tucked away next to the toilets or the stairs. Unless you're seriously allergic to tobacco you'll probably find it more pleasant to sit amid the smoke with the rest.

Smoking is banned in most theatres, cinemas and on public transport.

## Telephones

All French telephone numbers have ten digits. Paris and Ile de France numbers begin with 01, the rest of France is divided into four regional zones (02-05). If you are calling France from abroad leave off the 0 at the start of the ten-digit number. International dialling codes start with 00.

Most public phones in Paris use phonecards (*télécartes*) and accept major credit cards. Sold at *tabacs* (tobacconists), post offices, airports and train and Métro stations, cards cost 40F for 50 units and 96F for 120 units. Cafés have coin phones, while post offices usually have both coin and card phones. A three-minute call in a coin-operated call box within Paris is generally 1F or 2F.

In a phone box, the initial instructions on the digital dislay screen should read *décrochez* ('pick up'). Pick up the phone and insert your card into the slot when the instruction *introduire votre carte* appears. The screen should read *patientez SVP*. When *numérotez* appears, this is your signal to dial. *Crédit épuisé* means that you have no more units left. Finally, hang up (*raccrochez*), and don't forget your card.

If you are using a credit card, insert the card, key in your PIN number and then *patientez SVP* should appear. You then continue as above.

## Time & the Seasons

France is one hour ahead of Greenwich Mean Time (GMT), except between the end of September and the end of October (when it's the same). In France time is based on the 24-hour system. Thus, 8am is *8 heures*, noon is *12 heures* (*midi*), 8pm is *20 heures* and midnight is *0* (*zéro*) *heure* (*minuit*).

**Spring**: Paris in the spring is proverbially magical, but also crowded. The weather is usually fine, if a bit rainy.

**Summer**: A great time to visit so long as you don't expect to find too much going on. It's fairly easy to find a hotel room, traffic is relatively smooth and parking possible. It can get pretty hot and muggy by day, but evenings are just right, and it stays light late. *See chapter* **Paris by Season**.

**Autumn**: The weather is usually good; September and October are peak months for tourism and business visitors – finding a hotel can be difficult.

**Winter**: In spite of the cold (below-zero temperatures) and the rain (especially in February and March), there are more cultural events during the winter than in any other season.

### Average Temperatures

**January** 7.5°C (5.5°F); **February** 7.1°C (44.8°F); **March** 10.2°C (50.4°F); **April** 15.7°C (60.3°F); **May** 16.6°C (61.9°F); **June** 23.4°C (74.1°F); **July** 25.1°C (77.2°F); **August** 25.6°C (78.1°F); **September** 20.9°C (69.6°F); **October** 16.5°C (61.7°F); **November** 11.7°C (53.1°F); **December** 7.8°C (46°F).

## Tourist Information

The official tourist offices provide a wide range of basic information on attractions and events in and around Paris. For full information on what's on in the city at any time, the best sources are local listings magazines (*see chapter* **Media**). For details of recommended city maps and the public transport system, *see chapter* **Getting Around**. If you intend to do some serious sightseeing and museum-visiting in Paris the **Paris Carte Musées et Monuments** is a good buy (*see chapter* **Museums**).

### Office de Tourisme de Paris

*127 av des Champs-Elysées, 8th (01.49.52.53.54/ recorded information in English 01.49.52.53.56).* M° *Charles de Gaulle-Etoile.* **Open** *Information & ticket office* 9am-8pm daily. *Hotel reservations/bureau de change* 9am-7.30pm daily. Closed 1 May.

Brochures, guidebooks and information on sights and events in Paris and the suburbs. It has a souvenir and bookshop, and also sells phonecards, museum cards and travel tickets (*see chapter* **Getting Around**). There is also a ticket desk for museums, theatres, tours and other attractions, a bureau de change, and hotel and train reservation services (for which a fee is charged). All the staff are multi-lingual. The branch offices have more limited facilities.

**Branches: Eiffel Tower** (01.45.51.22.15). **Open** *May-Sept* 11am-6pm daily. **Gare d'Austerlitz** (01.45.84.91.70). **Open** 8am-3pm Mon-Fri; 8am-1pm Sat. **Gare de l'Est** (01.46.07.17.73). **Open** 8am-8pm Mon-Sat. **Gare de Lyon** (01.43.43.33.24). **Open** 8am-8pm Mon-Sat. **Gare Montparnasse** (01.43.22.19.19). **Open** 8am-8pm, Mon-Sat. **Gare du Nord** (01.45.26.94.82). **Open** 8am-8pm Mon-Sat.

# Essential Vocabulary

In French, as in other Latin languages, the second person singular (you) has two forms. Phrases here are given in the more polite *vous* form. The *tu* form is used with family, friends and young children, and you should be careful not to use it with people you do not know sufficiently well. You will also find that courtesies such as *monsieur*, *madame* and *mademoiselle* are used much more than their English equivalents. *See also* chapters **Study** for information on language courses and **Restaurants: A la carte** for help in deciphering menus.

## General Expressions

**good morning/good afternoon, hello** *bonjour*
**good evening** *bonsoir;* **goodbye** *au revoir*
**hi** (familiar) *salut;* **OK** *d'accord;* **yes** *oui;* **no** *non*
**Do you speak English?** *Parlez-vous anglais?*
**How are you?** *Comment allez vous?/vous allez bien?*
**How's it going?** *Comment ça va?/ça va?* (familiar)
**Sir/Mr** *monsieur (M);* **Madam/Mrs** *madame (Mme)*
**Miss** *mademoiselle (Mlle)*
**please** *s'il vous plaît;* **thank you** *merci;* **thank you very much** *merci beaucoup*
**sorry/excuse me** *pardon/excusez-moi*
**Do you speak English?** *Parlez-vous anglais?*
**I don't understand** *Je ne comprends pas*
**Speak more slowly, please** *Parlez plus lentement, s'il vous plaît*
**Leave me alone** *Laissez-moi tranquille*
**how much?** *combien?*
**Have you got change?** *Avez-vous de la monnaie?*
**I would like....** *Je voudrais....*
**good** *bon/bonne;* **bad** *mauvais/mauvaise*
**small** *petit/petite;* **big** *grand/grande*
**beautiful** *beau/belle;* **well/badly** *bien/mal*
**expensive/cheap** *cher/pas cher*
**It's too expensive** *C'est trop cher*
**very** *très;* **with** *avec;* **without** *sans*
**and** *et;* **or** *ou;* **because** *parce que*
**who?** *qui?;* **when?** *quand?;* **what?** *quoi?;* **which?** *quel?;* **where?** *où?;* **why?** *pourquoi?;* **how?** *comment?*
**at what time/when?** *à quelle heure?*
**forbidden** *interdit/défendu*
**out of order** *hors service (hs)/en panne*
**daily** *tous les jours (tlj)*

## On the Phone

**hello** (telephone) *allô;* **who's calling?** *C'est de la part de qui?/Qui est à l'appareil?* (familiar)
**Hold the line** *Ne quittez pas/Patientez s'il vous plaît*

## Getting Around

**Where is the (nearest) Métro?** *Où est le Métro (le plus proche)?;* **When is the next train for... ?** *C'est quand le prochain train pour... ?*
**ticket** *un billet;* **station** *la gare;* **platform** *le quai*
**entrance** *entrée;* **exit** *sortie*
**left** *gauche;* **right** *droite;* **interchange** *correspondence*
**straight on** *tout droit;* **far** *loin;* **near** *pas loin/près d'ici*
**street** *la rue;* **street map** *le plan;* **road map** *la carte*
**Is there a bank near here?** *Est-ce qu'il y a une banque près d'ici?*
**bank** *la banque;* **Post Office** *La Poste*
**tobacconist** *un tabac;* **a stamp** *un timbre*

## Sightseeing

**museum** *un musée;* **church** *une église*
**exhibition** *une exposition*
**ticket** (for theatre, concert) *une place*
**open** *ouvert;* **closed** *fermé*
**free** *gratuit;* **reduced price** *un tarif réduit*
**except Sunday** *sauf le dimanche*

## Accommodation

**Do you have a room (for this evening/ for two people)?** *Avez-vous une chambre (pour ce soir/ pour deux personnes)?*
**full** *complet;* **room** *une chambre*
**bed** *un lit;* **double bed** *un grand lit;*
**(a room with) twin beds** *une chambre à deux lits*
**with bath(room)/shower** *avec (salle de) bain/douche*
**breakfast** *le petit déjeuner;* **included** *compris*
**lift** *un ascenseur;* **with air-conditioning** *climatisé*

## At the Café or Restaurant

**I'd like to book a table (for three/at 8pm)** *Je voudrais réserver une table (pour trois personnes/à vingt heures)*
**lunch** *le déjeuner;* **dinner** *le dîner*
**coffee (espresso)** *un café;* **white coffee** *un café au lait/café crème;* **tea** *le thé;* **wine** *le vin;* **beer** *la bière*
**mineral water** *eau minérale;* **fizzy/still** *gazeuse/plat*
**tap water** *eau de robinet/une carafe d'eau*
**the bill, please** *l'addition, s'il vous plaît*

## Behind the Wheel

**give way** *ceder le passage*
**it's not your right of way** *vous n'avez pas la priorité;* **no parking** *stationnement interdit/stationnement gênant;* **deliveries** *livraison*
**toll** *péage;* **speed limit 40** *rappel 40*
**petrol** *essence;* **unleaded** *sans plomb*
**traffic jam** *embouteillage/bouchon;* **speed** *vitesse*
**traffic moving freely** *traffic fluide*
**dangerous bends** *attention virages*

## Numbers

0 *zéro;* 1 *un, une;* 2 *deux;* 3 *trois;* 4 *quatre;* 5 *cinq;* 6 *six;* 7 *sept;* 8 *huit;* 9 *neuf;* 10 *dix;* 11 *onze;* 12 *douze;* 13 *treize;* 14 *quatorze;* 15 *quinze;* 16 *seize;* 17 *dix-sept;* 18 *dix-huit;* 19 *dix-neuf;* 20 *vingt;* 21 *vingt-et-un;* 22 *vingt-deux;* 30 *trente;* 40 *quarante;* 50 *cinquante;* 60 *soixante;* 70 *soixante-dix;* 80 *quatre-vingts;* 90 *quatre-vingt-dix;* 100 *cent;* 1,000 *mille;* 1,000,000 *un million.*

## Days, Months & Seasons

**Monday** *lundi;* **Tuesday** *mardi;* **Wednesday** *mercredi;* **Thursday** *jeudi;* **Friday** *vendredi;* **Saturday** *samedi;* **Sunday** *dimanche.* **January** *janvier;* **February** *février;* **March** *mars;* **April** *avril;* **May** *mai;* **June** *juin;* **July** *juillet;* **August** *août;* **September** *septembre;* **October** *octobre;* **November** *novembre;* **December** *décembre.* **Spring** *printemps;* **Summer** *été;* **Autumn** *automne;* **Winter** *hiver.*

# Getting Around

**Getting from A to B is easy when you know how. Here are some handy hints to get you on your merry way.**

Because Paris proper is so concentrated and compact – rarely more than 10km across at any given point – it remains a wonderfully 'walkable' city. For tired feet there's a well-organised public transport system. If you come to Paris by car you're better off leaving it outside the *Périphérique*, in the outer *arrondissements* or in a hotel car park, as atrocious traffic and expensive parking can make driving hellish. Cycling in Paris can also be a death-defying feat, although new cycle lanes are on the increase (*see box below*). For details of leaving Paris by train and driving in Paris, *see chapters* **Getting Started** *and* **Survival**. Bike and car hire, and travel agencies are covered in *chapter* **Services**. For Seine boat trips and other organised city tours, *see chapter* **Sightseeing**.

### Crossing the road: essential tips

Crossing Paris' multi-lane boulevards can be lethal to the un-initiated. By law drivers are only fully obliged to stop when there is a red light. Where there is a crossing, whether it has a flashing amber light or a sign saying *Priorité aux Piétons*, most drivers will ignore pedestrians and keep going. Making eye contact may cause a driver to stop, but don't count on it.

### Maps

Free maps of the Métro, bus and RER systems are available at airports and all Métro stations. The Paris transport authority RATP also offers other free brochures, available from Métro stations: *Paris Visite – Le Guide* has details of transport tickets and a small map; the *Grand Plan de Paris* is a fold-out map that also indicates the Noctambus night

bus lines (*see below* **Buses**). Plans of the Métro and RER and street maps are also included at the back of this Guide.

If you're staying more than a few days it's worth buying a map book covering the city in detail. The Michelin *Paris-Plan, Paris par Arrondissement* (Editions l'Indispensable), the small paperback *Plan de Paris* (Editions Leconte) and the slightly larger *Collection Plan Net* (Ponchet Plan Net) are all available from kiosks and bookshops.

## Arriving & Leaving

### Roissy Charles de Gaulle airport

Most international flights arrive at Roissy-Charles de Gaulle airport, 30km (19 miles) north-east of Paris. Its two main terminals are some way apart, so it's important to check which is the right one for your flight. The airport has a 24-hour, English-speaking information service: 01.48.62.22.80.

The **RER** is the quickest and most reliable way to central Paris (about 45 minutes). A new station gives direct access from Terminal 2 (Air France flights); for Terminal 1 you have to take the free shuttle bus. Trains (45F) run every 15 to 20 minutes, 5am-11.45pm daily.

**Air France buses** (55F) leave every 12 minutes, 5.40am-11pm daily, from both terminals and stop at Charles de Gaulle-Etoile. Air France buses also run to Gare Montparnasse (70F), 7am-9am (hourly), 9am-2pm (every 30 min), 2-11pm (hourly). The RATP-run **Roissybus** (40F) runs every 25 minutes, 6am-11pm, between the airport and rue Scribe, near pl de l'Opéra (at least 45 minutes).

The least reliable and most expensive means of transport, a **taxi** to central Paris can take 30-60 minutes. Expect to pay 170F-230F plus 6F per piece of luggage.

### Orly airport

French domestic and several international flights use Orly airport, 18km (11 miles) south of the city. It also has two terminals, Orly-Sud and Orly-Ouest, although all forms of transport stop at both. Orly has an English-speaking information service on 01.49.75.15.15, and is open 6am-11.30pm daily.

The high-speed **Orlyval** shuttle train runs every 5-8 minutes to RER station Antony (50F), and takes about 30 minutes. Alternatively, catch the courtesy bus, **Orlyrail**, to RER station Pont de Rungis, where you can get a train to central Paris for 27F. Trains run every 15-20 minutes, 6.30am-11.30pm daily, and take about 50 minutes.

The **Air France bus** (40F) takes about 30 minutes, leaving both terminals every 12 minutes, 5.50am-11pm daily, and stopping at Invalides and Montparnasse.

The RATP-run **Orlybus** to Denfert-Rochereau leaves every 10-12 minutes, 6am-11.30pm daily. Tickets (30F) are available from machines in the airport hall.

A **taxi** into town takes 20-40 minutes and costs about 120F plus 6F per piece of luggage.

### By Eurostar train

The Eurostar train journey time is three hours, with little of the time wasting involved in getting to and checking in at airports, and on arrival you are of course right in the centre of each city. Eurostar trains from London (01233 617575) arrive at Gare du Nord (08.36.35.35.39/Minitel 3615 SNCF), offering easy access to public transport.

## Métro marvels

Métro stations worth a visit in their own right.
**Abbesses** (Line 12) has murals running alongside the spiral staircase which leads up to one of the more elaborate Art Nouveau Métro entrances.
**Arts et Métiers** (Lines 3, 11) Dramatic copper-covered art. Porthole exhibits of engineering inventions from the Musée des Arts et Métiers.
**Bastille** (Line 1, 5, 8) Decorated with colourful scenes of the storming of the Bastille.
**Concorde** (Lines 1, 8, 12) The tiles were designed by two women artists to spell out the *Déclaration des Droits de l'Homme*, letter by letter.
**Liège** (Line 13) has tiled panels on the platform walls.
**Louvre** (Line 1) has replicas and exhibits from the Louvre: Egyptian busts, Assyrian winged beasts.
**Varenne** (Line 13) has exhibits from the nearby Rodin Museum.

## By Coach

International coach services to Paris arrive at the Gare Routière International Paris-Gallieni at Bagnolet, 20th. Mº Gallieni. For information or reservations (English-speaking) call Eurolines on 01.49.72.51.51. Hoverspeed coaches arrive at 165 av de Clichy, 17th (01.40.25.22.00). Mº Brochant. For reservations, call 0800.90.17.77.

## Public Transport

The Parisian public transport system (**RATP**) consists of the **Métro** (underground/subway), bus routes and the **RER** suburban express railway which interconnects with the Métro inside Paris. Pick up a free map at any Métro station. **SNCF**, the French national railway system, serves both the French regions (*Grandes Lignes*) and the suburbs (*banlieues*) from the mainline stations. Paris and its suburbs are divided into five travel zones. Zones 1 and 2 cover the city limits. **RATP** information 6am-9pm daily, 08.36.68.77.14; 24-hour recorded service 01.43.46.14.14; English-language service 08.36.68.41.14.

### Tickets & Travel Passes

RATP **tickets** and passes are valid on the Métro, buses and RER. Tickets and carnets can be bought at Métro stations, tourist offices, the airports and at tobacconists (*tabacs*). Keep your ticket in case of spot checks and to exit from stations.

Individual tickets cost 8F; it's more economical to buy a block of ten tickets (*carnet*) for 46F. **Carte Orange** travel passes (passport photo needed) offer unlimited travel in the relevant zones for a week or month. *Coupon Hebdomadaire* – valid Mon-Sun inclusive, two zones: 72F. *Coupon Mensuel* – valid from the first day of the month, two zones: 243F. These are better value than **Paris Visite** tourist passes – three-day pass for zones 1-3 105F, five-day pass 165F, with discounts to some tourist attractions. A one-day **Formule 1** pass (unlimited travel on all systems) ranges from 30F for zones 1-2 to 100F for zones 1-5 (includes airports).

### Métro & RER

The Paris Métro is at most times the quickest, cheapest and most convenient means of travelling around the city. The trains run daily 5.30am-12.45am. The individual lines are numbered, with each direction named after the last stop on the line. So Line 4 running north is indicated as Porte de Clignancourt, while the same line southbound will be designated Porte d'Orléans. It is important to know the names of the final stations on the lines you are using, above all when changing lines. Follow the orange *correspondance* signs to change lines; the connecting passages can be very long. The exit (*sortie*) is indicated in blue. The new, high-speed line, Météor, due to start running late in 1997, will link up the new Bibliothèque Nationale in Tolbiac to Madeleine.

The four RER lines (A, B, C, D) run across Paris and into the Ile de France commuter land. Within Paris, the RER is useful for making faster journeys – Châtelet-Les Halles is, for example, only two stops on the RER compared with eight on Métro Line 1. The RER runs daily 5.30am-midnight, with trains about every 12 minutes.

### Buses

Buses can be more convenient for shorter trips, or those between places with no obvious Métro connection. Bus routes run 6.30am-8.30pm Mon-Sat (limited Sunday service), until the night buses take over. You can use either a single Métro ticket, a ticket bought from the driver (8F) or a Métro pass. Tickets should be punched by the machine next to the driver; travel passes should be shown to the driver. When you want to get off, press the request button and the *arrêt demandé* (stop requested) sign above the driver will light up.

After the Métro and normal bus services stop running, the only form of public transport available – apart from taxis – are the **Noctambus** night buses, which run hourly from 1.30am to 5am daily, between pl du Châtelet and the suburbs. Noctambus ranks A to H serve the Right Bank; J and R serve the Left Bank. Look out for the owl logo on bus stops. A journey costs three tickets; travel passes are valid. There is no service to south-west Paris.

### Useful routes

As well as the standard routes a special scenic **Balabus** service runs on Sundays and holidays during the summer (*see chapter* **Sightseeing**). The following normal routes also pass interesting places and, unless stated, run on Sundays:
**29** Gare St-Lazare, past Opéra Garnier, bd Haussmann, Centre Pompidou, the Marais, Bastille to Gare de Lyon (no service Sunday).
**38** Centre Pompidou to place du Châtelet, past the Palais de Justice and the St-Chapelle in one direction, Notre Dame in the other, up bd St-Michel past the Musée de Cluny, the Sorbonne and the Jardin du Luxembourg to the Catacombs.
**48** Montparnasse, St-Germain-des-Prés, Louvre, Palais Royal, Richelieu-Drouot (no service Sunday).
**67** From sleazy Pigalle via the Louvre to Porte d'Italie, taking in the Jardin des Plantes and the Mosque.
**68** From Place de Clichy via Opéra, the Palais Royal and the Louvre to Musée d'Orsay, bd Raspail to Montparnasse, the Catacombs and Porte d'Orléans.
**69** From Père Lachaise, via Bastille, the Hôtel de Ville and Châtelet along the *quais* to the monuments of the 7th *arrondissement*, the Musée d'Orsay, Invalides and Champ de Mars (no service Sunday).
**72** From the 16th *arrondissement* to the Hôtel-de-Ville along the Seine in one direction and the rue de Rivoli in the other.
**73** From La Défense past the Arc de Triomphe and along the Champs-Elysées to place de la Concorde and across the river to Musée d'Orsay (no service Sunday).
**82** From the smart residential districts of Neuilly to the Jardin du Luxembourg via the Eiffel Tower and Invalides.
**84** From chic Parc Monceau in the 17th *arrondissement* to the Grands Boulevards, the Madeleine, St-Germain-des-Prés and St-Sulpice, to finish at the Panthéon (no service Sunday).

**95** One arty hill to another: Montparnasse to Montmartre.
**PC** (or *Petite Ceinture*, the small belt) goes all the way around the outer boulevards, just within the *Périphérique*.
**Montmartrobus** Minibus service through Montmartre.

## Taxis

Taxi ranks are found on major roads and at stations. The large white light on the roof indicates the cab is free. A glowing orange light means the cab is engaged. If you try and hail a taxi, note that taxi ranks take precedence, as taxis are not allowed to stop for a fare within 50m of a rank.

Taxi charges are based on area and time: **a** (day 7am-7pm Mon-Sat; 3.36F per km); **b** (at night 7pm-7am Mon-Sat, all day Sun; 7am-7pm Mon-Sat suburban zone and airports; 5.45F per km); **c** (at night 7pm-7am daily suburban zone and airports; 7F per km). The tariff is shown on the meter. Most journeys in central Paris average 35F-70F; there's a minimum charge of 13F and a 6F surcharge for each piece of luggage. Most drivers will not take more than three people, and it's polite to round up the fare by 2F-5F. Taxi drivers provide receipts on request: ask for *un reçu*. The following taxi firms

(some have English-speaking operators) accept telephone bookings 24 hours daily:
**Alpha** 01.45.85.85.85; **Artaxi** 01.42.41.50.50; **G7** 01.47.39.47.39; **Taxis Bleus** 01.49.36.10.10.

## Disabled Travellers

Neither the Métro nor city buses are suitable for wheelchair users, except for bus line 20 which runs between Gare St-Lazare and Gare de Lyon. Some buses have seats for people with poor mobility. RER lines A and B and some SNCF trains are wheelchair accessible in parts. Ask station staff if access is possible. All Paris taxis are obliged by law to take passengers in wheelchairs. The following services offer transport services for the disabled.

**Aihrop** (01.40.24.34.76). **Open** 10am-3pm Mon-Fri. Operates adapted vehicles to and from the airports. Offers specific trips (book 24 hours in advance), and specialised hire services (fully adapted for wheelchairs), some of which are listed below. For more information on access and facilities in Paris for the disabled, *see chapter* **Survival**.
**GiHP** 24 av Henri Barbusse, 93000 Bobigny (01.41.83.15.15). **Open** 8.30am-noon, 2-6pm, Mon-Thur; 8.30am-noon, 2-5pm, Fri; 7am-7pm Sat, Sun. **Le Kangourou** 92500 Rueil-Malmaison (01.47.08.93.50). **Open** 9am-6pm Mon-Fri.

# Cycling lanes

If you thought *Flatliners* was the closest you'd get to a near-death experience, you obviously haven't tried cycling in Paris. However, things may be changing with the addition of new cycling lanes to the streets.

The idea is hardly new, and Paris has had it before; the last set of lanes were set in the middle of the road leaving cyclists wedged in traffic, and unsurprisingly had little success. Under pressure to ease the city's terrible pollution, Paris' mayor Jean Tiberi has relaunched the idea. This time the lanes (*pistes cyclables*) are at the edge of the road, but only a small percentage are actually separated from the rest of the traffic, most being shared with buses and sectioned off only by tiny markers set in the tarmac.

Neither are the chosen routes ideal; the north-south axis follows rue de Rennes, bd St-Michel and bd Sébastopol, with the east-west route taking the busy Champs-Elysées, bd St-Germain and rue de Rivoli. By far the nicest section is between place Daumesnil and Bois de Vincennes, where the lane follows the Promenade Plantée, on the tracks of an old railway line.

Elsewhere expect to encounter delivery vans, scooters, bumbling pedestrians and even roller-bladers blocking your way. The hefty 900F fine for obstructing a cycle lane is barely enforced,

and, amazingly, cyclists are also liable to get fined; 230F for not using the lane provided.

Another 50km are promised for 1997, but there's little hope as the original 50km promised by the end of 1996 are still not all completed. After a difficult start, one can only hope that the tiny network will be extended to make cycling in the city a practical choice.

# Accommodation

**Whether you're after cheap and cheerful or memorable setting for the holiday of a lifetime, Paris has that special hotel.**

Paris boasts a wonderfully curious mix of hotels. Many rate as cultural attractions in their own right, awash with historic or literary associations, as former mansions, abbeys and even tennis courts have been adapted to welcome travellers. Even the most bohemian artists' garrets today tend to offer modern conveniences and plumbing. What's more, many are right in the centre of Paris, in walking distance from famous sights and museums.

For those looking to live it up regardless of price, Paris' palaces aren't just for royalty. For traditional grandeur, the Crillon or the Ritz are as magnificent as ever, while the new Hôtel Costes, occupying what was merely another hotel in its past life, proclaims itself an Italian '*palazzo*', and has the buzz of a place which has become *the* Paris hot spot.

## STAR RATINGS

The French hotel classification system (from no stars to four-star de luxe) is based on set factors such as the size of rooms and public areas, the presence of a lift, guest services and so on, but not on aspects like cleanliness, warmth of welcome or tastefulness of décor. In addition, as many hotels don't bother to upgrade after renovation, a two-star hotel may well be better (but not necessarily cheaper) than a three-star one. While the four-star de luxe (L****) establishments are justly called 'Palace Hotels', with 24-hour hot and cold running service and very helpful concierges, even most two- or three-star hotels offer very reasonable accommodation. One-star and no-star hotels are more likely to have shared bathroom facilities and non-English speaking staff. Many don't accept credit cards (or travellers' cheques), and lock up for the night around 1am.

Hotels risk being booked to the hilt during high season, which generally constitutes May, June, September, October, and Christmas to New Year, and in particular for fashion weeks (January and early July for couture, March and October for *prêt-à-porter*) and trade fairs, which are similarly most common in spring and autumn. At these times it's best to book a room before setting off. During low season (late July, August, November, December), you may well be offered rooms at less than the price listed here – it's always worth asking.

Same-day reservations can be made in person only at all branches of the Office de Tourisme de Paris (*see chapter* **Essential Information**). A small fee is charged (8F-50F), depending on the category of the hotel. The prices quoted for a double room are for two people and, unless stated, all include private shower or bath. All hotels are also required to charge an additional room tax (*taxe de séjour*) of 1F-7F per person, per night, depending on the hotel category.

## Palace Hotels

### Hôtel Meurice

*228 rue de Rivoli, 1st (01.44.58.10.10/fax 01.44.58.10.15).* M° *Tuileries.* **Rates** *single* 2,400F-2,750F; *double* 2,750F-3,200F; *suite* 5,500F-8,500F; *breakfast* 150F-195F. **Credit** AmEx, DC, MC, V.

The Calais post-master Augustin Meurice, who had been in business transporting British tourists to Paris, took advantage of the blossoming tourism which met the end of the Napoléonic Wars and opened the Meurice. Originally located on rue St-Honoré, the 180-room hotel moved to its present address opposite the Tuileries in 1835, when it became the English nobility's home away from home. Before the war, it was a favourite for the eccentric antics of Salvador Dali more recently, the hotel has welcomed Kirk Douglas and soprano Kathleen Battle, but one gets the impression that the Meurice is happy to see showbiz stars stay at the Ritz, preferring royalty more in keeping with its 'Hotel of Kings' image. The opulent Salon Pompadour, with its chandeliers, golden furniture and rococo mouldings, is the closest you'll get to Versailles without leaving Paris.

**Hotel services** *Air-conditioning. Bar. Babysitting.*

## Pick of the best

Architecture **Hôtel du Jeu de Paume**, *see p15*.
Bargain **Hôtel Tiquetonne**, *see p25*.
Contemporary style **Le Montalembert**, *see p19*.
Conviviality **Hôtel de Nesle**, *see p27*.
Film theme **Hôtel du Septième Art**, *see p23*.
Garden **Hôtel des Grandes Ecoles**, *see p20*.
Gym **Le Royal Monceau**, *see p13*.
Home from home **Castex Hôtel**, *see p25*.
Location **Hôtel Malher**, *see p20*.
Luxury **Hôtel de Crillon**, *see p13*.
Star gazing **Hôtel Costes**, *see p15*.
View **Hôtel Ermitage**, *see p25*.

*Business & conference services. Jet rental. Laundry. Lift.
Parking. Restaurant. Tickets.* **Room services** *Hairdryer.
Minibar. Radio. 24-hour room service. Telephone. TV
(satellite).*

### Hôtel Ritz

*15 pl Vendôme, 1st (01.43.16.30.30/fax 01.43.16.31.78).
Mº Concorde or Opéra.* **Rates** *single 2,800F-3,400F;
double 3,400F-4,300F; suite 4700F-32,900F; breakfast
180F-330F.* **Credit** AmEx, DC, MC, V.
Reigning over elegant place Vendôme, the 142-room, 45-suite
Ritz has been home to Coco Chanel, the Duke of Windsor and
Marcel Proust, as well as Ernest Hemingway, who reputed-
ly said that he hoped heaven would be as good as the Ritz.
Hopefully, heaven is a bit less exclusive. It doesn't have a
lobby (no loitering for paparazzi), the Oriental-carpeted corri-
dors simply go on for ever and the windows overlooking the
place Vendôme are not only sound-proof, they're bullet-proof.
There's a sophisticated cocktail bar (the Hemingway, of
course) and a health club out of pre-Vesuvius Pompeii.
Guests are entitled to attend cooking classes at the *Ritz-
Escoffier Ecole Gastronomique Française*
**Hotel services** *Air-conditioning. Bars. Babysitting.
Business & conference services. Cookery school.
Hairdresser. Health spa. Nightclub. Restaurant. Shops.
Swimming pool. Tickets.* **Room services** *Hairdryer.
Jacuzzi. Minibar. Room service (24-hour). Stereo.
Telephone. TV (satellite). Video.*

### Le Bristol

*112 rue du Fbg-St-Honoré, 8th (01.53.43.43.00/fax
01.53.43.43.26). Mº Miromesnil.* **Rates** *single 2,500F-
2,950F; double 3,150F-4,500F; suite 4,600F-15,600F;
breakfast 165F-240F.* **Credit** AmEx, DC, MC, V.
Opened in 1924, the Bristol likes to pride itself on discreet
class rather than the flashy luxury of some of its palace
rivals, attracting a business rather than pop-star clientele.
Most of the 200 rooms are furnished in sober, traditional style
*à la* Louis XV. Many overlook gardens, and some suites have
private terraces. Those in La Résidence, the wing added in
1975, are more contemporary, with stunning Italian marble
bathrooms. There is a glassed-in summer restaurant in the
garden, and a winter restaurant occupying a tapestry-hung,
oak-panelled oval room. There's also a dramatic (if small)
indoor swimming pool on the glass-enclosed rooftop.
**Hotel services** *Air-conditioning. Bar. Business services.
Fitness centre. Hairdresser. Laundry/dry-cleaning.
Parking. Restaurant. Swimming pool. Tickets.* **Room
services** *Minibar. Room service (24-hour). Telephone.
TV (satellite).*

### Hôtel de Crillon

*10 pl de la Concorde, 8th (01.44.71.15.00/fax
01.44.71.15.02). Mº Concorde.* **Rates** *single 2,550F-
2,900F; double 3,200F-3,800F; suite 4900F-32,000F;
breakfast 150F.* **Credit** AmEx, DC, MC, V.
Vying with the palatial Ritz for the title of grandest hotel in
Paris, the Crillon is hard to match for the sheer magnificence
of its location, in a Neo-Classical palace built in 1752-70 by
Jacques-Ange Gabriel as part of the place de la Concorde,
with correspondingly spectacular views. The high-profile
clientele is eclectic, from film and pop stars to politicians, but
the hotel itself continues to stand on gilt-edged tradition. The
huge butterscotch marble lobby dripping with chandeliers,
the blue-draped Jardin d'Hiver *salon de thé*, the superb
Ambassadeurs restaurant and the magnificent presidential
suites that overlook the place all ooze prestige, echoed in all
123 rooms and 40 suites.
**Hotel services** *Air-conditioning. Babysitting. Bar.
Boutique. Business services. Conference services. Fitness
Centre. Restaurants. Ticket agency. Wheelchair access.*
**Room services** *Hairdryer. Minibar. Room service (24-
hour). Safe. Telephone. TV (Cable).*

### Hôtel Meurice: *'The Hotel of Kings'.*

### Hôtel George V

*31 av George V, 8th (01.47.23.54.00/fax 01.47.20.40.00).
Mº George V.* **Rates** *single 1,800F-2,300F; double 2,500F-
3,900F; breakfast 140F.* **Credit** AmEx, DC, MC, V.
The ornate and exclusive George V (part of the Forte chain)
continues to dazzle its guests with its opulence and the high
standards of service in its 300 rooms. The trappings could
scarcely be more lavish – the hotel is stuffed with antiques,
and in the Salon Louis XIII there is even a Renaissance fireplace from a Loire Valley château and a seventeenth-century
Aubusson tapestry. Despite the traditionalism, it attracts a
rock star clientele. Lennon and McCartney camped out here
in 1964 while they wrote some of the album *A Hard Day's
Night*, while more recently it has welcomed the Rolling
Stones and Meg Ryan.
**Hotel services** *Air-conditioning. Babysitting. Bar.
Boutiques. Bureau de change. Business services. Car
rental. Hairdresser. Laundry/dry-cleaning. Limousine
service. Restaurants. Tickets.* **Room services** *Minibar.
Room service (24-hour). Telephone. TV.*

### Le Royal Monceau

*37 av Hoche, 8th (01.42.99.88.00/fax 01.42.99.89.90).
Mº Charles de Gaulle-Etoile.* **Rates** *single 2,700F; double
3,300-3,500F; suite 4,800F-17,000F; extra bed 400F;
breakfast 140F-190F.* **Credit** AmEx, DC, MC, V.
The Monceau, with its pale grey and white marble floors and
sofas, cream walls, crystal chandeliers, and Gobelins tapestries in the lobby, is a temple to 1920s opulence. The 219
rooms and suites are more restrained, if still lavishly over
furnished. There are French and Italian restaurants, and Les
Thermes health club has a choice of classes, squash courts
and a marble room filled with high-tech exercise equipment.
There is a bar next to the small but elegant pool.
**Hotel services** *Air-conditioning. Babysitting. Bar.
Business & conference services. Hairdresser. Health
club/gym. Parking. Restaurants. Swimming pool. Tickets.*
**Room services** *Hairdryer. Minibar. Room service (24-
hour). Telephone. TV (satellite). Video.*

### Hôtel Plaza Athénée

*25 av Montaigne, 8th (01.53.67.66.65/fax 01.53.67.66.66).
Mº Alma-Marceau.* **Rates** *High season (May, June, Sept,
Oct): single 2,500F-2,950F; double 3,200F-4,000F; suite
7,200F-13,000F. Low season: single 2,300F-2,740F; double
3,310F-4,750F; suite 6,430F-9,440F; breakfast 160F-250F.*
**Credit** AmEx, DC, MC, V.
Surrounded by haute-couture houses, it's no wonder that the
red carpet is always on hand at the sumptuous *belle époque*
Plaza Athénée. Beyond the imposing entrance is an ample
table-lined corridor, where guests sit around to see and be

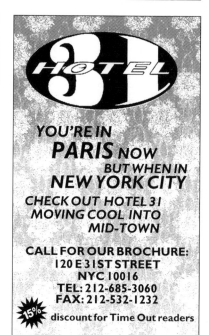

seen, while the 211 silk-and-satin clad rooms are rich with comfort. In summer, the Cour Jardin becomes a six-storey cascade of ivy, a perfect place for afternoon tea. La Régence restaurant is known for its haute cuisine, while more casual diners head for the brasserie.
**Hotel services** *Air-conditioning. Babysitting. Bars. Boutiques. Business services. Hairdresser. Laundry/dry-cleaning. Parking. Restaurants. Tickets.* **Room services** *Hairdryer. Minibar. Modem. Radio. Room service (24-hour). Telephone. TV (satellite).*

### Le Raphaël
*17 av Kléber, 16th (01.44.28.00.28/fax 01.45.01.21.50). Mº Kléber.* **Rates** *single* or *double* 1,850F-3,900F; *suite* 6,000F-23,000F; *breakfast* 120F-160F. **Credit** AmEx, DC, MC, V.
Opened in 1925, the Raphaël, is an echo of a more civilised age, with Oriental rugs, carved wooden panelling and club-like English bar, where powerbrokers from the adjacent conference centre come to unwind, and 90 elegant rooms stuffed with antiques. There's even a Turner in the lobby. December 1996 saw the opening of a roof garden on the 7th floor, from which you can have the unusual experience of looking down on the Arc de Triomphe.
**Hotel services** *Air-conditioning. Babysitting. Bar. Business and Conference services. Laundry/dry-cleaning. Restaurant. Tickets.* **Room services** *Hairdryer. Minibar. Room service (24-hour) . Telephone. TV (satellite).*

## De Luxe/Expensive

### Hôtel Costes
*239 rue St-Honoré, 1st (01.42.44.50.00/fax 01.45.22.78.87). Mº Tuileries.* **Rates** *single* 1,500F; *double* 1,700F-2,500F; *suite* 2,490-3,450F; *breakfast* 95F. **Credit** AmEx, DC, MC, V.
After the trend-setting Café Beaubourg and Café Marly (*see* chapters **Cafés & Bars** *and* **Restaurants**), Jean-Louis Costes has done it again with the instantly fashionable Hôtel Costes opened in 1995 and soon graced by top models, film stars and Fergie. This time, he teamed up with designer Jacques Garcia to create a mood of subtly contemporary historicism. A discreet entrance hall hides a labyrinth of concentrated luxury, from the Italianate central courtyard looked over by Roman Gods to the towering conservatory and a restaurant that fills nightly with media and film folk (*see* chapter **Restaurants**), as well as a new pool, fitness centre and hammam. Bedrooms and bathrooms, resplendent with maroon and mahogany, are firmly in the opulent age of Napoléon III's Second Empire.
**Hotel Services** *Air conditioning. Bar. Concierge. Lifts. Laundry. Restaurant. Ticket agency.* **Room services** *CD player. Fax. Hairdryer. Minibar. Radio. Room service. Telephone. Television (satellite).*

### Hôtel Regina
*2 pl des Pyramides, 1st (01.42.60.31.10/fax 01.40.15.95.16). Mº Pyramides or Tuileries.* **Rates** *single* 1,600F; *double* 1,900F-2,200F; *suite* 2,700-3,500F; *breakfast* 95F-145F. **Credit** AmEx, DC, MC, V.
Like the gilded statue of Joan of Arc in the centre of the square, the hotel itself, refurbished in 1995, is an extravagant relic of another age. The old panel clock which has a face for each of seven different cities and the free-standing wooden change kiosque evoke the excitement of the first days of transatlantic steamtravel. To the soothing sounds of harp music, subdued concierges will take your baggage up to your room. Upper rooms offer great views over the Jardin des Tuileries and Louvre.
**Hotel services** *Air conditioning. Babysitting. Bar. Change. Conference facilities. Conservatory. Laundry/dry cleaning. Lift. Porter. Restaurant. Tickets.* **Room services** *Minibar. Radio. Room service (24-hour). Safe. TV.*

**Hôtel Jeu de Paume**: *once a tennis court.*

### Pavillon de la Reine
*28 pl des Vosges, 3rd (01.42.77.96.40/fax 01.42.77.63.06). Mº Bastille.* **Rates** *single* 1,600F; *double* 1,800F-2,200F; *suite* 2,800F; *breakfast* 95F-120F. **Credit** AmEx, DC, MC, V.
Stepping off the otherworldly place des Vosges into the front garden of this ivy-covered mansion is a dreamlike experience, particularly at night when the facade is dramatically lit. The interior is full of soft-edged comfort, from the heraldic-themed hallway, tapestry-hung breakfast room and *trompe l'oeil* lift, to rustic, beamed corridors and 50 absurdly romantic, pastiche historic bedrooms, with lavishly draped four-posters. The split-level duplexes are particularly spacious.
**Hotel services** *Laundry. Lift.* **Room services** *Room service (24-hour). Safe. Telephone. TV (satellite). Wheelchair-adapted rooms.*

### Hôtel du Jeu de Paume
*54 rue St-Louis-en-l'Ile, 4th (01.43.26.14.18/fax 01.40.46.02.76). Mº Pont-Marie.* **Rates** *single* or *double* 895F-1,350F; *triple* 1,450F; *breakfast* 80F. **Credit** AmEx, DC, MC, V.
In 1634, when the Marais and the Ile St-Louis were built up as a fashionable home for the aristocracy, Louis XIII ordered the construction of the city's first *Jeu de Paume* (real tennis court) here on the island. Rescued and cleverly converted in 1988 to preserve ancient features, the galleried, timber-framed court today makes a wonderfully airy breakfast room and centrepiece of a romantic and comfortable 32-room hotel in this still exclusive-feeling enclave of the city. There's a salon on the second floor, and a serene secret garden.
**Hotel services** *Babysitting. Bar. Conference services. Laundry. Lift. Multi-lingual staff. Safe. Sauna.* **Room services** *Hairdryer. Minibar. Telephone. TV (satellite).*

### L'Hôtel

*13 rue des Beaux-Arts, 6th (01.43.25.27.22/fax
01.43.25.64.81). M° Mabillon.* **Rates** *single* or *double*
800F-2,500F; *suite* 2,200F-3,600F; *breakfast* 100F.
**Credit** AmEx, DC, MC, V.
Showbiz and fashion types, after Left Bank character, flock
to this just slightly over-the-top-hotel on a gallery-filled St-
Germain street. In its shabbier days as the Hôtel d'Alsace,
Oscar Wilde, disguised as Sebastian Melmoth, camped out
here until his death in 1900, claiming he was dying 'beyond
his means'. Guy-Louis Duboucheron acquired the place in
1968 and restored Wilde's room, as well as the Art Deco bedroom of music hall star Mistinguett, with an opulence that
borders on camp. An intriguing circular stone light well runs
the height of the building. Lower rates in July and August.
**Hotel services** *Air-conditioning. Laundry. Lift.*
**Room services** *Hairdryer. Minibar. Safe. Telephone.
TV (satellite).*

### Hôtel de l'Abbaye

*10 rue Cassette, 6th (01.45.44.38.11/fax 01.45.48.07.86).
M° St-Sulpice.* **Rates** *single* or *double* 980F-1,500F; *suite*
1,800-19,50F; *breakfast* included. **Credit** AmEx, MC, V.
Wood panelling, well-stuffed sofas and an open fireplace add
provincial charm to this tranquil eighteenth-century residence that was an abbey before the French Revolution. There
are three intimate drawing rooms, and best of all, a surprisingly large garden where breakfast is served in warmer
months. Completely renovated a couple of years ago to a
state of quiet luxury, the 46 rooms vary from small to grand,
but each is an exercise in good taste.
**Hotel services** *Air-conditioning. Babysitting. Bar.
Exchange. Garden. Laundry. Lift. Safe. Tickets.* **Room
services** *Hairdryer. Radio. Telephone. TV (cable).*

### Hôtel Buci Latin

*34 rue de Buci, 6th (01.43.29.07.20/fax 01.43.29.67.44).
M° St-Germain-des-Prés.* **Rates** *single* or *double* 900F-
1,170F; *duplex* 1,590F; *suite* 1,690F; *breakfast* included.
**Credit** AmEx, DC, MC, V.
In contrast to the ancient and mock-ancient endeavours of
most Paris hotels, the Buci Latin, above the lively rue de Buci
street market, is proudly postmodern. The lounge offers
wacky yellow sofas, curved pink-red walls and colourful

sculptures; designer graffiti decorates the stairwell and you
recognise your room by the painting on the key ring. Room
140 is a duplex with iron and wood furnishings, and upstairs
bathroom; suite 162 has an Olympic-size jacuzzi and terrace.
**Hotel services** *Air-conditioning. Babysitting. Bar.
Change. Coffee shop. Laundry. Lift. Safe. Tickets.* **Room
services** *Hairdryer. Minibar. Radio. Room service (24-
hour). Telephone. TV (satellite).*

### Left Bank Hôtel

*9 rue de l'Ancienne-Comédie, 6th (01.43.54.01.70/fax
01.43.26.17.14). M° Odéon.* **Rates** *single* 895F; *double*
990F; *suite* 1,400F; *extra bed* 100F; *breakfast* 50F. **Credit**
AmEx, DC, MC, V.
In a seventeenth-century building in St-Germain. The inte-
rior goes for neo-baronial with wood-panelled lobby, Old
Master repros, antique wooden chests and lots of tapestries.
The 31 beamed rooms are spacious with antique-style
furniture and thoroughly up-to-date pink marble bathrooms.
The street-side windows are sound-proofed.
**Hotel services** *Air-conditioning. Babysitting. Laundry
service. Lift.* **Room services** *Hairdryer. Minibar. Safe.
Telephone. TV (Cable). Wheelchair-adapted room.*

### Relais Saint-Germain

*9 carrefour de l'Odéon 6th (01.43.29.12.05/fax
01.46.33.45.30). M° Odéon.* **Rates** *single* 1,280F; *double*
1,530F-1,700F; *suite* 1950F; *extra bed* 250F; *breakfast*
included. **Credit** AmEx, DC, MC, V.
Down the street from the Odéon Theatre in the heart of the
Left Bank, this hotel has preserved the character of its seventeenth-century building. The 22 generously sized rooms
are individually decorated, combining antique furnishings,
beautiful fabrics and entirely modern fittings. Each room is
named after a French writer (ie. the 'Molière' suite).
**Hotel services** *Air-conditioning. Bar. Laundry. Lift.
Safe. Tickets.* **Room services** *Hairdryer. Minibar. Room
service (24-hour). Safe. Telephone. TV (cable). Video.*

### La Villa

*29 rue Jacob, 6th (01.43.26.60.00/fax 01.46.34.63.63).
M° St-Germain-des-Prés.* **Rates** *single* or *double* 900F-
1,800F; *suite* 2,000F; *breakfast* 80F. **Credit** AmEx, DC,
MC, V.

**Le Montalembert** *mixes contemporary chic with traditional touches.*

Through the glass facade of this postmodern hotel lie the daring purple walls and rugs, and intricate iron-railing of 'Le Bar'. Room numbers are projected onto the carpets and the 32 rooms are bold and bright, furnished in leather, burnished metals and sanded glass. All have flashy marble, chrome and glass bathrooms, the perfect place for your Philippe Starck toothbrush. The Villa also boasts a top-rate jazz club (*see chapter* **Music: Rock, Roots & Jazz**).
**Hotel services** *Air-conditioning. Babysitting. Bar. Jazz club. Laundry. Lift.* **Room services** *Hairdryer. Minibar. Non-smoking rooms. Radio. Room service (24-hour). Safe. Telephone. TV (cable).*

### Hôtel Lutétia

*45 bd Raspail, 7th (01.49.54.46.46/fax 01.49.54.46.00). M° Sèvres-Babylone.* **Rates** *single or double* 950F-1,650F; *suite* 1,950F-3,000F; *extra bed* 350F; *breakfast* 65F-125F. **Credit** AmEx, DC, MC, V.
The Lutétia, a masterpiece of Art Nouveau and early Art Deco architecture, opened in 1910 to serve provincial shoppers coming to the Bon Marché, and bringing Grand Hotel style to the Left Bank. In a less-glorious interlude it was used by the Gestapo during the German occupation. Its 271 rooms were luxuriously revamped by Sybille de Margerie, maintaining an elegant 1930s feel with shades of purple, gold and pearl grey, while the salons offer chandeliers, red velvet upholstery, bronze sculptures and a glass Art Deco ceiling.
**Hotel services** *Air-conditioning. Babysitting. Bar. Change. Conference services. Laundry. Lift. Parking. Restaurants.* **Room services** *Hairdryer. Minibar. Radio. Room service (24-hour). Safe. Telephone. TV (cable).*

### Le Montalembert

*3 rue de Montalembert, 7th (01.45.49.68.68/fax 01.45.49.69.49). M° Rue du Bac.* **Rates** *double* 1,675F-2,140F; *suite* 2,700F-3,700F; *breakfast* 100F. **Credit** AmEx, DC, MC, V.
Behind an elaborate Beaux-Arts-style facade lies a discreetly luxurious modern hotel that successfully mixes old with new. The spacious contemporary foyer is dotted with primitive art, the 56 rooms sport antique *armoires*, wooden bedheads and striking black and white striped bedcovers. The bathrooms are sleek, with black marble, sophisticated lighting and lots of chrome. The attic suite is Sir Terence Conran's Paris *pied à terre*.
**Hotel services** *Air conditioning. Babysitting. Bar. Change. Conference facilities. Laundry. Lift. Restaurant. Tickets.* **Room services** *Hairdryer. Minibar. Modem. Room service (24-hour). Telephone. TV (satellite).*

### Hôtel Astor Western Demeure

*11 rue d'Astorg, 8th (01.53.05.05.05/fax 01.53.05.05.30). M° St-Augustin.* **Rates** *single or double* 1,790F-2,650F; *suite* 2,950F-8,000F; *breakfast* 120F. **Credit** AmEx, DC, MC, V.
Classical music, white lilies and a besuited concierge give this Art Deco building a kind of elegance which, rare for its price range, is not intimidating. Reopened in 1996 after redecoration by fashionable designer Frédéric Méchiche, the marble floors and 15ft-sweeping curtains of the foyer are grand, and the bedrooms spacious and comfortable, with Bang & Olufson CD players in every room and a state-of-the art fitness room contrasting with the historicism. Star chef Joël Robuchon acts as consultant for the restaurant.
**Hotel Services** *Babysitting. Bar. Currency exchange. Health club. Laundry. Non-smoking floors. Parking (140F/day). Restaurant.* **Room services**. *CD player. Fax and computer outlets. Hairdryer. Minibar. Room service (24-hour). Safe. TV (cable).*

### Le 55

*55 av Reille, 14th (01.45.89.91.82/fax 01.45.89.91.83). M° Porte d'Orléans.* **Rates** *junior suite* 900F; *senior suite* 1200F; *breakfast included.* **No credit cards.**

A must for architecture buffs, this house and studio was built by Jean Delechette in 1925 for artist Georges Bracque, and is neighbour to the Maison Guggenbühl designed by Le Corbusier. Now restored and converted into an extremely intimate hotel – there are only two suites, each with private bathroom, sitting room and separate bedroom furnished with designs by Le Corbusier and Eileen Gray.
**Hotel services** *Laundry service.* **Rooms services** *Double glazing. Minibar. Radio. Telephone. TV (cable).*

## Moderate

### Hôtel Brighton

*218 rue de Rivoli, 1st (01.47.03.61.61/fax 01.42.60.41.78). M° Tuileries.* **Rates** *single* 540F-870F; *double* 570F-900F; *triple* 990F-1,070F; *suite* 1,300F; *breakfast included.* **Credit** AmEx, DC, MC, V.
Although it augurs old-fashioned splendour, this 70-room hotel has got slightly left behind by its luxurious neighbours, which means you can obtain rue de Rivoli status at fair prices. The uniformed porters, *faux* marble-columned *salon de thé*, chandeliers and a superb view over the Tuileries to the Eiffel Tower from the balconied rooms add a touch of grandeur.
**Hotel services** *Change. Laundry. Lift. Porter. Safe. Salon de thé.* **Room services** *Double glazing. Minibar. Telephone. TV.*

### Le Brittanique

*20 av Victoria, 1st (01.42.33.74.59/fax 01.42.33.82.65). M° Châtelet-Les Halles.* **Rates** *single* 646F; *double* 774F-887F; *breakfast* 52F. **Credit** AmEx, DC, MC, V.
Located off the place du Châtelet, this old-fashioned, 40-room hotel served as a Quaker mission during World War I. The redecorated lobby is smart, with antique-style floral print and red-leather sofas. Some rooms look onto a quiet courtyard, others on the tree-lined street.
**Hotel services** *Laundry. Lift.* **Room services** *Double glazing. Hairdryer. Safe. Minibar. Telephone. TV.*

### Hôtel Favart

*5 rue Marivaux, 2nd (01.42.97.59.83/fax 01.40.15.95.58). M° Richelieu-Drouot.* **Rates** *single* 510F; *double* 630F; *triple* 730F; *breakfast included.* **Credit** AmEx, DC, MC, V.
On the ravishingly pretty square of the Opéra Comique, this is the hotel where Goya stayed in his brief sojourn in Paris in the summer of 1824. Today the hotel remains reassuringly old-fashioned, drawing an international tourist clientele. The large reception area is just slightly fusty with its plump velvet tub chairs and loudly patterned carpets, the bedrooms are traditional: unexceptional, yet spacious.
**Hotel services** *Bar. Lift. TV lounge.* **Room services** *Radio. Telephone. TV (Cable).*

### Grand Hôtel de Besançon

*56 rue Montorgueil, 2nd (01.42.36.41.08/fax 01.45.08.08.79). M° Etienne-Marcel.* **Rates** *single* 520F; *double* 560F-590F; *breakfast* 40F. **Credit** AmEx, DC, MC, V.
Entirely renovated a couple of years ago, the Besançon occupies a nineteenth-century building, on the bustling, colourful rue Montorgueil, near Les Halles and the Pompidou Centre. The stained-wood and Louis-Philippe-style furniture, the large framed prints and tilting staircase make for a quaint, if a bit serious, feel. Although all 20 rooms have double-glazed windows, late risers might prefer the rooms facing the back.
**Hotel services** *First floor lift. Laundry. Safe.* **Room services** *Double glazing. Hairdryer. Radio. Telephone. TV (satellite).*

### Axial Beaubourg Hôtel

*11 rue du Temple, 4th (01.42.72.72.22/fax 01.42.72.03.53). M° Hôtel-de-Ville.* **Rates** *single* 450F-550F; *double* 560F-640F; *breakfast* 35F. **Credit** AmEx, DC, MC, V.

The hotel's electric glass doors slide open to reveal a sunny, modern reception area within a historic shell. Exposed wooden beams in the first-floor rooms, and the sixteenth-century cellar, which serves as a breakfast-room, add a touch of charm to this 39-room hotel, whose staff offer a warm welcome. Near the Pompidou Centre, it's very popular, so book in advance. **Hotel services** Babysitting. Laundry. Lift. **Room services** Double glazing. Hairdryer. Safe. Telephone. TV (satellite).

## Bastille Spéria

*1 rue de la Bastille, 4th (01.42.72.04.01/fax 01.42.72.56.38). M° Bastille.* **Rates** *single* 510F-544F; *double* 550F-616F; *triple* 740F; *breakfast* 40F. **Credit** AmEx, DC, MC, V.
Redecorated two years ago, the Bastille Spéria is in an ideal location for the Bastille or Marais, a few steps from the new Opéra on one side, the place des Vosges on the other. Behind a period facade with glass *porte-cochère* is a crisp, business-like modern interior with lots of plants and leather sofas in the lounge and 42 tasteful (pink and grey) rooms.
**Hotel services** Laundry. Lift. **Room services** Double glazing. Hairdryer. Ironing board. Minibar. Safe. Telephone. TV (satellite).

## Hôtel Caron de Beaumarchais

*12 rue Vieille-du-Temple, 4th (01.42.72.34.12/fax 01.42.72.34.63). M° Hôtel-de-Ville.* **Rates** *single* or *double* 660F-730F; *breakfast* 48F, *brunch* 78F. **Credit** AmEx, DC, MC, V.
A great Marais location, very helpful staff and attractive deep-blue facade and lobby, with antique furniture and Louis XVI fireplace, make staying in this hotel a pleasure. Renovated in 1993, the 19 charming, if small, wood-beamed rooms are hung with pages from first editions of *The Marriage of Figaro*, in tribute to former neighbour Beaumarchais. Breakfast is served in a stone cellar.
**Hotel services** Air-conditioning. Laundry. Lift. Safe. **Room services** Double glazing. Hairdryer. Minibar. Telephone. TV (satellite).

## Grand Hôtel Malher

*5 rue Malher, 4th (01.42.72.60.92/fax 01.42.72.25.37). M° St-Paul.* **Rates** *single* 470F-620F; *double* 570F-720F; *suite* 880F-980F; *breakfast* 45F. **Credit** AmEx, MC, V.
In the same family for three generations, the Malher has been brought upmarket to meet the needs of all types after a prime Marais position. The large windows and sparsely furnished lobby give the hotel a light, airy feel, while the 31 tastefully decorated rooms have pretty *armoire* wardrobes. Breakfast is served in a seventeenth-century vaulted wine cellar.
**Hotel services** Lift. Small conference room. No smoking rooms. Safe. **Room services** Double glazing. Hairdryer. Minibar. Telephone. TV (Cable).

## Hôtel St-Merry

*78 rue de la Verrerie, 4th (01.42.78.14.15/fax 01.40.29.06.82). M° Hôtel-de-Ville.* **Rates** *single* or *double* 400F-1,050F; *triple* 1,200F; *breakfast* 50F. **No credit cards.**
Growing out of the side of a sixteenth-century church, the St-Merry has a colourful past, first as a presbytery, later as a seedy brothel. Today it's an eccentric haven on a lively pedestrian thoroughfare near the Centre Pompidou. A winding wooden staircase leads up to the first-floor reception, where stone walls, wooden beams and bottle-green windows preserve the Gothic atmosphere. The twelve rooms are similarly styled: hair dryers are discreetly hidden, Gothic masonry pokes eerily through and the replica furnishings have been painstakingly collected by the owner, Christian Crabbe. Room No 9 is particularly unusual with the church's flying buttresses leaping across the space. Book well in advance, as it has a devoted following, in spite of the lack of lift and TVs.
**Hotel services** Change. Laundry. Safe. **Room services** Double glazing. Hairdryer. Telephone.

## Hôtel du Vieux-Marais

*8 rue du Plâtre, 4th (01.42.78.47.22/fax 01.42.78.34.32). M° Hôtel-de-Ville.* **Rates** *single* 400F-505F; *double* 510F-550F; *triple* 665F; *breakfast* 35F. **Credit** MC, V. Closed Aug.
The excellent location on a calm Marais street, clean rooms and an aim-to-please staff ensure the popularity of this 44-room hotel, which is gradually being redecorated floor by floor (*adieu* floral wallpaper).
**Hotel services** Lift. **Room services** Double glazing. Telephone. TV.

## Hôtel des Grandes Ecoles

*75 rue du Cardinal-Lemoine, 5th (01.43.26.79.23/fax 01.43.25.28.15). M° Cardinal-Lemoine.* **Rates** *single or double* 490F-570F; *breakfast* 40F. **Credit** MC, V.
This is the sort of hotel you dream of stumbling on. Entered through an archway on a hilly medieval street near place de la Contrescarpe in the Latin Quarter is what can best be described as a country manor standing within its own shady garden. Inside are a hallway with bronze chandelier, a charmingly fusty living room with parquet floor, piano and lacy tablecloths, and flowery bedrooms. They are in the process of converting the other buildings in the impasse to add 50 more rooms (due to open in the summer of 1997), which may lose some of the intimacy but should make reservations easier.
**Hotel services** Garden. Parking. **Room services** Telephone. TV.

## Select Hôtel

*1 pl de la Sorbonne, 5th (01.46.34.14.80/fax 01.46.34.51.79). M° Cluny-La Sorbonne/RER Luxembourg.* **Rates** *single* 530F; *double* 650F-780F; *triple* from 890F; *suite* 1250F; *breakfast* 30F. **Credit** AmEx, DC, MC, V.
Right on the place de la Sorbonne with its studenty cafés and bookshops, the Select offers an interesting combination of old and new. What from the outside appears to be a classic townhouse opens onto a dramatic lobby with granite floors and pillar and glassed-in atrium complete with palm tree, while the wooden beams, stone walls and vaulted breakfast cellar preserve original features. The 68 stylishly renovated rooms make clever use of limited space, partially through the use of mirrors, while there are fantastic views across town from the sixth floor.
**Hotel services** Air-conditioning. Bar. Laundry. Lift. Safe. Wheelchair access. **Room services** Double glazing. Hairdryer. Telephone. TV (satellite).

## Hôtel des Trois Collèges

*16 rue Cujas, 5th (01.43.54.67.30/fax 01.46.34.02.99). M° Cluny-La Sorbonne/RER Luxembourg.* **Rates** *single* 380F-600F; *double* 480F-650F; *triple* 750F; *breakfast* 42F. **Credit** AmEx, DC, MC, V.
On a small street near the Sorbonne, the Trois Collèges stands out from the other hotels in the neighbourhood with its ultra-modern lobby, done out in cool marble and contemporary wooden furniture, and *salon de thé*, which is open to the public. The 44 rooms are modern and clean.
**Hotel services** Laundry. Lift. Safe. Salon de thé. Tickets. Wheelchair access. **Room services** Double glazing. Hairdryer. Telephone. TV (cable).

## Hôtel Bonaparte

*61 rue Bonaparte, 6th (01.43.26.97.37/fax 01.46.33.57.67). M° St-Sulpice.* **Rates** *single* 450F-545F; *double* 575F-695F; *triple* 770F; *breakfast* included. **Credit** MC, V.
Fresh flowers are delivered weekly to this small, friendly hotel around the corner from St-Sulpice and its charming square. The Neo-Classical entrance is small, but the 29 rooms are spacious, many furnished with dark-wood antique-style *armoires*. The best are on the street side, with decorative fireplaces with gilt mirrors. The bathrooms have been redone recently, in rose-coloured marble.
**Hotel services** Lift. **Room services** Double glazing. Hairdryer. Minibar. Safe. Telephone. TV.

The **Hôtel Regent's Garden** *is an idyllic, historic hideaway.*

## Hôtel Louis II

*2 rue St-Sulpice, 6th (01.46.33.13.80/fax 01.46.33.17.29).*
*Mº Odéon.* **Rates** *single* or *double* 500F-700F; *triple* 850F;
*breakfast* 42F. **Credit** AmEx, DC, MC, V.
This 22-room hotel in an eighteenth-century building offers
charm at reasonable prices. Although the hotel could use
some freshening up, it is clean, and its lobby has exposed
wooden beams and tapestried-chairs. The top-floor rooms
are the most expensive, but the smaller rooms are just as
pleasant, with flowery wallpaper and white-knit bedspreads.
**Hotel services** *Lift.* **Room services** *Hairdryer.*
*Minibar. Safe. Telephone. TV.*

## Hôtel des Marronniers

*21 rue Jacob, 6th (01.43.25.30.60/fax 01.40.46.83.56).*
*Mº St-Germain-des-Prés.* **Rates** *single* 520F; *double* 715F-
765F; *triple* 940F-1040F; *breakfast* 45F. **Credit** MC, V.
Reached across a paved courtyard with the chestnut tree of
the name, this hotel is St-Germain charm personified. The
courtyard and garden make for a remarkably calm establishment; indeed the loudest things here are the colourful
walls of the spiral staircase and the rich wallpaper fabric.
**Hotel services** *Babysitting. Bar. Conference facilities.*
*Garden. Lift. Safe. Tickets.* **Room services** *Hairdryer.*
*Telephone. TV (satellite).*

## Hôtel de St-Germain

*50 rue du Four, 6th (01.45.48.91.64/fax 01.45.48.46.22).*
*Mº St-Sulpice.* **Rates** *High season* (Apr-Jun, Sept-mid-
Nov): *single* 585F; *double* 695F. *Low season: single* 415F;
*double* 520F; *breakfast* 45F; *extra bed* 120F. **Credit**
AmEx, DC, MC, V.
In a period building in the St-Germain fashion hub, this
30-room, recently renovated hotel has a cosy feel, with its
flowery sofa, pale salmon curtains, plants, winding metal
staircase and comfortable rooms.
**Hotel services** *Change. Laundry. Lift.* **Room services**
*Double glazing. Hairdryer. Minibar. Radio. Safe.*
*Telephone. TV (cable).*

## Hôtel Lenox

*9 rue de l'Université, 7th (01.42.96.10.95/fax*
*01.42.61.52.63). Mº Rue du Bac or St-Germain-des-Prés.*
**Rates** *doubles* 650F-1100F; *duplexes* 1500F; *breakfast*
45F. **Credit** AmEx, DC, MC, V.

Artists, photographers and designers Katherine Hamnett
and John Rocher are among fans of this stylish, relaxed hotel,
where thriving plants and oil paintings warm up the lobby.
Rooms are spotless and tastefully decorated in restrained
floral patterns. There is also a comfortable bar, where the
ubiquitous Hemingway is said to have wiled away the time.
**Hotel services** *Babysitting. Bar. Change. Laundry. Lift.*
*Porter.* **Room services** *Hairdryer. Modem. Radio.*
*Telephone. TV (satellite).*

## Hôtel Belle Epoque

*66 rue de Charenton, 12th (01.43.44.06.66/fax*
*01.43.44.10.25). Mº Ledru-Rollin.* **Rates** *Low season*
(mid-Jan-Mar, July-Aug): *single* 406F-656F; *double* 512F-
762F; *triple* 868F-900F. *High season: single* 530F-700F;
*double* 630F-950F; *triple* 1018F; *breakfast* 55F-70F.
**Credit** AmEx, MC, V.
An old facade hides this modern hotel near the Bastille which
pays homage to Art Deco style. 29 rooms are furnished with
reproductions of 1930s designs by Printz and Ruhlmann.
The recption areas offer marble floors and large club chairs,
opening onto a courtyard patio with vines and small tables.
**Hotel services** *Bar. Conference services. Courtyard*
*garden. Laundry. Lift. Restaurant. Safe.* **Room services**
*Double glazing. Minibar. Telephone. TV.*

## Hôtel Istria

*29 rue Campagne-Première, 14th (01.43.20.91.82/fax*
*43.22.48.45). Mº Raspail.* **Rates** *single* 470F-520F; *double*
530F-580F; *breakfast* 40F. **Credit** AmEx, DC, MC, V.
Tucked next to a block of dramatic tiled artists' studios,this
is a pretty little hotel with an illustrious past – the likes of
Man Ray and Hemingway parked their suitcases here during Montparnasse's arty heyday. Now rather more salubri-
ous than in those surreal days, rooms are neat and compact.
There's a stone breakfast cellar and tiny courtyard garden.
**Hotel services** *Courtyard. Laundry. Lift.* **Room**
**services** *Double glazing. Drinks. Hairdryer. Safe.*
*Telephone. TV.*

## Hôtel Regent's Garden

*6 rue Pierre-Demours, 17th (01.45.74.07.30/fax*
*01.40.55.01.42). Mº Charles de Gaulle-Etoile or Ternes.*
**Rates** *single* 650F-840F; *double* 700F-940F; *triple* 790F-
960F; *breakfast* 45F. **Credit** AmEx, DC, MC, V.

The thunder of traffic is plugged by a high wall of trees in this garden oasis just five minutes from the Arc de Triomphe. The boudoir-like foyer is a splendid reminder that the building was constructed for Napoléon III's personal physician and the 39 bedrooms are big and comfortable, the best with plush heavy curtains and grand mirrors. You can have breakfast in the pretty expanse of courtyard behind the hotel. **Hotel services** *Air Conditioning. Change. Garden. Lift. Laundry. Parking. Safe. Tickets.* **Room services** *Double glazing. Minibar. Radio. Telephone. TV (cable).*

## Inexpensive

### Hôtel Montpensier

*12 rue de Richelieu, 1st (01.42.96.28.50/fax 01.42.86.02.70). M° Palais-Royal.* **Rates** *single* 250F-295F; *double* 385F-450F; *triple* 520F; *shower* 25F; *breakfast* 35F. **Credit** AmEx, MC, V.
The hotel's 1970s-style entrance and lobby done in orange and black, and the lounge with tired brown sofas may not be to everyone's taste. Once the seventeenth-century *hôtel particulier* of the capricious Mademoiselle de Montpensier, cousin of Louis XIV, this often-renovated hotel offers an eclectic mix in its 43 rooms. Rooms range from large, high-ceilinged first-floor doubles to small singles with no shower or bath. Some rooms have been recently redone, others desperately need to be and a few, like No 36, with its historic painted wooden panelling and wall sconces, should never be touched. **Hotel services** *Café. Change. Safe. Tickets.* **Room services** *Double glazing. Hairdryer. Telephone. TV.*

### Hôtel Vertus

*5 rue des Vertus, 3rd (01.44.61.89.50/fax 01.48.04.33.72). M° Arts-et-Métiers.* **Rates** *single* 375F; *double* 480F; *suite* 600F; *breakfast* 35F. **Credit** AmEx, MC, V.
Occupying a renovated seventeenth-century building with all the requisite antique beams and exposed stone walls, this recently opened small hotel is decked out with pale wood furniture and plush blue-green carpets. Its nine rooms combine original architectural features with modern conveniences. The hotel is on a small pedestrian street, centrally based in the north of the Marais, where costume jewellers and Chinese wholesalers have yet to give way to gentrification. **Hotel services** *Laundry. Lift. Safe.* **Room services** *Double glazing. Hairdryer. Telephone. TV.*

### Grand Hôtel Jeanne d'Arc

*3 rue de Jarente, 4th (01.48.87.62.11/fax 01.48.87.37.31). M° St-Paul.* **Rates** *single* 295F-395F; *double* 305F-490F; *triple* 530F; *breakfast* 35F. **Credit** DC, MC, V.
This quiet Marais street, near the quirky place du Marché-Ste-Catherine has been home to a hotel since the seventeenth century. In 1994, new management removed the floral wallpaper and redid the public areas, but left the extraordinary Gaudi-esque mirror in the reception area. Most of the 36 rooms have also been tastefully renovated with salmon-pink wallpaper. The cheaper rooms are rather dark, so if you want a charming view, it's worth spending a little more. **Hotel services** *Lift. Safe.* **Room services** *Telephone. TV (cable).*

### Hôtel Place des Vosges

*12 rue de Birague, 4th (01.42.72.60.46/fax 01.42.72.02.64). M° Bastille or St-Paul.* **Rates** *single* 315F; *double* 450F-460F; *breakfast* 30F. **Credit** DC, MC, V.
Once a stables, this hotel, just off the place des Vosges in the Marais, has been elegantly renovated with plush red carpets and beamed ceilings carefully preserved. Although the 16 rooms tend to be small, they are tastefully decorated and the view from room No 60 is particularly picturesque. Some rooms look onto the back wall, but are quiet. **Hotel services** *Lift. Safe.* **Room services** *Telephone. TV (Satellite).*

### Hôtel Sansonnet

*48 rue de la Verrerie, 4th (01.48.87.96.14/fax 01.48.87.30.46). M° Hôtel-de-Ville.* **Rates** *single* 250F-365F; *double* 370F-400F; *shower* 20F; *breakfast* 33F. **Credit** MC, V.
In a historic Marais building, this small hotel is very centrally located. The listed facade and wrought-iron staircase with its Persian rug, and the high ceilings of the lobby make for a good first impression. The 26 immaculate, quiet rooms are less striking – most singles are without toilet or bathroom, but all doubles are en suite. The couple who've managed the hotel for 25 years offer a seasoned, patient welcome. **Hotel services** *Safe. Tickets.* **Room services** *Double glazing. Hairdryer. Room service (24-hour). Telephone. TV (Satellite).*

### Hôtel du Septième Art

*20 rue St-Paul, 4th (01.42.77.04.03/fax 01.42.77.69.10). M° St-Paul.* **Rates** *single* 295F-650F; *double* 410F-650F; *suite* 600F-650F; *breakfast* 45F. **Credit** AmEx, DC, MC, V.
A movie museum as much as a hotel, the Septième Art is a novelty establishment in the quiet St-Paul part of the Marais, stuffed full of Hollywood memorabilia. Stills of the Marx Brothers, Marilyn Monroe, Chaplin and Keaton prop up the bar, where's there's also a working fireplace, and each of the 23 rooms (guaranteed soundproof, in true gangster style) owes its character to a pre-1970s movie, with black and white tiled bathrooms to match. The jumble of artefacts represents just a fraction of the owner's huge private collection. **Hotel services** *Bar. Washer/dryer (30F/35F).* **Room services** *Telephone. TV (cable). Safe.*

### Hôtel Esmeralda

*4 rue St-Julien-le-Pauvre, 5th (01.43.54.19.20/fax 01.40.51.00.68). M° St-Michel or Maubert-Mutualité.* **Rates** *single* 160F-490F; *double* 450F-490F; *triple* 550F; *breakfast* 40F. **No credit cards.**
This small, basic, but extremely charming historic building in the lively Latin Quarter boasts superb views of Notre Dame, oozes beams, nooks and crannies, and has a resident cat. Individually designed rooms, antique beds, quirky bric-à-brac and an ancient wooden staircase (no lift) make this hotel very popular, even if the carpets and wallpaper are definitely on the shabby side, so it is best to book in advance. **Hotel services** *Safe.* **Room services** *Hairdryer. Telephone.*

### Familia Hôtel

*11 rue des Ecoles, 5th (01.43.54.55.27/fax 01.43.29.61.77). M° Maubert-Mutualité or Jussieu.* **Rates** *single or double* 370F-490F; *triple* 585F; *quad* 685F; *breakfast* 30F, 35F in room. **Credit** AmEx, DC, MC, V.
The floral-hung balconies are almost as effusive as the welcome at this newly renovated yet old-fashioned hotel near the Panthéon, the Sorbonne and Left Bank cinemaland. Amid a homely atmosphere, polyglot Eric Gaucheron and his staff will do their best to help and to tell you about Paris. There's an agreeable breakfast room with lace-covered tables, dried flowers, tapestries and antique furniture, while many of the 30 rooms have balconies. More expensive rooms have sepia murals of Paris, including Notre Dame and Hôtel du Nord. **Hotel services** *Lift. Safe. Tickets.* **Room services** *Double glazing. Hairdryer. Minibar. Telephone. TV (cable).*

### Hôtel de la Sorbonne

*6 rue Victor-Cousin, 5th (01.43.54.58.08/fax 01.40.51.05.18). M° Cluny-La Sorbonne.* **Rates** *single* 425F-465F; *double* 423F-500F; *breakfast* 35F. **Credit** AmEx, MC, V.
Geraniums pour out of the window boxes and a rubber plant swamps the cramped reception area at this charming hotel directly opposite the Sorbonne, in the scholarly heart of the Latin Quarter. Rooms are on the small side, but have all been pleasantly refurbished and are well equipped.

Hotel services *Lift. Safe.* **Room services** *Hairdryer. Radio. Telephone. TV (cable), Wheelchair access to ground-floor rooms.*

## Hôtel du Dragon

*36 rue du Dragon, 6th (01.45.48.51.05/fax 01.42.22.51.62). M° St-Germain-des-Prés.* **Rates** *single* 301F-326F; *double* 452F; *triple* 520F; *breakfast* 30F. **Credit** AmEx, MC, V.

Easy to miss from the street, this slightly delapidated, engagingly old-fashioned hotel offers bargain value in prime St-Germain shopping territory, attracting a young French crowd and impoverished intellectuals, while the turquoise lava lamp in the sitting room has come full circle into fashion. All rooms have showers.

**Hotel services** *Safe. Tickets.* **Room services** *Double glazing. Hairdryer. Room service (24-hour). Telephone. TV (satellite).*

## Hôtel du Lys

*23 rue Serpente, 6th (01.43.26.97.57/fax 01.44.07.34.90). M° Odéon or St-Michel.* **Rates** *single* 380F-450F; *double* 480F; *triple* 580F; *breakfast included.* **No credit cards.**

A seventeenth-century building near place St-Michel, with a flowered entrance (real and the wallpaper kind), wooden beams and a winding staircase. The 22 rooms are tastefully decorated in pinks and blues, sprinkled with antique furniture. Ask for a room at the front and high up if you want light. If you can brave the stairs, room 19 has a lovely terrace with plants. A faithful following makes reservations a must.

**Room services** *Double glazing. Hairdryer. Safe. Telephone. TV (cable).*

## Hôtel St-André-des-Arts

*66 rue St-André-des-Arts, 6th (01.43.26.96.16/fax 01.43.29.73.34). M° Odéon.* **Rates** *single* 235F-310F; *double* 350F-480F; *triple* 550F; *quad* 600F; *breakfast included.* **Credit** MC, V.

Housed in a building occupied by the king's musketeers in the seventeenth century, on one of the liveliest streets in St-Germain, this sociable, laid-back hotel is popular with a young, international clientele. With oak beams and an impressive, winding, half-timbered staircase, the only drawbacks are the old rugs, blankets, wallpaper and thin walls, although the hotel is beginning renovation and has recently installed a lift. The gregarious owner provides a steady stream of recorded jazz in the tiny lobby that doubles as a breakfast room. Most of the 33 rooms have private bathrooms.

**Hotel services** *Lift. Safe.* **Room services** *Telephone.*

## Hôtel de Nevers

*83 rue du Bac, 7th (01.45.44.61.30/fax 01.42.22.29.47). M° Rue du Bac.* **Rates** *single* 390F; *double* 420F-430F; *breakfast* 30F. **No credit cards.**

On a lovely boutique-filled street, this small seventeenth-century house offers unpretentious charm. The lobby's rugs, stone wall, and fresh flowers make for a cozy beginning. The nine rooms are tiny, but bright and spotless. Top floor rooms have private roof terraces, if you don't mind the climb.

**Hotel services** *Safe.* **Room services** *Telephone. Minibar.*

## Hôtel-Résidence Orsay

*93 rue de Lille, 7th (01.47.05.05.27/fax 01.47.05.29.48). M° Solférino or Assemblée Nationale.* **Rates** *single* or *double* 230F-480F; *breakfast* 35F. **Credit** MC, V.

Just a stone's throw from the Musée d'Orsay and with an elegant, historic facade, it's probably just pure coincidence that this 32-room hotel, resembling a French version of Soviet planning, with its 1970s lobby and formica-led fittings, is around the corner from the Socialist Party headquarters. But it's a cheap, clean sleep in a pricey area. Friendly staff.

**Hotel services** *Lift.* **Room services** *Double glazing. Telephone. TV.*

## Hôtel de Turenne

*20 av de Tourville, 7th (01.47.05.99.92/fax 01.45.56.06.04). M° Ecole-Militaire.* **Rates** *single* 320F; *double* 380F-450F; *triple* 525F; *breakfast* 38F. **Credit** AmEx, DC, MC, V.

Inexpensive rooms are scarce in this neighbourhood of wide boulevards and government ministries. However, this hotel, down the street from Napoléon's tomb and the Eiffel Tower, manages to keep up appearances at very reasonable rates. The downstairs lounge is not for aesthetes, but the 34 rooms in this old building are clean, sunny and comfortable. The Eiffel Tower is visible from some rooms on the sixth floor.

**Hotel services** *Change. Laundry. Lift. Safe. Tickets.* **Room services** *Double glazing. Hairdryer. Telephone. TV (satellite).*

## Hôtel des Arts

*7 cité Bergère, 9th (01.42.46.73.30/fax 01.48.00.94.42). M° Rue Montmartre.* **Rates** *single* 355F; *double* 355F; *triple* 475F-500F; *breakfast* 30F. **Credit** AmEx, DC, MC, V.

The best of several hotels in a celebrated passageway-courtyard in a late-night part of town, this friendly, family-run 26-room hotel has reams of theatre and museum posters plastered on the halls and a talkative, 35-year-old parrot called Babar ruling the reception area. Rooms are larger than average; those upstairs have been modernised. The attics combine the charm of sloping ceilings with minuscule windows.

**Hotel services** *Laundry. Lift. Parking. Safe. Tickets.* **Room services** *Double glazing. Hairdryer. Radio. Telephone. TV.*

## Hôtel Chopin

*46 passage Jouffroy, 9th (01.47.70.58.10/fax 01.42.47.00.70). M° Rue Montmartre.* **Rates** *single* 355F-435F; *double* 375F-390F; *triple* 565F; *breakfast* 38F. **Credit** AmEx, DC, MC, V.

If you like Paris' network of nineteenth-century glass-roofed passages, you'll adore this place buried in a historic *passage* built in 1846, among antiquarian bookshops, printsellers, old-fashioned toy shops and the Musée Grévin. The 36 bedrooms, with wooden *armoires* and tables, and pretty printed curtains, have been pleasantly modernised and redecorated, but the entrance hall remains a rosy, turn-of-the-century fuss of leather Chesterfields and lace curtains.

**Hotel services** *Lift. Safe.* **Room services** *Telephone. TV.*

## Résidence du Pré

*15 rue Pierre-Sémard, 9th (01.48.78.26.72/fax 01.42.80.64.83). M° Cadet.* **Rates** *single* 425F; *double* 460F-485F; *triple* 600F; *breakfast* 50F. **Credit** AmEx, DC, MC, V.

On a street of nineteenth-century buildings festooned with ornate wrought-iron balconies, the recently renovated, 40-room Résidence du Pré is the least expensive of three Hôtels du Pré, and benefits from the group's efficient management. Rooms vary from serious beige and ochre tones, to yellow, pastel-flowered comforters with wicker furniture. The hotel is not far from the Gare du Nord with good access to the RER.

**Hotel services** *Bar. Lift. Safe. Parking (60F).* **Room services** *Double glazing. Telephone. TV (satellite).*

## Hôtel Apollo

*11 rue de Dunkerque, 10th (01.48.78.04.98/fax 01.42.85.08.78). M° Gare du Nord.* **Rates** *single* 180F-325F; *double* 380F-425F; *triple* 430F-480F; *quad* 600F; *breakfast* 30F. **Credit** AmEx, DC, MC, V.

Opposite the Gare du Nord, the Apollo is a great find, in an area full of doubtful cheap hotels. The 45-room hotel has true charm, with its iron lift, red carpets, Persian rugs, and panther statues on every floor. Its rooms are decorated country-style, with large *armoires* and florid wallpaper.

**Hotel services** *Laundry. Lift. Safe.* **Room services** *Double glazing. Minibar. Telephone. TV.*

*Hippy vibes hang on at **Hôtel de Nesle**.*

Sacré-Coeur, it is on a peaceful street protected from the tourist madness. The hallways run amok with blue-green walls, paintings and chandeliers, while the bedrooms are large, endearingly over-decorated and characterful. The ground-floor rooms give directly onto a garden, while the back rooms on upper-floors have exceptional views of the city. **Hotel services** *Garden.* **Room services** *Double glazing. Hairdryer. Telephone.*

### Prima Lepic
*29 rue Lepic, 18th (01.46.06.44.64/fax 01.46.06.66.11). M° Abbesses or Blanche.* **Rates** *single* 350F; *double* 380D-400F; *triple* 450F-500F; *quad/quin* 600F-700F; *breakfast* 30F. **Credit** MC, V.
Located on a winding street that leads up to the top of the Butte Montmartre, and just five minutes from Sacré-Coeur, the 38-room Prima Lepic is nostalgic bohemian Montmartre. Decorated with a floral theme, there are potted plants and flowers in the foyers and florid wallpaper in the bedrooms, many of which look over a pretty courtyard.
**Hotel services** *Lift. Safe.* **Room services** *Double glazing. Hairdryer. Telephone. TV.*

## Budget

### Hôtel de Lille
*8 rue du Pélican, 1st (01.42.33.33.42). M° Palais-Royal-Louvre.* **Rates** *single* 200F; *double* 230F-280F; *shower* 30F. No breakfast. **No credit cards.**
The yellow vases with fake flowers, and crooked winding staircase with a worn Persian rug are hardly glamorous, but with the Louvre just a minute away, this hotel makes up in convenience what it may lack in comfort and services. Of the 13 rooms, the six most expensive have showers.

### Hôtel Tiquetonne
*6 rue Tiquetonne, 2nd (01.42.36.94.58/fax 01.42.36.02.94). M° Etienne-Marcel.* **Rates** *single* 133F-203F; *double* 236F; *breakfast* 22F. **Credit** MC, V.
Basic but central, clean, and superb value on a small and upwardly mobile street near Les Halles, this is the sort of budget hotel where international backpackers rub shoulders with French provincial salesmen. Many of the 45 recently redecorated rooms are high-ceilinged and surprisingly spacious, with modern bathrooms and a mishmash of furniture.
**Hotel services** *Lift.* **Room services** *Telephone.*

### Hôtel Castex
*5 rue Castex, 4th (01.42.72.31.52/fax 01.42.72.57.91). M° Bastille.* **Rates** *single* 220F-270F; *double* 300F-340F; *triple* 440F; *breakfast* 25F. **Credit** MC, V.
Young and enthusiastic Blaise Bouchand will bend over backwards for guests in this well-maintained hotel which has been in his family for four generations. A home from home, the 27 larger-than-average rooms are quiet and spotless, and regularly spruced up; even the singles here offer enough space to walk around an open suitcase. All rooms have a shower or bath, and most have their own toilet. Well located between the Bastille and the Ile St-Louis.
**Hotel services** *Safe. TV.* **Room services** *Telephone.*

### Hôtel de la Herse d'Or
*20 rue St-Antoine, 4th (01.48.87.84.03/fax 01.48.87.94.01). M° Bastille.* **Rates** *single* 160F-280F; *double* 200F-280F; *shower* 10F; *breakfast* 25F. **No credit cards.**
On the main artery between Hôtel de Ville and the Bastille, among excellent food shops. Don't be misled by the stone corridor leading to the reception, which is infinitely grander than the rest of the hotel. The no-frills rooms, most looking onto a wall (dark) or the noisy street (bright), are acceptable for the price, and some have a private bathroom.
**Room services** *Telephone.*

### Résidence Magenta
*35 rue Yves-Toudic, 10th (01.42.40.17.72/fax 01.42.02.59.66). M° Jacques-Bonsergent.* **Rates** *single* 330F; *double* 370F-390F; *triple* 450F; *quad* 530F; *breakfast* 38F. **Credit** AmEx, DC, MC, V.
Like some strange George Segal sculpture fantasy, plaster sheets drape the reception of this otherwise sane hotel on a quiet street near place de la République. Genial staff welcome young travellers who can double, triple or even quadruple up in large, spotless rooms. All 32 have bathrooms, and those on the ground floor are accessible from the courtyard.
**Hotel services** *Laundry. Lift.* **Room services** *Safe. Telephone. TV (satellite). Wheelchair access to ground-floor rooms.*

### Hôtel Keppler
*12 rue Keppler, 16th (01.47.20.65.05/fax 01.47.23.02.29). M° Charles de Gaulle-Etoile.* **Rates** *single* or *double* 450F; *triple* 520F; *breakfast* 30F. **Credit** AmEx, MC, V.
The 49-room Keppler is tucked away on an elegant, quiet street behind the chic avenue Marceau, and everything about it whispers 16th *arrondissement*. A vintage, wonderfully ornate nineteenth-century lift and well-sized rooms are to be expected in this neighbourhood – but not often at these prices. Efficient and just slightly stuffy, like the district.
**Hotel services** *Bar. Lift.* **Room services** *Hairdryer. Room service (24-hour). Safe. Telephone. TV (satellite).*

### Hôtel Ermitage
*24 rue Lamarck, 18th (01.42.64.79.22/fax 01.42.64.10.33). M° Lamarck-Caulaincourt.* **Rates** *single* 410F; *double* 470F; *triple* 590F; *quad* 670F; *breakfast* included. **No credit cards.**
Although this twelve-room hotel is only five minutes from

## Hôtel Pratic

*9 rue d'Ormesson, 4th (01.48.87.80.47/fax 01.48.87.40.04). M° St-Paul.* **Rates** *single* 180F; *double* 244F-340F; *breakfast* 25F. **No credit cards**.
It's hard to beat this hotel's price, and its location – overlooking the charming restaurant- and café-filled place du Marché-Ste-Catherine in the heart of the Marais. A recent renovation has created a breakfast room, freshened up the halls and added new if mismatched touches to the 24 rooms, but left the remarkable egg-shaped loo between the first and second floors intact. Pricier rooms have a private bathroom.
**Room services** *Double glazing. Telephone.*

## Hôtel Gay-Lussac

*29 rue Gay-Lussac, 5th (01.43.54.23.96/fax 01.40.51.79.49). RER Luxembourg.* **Rates** *single* 185F; *double* 240F-360F; *triple* or *quad* 400F-540F; *breakfast included*. **No credit cards**.
This turn-of-the-century building has the air of an old-fashioned provincial hotel. On the corner of a busy thoroughfare near the Luxembourg Gardens and the Panthéon, the Gay-Lussac got lost somewhere in the 1970s, but offers large, simple, reasonably priced rooms, nearly all with private bathroom, and a friendly welcome.
**Hotel services** *Breakfast room. Lift. TV lounge.* **Room services** *Telephone.*

## Hôtel de Nesle

*7 rue de Nesle, 6th (01.43.54.62.41). M° Odéon.* **Rates** *single* 250F; *double* 300F; *shower* 25F; *triple* 500F; *breakfast* 25F. **No credit cards**.
Expect a wonderfully eccentric welcome from Mme Renée who introduces her international backpacker clientele to the two ducks in the garden of this charming, former hippy hangout in a tiny St-Germain backstreet. Then, climb the staircase to rooms decorated with wacky murals: Ancient Egypt nestles alongside India, while across the hall blazes Molière's France. If your French is up to it, ask about the Nesle (pronounced 'nell') and she'll entertain you with tales and photos from when the place looked (even) more like an opium den. Showers only, no private bathrooms and no advance reservations make it tricky, but lots of fun. Be sure to arrive early, and beware, loners might have to share a room.
**Hotel services** *garden.* **Room services** *Telephone*

## Hôtel le Petit Trianon

*2 rue de l'Ancienne-Comédie, 6th (01.43.54.94.64). M° Odéon.* **Rates** *single* 170F; *double* 350F; *triple* 450F; *breakfast* 25F. **No credit cards**.
Although tiny and simple, the white rooms up the old winding staircase (with equally ancient carpet) of this small hotel on a busy street in St-Germain, hit the spot for those on a small budget. Eight of the 15 rooms have showers. Possible discounts for longer stays.

## Hôtel St-Michel

*17 rue Gît-le-Coeur, 6th (01.43.26.98.70). M° St-Michel.* **Rates** *single* or *double* 190F-375F; *triple* 490F-535F; *shower* 12F; *breakfast* 25F. **No credit cards**.
On a rare, quiet street off the agitated heart of boulevard St-Michel, this modest 25-room hotel offers good value. The rooms are badly lit and the wallpaper is ancient, but clean; higher-priced rooms come with twin beds and bathrooms.
**Hotel services** *Safe.* **Room services** *Double glazing. Telephone.*

## Grand Hôtel Lévêque

*29 rue Cler, 7th (01.47.05.49.15/fax 01.45.50.49.36). M° Ecole-Militaire.* **Rates** *single* 225F; *double* 335F-380F; *triple* 480F; *breakfast* 30F. **Credit** MC, V.
Located on an excellent market street in a residential part of town near the Eiffel Tower, the Lévêque is a good bet if you want to mix with the locals. The long, old-tiled entrance is charming, while many of the 50 simple and dark rooms have

been nicely redone in the last few years, and most have private bathrooms. The hotel has a following, so reserve ahead.
**Room services** *Double glazing. Safe. Telephone.*

## Hôtel de Nevers

*53 rue de Malte, 11th (01.47.00.56.18/fax 01.43.57.77.39). M° République.* **Rates** *single* 150F-245F; *double* 170F-260F; *triple* 310F; *quad* 380F; *shower* 20F; *breakfast* 25F. **Credit** MC, V.
Located on a small street with three other budget hotels, the Nevers is definitely the best kept, with very clean, spacious rooms, awesome owners and bossy cats. It's worth paying a bit extra for the rooms with a shower. An unexciting but handy location, with the Marais only a ten-minute walk.
**Hotel services** *Lift.* **Room services** *Telephone.*

## Hôtel Tolbiac

*122 rue de Tolbiac, 13th (01.44.24.25.54/fax 01.45.85.43.47). M° Tolbiac.* **Rates** *single* 110F-155F; *double* 160F-200F; *studio with kitchenette* 800F-1500F a week (July, Aug); *breakfast* 15F, 25F. **No credit cards**.
In the heart of Chinatown, the seven-storey Tolbiac may not be the most convenient but is certainly among the nicest of the budget hotels. Renovated in 1995-1996, the 47 bright, clean rooms have hardwood floors, mercifully plain walls, cheery bedspreads and sinks, while many also offer a shower. As well as a breakfast room, there's a small courtyard with flowers and colourful tiled tables for the warmer months.
**Room services** *Double glazing. TV.*

## Hôtel des Batignolles

*26-28 rue des Batignolles, 17th (01.43.87.70.40/fax 01.44.70.01.04). M° Rome.* **Rates** *single or double* 320F; *breakfast* 25F. **Credit** DC, MC, V.
Two blocks away from the iniquitous Place de Clichy, this former girls' boarding house is a wholesome alternative to the array of sleazier establishments in the area. It has plenty of character, with a plant-filled courtyard patio and 35 pleasantly spacious rooms, all with phones and ensuite bathrooms. The interior retains an air of the building's institutional past, but together with the uneven corridors and the *tromp l'oeil* facade, the effect is cheerfully cock-eyed. Reductions are available for stays of longer then six days.
**Hotel services** *Safe.* **Room services** *Double glazing. Telephone.*

# Youth Accommodation

For more information on youth and student accommodation, see *also chapter* **Study**.

### BVJ

*44 rue des Bernadins, 5th (01.53.00.90.90). M° Maubert-Mutualité.* **Open** 24-hour, all year. **Rates** 120F (incl breakfast). **No credit cards**.
BVJ hostels offer single or shared rooms (for up to eight people) for 120F per night (plus 10F for a single); 100F (without breakfast). Branches open all year round, and offer special rates for extended stays.
**Branch: Paris/Louvre** 20 rue J-J Rousseau, 1st (01.42.33.55.00).

### MIJE

**Le Fourcy** *6 rue de Fourcy, 4th (01.42.74.23.45/fax 01.40.27.81.64). M° St-Paul.* **Open** *reservations* 7am-10pm daily; *hostels* 7am-1am daily. **Rates** 120F per person in dorms; *single* 195F (18-30 age limit); *double* 300F; *breakfast included* (plus 10F membership). **No credit cards**.
Two seventeenth-century aristocratic residences and a former girls' convent are surely the best hostels in Paris, with a charm rarely found in a low-budget hotel. Located in the historic Marais, the plain but clean rooms sleep from three

to eight people, and all have a shower and washbasin. Le Fourcy's dining hall is open to guests at all three MIJE hostels, while its quiet, leafy courtyard is great for picnics. With a young and international clientele and a riotously sociable atmosphere, they are understandably popular, so come early – only groups can book in advance.
**Branches: Le Fauconnier** 11 rue du Fauconnier, 4th (01.42.74.23.45); **Maubisson** 2 rue des Barres, 4th (01.42.72.72.09.

## Association des Etudiants Protestants de Paris
*46 rue de Vaugirard, 6th (01.46.33.23.30/fax 01.46.34.27.09). M° Mabillon or St-Sulpice.* **Open** *Office* 8.45am-noon, 3-7pm, Mon-Fri; 8.45am-noon, 6-8pm, Sat; 10am-noon Sun. *Hostel* 24 hours daily. **Rates** 75F per person per night in dorm; *single* 93F; *double* 86F per person, available July-Sept only; *breakfast included.* **No credit cards.**
In a good location by the Luxembourg gardens, the AEPP, which has occupied this building for over 100 years, offers accommodation mainly in dormitories for students aged 18-26. No reservations are accepted, and membership is 10F, payable upon arrival in addition to a 100F deposit. There are basic cooking facilities, a café, and a lounge with a TV. The maximum stay is five weeks.

## Résidence Bastille
*151 av Ledru-Rollin, 11th (01.43.79.53.86/fax 01.43.79.35.63). M° Voltaire.* **Open** 7am-12.30pm, 2pm-1am daily. **Rates** (incl breakfast) 115F per person per night. **No credit cards.**
Slowly being renovated floor by floor, this modern hostel has 150 beds in dormitory-style rooms for people aged under 35. Some of the triples and quads have their own bathroom, others share hall facilities.

## HI (Hostelling International)
**Le D'Artagnan** *80 rue Vitruve, 20th (01.40.32.34.56/fax 01.40.32.34.55). M° Porte de Bagnolet.* **Open** *Office* 8am-1am. *Hostel* 24-hours, rooms closed noon-3pm. **Rates** *dormitory* 113F; *double* 258F; *breakfast included.* **Credit** MC, V.
The four official youth hostels in and around Paris are part of the International Youth Hostel Federation booking network, which allows members of affiliated organisations in other countries to book from home (up to six consecutive nights) and pay in advance in their local currency. For details contact your local HI association. The Jules Ferry, near place de la République, is the only one with a fairly central location. The D'Artagnan, the biggest youth hostel in Europe, is a 440-bed complex with a restaurant, a bar and a mini-cinema.
**Branches: Jules Ferry** 8 bd Jules-Ferry, 11th (01.43.57.55.60/fax 01.40.21.79.92); **Cité des Sciences** 24 rue des Sept-Arpents, 93310 Le Pré St-Gervais (01.48.43.24.11/fax 01.48.43.26.82); **Léo Lagrange** 107 rue Martre, 92110 Clichy (01.41.27.26.90/fax 01.42.70.52.63).

## Chain Hotels

### Novotel
*8 pl Marguerite de Navarre, 1st (from the UK 0171 7241000/from France 01.42.21.31.31/fax 01.40.26.05.79). M° Châtelet-Les Halles.* **Rates** *single* 780, plus 40F per person; *double* 915F; *suite* 1,200F-1,500F; *breakfast* 64F. **Credit** AmEx, DC, MC, V.
A major French chain, with seven ultra-modern Paris hotels. Many rooms in the Châtelet branch look out onto the Forum des Halles and the St-Eustache Church. The huge lobby, restaurant and bar feel somewhat like a fancy airport. There are also branches at 2/8 rue Hector Malot, 12th (01.44.67.60.00); 85 rue de Bercy, 12th (01.43.42.30.00); 15/17/19 bd Romain Rolland, 14th (01.41.17.26.26).

### Holiday Inn
*Central reservations across Europe UK 0800-897121; France 0800-905999/01.43.55.44.34/fax 01.47.00.32.34.* **Rates** prices vary according to hotel: *single* or *double* 310F-1395F; *executive* 1595F; *breakfast* 80F-87F. **Credit** AmEx, DC, MC, V.
A dependable American-owned chain, with 16 hotels in Paris and suburbs, offering good facilities. Much the grandest is the vast establishment running along one side of place de la République, with apartments, business facilities, non-smoking rooms and a Napoléon III-style courtyard garden.

### Hôtel Ibis
*Central reservations from the UK 0171 7241000; from France 01.60.77.52.52/fax 01.69.91.05.63.* **Rates** *single* 395F; *double* 540F; *triple* 590F; *breakfast* 39F. **Credit** AmEx, DC, MC, V.
This mid-price French chain has 17 hotels around Paris, with large branches at Montparnasse, Montmartre and La Villette.

### Timhotel
*Central reservations 01.44.15.81.15/fax 01.44.15.95.26.* **Rates** *single* or *double* 440F-650F; *triple* 570F-850F; *breakfast* 49F-55F. **Credit** AmEx, MC, V.
A bit different from the hotel chain norm, Timhotels are usually quite small, individually decorated and well located. There are 21 in Paris, all offering good amenities for the price range. There's a particularly charming one on place Emile Gondeau in Montmartre. Other good branches near the Jardin des Plantes and the Bourse.

## Bed & Breakfast

### Café Couette et Châteaux
*8 rue d'Isly, 8th (01.42.94.92.00/fax 01.42.94.93.12). M° Gare St-Lazare or Havre-Caumartin.* **Rates** (including breakfast, 2 night minimum) *single* 220F-370F per night; *double* 280F-520F per night. **Open** 10am-6pm Mon-Sat. **Credit** AmEx, MC, V.
The vast number of hotels and the Parisian reserve about inviting strangers into their home make staying in a B&B an unlikely option. Nonetheless, Café Couette has 80 participating hosts in Paris (and 420 more throughout France), with varying levels of privacy and luxury as indicated by their coffee-pot rating system. B&B's with three or four *cafetières* have private bath and toilet, those with two involve sharing. Reserve at least 24 hours in advance.

## Short-term Rentals

Studios and one- or two-bedroom flats with kitchenettes, are generally let by the week. Towels, sheets and kitchenware are provided, and there is maid service. A refundable deposit (1,000F-3,500F) is usually payable on arrival. The following is a list of residence hotels:

### Hôtel Résidence des Halles
*4 rue des Halles, 1st (01.40.13.85.80/fax 01.40.13.85.78). M° Châtelet-Les Halles.* **Rates** *studios: 1-2 persons* 550F-650F per night; *3-5 persons* 1,010F per night. *Breakfast* 45F. **Credit** AmEx, DC, MC, V.
Completely renovated in 1996, there are 11 rooms for rent by the day, week or month. Although they lack character, all studios are clean, with a fully equipped kitchen and plenty of light. Some floors have balconies. Lower rates for stays of one week or longer. Centrally located.
**Hotel services** *Conference services. Fax. Laundry. Lift. Minitel.* **Room services** *Kitchen. Room service (24-hour). Safe. Telephone. TV (cable).*

### Le Claridge

*74 av des Champs-Elysées, 8th (01.44.13.33.00/fax 01.42.25.04.88). M° Franklin D Roosevelt.* **Rates** *studios* from 1,080F per night; *two-room flats* from 1,700F; *three-room flats* from 2,700F. **Credit** AmEx, DC, MC, V.

Two hundred clean-cut, rather standard apartments above the Claridge mall, in what was once one of the grandest mansions on the Champs-Elysées. Discounts for longer stays. **Hotel services** *Air-conditioning. Conference services. Fax. Minitel. Laundry. Lift.* **Room services** *Room service (breakfast only). Safe. Telephone. TV (Satellite).*

### Home Plazza Bastille

*74 rue Amelot, 11th (01.40.21.20.00/fax 01.47.00.82.40). M° St Sébastien-Froissart.* **Rates** *studios 1 person* 787F per night; *2 persons* 894F; *3 persons* 1,180F; *4 persons* 1,50F; *5 persons* 1,815F. **Credit** AmEx, DC, MC, V.

Rooms by the day, week or month in this 289-unit residence aimed at the business traveller. Standard rooms are small but attractively decorated. Discounts for longer stays. **Hotel services** *Bar. Babysitting. Business and secretarial services. Health spa. Garden. Restaurant. Parking.* **Room services** *Hairdryer. Telephone. TV (satellite).* **Branch: Home Plazza St-Antoine** 289 bis rue du Fbg-St-Antoine, 11th (01.40.09.40.00).

### Pierre et Vacances Montmartre

*10 place Charles Dullin, 18th (01.42.57.14.55/fax 01.42.54.48.87). M° Anvers.* **Rates** *studios* 555F-890F; *2-room flats* 865F-1,090F; *3-room flats* 1,135F-1,290F. **Credit** AmEx, DC, MC, FTC, V.

A 76-unit, modern complex close to Sacré-Coeur, with apartments that sleep from one to six people. Garden with a few tables, pool table in lobby. Discounts for longer stays. **Hotel services** *Lift. Laundry. TV.* **Branch: Pierre et Vacances Porte de Versailles** 20 rue Oradour-sur-Glane, 15th (01.45.58.45.58). 188 units.

## Rental Agencies

Several agencies specialise in short-term rentals of furnished flats for foreign temporary residents.

### RothRay

*10 rue Nicolas-Flamel, 4th (01.48.87.13.37/fax 01.40.26.34.33). M° Châtelet Les-Halles.* **Open** 8am-6pm Mon-Fri; 8am-1pm Sat. **No credit cards.**

Fully-furnished apartments for lease by the week or longer. All are centrally located – in the Marais, Châtelet or Ile St-Louis. Studios from 9,000F per month.

### De Circourt Associates

*170 rue de Grenelle, 7th (01.47.53.86.38/fax 01.45.51.75.77). M° Latour-Maubourg.* **Open** 9.30am-6.30pm Mon-Fri. **Credit** MC, V.

A professional organisation catering to corporate clients as well as individuals, with over 5,000 furnished long- and short-term flats from 3,500F to 40,000F a month.

### Apalachee Bay

*56 rue Galilée, 8th (01.49.52.01.52/fax 01.40.70.01.37). M° George V.* **Open** 9am-7pm Mon-Fri; 10am-4pm Sat. **Credit** AmEx, DC, MC, V.

Run by two young Englishmen, this agency has flats available for long- or short-term rental. Details on the Internet. http://www.apalachee.com

### Paris Appartements Services

*69 rue d'Argout, 2nd (01.40.28.01.28/fax 01.40.28.92.01). M° Sentier.* **Open** 9am-6pm Mon-Fri. **Credit** AmEx, MC, V.

Forty furnished (IKEA-style) studios and flats in the 1st to the 4th *arrondissements*. Studios from 3,500F per week, one-room flats from 5,250F per week, with maid service: weekly cleaning and changing of linen are included, breakfast can also be arranged, and a 24-hour helpline is available. Lower rates for periods of more than one month. Bilingual staff. *Web Page address: http:www.pariserve.tm.fr/paris-apt/*

## Camping

### Camping du Bois de Boulogne

*2 allée du Bord de l'Eau, Bois de Boulogne, 16th (01.45.24.30.00; fax 01.42.24.42.95). M° Porte Maillot* (free shuttle-bus to campsite during summer) or bus 43. **Open** 24 hours daily. **No credit cards.**

It's unlikely that you'd really come to Paris to camp, but a campsite does exist on the western side of the Bois de Boulogne. Operated on a no-reservations policy, there is no demand in the winter, and huge queues every day during summer. A one- to two-person plot with electricity and water for a tent or caravan costs 125F-132F per night, or 85F-108F per night for a pitch without electricity. Add 22F for each additional person. Reservations are sometimes accepted for large groups.

# Paris by Season

**An all-weather guide to the funkiest festivals, festive foods, farm favourites and keeping up with all things French.**

The national holiday **Bastille Day** (14 July) shows what Republicanism is all about, but although France is a proudly lay state, Catholic tradition also features – especially if, as with the **Fête des Rois**, there's a food angle. French love categorising events into festivals, to cater to all tastes from streetwise hip hop to the most demanding contemporary music. While summer may be the best time for discovering Paris by foot and by the café terrace, it is in winter that the serious arts season takes off with the major exhibitions and heavyweight theatrical productions.

Look out also for promotions such as *La Mairie de Paris vous invite au théâtre*, which offers two seats for the price of one. The Office de Tourisme de Paris at 127 avenue des Champs-Elysées, 8th/ 01.49.52.53.54 (*see chapter* **Essential Information**) should have additional information on the events below closer to the date. For details on each week's events, see listings magazines in **Media**. For additional dance, film, music and sporting events, *see chapters* **Dance, Film, Music: Classical & Opera, Music: Rock, Roots & Jazz** *and* **Sport & Fitness**.

*Political bull at the* **Salon de l'Agriculture**.

## Spring

### Salon de l'Agriculture

*Parc des Expositions de Paris, Porte de Versailles, 15th (01.49.09.60.00). M° Porte de Versailles.* **Dates** late February-early Mar. **Open** 9am-7pm. **Admission** 50F.
Rural France comes to town to create the largest farm in the world. Farmers inspect perfectly groomed sheep, manicured pigs and subsidy-hungry machinery, then repair to the food and drink hall to sample regional produce. If there's an election on the horizon, politicians will also be out in force.

### La Nuit des Publivores

*Rex or Palais des Congrès (01.42.89.23.28).* **Date** March.
An unmissable treat for ad addicts – new and old ads from around the world are screened all night, with breaks for ice cream. The atmosphere is like a joyous pop concert, with applause for faves and hisses for the cheesy.

### Foire du Trône

*Pélouse de Reuilly, Bois de Vincennes, 12th (01.46.27.52.29). M° Porte Dorée.* **Dates** end Mar-end May. **Open** 2pm-midnight Mon-Thur, Sun; 2pm-1am Fri, Sat, eve of public holidays. **Admission** free; rides 10F-20F.
The largest funfair in France arrives with all the thrills of a huge Ferris wheel, haunted houses, plus *barbe à papa* (candy floss) and other sticky treats, plus old-fashioned (and surely not politically correct) fairground attractions and freak shows from fortune tellers to bearded ladies.

### Le Chemin de la Croix

*square Willette, 18th. M° Anvers or Abbesses.* **Date** 12.30pm Good Friday.
A large crowd follows the Archbishop of Paris, Cardinal Lustiger, from the bottom of the hill of Montmartre up the steps to the Sacré Coeur, as he performs the fourteen traditional stations of the cross.

### Festival EXIT

*Maison des Arts et de la Culture de Créteil, pl Salvador Allende, 94000 Créteil (01.45.13.19.19). M° Créteil-Préfecture.* **Dates** late Mar-early Apr. **Tickets** 100F.
A festival of avant-garde dance, theatre and performance, launched in 1994, has made an immediate impact with its radical multi-national programming.

### Banlieues Bleues

*Seine St-Denis and area.* **Information** (01.43.85.66.00). **Dates** late Mar-early Apr. **Admission** 70F-150F.
Held in the Paris suburbs, this festival draws some of the greatest names in jazz, blues, r'n'b, soul and funk. Noted for quirky world-jazz acts and cross-cultural collaborations.

### April Fool's Day

*All over France.* **Date** 1 Apr.
Known to the French as *Poisson d'Avril*, the April fish. The big idea is to try to stick a paper fish to some unsuspecting sucker's back. French journalists pride themselves on putting April Fool's tricks on the public.

### Paris Marathon

*Starts around 9am av des Champs-Elysées, first runners finish about 11am av Foch.* **Information** *AMSP, 17 rue de Sévigné, 4th (01.53.17.03.10).* **Date** one Sun, mid-late Apr.
One of the world's biggest marathons, with a route that takes in some of the city's most famous sites. Huge crowds encourage the runners. *See also chapter* **Sport & Fitness**.

### Foire de Paris

*Parc des Expositions de Paris, Porte de Versailles, 15th.*
*M° Porte de Versailles.* **Information** *(01.49.09.60.00).*
**Dates** end Apr-early May. **Admission** about 50F.
This giant fair is a sort of amalgam of the Ideal Home and
the Food & Wine fairs. Also has sport and leisure sections.

### May Day

**Date** 1 May. **Information** *(01.45.51.22.15).*
Labour Day is the most ardently maintained of all public
holidays, far outdoing Christmas or New Year. All museums
and monuments (not the Eiffel Tower) are closed and unions
and leftist groups stage a colourful march through working-
class eastern Paris. The Bastille is a popular place to watch.

### Vintage Car Rally, Montmartre

*Departure 10am rue Lepic. arrive pl du Tertre, 18th.*
*M° Abbesses or Anvers.* **Information** *(01.46.06.79.56).*
**Dates** Sun closest to 15 May.
This is one of the oldest annual vintage car races in the
world. Crowds line the streets to cheer beautiful old vehicles
up the steep streets of Montmartre. 1998 is a bumper year
for Renault, date of its 100th birthday.

### Les Cinq Jours de l'Objet Extraordinaire

*rues du Bac, de Lille, de Beaune, des Sts-Pères, de*
*l'Universite and quai Voltaire, 7th. M° Rue du Bac or*
*St-Germain-des-Prés.* **Information** *(01.42.60.36.47).*
**Date** third week of May. **Admission** free.
For five days, antique dealers each showcase one item, all
chosen around a theme. Participating shops are decorated
with flowers, and red carpets down the pavements mark out
the relevant streets. Special evening and Sunday openings.

## Summer

### Salon d'Art Contemporain de Montrouge

*Mairie de Montrouge, 43 rue Emile Boutrouq, 92000*
*Montrouge (01.46.12.75.73). M° Porte d'Orléans, then*
*bus 68, 126 or 128.* **Dates** May. **Admission** free.
Contemporary art exhibition for new artists held in a
working-class suburb. Some 2,000 painters, sculptors and
photographers submit work, but only a few end up on show.

### French Tennis Open

*Stade Roland Garros, 2 av Gordon Bennett, 16th*
*(01.47.43.48.00). M° Porte d'Auteuil.* **Dates** late May-
early June.
The international tennis circus descends on Paris for the
French Grand Slam tournament. A very glitzy event.

### St Denis Festival

*Various venues in St-Denis. M° St-Denis Basilique.*
**Information** *(0148.13.06.07).* **Dates** June-early July.
Classical music festival offers the pleasure of hearing top-
class choirs and orchestras amid the Gothic splendour of St-
Denis Basilique and in other historic buildings in the suburb.

### Open Weekend at the Garde Républicaine

*12 bd Henri IV, 4th (01.42.76.13.13). M° Sully-Morland.*
**Date** one weekend in mid June.
Polished horses, gleaming weaponry, booming brass as the
historic regiment and presidential guard opens its doors.

### Festival Chopin à Paris

*Orangerie de Bagatelle, parc de Bagatelle, Bois de*
*Boulogne, 16th. M° Porte Maillot, then bus 244.*
**Information** *(01.45.00.22.19).* **Dates** mid June-
mid July, 8.45pm Mon-Fri; 4.30pm, 8.45pm Sat, Sun.
**Admission** 100F-150F plus 10F entry to park.
An annual treat for piano lovers, staged in the Orangerie of
the Bagatelle gardens. Evening concerts are candlelit.

### Fête de la Musique

*All over Paris.* **Information** *(01.40.03.94.70).*
**Date** 21 June, noon on.
Steel bands, salsa parades, wandering accordionists and
classical string quartets are just part of the fun on the longest
day of the year, when thousands of musicians give free concerts all over the city. Traditionally there is a big name free
rock concert at place de la République, indie rock bands at
place Denfert-Rochereau and a top-class classical orchestra

# That August feeling

You may be surprised to arrive in a city where
every shop window appears to consist of brown
paper and where you'll hear English, German,
Italian, Japanese but not much French. In
August, the city is as beautiful as ever, but ever
since 1936, when paid holidays
were first granted by the Front
Populaire, Parisians have fled en
masse in August and the city
abandons any pretence of being
a cultural, shopping or gourmet
capital. For some signs of indige-
nous life, try Paris' poorer
*quartiers* (mainly in the east),
where the population is less able to afford holidays. The orchestras are on the Riviera, impoverished artists have left their garrets for some
southern château, DJs will have decamped to
Ibiza, St Tropez, La Baule or Biarritz, and restau-

rants, except those aiming firmly at tourists, pull
down their blinds. What cars there are are even
more dangerous than usual, as they speed along
half-empty streets (much parking is free). Worst
of all, there's the crisis of the *baguette* (remember that the French Revolution
began with a shortage of bread),
as you're forced tramp the pavements in search of a baker who
is open. By law, bakers within an
area have to arrange among
themselves, so that at least one
remains open, but an unfamiliar
*baguette*, a change of flour in a
*pain de campagne*, such details constitute a crisis. The French love their holidays, but there's a
palpable sense of relief in the streets, and a feeling that life can begin again, on the last weekend
of August, when everyone is back in town.

in the courtyard of the Palais-Royal. Many more anarchic gigs are put on by local cafés or bars or by street musicians.

## Feux de la St-Jean/Fireworks at La Villette
*Quai St-Bernard, 5th. Mᵒ Gare d'Austerlitz. Parc de la Villette, 19th (01.40.03.75.03). Mᵒ Porte de la Villette or Porte de Pantin.* **Dates** mid June. **Admission** free.
The feast of St John the Baptist is traditionally celebrated in France with fireworks, in Paris along the Seine. At roughly the same date, there's an arty fireworks affair at La Villette on the banks of the Canal de l'Ourcq, designed by a leading designer or architect, working with a team of pyrotechnic wizards.

## Gay Pride March
**Information** *(01.47.70.01.50).* **Date** 28 June.
The colourful parade by gays and lesbians traditionally goes from République via the Marais to Beaubourg, but on some years takes in Montparnasse and St-Germain. *See also chapter* **Gay & Lesbian Paris**.

## La Course des Garçons de Café
*Starts and finishes Hôtel de Ville, pl de l'Hôtel de Ville, 4th. Mᵒ Hôtel-de-Ville. Information (01.46.33.89.89).* **Date** a Sunday in late June-early July.
A highlight of the alternative sporting year as over 500 bona fide café waiters and waitresses in uniform – bow-ties, aprons, the lot – and tray in hand race over an 8km circuit via the Grands Boulevards and St-Germain-des-Près. Any breakage during the race disqualifies the participant.

## Fête du Cinéma
*All over Paris.* **Dates** 3 days, end June.
Movie-goers get a passport which allows them to see as many films as they like for 10F each time, after paying normal entry for the first film.

## Grandes Fêtes de Nuit de Versailles
*Bassin de Neptune, Parc du Château de Versailles. RER C Versailles Rive Gauche. Information (01.39.50.36.22).* **Dates** 10.30pm, two Saturdays in July; 10pm, two Saturdays in Sept. **Admission** 70F-185F.
The sound and light spectacular in the gardens of the Château de Versailles attempts to recreate the spirit of the lavish court pageants given by Louis XIV. Costume scenes, dance and music are acted out against a background of fireworks and Le Nôtre's Baroque fountains. For further details on Versailles, *see chapter* **Trips Out of Town**.

## La Goutte d'Or en Fête
*pl Léon, 18th. Mᵒ Barbès-Rochechouart.* **Information** *(01.42.62.11.13).* **Dates** usually first week of July. **Admission** free.
This music festival was initiated to restore pride to the poor, largely Arab and African Goutte d'Or district (*see chapter* **The Right Bank**), and has been so successful that external promoters have begun to move in on it. *Raï*, rap and reggae, with young local performers playing alongside established names on the world music scene.

## La Villette Jazz Festival
*Parc de la Villette, 211 av Jean-Jaurès, 19th (01.40.03.75.75). Mᵒ Porte de Pantin.* **Dates** end June-early July. **Admission** 140F; 110F unemployed, students; some concerts free.
After a whole decade, the Halle that Jazz festival has been renamed to mark its colonialisation of the entire La Villette complex. Big jazz, blues and Latin names perform in the Grande Halle, more experimental crossover types at the Hot Brass or Cité de la Musique and freebie events in smaller bar spaces or in the park itself.

## Bastille Day (Le Quatorze Juillet)
*All over France.* **Information** *(01.49.52.53.54).* **Dates** 13 July (evening), all day 14 July.
Bastille Day, the French national holiday, commemorates 14 July 1789, the date of the storming of the Bastille prison, the start of the French Revolution and a foretaste of much bloodier events to come. The day has come to symbolise the uprising and the republican ideals of *liberté, egalité* and *fraternité*. Celebrations start on the evening of 13 July, when Parisians dance and revel in the Bastille square, and in other parts of the city, particularly the Trocadéro-Champ-de-Mars area. Less dangerous partying takes place at the firemen's balls organised in local *casernes de pompiers*. The fire stations of rue de Sévigné, rue du Vieux-Colombier, rue Blanche and boulevard de Port-Royal are renowned for throwing a mean *bal* (usually on both 13 and 14 July). There's a big Gay Ball outside along the quai de la Tournelle in the 5th.
At 10am on the 14th crowds line the Champs-Elysées to watch the President lead a military parade from the Arc de Triomphe to the place de la Concorde. Colourful jet formations roar overhead, and deafening tanks, elite regiments and weaponry galore pay testimony to France's military might. The biggest round of applause is reserved for the fire brigade bringing up the rear. Arrive early if you want a view, and note that the Métro stops along the Champs are closed. Thousands gather at the Champ-de-Mars for the best view of the evening firework display at Trocadéro.

## Paris, Quartier d'Eté
*Various venues around Paris.* **Information** *L'Eté Parisien, 43 rue de Rivoli, 1st (box office 01.44.83.64.40).* **Dates** 14 July-15 Aug. **Admission** Varies, some events free.
Proof that life does go on in Paris after Bastille Day. Most venues are outdoors with classical and world music concerts, dance and other entertainment in parks and squares such as the Arènes de Lutèce, the Luxembourg gardens, the Palais Royal and the Tuileries, and a wildly eclectic international array of participants.

**Bastille Day** *is celebrated with a bang.*

**Tour de France** *cyclists race to the finish.*

### Le Cinéma en Plein Air
*Parc de la Villette, 19th (01.40.03.75.03). M° Porte de Pantin.* **Dates** 15 July-15 Aug approx. **Admission** free.
Outdoor film festival where movie greats are projected on to a huge screen in the park.

### Tour de France
*Finishes on the Champs-Elysées.* **Information** *(01.49.35.69.00).* **Date** third or fourth Sun in July.
As much a fixture of French life as the *képi* and the *quatorze juillet*. The cyclists enter Paris by different routes each year, but the race always finishes on the Champs-Elysées. *See also* chapter **Sport & Fitness.**

### Fête de l'Assomption
*Cathédrale Notre Dame, pl Notre Dame, 4th (01.42.34.56.10). M° Cité.* **Date** 15 Aug. **Admission** free.
Assumption Day renders Notre Dame a place of religious rather than touristic pilgrimage. A huge procession parades around the Ile de la Cité behind a statue of the Virgin.

## Autumn

### Fête de L'Humanité
*Parc de la Courneuve, 93 La Courneuve. RER B Aubervilliers-La Courneuve-Aubervilliers, then bus 150 or 249.* **Information** *(01.49.22.72.72).* **Dates** second weekend of Sept. **Admission** 50F; free under-12s.
The vast annual Communist Party bash put on by its newspaper *L'Humanité* is not what it used to be, although a right-wing government in power helps. Expect political debates, political literature, street theatre and lots of food stalls. Best of all, though, are the concerts played by big names plus lots of home grown pop, jazz and world music talent.

### Journées Portes Ouvertes
*Various venues in Paris and the rest of France.* **Information** *(01.44.61.20.00).* **Date** weekend closest to 15 Sept.
A chance to visit a government office or ministry. The extra-ordinary popularity of this annual two days of 'Open Doors' is demonstrated by the thousands of Parisians who queue for hours for the right to enter the Elysée Palace (home of the President), Matignon (home of the Prime Minister), Palais Royal or Palais du Luxembourg, driven by curiosity and the democratic need to step on their leaders' carpets. If you don't like waiting, seek out some of the more obscure embassies, ministries and private mansions normally off-limits to the public. *Le Monde* and *Le Parisien* give detailed information, as does the Hôtel de Sully, 62 rue St-Antoine, 4th.

### Festival d'Automne
*Various venues.* **Information** *56 rue de Rivoli, 1st (01.42.96.96.94).* **Dates** 15 Sept-31 Dec. **Admission** 100F-250F.
A high-brow challenge to the senses as world-class performers present experimental theatre, music and contemporary dance productions at such prestige venues as the Théâtre de la Ville, Odéon-Théâtre de l'Europe and the big public theatres in the suburbs (*see chapter* **Theatre**). The Festival regularly features leading international directors. Programmes are available by mail.

### Fêtes des Vendanges à Montmartre
*All over Montmartre and in the Mairie of the 18th arrondissement, 1 pl Jules-Joffrin, 18th. M° Abbesses, Lamarck-Caulaincourt or Jules-Joffrin.* **Information** *Syndicat d'Initiative, pl du Tertre, 18th (01.42.62.21.21).* **Date** first Sat in Oct.
The grape harvest at the last remaining vineyard of the many that once covered the hill of Montmartre is celebrated with much pomp in a colourful parade from the Mairie to the vineyard and back again. Local residents dress up in nineteenth-century garb, bands parade and speeches are made.

### Prix de l'Arc de Triomphe
*Hippodrome de Longchamp, Bois de Boulogne, 16th (01.49.10.20.30). M° Porte d'Auteuil.* **Date** first weekend in Oct. **Admission** *lawns* free, *enclosure* 50F.
France's première horse race, when *le tout-Paris* take their best frocks and champagne coolers out for a canter. *See also* chapter **Sport & Fitness**.

### FIAC (Foire Internationale d'Art Contemporain)
*Espace Eiffel Branly, 29-55 quai Branly, 7th (info OIP 01.41.90.47.80). M° Bir-Hakeim/RER Champ-de-Mars-Tour Eiffel.* **Dates** early Oct. **Admission** 60F.
One of the main events on the international contemporary art calendar: over 150 galleries are represented, around half of them foreign. FIAC has moved to the temporary Espace Eiffel-Branly while repairs are carried out on the Grand Palais. After some dismal, staid years, things looked up in 1996 as a slimmed-down fair put the emphasis back on the contemporary. *See also* chapter **Galleries**.

### Artistes à la Bastille/Le Génie de la Bastille
*Artists' studios in the Bastille area. M° Bastille.* **Information** *Artistes à la Bastille (01.47.00.80.78). Génie de la Bastille (01.40.09.84.03).* **Dates** four days mid-Oct. **Admission** free.
The best established of the many artists' studio open weekends takes place in the Bastille area, where thousands of artists moved into old furniture workshops since the seventies. Currently put on by two rival organisations, it's an interesting way to see the varied work of hundreds of painters, sculptors, engravers, photographers and designers and the places where they work. *See also* chapter **Galleries.**

### Salon du Champignon
*Jardin des Plantes, 36 rue Geoffroy-St-Hilaire, 5th (01.40.79.36.00). M° Gare d'Austerlitz.* **Dates** mid Oct-late Oct. **Admission** free.
Autumn means wild mushroom season and even in the Paris area, keen mushroom hunters head off to the Forest of Fontainebleau to seek them out. This festival is of scientific and culinary interest, with hundreds of specimens on show and mycologists on hand to help identify those safe to eat.

### All Saint's Day
*All over France.* **Date** 1 Nov.
Halloween celebrations are seen as an American import, but 1 Nov is a public holiday, and cemetery visiting is big business, traditionally accompanied by chrysanthemums.

### Festival Fnac-Inrockuptibles
*La Cigale and other venues.* **Dates** four days beg Nov.
**Admission** tickets from Fnac.
Indie rock and retro pop are the name of the game at the annual rock festival, which has introduced such acts as Beck, Fiona Apple and Gorky's Zygotic Mynci to Paris. *Les Inrocks* has also proved itself open to new influences like easy listening and trip hop.

### Marjolaine
*Parc Floral de Paris, Bois de Vincennes, 12th.*
*M° Château de Vincennes, then shuttle bus.*
**Information** *(01.43.43.92.95).* **Date** Ten days early Nov. **Admission** 45F.
Paris is hardly famed as a green destination but this annual Salon for the ecologically minded has existed since the 1970s and – helped by a few mad cows, nuclear tests, etc – grows bigger by the year. Some 450 stands dispense organic foods and wines, handmade gifts, household, health and beauty products and inform on environmental organisations from Greenpeace to cycling campaigns.

### Armistice Day
*Arc de Triomphe, 8th. M° Charles de Gaulle-Etoile.* **Date** 11 Nov.
There is no military parade at the remembrance ceremony for the dead of both World Wars. Wreaths are laid by the President and others at the Tomb of the Unknown Soldier under the Arc de Triomphe.

### Fête du Beaujolais Nouveau
*All over France.* **Date** third Thur in Nov.
The first day of the arrival of each year's Beaujolais Nouveau is no longer the event it was a few years ago, but wine bars and cafés still attract the crowds (some of them from midnight on Wednesday, but especially on Thursday evening) who gather to assess the new vintage and deem its bouquet banana or blackberry.

*All dressed up for the* **Fête de Vendanges**.

## Winter

### La Crèche sur le Parvis
*pl de l'Hôtel de Ville, 4th (01.42.76.40.40). M° Hôtel-de-Ville.* **Dates** early Dec-early Jan. **Admission** 30F.
Every year the City Hall of Paris invites a city to install life-size Nativity scenes under a tent at the place de l'Hôtel de Ville. Proceeds go to charity.

### Africolor
*Théâtre Gérard Philippe, 59 bd Jules-Guesde, 93 St-Denis (01.48.13.70.00). M° St-Denis Basilique.* **Dates** three or four days leading up to 24 Dec. **Admission** 110F.
African music fest promises a melting pot of traditional and Western-influenced sounds from across the African continent, culminating in a big all-night party on Christmas Eve.

### Christmas
**Date** *Christmas Eve* 24 Dec, *Christmas Day* 25 Dec.
Christmas is a family affair, with a dinner (on Christmas Eve) that traditionally includes *foie gras* or oysters, goose or turkey and a rich yule log *(bûche de Noël)* of chocolate, sponge and/or ice cream. On Christmas Eve, the **Cathédrale Notre Dame de Paris** is packed for the 11pm service.

### New Year's Eve
*av des Champs-Elysées and all over Paris.* **Date** 31 Dec.
On the *Fête de St Sylvestre,* tourists and teenagers crowd the avenue des Champs-Elysées and let off bangers.

### La Grande Parade de Montmartre
*Departs pl Pigalle, 18th, M° Pigalle. Arrives 3pm pl Jules-Joffrin, M° Jules Joffrin.* **Information** *(SIVM 01.42.62.21.21).* **Date** 1 Jan, 2pm.
This colourful parade does its best to rouse Paris out of its post-New Year's Eve hangover.

### Epiphany (Fête des Rois)
*All over France.* **Date** 6 Jan.
On the Feast of the Three Kings pâtisseries sell thousands of *galettes des rois,* a flaky pastry cake with an almond filling in which a *fève* or tiny charm is hidden. Whoever finds the charm dons a cardboard crown (given with each *galette*), becomes king or queen for a day, and chooses a consort.

### Commemorative Mass for Louis XVI
*Chapelle Expiatoire, 29 rue Pasquier, 8th (01.42.65.35.80). M° St-Augustin.* **Date** Sun closest to 21 Jan.
Members of France's aristocracy gather with die-hard royalists and assorted other far-right crackpots to mourn the beheading of Louis XVI on 21 January 1793. Firm republicans are supposed to mark the day by eating *tête de veau.*

### Festival Mondial du Cirque du Demain
*Cirque d'Hiver Bouglione, 110 rue Amelot, 11th. M° Filles du Calvaire.* **Information** *(01.48.04.30.30).* **Dates** five days end Jan. **Admission** 70F-150F.
Young circus *artistes* teeter on high wires, clown, juggle or contort to catch the eye of any ring master in the audience. This is the springboard for many innovative talents who go on to join top modern troupes like Plume or Archaos.

### Chinese New Year Festival
*Around av d'Ivry and av de Choisy, 13th. M° Porte de Choisy or Porte d'Ivry.* **Information** *Association Culturelle Franco-Chinoise (01.45.20.74.09).* **Date** in Jan or Feb.
Chinatown comes alive to the sound of fireworks and the clash of cymbals, as dragon dancers snake between the tower blocks to usher in the Chinese New Year. Whatever day the New Year actually falls, the main festivities take place on the nearest weekend. Belleville, the right-bank Chinese area, is quiet by comparison.

# Sightseeing

**A run-down of Paris' sights: the stunning palaces, colossal cathedrals, spectacular squares and historic bridges.**

You may think you know Paris' best sights; but no matter how often you've seen the **Eiffel Tower** or **Arc de Triomphe** in photos or on television, nothing diminishes the power of discovering the real thing for yourself. What's more, visiting them is usually easy, since most places are within walking distance of each other, or a short Métro ride. The major museums included below are mainly covered in their architectural and historical context; for more on the collections within, *see chapter* **Museums**. For more about the places listed here in their Parisian context, *see chapters* **The Islands, The Right Bank** *and* **The Left Bank**.

If you are visiting several sights in a short period, the **Paris Carte Musées et Monuments** pass is a good investment, *see chapter* **Museums**.

## Focal Points

### Arc de Triomphe

*pl Charles de Gaulle (access via underground passage), 8th (01.43.80.31.31). M° Charles de Gaulle-Etoile.* **Open** *Oct-Mar* 10am-5.30pm daily; *Apr-Sept* 9am-6.30pm Mon-Thur, Sat, Sun; 9.30am-9.30pm Fri. Closed public holidays. **Admission** 32F; 21F 18-25s; 15F 12-17s; free under-12s. **Credit** (shop only) AmEx, MC, V.

At the western end of the **Champs-Elysées**, the Arc de Triomphe forms the centrepiece of Paris' grand east-west axis from the **Louvre**, through the Arc du Carrousel and the **place de la Concorde** on one side, and up to the **Grande Arche de la Défense** on the other. The Arc – a modest 50m (164ft) tall, 45m (148ft) wide and decorated with a giant frieze of battle scenes and sculptures on its flanks, including Rude's famous *Le Départ des Volontaires*, also known as *Le Marseillaise* – was commissioned by Napoléon in 1806 as a tribute to his own military victories, but was only completed in 1836. In 1920 the Tomb of the Unknown Soldier was laid at the arch's base, and an eternal flame burns to commemorate the dead of World Wars I and II. The manic drivers zooming around the arch turn place Charles de Gaulle into a race track, but fortunately there's a subway. You can reach the top of the arch via lift or steps, from where you can appreciate the masterful geometry of Haussmann's subsequent great redesign of Paris, with its uniform facades designed by Hittorff and twelve radiating avenues, which include some of the smartest residential streets in the city. Queues build up at the foot of the arch, so try to arrive early.

### Cathédrale Notre Dame de Paris

*pl du Parvis-Notre-Dame, 4th (01.42.34.56.10). M° Cité.* **Open** 8am-6.45pm Mon-Fri, Sun; 8am-12.30pm, 2-6.45pm, Sat. **Admission** free. *Towers* (01.44.32.16.70) entrance at foot of north tower. **Open** *from June 1997,* probably 9.30am-6pm daily. **Admission** ring for details. **No credit cards.**

It's said that all the roads of Paris lead to the *Kilomètre Zéro* in the square in front of Notre Dame Cathedral on the Ile de la Cité. Catholics and, equally devoutly, tourists from all over the world come to pay homage to the Gothic masterpiece. Begun in 1163 by Bishop Maurice de Sully, keen to outdo the impressive new abbey at **St-Denis**, it was not completed until 1345, and has since been altered and renovated many times. The cathedral straddles two architectural eras, echoing the great galleried churches of the twelfth century and looking forward to the buttressed cathedrals, such as **Chartres**, which were to follow. Among its most famous features are the three glorious rose windows on the transepts and on the west front.

During the Revolution, the cathedral was turned into a temple of reason and a wine warehouse, and the statues of the kings were destroyed by anti-royalists – those seen today are nineteenth-century replicas. Unexpectedly, several of the originals were discovered in 1979 and are now on show at the **Musée National du Moyen Age**. The structure had fallen into such a state of delapidation by the early nineteenth century that artists, politicians and writers, among them Victor Hugo, petitioned King Louis-Philippe to restore the cathedral, which was masterfully done by Viollet-Le-Duc. During the Nazi occupation, all the panes from the stained-glass windows were removed, numbered and replaced with sandbags to save them from destruction. Renovation work continues today, as sculptures are being cleaned and in places replaced, but once the tower visit reopens (probably

**Cathédrale Notre Dame** *inspires high jinks.*

# carte musées monuments
## the Paris museum pass

Valid for 1, 3 or 5 days, the museum pass gives wait-free admission to see the permanent collections of 70 museums and sights in and around Paris.

On sale in museums, monuments, metro stations, at the Tourist Information Bureau (Carrousel du Louvre), and at the Paris Tourist Office.

## LA VUE PARISIENNE

TO THE TOP IN 38 SECONDS

OPEN DAILY
9.30am -11pm

### TOUR MONTPARNASSE
Tous les jours, tous les soirs.
56e étage et terrasse.
M° Montparnasse-Bienvenüe

### PANORAMIC VISIT
Every day, every night.
56th floor and terrace.
Tel: (33-1) 45 38 52 56

June 1997) you can once again take the dim staircase up the north bell tower, leading to a gallery adorned with gargoyles who peruse the surrounding view with weary malice. Walk around the back of the cathedral for the best view of its arched flying buttresses. *See also chapter* **The Islands**.

## Eiffel Tower

*Champ de Mars, 7th (01.44.11.23.45/recorded information 01.44.11.23.23). M° Bir-Hakeim/RER Champ-de-Mars.* **Open** *1 Jan-12 June* 9am-11pm; *13 June-31 Aug* 9am-midnight; *Sept-Dec* 9am-11pm daily. **Admission** *By lift* 1st storey 20F/10F (4-12s); 2nd storey 42F/21F (4-12s); 3rd storey 57F/28F (4-12s). *By stairs* 1st & 2nd storeys only 12F. **No credit cards.**
What for many is the symbol of Paris was the tallest building in the world at 300m (984ft) when built in 1889 for the Exposition Universelle on the centenary of the Revolution. Now, with the addition of an aerial, it reaches to 321m (1,053ft). The view of it from Trocadéro across the river is monumental, but the distorted aspect from its base most dramatically shows off the graceful ironwork of Gustave Eiffel. Be prepared for a long wait for a ride in the lifts, as the tower gets four million visitors a year, its present popularity contrasting with the spluttering indignation which greeted its construction. To save time and money you can stop at the first or second platform, but those who travel all the way to the top can view Gustave Eiffel's cosy salon and enjoy amazing panoramas: up to 67km (42 miles) on a good day. The queue is not so long at night, when the city lights against the Seine live up to their romantic image. There's a brasserie on the first level, and the smart Jules Verne restaurant on the second, as well as a post office and souvenir shops.

## La Grande Arche de la Défense

*Paris la Défense (01.49.07.27.57). M° Grande Arche de la Défense.* **Open** *Apr-Oct* 9am-8pm daily (roof-top closes one hour later); *Nov-Mar* 10am-6pm Mon-Sat; 9am-7pm Sun, public holidays (roof-top closes one hour later). **Admission** 40F; 30F under-18s, students, unemployed. **No credit cards.**
Planned to complete the axis of the Champs-Elysées and the Arc de Triomphe – and then skewed at a slight angle – the Grande Arche is simultaneously one of the most pointless and most successful of the *Grands Projets*, providing a landmark amid the previously featureless towers of Paris' modern business reservation in the western suburbs. It also catapulted the obscure Danish architect Johan Otto von Spreckelsen to fame, although he died before it was completed. British engineer Peter Rice finished the work and designed the canvas 'clouds' suspended in the arch's aperture. Only from close up do you realise quite how vast the structure is, as the arch's cuboid form disguises its immense height. A stomach-churning ride in high-speed glass lifts takes you up through the 'clouds' to the roof where there is an exhibition space and a bird's eye view into Paris and out to the city's western reaches. *See also chapter* **Paris by Area: Beyond the Périphérique**.

## Palais & Musée National du Louvre

*entrance through Pyramid, Cour Napoléon, 1st (01.40.20.50.50/recorded information 01.40.20.51.51). M° Palais-Royal.* **Open** 9am-9.45pm Mon (only the Aile Richelieu) & Wed (last tickets 9.15pm); 9am-6pm Thur-Sun (last tickets 5.15pm). *Temporary exhibitions* 10am-10pm Mon, Wed-Sun. *Medieval Louvre* 9am-9.30pm Mon, Wed-Sun **Admission** 45F (until 3pm) 26F (Mon, Wed-Sat after 3pm, Sun); free under-18s, first Sun of month. *Temporary exhibitions* admission varies. **Credit** (bookshop only) AmEx, MC, V.
Arguably the greatest art collection in the world. The Louvre's miles of galleries take in the sculptures of ancient Syria, Rome and Greece, and such cultural icons as the *Mona Lisa*, the Venus de Milo, Géricault's *Raft of the Medusa* and Delacroix's *Liberty Leading the People*. The palace itself is the largest in Europe, and was home to generations of French monarchs from the fourteenth century onwards. Although it looks homogeneous, it was built over several centuries. One consequence of the recent renovation is that a section of its massive walls of the original twelfth-century keep built by King Philippe-Auguste and still hidden within the later building, is now open to view in the underground complex that forms the new main entrance to the museum. In the 1540s, François 1er asked Pierre Lescot to begin constructing a new Renaissance palace; continued by his successors, it is now the enclosed Cour Carrée, at the eastern end of the building, its walls etched with royal monograms – H interlaced with C and D for Henri II, his queen Catherine de Médicis and favourite Diane de Poitiers. Henri IV and Louis XIII completed the Cour Carrée and built the wing along the Seine. Napoléon built the galleries along the rue de Rivoli, complete with matching figures – now houses the independently run **Musée des Arts Décoratifs**, newly expanded **Musée de la Mode et du Textile** and **Musée**

---

# Walk the meridian way

Keep your eyes to the ground. Paris' most minimalist monument is also its longest. In 1806, François Arago, French astronomer and politician, was commissioned to continue plotting the French meridian from France to the Balearic Islands, soon to become an invaluable source to geographers and the French navy – until, that is, the British declared Greenwich in London as the new meridian.

In his honour, a bronze statue of Arago was erected in 1893 and dominated the little square of l'Ile-de-Sein – where the meridian crosses boulevard Arago – until 1942, when it was one of many to be melted down during the war. Today, only the statue's socle remains on this spot. Fascinated by Arago's achievements, Dutch artist Jan Dibbets wanted to create a new memorial with a modern twist, or what he saw as 'an imaginary monument realised along the length of an imaginary line, the Paris meridian'. Dibbets set to work on his non-monumental monument, and embedded 135 bronze medallions, carrying both the name of Arago and the north-south axis, along the Paris meridian line. Individually, the medallions may be small, but they cover the entire length of Paris, running through the 18th *arrondissement*, the 9th, 2nd, 1st, 6th and 14th, and just happening to pass through some of the city's most celebrated sights, among them the **Jardin du Luxembourg**, the **Louvre**, **Palais-Royal**, **Sacré-Coeur**, **Parc Montsouris**, boulevard Haussmann, rue de Rivoli, rue de Seine, and boulevard St-Germain.

---

de la Publicité (entrance on rue de Rivoli); and his nephew Napoléon III added the Cour Napoléon.

After the court left for **Versailles** under Louis XIV, most of the Louvre was given over to offices and apartments for a multifarious variety of state servants. The museum collection was first opened to the public in 1793, but the last government department, the Ministry of Finance, remained in the palace until the 1980s, when the Louvre's latest great transformation, the *Grand Louvre* project, began. One major feature of it has been the opening of the Richelieu Wing in 1993, which doubled the exhibition area; another, the best-known and most controversial, is IM Pei's wonderful glass pyramid in the Cour Napoléon, opened in 1989 on the bicentenary of the Revolution. It now dominates and provides the main entrance to the museum. West of the pyramid, the little Arc du Carrousel, with its rose-coloured marble columns, was erected in 1806-9 to commemorate Napoléon's victories in 1805. It served as a gateway to the Tuileries Palace, burned down in 1871, and is linked visually to the greater Arc de Triomphe by the Champs-Elysées and the Tuileries. The arch now triumphs above an underground shopping and restaurant development, the Carrousel du Louvre, opened in 1993, the new venue for the fashion shows and another dramatic element in the *Grand Louvre* project. To avoid the queues you can also enter direct from the Carrousel du Louvre, at 99 rue de Rivoli or direct from Palais-Royal Métro.

## Attractions

### Forum des Halles
*1st. M°/RER Châtelet-Les Halles.*
Pickpockets, drug dealers, pleasure-seekers and the homeless prowl around what was the site of the old central produce market of Paris, transferred to suburban Rungis in 1969. There had been markets here since 1181, but their heyday came last century, when Haussmann commissioned Baltard to construct large pavilions of cast iron and steel to house them. What now stands in their place is the Forum des Halles, a giant underground shopping mall which incorporates the **Ciné Cité** multiplex cinema, the **Vidéothèque de Paris** and a swimming pool, as well as lots of mainly mass-market clothing chains and large branches of **Fnac** and Habitat. The first part of the centre was completed in 1979, and the second phase near the Bourse du Commerce added in 1986. Both are now severely shabby, but as much as you may try to avoid them, you're bound to end up here at sometime if only because of the vast Métro and RER interchange which emerges through the Forum's depths.

### Manufacture des Gobelins
*42 av des Gobelins, 13th (01.44.08.52.00). M° Gobelins.*
**Open** 2-3pm Tue-Thur. **Admission** 45F; 35F 7-25s, over-60s; free under 7s. **No credit cards.**
Tapestries have been woven on this site almost continuously since 1662 when Colbert, Louis XIV's gifted jack of all trades, set up the Manufacture Royale des Meubles de la Coronne. Also known as the Gobelins after Jean Gobelin, a fifteenth-century dyer who previously owned the site, the factory was at its wealthiest during the *ancien régime* when thousands of tapestries were produced for royal residences under the direction of artists such as Le Brun and Oudry. Today tapestries are still woven (almost) exclusively for the state and visitors can watch weavers at work on pieces destined for French ministries and embassies around the world. The guided tour (in French) through the 1912 factory gives you a chance to understand the time-consuming weaving process and includes a visit to the Savonnerie carpet workshops next door. The tour also takes in the eighteenth-century chapel and the Beauvais tapestry workshops.

*The **Palais du Louvre** is the paradigm of pyramid power.*

### Marché aux Puces de St-Ouen (Clignancourt)
*93400 St-Ouen. M° Porte de Clignancourt.* **Open** 7.30am-6.30pm Mon, Sat, Sun.
Irrestible for lovers of antiques and bric-a-brac, the Puces de St-Ouen is the city's largest flea market, composed of several small arcades of semi-permanent stalls, most of them running off the rue des Rosiers. You can find almost anything here, and quality (and prices) at many of the antiques dealers is high, from Louis XV armchairs and Art Deco sideboards to '50s bar stools, as well as a rather seedier section devoted to new and second-hand garments. Arrive early if you want to find any bargains, or just wander around and take in the atmosphere; there are plenty of small cafés to offer sustenance while you hunt. *See also chapter* **Specialist Shops.**

### Le Viaduc des Arts
*15-121 av Daumesnil, 12th. M° Bastille, Ledru-Rollin or Gare de Lyon.*
Under the arches of a disused railway viaduct, chic glass-fronted workshops opened in 1995 now provide a showroom for designers and craftsmen, continuing the long tradition of furniture trades in the Faubourg-St-Antoine. Some outlets are rather twee, but the variety is fascinating: from contemporary furniture designers to picture frame gilders, tapestry restorers, porcelain decorators, architectural salvage and a French hunting horn maker, as well as design gallery **VIA**. Along the top of the viaduct, the planted promenade offers a traffic-free view into Parisian lives and continues eastward to the Bois de Vincennes. *See also* **Parks & Cemeteries.**

### La Villette
**Cité des Sciences et de l'Industrie** *30 av Corentin-Cariou, 19th (01.40.05.70.00/recorded information 01.36.68.29.30). M° Porte de la Villette.*
**Cité de la Musique** *(01.44.84.45.00), Grande Halle de la Villette (01.40.03.75.03), 211-219 av Jean-Jaurès, 19th M° Porte de Pantin.*
**Guided tours of park** *(01.40.03.75.05).* 3pm Wed from intersection of Canal de l'Ourcq and Canal St-Martin. **Price** 35F; 30F under-26s, students, over-60s.
A postmodern park (*see chapter* **Parks & Cemeteries**) and giant arts and science complex running either side of the Canal de l'Ourcq in north-east Paris, La Villette has proved an enormously successful example of urban renewal, and now gets more visitors a year than Disneyland Paris. It was the site of Paris' principal cattle market and abattoir, and was going to be replaced by a high-tech slaughterhouse, until half-way through construction it was turned remarkably successfully into the **Cité des Sciences et de l'Industrie**, an ultra-modern science museum full of interactive exhibits, that is great for kids. Outside are the shiny spherical **Géode** cinema and Argonaute submarine and the park, dotted with little red *folies*, is a big draw for varied entertainments (from fireworks to outdoor film, *see chapter* **Paris by Season**); while across large lawns or '*prairies*' on the southern side of the canal are the aircraft-hangar-like **Zénith** spot for pop concerts, **Hot Brass** jazz club, and the **Grande Halle de la Villette**, used for trade fairs, exhibitions and the Villette Jazz Festival, which is the last remaining part of the old iron abattoir structure. It is winged by the Conservatoire de la Musique music school on one side and the **Cité de la Musique**, designed by Christian de Portzamparc, with its concert halls, rehearsal rooms and **Musée de la Musique** and **Café de la Musique** on the other.

## Archeological Sights

### La Crypte Archéologique
*parvis de Notre-Dame, 4th (01.43.29.83.51). M° Cité.*
**Open** Apr-Oct 10am-5.30pm; Oct-Mar 10am-4.30pm.
**Admission** 32F; 21F 12-25s; free under-12s.
**No credit cards.**

# Under the bridges of Paris

Like an artery through the city, the Seine invigorates Paris, crossed by fine bridges and lined with some of its most impressive monuments. When building houses on bridges was banned in the sixteenth century, the river was confirmed as an aesthetic as well as functional asset.

Even though the river is now lined with expressways, between the Invalides and the Bastille the tree-lined, paved *quais* are still ideally walkable and can be a refreshing relief after the crush at street level. Between the Louvre and Notre-Dame, you can also stop to browse through the old books and postcards sold by *bouquinistes* from bottle-green boxes. In the summer, the *quais* turn into Paris Beach, full of aspiring tanners. For serious sunbathing hit the stretch below the Louvre near **Pont du Carrousel**.

In the west of the city, the **Pont Mirabeau** inspired Apollinaire to write his famous poem of the same name, meditating on the passage of time. It also offers great views of the Eiffel Tower. Going east, beneath the **Pont de Grenelle**, is the Allée des Cygnes, a thin strip of an island where horses' bones and dead Protestants were dumped in the sixteenth century. Now the island is a delightful tree-lined pathway with its own copy of the *Statue of Liberty*. At its eastern end, the double-decker **Pont Bir-Hakeim** is a curiosity: raised Métro line up above, road traffic and pedestrians below.

The **Pont de l'Alma** commemorates victory over the Russians at Alma during the Crimean war. Originally adorned with four massive soldiers, the bridge was rebuilt in the 1970s but the figure of the Zouave was preserved and is still used to measure the height of the Seine when it floods. Back towards the centre of Paris, the glittering **Pont Alexandre III** comes into view, connecting the Invalides and the Grand Palais. All cast-iron lamp-posts, gilded statues and precious putti, the city's most exuberant bridge was unveiled for the 1900 Exhibition. Lining the Right Bank are some house boats inhabited by a few artists and modern-day

bohemians, overlooked by the stern facade of the Assemblée Nationale across the river.

Between the Louvre and the Institut de France, is the wonderfully romantic iron footbridge the **Pont des Arts**, from which you can enjoy superb views over the Ile de la Cité. Torn down to facilitate boat traffic, it was rebuilt with wider-spaced pylons in the 1980s. Easily recognisable with its turret-shaped recesses, the **Pont Neuf** at the tip of the island is the longest and oldest surviving bridge in Paris. When Henri IV opened it in 1605, it was the first crossing over the Seine without houses crowded along it and the first with raised pavements. Its views soon made it popular for promenades. If you take a boat trip, you'll be able to see the grinning gargoyles carved on its arches, supposedly portraying members of Henri IV's court.

The **Petit Pont**, linking the Ile de la Cité to the Latin Quarter, has a far longer history, stretching back to the earliest settlement of Lutétia by the Parisii (*see chapter* **Roman & Dark Age Paris**). It has been rebuilt many times and was originally defended by a small fortress. The present bridge dates from 1852.

Continuing east, the **Pont de Sully** crosses over the Ile-St-Louis offering views which span several centuries of Paris history: Notre Dame and seventeenth-century aristocratic dwellings from one side, the Bastille column and high-tech Institut du Monde Arabe at either end. Here the quai St-Bernard drifts into the Musée de Sculpture en Plein Air, where modern sculptures lurk sheepishly amongst kissing couples. Beyond Austerlitz is Paris' 36th and newest bridge, the **Pont Charles de Gaulle**, opened in August 1996. Low-lying and functional, architects Arretche and Karaskinki liken its minimalism to the wing of an aeroplane. Fans of modern architecture will also find plenty to interest them from the **Pont de Bercy**, where the Orwellian Finance Ministry has its feet in the water and the turf-covered Palais des Omnisports squats across the river from the glass towers of the new Bibliothèque Nationale.

The excavations unearthed under the cathedral parvis span a period of sixteen centuries running from the remains of Gallo-Roman ramparts and a hypocaust, complete with furnace and brick piles, to part of a mid-nineteenth-century drain. They give a good idea of the city's continuing evolution with fifteenth-century cellars built into old Roman walls and remains of medieval streets alongside foundations of the eighteenth-century Foundling hospital. A system of maps, models and labels made sense of the excavations, while objects and prints emphasise the area's historical significance, reflected in the fact that the parvis still marks the *Kilomètre Zéro* from which all road distances in France are measured.

### Arènes de Lutèce

*entrances rues Monge, Navarre, 5th. M° Cardinal-Lemoine.* **Open** *May-Sept* 10am-8.30pm; *Oct-Apr* 10am-5.30pm, daily.
This was once the Roman arena, where roaring beasts and wounded gladiators met their deaths. The site was discovered in 1869, and if you enter via the passageway at 49 rue Monge you may feel you've stumbled on a secret. But so have the gangs of kids playing football, skateboarders, *boules*-players and drunks, so don't expect romantic seclusion.

### Fortified Wall of Philippe-Auguste

*rue des Jardins-St-Paul, 4th. M° Pont Marie or St-Paul.*
King Philippe Auguste (1165-1223) was the first great builder Paris had known since Roman times. Not only did he order the major roads of his capital to be paved, he also enclosed the growing city on both the Left and Right banks of the Seine within a great defensive wall – the western defence being the Louvre. The largest surviving section of this wall, complete with towers, stands along the rue des Jardins-Saint-Paul, between the rue Charlemagne and the rue de l'Avé-Maria. Another chunk of the wall can still be seen at 3 rue Clovis in the **Latin Quarter**, and odd remnants of towers are dotted around the Marais and St-Germain-des-Prés.

## Centres of Learning

### Bibliothèque Nationale Richelieu

*58 rue de Richelieu, 2nd (01.47.03.81.26). M° Bourse.* *(Galerie Colbert annexe, 6 rue Vivienne)* **Open** *Galerie Mansart/Galerie Mazarine* 10am-7pm Tue-Sun. *Cabinet des Médailles* 1-5pm Mon-Sat; noon-6pm Sun. *Galerie Colbert* noon-7pm Mon-Sat. **Admission** *Galerie Mansart/Mazarine* 30-45F. *Cabinet des Médailles* 22F; 15F students, over-60s, under-26s. *Galerie Colbert* free (over 750F only) V.
The genesis of the French National Library dates from the 1660s, when Louis XIV's finance minister Colbert brought together the manuscripts of the royal library in the lavish town house which had belonged to Cardinal Mazarin. First opened to scholars in 1720, by 1724 the institution had received so many new acquisitions that the neighbouring Hôtel de Nevers was added to it. Some of the original painted decoration can still be seen in the Galeries Mansart and Mazarine, originally Mazarin's private art gallery and library, and open to the public for exhibitions of manuscripts, drawings and prints, but most of the present complex was transformed in the 1860s, including the circular, domed grand reading room. Architect Henri Labrouste's metal columns, vaulting and ceramic domes were very innovative in their time, and are still impressive, although generally open only to researchers in possession of an elusive reader's pass. Visitors can also visit the Cabinet des Médailles et des Antiques, to which all ancient coins discovered in France must be submitted. Although the main part of the library has now been transferred to the gigantic new **Bibliothèque Nationale François Mitterrand** (*see below*), the precious manuscripts remain here as do the priceless collections of engravings, drawings, musical scores and photographs. *See also chapter* **Museums**.

### Bibliothèque Nationale de France François Mitterrand

*11 quai François-Mauriac, 13th (01.53.79.53.79). M° Quai de la Gare.* **Open** 10am-7pm Tue-Sat; noon-6pm Sun. **Admission** *Day pass* 20F. *Annual pass* 200F.
Opened on 17 December 1996 by President Chirac, the new Bibliothèque Nationale de France is now officially named after François Mitterrand. The last of Mitterrand's *Grands Projets*, the *Très Grande Bibliothèque*) is now officially named after François Mitterrand. The last of Mitterrand's *Grands Projets*, the 'biggest library in the world', was also the most expensive and the most controversial. Much of the criticism has been aimed at the design of architect Dominique Perrault, chosen directly by the former President himself. Perrault had the curious idea of storing books in four L-shaped glass towers; when it was pointed out that keeping precious documents behind glass meant that sunlight could destroy them, wooden shutters had to be installed, at more expense. Perrault's plan created a central void filled with a garden of 140 trees, which have been uprooted from Fontainebleau at a cost of 40 million francs. Open to view from above by everyone, the gardens will be open only to those with research passes, when the research section, below the public reading rooms, opens in 1998. The height of each tower, the layout of the reading rooms and the use of rare wood for the esplanade have also caused criticism. The library houses over ten million volumes, 420 kilometres of shelves and room for 3,000 readers. Books, newspapers and periodicals are on public access to anyone over 18. An audio-visual room allows the public to browse through photo archives, film documentaries or sound recordings, and there are regular exhibitions. *See also chapter* **Museums**.

### Ecole Nationale Supérieure des Beaux-Arts

*14 rue Bonaparte, 6th (01.47.03.52.15). M° St-Germain-des-Prés.* **Open** 8.30am-8pm Mon-Fri. **Exhibitions** entrance at 13 quai Malaquais, 6th. **Open** *Exhibitions* 1-7pm, Mon-Fri. **Admission** 20F; 10F groups; free students, over-60s. **No credit cards.**
Paris' most prestigious fine arts school is installed in what remains of a seventeenth-century convent, the eighteenth-century Hôtel de Chimay and some nineteenth-century additions. After the Revolution, the buildings were transformed into a museum of French monuments, and then into the Ecole in 1816. Today, it is often used as a venue for exhibitions, but at other times only the courtyard is open to visitors.

### Institut de France

*23 quai de Conti, 6th (01.44.41.44.41). M° St Germain-des-Prés.* **Guided tours** 3pm, first Sat of the month. **Admission** 20F. **No credit cards.**
The classical Baroque building, designed by Le Vau, which houses the Institut de France, dates from 1663-84. Overlooking the Seine, the semi-circular structure dominated by its dome, was founded by Mazarin as a school for provincial children. In 1805 the five academies of the institute were transferred here from the Louvre by Napoléon. Most prestigious is the Académie Française, renowned for outbursts against Franglais, whose 40 eminences work steadily away on their dictionary of the French language. Inside the building is Mazarin's tomb, as well as the Bibliothèque Mazarine, which holds 500,000 volumes. To visit at any other time, call ahead to make an appointment.

### La Sorbonne

*47 rue des Ecoles, 5th (01.40.46.20.15). M° Cluny-La Sorbonne.* **Open** courtyards 9am-4.30pm Mon-Fri. **Admission** limited public access.
Founded in 1253 by the cleric Robert de Sorbon as one of several separate theological 'colleges' in this area (*see chapters* **Middle Ages to Renaissance** *and* **The Left Bank**), the University of the Sorbonne was at the centre of the Latin Quarter's intellectual activity from the Middle Ages until

May 1968, when its premises were occupied by students and stormed by the CRS (riot police). The authorities subsequently splintered the University of Paris into less strategically threatening suburban outposts, but the Sorbonne remains home to the Faculté des Lettres. Rebuilt one time by Richelieu, reorganised by Napoléon, the present buildings mostly date from 1885 to 1900 and include a labyrinth of classrooms and quaint lecture theatres, as well as an observatory tower, visible from the rue St-Jacques. The elegant dome of the seventeenth-century chapel dominates the place de la Sorbonne. The chapel is closed to the public except for occasional concerts and exhibitions; Cardinal Richelieu is buried in an ornate tomb inside. Members of the public who wish to visit the Sorbonne must make reservations one month in advance; phone 01.40.26.20.15, and confirm in writing to Mme Bolot, 47 rue des Ecoles, 5th.

## Monuments

### Mémorial des Martyrs de la Déportation

*sq de l'Ile de France, 4th (01.46.33.87.56). M° Cité.*
**Open** 10am-noon, 2-5pm daily.
Approached via a small park at the top of the Ile de la Cité, this is a simple, sober monument to World War II victims (virtually all Jews) of Nazi deportations.

### Le Panthéon

*pl du Panthéon, 5th (01.43.54.34.51). RER Luxembourg.*
**Open** *1 Apr-30 Sept* 9.30am-6.30pm; *1 Oct-31 Mar* 10am-6.15pm daily. **Admission** 32F; 21F 12-25s; free under-12s. **No credit cards.**
Designed by Soufflot, who also planned the surrounding square, this Neo-Classical megastructure was the architectural *Grand Projet* of its day. A grateful Louis XV had it built to thank Ste-Geneviève, patron saint of Paris, for helping him recover from an illness. But events caught up with its completion in 1790, and in post-Revolutionary spirit it was re-dedicated as a temple of reason and the resting place of the nation's great men. It was definitively secularised in 1885, in a neat reversal of the history of Rome's famed Pantheon, upon which it was modelled, which started as a pagan temple only to be turned into a Catholic church. In the recently restored church you can admire the elegant Greek columns and numerous domes, which give the building an airy grandeur, as well as the nineteenth-century murals by Puvis de Chavannes depicting the life of Ste-Geneviève, but it is the crypt full of great men that is most interesting. Statesmen, politicians and thinkers, as well as Voltaire, Rousseau, Victor Hugo and Zola are among those who repose in the barrel-vaulted crypt. New heroes are added extremely rarely: Pierre and Marie Curie's remains were transferred here in 1995, the latter being the first women to be interred in the Pantheon in her own right; André Malraux was transferred here in November 1996. The steep spiral stairs to the colonnade around the dome are worth the climb for the views.

## Notable Buildings

### Centre Pompidou

*Centre National d'Art et de Culture Georges Pompidou, rue Beaubourg, 4th (01.44.78.12.33). M° Châtelet-Les Halles, Hôtel-de-Ville or Rambuteau.* **Open** noon-10pm Mon, Wed-Fri; 10am-10pm Sat, Sun, holidays. Closed 1 May. **Admission** *Musée National des Art Moderne* 35F; 24F 16-25s; free under-16s. *Temporary exhibitions* fee varies. *Day pass to museum and all exhibitions* 70F; 45F students, 16-25s; free art students, unemployed, under-16s. **Guided Tours** (phone for details) 35F; 24F 16-25s; free under-16s. **Credit** Bookshop (over 100F) AmEx, MC, V.
The primary colours and exposed pipes and air ducts make the Centre Pompidou one of the most instantly recognisable buildings of Paris. Commissioned in 1968 by President Georges Pompidou, and opened in 1977, it was bravely slotted into a then run-down historic district, ironically called Beaubourg ('beautiful village'). The Italo-British architectural duo of Renzo Piano and Richard Rogers won the competition for its design with their notorious 'inside-out', boilerhouse approach, which put all the services such as air-conditioning, lifts and escalators on the outside, leaving a freely adaptable space for the galleries within. The Centre, often known simply as 'Beaubourg', was a pioneer in the concept of a multi-media space; it includes a vast public library and music library, the CCI, specialising in industrial design and architecture, the Salle Garance cinema and the centre for research in contemporary music IRCAM, housed in the red-brick building across the place St-Merri. There's also the treasure-packed **Musée National d'Art Moderne**, which continues the history of twentieth-century art from where the Musée d'Orsay leaves off in 1914. The fifth-floor exhibition area is used for blockbuster theme shows and retrospectives, while smaller contemporary art and design exhibitions are staged on the mezzanine levels and in the central forum space. With eight million visitors each year, it is unfortunate that the building is to undergo a major renovation programme from October 1997 to late 1999, which will involve closure of most of the Centre, although an exhibition space will remain open, as will the escalators offering one of the best views in Paris. A teepee on the piazza will explain the changes going on inside. *See also chapters* **Museums, Music: Classical & Opera** *and* **Study.**

### La Conciergerie

*1 quai de l'Horloge, 1st (01.53.73.78.50). M° Cité.* **Open** 10am-5pm daily. **Admission** 32F; 21F 12-25s; free under-12s. **No credit cards.**
Viewed from the Right Bank, the Conciergerie looks just like the forbidding medieval fortress and prison it once was. However, much of the gloomy facade was added by nineteenth-century neo-Gothic restorers, although the thirteenth-century Bonbec tower (furthest to the west) was part of the palace of the Capetian kings. A visit takes you through the massive medieval kitchens and the Salle des Gens d'Armes, an impressive vaulted Gothic hall built for Philippe le Bel at the beginning of the fourteenth century. It gradually became a prison under the watch of the Concierge. Inside you can see the cell where Marie Antoinette was held during the Revolution. Her enemies Danton and Robespierre later ended up here too, following thousands of others who had passed through on their way to the guillotine under the Terror. The Chapelle des Girondins contains some grim souvenirs, such as Marie Antoinette's crucifix and a guillotine blade, ready to replace its blunted predecessor. On the outside, have a look at the Tour de l'Horloge. Built in 1370 and carefully restored, it was the first public clock in Paris.

### Grand Palais

*av Winston Churchill, av du Général Eisenhower, 8th (recorded information 01.44.13.17.17/exhibition information 01.44.13.17.30). M° Champs-Elysées Clemenceau.* **Open** 10am-8pm Mon, Thur-Sun; 10am-10pm Wed, last tickets 45min before closing. **Admission** varies. **Credit** AmEx, MC, V.
The Grand Palais was built for the Exposition Universelle of 1900, and covers a wide tract of land between the Champs-Elysées and the Seine – it's impossible to miss its immense glass dome, and galloping bronze horses pulling chariots. Its three different facades were designed by three different architects, which explains the rather eclectic wealth of decoration. Today the Palais is divided into three main exhibition spaces. The entrances on avenue du Général Eisenhower lead into spaces for blockbuster art shows; the wing nearest to the Seine holds the **Palais de la Découverte** science museum. The avenue Winston Churchill wing, long used for major art salons and book fairs, had to be closed for restoration in 1994 when bits started to fall off the dome, and is due

to reopen in 1998. Facing the Grand Palais across avenue Winston Churchill is the smaller **Petit-Palais**, also built for the Exhibition and now an art museum and exhibition space. *See also chapter* **Museums**.

## Institut du Monde Arabe

*1 rue des Fossés St-Bernard, 5th (01.40.51.39.53). Mᵒ Jussieu.* **Open** 10am-6pm Tue-Sun. *Library* 1-8pm Tue-Sat. *Café* 2.30-6.30pm Tue-Sat; noon-3pm Sun. . **Admission** *Building, roof-top terrace, library* free. *Museum* 25F; 20F students, over-60s. *Exhibitions* 30F; 25F students, unemployed, over-60s.

One of the *Grands Projets*, this wedge-shaped building was purpose-designed by French architect Jean Nouvel in 1980 as an Arab cultural centre. Nouvel took his inspiraton for its distinctive windows from the screens of Moorish palaces and devised an intriguing high-tech version based on the principle of of a camera aperture, so that they would adjust automatically always to admit the same amount of daylight. However, a mix of technical and financial problems has led to this gadget being shut down. A clever blend of high-tech steel and glass architecture and Arab influences, it's still one of the finer buildings of 1980s Paris. Inside is a permanent collection of Middle Eastern art, temporary exhibition spaces that present work ranging from ancient civilisations to contemporary design and photography, a specialist library, and café. There is a performing arts programme of dance and classical Arab music, and a great view from the roof-top terrace.

## Les Invalides

*Esplanade des Invalides, 7th (01.44.42.54.52/Musée de l'Armée 01.44.42.37.67). Mᵒ Invalides.* **Open** *Apr-Sept* 10am-6pm; *Oct-Mar* 10am-5pm daily. **Admission** (valid 2 days) 37F; 29F under-26s, students; free unemployed, under-12s. **No credit cards.**

Visible from miles away because of the gleaming golden Eglise du Dôme (regilded for the 1989 bicentenary of the Revolution), Les Invalides is actually a collection of buildings. The huge classical-style Hôtel des Invalides, constructed between 1671 and 1676 for Louis XIV, was built as a military hospital for the King's soldiers. It was also a retirement home for wounded soldiers that at one time housed up to 6,000 invalids, hence the name. Other buildings on the site

include the Musée de l'Armée (*see also chapter* **Museums**), the Musée de l'Ordre de la Libération and the Eglise St-Louis. The army museum has a staggering display of weapons, maps and war-time paraphernalia from the *ancien régime* to World War I and II. The church of the Dôme is a typical, highly decorated example of French architecture from Louis XIV's time. Designed by Hardouin-Mansart, with a square ground plan, it is one of the grandest Baroque churches in the city. Since 1840 it has been dedicated to the worship of Napoléon, whose body was brought here from the island of St Helena 19 years after he died there. It now lies beneath the coffered Baroque dome, in a red porphyry sarcophagus in a hushed circular crypt. The church of St-Louis is also known as the Church of the Soldiers, decorated with captured flags, and with a crypt filled with the remains of military men.

## Musée National du Moyen Age – Thermes de Cluny

*6 pl Paul-Painlevé, 5th (01.53.73.78.00). Mᵒ Cluny-La Sorbonne.* **Open** 9.15am-5.45pm Mon, Wed-Sun. **Admission** 28F; 18F 18-25s, students, over-60s; free under-18s. **Guided tours** *Medieval collections* 3.30pm Wed, Sat, Sun. *Baths* 2pm Wed, Sat, Sun. 36F; 21F under-18s, plus entry charge. **Credit** (shop only) MC, V.

Along with the Hôtel de Sens in the Marais, this crenellated building is one of only two remaining examples of important fifteenth-century secular architecture in Paris. It was built – on top of an earlier Gallo-Roman baths complex dating from the second and third centuries – by Jacques d'Amboise in 1485-1498 at the request of the Abbé de Cluny, who wanted somewhere to lodge priests passing through the capital. These are the most important Roman remains in Paris, and three large rooms are visible – the frigidarium, tepidarium and caldarium. After the Revolution, a printer, a laundry and coopers set up shop here in 1807, before it was turned into a museum in 1844. Today, still commonly referred to as Cluny, it houses an exceptional collection of Medieval art, with the *Lady & the Unicorn* tapestries and superb goldwork, architectural fragments and artefacts. Some of the Roman remains can be seen from the street; wander too into the main courtyard and admire the magnificent staircase, Gothic mullioned windows and balustrade lined with dramatic gargoyles.

**La Conciergerie** *was home to the Capetian kings, before it became a prison.*

## Musée d'Orsay

*1 rue de Bellechasse, 7th (01.40.49.48.14/recorded
information 01.45.49.11.11). M° Solférino/RER Musée
d'Orsay.* **Open** 10am-6pm Tue, Wed, Fri, Sat; 10am-
9.45pm Thur; 9am-6pm Sun. **Admission** 39F; 27F 18-25s,
over-60s, Sun; free under-18s. **Credit** (bookshop only) V.
The Musée d'Orsay was originally a train station, designed
by Victor Laloux as part of the enormous works for the 1900
Exposition Universelle. You can still see the names of towns
it once served on the Seine-side facade. Trains ceased to run
there in the 1950s as its platforms proved too short, and for
a long time it was threatened with demolition, until in the
late 1970s President Giscard bowed to public pressure and
scrapped plans to demolish the fine Beaux-Arts edifice with
its distinctive twin clock towers. It was decided instead to
turn it into a museum of the nineteenth century, housing the
splendid Impressionist canvases formerly crammed into the
Jeu de Paume, plus paintings and sculpture from the Louvre
and other museums, in a boldly redesigned interior by Italian
architect Gae Aulenti. Opened in 1986, the crowds snaking
their way into the building attest to the project's success: a
perfect fusion of form and content. The collection spans the
period from around 1830 to 1914, and the main attraction,
besides Manet's *Olympia* on the ground floor, is the skylit
Impressionist gallery on the upper floor, filled with masterpieces by Monet, Dégas, Renoir, Pisarro and Van Gogh.

## Opéra Bastille

*pl de la Bastille, 12th (01.44.73.13.00/recorded
information 01.43.43.96.96). M° Bastille.* **Open** *guided
tours* phone for details. **Admission** 50F; 30F students,
unemployed, under-16s, over-60s. **No credit cards.**
The megalithic Opéra Bastille has been one of the most
controversial of all François Mitterrand's *Grands Projets,*
whether because of the cost of its upkeep, its scale, the quality of the architecture or the opera productions put on here.
Opened in 1989, some described it as a stroke of socialist
genius to deliberately implant a high-culture edifice in a traditionally working-class district; others suggested it was a
typical piece of Mitterrand skulduggery, an extravagant
piece of diversionary propaganda. There's no doubt that the
curved, marble-faced structure has contributed to the renewal of the *quartier.* However, recent attention has centred on
the shortcomings of the building: netting was hurriedly put
up to stop granite slabs falling on on pedestrians below, suggesting that major repairs are needed to a building not yet
ten years old. Also, although it was intended as an 'opera for
the people', that has never really happened and opera and
ballet productions are now shared between Bastille and the
Opéra Garnier (*see below*). It has been called the world's
largest public toilet; you'll have to make up your own mind.

## Palais Garnier

*pl de l'Opéra, 9th (01.44.73.13.004). M° Opéra.* **Open**
*Visits* 10am-5pm daily (except when morning concerts).
*Museum* 10am-5pm daily. **Guided tours** in French
(01.40.01.22.63) 1pm Tue-Sun (60F). **Admission** 30F, incl
museum; 20F students, unemployed; free under-10s.
**No credit cards.**
Awash with gilt, satin, red velvet and marble, the opulent
Palais Garnier, with its sumptuous grand staircase, mass of
sculptures and glittering chandeliers is a monument to the
ostentation of the French *haute bourgeoisie* under the Second
Empire. Designed by Charles Garnier in 1862, it has an
immense stage and an auditorium that holds more than 2,000
people. It even had a ramp up the side of the building on rue
Scribe for the Emperor to drive his carriage straight to the
royal box. The facade is equally opulent, and in its time a
source of controversy. The sculpture of a group of dancers
by Carpeaux to the right of the entrance shocked Parisians
with its frank sensuality, and in 1869 someone threw a bottle of ink over their marble thighs; the original is now safe
in the **Musée d'Orsay**. Since it reopened the Garnier again
hosts opera productions as well as ballet. Visitors can see

the controversial false ceiling of the auditorium dome, painted with scenes from opera and ballet by Chagall in 1964, the
library, museum, Grand Foyer and Grand Staircase.

## Palais de Chaillot & Trocadéro

*pl du Trocadéro, 16th. M° Trocadéro.*
Looming across the river from the Eiffel Tower, the immense
Palais de Chaillot in the place du Trocadéro is home to cultural institutions and four very different and underrated
musuems: the **Musée de la Marine** (marine and naval history); the **Musée de l'Homme** (enthnology, anthropology
and human biology); the **Musée des Monuments
Historiques** (with plaster casts of architectural treasures
from all over France); and the **Musée du Cinéma-Henri
Langlois** (the history of cinema). The complex also contains
the **Cinémathèque** and the **Théâtre National de
Chaillot**. It's an intimidating, pseudo-classical building that
was built for yet another international exhibition, in 1937,
and is typical of the monumental neo-totalitarian architecture of the time, although it was actually built on the foundations of an earlier complex put up for the World Fair of
1878. The Trocadéro gardens below it are a little dilapidated, but the impressive tiered terraces and pool with bronze
and stone statues showered by powerful spraying fountains
form a spectacular ensemble with the Eiffel Tower and
Champ de Mars across the river, especially when floodlit at
night. Watch out for roller-skaters coming towards you from
all directions as you walk across the esplanade.

## Tour Maine-Montparnasse

*33 av de Maine, 15th (01.45.38.52.56). M°
Montparnasse-Bienvenüe.* **Open** 9.30am-10.30pm daily.
**Admission** lift to 59th storey 42F; 36F over-60s; 33F 18-
25s; 26F under-17s; free under-5s. **No credit cards.**
This steel-and-glass skyscraper was built in 1974 on the site
of the former Gare Montparnasse, and at 209m high, it's
lower than the Eiffel, but more central, and offers some excellent views over Right and Left Banks. A lift whisks you up

*Second Empire kitsch at* **Palais Garnier**.

# RIGHT BANK?
# LEFT BANK?

## It's all the Seine to us!
## Two English pubs with
## a difference.

116 RUE ST DENIS, 2ND.
TEL: 01.42.36.34.73
M° ETIENNE MARCEL, LES HALLES,
RÉAUMUR SÉBASTOPOL

9 RUE PRINCESSE, 6TH.
TEL: 01.40.51.77.38
M° MABILLON, ST SULPICE,
ST GERMAIN-DES-PRÉS

**REAL ALES BREWED ON THE PREMISES.**
**DELICIOUS FOOD INCLUDING WEEKEND BRUNCH.**
**FRIENDLY, ENGLISH-SPEAKING STAFF.**
**OPEN EVERY DAY, NOON - 2AM.**

*Daniel Buren's characteristically stripey masterpiece at the* **Palais-Royal**.

to the 56th floor in just 40 seconds, where you'll find a display of aerial views of Paris, some of which date back to 1858, allowing you to see how the city has changed.

## Palaces & Mansions

### Château de Malmaison

*av du Château, 92500 Rueil-Malmaison (01.41.29.05.55).* RER La Défense, then bus 258. **Open** *Apr-Sept* 9.30am-noon, 1.30pm-5pm, Mon-Fri; Sat, Sun. *Oct-Mar* 10am-noon, 1.30pm-5pm, Mon, Wed-Sun. **Guided tours** Sat, Sun. **Admission** 30F, plus over-60s; 20F 18-25s, Sun; free under-18s, unemployed.

The château at Malmaison, today within Paris' smart western suburbs, owes its renown to its Napoleonic connections. Bought in 1799 by Josephine, it was the Emperor's favourite retreat during the Consulate (1800-03) and one of the few places he could feel at ease. Most of the building dates from the seventeenth century, but the entrance was turned into the form of a military tent by the couple, who also enlarged and decorated the reception rooms in neo-Roman style and added an orangery, greenhouse, stables and theatre. After their divorce in 1809 Napoléon left the château to Josephine, who died there in 1814. Following his defeat at Waterloo, he stopped off at Malmaison on his way to exile. In 1896, the sadly-decayed château was bought by a banker who restored it and left it to the state in 1904 on condition that it be made a Napoleonic museum. Inside you can see portraits of Napoléon by Gros and David, as well as the Salle du Conseil, in which the Emperor took many of his most important decisions, the Grecian dining room and the billiard room. Next to the house is Josephine's rose garden, and a cedar which she is supposed to have planted in celebration of victory at the Battle of Marengo. Napoléon's coach, seized by Marshal Blücher at Waterloo, is on display in the stables. There is an annexe of the museum in the nearby Château de Bois Préau.

### Hôtel de Sens (Bibliothèque Forney)

*1 rue du Figuier, 4th (01.42.78.14.60). M° St-Paul.* **Open** *Library* 1.30-8.30pm Tue-Fri; 10am-8.30pm Sat. *Exhibitions* 1.30-8pm Tue-Fri; 10am-8pm Sat. **Admission** *Exhibitions* 20F; 10F students, under-12s, over-60s. **No credit cards.**

One of the oldest private residences in Paris, this enchanting and rare example of Parisian medieval architecture was built in 1475-1519 for the wealthy Archbishops of Sens. It's a fanciful ensemble of turrets, and is remarkable for its superb windows, elaborately carved dormers and Gothic entrance-ways which feature magnificent vaulting. During the sixteenth century Wars of Religion, the Guise brothers hatched many an anti-royalist plot within its walls. Its most famous tenant, however, was the reine Margot, who lived here after she was repudiated by Henri IV, having failed to provide him an heir. Today, the *hôtel* is home to the **Bibliothèque Forney**, one of the richest libraries in Paris, devoted essentially to applied and graphic arts, which holds fascinating temporary exhibitions, and provides guided tours for visitors on demand (01.42.78.14.60).

### Hôtel de Sully

*62 rue St-Antoine, 4th (01.44.61.20.00/information 01.44.61.21.69). M° St-Paul or Bastille.* **Open** *courtyards* 10am-7pm daily. **No credit cards.**

This perfectly restored Louis XIII-style *hôtel particulier* is one of the most distinguished mansions still standing in the Marais. Designed by Jean Androuet du Cerceau in 1624, it was bought by Henri IV's former minister the Duc de Sully, who lavished money on decorating and extending it. The *hôtel* has been carefully restored. Today it's home to the Caisse Nationale des Monuments Historiques, which has an excellent bookshop and offers a vast array of guided tours (in French) of Paris, and to the **Mission du Patrimoine Photographique**. The interior is closed to the public, but you can walk through the two beautifully proportioned courtyards, with allegorical relief sculptures of the seasons and the elements. At the rear of the second courtyard is a pretty orangery, one of the few to survive in the district; next to it a small arch leads through into the **place des Vosges**.

### Palais-Royal

*main entrance pl du Palais-Royal, other entrances in rue de Montpensier, rue de Beaujolais, rue de Valois, 1st. M° Palais-Royal.* **Open** *Gardens only* dawn-dusk daily. **Admission** free.

The Palais-Royal has a rich and racy history. It was built for Cardinal Richelieu by Jacques Lemercier as his own private residence, and known as the Palais Cardinal. Richelieu left the palace to Louis XIII, whose widow moved in, preferring it to the vast halls of the Louvre and giving it its present name. It was, however, in the 1780s, when the Duc d'Orléans, known as Philippe-Egalité, enclosed the gardens within a three-storey peristyle, that the building's most remarkable era began. Housing cafés, theatres, sideshows and shops, its arcades came into their own as a popular society trysting place. Its cafés saw revolutionary plotting before the Revolution, and the Palais-Royal also became known once again for its depravity, as a hot-bed of gambling and prostitution. Of the old cafés, the **Grand Véfour** remains, now one of the best restaurants in town. Today the gardens offer a surprisingly tranquil spot in the heart of Paris, while many of the little shops in the arcades specialise in prints and antiques. The former palace houses the Conseil d'Etat and

*Greek and Gothic shrines at the* **Madeleine** *and* **St Germain-des-Prés**.

the Ministry of Culture, and is one of the most-visited sites during the Journées Portes Ouvertes (*see chapter* **Paris by Season**). The main courtyard, after years of ignominy as a car park, now contains Daniel Buren's sculpture of 280 black and white striped columns of different heights. Some are hidden underground below grates; others are just the right height to sit on. *See also chapter* **The Right Bank**.

## Places of Worship

### Alexandre Nevsky Cathedral

*12 rue Daru, 8th (01.42.27.37.34). M° Courcelles.* **Open** 3-5pm Tue, Fri. *Service* 6pm Sat; 10.30am Sun.

There are enough onion domes and gilding, icons and frescoes here to make you think you are in Moscow, but no wonder it looks so convincing, for this Russian Orthodox church was built 1859-61 in Neo-Byzantine style on a Greek-cross plan by the Tsar's architect Kouzmine, architect of the St Petersburg Beaux-Arts Academy, and Strohm, and is still at the heart of Paris' little Russia today.

### Basilica of St-Denis

*2 rue de Strasbourg, 93200 St-Denis (01.48.09.83.54). M° St-Denis-Basilique.* **Open** *Apr-Sept* 10am-7pm Mon-Sat; noon-7pm Sun. *Oct-Mar* 10am-5pm Mon-Sat; noon-5pm Sun. **Admission** *Cathedral* nave free. *Royal tombs* 32F; 21F 12-25s, students; 10F 12-17s; free under-12s, unemployed. **Guided tours** 3pm daily (phone for tour in English: 01.42.43.33.55). **No credit cards.**

Legend has it that when St-Denis, first Bishop of Paris, was beheaded, he rose to his feet, picked up his head and, accompanied by a choir of angels, walked to Vicus Catulliacus (now St-Denis), where he wished to be buried. The first church on this site was built over his tomb in around 475. However, the present edifice dates from the thirteenth century, and is commonly regarded as the first example of true Gothic architec-

ture, as well as one of the finest. It stands today at the heart of the old town of St-Denis, now surrounded by one of Paris' most sprawling industrial suburbs (*see chapter* **Beyond the Périphérique**). Much more impressive inside than the damaged facade suggests, the basilica was begun by Abbot Suger in the twelfth century, although it was only in the middle of the following century that the architect Pierre de Montreuil erected the spire and rebuilt the choir, nave and transept. This was the burial place for all monarchs of France between 996 and the end of the *ancien régime*, with the exception of three, so the ambulatory amounts to a veritable museum of French funerary sculpture, including the fanciful Gothic tomb of Dagobert, the Renaissance tomb of François 1er and two different tombs designed for Henri II and Catherine de Médicis. The basilica was greatly damaged during the Revolution in one giant explosion of popular anger in 1792 when the tombs were desecrated and the royal remains thrown into a communal pit nearby. In 1805, Napoléon ordered the restoration of the building, which was completed by Viollet-le-Duc in 1875. Part of the fifth-century church can still be seen in the crypt. Beside the basilica is the former abbey, which is now a girls' high school.

### La Madeleine

*pl de la Madeleine, 8th (01.44.51.69.00). M° Madeleine.* **Open** 8am-7pm Mon-Sat; 9am-1pm, 3.30-7pm, Sun. **Admission** free.

The building of a giant church on this site was begun in 1764, but little had been completed by the time of the Revolution. In 1806 Napoléon decided to continue the project as a 'Temple of Glory' dedicated to his Grand Army, and commissioned Barthélemy Vignon to design a semi-Athenian temple that is the epitome of the Neo-Classicism that fascinated Paris in the early nineteenth century. Following the Emperor's fall the building suffered from a severe lack of public support, but it was finally consecrated as a church in 1845. The gigantic colonnades of the facade, recently cleaned,

*Glorious glass at the* **Sainte-Chapelle** *and Italianate piazza-style at* **St-Sulpice**.

are mirrored by those of the Assemblée Nationale across the river, with the Concorde obelisk as midpoint. Inside are three and a half giant domes and psuedo-Grecian side altars amid a sea of multi-coloured marble. The unofficial parish church of Paris' showbiz community, the Madeleine hosts celebrity weddings and funerals, filling the surrounding place with weeping fans. A greater attraction though might be the luxury food shops that line the square.

### La Mosquée de Paris

*pl du Puits-de-l'Ermite, 5th (01.45.35.97.33/Tea room 01.43.31.38.20/Turkish baths 01.43.31.18.14). Mº Censier-Daubenton.* **Open** *Guided tours* 9am-noon, 2-6pm Mon-Thur, Sat, Sun (closed during Muslim holidays). *Tea room* 9am-11pm daily. *Turkish baths women* 10am-9pm Mon, Wed-Sat; *men* 10am-9pm Tue, Sun. **Admission** 15F; 10F 7-25s, over-60s; free under-7s. *Tea room* free. *Turkish baths* 85F. **No credit cards.**
Opposite the **Jardin des Plantes**, the green-and-white minaret comes as a surprise against the Parisian skyline. The mosque was built in 1922, and is now the centre of the largely Algerian-dominated Moslem community in France. Partly modelled on the Alhambra in Granada, it has a beautiful interior patio and a series of flamboyant domes. At the entrance on rue Geoffroy St-Hilaire there are splendid Turkish baths, which also contain a very enjoyable Moorish tearoom. It also houses a library.

### Sacré Coeur

*35 rue du Chevalier-de-la-Barre, 18th (01.53.41.89.00). Mº Abbesses or Anvers.* **Open** *Crypt/dome* Oct-Mar 9am-6pm; *Apr-Sept* 9am-7pm, daily. **Admission** *Crypt* 15F; 8F 6-16s, students; free under-6s. *Dome* 15F; 8F 6-25s, students; free under-6s. *Crypt/dome* 25F; 13F 6-25s; free under-6s. **No credit cards.**
The icing sugar-white dome is one of the most visible landmarks in Paris, and dominates the butte Montmartre. It can

be reached from place St-Pierre-Valadon by steep steps or by a the modern funicular beside. Building was started on the Sacré Coeur as an act of penance after the nation's defeat by the Prussians in 1870 (and the take-over of Paris by the pagan Commune the following year), but wasn't finished until 1914, when another brush with the enemy to the east meant it wouldn't be consecrated before 1919. A jumble of architects worked on the mock Romano-Byzantine edifice, but its kitsch style is held in great affection by many. The lavishly adorned church, the crypt and the gallery in the dome, where the view is even better, are all open to visitors.

### Sainte-Chapelle & Palais de Justice

*4 bd du Palais, 1st (01.53.73.78.50). Mº Cité.* **Open** *Apr-Sept* 9.30am-6.30pm; *Oct-Mar* 10am-5pm, daily. **Admission** 32F; 21F 12-25s, students, unemployed; free under-12s. **Credit** (bookshop only) MC, V.
Tucked away inside a courtyard of the Palais de Justice is the exquisite Sainte-Chapelle. France's devout King Louis IX (1226-70), later canonised as Saint Louis, was an enthusiastic collector of holy relics – some of them of very doubtful authenticity, as the king was the target for every conman in Europe. In the 1240s he ordered Pierre de Montreuil to design a suitable church in which to house them. Seemingly built almost entirely of stained glass, the two-level chapel is a monument to high Gothic style, with beautiful star-painted vaulted ceilings. Bring binoculars, and come on a sunny day to view the fine details of the stained glass, which depicts Biblical scenes. The chapel is regularly used for concerts by early music ensembles. It is surrounded by the warren of buildings that form the Palais de Justice, the seat of authority from Roman times until 1358, although most of the present buildings date from the eighteenth and nineteenth centuries. It is still the focal point of justice in Paris – after going through the security system, you can walk through the marble corridors, full of black-gowned lawyers, and sit in on cases in both the civil and criminal courts.

Featured above are clothes from: RICCI, MUGLER, SAINT-LAURENT,
LACROIX, ALAIA, CHANEL (except the model in salmon)

# RECIPROQUE
## Nicole Morel

| HIGH FASHION | | TRINKETS-GIFTS |
| CLOTHING | | ACCESSORIES |
| WOMEN | **CONSIGNMENT SHOP** | JEWELLERY |
| MEN | **700m² Retail Space** | FURS |

The best and biggest second-hand boutique in Paris. Ladies' and
men's clothing by famous fashion designers, all in perfect condition.

ALAIA - ARMANI - BOSS - CALVIN KLEIN - CHANEL - CHURCH'S
DIOR - DONNA KARAN - FAÇONNABLE - GAULTIER - GUCCI
HERMES - HERVE LEGER - KENZO - MUGLER - MONTANA - LACROIX
PRADA - RALPH LAUREN - SAINT-LAURENT - VERSACE
VIVIENNE WESTWOOD - VUITTON - YAMAMOTO

Housewares and gifts.

89, 92, 93, 95, 97, 101, 123 Rue de la Pompe, 16th.
Métro: Pompe. Telephone: 01.47.04.82.24 / 01.47.04.30.28

## St-Etienne-du-Mont

*pl Ste-Geneviève, 5th (01.43.54.11.79). M° Cardinal-Lemoine/RER Luxembourg.* **Open** *Sept-June* 8am-noon, 2-7pm, Mon-Sat; 9am-noon, 2.30-7pm, Sun. *July, Aug* 10am-noon, 4-7pm, Tue-Sat; 9am-noon, 3-7pm, Sun. **Admission** free.

The ornate shrine of Ste Geneviève, the city's patron saint, is inside the church, to the right of the choir. The stained glass windows show scenes from her life, including her restoration of her mother's sight by washing her eyes with well water. The present church was built – in an amalgam of styles – between 1492 and 1626, and originally adjoined the abbey church of Ste-Geneviève. It has a Gothic rose window and a stunning Renaissance roodscreen with double spiral staircase and ornate stone fretwork, the only remaining rood screen in Paris, and ornate 1651 wooden pulpit by Germain Pillon with massive female figures of the virtues.

## St-Eustache

*rue du Jour, 1st Paris (01.40.26.47.99). M° Châtelet-Les Halles.* **Open** *May-Oct* 8am-8pm Mon-Sat; 8am-1pm, 2.30-7pm, Sun. *Nov-Apr* 8am-7pm, Mon-Sat; 9am-12.30pm, 3-8pm, Sun. **Guided tours** 3pm, free (phone ahead). **Organ recitals** 5.30pm Sun, free.

This barn-like, cathedral-sized church dominates Les Halles. Its structure is essentially Gothic, but the classical decoration is just as distinctively Renaissance. During the Revolution it became the Temple of Agriculture, appropriately enough, given the proximity of the market. A favourite with music-lovers, it boasts a magnificent 8,000-pipe organ.

## St-Germain-des-Prés

*pl St-Germain-des-Prés, 6th (01.43.25.41.71). M° St-Germain-des-Prés.* **Open** 8am-7pm daily. **Guided tours** *informal* 1.30-5.30pm Tue, Thur (except July, Aug). *formal* 3pm third Sun of the month. **Admission** free.

On the advice of St-Germain, who would become bishop of Paris in 555, Childebert, son of Clovis, had a basilica and a monastery built towards 543. The oldest church in Paris, for many years it was known as St-Germain-le-Doré ('Saint-Germain the Golden') because of its copper roof. The original church was destroyed and pillaged by Normans, to be rebuilt around the year 1000 in Romanesque style, although most of the present structure is twelfth century, albeit heavily altered after its tumultuous history during the Revolution, when the abbey was burnt and a saltpetre refinery installed in the church. Today, only some ornate carved capitals and the tower remain of the eleventh-century church, the top of which was, however, also altered during clumsy restoration work last century, when a spire was added, as were the frescoes in the nave by Hippolyte Flandrin. The twelfth-century Gothic choir was inspired by the one at St-Denis. The village-like charm of the outside of the church is not matched by the rather disparate interior, although there are several interesting tombs. Under the window in the second chapel is the funeral stone of the philosopher Descartes, whose ashes (bar his skull) have been in the church since 1819.

## St-Séverin

*1 rue des Prêtres-St-Séverin, 5th (01.42.34.93.50). M° Cluny-La Sorbonne or St-Michel.* **Open** 11am-7.30pm Mon-Fri; 11am-8pm Sat; 9am-9pm Sun. **Admission** free.

The Primitive and Flamboyant Gothic styles merge in this complex, composite little church, mostly built between the thirteenth and fifteenth centuries, although further alterations were carried out in the 1680s, paid for by Louis XIV's cousin the 'Grande Mademoiselle'. The double ambulatory is famed for its remarkable 'palm tree' vaulting and the unique double spiral column.

## St-Sulpice

*pl St-Sulpice, 6th (01.46.33.21.78). M° St-Sulpice.* **Open** 8.30am-7.30pm daily. *Guided tours* 3pm the second Sunday of every month. **Admission** free.

Work on this giant church started in 1646, but it was only completed 120 years later after six architects had worked on the building. The grandiose Italianate facade is the work of Jean-Baptiste Servandoni, from 1733-45, although the two towers remained unfinished at his death. The south one has never been completed, and is still five metres short of its neighbour. Servandoni had originally planned to construct a semi-circular place in front of the church, but this was never carried out and the present one was designed in the last century by Visconti, who also designed the fountain. The church's interior is famed for the three murals by Delacroix in the first chapel on the right of the entrance, depicting Jacob's fight with the Angel, Heliodorus chased out of the temple and St Michael killing the Dragon. Don't miss the two giant shell water stoops – a gift from the Doge of Venice to François 1er in the sixteenth century.

## Tour St-Jacques

*pl du Châtelet, 4th Paris. M° Châtelet-Les Halles.*

Much-loved by the Surrealists and complete with gargoyles, this solitary Flamboyant Gothic bell-tower is all that remains of the church of St-Jacques-La-Boucherie, built for the powerful Butchers' Guild in 1523. Pascal carried out experiments into the weight of air here in the seventeenth century. A weather station now crowns the 52-metre high tower, which can only be admired from outside.

## Val-de-Grâce

*pl Alphonse-Laveran, 5th (01.40.51.47.28). RER Port-Royal.* **Open** *from Dec 1997* 10am-noon, 2-5pm, daily.

This church and its surrounding Benedictine monastery – now a hospital and a small medical museum – were built by François Mansart and Jacques Lemercier, in fulfilment of Anne of Austria's vow to erect 'a magnificent temple' if God blessed her with a son. He promptly presented her with two. Extraordinarily expensive and built over several decades, the recently restored Val-de-Grâce is the most luxuriously Baroque of the city's seventeenth-century domed churches, closely influenced by the Redentore in Venice, with a few Bernini-esque touches like the baldaquin with spiral columns borrowed from St Peter's in Rome. Bernini himself greatly admired Mignard's dome fresco, saying that it was 'the masterpiece of French art'. Its swirling colours and forms are meant to give the viewer a foretaste of heaven. The church is closed until Dec 1997.

# Seats of Power

## Assemblée Nationale

*33 quai d'Orsay, 7th (01.40.63.60.00). M° Assemblée Nationale.* **Open** *Guided tours only* 10am, 2pm, 3pm Sat when Chamber is not in session; ID required; arrive early.

The Palais Bourbon has been home to the Assemblée Nationale, the lower house of the French parliament, since 1827, and was the seat of the German military administration during the Occupation in World War II. Originally built in 1722 for Louis XIV's daughter, the Duchess of Bourbon, the palace was later extended by the Prince de Condé, who added the Hôtel de Lassay, today official residence of the Assembly's president. The Greek-style facade facing the Seine was simply stuck onto the building under Napoléon in 1806 to echo that of the Madeleine across the river; the real entrance is via the place du Palais Bourbon. Inside, the library is decorated with Delacroix's *History of Civilisatio*n.

## La Bourse

*Palais Brongniart, pl de la Bourse, 2nd (01.40.26.41.12). M° Bourse.* **Guided tours** every 15 minutes, 1.15-4pm Mon-Fri. **Admission** 30F; 15F students.

It was Napoléon who gave Paris its temple of business, Paris' stock exchange, also known as the Bourse des Valeurs, to differentiate it from the former corn exchange at Les Halles, the Bourse du Commerce (*see chapter* **Business**). After

being housed at different times in the rue Vivienne, the Louvre and the Palais-Royal, the stock exchange moved to the building designed for it by Alexandre Brongniart in 1808. Its grandiose columned frontage is typical of First Empire Neo-Classical taste; two new wings were added in 1902 to give the building the shape of a cross. The steps to the east and west are flanked by four allegorical statues representing Business, Justice, Agriculture and Industry.

## Hôtel de Ville

*pl de l'Hôtel de Ville (main public entrance 29 rue de Rivoli), 4th (01.42.76.50.49). M° Hôtel-de-Ville.* **Open** for tour groups and during exhibitions only.

The fanciful confection of the Hôtel de Ville, the city hall, symbolises the power of the City of Paris rather than state government. There has been a town hall here since 1260, but it's best remembered for the part it played in the Revolution. King Louis XVI was obliged to kiss the tricolore here in 1789, and three years later Danton, Marat and Robespierre made the Hôtel their seat of government. Revolutionaries again made it their base in 1871, when the Commune was proclaimed, but in May, the building was recaptured by the government and wrecked in savage fighting. It was rebuilt in 1873-82, and much enlarged in a fanciful neo-Renaissance style. Guided tours view the seven different types of wood on the dining-room floor, the 24 lavish chandeliers and the statue on the roof symbolising the city of Paris.

## Palais du Luxembourg

*rue de Vaugirard, 6th. M° Odéon/RER Luxembourg.*

The Palais du Luxembourg, which now houses the French Senate, was originally built for Henri IV's widow Marie de Médicis in the 1620s by Salomon de Brosse, on the site of the former mansion of the Duke of Luxembourg. Its Italianate style was intended to resemble the Pitti Palace in her native Florence, although she did not live here for long, as Richelieu had her exiled to Cologne. The palace and its grounds, the **Jardins du Luxembourg**, remained in royal hands until the 1789 Revolution, when they passed to the state. The palace now houses the French Senate.

# Streets & Squares

## Avenue des Champs-Elysées

*8th. M° Concorde, Champs-Elysées-Clemenceau, Franklin D Roosevelt, George V, Charles de Gaulle-Etoile.*

The most famous street in Paris, the Champs-Elysées (the 'Elysian Fields') can be a disappointment on first tourist-filled sight. Nonetheless, despite the proliferation of burger bars, over-priced cafés, car showrooms and shopping malls, vestiges of the street's grandeur remain, whether in the vivacity of its night life, the queues outside the cinemas, the pomp and ceremony of the 14 July parade, the New Year celebrations, the excitement of the final stage of the Tour de France, or quite simply the impressive vista at night stretching from the floodlit place de la Concorde at one end to the Arc de Triomphe at the other. One of Jacques Chirac's worthier efforts as mayor was a major facelift for the avenue, with new underground car parks and smart granite paving.

Despite some early landscaping in the seventeenth century as a continuation of the **Jardin des Tuileries**, the Champs-Elysées long remained pretty rural, and shortly before the Revolution the local guard worried that the area's dark corners offered 'to libertines and people of bad intentions a refuge that they can abuse'. During the Second Empire, the Champs-Elysées became a focus of fashionable Parisian society, and smart residences and hotels were built along its upper half. The Prussian army in 1871 and Hitler's troops in 1940 both made their point by marching down it,

*Ladies of the* **place de la Concorde** *fountains get an eyeful of the Eiffel Tower.*

amid a silently hostile reception, but loud celebrations accompanied the victory march along the avenue in 1944. The English Gardens by place de la Concorde, the Grand Palais and Petit Palais, the Arc de Triomphe, the gourmet restaurants **Laurent** and **Ledoyen** and the elegant houses at the Rond-Point are some of the area's major highlights.

## Place de la Bastille

*11th/12th/4th. M° Bastille.*

Nothing remains of the infamous Bastille prison which, on 14 July 1789, was stormed by the assembled forces of the plebeian revolt. Although by that time only a handful of prisoners were incarcerated there, the event provided the rebels with gunpowder, and gave the insurrection momentum. It remains the eternal symbol of the Revolution, which is still celebrated here with a particularly lively street *bal* every Bastille Day. The prison was quickly torn down, and most of its stones were used to build the Pont de la Concorde, although supposed bits and pieces of it could be bought from local entrepreneurs for months afterwards. In the Bastille Métro station vestiges of the prison's foundations can be seen. The Colonne de Juillet, topped by a gilded *génie* of Liberty, in the middle of the square, commemorates the Parisians killed during the later revolutions of July 1830 and 1848. The place has traditionally been a boundary point between central Paris and the more proletarian east, but this is an area which has been undergoing enormous rejuvenation, sparked off partly by the vast new **Opéra Bastille** and by the creation of the Port de l'Arsénal marina to the south, to become one of the most buzzing areas in town.

## Place de la Concorde

*8th. M° Concorde.*

Planned by Jacques-Ange Gabriel for Louis XV in 1753, the place de la Concorde is the largest square in Paris, a great hub of the city, with grand perspectives stretching east-west from the Louvre to the Arc de Triomphe, and north-south from the Madeleine to the Assemblée Nationale across the Seine. The construction of this giant space took several years, and disaster marred the fireworks planned here to celebrate the marriage of the Dauphin to Marie-Antoinette in 1770, when over a hundred people were crushed falling into a ditch in the unpaved place. Gabriel also designed the two grandiose colonnaded mansions on either side of rue Royale: the one on the west now houses the exclusive Crillon hotel (*see chapter* **Accommodation**), while the other is the Navy Ministry. The place was further embellished in the nineteenth century when the fountains, depicting river and maritime navigation, sturdy classical lamp-posts and the obelisk from Luxor were added. It's at its most beautiful at sunset or when lit up at night, the best view being from the terrace by the Jeu de Paume at the end of the Jardin des Tuileries.

## Place de la Contrescarpe

*5th. M° Place Monge or Cardinal-Lemoine.*

Originally a medieval square by the city wall, picturesque place de la Contrescape has been a famous rendezvous since the 1530s, when writers Rabelais, Ronsard and Du Bellay frequented the cabaret de la Pomme de Pin at No 1. Today, it's still popular with students and tourists, who flock into the bars and cheap restaurants of nearby rue Mouffetard.

## Place Dauphine

*1st. M° Pont-Neuf.*

This square at the tip of the Ile de la Cité was commissioned, like the place des Vosges, by Henri IV (*see also chapter* **Architecture**). A leafy oasis amongst the surrounding grand buildings, home to several small art galleries and restaurants, it feels peculiarly insulated from the city, and was a great favourite of Surrealist André Breton. André Malraux had a Freudian analysis of its appeal – 'the sight of its triangular formation with slightly curved lines, and of the slit which bisects its two wooded spaces. It is, without doubt, the sex of Paris which is outlined in this shade.'

# Crime & Intrigue

Paris offers plenty of shady history for budding Sherlocks and Maigrets, with celebrity scandals and political intrigue high on the agenda, in some of Paris' most respectable-seeming *quartiers*. You only need to look at a copy of *Paris Match* to realise that little has changed. Aspiring sleuths should also take in the **Musée de la Contrefaçon** and the **Musée de la Préfecture de Police**, while tap in the word 'meurtre' into the database of the **Vidéothèque de Paris** and you'll get a cool 119 responses to murder in the Paris film archives.

### Deadly Potions

Chic Marais resident, the Marquise de Brinvilliers, set out on her career as France's most notorious poisoner on 12 rue Charles V, 4th. She learned the art from her lover, who had picked up the basics in the Bastille, and then practised on several unfortunate patients she visited at the Hôtel Dieu hospital and on her servants before eliminating her prime target, *cher papa*. She then worked her way through her brothers to obtain the family fortune. Ironically, it was the natural death of her lover which revealed an account of her activities and several lethal phials secreted *chez lui*. She was beheaded in the place de Grève in 1672, now the place de l'Hôtel de Ville. Records of her arrest can be seen in the **Musée de la Préfecture de Police**.

### Queenly Gems

Even the most richly adorned cleavage in the kingdom was not scandal-free. The scandal of Marie-Antoinette's necklace involved the Cardinal de Rohan, who resided in palatial style at 87 rue Vieille-du-Temple. In 1785, Rohan purchased a bauble for the Queen for the colossal sum of 1.5 million *livres*. It was suspected that royal subterfuge had been used to obtain the jewels at the expense of her good subjects; it was even rumoured that her majesty was not above swapping sexual favours for costly gems. The Cardinal was exonerated, but his coterie remained mired in intrigue. During the Revolution, the residence housed a group that helped plot the fall of Robespierre.

### Royal Heads

Louis XVI's may have been the most famous head to roll under the Revolution in 1793, but he was only one of a long line of monarchs to die an unnatural death. Poor Henri IV survived at least 23 attempts on his life, before he was finally assassinated in rue de la Ferronerie near Les Halles by François Ravaillac, a fanatical Catholic, who had followed the royal carriage since the Louvre. The mobbed streets of Les Halles (nothing changes), allowed him to get near enough to Henri IV to stab him three times. The king died an excruciating death, Ravaillac languished in the **Conciergerie**.

Post Revolution rulers weren't immune either, although King Louis-Philippe had a lucky escape in 1835 at 50 boulevard du Temple, when the Corsican conspirator Fischi and cronies fired a primitive machine gun from here in an attempt to assassinate the king on his way to Bastille Day festivities. Unfortunately for them, they merely succeeded in killing some of the entourage and were subsequently executed.

### Politics & Intrigue

French politics have continued to be a colourful, stunt-filled affair this century. The Café du Croissant, 146 rue Montmartre, 2nd, is a café with a past, where Socialist leader Jean Jaurès was assassinated on 31 July 1914. Only a few years later in 1932, at the **Hôtel** Saloman de Rothschild, 11 rue Berryer, 8th (now the **Centre National de la Photographie**), the Russian Gorguloff fatally injured French President Paul Doumer. The pistol concerned can be seen in the **Musée de la Préfecture de Police**. The intrigue continued. Charles de Gaulle is said to have survived his real-life Day of the Jackal in place du 18 juin at Montparnasse. Arch-intrigue artist François Mitterrand claimed he was nearly victim of a gun ambush near the Observatoire behind the Lumembourg Gardens in 1957. One-time friend and adviser to Mitterrand, Peter Greenaway's documentary *Les Morts de la Seine* looks at their watery misery.

Drowning in the Seine isn't the only route to a water, death: Parisians seem to have a special proclivity for meeting the Grim Reaper in their bathrooms. Revolutionary Marat met his waterloo in the tub, at his home in rue des Cordeliers (now rue de l'Ecole de Médecine, 5th). He was stabbed to death in 1793 by Charlotte Corday, but gained eternity through David's celebrated painting of his wet demise. The scene is commemmorated in wax at the **Musée Grévin**.

Nearly 200 years later, disco diva Claude François (best known for singing the original French version of 'My Way') expired suddenly while having a soak in his luxury flat at 46 bd Exelmans, 16th. Though no pictorial record commemorates it, there's no lack of lurid images in the public's mind, as rumours he electrocuted himself with a mysterious electrical appliance refuse to die.

If you've overcome the desire to crowd the most visited tomb in the **Cimetière Père Lachaise**, you might pay homage at 17 rue Beautreillis, 4th, from where Jim Morrison was taken feet first after allegedly suffering a drug overdose in his bathtub.

### Soggy Endings

Between 1795 and 1801, 306 bodies were fished out of the Seine. Even for violent times, this was remarkble. Whether suicides, accidental deaths or villainous murders, Peter Greenaway's documentary *Les Morts de la Seine* looks at their watery misery.

## Place Vendôme
*1st. M° Tuileries or Opéra.*

The wonderfully elegant place Vendôme got its name from the *hôtel particulier* built by the Duc de Vendôme previously on this site. Inaugurated in 1699, the eight-sided *place* was conceived by Hardouin-Mansart to show off an equestrian statue of the Sun King. This statue was torn down in 1792, and in 1806 a Colonne de la Grande Armée, modelled on Trajan's column in Rome and with a bronze frieze made out of 1,250 Russian and Austrian cannons captured at the battle of Austerlitz, was erected by Napoléon to celebrate his own martial triumphs. During the 1871 Commune this symbol of 'brute force and false glory' was pulled down by the revolutionaries, among them the painter Courbet. The present column is a replica, put in place only three years later, with most of the original frieze. Today the square is home to Paris' most exclusive jewellers, international banks, the Justice Ministry and the Ritz hotel, at No 15. Chopin died at No 12, in 1849. The place was recently given a face-lift, and an underground car park has removed cars from its surface.

## Place des Victoires
*1st, 2nd. M° Bourse.*

Louis XIV introduced the grand Baroque square to Paris. The first Parisian square built in his honour was the circular place des Victoires, designed in 1685, like place Vendôme (*see above*), by Hardouin-Mansart to set off an equestrian statue of the Sun King. The original disappeared during the Revolution, and the current statue dates from 1822. Today, the sweeping facades shelter some of the most prestigious names in fashion, such as Kenzo and Thierry Mugler.

## Place des Vosges
*4th. M° St-Paul.*

Ruling at the heart of the historic Marais, the first planned *grande place* in Paris, was built between 1605 and 1612 by Henri IV, and inspired the nobility to build lavishly in the surrounding district (*see chapter* **The Right Bank**). Originally called the place Royale, the square's modern name dates from the Napoleonic Wars, when the Vosges was the first region of France to pay its war taxes. Mme de Sévigné, the famous salon hostess and letter writer, was born here in 1626. With its beautifully harmonious red brick and stone arcaded facades and steeply pitched roofs, the square is intimate, and quite distinct from the more pompous grandeur of later Bourbon Paris. In Mme de Sévigné's time the garden reputedly saw duels and romantic trysts; it now attracts a mix of boules players and children.

## Place du Tertre
*18th. M° Abbesses.*

Formerly a real village square and now one of the biggest tourist traps in Paris at the top of Montmartre, full of hustling quick-portrait sketchers and tacky restaurants, it remains an awesome warning of what tourism can do to village life. According to popular myth, Russian soldiers invented the word 'bistro' at the restaurant La Mère Catherine, during the Russian occupation in 1814, when they ordered their coffee to be brought to them *bistro* – fast.

# Underground Paris

## Les Catacombes
*1 pl Denfert-Rochereau, 14th (01.43.22.47.63).*
*M° Denfert-Rochereau.* **Open** 2-4pm Tue-Fri; 9-11am, 2-4pm, Sat, Sun. Closed public holidays. **Admission** 27F; 19F under-25s, students, over-60s; free under-7s. **No credit cards.**

These dank, subterranean passages stretching for miles have existed since Roman times. Towards the end of the eighteenth century many of the old, over-crowded Paris cemeteries were emptied out, and their contents transferred here, to what had been the stone quarries of Montrouge. Stacks of

bones are neatly arranged in patterns, interspersed with tidy rows of skulls, while mottoes and macabre quotations inscribed on stone tablets add philosophical reflections on death. There are supposedly bits of some six million people down here, including victims of the revolutionary Terror.

## Les Egouts de Paris (The Sewers)
*Entrance by the Pont de l'Alma, opposite 93 quai d'Orsay, 7th (01.47.05.10.29). RER Pont de l'Alma or M° Alma-Marceau.* **Open** Oct-Mar 11am-5pm. Apr-Sept 11am-4pm Mon-Wed, Sat, Sun. Closed for three weeks in Jan. **Admission** 25F; 20F students, under-16s.

Truly the city's underbelly. Part of its sewers have been made into one of the smelliest museums in the world, leading through several tunnels, with huge metal pipes overhead and murky green water flowing rapidly beneath the grating underfoot. On display there are various pieces of equipment used in the purifying process, while a slide show and display recount the history of the Parisian water and sewer systems. You can find out that a certain M. Poubelle (who gave the dustbin its French name) first initiated household waste collection, and that each Paris sewer is marked with a replica of the corresponding street sign above it, making the 2,100 kilometre system a real city beneath a city.

# Tours & Guided Visits

## Paristoric
*11bis rue Scribe, 9th (01.42.66.62.06). M° Opéra.* **Shows** Apr-Oct hourly 9am-9pm daily; Nov-Mar hourly 9am-6pm Mon-Thur, Sun; hourly 9am-9pm Fri, Sat. **Admission** 50F; 40F unemployed, over-60s; 30F under-18s, students.

A 45-minute, armchair ride which flashes through 2,000 years of Paris history, from Roman Lutétia to the Louvre Pyramid. Images are beamed from 26 projectors onto a huge screen, accompanied by music and Dolby cannon fire. Headset commentary in English and other languages.

## Paris-Vélo
*2 rue du Fer-à-Moulin, 5th (01.43.37.59.22). M° Censier-Daubenton.* **Open** 10am-12.30pm, 2-7pm Mon-Sat; 10am-2pm Sun. **Tickets** 150F; 120F under-26s; 180F/150F *night-time tours*; includes tour, bike rental, insurance. **Credit** MC, V.

Gentle three-hour bike tours around Paris accompanied by a bilingual guide, including a Paris-by-night ride.

## Canal Trips
**Canauxrama** *(01.42.39.15.00). Departs* Bassin de la Villette, 13bis quai de la Loire, 19th, M° Jaurès 9.45am, 2.25pm daily; and Porte de l'Arsenal, 12th, M° Bastille 9.45am, 2.30pm daily. Trips (fewer in winter) last 2-3 hours. **Tickets** 75F; 60F stuents, unemployed, over-65s; 45F 6-12s; free under-6s. Live commentary in French, and in English if enough foreigners, otherwise a written text. **Navettes de la Villette** *(01.42.39.15.00). Shuttle service between Parc de la Villette, M° Porte de Pantin and Rotonde deLa Villette, M° Jaurès.* **Departs** every 30 mins: Apr-Sept 11am-12.30pm Wed; 1.30-6.30pm, Sat, Sun, holidays; Jul-Aug 11am-12.30pm, 1.30-6.30pm, daily. **Tickets** 10F single; 15F return.
**Paris Canal** *(01.42.40.96.97). Departs* Musée d'Orsay, M° Solférino 9.30am, arrives Parc de la Villette, M° Porte de Pantin 12.30pm, daily. **Departs** 5 Mar-11 Nov Parc de la Villette 2.30pm, arrives Musée d'Orsay 5.30pm, daily. **Tickets** 95F; 70F 12-25s, over-60s (except Sun afternoons and Bank Holidays); 55F 4-11s; free under 4s.

## Coach Tours
**Balabus Hours** *Apr-Sept* 12.30-8pm, Sun and public holidays. **Tickets** four RATP tickets or fewer depending

on the length of the journey.
Bus along sites between La Défense and Gare de Lyon.
**Cityrama** *4 pl des Pyramides, 1st (01.44.55.61.00). M°
Palais Royal.* **2-Hour Tour** *Summer* hourly 9.30am-
4.30pm hourly daily; *winter* 9.30am, 10.30am, 1.30pm,
2.30pm daily. **Ticket** 150F; 75F 4-11s (under -12s free in
winter). **Credit** AmEx, DC, MC, V.
Tours of the classic sites of Paris. Recorded commentary in
English. Also longer artistic and panoramic tours.
**Parisbus** *(01.42.30.55.50).* First and last bus leave from
Eiffel Tower, quai Branly, 7th; stops include Notre-Dame,
Musée d'Orsay, Opéra, Arc de Triomphe, Grand Palais.
Bus runs every 50 minutes. **Trips** every 50 minutes
*Easter to end July* 10am-5pm; *Aug-mid Oct* 9.45am-
4.50pm; *mid Oct-Easter* 9.55am-2.55pm, daily. **Tickets**
125F; 100F students, unemployed, over-60s; 60F under-
12s; free under-4s. **No credit cards.**
Red London doubledeckers with a pre-recorded commentary
in English. You can get off and on at will at any of nine stops
and tickets are valid for two days.
**Paris Vision** *214 rue de Rivoli, 1st (01.42.60.31.25). M°
Tuileries.* **Trips** hourly 9.30am-3.30pm daily. **Tickets**
150F; 75F 4-11s; free under-4s. **Credit** AmEx, DC, MC, V.
Tickets are available from the departure point 15 minutes
before the trip. Pre-recorded commentaries.

## Seine Boat Trips

A Seine trip is an ideal way to see the city from river level.
Apart from Batobus which is a summer river bus service, all
offer commentary in French, English and sometimes other
languages, and vary in size from vast 800-seat Bateaux
Mouches to the smaller Vedettes du Pont-Neuf.
**Bateaux-Mouches** *pont de l'Alma, right bank, 8th
(01.40.76.99.99/recorded info/01.40.76.99.99/lunch or
dinner booking 01.42.25.96.10). M° Alma-Marceau.*
**Departs** every 30min from 10am-12.30pm, 1.30-11pm,
daily; trip lasts one hour. **Tickets** 40F; 20F under-14s;
free under-5s. **Book** ahead for lunch 1pm departure (300F;
150F) and dinner 8.30pm departure (500F, smart dress)
cruises. **Credit** AmEx, DC, MC, V.
**Bateaux Parisiens Tour Eiffel** *port de la
Bourdonnais, 7th (01.44.11.33.55). M° Bir-Hakeim or
Trocadéro.* **Departs** half-hourly; *summer* 10am-10pm
daily; *winter* 10am-9pm, daily. **Tickets** 45F; 20F under-
12s. *Lunch cruises* 300F; *dinner cruises* 550F. **Credit** (for
meal cruises only) MC, V.
**Bateaux Vedettes de Paris** *port de Suffren, 7th
(01.47.05.71.29) M° Bir-Hakeim/RER Champ de Mars.*
**Departs** half hourly; *summer* 9am-11pm; *winter* 9am-
6pm, daily. **Tickets** 45F; 20F 5-12s; free under-5s.

**Credit** AmEx, V.
**Batobus** *stops at Eiffel Tower, Musée d'Orsay, the
Louvre, Notre Dame and quai de l'Hôtel de Ville.
(01.44.11.33.44).* **Departs** *Apr-Sept* half hourly 10am-
7pm daily. **Tickets** per station 12F; day pass 60F. **No
credit cards.**
**Les Vedettes du Pont Neuf** *1 square du Vert-Galant,
1st (01.46.33. 98.38). M° Pont-Neuf.* **Departs** *summer*
every 30 mins: 10am-noon, 1.30-6.30pm, daily; floodlit
evening trips 9-10.30pm daily; *winter* times depend on
demand. **Tickets** 45F; 20F 4-10s; free under-4s.

## Walking Tours

There are many individual guides who organise walks (in
French), details of which are published weekly in *Pariscope*.
The Caisse Nationale des Monuments Historiques et des
Sites (Hôtel de Sully, 62 rue St-Antoine, 4th/01.44.61.20.00),
does tours of monuments, museums and historic districts (in
French). The tours listed below have English-speaking
guides; their walks are usually listed in *Time Out Paris*, but
most will also organise walks for groups on demand. Walks
usually last around 90 minutes; prices do not include additional entrance fees for museums or other sights visited.
**Anne Hervé** *(01.47.90.52.16).* **Tours** Sat and Sun in
summer; fortnightly in winter. **Tickets** 50F.
**Paris Contact** *Jill Daneels (01.42.51.08.40).* **Tours**
2.30pm Mon, Fri; otherwise phone for details. **Tickets**
60F; 50F students, over-60s.
**Paris Walking Tours** *Oriel and Peter Caine
(01.48.09.21.40).* **Tours** last 90 minutes, usually Tue,
Thurs, Sat, Sun, phone for details. **Tickets** 60F; 40F
students; free under-10s (except sewers).
**Walking the Spirit** *(01.42.29.60.12).* **Tours** 9.30am
Sat, Sun. **Tickets** 100F. Tours associated with African-
Americans in Paris.

## Le Petit Train de Montmartre

*Leaves from pl Blanche, 18th (01.42.62.24.00). M° Blanche.*
**Trips** *summer* every 20 mins, 9.30am-2am daily; *winter*
every 40 mins, 10am-6.30pm, daily. **Tickets** 30F; 18F
under-12s.
Miniature train tours around Montmartre.

## Hélifrance

*4 av de la Porte de Sèvres, 15th (01.45.54.95.11/
01.45.57.53.67). M° Balard.* **Open** 8am-8pm Mon-Fri;
9am-6pm Sat, Sun. **Price** 30min flight 850F; 1,200F 45-
min scenic tour. **Credit** AmEx, MC, V.
Five passengers can take off for a helicopter trip over the St-
Cloud forest, then back via the Chevreuse Valley.

*The* **Ile de la Cité** *still ruling the waves.*

# Parks & Cemeteries

*Paris looks set for a new image as a garden city, as a spate of park building adds to Haussmann's foundations.*

Over the past two decades Paris has been making up for its lack of green space. Derelict industrial sites, and even aerial spaces, have been converted in a fervour for garden-building that beats anything since Baron Haussmann under the Second Empire. Beyond his notorious boulevards, the unsung Haussmann also aimed to 'ventilate' the city. Together with his engineer Adolphe Alphand, Haussmann spruced up the royal hunting forests of **Bois de Boulogne** and **Bois de Vincennes**, redesigned **Parc Monceau** and created the **Parc Montsouris** and **Buttes-Chaumont**, as the informal *jardin à l'anglaise* vied for popularity with the paths and terraces of Le Nôtre's *jardin à la française* in the **Tuileries**. Today's adventurous new gardens, like the **Parc André Citroën**, take both these traditions but are strictly contemporary. Other gardens lurk secretly behind palatial *hôtels particuliers* or within courtyards, but those that can be visited include the gardens of the **Musée Rodin** and the **Hôtel de Sens**.

Most parks are open daily from early morning until early evening. The Mairie de Paris publishes a brochure of guided visits to Paris gardens (in French), available from the Service des Visites, 3 av de la Porte d'Auteuil, 16th/01.40.71.75.23.

## Classic Parks

### Jardin du Luxembourg

*pl Auguste-Comte, pl Edmond-Rostand or rue de Vaugirard, 6th. M° Odéon/RER Luxembourg.*
Part formal garden with its terraces and gravel paths, part 'English garden' of lawns and part amusement centre for gardenless Parisians, the Jardin du Luxembourg is the quintessential Paris park. The gardens were created for Marie de Médicis at the same time as the Palais du Luxembourg (*see chapter* **Sightseeing**), but were much reworked by Chalgrin last century. Dotted around the park is a veritable gallery of French sculpture from the looming Cyclops on the 1624 Fontaine de Médicis to the right of the palace, to wild animals, queens of France, a mini-version of Bartholdi's *Statue of Liberty* and a monument to Delacroix by Dalou. There are apple orchards, containing over 300 varieties of apple, and an apiary where you can take courses in the art of beekeeping. The Luxembourg is also a park of action: children can enjoy pony rides, sandpits and roundabouts, and sail toy boats on the large octagonal pond; there are tennis courts, boules pitches, a café and a bandstand, while the green park chairs are beloved of both booklovers and *drageurs*. The perspective from the palace continues south across rue Auguste-Comte in the Jardins de l'Observatoire.

### Jardin des Plantes

*pl Valhubert, rue Buffon or rue Cuvier, 5th (01.40.79.30.00). M° Gare d'Austerlitz or Jussieu.*
Although small and slightly rundown, the Jardin des Plantes contains over 10,000 species of plants, including winter and

*Conserving energy at the **Jardin des Tuileries**.*

Alpine gardens and tropical greenhouses (open selected days and hours). Originally planted by Louis XIII's doctor Guy de La Brosse as the royal medicinal plant garden in 1626, the Jardin opened to the public in 1640, and also contains a small zoo and the assorted pavilions of the Muséum National d'Histoire Naturelle (*see chapters* **Museums** *and* **Children**), of which the magnificent Grande Galerie de l'Evolution sits resplendent like a palace at the end of formal beds. Behind, a charming eighteenth-century yew maze, designed by the botanist Buffon, spirals up a little hill to an iron gazebo. Several ancient trees include a cedar planted in 1734.

### Jardin des Tuileries
*rue de Rivoli, 1st. M° Tuileries or Concorde.*
Stretching between the Louvre and the place de la Concorde, the gravelled alleyways here have been a fashionable promenade ever since opened to the public in the sixteenth century. The gardens were laid out in roughly their present form by André Le Nôtre, who began his illustrious career as royal gardener here in 1664 (*see also* Versailles *and* Vaux-le-Vicomte *in chapter* **Trips out of Town**), creating the prototype *jardin à la française* with its terraces and central vista running through round and octagonal ponds, and continuing along what would become the Champs-Elysées. By the nineteenth century, cafés and other entertainments flourished and when the Tuileries palace was burnt down by the Paris Commune in 1871, the park was expanded rather than rebuild the palace. As part of the *Grand Louvre* project, the most fragile sculptures, including Coysevox's winged horses, have been transferred to the Louvre and replaced by copies, the 18 Maillol sculptures have returned to the Jardin du Carrousel (the part nearest to the Louvre), while replanting has restored parts of Le Nôtre's design and renewed trees damaged by pollution. Today, the Tuileries still have a pleasure-garden feel, with pony rides, boules players, cafés and ice cream kiosks and a big funfair every summer.

### Parc des Buttes-Chaumont
*rue Botzaris, rue Manin, rue de Crimée, 19th. M° Buttes-Chaumont.*
This fantasy wonderland is the perfect, picturesque meeting of nature and the artificial with meandering paths and vertiginous cliffs. It was designed by Alphand in the 1860s for Haussmann on the site of a gypsum quarry, rubbish tip and sinister public gibbet. From the summit, waterfalls cascade out of a man-made cave, complete with fake stalactites, while out of the artificial lake rises a 50 metre-high rock reached by impressive suspension bridge. Climb to the little classical gazebo, modelled on the Temple of the Sibyl at Tivoli, at the top of the island, from where there are superb views of the Sacré-Coeur and the surrounding area.

### Parc Monceau
*bd de Courcelles, 17th. M° Monceau*
Surrounded by grand *hôtels particuliers*, the Monceau is a favourite with well-dressed *BCBG* children and their nannies. It was laid out in the late eighteenth century for the Duc de Chartres (Philippe Egalité) in the English style that was then so fashionable, with an oval lake, spacious lawns and a variety of follies – an Egyptian pyramid, a Corinthian colonnade, Venetian bridge and ancient tombs. Alphand transformed it into a public park and added a fragment of the old Hôtel de Ville. At the main entrance is one of the tax pavilions constructed by Ledoux.

### Parc Montsouris
*bd Jourdan, 14th. RER Cité-Universitaire.*
Another of Alphand's parks for Haussmann, on the southern edge of the city, with obligatory lake and artificial cascades. Its gently sloping lawns descend towards a lake, with turtles and ducks, and the variety of its bushes and trees and beautiful flowerbeds make it the most colourful of all the capital's parks. Spot the bed planted with different roses for French newspapers and magazines.

*The romantically rundown* **Serres d'Auteuil**.

### Les Serres d'Auteuil
*3 av de la Porte d'Auteuil, 16th (01.40.71.75.23).*
*M° Porte d'Auteuil.* **Open** 10am-5pm daily.
**Admission** 5F; 2.50F 6-18 years, free over-60s, under-6s.
**No credit cards.**
These wonderfully romantic glasshouses were opened in 1895 to cultivate plants for parks and public spaces across Paris. Today there are special seasonal displays of orchids and begonias, but best of all is the steamy tropical central pavilion with palm trees, twittering birds and a pool of Japanese ornamental carp.

## Beyond the Périphérique

### Les Jardins Albert Kahn
*14 rue du Port, 92100 Boulogne (01.46.04.52.80).*
*M° Marcel-Sembat.* **Open** May-Sept 11am-7pm Tue-Sun;
Oct-Apr 11am-6pm Tue-Sun. **Admission** 22F; 15F
students, over-60s; free under-8s. **No credit cards.**
With its painted red bridges, coloured maples, bamboos, Japanese shrines and houses, cascading streams and geometric landscaping, the Jardins Albert Kahn should be twee, but remarkably aren't. Instead they pack an enormous variety of habitats, species and, quite simply, moods into a small space. The famed Japanese garden is followed by a quadrangle of roses and fruit trees, and then leads via the Blue Forest – where misty spruces and tall cedars cast an undeniably blue haze – via marshy Marais to the boulders, ferns and pines of the Vosgeian forest, like a lump of Alsace transplanted. Water and evergreens dominate the gardens, making them interesting even in winter.

### Parc de St-Cloud
*92100 St-Cloud (01.45.66.57.89). M° Pont de Sèvres and
cross river.* **Open** Mar-Oct 7.30am-9pm; Nov-Feb 7.30am-
8pm. **Admission** free; 13F for cars.
This is a rare park where you can walk, picnic, play football or frisbee on the grass, cycle or hire a peddle car, making an ideal weekend escape route. But underneath is another classic French park laid out by Le Nôtre, now all that remains of a royal château that once belonged to 'Monsieur', brother of Louis XIV, and was destroyed by fire in 1870, three months after the Franco-Prussian war was declared in the château. There are complex arrangements of avenues that meet in stairs, long perspectives, stepped terraces, a great view over Paris from the Rond-Point du Balustrade and a

series of pools and fountains, of which the most spectacular is the Grande Cascade, a multi-tiered feast of dolphins and sea beasts, switched on at 4pm on the second and fourth Sundays of the month from May to September.

## Into the Twenty-First Century

From sound gardens to ornamental vegetables, these adventurous futurist parks may occasionally allow you to walk on the grass, but don't ever forget their intellectual flavour.

### Jardin de l'Atlantique

*entry from Gare Montparnasse or pl des Cinq-Martyrs-du-Lycée-Buffon, 15th. M° Montparnasse-Bienvenüe.*
Perhaps the hardest of all to find, the Jardin de l'Atlantique, opened in 1995, takes the Parisian quest for space airbound with an engineering feat suspended 18 metres over the railway tracks of Montparnasse station to provide a small oasis of paths, trees and bamboo in an urban desert.

### Parc André Citroën

*rue Balard, rue St-Charles, quai Citroën, 15th. M° Javel or Balard.*
Laid out on the site of the Citroën car factory in western Paris, this park is the twenty-first-century equivalent of a French formal garden, comprising two large glasshouses, computerised fountains, waterfalls, black and white gardens, a wilderness and a series of small glasshouses and gardens planted with different-coloured plants and even sounds. What at first seems rather cold merits exploration, for modern-day Le Nôtres (Gilles Clément and Alain Prévost) have been at play: stepping stones and kids rushing between water jets prove that this is a garden for pleasure as well as philosophy. Opened in 1993 and still developing, the park will eventually extend to the Seine.

### Parc de Bercy

*rue de Bercy, 12th. M° Bercy.*
Taking shape on the site of the Bercy warehouses across the river from the new national library, Bercy combines the French love of geometry with that of food. There's a large lawn crossed by paths with trees and pergolas, and a grid with square rose, herb and vegetable plots, an orchard, and gardens representing the four seasons. Brick paths still with

**Les Jardins Albert Kahn**: *a garden idyll.*

iron wagon tracks have been preserved to guard the memory of barrels wheeled in from boats on the Seine. While you're here take a look at the cascading exterior of the American Center, designed by Californian architect Frank Gehry, and now sadly closed and seeking a buyer.

### Parc de la Villette

*av Corentin-Cariou, 19th. M° Porte de la Villette. or av Jean-Jaurès, 19th. M° Porte de Pantin.*
Dotted with the quirky bright red pavilions or *folies* designed by Swiss architect Bernard Tschumi, the Parc de la Villette is a postmodern feast between the Cité des Sciences et de l'Industrie in the north and the Cité de la Musique in the south, all on the site of former abattoirs, of which only the Grand Halle remains. The design may have originated from a complicated theory of points, lines and surfaces, but the result is fun. The *folies* serve as glorious climbing frames in additions to such uses as first aid post, burger bar, children's art centre and Hot Brass jazz club. Children shoot down a Chinese dragon slide and a meandering suspended path follows the Canal de l'Ourcq that bisects the park. As well as big lawns or prairies, ten themed gardens have evocative names such as the Garden of Mirrors, of Mists, of Acrobatics and of Childhood Fears.

### La Promenade Plantée

*av Daumesnil, 12th. M° Bastille, Ledru-Rollin, Gare de Lyon or Daumesnil.*
There's life above art as the railway tracks above the Viaduc des Arts (*see chapter* **Sightseeing**) have been replaced by a promenade planted with roses, shrubs and clumps of rosemary by architect Philippe Mathieux and landscape designer Jacques Vergely. The walk offers great high-level views into neighbouring apartments. It continues through modern housing, the Jardin de Reuilly and the Jardin Charles Péguy on to the **Bois de Vincennes** at the Porte Dorée in the east. Roller bladers are banned but no one seems to have noticed.

## The Bois

### Bois de Boulogne

*16th. M° Porte-Dauphine or Sablons.*
Covering over 865 hectares, the Bois is a series of gardens within sometimes-scrubby woodland. Most pleasant is the Parc de Bagatelle (route de Sèvres à Neuilly, 16th/ 01.40.67.97.00. open 9am-5.30pm), surrounding a château that formerly belonged to Richard Wallace, the Marquis of Hertford. The gardens are famous for their roses, spring daffodils and water lilies. The Jardin d'Acclimatation is an amusement park for kids (*see chapter* **Children**). The Bois also has two lakes, racecourses (Longchamp and Auteuil), several restaurants, 140,000 trees and many tracks and paths to accommodate horse riders and cyclists. Packed at weekends with dog walkers, picnickers and sports enthusiasts, at night it's much more seedy, and despite clean-up attempts is still associated with kerb-crawling and prostitution.

### Bois de Vincennes

*12th. M° Porte-Dorée or Château de Vincennes.*
East of the city is Paris' biggest park. Formerly the royal forest of the Valois, it was made into a park in 1860 by Napoléon III, and owes much to Haussmann's landscape architect Alphand, who added the lake and cascades that are a major part of its charm. Boats can be hired on the lake, and there are various cycle paths, a Buddhist temple, a racetrack, baseball field and flower gardens. It also contains Paris' **Zoo** (*see chapter* **Children**), and the Cartoucherie theatre complex (*see chapter* **Theatre**), while next to the park is the imposing **Château de Vincennes**, where England's Henry V died in 1422. The **Parc Floral de Paris** (esplanade du Château, 12th/01.43.43.92.95) boasts horticultural displays, summer concerts, a picnic area, exhibition space, children's amusements and crazy golf.

Remember furry loved ones at the **Cimitière des Chiens**.

# Dead & Buried

Under Napoléon I, the prefect Frochot created new cemeteries at the gates of the city: Père Lachaise in the east, Montparnasse in the south and Montmartre in the north, all of which came within the capital when the city's boundaries were extended in 1860. Unless stated, cemeteries are generally open from 8am or 9am daily to around 6pm (5pm in winter).

## Cimetière de Montmartre

*20 av Rachel, access by stairs from rue Caulaincourt, 18th (01.43.87. 64.24). Mº Blanche.*

A small, romantic ravine – which was once quarries, then a communal burial pit before moving up in the world intellectually – on the slopes of the Butte Montmartre. Here you will find playwright-actor Sacha Guitry, François Truffaut, Emile Zola, Nijinsky, Berlioz, Dégas, Greuze, Offenbach, Feydeau, Alexander Dumas *fils*, German poet Heine and many other writers and artists, reflecting the theatrical and artistic past of the area. There's also *La Goulue*, real name Louise Weber, first great star of the Can-Can and model for Toulouse Lautrec, celebrated beauty Mme Récamier, and the consumptive heroine Alphonsine Plessis, inspiration for Dumas' *La Dame aux Camélias* and Verdi's *La Traviata*. Flowers and poems are still left daily for Lebanese diva Dalida, who lived nearby.

## Cimetière de Montparnasse

*3 bd Edgar-Quinet, 14th (01.44.10.86.50). Mº Edgar-Quinet or Raspail.*

Pay homage to writers Jean-Paul Sartre and Simone de Beauvoir, Baudelaire, Maupassant and Tristan Tzara, composers César Frank and Saint-Saëns, sculptors Dalou, Rude, Batholdi, Laurens (with a black marble mourner) and Zadkine, the unfortunate Captain Alfred Dreyfus, André Citroën of car fame, and the delightful M and Mme Pigeon reposing in their double bed. More recent occupants of this 44-acre cemetery include Jean Seberg, waiflike star of *A bout de souffle*, beloved comic Coluche and *provocateur* Serge Gainsbourg. In the northeast corner is one of Brancusi's best known sculptures, *Le Baiser*, adorning one of the tombs. The ruins of a windmill are a relic of a more rural past.

## Cimetière de Passy

*2 rue du Commandant-Schloesing, 16th (01.47.27.51.42). Mº Trocadéro.*

The Grim Reaper comes even to the wealthiest districts. Tombs include those of composers Debussy and Fauré, painters Manet and his sister-in-law Berthe Morisot and writer Giraudoux among numerous generals and politicians.

## Cimetière du Père Lachaise

*Main entrance bd de Ménilmontant, 20th (01.43.70.70.33). Mº Père-Lachaise.*

With its thousands of tightly packed tombs arranged along cobbled lanes and tree-lined avenues, this vast cemetery is almost like a miniature city in itself and is supposedly the most visited cemetery in the world. Its hilly site gives a great perspective over Paris. Funerary memorials and family vaults range from the plain and sombre to the grandiose, and plots can still be leased. Named after the Jesuit priest Père de la Chaise, Louis XIV's confessor, the first part of the cemetery was laid out by the architect Brogniart in 1804 with trees and natural curving alleys. The *Colombarium* (crematorium) was added in 1889. The presumed remains of the medieval lovers Abélard and Héloïse were moved here in 1817 along with Molière and La Fontaine in a bid to gain public popularity for the cemetery. This was clearly effective as the famous inhabitants soon multiplied, among them Sarah Bernhardt, Colette, Edith Piaf, Delacroix, Ingres, Géricault, Bizet, Balzac, Proust and Chopin (his empty tomb), as well as lesser-known figures who have contributed to Parisian history. The biggest draw is Jim Morrison, who was buried here in 1971. His grave still attracts a flow of spaced out pilgrims; the graffiti will show you the way. Also visit Oscar Wilde's tomb, whose headstone was carved by Epstein. It's a winged, naked, male angel which was considered so offensive when first erected (the *mot juste*), that it was neutered by the head keeper, who subsequently used the offending part as a paper-weight. The north-east corner of the cemetery wall, the '*Mur des Fédérés*', got its name after 147 members of the Paris Commune of 1871 were shot against it (*see* chapter **Empires & Revolutions**). Nearby is a memorial to members of the resistance deported during World War II.

## Cimetière des Chiens

*4 pont de Clichy, 92600 Asnières (01.40.86.21.11). Mairie de Clichy.* **Open** Mar-Oct 10am-noon, 3-7pm, Mon, Wed-Sun; Nov-Apr 10am-noon, 3-5pm, Mon, Wed-Sun. **Admission** 15F; 5F children. **No credit cards**.

'Deceived many times by humans, never by my dog.' Paris has 200,000 dogs and some of them, along with many cats, a horse and a monkey, end up here at the dog cemetery of Asnières, on a brightly forlorn island in the Seine. A rather decaying neo-Byzantine entrance points to a grander past, although efforts are being made to restore some of the finest tombs. Just within the portals lies a grand monument, a small girl draped over a large dog: Barry the St Bernard 'who saved the lives of 40 persons. He was killed by the 41st.' Here we are in a poignant otherworld of beloved Trixies, Oscars and much-missed Fidos, redolent both of beloved animals and of lonely lives. There is even room for the wicked: 'the errant dog', who one summer day in 1958 died at the gates of the cemetery and was the 40,000th beast to be buried here.

# History

# Key Events

## Roman Paris & the Dark Ages

**c 250** BC *Lutetia* founded on the Ile de la Cité by a Celtic tribe, the Parisii
**52 BC** Paris conquered by the Romans
**260** St Denis executed on Montmartre
**361** Julian, Governor of Lutetia, becomes Roman Emperor
**451** Attila the Hun nearly attacks Paris
**508** Frankish king Clovis makes Paris his capial
**635** first Fair of St-Denis
**800** Charlemagne, first Holy Roman Emperor. Moves capital from Paris to Aix-la-Chapelle
**840-880** Paris sacked by the Vikings
**987** Hugues Capet, Count of Paris, first King of France

## Middle Ages to Renaissance

**1136** Abbot Suger begins Basilica of St-Denis
**1163** Building of Notre Dame begun
**1190-1202** Philippe-Auguste constructs new city wall enclosing Left and Right banks
**1215** University of Paris recognised with Papal Charter
**1340** Beginning of Hundred Years' War with England
**1357** Revolt by Etienne Marcel
**1364** Charles V moves royal court to the Louvre
**1420-1436** Paris under English rule
**1473** First printing press in Paris
**1528** François 1er begins rebuilding of Louvre
**1572** St Bartholemew's Day massacre of Protestants
**1593** Henri IV becomes a Catholic, ending Wars of Religion

## Ancien Régime

**1605** Building of Place des Vosges begun
**1610** Henri IV assassinated
**1634** Académie Française founded by Cardinal Richelieu
**1643** Cardinal Mazarin becomes Regent
**1648-1653** Paris occupied by the *Fronde* rebellion
**1661** Louis XIV begins personal rule
**1667** Paris given its first street lighting
**1672** Creation of Grands Boulevards on line of Charles V's city wall. Portes St-Denis and St-Martin built.
**1682** Louis XIV transfers Court to Versailles
**1700** Beginning of War of the Spanish Succession
**1715** Death of Louis XIV
**1720** John Law's bank scheme collapses
**1751** First volume of Diderot's *Encyclopédie* published
**1753** Place Louis XV begun, later Place de la Concorde
**1785** Tax Wall built around Paris
**1789** First meeting of Estates-General called since 1614

## Revolutions & Empires

**1789** 14 July: Paris mob takes the Bastille. October: Louis XVI forced to leave Versailles for Paris. Population of Paris is then about 600,000
**1791** 20 June: Louis XVI attempts to escape from Paris
**1792** September Massacres. 22 September: Republic declared
**1793** Execution of Louis XVI and Marie-Antoinette. Louvre museum opens to the public
**1793-1794** The Terror in Paris.

**1794** July: Jacobins overthrown; Directory takes over
**1799** Napoléon stages coup, and becomes First Consul
**1804** Napoléon declares himself Emperor
**1806** Napoléon orders building of the Arc de Triomphe
**1814** Napoléon defeated; Russian army occupies Paris
**1815** Napoléon regains power for the 'Hundred Days'. Napoléon defeated at Waterloo, abdicates for second time. Bourbons restored, with Louis XVIII
**1828** Paris given first horse buses
**1830** July: Charles X overthrown: Louis-Philippe of Orléans becomes king
**1837** First railway line in Paris, to St-Germain en Laye
**1848** Louis-Philippe overthrown: Second Republic, most men get the vote. Louis-Napoléon Bonaparte is elected President
**1852** Following coup, Louis-Napoléon declares himself Emperor Napoléon III: Second Empire.
**1853** Haussmann appointed Prefect of Paris
**1862** Construction of Opéra Garnier begun
**1863** Manet's *Déjeuner sur l'Herbe* first exhibited
**1870** Prussian victory at Sedan. Napoléon III abdicates

## The Third Republic

**1871** Commune takes over Paris after the Prussian siege
**1889** Paris Exhibition on centenary of Revolution: Eiffel Tower built
**1895** Dec: First public cinema screening in Paris by the Lumière brothers
**1900** Paris World Exhibition: population of Paris then two million. First Métro line opens.
**1904** Pablo Picasso moves to Paris
**1914** As World War I begins, Germans beaten back from Paris at Battle of the Marne
**1919** Peace conference held at Versailles
**1936** France elects Popular Front government
**1940** Germans occupy Paris
**1942** Mass deportation of Paris Jews
**1944** 25 August: Paris liberated. Women given the vote.

## De Gaulle to Chirac

**1946** Fourth Republic established
**1947** Dior's New Look.
**1949** Simone de Beauvoir publishes *The Second Sex*
**1955-1956** Revolt begins in Algeria
**1957** Opening of CNIT in new La Défense business district
**1958** De Gaulle President: Fifth Republic
**1959** France founder member of EEC (European Economic Union)
**1968** May: student riots and strikes in Paris and across France
**1969** De Gaulle resigns; Les Halles market closes
**1973** Boulevard Périphérique around Paris inaugurated
**1977** Centre Pompidou opens. Jacques Chirac elected Mayor of Paris
**1981** François Mitterrand elected President
**1989** Bicentenary of the Revolution celebrated: Louvre pyramid and the Opéra Bastille both completed
**1992** Disney theme park opens outside Paris
**1995** May: Jacques Chirac elected President
**1996** December: Openig of new Bibliothèque Nationale François Mitterrand.

# Roman Paris & the Dark Ages

**Early tribes and Roman invaders set the framework of Paris, and saintly miracles abound.**

In about 250BC a Celtic tribe called the Parisii first established a fishing settlement on the Ile de la Cité, probably driven from lands further east by the more powerful Belgae. Their new settlement on a road linking Germany to Spain and at the confluence of three rivers, the Seine, the Marne and the Oise, was a natural crossroads. Rich in agricultural land and stone quarries, the community flourished. The Celts were canny traders, and grew prosperous, as a hoard of local gold coins from the first century BC – now in the Musée des Antiquités Nationales in St-Germain-en-Laye (pl du Château /01.34.51.53.65) – indicates.

Its strategic position also made the city a prime military target. By the first century BC the Romans had arrived in northern Gaul. Julius Caesar mentions 'the city of the Parisii, situated on an isle in the Seine', known as *Lutetia*, in his *Gallic Wars*.

In 53 BC when the Celtic tribes, the Senones and the Carnutes, refused to send delegates to Julius Caesar's Assembly of Gaul at Amiens, Caesar ordered the assembly to the Ile de la Cité to keep watch over the rebellious tribes. The following year, the Celt Vercingétorix spearheaded a countrywide revolt, joined by Camulogenus, who took control of Lutétia, while his army camped on Mons Lutetius, later site of the Panthéon. Labienus, Caesar's lieutenant crushed the rebels at Melun, then crossed the Seine and marched downstream, his four legions camping in an area now occcupied by the Louvre's Cour Carrée. In a brief, but cataclysmic battle on the approximate site of the Champ de Mars, Camulogenus and his army were massacred, and Vercingétorix was captured; thereafter the Parisii tribe was under Roman rule, as indeed was the rest of Gaul.

Lutétia thrived under Roman rule. The town spread from the Cité across the **Petit Pont** to the Left Bank, fanning out on either side of the *cardus maximus* (main thoroughfare), the present-day **rue St-Jacques**. Many of its villas were of masonry, brick and mortar, some embellished with carving, stucco, frescoes and mosaics. A model of the ancient city, along with architectural vestiges, is on view at **Musée Carnavalet**. It was during the golden age of Gallo-Roman architecture (around AD50-200) that Lutétia acquired its grandest public buildings. The remains have been uncovered of a forum on **rue Soufflot** and a trio of bathing establishments (rue des Écoles, rue Gay-Lussac and boulevard St-Michel). Parts of the city wall and a hypocaust have been uncovered at the **Archaeological Crypt** of Notre Dame. There was also a temple to Jupiter nearby, where the cathedral now stands. Only the 10,000-seat arena **Arènes de Lutèce**, where Romans watched Christians being slaughtered by lions, and the baths at the **Thermes du Cluny** reflect anything of their former glory today.

## ST DENIS

Christianity made its first appearance in the city in the third century AD, when the Athenian St Denis, first bishop of Lutétia, was sent to evangelise its people. Legend has it that one day, he and two companions began to knock pagan statues off

*Roman bathing at the **Thermes du Cluny**.*

their pedestals. They were immediately arrested, and the Roman governor decreed that they should be decapitated on Mount Mercury, thereafter known as Mons Martis or Mount of Martyrs, later Montmartre. Headless and bleeding, the plucky Denis picked up his bonce and walked away, his lips chanting psalms. He finally fell at a seemingly predestined site north of Paris, where a pious Christian woman buried him. A sanctuary was later erected on the spot where this was believed to be, since replaced by the **Basilica of St-Denis**.

By the time of Denis, around 260, Roman power was weakening, and Lutétia was under increasing attack from barbarian invaders from the east. Many of its inhabitants retreated to their ancestral island in the Seine, and a wall was built around the Cité. Lutétia, however, would still be able briefly to become one of the capitals of the Roman Empire.

In 313 the Emperor Constantine effectively made Christianity the new religion of the Empire. In 357, a new governor and military commander arrived in Lutétia, Constantine's nepthew Julian. He did a great deal to improve the city and its defences; he could also be said to be the first independent Parisian intellectual, seeking to return to Platonic ideals in opposition to what he saw as the brutality of Constantine and subsequent Christian emperors. Julian continued to call the town Lutétia, even though an imperial decree of 212 resulted in Lutétia being renamed Paris, after the Parisii. In 361, following a series of victories against the barbarians, his army declared him Roman Emperor in Paris. Condemned by Christian historians as 'Julian the Apostate', he could do little to turn back the new faith or the decline of Rome, for he was killed in battle in 363.

## THE MEROVINGIANS

By the beginning of the fifth century, Roman rule had effectively collapsed in northern Gaul, and its cities were left to fend for themselves. In the chaos that followed, it was the exemplary life of St Geneviève and the threat of war – that helped confirm many converts in the new faith. As the legend goes, in 451 Attila the Hun and his army were approaching Paris. Its people panicked, and prepared to flee. But Geneviève, a saintly Christian girl, urged them to stay put. She told them the Hun would spare them so long as they repented of their sins and prayed with her. And miraculously, Attila did not attack but moved off to the south. Geneviève was acclaimed as the saviour of Paris.

Her powers of resistance were not limitless. In 464 another barbarian, the Frank Childeric, attacked Paris, and in 508 his son Clovis made it his capital, using the former Roman governor's palace on the Ile de la Cité as the seat of his realm. The now-aged Geneviève was, however, successful in converting the new king to Christianity. He was baptised by St Rémi in Reims in 996 (*see chapter* **Trips Out of Town**).

Clovis (ruled 481-511) began the Merovingian dynasty, known as the 'Long-haired kings' because they never cut their hair. On the Left Bank he founded the abbey of St Pierre and St Paul (later renamed the abbey St Geneviève), where he, his queen Clotilde and Geneviève could be buried side by side. The Tour de Clovis, within the Lycée Henri IV is a last relic of the basilica. St Geneviève who died in around 512 is regarded as the patron saint of Paris; there is a shrine and her relics in the church of St-Etienne-du-Mont. His son and successor Childéric II founded the equally renowned abbey of **St-Germain-des-Prés**. This did not mean that the Merovingians were especially pious. Rather, they were extremely brutal, particularly to each other. Under their law an inheritance had to be divided equally among any heirs. This led to regular bloodletting and infanticide between royal princes, dowager queens and uncles, in fratricidal antics that would finally snuff out the line in 751. Most productive of the dynasty for Paris was Dagobert (628-638), who established the important annual Fair of St-Denis just outside the city, which would play a major part in cementing Paris' position as the commercial – and cultural – hub of northern France.

## CAROLINGIANS & VIKINGS

The Merovingians were succeeded by the Carolingians, after Charles Martel ('the Hammer'), credited with having halted the spread of Islam by his victory over the Moors at Tours in 732. In 751 his son Pepin 'the Short' was proclaimed King of all the Franks. His heir Charlemagne extended the Frankish kingdom and was crowned Holy Roman Emperor by the pope in 800. Charlemagne, however, moved his capital to Aix-La-Chapelle (Aachen), which led Paris to become something of a backwater, entrusted to a hereditary Count.

After Charlemagne, the Carolingian empire gradually fell apart, as its predecessors had done. Over the next century, Paris suffered from famine, floods and marauding Vikings (the Norsemen or Normans), who sacked the city repeatedly between 845 and 885 and looted wealthy abbeys like St-Germain-des-Prés. The local aristocracy and clergy were ever-more frustrated at the inability of their 'emperors' to help them against the Norsemen and sought a leader of their own. When the Emperor Charles II the Bald showed little interest in defending the city, the Parisians sought help from Robert the Strong, Count of Anjou and a renowned warrior. His son Eudes (Odo), succeeded him as Count of Paris, and led the defence of the city in a ten-month long Viking seige in 885, sharing the throne 893-898 with Charles III the Simple. The feudal lords thus came to outpower their masters and in 987, the Count of Paris, Hugues Capet, great-grandson of Robert the Strong, was elected King of France by his peers at Senlis, and made Paris his capital. A new era was beginning.

# Middle Ages to Renaissance

***The Capetians put Paris at the heart of France and, despite wars and rebellions, the city's intellectual reputation is established.***

The ascension of Hugues Capet, founder of the Capetian dynasty, is the point from which 'France' can be said to exist. For a long time, however, the 'kingdom' consisted of little more than the Ile-de-France, and powerful local lords – in Normandy, Burgundy, the south, and later the possessions of the Kings of England – would defy the royal authority for centuries. France would largely be created through the gradual extension of Parisian power. Equally, the entire country's history is peculiarly inseparable from that of its capital city.

The early Capetians made very slow progress, although Paris continued to grow in importance, thanks in good part to its many powerful abbeys, and to the important fairs of St-Germain and St-Denis. In the twelfth century, the city became the centre of a spectacular renaissance, as a boom in commerce and construction made Paris into a political, economic, religious, and cultural capital.

A major figure in this expansion was Suger, Abbot of St-Denis and minister to a series of weak monarchs, Louis VI (the Fat) and Louis VII (the Younger). The latter unwisely divorced the first of his three wives, Eleanor of Aquitaine, who subsequently married Henry II of England, bringing a vast portion of southwest France under English control. Abbot Suger did much to hold the state together and give it an administration; as a priest, in 1136 he commissioned the new **Basilica of St-Denis**, since the old church could no longer house the pilgrims who flocked to the shrine. Considered the first true Gothic building, St-Denis had a prodigious influence across France and beyond, setting the style for ecclesiastical building for the next four centuries. Gothic spires began to soar above the Paris skyline. In 1163, Bishop Sully of Paris began the construction of **Notre Dame**, the embodiment of the High Gothic aesthetic.

## ABELARD & HELOISE

Paris also developed a reputation as a centre of learning. The abbeys had kept scholastic traditions alive during the preceding centuries, and by the eleventh century the Canon school of Notre Dame was already widely admired for its schol-

**Charles VII** *by Jean Fouquet.*

arship. By about 1100, scholars began to move out from the cathedral school and teach independently in the Latin Quarter.

One of the first independent teachers was a brilliant logician and dialectician called Peter Abélard, who had rooms in **rue Chanoînesse**, behind Notre Dame, a rare part of the Ile de la Cité where the street plan today remains much as it did when trod by Medieval scholars. In 1118, when he was 39, he was employed by Canon Fulbert of Notre Dame as tutor to his 17-year-old niece Héloïse. They began a passionate affair, which was discovered by the Canon. Twice he enjoined them to remain celibate; twice they failed to obey him, until Fulbert, enraged, had Abélard castrated and Héloïse consigned to a convent. During the rest of their lives, Abélard wrote some of the most refined works of Medieval philosophy, while Héloïse wrote ardent, poetic letters to her lost lover. The two were reunited in death and today occupy a fanciful neo-Gothic tomb in **Père Lachaise** cemetery.

The Paris schools gradually became more formally organised, and in 1215 combined to form a 'university', under papal protection. The greatest Medieval thinkers studied and taught in this 'New Athens'; the German theologian Albert the Great, the Italians Thomas Aquinas and Bonaventure, the Scots Duns Scotus and the Englishman William of Ockham. Most famous of its colleges was the **Sorbonne**, founded in 1253 by Robert de Sorbon, chaplain of King Louis IX (*see below*).

## PHILIPPE AUGUSTE

The first great Capetian monarch was Philippe Auguste (1180-1223), the great rival of Richard the Lionheart of England. Philippe greatly extended the power of the French crown, winning Normandy off John Lackland and adding the Auvergne and Champagne to his kingdom. He was also the first great royal builder to leave his mark on Paris. Abandoning the city's old Roman defences, he built a new, larger fortified city wall, chunks of which can still be seen in **rue des Jardins-St-Paul** in the Marais and **rue Clovis** in the Latin Quarter. He also began a new royal fortress on the Right Bank, the **Louvre**, although his main residence was still on the Ile de la Cité. In 1181, he established permanent covered markets, *Les Halles*, on the site they would occupy until 1969. He also sought to do something about the city's putrid mud and foul odours, ordering the first paving of streets in post-Roman Paris, and closing the most pestilential cemeteries.

Paris' merchants and trade guilds flourished and established a position of power they would retain for centuries. The centre of city (rather than Court) institutions were the place de Grève, now **place de l'Hôtel de Ville**, and the **Châtelet** fortress.

## ST LOUIS & THE LAST CAPETIANS

Philip's grandson Louis IX (1226-70, St Louis) was famed for his extreme piety. When not on crusade, or scouring Europe for holy relics, he also put his stamp on Parisian architecture, commissioning the **Sainte-Chapelle**, convents, hospices and even student hostels. But it was his grandson, Philippe IV (the Fair, 1285-1314) who transformed the inelegant fortress on the Cité into a palace fit for a king, with the monumental Salle des Gens d'Armes in the **Conciergerie**, built to receive royal petitioners, reputedly the most beautiful hall in France.

The fourteenth century signalled troubled times for the French crown. Philippe IV died in 1314, the end of his reign marred by the debasement of the currency, insurrection in Paris and riotous debauchery at Court. In suspiciously quick succession, his three sons ascended the throne. The last, Charles IV, died in 1328 leaving no male heir.

## THE VALOIS KINGS

All this proved irresistible to the English, who claimed the French crown for young Edward III,

**François 1er** *immortalised by Jean Clouet.*

son of Philippe IV's daughter. The French refused to recognise his claim, since the traditional Salic law of the Franks barred inheritance via the female line. Philippe de Valois, the late king's cousin, claimed the crown for himself (Philippe VI, 1328-50), and thus began the Hundred Years' War.

The Black Death arrived in Europe in the 1340s and, in Paris, outbreaks of the plague alternated with battles, bourgeois revolts, popular insurrections and bloody vendettas between aristocratic factions. In 1355, Etienne Marcel, a rich draper, *prévôt* of the Paris merchants (sort of forerunner of the mayor of Paris) and member of the *Etats-généraux*, which had met for the first time in Paris in 1347, seized Paris, aiming to limit the power of the throne and to gain a city constitution for Paris from the Dauphin Charles (then regent as his father Jean II had been captured by the English). In 1358 Charles' supporters retook the city, and Marcel and his supporters were savagely executed. As king, however, Charles V 'The Wise' (1364-80), mindful of the city's defiance of royal authority, transferred his residence to the safety of the Louvre, where he installed both his library and precious works of art. He further extended the city walls and had a new stronghold built on the eastern edge of Paris, the **Bastille**. Despite the turmoil in the country, the arts were still able to flourish, and during this period Parisian artisans produced peerless miniatures, tapestries, manuscripts, and objects carved in ivory or wrought in silver and gold.

After the battle of Agincourt in 1415 the English, in alliance with the Dukes of Burgundy, seemed to have won, and from 1420 to 1436 Paris was under English rule (as was most of France), with the Duke of Bedford as governor. In 1431, Henry VI of England was crowned King of France in Notre Dame. However, for much of this time the city was virtually under siege by the French, at one time by Joan of Arc. Eventually, Charles VII (1422-61) was able to retake his capital.

## RENAISSANCE & HERESY

The last decades of the fifteenth century saw a rapid extension of royal authority, as the restored Valois monarchs sought to reaffirm their position. They also saw prosperity return to the capital, in the form of trade and the expansion of all kinds of crafts. Masons erected churches in the Flamboyant Gothic style (*see chapter* **Architecture**), as well as an impressive array of *hôtels* commissioned by nobles, prelates and the wealthy bourgeoisie, such as the **Hôtel de Cluny** and the **Hôtel de Sens**. Even in relatively humble households glass began to replace greased cloth and paper in windows, and forks appear for the first time on tables. The city's population tripled over the sixteenth century and the *faubourgs* outside the city walls also grew.

Printing was also introduced, largely thanks to two booksellers, Fust and Schöffer, who brought printed books to the city in 1463, supported by wily Louis XI (1461-81) against the opposition of the powerful scribes and booksellers' guilds. In 1470, Guillaume Fichet and Jean de la Puin of the Sorbonne invited Swiss printers to set up a press in Fichet's college rooms, and other printers followed. Soon books were no longer the reserve of the wealthy – by the end of the sixteenth century Parisian printers had published 25,000 titles.

## FRANCOIS IER

Most spectacular of the Valois kings was François 1er (1515-47), the epitome of a Renaissance monarch. He spent much of his time in endless wars with his great rival the Emperor Charles V, but also built sumptuous châteaux at **Fontainebleau**, **Blois** and **Chambord** (*see chapter* **Trips Out of Town**), and gathered about him a glittering court of knights, poets and Italian artists, such as Leonardo da Vinci and Benvenuto Cellini. He also set about making the Louvre habitable, beginning the palace that we can see today. Inside, he hung his favourite Titians, some Raphaels and the *Mona Lisa*. A native school of portraiture also developed with François Clouet preeminent.

All François' grandeur, however, was unable to prevent the advance of Protestantism. The strongholds of the Huguenots, or French Protestants, were mostly in the west; Paris, in contrast, was a citadel of virulent and often bloodthirsty Catholic orthodoxy, complicated by the interwoven aristocratic squabbles between the factions of the Huguenot Prince de Condé and the Catholic Duc de Guise, supported by François 1er's successor Henri II (1547-60). During the 1530s and '40s an increasing number of heretics were sent to the stake in the place de Grève, as the Renaissance and its carefree ambiance went up in smoke.

## THE WARS OF RELIGION

By the 1560s, the situation had degenerated into open warfare. Henri II's scheming widow Catherine de Médicis, regent for the young Charles IX (1560-74), was the real power behind the throne. Savagery was seen on both sides, and paranoia was rife. In 1572, Paris itself became a blood-bath. A rumour ran round that Huguenots were plotting to murder the royal family and sack the city; in anticipation, on 23 August, St Bartholomew's Day, Catholic mobs turned on anyone suspected of Protestant sympathies, killing over 3,000 people in the capital. When King Henri III (1574-89) sought to find a compromise between the two sides, Paris turned on its sovereign and forced him to flee the Louvre. In August 1589 he was assassinated by a fanatical monk, bringing the Valois line to an end.

Henri III had recognised his ally Henri of Navarre, a Huguenot, as heir. Henri of Navarre proclaimed himself King Henri IV, founding the Bourbon dynasty. Fervently Catholic Paris continued to resist in a siege that dragged on for almost four years. Inside the city, people ate cats, rats, horses, donkeys and even grass. Finally, in 1593 Henri IV agreed to become a Catholic and was received into the church at **St-Denis**, declaring that *'Paris vaut bien une messe'* (Paris is well worth a mass). On 22 March 1594, Henri entered the city; whatever the doubts over his sincerity, the Parisians were exhausted, and prepared to let the 'Wars of Religion' come to an end.

The tomb of **Henri II and Catherine de Médicis** at St-Denis.

# Ancien Régime

**Powerful cardinals pave the way for absolutism and French monarchy reaches its apotheosis under the Sun King.**

Henri IV undertook to unify the country and re-establish the power of the monarchy, considerably weakened by the Wars of Religion, aided by his able minister Sully. In Paris, he set about changing the face of his ravaged capital, giving it some of its most familiar and enduring features. He commissioned **place Dauphine** on the Ile de la Cité and, across the Seine, ordered the construction of Paris' first enclosed, geometrical square – the place Royale, now **place des Vosges**. Although nobles had started colonising the once-marshy area the previous century with Diane de France's **Hôtel Lamoignan** and the **Hôtel Carnavalet**, it was the royal sanction given by the place Royale which really set in motion the building of an entire elegant neighbourhood around it, the Marais.

Among his many improvements in Paris, Henri IV unfortunately never got round to improving the city's congested streets, habitually clogged with pedestrians, horses, donkeys and the latest innovation, the coach. On 14 May 1610, after at least 23 other assassination attempts had failed, the King was stabbed to death by a Catholic fanatic while caught in a bottleneck on the **rue de la Ferronnerie**. The *ancien régime* began as it would end: with regicide.

## CARDINAL RICHELIEU

When Henri died his son, Louis XIII (1610-43) was only eight years old, and Henri's widow, Marie de Médicis, was installed as regent. Her idea of her own importance can be seen in the retirement home she commissioned for herself, the **Palais du Luxembourg**, and the extraordinary series of 24 panels glorifying her role in history she had painted by Rubens, now in the Louvre. In 1617 Louis XIII, still only 16, was encouraged to take over power himself. The real head of his government, however, was Cardinal Richelieu, who in 1624 became the king's chief minister.

Richelieu won the confidence of anxious, tormented Louis XIII, who stuck by his minister through numerous plots hatched by his mother, his Queen, Anne of Austria, assorted royal princes and disgruntled grandees. A brilliant administrator, Richelieu returned the favour by creating a strong, centralised monarchy, effectively paving the way for the absolutism of Louis XIV, and steadily grinding down what he perceived as the two major enemies of the French monarchy:

abroad, Spain, and at home the independent power of the aristocracy, in particular, the Huguenots.

Richelieu was also one of the great architectural patrons of the age. He commissioned Jacques Lemercier to build him a palace, then known as the Palais Cardinal, later a royal residence as the **Palais-Royal**, and rebuilt the **Sorbonne** (Richelieu's tomb is in the chapel). This was also the height of the Catholic Counter-Reformation, and architects were given lavish commissions to create splendid Baroque churches, such as the **Val-de-Grâce**.

In the Marais, the aristocratic *hôtel particulier* flowered into a distinctive genre (*see chapter* **Architecture**). The literary lights of France's *Grand Siècle* often found their patrons in this area, where salons hosted by lettered ladies, like Mlle de Scudéry, Mme de la Fayette, Mme de Sévigné and the erudite courtesan Ninon de l'Enclos, rang with saucy wit, pithy asides and political intrigue. By comparison, Richelieu's Académie Française (founded in 1634) was a fusty and rather pedantic reflection of the establishment.

Similarly elegant *hôtels* to those of the Marais were built on the Ile St-Louis, urbanised in just 20 years, and in the quarter around the Cardinal's Palais-Royal, while slightly more modest residences appeared on the Left Bank, around the rue de Seine. Everybody who was anybody in France needed a suitably modern house in Paris, and speculators were eager to provide them.

## CARDINAL MAZARIN

Richelieu died in 1642. The following year Louis XIII also died, leaving once again an under-age heir, five-year-old Louis XIV. His mother, Anne of Austria, became regent, with as chief minister a follower of Richelieu, Cardinal Mazarin, whose palace forms part of the old **Bibliothèque Nationale** in rue de Richelieu.

From 1648 to 1653 the royal family was forced to flee Paris by the Fronde, a rebellion of peasants and some of the aristocracy against taxes and the growth in royal power. This incident has traditionally been believed to be one of the roots of Louis XIV's persistent dislike of his capital. For a time, Parisians supported the principal leader of the Fronde, the prince of Condé. However, they soon tired of anarchy and violence. When Mazarin and the boy-king Louis XIV entered Paris in 1653 behind an army raised by Mazarin himself, they

*The sun never sets on Rigaud's* **Louis XIV**.

were warmly received by the populace. Mazarin died in 1661, shortly after Spain, France's enemy since the days of François 1er, had been decisively defeated, leaving France more powerful than ever and with military capacity to spare.

## LOUIS XIV THE SUN KING

This was the launching pad for the personal rule of Louis XIV, who after the death of Mazarin announced that he would be his own chief minister, with the classically megalomaniac statement *'L'Etat, c'est moi'* ('The State is me'). Military expansion was essential to Louis XIV's concept of greatness, and so France engaged in continual wars, with the Dutch, Austria and England. Loyal theorists developed the idea of the absolute monarchy, and poured praise upon the 'Sun King'.

An essential figure in Louis' years of triumph was Jean-Baptiste Colbert, his minister of finance. Colbert took a particular interest in Paris. Steeped in the Classics, he envisaged Paris as a 'new Rome', with grand, symmetrical vistas. In the 1680s, the finely proportioned **place des Victoires** and **place Vendôme** were commissioned, both originally augmented by statues glorifying the king, and the first boulevards opened up with triumphal arches at the **Porte St Denis** and **Porte St Martin**. The Baroque city thus functioned as a kind of grand theatre, an expression of absolute monarchy in stone calculated to impress an already overawed populace still further.

Louis XIV, however, took little interest in Colbert's schemes. Such was his aversion to Paris that from the 1670s the focus of his interest was **Versailles**, to which he had decided to transfer the court, and into which he poured vast quantities of wealth. A place at court was essential for a successful career and the ambitious had no choice but to follow the monarch.

Culture and the arts flourished. In 1659 Molière's troupe of wandering actors settled in Paris under the protection of the King, presenting plays for both court and public. After the playwright's death in 1673, they became the **Comédie Française**. Favoured composer at Versailles was the Italian Lully, who was granted sole right to compose operas – in which the King himself often appeared – but other composers included Rameau and Charpentier, while Madame de Maintenon encouraged the tragedies of Racine.

For all its endlessly proclaimed grandeur, however, Louis XIV's regime already had within it elements of its own destruction. The royal finances were in permanent disorder, despite the best efforts of Colbert, and as the wars dragged on, the demands of the state in taxes were reflected in growing poverty and rising vagrancy, while endless wars left a legacy of a great many crippled veterans reduced to begging in the streets. The **Invalides** was built to house them, but it was never enough. It was estimated that about a tenth of the population of Paris were vagrants, vagabonds, delinquents, women of easy virtue *et al.* To deal with them in 1667 Colbert appointed Paris' first Lieutenant of Police, Gabriel de La Reynie. The **Salpêtrière**, a veritable city within a city, was erected to shelter women who were rounded up in Paris. Thus the administration tried to camouflage the misery of its underside – beneath domes and colonnaded façades.

France was increasingly exhausted in the last years of the Sun King's reign. Louis lost his most able assistant with the death of Colbert in 1683, and the military triumphs of earlier years gave way to the grim struggles of the War of the Spanish Succession. Life at Versailles soured under the dour Mme de Maintenon, Louis' last mistress, who he secretly married in 1684. Nobles started to sneak away from Versailles to build handsome *hôtels particuliers* in the fashionable new Faubourg-St-Germain.

## LOUIS XV

Louis XIV had had several children, but within a very short time, not long before his own death, both his son and grandson had died, leaving his five-year-old great-grandson, Louis XV (1715-74), as heir. The Regent, Philippe d'Orléans, speedily moved the Court back to Paris. Parisians were more than ready for a *bon vivant* after the deprivations of the recent past. The Regent, an able general and diplomat, was also known as a drinker, blasphemer and all-round rake, who liked to frequent Parisian gambling dens. Installed in the Palais-Royal, he regularly threw lavish dinners that degenerated into orgies.

The lives led by pleasure-loving courtiers and the Parisians who aped them spawned a large service population of dressmakers, jewellers, hairdressers, decorators and domestics of every degree. Tales of country youths corrupted by the city where they came to seek their fortune inspired writers from Marivaux to Rousseau, Restif de la Bretonne to the Marquis de Sade: Paris was the *nouvelle Babylone*, the modern Sodom.

The state, however, was by now chronically in debt, even though the Regent sought to avoid further military entanglements. The main form of taxation was in duties on commodities, especially salt. Collection was 'farmed out' to a kind of private corporation, the *Fermiers généraux*', who passed on an amount to the state and kept a profit for themselves. This system bore down disproportionately on the poor, was riddled with corruption and never produced the resources the state needed; nevertheless, so many interests were involved that none of the *ancien régime*'s ministers was ever able to abolish it.

The Regent Orléans thought he had found one remedy for the state's debts when he gave his support to a Scottish banker, John Law, for an investment scheme in France's colonies, known as the 'South Sea Bubble'. For a while, it inspired a mania of wheeling and dealing. Predictably, the bubble burst. In 1720, a run on the bank revealed that very little gold and silver was on hand to back up the paper bills. Panic ensued. Law was expelled from France, and the Regent, and to some extent royal government itself, were deeply discredited.

## THE AGE OF ENLIGHTENMENT

As soon as he was his own man, Louis XV quit Paris for Versailles, which once again saw sumptuous festivities. But in the Age of Enlightenment, Paris was the real capital of Europe, where the era's most brilliant minds met and matched wits. 'One lives in Paris; elsewhere, one simply vegetates', wrote Casanova. Intellectual activity was matched by a flourishing of the fine and decorative arts with fine *ormolu* furniture, the royal porcelain manufacture at Sèvres and painters like Boucher, Van Loo and Fragonard setting the style.

Paris' salons, hosted by a select group of influential women, became the most important forums for intellectual debate, under renowned hostesses like the Marquise du Deffand on rue de Beaune, Julie de Lespinasse, who held court on rue de Bellechasse, and Madame Geoffrin on rue St-Honoré. Their influence was such that on his arrival in the city Rousseau was told, 'You can't do anything in Paris without women'. It was to this lettered milieu that the King's mistress, the beautiful and cultivated Marquise de Pompadour (1721-64), belonged. She was a friend and protectress of Diderot and the *encyclopédistes*, of Marivaux and of Montesquieu; she also corresponded with Voltaire. She encouraged Louis XV to embellish his capital with monuments, such as Jacques-Ange Gabriel's **Ecole Militaire** and the place Louis XV (now **place de la Concorde**).

## LOUIS XVI, PRELUDE TO REVOLUTION

The great failure of Louis XV's reign was the defeat of the Seven Years' War (1756-63), in which France lost most of its colonies in India and Canada to Britain. His successor Louis XVI (1774-93), began his reign auspiciously enough.

Even though dire poverty could easily be found both in city and country, France was expanding economically and culturally and across Europe, people craved Parisian luxuries. The capital itself looked sprucer than ever. Roads were widened, lamps erected, gardens and promenades created, while there were an ever-wider selection of distractions. Nobs indulged in horse racing (a taste acquired from the English) at **Vincennes** and the **Bois de Boulogne**. On the boulevard du Temple, all classes rubbed shoulders to watch dancers, singers, acrobats and trained monkeys.

The city was obsessed with the new, whether it was ballooning (first demonstrated by the Montgolfier brothers in 1783) or the works of Rousseau, exalting 'Nature' and scorning aristocratic convention. Even royal princes flirted with the new sensibilities, as the Duc d'Orléans developed the **Palais-Royal** as a kind of open house for different classes, entertainments and ideas.

Meanwhile, Louis XVI's problems were made acute by having won a war. France's intervention in the American War of Independence regained several colonies; but also meant giving support to rebels, thus driving the royal finances towards total bankruptcy. Indecisive Louis XVI was his own worst enemy; as the 1780s wore on a series of ministers attempted sometimes radically different solutions to the financial situation, without ever being given adequate royal support. In 1785, at the behest of the *Fermiers généraux*, a tax wall was built around Paris, but only served to increase popular discontent (*see* chapter **Architecture**).

Louis' only remaining option was to appeal to the nation for help in maintaining the national finances, in the first place through the *parlements* or regional assemblies of lawyers, and if all else failed the *Etats-généraux*, the representation of the Nobility, Clergy and Commoners, which had not met since 1614. Given the mood in the country, this would inevitably involve altering the entire relationship between society and a monarchy that believed it had an absolute right to command. Louis XVI continued to prevaricate, as 1789 began.

# Revolutions
# & Empires

**The downfall of the monarchy, the advent of Liberté, Egalité and Fraternité: the first Revolution gives a taste for more.**

The spring of 1789 found Louis XVI increasingly isolated as unrest swept through France. In Paris, the people were suffering the results of a disastrous harvest, and there were riots in the Faubourg St-Antoine. When he finally agreed to convene the *Etats-généraux* at Versailles in May, the King was understandably apprehensive.

The members of the Third Estate, the commoners, aware they represented a far larger proportion of the population than nobility and clergy, demanded a system of one vote per member. Discussions broke down, and a rumour went round that the King was sending troops to arrest them. On 20 June 1789, at the Jeu de Paume at Versailles, the Third Estate took an oath not to separate until 'the constitution of the kingdom was established'. Louis finally backed down, and the Estates-General renamed itself the National Assembly and set about discussing a Constitution.

The debate, however, had gone beyond the Assembly into the Paris streets, among the poor *sans-culottes* (literally, without breeches, as only the poor then wore long trousers). It was assumed that any concession by the King was intended to deceive. Louis had posted foreign – Swiss and German – troops around Paris, and on 11 July dismissed his minister, Jacques Necker, considered the sole ally of the commoners. On 13 July an obscure lawyer named Camille Desmoulins leapt up on a café table in the **Palais-Royal** to speak. Likening Necker's dismissal to another St Bartholomew's Day, he called on all patriots to throw off slavery for ever. *'Aux armes!'* he exhorted the excited crowd: 'To arms!'

## STORMING THE BASTILLE

A crowd stormed the **Invalides**, carrying off thousands of guns, and then moved on to the **Bastille**, symbol of royal repression. Its governor, the Marquis de Launay, refused to surrender, but the huge crowd outside were ever more aggressive. What seems to have happened next is that a nervous Bastille sentry fired a shot, and within minutes they were all firing on the crowd. The mob, incensed, brought up cannon to storm the fortress.

*The guillotine: tool of the Terror.*

After a brief battle, during which 87 revolutionaries were killed, Launay offered his surrender. The crowd were in no mood to be forgiving, and he was immediately killed, his head paraded through Paris on a pike. Inside the hated Bastille the insurgents famously found only seven prisoners. Nevertheless, the Revolution now had the symbolic act of violence that marked a break with the past.

## REVOLUTIONARY PARIS

With the Revolution in motion, political debate in Paris proliferated on every side, above all in the rapidly multiplying political clubs, such as the

# Revolutionary treasure trail

Reminders of the Revolution exist all over Paris, for if the workers of popular *quartiers* like the Faubourg-St-Antoine provided the mob, lawyers and intellectuals preferred the cafés of the Palais Royal and St-Germain for plotting.

### Palais Royal
*1st. M° Palais-Royal.*
Owned by Louis XVI's cousin, the Duc d'Orléans, a revolutionary sympathiser known as Philippe Egalité, the palace sheltered many a political club. On 13 July 1789 political agitator Camille Desmoulins stood on a table in Café Foy (56-60 Galerie Montpensier), calling the crowd to arms and taking leaves from the garden's chestnut tree to make the first cockades. At 177 Galerie de Valois, Charlotte Corday bought the knife used to stab Marat.

### Tuileries
*1st. M° Tuileries or Concorde.*
The royal family were virtual prisoners in the Tuileries palace from October 1789 until 1792 when moved to the Temple prison. The Convention then moved in renaming it the Palace National. The palace burnt down under the Commune. Robespierre lived nearby at 398 rue St-Honoré.

### Conciergerie
*1 quai de l'Horloge, 1st (01.43.54.30.06). M° Cité or Châtelet-Les Halles.*
Prisoners awaited the guillotine in this medieval fortress. As a stone tablet inscribed with prisoners' names reveals, far from all, including a florist and a hairdresser, were of noble birth. Marie-Antoinette was held here from 11 September to 16 October 1793 (her cell is now a chapel), followed by many who had condemned her, including Robespierre. Under the Terror, the Salle des Gardes was so full it was divided vertically to house more prisoners.

### Bastille
*4th, 11th, 12th. M° Bastille.*
A plaque at 4 rue St-Antoine marks the entrance to the much-hated fortress prison stormed on 13 July 1789 and razed to the ground soon after. A fragment of the foundations can be seen on the platform of line 5 of the Métro, while those who stumble upon square Henri-Galli, will find a modest monument of foliage-covered stones.

### Hôtel de Ville
*4th. M° Hôtel de Ville.*
On 13 July, the city's electorate threw the monarch's city government out of the Hôtel de Ville and elected a Permanent Committee in its place. On 5 October, a swarm of women armed with pitchforks stormed the Hôtel de Ville against the bread shortage, but were diverted to Versailles with a petition for the king. During the Terror, the Hôtel de Ville was the seat of the government, a committee of twelve men, including Robespierre and St-Just, who sent an estimated 20,000 people to the guillotine.

### Couvent des Cordeliers
*15 rue de l'Ecole de Médecine, 6th. M° Odéon.*
Hotbed of plotting by the Club des Cordeliers, the former refectory of this convent remains within the Faculty of Medecine. A few doors down the street, then named rue des Cordeliers, Jacobin propagandist Jean-Paul Marat was stabbed in his bathtub by Charlotte Corday in 1793.

**La Chapelle Expiatoire**: *royal memorial.*

### Passage St-André des Arts
*6th. M° Odéon.*
Here Dr Guillotine, doctor of medecine, tried out his infamous tool, in a very French take on the industrial revolution, supposedly in the cellar of what is now the Pub St-Germain (*see chapter* **Cafés & Bars**).

### Champ de Mars
*7th. M° Ecole-Militaire.*
On 14 July 1790 Louis and Marie-Antoinette were among 200,000 celebrants of the Fête de la Fédération on the Champ-de-Mars, the first Bastille Day celebration. Prince Talleyrand, bishop of Autun and a member of the Assembly, celebrated mass at the Altar of the Fatherland.

### Place de la Concorde
*8th. M° Concorde*
Renamed place de la Revolution, the guillotine was set up here, for the executions of Louis XVI, Marie Antoinette, Philippe-Egalité, Danton, Mme de Barry and many more. Later transferred to the place de la Nation, it was back in place for the demise of Robespierre in 1794.

### Chapelle Expiatoire
*29 rue Pasquier, 9th (01.42.65.35.80). M° Madeleine.*
**Open** 10am-1pm, 2-5pm Wed.
Louis XVIII commissioned Fontaine to build a memorial chapel to the deposed monarchs, on the site of a cemetery where almost 3,000 victims of the Revolution were buried, including Philippe-Egalité, Charlotte Corday, Madame Roland, Mme du Barry, Camille Desmoulins, Malesherbes, Danton and Lavoisier, as well as Louis XVI and Marie-Antoinette, whose remains were found on the exact spot where the altar stands. Two marble statues represent Louis XVI supported by an angel and Marie-Antoinette, kneeling at the feet of Religion, represented by the King's sister, Mme Elisabeth.

Cordeliers, who met in the Franciscan monastery of the same name, or the radical Jacobins, who had taken over a Dominican convent on rue St-Honoré. Thousands of pamphlets were produced, read avidly by a remarkably literate public.

But there was also a very real level of hardship among the poor and a violence that came to the surface more and more frequently. Moreover, the disruption spreading through the countryside interrupted deliveries of wheat to Paris, raising bread prices still further. In October, an angry crowd of Parisian women, among them early feminist Théroigne de Méricourt, marched to Versailles to protest at the price of bread, the incident when Marie-Antoinette supposedly suggested they should try a *brioche*. The women ransacked part of the palace, killing some of its Guards, and were only placated when Louis XVI appeared with a revolutionary red-white-and-blue cockade and agreed to be taken to Paris. From then on, the royal family were virtual prisoners in the Tuileries.

In the Assembly, the prevalent political tendency was initially promulgated by the Girondins, who favoured some sort of agreement with the monarchy, but they were under ever-more intense attack from openly Republican groups like the Jacobins. By 20 June 1791, Louis decided he had had enough. He and his family sought to leave Paris by night, hoping to escape from France and organise resistance from safety abroad. They got as far as the town of Varennes, where they were recognised, and were returned to Paris as captives.

The following year, the monarchies of Europe formed a coalition to save Louis and his family. A Prussian army marched into France, and the Duke of Brunswick threatened to raze Paris if the King came to any harm. Paranoia was a fundamental element in events, for not just Louis but anyone who showed sympathy for him could be accused of conspiring with foreign powers against the people. On 10 August, an army of *sans-culottes* demanded that the Assembly officially depose Louis. This was refused, and the crowd attacked the Tuileries. The royal family were imprisoned by the radical Commune de Paris, led by Danton, Marat and Robespierre, which thus became the dominant force in the Revolution.

## THE TERROR

The next month, as the Prussians approached Paris, saw the 'September Massacres'. Revolutionary mobs invaded the city's prisons to eliminate anyone who could possibly be a 'traitor', in an orgy of bloodletting that accounted for close to 2,000 people. The monarchy was formally abolished on 22 September 1792, a day proclaimed the first day of 'Year I of the French Republic' in the radicals' all-new calendar. Almost immediately the French citizen army defeated the Prussians at Valmy. The Republic, it seemed, could be triumphant.

This was the beginning of the most radical phase of the Revolution. The Jacobins proclaimed the need to be implacable with 'the enemies within', and so Dr Guillotin's new invention took its place in the *place de la Révolution* (formerly Louis XV, now Concorde). Louis XVI was executed on 21 January 1793, to be followed in October by Marie-Antoinette.

They might have taken solace in the knowledge that the same fate awaited their executioners. In September 1793 the Revolutionary Convention, which had replaced the National Assembly, put 'terror on the agenda', in response to demands from the mob for more decisive action against foreign spies. An infernal machine was wound up that would claim thousands of victims before its energy expired. The Revolution, as the Jacobin St-Just said, 'devoured its own children': most of the leading Girondins, *Philippe-Egalité* of Orléans, and then even Jacobins such as Danton and Camille Desmoulins all travelled the same road from the Conciergerie to the scaffold. During the *Grande Terreur* of 1794, 1,300 heads fell in just six weeks.

## THE AGE OF REASON

The cultural transformation associated with the Revolution was also proceeding apace; churches were confiscated in November 1789, to be made like Notre Dame into 'Temples of Reason' or be put to practical uses. Many were vandalised, including transferring the carved bookcases from the Celestins convent to the Bibliothèque Nationale and transforming the Sainte-Chapelle into a storehouse for flour. The place du Trône (now place de la Nation) became place du Trône Renversé (place of the Overturned Throne) and an 'Altar of the Fatherland' was installed on the Champ de Mars. All titles were abolished – even *monsieur* and *madame* became *citoyen* and *citoyenne*. Artists also participated in the revolutionary cause. As well as painting portraits of revolutionary figures and the *Death of Marat*, David organised the Fête de la Régénération in August 1793 at the Bastille.

## THE DIRECTOIRE

The collective psychosis that was the Terror was unable to sustain itself forever. In July 1794 a group of moderate Republicans led by Paul Barras succeeded in arresting Robespierre, St-Just and the remaining Jacobins. They were immediately guillotined themselves, amid expressions of generalised hatred for these erstwhile popular heroes. With this, the Terror ended.

The wealthy of Paris, among them some Revolutionary *nouveaux riches*, emerged blinking into the fashionable corners of the city. Barras and his colleagues set themselves up as a five-man 'Directory' to rule the Republic. In 1795, they were saved from a revolt in Paris by an ambitious young Corsican general called Napoléon Bonaparte. France might no longer be the fire-breathing Republic of the Jacobins, but it was still at war with most of the monarchies of Europe. Bonaparte was sent to command the army in Italy, where he covered himself with unprecedented glory. In 1798, he took his army to Egypt, which he almost succeeded in conquering.

## EMPEROR NAPOLEON

When he returned to France, he found a Republic in which few had any great faith, while many were prepared to accept a dictator who had emerged from the Revolution. There had always been two potentially contradictory impulses behind the Revolution: a desire for a state that would be a democratic expression of the people, but also for one that would be an effective, powerful defender of the nation, for the Revolutionaries were intensely patriotic. Under Napoléon, the former impulse was put on hold, while France was given the most powerful centralised, militaristic state it had ever seen.

In November 1799 Bonaparte staged a coup, and in 1800 he was declared First Consul. Between continuing military campaigns, he set about transforming France with extraordinary energy – the education system (with the *Grandes Ecoles*), civil law (the *Code Napoléon*), the administration, all bear the Napoleonic stamp to this day. In 1804, he crowned himself Emperor in an ostentatious ceremony in Notre Dame.

Napoléon was also the second great megalomaniac to leave his mark on Paris, leaving his stone 'N' carved even into buildings that he had not had built, although he had much greater regard for his capital than did Louis XIV. His first additions to the city were characteristically practical: the canals, the *quais* along the Seine, and some fine bridges, notably the **Pont des Arts**. These projects created a great deal of employment, which was one reason why his regime was for a good while very popular. He also desired to be master of the 'most beautiful city in the world', complete with palaces, broad boulevards, colossal monuments and temples evoking the monumental splendour of Augustan Rome – as seen in the **Madeleine** or the **Bourse**, a temple of money. The Emperor's official architects, Percier and Fontaine, also designed the **rue de Rivoli** and put up fountains all over the city.

Parisian society regained its *brio*. Egyptomania swept town after Bonaparte's Egyptian campaign, seen in Empire-Style furniture and in architectural details in the new area around rue and passage du Caire, while fashionable ladies mixed transparent Greek draperies and couture *à l'égyptienne*.

The Napoleonic epic was inseparable from military expansion. For years, he seemed invincible. In 1805, he crushed the Austrians and Russians at Austerlitz, the victory he wished to commemorate with the **Arc de Triomphe**. By the time of his marriage to the Empress Marie-Louise in 1810,

only the foundations had been completed, and the imperial household had to make do with an artificial one made of wood. It was only thanks to the royalist Louis-Philippe that the Arc was completed in 1836. By 1807, Napoléon was on the borders of Russia. His victories – Wagram, Eylau, Ièna, Rivoli, Friedland – have become inseparable parts of the Paris street plan. However, even he overreached himself, in Spain, from 1808, and in the disastrous invasion of Russia in 1812. By 1813 his army was exhausted and in retreat, and in 1814 Paris was occupied for the first time since the Hundred Years' War, by the armies of the Czar.

Napoléon did of course have one last throw, with his escape from confinement in Elba, return to Paris, and the 'hundred days' that ended with defeat by Wellington at Waterloo in 1815.

## MONARCHY RESTORED

In 1814, and then again in 1815, after Waterloo, the Bourbons were restored to the throne of France, in the shape of an elderly brother of Louis XVI, as Louis XVIII. Although they realised that the pretensions of the *ancien régime* were lost forever, and France now had a Constitution, he and his ministers still sought to establish a repressive, Catholic regime, that would in some way turn back the clock after the Revolution. In this they could hope to find much support in large areas of rural France, where conservative values remained strong.

Paris, however, still nurtured a strong feeling of rebellion. Over the next 60 years, a pattern would be repeated, already seen to some extent in 1789: Paris, especially working-class districts like the **Faubourg St-Antoine** or **Belleville**, was far more radical than anywhere else in the country. The peculiar weight of Paris in French affairs meant that it could often be seen to be seeking to impose its radicalism on the rest of the nation. At the same time, the radicalism of Paris was fed by a progressive press, liberal intellectuals – including many Romantic artists and authors, such as Hugo, Daumier, Delacroix and Lamartine – radical students and a growing, desperately poor and dangerously anarchic underclass. When provoked, this volatile coalition could explode into revolutionary violence.

## THE 1830 REVOLUTION

Another brother of Louis XVI, Charles X became king in 1824 – ruling but for six short years. As king, he was a reactionary, aided – to his downfall – by absolutist minister Prince Polignac who on 25 July 1830 abolished freedom of the press, dissolved the Chamber of Deputies and altered the election laws, all in violation of the Charter of Liberties granted in 1814 by Louis XVIII. The next day, 5,000 printers and other press workers were in the streets shouting, '*A bas les ministres! Vive la Charte!*' (Down with the ministers! Long live the

*The Tricolore rules:* **28 July 1830: Liberty leading the People** *by Delacroix.*

Charter!) Three newspapers defied the press ban and published. When the police tried to seize the copies, artisans and shopkeepers joined the riot. On 28 July, barricades went up, the disbanded National Guard came out rearmed, Republicans organised insurrection committees, and whole regiments of the Paris garrison defected. While Charles hid out in St-Cloud, hoping that the storm would blow over, inside the city a provisional government was formed, which ordered the tricolore to be raised at the Hôtel de Ville, Notre Dame Cathedral and on various bridges. Then followed three days of fighting, known as 'Les Trois Glorieuses', until Maréchal Marmont, who had been put in charge of the Paris garrison, realised he could not bring order to the capital, and Charles was forced to abdicate in favour of his heir.

Yet another eccentric left-over of the *ancien régime* was winched onto the throne. Louis-Philippe, Duc d'Orléans, son of *Philippe-Egalité*. A father of eight, who never went out without his umbrella and considered it his duty to carve the Sunday roast, he was eminently acceptable to the Parisian bourgeoisie. But the workers, who had spilled their blood in 1830 only to see quality of life worsen, simmered with rancour and frustration throughout the 'July Monarchy'.

## LES MISERABLES

At the time of the Restoration and the July Monarchy, Parisians of all classes often inhabited the same streets, and sometimes the same buildings, with the well-heeled on the first floor (the *étage noble*) and the less privileged under the rafters, or in obscure alleys and culs-de-sac.

In the first half of the century, the population of Paris doubled to over a million, as a building boom – in part appropriating lands seized from the nobility and clergy under the Revolution – flooded the capital with droves of workers from the provinces. After 1837, when France's first railway line was laid between Paris and St-Germain-en-Laye, there were also railway stations to build. The overflow emptied into the poorest quarters. Novelists such as Balzac, Hugo and Eugène Sue were endlessly fascinated by the city's underside, and penned hair-raising accounts of dank, tomb-like hovels where the sun never shone, and of dismal, dangerous streets in central Paris whose denizens subsisted on pauper's wages.

The well-fed, complacent bourgeoisie (mordantly caricatured in Daumier's lithography) regarded this populace with fear. For while the **Bourse**, property speculation and industry flourished after 1830, workers under Louis-Philippe were still forbidden from forming unions or striking. Gaslight, which made city streets so much more pleasant, also enabled the working day to be extended to 15 hours or more. Factory owners pruned salaries to the limit, exploited children and were unfettered by any legislation. Unemployed or disabled workers and their families were obliged to beg, steal or starve.

A cholera epidemic in 1831 claimed 19,000 victims in just three months, and aggravated the already bitter class divisions. The rich blamed workers, beggars and immigrants for breeding disease; the poor hated the bourgeoisie who could afford to escape the city's fetid air, or move to the spacious new neighbourhoods developing in the 8th and 9th *arrondissements*. The stage was set for a battle, and it was to have an even more ferocious edge than that of 1830.

Louis-Philippe's *Préfet*, Rambuteau, was no Baron Haussmann (*see below*), but he made a pitch to win Bonapartist support, finishing the **Arc de Triomphe** and the **Madeleine** and also initiated some projects of his own, notably the **Pont Louis-Philippe** and **Pont du Carrousel**.

## 1848: REVOLUTION AGAIN

On 23 February 1848 nervous troops fired on a crowd on the boulevard des Capucines. Once again, demonstrators demanded blood for blood. Paris reaffirmed its right to the title *capitale des révolutions*, as barricades again covered the city. The National Guard – called out to put down the insurrection – defected to the rebels' side. In the Tuileries, Louis-Philippe abdicated, and abandoned his palace, his capital, and his country, just as Charles X had done 18 years earlier.

The workers' revolution of 1848 made France a republic again – but not for long. The Second Republic was given a progressive provisional government, which included the Romantic poet Lamartine and a mechanic – the first French proletarian to hold such a position. They abolished slavery in the colonies and the death penalty for political crimes; gave most French men (but only men) the vote and set up 'National Workshops' to guarantee jobs for all workers. The capital, however, had not counted on the reaction of the provinces. In May 1848, general elections put a conservative commission at the head of the Republic. One of its first official acts was to liquidate the 'make work' scheme, as too costly and allied with socialism.

Desperate workers took to the streets in the 'June Days'. And this time the insurgents got the worst of it: thousands fell under the fire of the troops of General Cavaignac, and others were massacred in reprisals after the combat had ended.

## SECOND EMPIRE

At the end of 1848, to widespread surprise, new elections gave an overwhelming mandate to a new President of the Republic, Louis-Napoléon Bonaparte, nephew of the great Emperor. After a couple of years consolidating his position, he decided that he didn't merely want to preside, but to reign, seizing power in a *coup d'état* on 2 December 1851. His troops met with little resistance, but nonetheless somehow contrived to fire on an unarmed crowd and kill at least 100 innocent people. A year later, in 1852, the Prince-Président moved into the Tuileries Palace as Emperor of France: *Vive Napoléon III*.

The Second Empire was an often decadent, sometimes ramshackle affair. At home, Louis-Napoléon combined authoritarianism with crowd-pleasing social welfare, in the Bonapartist style. Abroad, his policies included absurd adventures such as the attempt to make Austrian Archduke Maximilian Emperor of Mexico.

Still more than his illustrious uncle, though, Louis-Napoléon had grandiose plans for Paris, and it is they that are his most lasting legacy. His ideas included completing the Louvre, landscaping the Bois de Boulogne, constructing new iron market halls at Les Halles, and, above all, opening up a whole series of new boulevards and train stations. To carry out these daunting tasks he appointed an Alsatian Protestant named Baron Haussmann, Prefect of the Seine from 1853. Haussmann set about his programme with unprecedented energy, giving the aged, malodorous city its greatest-ever transformation (*see chapter* **Architecture**). Haussmann's bulldozer did not escape controversy. *Hôtels particuliers* in the Faubourg-St-Germain, ancient vestiges of the Latin Quarter, and the much-loved *boulevard du crime* with its theatres, all fell before the axe. Baudelaire lamented that '*Le vieux Paris n'est plus*' (the old Paris is no more).

The new Paris was a showcase city, with the first department stores and the International Exhibition of 1867. With so much building work, there was naturally plenty of opportunity for speculation, which Louis-Napoléon's regime, always ready to accommodate bankers, was concerned to see taken up. Paris confirmed its reputation as the world capital of sensual pleasure, a place where everything was for sale, and moralists again decried it as a 'New Babylon'. Even the unchallengeable Haussmann was not above reproach, and he was forced to resign in 1870 after it was shown that some of his projects were based on highly questionable accounts. The combination of sensuality and indulgent opulence of the Second Empire can well be seen in the regime's most distinctive single building, Charles Garnier's **Palais Garnier**, even though Louis-Napoléon did not see it completed.

In 1870, Louis-Napoléon was maneouvred into war with the German states, led by Bismarck's Prussia. At Sedan, in September, the French army was crushed, and Louis-Napoléon abdicated. The Second Napoleonic interlude was over.

# The Third Republic

**Despite sieges and occupation, the new Republic survives to see in Impressionism and the Naughty Nineties.**

Days after Napoléon III's defeat at Sedan, on 4 September 1870, a Parisian crowd demanded and won a new Republic, proclaimed to much cheering at the **Hôtel de Ville**. A provisional government was formed, yet within weeks Paris was under siege by the Prussians. Beleaguered Parisians shivered and starved through the winter. In addition to horses, dogs, cats, and rats, animals from the zoo in the **Jardin des Plantes** ended up in the city's butcher shops. Christmas dinner at the fashionable Restaurant Voisin featured a *consommé d'éléphant* for the soup course, followed by *civet de kangourou* and *cuisson de loup sauce chevreuil*.

In January 1871, Prussian artillery bombarded the southern *arrondissements*. The French government negotiated a temporary armistice with Bismarck, then hastily arranged elections for a National Assembly mandated to make peace. Paris

**Hôtel de Ville**: *the home of revolution.*

voted republican, but the majority went to conservative monarchists. The peace terms signed at **Versailles** on 28 January 1871 – a five billion-franc indemnity, occupation by 30,000 German troops and the concession of Alsace-Lorraine to the newly united Germany – were viewed as a betrayal by disgusted Parisian patriots. Worse still, the new Assembly under Adolphe Thiers spurned the left-leaning, mutinous capital and chose to set up in Versailles instead. Paris understandably regarded this *décapitalisation* as an act of hostility and the climate of insurrection grew.

## THE PARIS COMMUNE

Although Paris was marked by revolution in the nineteenth century, none proved bloodier nor more consequential than the last, which continued for nine weeks from March to May 1871 and remains engraved in the collective memory of the Left and the French working class.

The turning point came on 18 March 1871, when Thiers sent a detachment of soldiers to Montmartre to collect 200 cannons from the Garde Nationale. The mission ended disastrously with the insurrectionists fending off the troops, and killing two generals; a plaque on **rue Chevalier-de-la-Barre**, behind Sacré-Coeur, describes the executions.

Thiers immediately ordered all government officials and the regular army to leave Paris for Versailles, leaving the city in the hands of the poor and radicals, which reflected nearly every spectrum on the Left, including Marxist trade unionists, veteran Jacobins, anti-clericals and members of the Garde Nationale. On 26 March, the Commune of Paris was proclaimed at the Hôtel de Ville. Overwhelmingly populist, the Commune's Assembly comprised 33 workers, 14 clerks and accountants, a dozen journalists, a dozen or so lawyers, teachers, artists and doctors, and a handful of small business owners.

Its simplistic political platform decreed the separation of Church and State, the secularisation of schools, abolishing night work in bakeries, turning abandoned companies into workers' cooperatives, and extending the moratorium on debts and rents. Yet, there was never any question of abolishing private property, since the worker's fundamental aim was to become the sole proprietor of an atelier.

Even artists like Gustave Courbet got swept up in the Commune's fever. A federation of artists was established in April 1871, which attracted such major talents as Corot, Daumier, Manet, Millet and the caricaturist André Gill (later of the famed **Lapin Agile** cabaret in Montmartre).

While support for the Commune was palpable among thousands of disenfranchised workers and inflamed intellectuals, their lack of organisation and political experience proved fatal to their cause. Moreover, they were significantly outnumbered: while the Thiers government had constituted an army of 130,000 well-equipped and indoctrinated men, the Commune could only count on at best 40,000 men of various stripes and affiliations.

It was only a matter of days until Thiers and his *Versaillais* troops began their assault on the city. Barely two weeks after the Montmartre rebellion, the Commune's two principal military strategists, Gustave Flourens and Emile Duval, were taken prisoner and executed on 4 April. By 11 April, Thiers' troops had taken back the suburbs of Colombes, Asnières, Montrouge and Boulogne, and by early May had overtaken Meudon and Châtillon and successfully dismantled forts at Issy and Vanves.

## LA SEMAINE SANGLANTE

Soon, barrages of artillery encircled the city, while inside Paris barricades of sandbags and barbed wire sprung up everywhere. Men, women, and even children were caught up in house-to-house street fighting. On 21 May, in the week that would go down as the '*Semaine sanglante*' (Bloody Week),

*The futuristic 1889* **Exposition Universelle**.

Thiers' *Versaillais* occupied the west of the city, where the rich lived. Within three days of fighting, more than half the city was retaken. Marquis Gallifet, 'the butcher of the Commune', did a brutal 'mop-up' job in the **parc des Buttes-Chaumont**. On 28 May, among the tombs of **Père Lachaise Cemetery**, 147 Communards were cornered and executed, against the '*Mur des Fédérés*', today a moving memorial to the insurrection. The last serious resistance ended in the afternoon on the Fontaine-au-Roi, by the place de la République.

It is estimated that between 3,000 and 4,000 Communards or '*fédérés*' were killed in combat, compared with 877 *Versaillais*. Numerous atrocities were committed on both sides. The Commune kidnapped and killed the Archbishop of Paris and set fire to a third of the city. 'Paris will be ours or Paris will no longer exist!' vowed 'the red virgin', Louise Michel. The Hôtel de Ville was set ablaze, as well as the Tuileries, the Cour des Comptes and the Palais de la Légion d'Honneur. Although the Hôtel de Ville was rebuilt, the Tuileries was not and was ultimately torn down in 1880.

Thousands of insurrectionists were singled out and shot, often on the flimsiest of pretexts. At the Châtelet, Mazas and Roquette prisons, in the Luxembourg Gardens, at the Ecole Militaire, even on the steps of the Panthéon, Communards were shot en masse: a minimum of 10,000, more likely 20,000, if not more. Many of the victims were buried under public squares and pavements; some were incinerated, partly out of fear of an epidemic.

Perhaps the most potent and illuminating account of the Commune can be found in the **Musée d'Art et d'Histoire de St-Denis,** where posters, satirical prints by Klenck, Faustin and Steilen, lithographs by Manet and the newspaper *Cri du Peuple*, bring this period to life.

## EXPOSITIONS UNIVERSELLES

The regime established after 1871, the Third Republic, was an unloved compromise. The right yearned for the restoration of some kind of monarchy; on the left, the Republic was seen as tainted because of its suppression of the Commune. During its early years, its collapse was confidently predicted, but the Third Republic would actually survive for 70 years, making it the longest-lasting French political system since the Revolution.

Paris celebrated its faith in science and progress with two World Exhibitions. The 1889 exhibition was designed to mark the centenary of the Revolution and to confirm the respectability of the Third Republic, with festivities that combined elements of a trade fair and a patriotic paean to Republican values. Centrepiece was a giant iron structure, the **Eiffel Tower**, erected in the face of protests, such as that of writer Maupassant, who denounced it as a 'barbaric mass'. Despite prophesies of disaster, the Exhibition was a great suc-

# Impressionist Paris

Excited by the nightlife, low-life and all the new paraphernalia of nineteenth-century life, the Impressionists were the ultimate urban painters. Rejected by the official Salon, their first group exhibition took place in 1874 in the atelier of the photographer Félix Nadar, on the boulevard des Capucines. Rapidly changing Paris provided the perfect subject matter for these artists intrigued by light conditions and a certain concept of depicting 'reality'. If the Realists Courbet and Millet had concentrated on rural life and Claude Monet could paint Rouen cathedral or haystacks at all times of day, he was equally inspired by the sunlight falling on St-Germain l'Auxerrois or by the smoky conditions and iron and glass architecture of the hectic Gare St-Lazare; while café life was perfect creative fuel for Renoir or Manet. In his bold compositions, Gustave Caillebotte broke with careful framing and concentrated on action and bustle, as figures cross the streets in all types of weather.

Degas was, of course, a regular at the rehearsals of the corps de ballet at the new Paris opera, producing wonderful backstage scenes using techniques of composition taken from Japanese woodcuts. Both he and Renoir lived on or near still

**Degas** *was impressed by ballerinas.*

semi-pastoral Montmartre, and left vivid records of *La Vie montmartroise*, such as *La Chanson du chien*, *La Chanteuse au gant*, *Le Café-concert* and Renoir's classic *Moulin de la Galette*.

---

cess, while the Tower, of course, became something without which Paris is unimaginable.

On 1 April 1900, another World Exhibition greeted the new century. On the banks of the Seine a futuristic city sprang up, of which the **Grand** and **Petit Palais**, the ornate **Pont Alexandre III** and grandiose Gare d'Orsay (now **Musée d'Orsay**) remain. In July 1900, the first line of the Paris Métro ferried passengers from Porte Maillot to Vincennes, in the unheard-of time of 25 minutes. The 1900 Exhibition drew well over 50 million visitors, who marvelled at the wonders of electricity, rode on the exciting new Ferris wheel, and drank in the heady atmosphere of Paris.

### THE DREYFUS CASE

The period was not, however, devoid of tensions. After the defeat of 1870, many circles were obsessed with the need for 'revenge' and the recovery of Alsace-Lorraine; a frustration also expressed in xenophobia and anti-semitism. These strands came together in the Dreyfus case, which polarised French society for years. In 1894, a Jewish army officer, Captain Alfred Dreyfus, was accused of spying for Germany, quickly condemned and sent to Devil's Island. As the facts emerged, suspicion pointed clearly at another officer. Leftists and lib-

erals, such as Emile Zola, took up Dreyfus' case; rightists were bitterly opposed, sometimes taking the view that even if he were innocent it was imperative that the honour of the army should not be questioned. Such were the passions mobilised that fights broke out in the street; nevertheless, Dreyfus was eventually vindicated, and released in 1900.

Paris of the naughty nineties was synonymous with illicit pleasures inaccessible elsewhere. In 1889, impresario Maurice Zidler opened the **Moulin Rouge**, which successfully repackaged a half-forgotten dance called the *chahut* as the can-can. In 1894, what is believed to have been the world's first strip joint opened nearby on rue des Martyrs, the Divan Fayouac, with a routine titled *Le Coucher d'Yvette* ('Yvette Goes to Bed').

The *belle époque* ('beautiful era', a phrase coined in the 1920s in a wave of nostalgia after the horrors of World War I) was a time of prestigious artistic activity in Paris, the world centre of painting, music, dance and almost every other art.

### THE GREAT WAR

On 2 August 1914, France learned that war with Germany was imminent. In the streets of Paris, there was genuine rejoicing, for to many it seemed simply that the long-awaited opportunity for 'revenge' had finally come. However, the Allied armies were steadily pushed back. By 2 September the Germans were on the Marne, just 15 miles from Paris. The government took refuge in Bordeaux, entrusting the defence of the capital to General Galliéni. What then occurred was later glorified as the 'Miracle on the Marne'. Troops were ferried to the front in Paris taxis, one of which is now in the **Musée de l'Armée.** By 13 September, the Germans were pushed back to the Oise, and Paris was safe.

After the catastrophic battle of Verdun in 1916 had inflicted appalling damage on the French army, a strong current of defeatism emerged. Parisian spirits were further sapped by a raging flu epidemic and the shells of 'Big Bertha' – a gigantic German cannon levelled at the city from over 75 miles away. Georges Clemenceau, a veteran Parisian radical, was made prime minister in 1917 to restore morale. On 11 November, the Armistice was finally signed in a clearing in the forest of **Compiègne.** Celebrations lasted for days, but the war had cut a swathe through France's male population, killing over one million men.

## THE INTERWAR YEARS

Paris emerged from the war with a restless energy expressed in an artistic scene that was more dynamic and cosmopolitan than ever. The city's continuing fascination with the new was seen in its enthusiastic embrace of Art Deco. Artistic life centred on Montparnasse. Throughout the '20s the area was an international focus, attracting refugees from the Russian Revolution like Zadkine and artists and writers from across the Atlantic like Man Ray and Hemingway.

The Depression did not hit France until after 1930, but when it arrived, it unleashed a wave of political violence. On 6 February 1934, Fascist and extreme right-wing groups demonstrated against the Republic and tried to invade the **Assemblée Nationale.** Fire hoses and bullets beat them back. Fifteen were killed, and 1,500 wounded. On the left, socialists and Communists united in the face of Fascism and the economic situation to create the Popular Front. In 1936, socialist Léon Blum was elected to head a Popular Front government. In the euphoric 'workers' spring' of 1936, workers were given higher salaries, the right to form unions, a 40-hour week and, for the first time, paid holidays.

By the autumn, however, debates about the Spanish Civil War had split the coalition, and the economic situation was deteriorating. Blum's government fell in June 1937. France seemed within an inch of revolution. The working class was disenchanted, and right-wing parties grew on the back of people's visceral fear of Communism, which to many seemed a far more immediate threat than Hitler. Tragically, each camp feared the enemy within far more than the real enemy that was waiting on its doorstep.

## THE SECOND WORLD WAR

Britain and France declared war on Germany in September 1939, but for months this meant only the *drôle de guerre* (phoney war), characterised by rumour and inactivity. Life continued much as before, except that curfews and black-outs put a brake on the capital's usual *joie de vivre.*

On 10 May 1940, the Germans launched their attack into France, Belgium and Holland. By 6 June, the French armies had been crushed and the Germans were already near Paris. A shell-shocked government left for Bordeaux, while archives and works of art such as the *Mona Lisa* were hurriedly hidden or bundled off to safety. Thousands of ordinary Parisians threw belongings into cars, carts, prams and bikes and began their own exodus south. Almost overnight the city emptied itself out. The population of Greater Paris in 1936 was 5 million; by the end of May 1940, it was 3.5 million, and by 27 June, it stood at 1.9 million.

Paris fell on 14 June 1940 with virtually no resistance. Units of the German Army marched along the **Champs-Elysées** and paraded in the Place de la Concorde. At the Hôtel de Ville, the tricolore was lowered and the swastika raised. The French cabinet voted to request an armistice, and Marshal Pétain, an elderly hero of the first war, dissolved the Third Republic and took over the government. The Germans occupied two-thirds of France, while the French government moved south to Vichy. Some cabinet members left for North Africa to try to set up a government-in-exile, while a young, autocratic general, Charles de Gaulle, went to London to organise a Free French movement in open opposition to the occupation.

Nazi insignia soon hung from every public building and monument, including the Eiffel Tower. As for the Parisians, some cried, some applauded and 15 committed suicide. The rest took the path of least resistance and stayed open for business – only this time with the Germans.

Hitler visited Paris only once, on 23 June 1940. He visited the Opéra Garnier, the Madeleine, the Eiffel Tower and Napoléon's tomb at the Invalides. Leaving the city, he observed: 'Wasn't Paris beautiful?... In the past, I often considered whether we would not have to destroy Paris. But when we are finished in Berlin, Paris will only be a shadow. So why should we destroy it?' (Later, when Germany was losing the war, Hitler ordered that Paris be burned, an order his generals refused to heed.)

## THE OCCUPATION

Paris was the Germans' western headquarters and a very attractive assignment compared to, for example, Russia. There was no shortage of Parisians who accepted the Germans, and warmed to an enemy who offered a champagne lifestyle and sustained Paris' traditional glitter. Maurice Chevalier and the actress Arletty were among

*The **Popular Front** and their **Fascist** counterparts take to the streets in 1934.*

those who were later condemned for having performed for, or having still closer contacts with, the Germans. So, too, was couturier Coco Chanel.

For the average Parisian, life under the occupation was full of deprivations. Private cars were banned. Bread, sugar, butter, cheese, meat, coffee, pork and eggs were rationed. People made do by turning city parks and rooftops into vegetable gardens, catching pigeons or keeping rabbits in bathtubs. A coffee substitute, dubbed *'café national'*, was made with ground acorns and chickpeas.

Occupied Paris also had its share of pro-Vichy bureaucrats who preferred to work with the Germans than embrace what many saw as a futile opposition. There were also *attentistes* (the wait and see-ers), and the black marketeers, who became rich on the back of Nazi rationing. Even so, many were prepared to risk being hauled off to the torture chambers of the Gestapo. By the summer of 1941, the first executions of French underground fighters by the Germans had begun, in response to the activities of the patriots, organised from Britain. Treachery and heroism, submissiveness and resistance, co-existed in a city of torn allegiances.

There was also the rounding-up and deportation of Jews, an area in which the role of the Vichy authorities was particularly shameful, and which remains a highly sensitive issue in France to this day. On 29 June 1940, Jews were ordered to register with the police; on 11 November, all Jewish businesses were required to post a yellow sign indicating *Entreprise juive* (Jewish business). The wearing of the yellow star was introduced in May 1942, soon followed by regulations prohibiting Jews from restaurants, tea-rooms, bars, concerts, cinemas, theatres and music halls, from going to markets, fairs, museums, beaches, race-courses, sports-grounds or campsites, as well as most jobs.

The first deportations of Jews (most foreign-born) took place on 14 May 1941. In August, 6,000 Jews were rounded up in the 11th *arrondissement*, before being sent on to Auschwitz. In July 1942, 12,000 Jews were summoned to the Vélodrome

d'Hiver (the winter cycling stadium). The Vichy Chief of Police ensured that not only Jews aged over 18, but also thousands of young children not on the original orders, were deported in what is known as the *Vél d'Hiv*. A monument to the event was commissioned by the French government and installed on the quai de Grenelle in July 1994, near where the Vélodrome once stood.

Still, it's important to note that not all Parisians stood for the persecution of the Jews. Many Jews were hidden, and a number of government officials tacitly assisted them with ration cards and false papers. While one-third of French Jews were deported and killed in concentration camps, the remaining two-thirds were saved, largely through the efforts of French citizens and the Resistance.

## LIBERATION

In June 1944, the Allies invaded Normandy. German troops began to retreat eastwards, and Parisians saw a real opportunity to retake their city. First came strikes – from 10 to 18 August – on public services. Parisians were bereft of Métro services, gas and electricity, and there was no radio broadcasting and no news, but people began to sense that liberation was finally at hand.

On 19 August, a *Tricolore* was hoisted at the Hôtel de Ville, and the Free French forces launched an insurrection. On 23 August, Hitler ordered Von Choltitz, the German commander, to destroy the French capital. Von Choltitz stalled, for which inaction he would later be honoured by a grateful French government. On 25 August, General Leclerc's French 2nd Armoured Division, which had been carefully put at the head of the US forces approaching Paris in order that it would be French troops who would first enter the city, made their way into Paris by the Porte d'Orléans.

The city went wild. Late in the afternoon, de Gaulle arrived to make his way down the Champs-Elysées to the Hôtel de Ville. 'We are living minutes that go far beyond our paltry lives,' he cried to an ecstatic crowd.

# De Gaulle to Chirac

*Paris rises from the wartime ashes and, despite the end of empire, a new monarchical style of presidency is born.*

In the immediate post-war years, those who had led the fight against the Vichy government and the Germans felt that now was the time to build a new society and a new republic. The National Resistance Council's post-war programme of reforms was approved by most parties from left to right, and Charles de Gaulle was proclaimed provisional President. Life began to resemble normality, although there were ugly accounts to settle in those post-liberation days. Vigilante justice prevailed as neighbour turned against neighbour, and accusations of collaboration began to fly. Mock trials were set up, and severe punishments doled out to *collabos,* although in a general desire to smooth over cracks and convince the nation that France had been resistant, many former Vichy officials, including former Bordeaux préfet Maurice Papon, who may only now come to trial, escaped trial and rose within the administration.

As the economy began to revive, post-war Paris became a magnet for thousands of French men and women for whom the capital represented a new opportunity. The population rose dramatically: in 1946, there were 6.6 million inhabitants in greater Paris, but by 1950 that number had increased by 700,000. In response, the state built *villes nouvelles* (new towns) and low-income housing.

## COLONIAL WAR

De Gaulle relinquished office in 1946, and the Fourth Republic was established. Thereafter, French troops were constantly engaged in a losing battle to save France's disintegrating Empire. Vietnam was lost in 1954, but after revolt broke out in Algeria in 1956 the socialist prime minister Guy Mollet sent in almost half a million French troops, the largest French expeditionary force since the Crusades. The army was demoralised, and many of the troops sent to Algeria were young conscripts. Algeria also became a major issue for intellectuals, and it was only a matter of time before the battles were reflected in Paris.

During the winter of 1955-56, riot police prowled Paris trying to keep the peace. France, so jingoistic in the first bellicose flush of *après-guerre,* was

becoming divided. Mutinous army officers, determined to oppose any 'sell-out' of the French settlers or *colons* in Algeria, took over government headquarters in Algiers. It was time, decided the Fourth Republic, to admit defeat and wheel the old demagogue out of retirement. In 1958 De Gaulle came back, with the understanding that he was to be allowed to rewrite the constitution and give France the republic he thought she deserved.

## DE GAULLE VICTORIOUS

De Gaulle used time-honoured tactics, appearing to promise one thing to the settlers in Algeria, while negotiating with Algerian rebel leaders for their country's independence. In 1962 Algeria was proclaimed independent, and some 700,000 embittered colonists came straggling back to France. Yet De Gaulle emerged crowing victory and the Gaullists were established as ruling the French roost.

France was at peace and economically prosperous. De Gaulle beamed down from his presidential throne like the monarch he wasn't. He commanded foreign policy, intervened in domestic policy when he felt like it, and reported to the nation by means of carefully orchestrated press conferences or appearances on television, which had by now muscled its way into many French homes.

The state was again under pressure to provide new housing. In Paris, radical urbanisation plans were hastily drawn up. Although historic areas were considered sacrosanct, large sections of the city succumbed to the demolition ball and chain. The 'Manhattanisation' of Paris was under way. André Malraux, Minister of Culture, did however undertake one major series of measures, to ensure the preservation of the historic buildings of the **Marais**.

The post-war mood of crisis was over, and into the breach thundered a sharp, fresh 'new wave' of cinema directors, novelists and critics: Truffaut, Godard and Resnais were among the filmmakers who quickly gained international status.

By 1968, youth chaffed against their yokes, as their numbers swelled the over-stretched French educational system. Dissatisfaction was widespread, not just with education, but also with the

*The Mitterrandian mark,* clockwise from left: *triumphal arch, museum, library and opera.*

authoritarian nature of the state and of French society, in contrast to the general, '60s mood of counter-culture radicalism. In May the students erupted, and, in the time-honoured way, took to the streets (*see page 84,* **May '68**). By mid-May, workers and trade unions had joined the protest.

Disaster was avoided, but only just, and confidence in De Gaulle was sorely shaken. He continued to hold office for another ten months. Then, after losing a referendum, he resigned and went back to his provincial retreat, where he died in 1970 at the age of 79. The cobblestones in Paris were replaced and paved over, so that they could never again serve as ammunition for the mob.

## POMPIDOU & GISCARD D'ESTAING

Georges Pompidou or Pom-Pom – as De Gaulle's successor was often called – didn't preside over any earth-shattering political developments during his time in office. What he did do was begin the process that changed the architectural face of Paris radically, and which affixed the state's signature on some of the most monumental building schemes since those of Haussmann and the Third Republic. It was Pompidou, a right-winger, who took the decision to implant an uncompromisingly avant-garde building, the **Centre Pompidou**, in the heart of one of Paris' oldest neighbourhoods, to the opposition of conservatives and socialists alike. Pompidou also gave the go-ahead to the redevelopment of **Les Halles**. This same period, not entirely unconnectedly, also saw fast food make its first appearance on the Parisian scene.

Valéry Giscard d'Estaing became president in 1974, on the sudden death of Pompidou. He made clear his desire to transform France into an 'advanced liberal society'. In Paris, although he

had hated the Centre Pompidou, notable decisions were to turn the **Gare d'Orsay** into a museum, and create a high-tech science museum in the vast old abattoirs at **La Villette** in north-east Paris.

## MITTERRAND'S *GRANDS PROJETS*

France was getting tired of the Gaullist élite. In an abrupt political turn-around, the socialists, led by François Mitterrand, swept into power in 1981. The mood in Paris was initially euphoric, but Socialist France turned out to be not wildly different from Gaullist France. After abolishing the death penalty and nationalising some banks and industries, the Socialists settled into a comfortable bourgeois rule. Life in France was pretty stable and prosperous during the 1980s. In Paris, these years were defined politically by the continuing feud between Mitterrand and Paris' right-wing mayor since 1977, Jacques Chirac.

From the very beginning of his presidency, Mitterrand cherished very distinctive ambitions for transforming the landscape of Paris. Both politically, and personally, Mitterrand had the airs of a monarch. His first operation was the most daring: open-heart surgery on the **Louvre**. This in turn carried with it a corollary, the transfer of the Ministry of Finance, formerly in the Louvre, to a new complex at **Bercy** on the Seine, viewed by many officials as banishment to a Gulag.

If the **Grande Arche** gave a monument to La Défénse in the west, choice of the Bercy site was part of a vast programme for the urban renewal of eastern Paris, as were Mitterrand's 'opera for the people' **Opéra Bastille** and the new national library, completed after Mitterrand's death (in January 1996) and renamed the **Bibliothèque Nationale François Mitterrand** in his honour.

# May '68

Even today, barely a week goes by without you hearing a French person evoke *soixante-huit*. If not a political revolution, May '68 was a cultural and social uprising that surprisingly allied France's students and intellectuals with working-class trade unionists. It was also the biggest strike in the history of France, when demonstrations stretched for seven kilometres through the streets of Paris.

On 2 May, students at the campus of Nanterre, west of Paris, attempted to occupy a college building, and the dean of the university decide to close the entire campus down. Dissent spread: the following day, the **Sorbonne's** rector asked students to evacuate its Grand Amphithéâtre, after confrontations between Trotskyist students and an extreme right group.

The students refused, and by the end of the afternoon, 2,000 students found themselves face to face with 1,500 policemen.

Paving stones were torn up, perhaps inspired by the Situationist group's slogan '*sous les pavés, la plage*' ('beneath the paving stones, the beach'). The confrontations continued all week along **boulevard St-Michel** and rue Gay-Lussac in the Latin Quarter. The government's reaction was to rule with an iron rod, and the violence of the police outraged the public and led to unions calling a one-day strike on Monday 13th. The same day, students took over the Sorbonne and the faculty at Censier, and workers from Renault and Sud-Aviation went on strike. By the 20th, over 6 million people were on strike in France. After negotiations failed, De Gaulle's proposal to hold a referendum was rejected with the worst night of violence. However, by the end of the month, the tide began to turn with an anti-strike demonstration on the Champs-Elysées on 30 May. By 5 June, workers began to go back to their factories.

The May events did, in effect, topple De Gaulle, though he managed to hang on for almost another year. Their main effect in modern France, though, has been psychological: they profoundly shook the country's institutions and its ruling classes, forcing a previously unheard-of attitude of open debate. Equally, May '68 is also the defining point of a generation, many of whom now constitute the establishment in large sections of, for example, the media, and, some would say, are as well-ensconced as any that went before them.

---

The *Grands Projets* have not necessarily met with universal acclaim. Even so, scarcely anyone has questioned the right of the President to devote huge sums to the embellishment of the French capital, or Mitterrand's belief that to keep Paris alive, new blood must be injected into it regularly.

Despite policies of decentralisation especially in the arts, Paris remained very much the intellectual and artistic hub of France, helped in part by the rivalry between left-wing central government and Jacques Chirac's right-wing Mairie de Paris, that helped see Paris-funded exhibitions at the **Petit Palais** and **Musée d'Art Moderne de la Ville de Paris** stand up against national **Grand Palais** and Centre Pompidou and Châtelet develop as a veritable rival to the Opéra Bastille.

## THE CHIRAC ERA OPENS

The last years of the Mitterrand era were marked by the President's ill health and a steady seeping away of his prestige. When the 1995 elections were held it was no surprise that Jacques Chirac won. Famous for being all things to all men (and women, he makes a great play for women's votes), Chirac came into power in an atmosphere of unemployment and recession very different to the expansive mood of the early 1980s. The first 18 months of his reign were marked by social strife, notably the infamous strikes of the winter of 1995, terrorist attacks, corruption scandals and a prime minister, Alain Juppé, whose unpopularity exceeded even that of previous record holder: France's only woman prime minister, Edith Cresson.

# Paris Today

**While Paris is more liveable in than ever, the response to a global market seems to be Luddism and government bewilderment.**

In the 1980s and early '90s, Paris was kept in trim by a creative tug-of-war between the Socialist President François Mitterrand, indulging his taste for monumental *grands travaux*, and the Gaullist mayor, Jacques Chirac. Chirac, occasionally snarling at or even obstructing Mitterrand's grandiose plans, kept his voters and built up his own credibility for the presidency simply by making the city a better place to live in, giving it attractive and cheap new nurseries for working mothers and cleaning up the districts that needed cleaning up. Now, although Paris is anything but dormant, the emphasis is changing. The *grands travaux* are over. The stress is on restoration work, like the plan to spruce up the *Grands Boulevards*. This operation to remove garish neon and install Third Republic-style street furniture resembles the exercise already carried out on the Champs-Elysées. At the same time, the *Grands Projets*, often described as 'pharaonic' are wearing less well than the pyramids, belying shoddy construction, too much corner cutting, or both. A good part of the city's and nation's public works budget will go into re-cementing the tiles to the Opéra Bastille.

Beneath the paving stones, there is an ambitious programme for adding underground car parks at strategic points around the centre. This way, it is hoped, those cars which once mirrored the basic anarchy of the average Parisian as they were jammed into any (illegal) nook or cranny will politely disappear. Although, ironically, 20 years of rampant car park building has only served to increase the number of cars. For the truly courageous more cycle-tracks are planned.

Now that Chirac is President, Paris like all of France has lost much of its earlier self-assurance and the loss is almost palpable. The overall crime statistics may be down, but the incidence of often aimless personal violence is up, reflecting the frayed tempers of a nation facing an unrelenting rise in unemployment. The inevitable social uncertainty is underscored by the brooding resentment of youth, whose jobless rate is double the national average, particularly among immigrants. Every winter, the plight of the homeless, usually estimated at 50,000 in Paris alone, hits the headlines. Yet it is still a city where, as many illegal but wily Eastern European immigrants were quick to discover, it is possible to find two free meals a day in the soup kitchens which dot the capital.

Even the social cloud, however, has its silver lining. The sluggish economy and new poverty have stopped the rise in property prices and rents, making living in Paris *intra-muros* more accessible to all and slowing the trend of migration to the suburbs. Central Paris has never been the exclusive preserve of the rich, although it was threatening to become so, and the mixture of social classes makes it a uniquely pleasant place to inhabit. It combines the advantages of a sophisticated major capital with some of the simple pleasures of a village, albeit minus the green fields. The Parisian really lives in his or her *quartier*. It is not just a place for going home to bed.

This is reflected to a large degree in shopping habits. Giant supermarkets have only made serious inroads into the *banlieue*, or suburbs; most Paris households still do a lot of their daily food

shopping in the old street markets and small neighbourhood shops. This reinforces the sense of a local community, with the shopkeepers knowing their customers' faces and, often, their names. The local café, though under seige from fast-food trends and high taxes, remains a cornerstone of urban life.

One of the great victories of Paris has been to contain the city proper within the *Périphérique* ring road, holding the strictly Parisian population at around two million and keeping the city a manageable size. Meanwhile the scruffy suburbs, with the honourable exception of the leafy upmarket districts to the west, sprawl towards the horizon. Their concentration of late twentieth-century ills prompts regular outbursts of violence between youths and police, sometimes for nights in succession, that have yet to spill over from ugly dormitory suburbs to Paris proper. Although the *banlieue* still makes itself felt, most visibly in Les Halles at weekends when the RER disgorges thousands of youngsters in search of distraction into the centre of Paris.

Despite Chirac's 1995 election promise that he would end the 'social fracture', the fulfilment of this pledge is a long time coming. Instead, the country has been treated to continuing austerity policies to make France elegible for European monetary union. Shocked by a militant public reaction to its first attempt to change the welfare system in December 1995, the Gaullist-conservative government coalition subsequently seemed to do little more than mark time, an unexpected lack of a firm hand that has created a fertile terrain for the extreme right anti-immigration National Front party of Jean-Marie Le Pen. With its message of 'The French First' and law and order, the National Front attracts the sympathies, and perhaps soon the vote, of more than a fifth of the population. Unless there is some unexpected reversal, this could make it the arbiter if future parliamentary elections fail to return a solid majority.

Since the bruising 1992 campaign for the referendum to ratify the Maastricht Treaty, the average French citizen has learned the name of his modern enemy. This is *mondialisation* or globalisation. The French know they do not like it and they know they want to continue living in the style to which they have become accustomed. Above all, they know they hate *le modèle anglo-saxon*, which they see as a hire-and-fire culture marked by rampant deregulation and contempt for the weak. Deregulation is arriving later than elsewhere, meaning that many of the industrial or service sectors are less competitive than those of their neighbours. Never known for eagerness to compromise, the French are showing little talent to adapt or to seek ways of softening the impending changes. When threatened, they block roads or occupy their workplaces, campaign for earlier and earlier retirement and go for other gestures that, in the end, do

little more than hurt an already fragile economy and make painful transition all the more inevitable.

Internationally, France has lost much of its political sway now that a unified Germany is taking a more forceful stance on the world stage. In Africa, France's traditional interventionist policy – usually the dispatch of the Foreign Legion to shore up friendly regimes – is challenged by an American promise to fill the vacuum left by the end of superpower tensions. The result is that the French tend to be more inward-looking and nationalistic than before. Flowing with the tide, the government has tried to tighten up immigration laws but its attempts to do so have been cack-handed. It has been slow to remove the flagrant injustices that leave many immigrants in a sort of limbo. A classic example is an illegal immigrant who has a child by a French partner. As the parent of a French national, he or she cannot be expelled; as an illegal, that same immigrant cannot obtain a work permit and live normally.

In Paris itself, only 85% of the population is estimated to be of strictly French origin. Earlier waves of immigrants from Mediterranean Europe, Africa and the Maghreb are being swelled by Eastern Europeans. They include seasonal visitors like the Romanian music teachers who play a Gallic accordion in the Métro to earn some precious foreign currency during their summer break, or more permanent settlers like the Poles, who no longer need a visa to enter France, often setting up teams of house decorators, who cheerfully bypass the tax system and undercut regular building firms, which are groaning under the weight of social charges that add over 40 per cent to their wage bills.

Culturally, there has been little memorable innovation in Paris in the first years of the 1990s. Publishing houses' fiction lists are weighed down by American or British works. Often the most talked- about plays in the theatres are from abroad and Sylvie Guillem, France's most talented ballerina, created a stir by stating forcefully on national television that she found artistic fulfilment easier to attain in London than Paris.

The positive side is that this leaves Paris with a wide ethnic and cultural diversity. Even where national predominance might be expected – in food – times are changing. There are now more foreign than French restaurants in Paris. In 1975, there was only one Indian restaurant in the city. Now the Minitel, electronic telephone directory, lists a dozen, certainly far below the real figure.

All the clichés about the uncertainties of the post-Cold War world apply to France. The question is how long it will take to absorb change and at what cost. In the meantime, a prevailing view among sociologists is that little will really happen without *jacqueries*, or peasant revolts, like those that have marked French history throughout the centuries. Perhaps they have already begun.

# Architecture

*The Grands Projets were nothing new: many ambitious rulers have left their mark on Paris.*

Paris owes its elegance to conscious planning, as the city grew outwards in concentric rings and powerful visions laid out squares and boulevards. The city's apparent homogeneity is largely the effect of the same materials – local yellow limestone and slate – later zinc roofs – being used for centuries. In fact, its architecture encompasses a huge variety of styles, from Gothic churches to '30s schools to controversial contemporary intrusions.

## The Romanesque

The medieval city was centred on the Ile de la Cité and the Latin Quarter. The main thoroughfares rue St-Jacques and rue Mouffetard, and even the modern street plan, followed those of Roman Paris. Paris had several powerful Romanesque abbeys outside the city walls, but existing remains of this style are sparse. **St-Germain-des-Prés** still has its rounded arches on the tower, while some decorated capitals survive in the solid-feeling nave.

## Gothic Paris

It was in the **basilica of St-Denis**, begun in 1136, under the patronage of the powerful Abbot Suger, that the Gothic trademarks of pointed arches, ogival vaulting and flying buttresses were com-bined for the first time. Today some of Suger's twelfth-century porch and his choir remain.

In technical terms, Gothic vaulting allowed buildings to span large spaces and let light in; this brought with it a new aesthetic of lightness and verticality and new styles of ornament. A spate of church building began with new cathedrals at **Chartres**, Sens and Laon, as well as **Notre Dame**, which incorporated all the features of the new style: twin-towered west facade, soaring nave, intricate rose windows and buttressed east end.

In the following century, ribbed vaulting be-came ever more refined and columns more slender, in the Rayonnant or 'High' Gothic style. One of the few master mason/architects whose name is known is Pierre de Montreuil, whose masterpiece, the **Ste-Chapelle** is virtually a wall of stained glass. An impressive secular building of the time is the *Salle des Gens d'Armes*, the huge vaulted hall in the **Conciergerie**, completed in 1314.

The later Flamboyant Gothic style of the late fourteenth century saw little structural innovation, but a wealth of decoration. The small church of **St-Séverin** is particularly original. The pinnacles and gargoyles of the early sixteenth-century **Tour St Jacques** and the wonderful porch of **St Germain l'Auxerrois** are also typically Flamboyant.

Paris' two finest surviving medieval mansions are from the end of the fifteenth century. The Hôtel

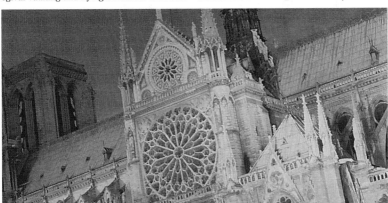

**Notre-Dame**, *with its intricate rose windows, followed St-Denis in Gothic style.*

de Cluny (**Musée de Cluny**) and **Hôtel de Sens** were urban palaces, built for powerful abbots. With living quarters at the rear of an enclosed forecourt, Cluny is a precursor of the domestic style of the sixteenth century. On a more humble note, the 1407 house of Nicolas Flamel, who was condemned for alchemy, at **51 rue de Montmorency** is one of the earliest surviving private houses in Paris.

## The Renaissance

The influence of the Italian Renaissance came late to Paris, and when it did it seems to have been largely due to the personal impetus of François 1er. He installed Leonardo da Vinci at Amboise (*see chapter* **Trips Out of Town**) and brought over Rosso and Primaticcio to work on his palace at Fontainebleau. It was not until 1528, however, that he moved his court in Paris and set about updating the **Louvre**, with the *Cour Carrée*, by Pierre Lescot. In the 1560s, Catherine de Médicis, widow of Henry II, commissioned Philibert Delorme to begin work on another palace at the Tuileries, burnt down during the Paris Commune in 1871.

The pretty church of **St Etienne-du-Mont** shows that Renaissance style remained a superficial effect: the structure is Flamboyant Gothic, but the balustrade of the nave and the elaborate roodscreen, with its spiral staircases and lacy fretwork, are Renaissance. Another, heavier hybrid is the massive **St-Eustache**. The Hôtel Carnavalet (**Musée Carnavalet**), altered by Mansart next century, is Paris' best example of a Renaissance mansion; the **Hôtel Lamoignan**, also in the Marais, still has its giant order pilasters in the courtyard.

## The Ancien Régime

France's first Bourbon king Henri IV had great plans for modernising his capital; he built the **Pont-Neuf** and laid out two major squares, the **place Dauphine** on the Ile de la Cité and the **place des Vosges** in the Marais, with new roads leading to them. Both followed a symmetrical plan, with vaulted galleries and steeply pitched roofs, and represented a clear departure from the untidy squares of medieval Paris. Their use of red brick, though, was short-lived. The place des Vosges, with its two pavillions to the north and south intended for the king and queen, seems a last flourish of the northern Renaissance in contrast with the classical stone buildings soon built around it.

The seventeenth century, the *Grand Siècle*, was a high point in French power, and also in architecture, painting and drama. The monarchy desired buildings that emphatically declared its own grandeur and greatness and the Baroque style satisfied this need perfectly. Some great architects emerged under court patronage, including Salomon de Brosse, François Mansart, Jules

Hardouin-Mansart (his nephew), Libéral Bruand and Louis Le Vau, the decorator Charles Lebrun and landscape architect André Le Nôtre.

Even in its most splendid at **Versailles**, French Baroque never reaches the level of excess of decoration of the Baroque in Italy or Austria. As with Poussin's paintings, French architects followed the Cartesian principles of harmony, order and balance, with a preference for symmetry that can be seen both in royal palaces and in the plan of the grand private houses put up in the Marais.

The **Palais du Luxembourg**, built in Italianate style for Marie de Médicis by Salomon de Brosse, combines simple, classic French château design with elements of the Pitti Palace in Marie's native Florence. Churches like **St-Paul-St-Louis** on rue St-Antoine and the **Chapelle de la Sorbonne** followed the Jesuit model of the Gesù in Rome. The **Val de Grâce** is one of the best examples of Baroque architecture in Paris. It was designed by François Mansart, a perfectionist who took so long he was replaced by Jacques Lemercier, who largely followed the former's plans. In the adjoining grand monastery, one can see the characteristic double-pitched 'Mansart roofs', a feature of Parisian and French architecture almost ever since. Libéral-Bruand's **Chapelle de la Salpêtrière** showed ingenious adaptation of the Classical ideal to very specific needs.

Domestic architecture also saw a boom as the nobility and *nouveaux-riches* of the royal bureaucracy flocked to build mansions for themselves. Henry IV had started the fashion in the Marais, and the previously unbuilt Ile-St-Louis soon filled up with *hôtels particuliers*. They follow a symmetrical U-shaped plan, with a secluded courtyard, combining both privacy and ostentation. Look through the archways to the *cour d'honneur*, where facades are richly decorated, in contrast with their street faces. The **Hôtel de Sully** has a fine facade and still has its Orangerie at the rear of the garden court; the Hôtel Salé (**Musée National Picasso**) is notable for its sphinx-adorned entrance and magnificent staircase with ornate ironwork and carved stone figures.

Along **rue du Faubourg-St-Antoine** a very different style of architecture developed. Most of the buildings one can see today date from the nineteenth century, but their style is much older. This was a working district, occupied by furnituremakers. The buildings they lived and worked in were tall, with arches from the street giving way to cobbled courtyards lined with workshops.

The work of Jules Hardouin-Mansart, official architect for Louis XIV, epitomises the use of architecture for the aggrandisement of the monarchy, with the creation of virtual stage sets to magnify the Sun King's absolute power. His 1685 **place des Victoires**, a perfect circle, and **place Vendôme** (1698), an elegant octagon of decorated arches and light Corinthian columns set off by

*Utopian Ledoux played taxing games with geometry at **La Rotonde de la Villette**.*

classical pediments, were both created to show off equestrian statues of the king. At the same time, the first *grands boulevards* were cut through in place of the old city wall.

The Louvre continued to grow, and Claude Perrault created the sweeping west façade. Libéral Bruand began the military hospital of **Les Invalides**, which, in contrast to his charming house in the Marais (**Musée de la Serrurerie**), is Baroque at its most official and monumental.

## Rococo & Neo-Classicism

In the eighteenth century, the Faubourg-St-Germain replaced the Marais as a fashionable address. Grand mansions were built along the rue de Grenelle, rue St-Dominique and rue de Varenne. Most can be viewed only from the street, except for the Hôtel Bouchardon (**Musée Maillol**), which still has some original carved panelling.

Under Louis XV, the severe lines of the previous century were softened by rounded corners and decorative detailing, such as satyr masks on doorways (as at Hôtel Chenizot, 51 rue St-Louis-en-l'Ile or Hôtel d'Albret, 31 rue des Francs-Bourgeois). The main developments, though, came in interior decoration, with the light, frivolous French version of Rococo style. The best examples are the interiors of the Hôtel Soubise (**Musée de l'Histoire de France**), with panelling, plasterwork and

paintings by leading craftsmen and artists of the day, including Boucher, Natoire, Restout and Van Loo, or the panelling and period furnishings at the Hôtel Denon (**Musée Cognacq-Jay**).

At the same time, the pomp of the *ancien régime* reached a peak with the **place de la Concorde**, Paris's largest square, created by Jacques Ange Gabriel in honour of Louis XV. Under Louis XVI, from the 1770s, curves again fell from fashion, as the Classicism of Ancient Rome became the leading source of inspiration. Soufflot's **Panthéon** (1755-92) was the *Grand Projet* of its day, a huge domed structure set over a Greek cross plan, inspired by the Pantheon in Rome.

One very late addition by the old regime to Paris was the tax wall, the *Mur des Fermiers Généraux*, built around the city in 1785. Some of Claude-Nicolas Ledoux's **toll gates** survive. In them he played games with pure geometrical forms; circular at Parc Monceau and **La Rotonde de la Villette** (place de Stalingrad), and rectangular pairs at place Denfert-Rochereau and place de la Nation.

## The Nineteenth Century

In its brief span the Revolution largely confined itself to pulling buildings down or appropriating them for new purposes. Royal statues bit the dust and churches became 'Temples of Reason' or grain stores. Napoléon, however, soon brought Paris back to a proper sense of its grand self. New land came on the market confiscated from aristocracy and church as new areas, especially in the eighth and ninth *arrondissements,* were built up.

Since the Emperor naturally compared himself to the Caesars, a stern classicism was the preferred style for great monuments and public buildings, as seen in the **Arc de Triomphe**, the **Madeleine** and the new **Bourse**. The Arc de Triomphe and the Madeleine were only finished under Louis-Philippe, in awe of the Napoleonic legacy, after 1830. Their classical style thus continued prominent on the streets of Paris, even though by the 1840s it was under challenge from a revival of Gothic, as seen in the church of **Ste-Clotilde** (1846-57) in the Faubourg St-Germain.

The Gothic revival in Paris, never as important as it was in Britain, was particularly associated

with the restoration of medieval buildings. Controversial standard-bearer of Gothic in France was Viollet-le-Duc. Despite his detailed research, his critics accused him of creating a fairy-tale, romanticised notion of the medieval, and his use of colour was felt to pollute these monuments with decoration. You can judge for yourself inside Notre Dame and the Ste Chapelle, or visit the castle he did build largely from scratch at **Pierrefonds**.

## Baron Haussmann

Under the Second Empire after 1848 Paris underwent perhaps its most radical transformation. Baron Georges-Eugène Haussmann, Napoléon III's *Préfet de la Seine* from 1853, was not an architect but an administrator, but he did most to make Paris the most modern city of its day. Straight,

# Glass houses

From stained glass games with colour reflections to the quest for ultimate transparency and the invisible facade, glass has appropriately made its mark on the city of light.

### 1246-48: La Sainte-Chapelle
*4 bd du Palais, 1st. M° Cité.*
Pierre de Montreuil's masterpiece built for St-Louis to house holy relics takes the Gothic ideal to its summit with 15 stained glass windows, each 15.4m x 4.25m, taking up almost the entire surface of the upper chapel and stone tracery reduced to a minimum. Put up so quickly, the glass while intensely beautiful was, apparently, in places inadequately fired and of shoddy quality, necessitating rescue in the nineteenth century.

### 1861-65: Gare du Nord
*pl Napoléon-III, 10th. M° Gare du Nord.*
Hittorrf – Haussmann's eclectic emissary, also responsible for place Charles-de-Gaulle (Etoile) and the Cirque d'Hiver – built Paris' best-preserved example of iron and glass train station architecture; behind a stone facade adorned with statues representing the towns of northern France, is a massive central vault in iron and steel that let light pour through onto the steam age.

### 1928-32: La Maison de Verre
*31 rue St-Guillaume, 7th. M° Rue du Bac.*
Built by Pierre Chareau for Dr Dalsace, in this icon of the Modern Movement, there is no longer a traditional wall nor windows, simply a wall in glass block, framed by metal, that made the interior a continuation of the exterior. Within, interior walls (also in glass) and a metal staircase were intended to be moveable. Still a private residence, and extremely difficult to visit, it may be, but you only have to see a building, be it garage or school, that uses glass block to know that somewhere it took its influence from Chareau's masterpiece.

### 1968-71: Parti Communiste Français
*2 pl du Colonel-Fabien, 19th. M° Colonel-Fabien.*
The French Communist Party headquarters were

**Fondation Cartier**: *Nouvel jewel in glass.*

designed by Oscar Niemeyer – the architect of Brasilia – with Paul Chemetov and Jean Deroche, as a 'foyer of the working class'. A curving glass curtain wall facade is raised on a sort of concrete wing 1.5m above ground.

### 1989: The Louvre Pyramid
*Palais du Louvre (Cour Napoléon), 1st. M° Palais-Royal.*
First of the *Grands Projets*. I M Pei used specially manufactured ultra-transparent glass, and the contrast with the historic facades is extraordinarily effective. Incidentally, it was not the first time a pyramid – the ultimate early building block – had been proposed for the Louvre. Pei also designed the high-tech glazing system that enclosed the Marly and Puget sculpture courts.

### 1994: Fondation Cartier
*261 bd Raspail, 14th. M° Raspail.*
Jean Nouvel's glass and steel structure takes the concept of *'la transparence'* – a buzzword among many French architects – to its maximum. The building comprises exhibition spaces on the ground floor and basement and six floors of offices for Cartier above. Nouvel had to design the building round a listed cedar tree planted by the writer Chateaubriand in the seventeenth century, a problem solved by outer wings of glass either side of the entrance.

broad boulevards were cut through the old city, often taking the eye to a focal point such as the new Opéra, the Gare de l'Est or the Arc de Triomphe, thus continuing the principal established by Hardouin-Mansart and Le Nôtre and perhaps a prescient prediction of Parisian driving habits. While the Ile de la Cité was decimated, many old districts were left largely unaltered; it is estimated that 27,000 houses were demolished and some 100,000 were built during this period.

The motives for this unprecedented exercise in urban and social engineering were a mixture of authoritarianism and paternalism characteristic of Napoléon III's regime. The wide boulevards, and the removal of the narrowest, shabbiest old streets of the city centre, were in part anti-revolutionary measures, since they made the construction of barricades far more difficult. However, the new streets also answered real communication and health problems in a city that had grown from a population of around 500,000 in 1789 to 1 million in 1850, was disease-ridden, and had new railway stations needing transport links. From an aesthetic viewpoint, they added the varied vistas, and quality of light, characteristic of Paris today. Haussmann's vision is best appreciated from the top of the Arc de Triomphe, where you can see twelve radiating avenues fanning out below.

There were more prosaic measures too; Haussmann constructed asylums, prisons, schools, hospitals, markets, water and sewage systems, and gave Paris an entirely new series of parks. The city also acquired the Haussmannian apartment block, which has lasted well into this century, with some differences in decoration. It's a form that has been highly adaptable – to different styles, budgets and sites. Typically, there is a grand balcony across the façade on the second and top floors, and only small balconies on intermediate storeys. Regulations of 1859 controlled the pitch of the roof, and ratio of building height to street width.

In amongst this upheaval, one particular building went up that epitomised Second-Empire style, even though it was not finished until after both Napoléon III and Haussmann had fallen from power: Charles Garnier's sumptuous **Palais Garnier** of 1862-75 perfectly expresses the ostentation and ambition of mid-century Paris.

## The Iron Age

As the nineteenth century progressed, engineering innovations made the use of iron frames in buildings increasingly common. Victor Baltard built market pavilions at Les Halles, demolished in 1969, that proudly proclaimed their structure, but more often than not ironwork was hidden behind stone exteriors, giving spacious interiors full of light. Even such apparently massive stone structures as the Galerie d'Evolution of the **Muséum d'Histoire**

**Naturelle** or the **Musée d'Orsay** are only shells around an iron frame. Henri Labrouste's innovative reading room at the **Bibliothèque Ste-Geneviève**, in place du Panthéon, was one of the first, prefiguring his **Bibliothèque Nationale**. Baltard's **St-Augustin**, on boulevard Malesherbes, is one of the strangest churches in Paris – its structure is entirely in metal, the stone exterior is only an envelope. The daring, open use of iron was most often seen in buildings erected for the great exhibitions, such as the most emphatic iron structure of them all, the **Eiffel Tower**.

## Art Nouveau & Belle Epoque

Genuine Art Nouveau architecture in Paris is actually quite rare, although some fine interiors exist, particularly those spruced up as part of the 1900 World Exhibition, such as **Brasserie Julien**. The heavier official Beaux-Arts floral style – directly descended from the work of Garnier – continued at the same time, seen in apartment buildings and bistros or in the Gare d'Orsay. The **Grand Palais** itself has elements of the new style in its sinuous metal stairway, but the heavily sculptured exterior is firmly within official monumental style.

Art Nouveau at its most fluid and flamboyant can be seen in Guimard's Métro stations, and the whiplash metalwork balconies of his 1901 **Castel Béranger** (14 rue de la Fontaine), or in the entrance to Jules Lavirotte's luxury apartments at **29 avenue Rapp**. Rue Réaumur has several Art Nouveau facades, or visit weird **14 rue d'Abbeville**, where glazed ivy climbs up the front.

At the same time, Henri Savage, architect of La Samaritaine, designed the unusual tiled building at **6 rue Vavin** (1911-12), using stepped-back terraces for the first time. From this he went to a bigger social housing project in rue des Amiraux, which even included a swimming pool. Social housing went up in many areas of Paris, funded by philanthropists like the Rothschilds in **rue de Prague**, or by the city as the former Thiers fortifications surrounding the city (just inside today's Périphérique ring road) were demolished.

## The Modern Movement

Two names stand out after World War I for their technical and aesthetic innovation, and influence – Auguste Perret and Le Corbusier. A third, Robert Mallet-Stevens, stands unrivalled for his elegance, notably the six houses of rue Mallet-Stevens in the 16th *arrondissement*. Paris is one of the best cities in the world for examples of Modern Movement architecture, especially in houses and studios, but also in a more diluted form in public buildings and low-cost public housing. At a decorative level, the geometrical influence and love of chrome, steel and glass found its way into Art Deco cafés and brasseries, like **La Coupole**, especially after the 1925 exhibition of decorative arts.

Perret stayed largely within a classical aesthetic, but his frank use of reinforced concrete gave scope for more varied facades than traditional load-bearing walls. Perhaps most interesting is his **Conseil Economique et Social** at place d'Iéna, a circular pavilion with an open horseshoe staircase. Fortunately Paris was spared his 1922 Maisons-Tours scheme, which would have transformed the city into an avenue of skyscrapers.

Le Corbusier first tried out his ideas in early private houses such as the **Villa La Roche and Villa Savoy** (*for both, see chapter* **Museums**), with their use of interesting volumes and terraces and functional built-in furniture. His Pavillon Suisse at the **Cité Universitaire** can be seen as an intermediary point between these villas and the mass housing schemes of his *Villes Radieuses*, which were to be so influential and so debased in postwar Europe. The Cité Universitaire, a sort of interwar paean to internationalism, inspired by garden cities, Oxbridge and American campus universities, although purely residential, is an interesting mix of International Modern and internationally vernacular. Willem Dudok's College Néerlandais is a perfect example of purist geometric De Stijl style; but the Maison d'Asie du Sud-Est (originally Cambodia) is an amusing blend of modernism and Far Eastern pastiche, with Khmer sculptures and a bird-beaked roof.

Other notable Modern Movement houses and apartments include Adolphe Loos' house for Dadaist poet Tristan Tzara, supposed fulfilment of his maxim 'ornament is crime', the Maison de Verre (*see p90* **Glass houses**), houses by Lurçat, Le Corbusier and Perret near Parc Montsouris, Pierre Patout's steamboat-style apartments at 3 boulevard Victor, 15th (the machine was part of the modern aesthetic, and Patout really had fitted

**Le Corbusier** designs for modern living.

out luxury liners) and the Studio Raspail at 215 bd Raspail by Elkouken: mock artists' studios for the enlightened bourgeoisie. The '30s also saw a return to vaguely totalitarian looking neo-classical monumentalism in public buildings, such as the **Palais de Tokyo** and **Palais de Chaillot** put up for Paris' 1937 Exhibition; or the Ministère du Travail in the 7th *arrondissement*, alongside a more socially inspired wave of school building.

## Post-War Paris

As France revived from the trauma of World War II, the 1950s saw the beginnings of La Défense, with the construction of the **CNIT** centre, and the 1958 **UNESCO** building, by Bernard Zehrfuss, Pier Luigi Nervi and Marcel Breuer. What was most needed at this time, however, were solutions to the problem of the shanty towns around the city, many occupied by immigrant workers. In the '60s, slab-like tower blocks sprouted in the ring of suburbs and new towns that were spreading around Paris. Redevelopment in the city proper was more limited, although changes in building regulations allowed taller buildings, noticeably in Montparnasse and in the 13th and 19th *arrondissements* (since altered, to prevent another **Tour Montparnasse** in central Paris).

The **Centre Pompidou**, opened in 1977, was in many ways the first of the radical, large-scale schemes that have become a trademark of modern Paris, introducing international architects into the city, and establishing the pattern of public competitions for big commissions. As Eiffel's Tower had done before, the glass and metal structure imposed within the stone fabric of Paris created initial scandal and then became quickly absorbed.

## The 1980s and Beyond

The 1980s and early '90s were, of course, dominated by Mitterrand's *Grands Projets*, with which the President sought to leave his stamp on the city. The **Louvre** Pyramid, **Institut du Monde Arabe** and **Grande Arche de la Défense** represent monuments of genuine worth, while the **Opéra Bastille**, the **Bibliothèque Nationale François-Mitterrand** and the **Ministry of Finance** are merely monumental.

Contemporary Paris also boasts interesting private commercial/cultural buildings in a multiplicity of styles, such as **Canal +** (Richard Meier) on rue de Cévennes, the (closed) **American Center** (Frank Gehry), or the **Fondation Cartier** (Jean Nouvel). If the era of *Grands Projets* is over, Paris still invests in public housing, and the roster of names involved is surprisingly international, with Aldo Rossi, Renzo Piano, de Portzamparc and younger French architects like Frédéric Borel, Architecture Studio or Valode & Pistre.

# Paris by Area

# Introduction

Look at a map and Paris seems deceptively uniform: its shape is a more or less regular oval, its boulevards form concentric rings spanning out evenly from the centre and the Seine runs through the middle in an elegant curve. Since the last century, the city has been divided into 20 *arrondissements* or districts which form a tight snail-shell spiral beginning at Notre Dame and finishing at the Porte de Montreuil, on the eastern edge of the official city limits.

Throughout Paris' history, city planners have deliberately created this sense of order and uniformity – usually in order to weed out political dissent and make the streets easier to police. But down the centuries Parisians have proved too resilient to submit entirely to such schemes, and beneath the surface their city is surprisingly diverse in style, structure and atmosphere.

Traditionally Paris is divided into two, like two halves of a brain: the practical, materialistic Right Bank, with its department stores, wholesale markets, designer shops and bustling avenues; and the intellectual, more refined Left Bank, site of university buildings, bookshops, cinemas and narrow streets stuffed with student garrets. In reality the divisions are more complex, with the grand and the intimate, the old and the new, the sacred and the profane mingling on both sides of the river.

Working out from the islands, the ancient centre of the city and now a major tourist magnet, this section explores the different themes of the city through its different districts, from the curious alleyways of the Faubourg-St-Antoine to the stiff-collared, bourgeois elegance of the 16th *arrondissement*. This is a city that is changing fast: the Latin Quarter and St-Germain have lost most of their students and become delightful but definitely upmarket strolling grounds, while the once down-at-heel streets north of the Palais-Royal have been spruced up to reveal a rabbit-warren of picturesque back alleys intertwined with grandiose glass-roofed arcades. Away from the centre, this famously compact city reveals individual townhouses, small but pretty parks, fine examples of avant-garde architecture, lively multi-racial communities and areas like the Butte-aux-Cailles and Ménilmontant that still preserve a distinctly villagey character.

However historic the city may seem, Paris continues to evolve. The La Défense business district to the west is one example, while development schemes at La Villette, Bercy and around the new Bibliothèque Nationale de France François Mitterrand are yet more attempts at social engineering, trying to breathe new life into previously neglected corners of the city.

# The Islands

*Paris' two islands in the Seine still conjure up wonderfully romantic images of time past.*

These islands may nestle alongside each other in the very centre of the city, connected by the Pont St-Louis, but they have very divergent histories and, and consequently, quite distinctive and separate characters.

## Ile de la Cité

*In the 1st and 4th arrondissements.*

The more westerly and larger of the two islands, the Ile de la Cité was the site of the original settlement that grew into Paris (*see chapter* **Roman Paris & the Dark Ages**). It was first inhabited in around 250 BC by the Parisii, and when it was conquered by the Romans two hundred years later it also became the centre of their city. Today, it is most visited for two major attractions, the **Sainte-Chapelle** and **Notre Dame** cathedral.

When Victor Hugo wrote *Notre Dame de Paris* in 1831, the Ile de la Cité as he described it was a bustling medieval quarter of narrow streets and hundreds of tall wooden houses: 'the head, heart and very marrow of Paris'. Baron Haussmann quickly put paid to that. During the Second Empire he supervised the expulsion of 25,000 people from the island, razing their homes, flattening some 20 churches and obliterating most of the streets. Rarely has a city centre been swept away with such ferocity. The lines of the old streets in front of Notre Dame are traced into the new parvis.

The people of the Ile were forced to resettle in slums in the east of the city, leaving behind a lot of empty space and a few large buildings – the **Conciergerie**, the law courts, the Hôtel Dieu hospital, the police headquarters and, of course, Notre Dame. The island now also plays host to hordes of tour coaches during the day, but otherwise it can often seem rather sad and soulless.

The most charming spot is the western tip, where the **Pont Neuf** spans the Seine above a leafy triangular garden known as the **square du Vert-Galant**. With a wonderful view of the river, it's a great spot for summer picnics. In the centre of the bridge is a statue of Henri IV on his horse, first erected in 1635, destroyed in the Revolution, and then replaced in 1818 with a replica made with bronze from an out-of-favour statue of Napoléon in place Vendôme. On the island-side of the Pont Neuf is the strangely secluded, triangular **place Dauphine**, once a haunt for lovers. Built in red brick and stone, it was – like the place des Vosges, commissioned by Henri IV, who named it in honour of his son, the Dauphin and future King Louis XIII, although few of its buildings today look as they did in 1607 (No 14 is one that does).

Moving along the *quais* towards the centre of the island, the view is dominated by the severe classical expanses of the **Palais de Justice** and, lining the Seine on the island's north bank, the medieval towers of the **Conciergerie**, both originally parts of the palace complex of the Capetian kings (*see chapter* **Middle Ages & Renaissance**), on what had been the Roman governor's house. In 1358, after Etienne Marcel's uprising caused Charles V to move the royal retinue into the Louvre, it gradually became a prison where people were tortured and incarcerated before being executed. Among those who contemplated the next world from here were Danton, Robespierre and Marie-Antoinette. Much of the facade is a nineteenth-century pseudo-medieval reconstruction, but the original fourteenth-century clock tower, the Tour de l'Horloge, remains, and the interior is well worth visiting for the magnificent, vaulted Salles des Gens d'Armes, vast kitchens and recreated prison cells.

Nearby, surrounded by the law courts of the Palais de Justice, is the Sainte-Chapelle, Pierre de Montreuil's masterpiece of stained glass and slender Gothic columns. It was built in the middle of the thirteenth century as a royal chapel to house the holy relics of often dubious origin that were acquired at huge expense and brought back from the Crusades by France's sainted king Louis IX. The two-tiered structure is awash with colour and light. The windows in the upper chapel, some of the finest original medieval stained glass in existence, recount stories from the Bible. Now the centre of the French legal system, the Palais de Justice slowly evolved alongside the Conciergerie, enclosing the Sainte-Chapelle and even, during some particularly thoughtless reconstruction after a fire in 1776, entirely blocking off the chapel's north side.

Across the boulevard du Palais, **place Louis Lépine** is now filled by the city's best flower market (8am-4pm Mon-Sat), partially transformed into a twittering bird market on Sundays. To the south is the impersonal facade of the Préfecture de Police, often known simply by its address, quai des Orfèvres, as immortalised in Simenon's Maigret detective novels. Straight ahead to the east is the

Hôtel Dieu, site of the oldest hospital in Paris, founded in the seventh century, although the present building dates from 1866-78. During the Middle Ages it had a reputation as the hospital from hell: if you were admitted, your chances of survival were slim. Today it's still the main hospital for central Paris, but a much quieter and safer place.

The eastern end of the island is dominated by the looming towers and flying buttresses of **Notre Dame**. Don't let the crowds put you off. Although heavily restored, the facade, with its three portals, remains a masterpiece of Gothic design, begun in 1163 but only completed in the 1340s. It was badly damaged by Revolutionaries in 1793, before being returned to its ceremonial role for the coronation of Napoléon as Emperor in 1804. Later, it was only saved from demolition by an active campaign led by Victor Hugo, and beginning in the 1840s extensive restoration was carried out by the Gothic Revivalist architect Eugène Viollet-le-Duc, who was responsible for much of the present-day interior. Don't miss the ascent to the roof (from the corner of rue du Cloître-Notre-Dame) to admire the wonderfully ghoulish gargoyles and fine view.

Back on terra firma, look for the bronze marker in front of the cathedral, showing the spot that is considered the centre of the city, and the point from which all distances are officially measured. Make sure you walk round the back of the building, too, for the best views of its structure, which looks especially surreal when floodlit at night.

To the north-east of the cathedral are a few medieval streets untouched by Haussmann, such as **rue Chanoinesse** – built to house canons of Notre Dame, **rue des Ursins** and the narrow **rue des Chantres**. Steps away from the cathedral at rue du Cloître Notre Dame is Le Vieux Bistro, one of the best traditional bistros in Paris (*see chapter* **Restaurants**). At **9 quai aux Fleurs**, marked by a plaque, Héloïse lived with her uncle Canon Fulbert, who had her lover Abélard castrated.

On the very eastern tip of the island, through a pretty garden, the square de l'Ile de France, is the **Mémorial de la Déportation**, a memorial to the thousands, mostly Jews, deported to death camps during World War II. Visitors descend a blind staircase to river level, where there are simple chambers inscribed with the names of the deportees.

## Ile St-Louis

*In the 4th arrondissement. Best M° stations Pont-Marie, Sully-Morland.*

Today, the Ile St-Louis is one of the most exclusive residential addresses in the city. Delightfully unspoiled, it has a mix of fine architecture, narrow streets and magnificent views from the tree-lined *quais* across the Seine.

**Ile St-Louis'** *well-preserved architecture.*

For hundreds of years, however, the island was entirely unbuilt, a swampy pasture belonging to Notre Dame and a retreat for fishermen, boaters, swimmers and lovers, known as the Ile Notre Dame. In the fourteenth century Charles V briefly disturbed its tranquility by building a fortified canal through the middle, thus creating a second island the Ile aux Vaches ('Island of Cows'). Its real-estate potential wasn't realised until the seventeenth century, when speculator Christophe Marie (after whom the Pont Marie is named) persuaded Louis XIII to let him fill in the canal and make plans for streets, bridges and houses. The island was renamed in honour of the King's pious predecessor, and eventually the venture proved a huge success, although Marie himself went bankrupt in the process. It became highly fashionable as a site for elegant new residences from the 1630s onwards, in great part thanks to the interest shown by society architect Louis Le Vau, who himself lived on the island; by the 1660s the entire island was filled.

Nowadays the Ile St-Louis is like a set from a *grand siècle* period drama, without a Métro or many modern shops. Instead there are *quais* lined with plane trees and poplars, fine houses with wrought-iron balconies and carved stone doorways, quirky gift shops, quaint tea shops and some lively bars and restaurants.

Running lengthways through the island is the **rue St-Louis-en-l'Ile**. At No 19bis is the little Baroque church of St-Louis-en-l'Ile, a popular venue for classical concerts. No 54 was once a tennis court, now the unusual Hôtel du Jeu de Paume (*see chapter* **Accommodation**). At No 31 is Berthillon, by general agreement purveyor of the best ice cream in town (*see chapter* **Food & Drink**), while at the western end is the Flore en l'Ile tea room with a great view across to Notre Dame, and the popular Brasserie de l'Isle St-Louis (*see chapter* **Restaurants**) which draws a mix of refined islanders, other Parisians and foreigners.

Among the finest buildings on the island are the **Hôtel Chenizot**, just down from Berthillon at 51 rue St-Louis-en-l'Ile, with its doorway adorned by a bearded faun and a balcony decorated with grim-faced monsters; the **Hôtel Lambert** at No 2, built by Le Vau in 1641 for Louis XIII's secretary, with its stone lions and palm trees; and the **Hôtel de Lauzun**, at 17 quai d'Anjou.

The Lauzun has an outstanding, largely original seventeenth-century interior and a fascinating history. Built by Le Vau in 1656, it once housed a salon frequented by Racine, Molière and La Fontaine. Later, in the 1840s, it was owned by literary aficionado Jérôme Pichon, who rented out rooms to artists and writers. Baudelaire first saw his lover and 'Black Venus' Jeanne Duval from his window, and wrote much of *Les Fleurs du mal* here. Lauzun is open to the public (01.43.54.27.14; Easter-Nov 10am-5.30pm Sat, Sun).

# The Right Bank

*Regal palaces and riotously revolutionary quartiers make the Right Bank an area of contrasts.*

## The Louvre & the Palais-Royal

*In the 1st, 2nd and part of the 8th arrondissement.*

Finding a reliable residence in Paris was a hazardous business for France's kings and emperors. Ever fearful of street riots, they first moved off the Ile de la Cité in the fourteenth century, then hopped between the Louvre, the place des Vosges and Versailles. The area round the Louvre remains full of royal and imperial survivals.

Although the main attraction of the **Louvre** is its works of art, it remains the Parisian palace *par excellence*, with its fine courtyards and galleries stretching towards the **Jardin des Tuileries**. One major consequence of all the recent renovation has been that part of Philippe-Auguste's original twelfth-century fortress, which Charles V made into a royal residence in the mid-fourteenth century, can now be seen within the walls of the surrounding palace. Over the sixteenth century, François 1er and his successors replaced the old fortress with a more luxurious residence, the Cour Carrée, perhaps the best example of Renaissance architecture in Paris, and the gallery along the Seine leading to the Tuileries Palace to the west. The wing along the rue de Rivoli and the Cour Napoléon were built by Napoléon and Napoléon III.

The Louvre was first opened to the public as a museum by the Revolutionary Convention in 1793, although the last vestige of state administration, the Finance Ministry, only moved out in 1989, as the museum again came to public attention with the *Grand Louvre* scheme, which added the notorious pyramid by IM Pei in Cour Napoléon, doubled the exhibition space and added the new subterranean **Carrousel du Louvre** shopping mall, exhibition centre and fast food halls. Initially opposed, the pyramid has surprisingly quickly become a part of the Paris landscape. The steel and glass structure is fascinating both for its technical brilliance and the tricks it plays with the light and water of the surrounding fountains. If you're not convinced, come back at night when, floodlit, it has a mesmerising glow, or ponder over the pyramid from a table under the arcades at the stylish **Café Marly**.

The *Grand Louvre* has also rejuvenated the **Musée des Arts Décoratifs**, **Musée de la Mode et du Costume** and shortly-to-open **Musée de la Publicité**, and restored the **Arc du Carrousel**, a mini-Arc de Triomphe built by

Napoléon. On top of it, he placed the famous Roman bronze horses he had taken from St Mark's in Venice. France was obliged to return them in 1815 and they were replaced with replicas in 1828. Through the arch you can now appreciate the extraordinary perspective through the **Jardin des Tuileries** – replanted to breathe new life into Le Nôtre's Baroque gardens – all along the **Champs-Elysées** up to the **Arc de Triomphe** and beyond to the **Grande Arche de la Défense**.

Most people now approach the Louvre by the Cour Napoléon, but it's also worth walking through the Cour Carrée out to rue du Louvre. On place du Louvre, opposite the eastern facade of the palace, is **St-Germain-l'Auxerrois**, once the parish church of the kings of France, and home to the only original Flamboyant-Gothic porch in Paris, built in 1435.

Along the north side of the Louvre, the **rue de Rivoli**, created by Napoléon for military parades, is remarkable for its uniform, arcaded facades, designed by the Imperial architects Percier and Fontaine. It runs in a perfect straight line to the **place de la Concorde** in one direction, to the Marais in the other, where it merges into the rue St-Antoine. Although most shops here now sell souvenirs, elegant, old-fashioned hotels still remain, like the **Meurice**, **Regina** and **Brighton**, as do gentlemen's tailors, the bookshops **W H Smith** and **Galliani** and the famous tea room **Angelina**, which somehow bypasses all modes.

Halfway along, at the end of the Louvre, have a look at **place des Pyramides**, at the junction of the rue de Rivoli and rue des Pyramides. The shiny golden equestrian statue of Joan of Arc is one of four statues of her in the city – designed, along with Rodin's *Burghers of Calais*, to make Brits feel guilty. To the north on rue St-Honoré, you come to the Baroque church of **St-Roch** (at No 292), begun for Louis XIV in 1653. It contains many works of French religious art, but is most noticed for the bullet holes in its facade left by Napoléon's troops when they put down a royalist revolt here in 1795. Writers Corneille and Diderot, and André Le Nôtre, genius of garden design, are all buried inside. Two streets further west is the rue du Marché St-Honoré, where the **Le Rubis** wine bar hosts the scrum to taste Beaujolais Nouveau every November.

*Nineteenth-century elegance lingers on in the* **rue de Rivoli**.

The old covered market in the place du Marché-St-Honoré has been replaced by a shiny new glass and steel construction by Spanish architect Ricardo Bofill, with shops downstairs and offices of the Paribas bank above. If you want to eat around here, there's **L'Absinthe** and a branch of bistro chain Batifol in the square. Behind are quiet streets such as rue Danielle-Casanova containing some fine, rather forgotten *hôtels particuliers*.

## Place Vendôme & Place de la Concorde

Further along the rue St-Honoré to the right you can see the eight-sided **place Vendôme**, one of the most beautiful squares in Paris and one of Louis XIV's major contributions to the city, with a perspective that now goes from the rue de Rivoli up to Opéra. Thanks to recent refurbishment, cars now park underground, so you can appreciate the square's formal geometry. It is dominated by a bronze-covered column modelled on Trajan's Column in Rome, and similarly illustrated with a spiral comic-strip of military exploits. On the top is a statue of Napoléon as Caesar.

A place Vendôme address has, perhaps, the highest snob-value in the city; the swish town houses have attracted bankers and jewellers since they were built. Cartier, Boucheron, Van Cleef & Arpels and other smart names enjoy the company of the Ministry of Justice and the Ritz hotel at No 15, the place Hemingway claimed to have personally 'liberated' in 1944 (in fact, he merely ordered a drink there after the fighting was over), while Charvet at No 28 is reputed for the best handmade shirts.

At the far end of the Tuileries, the **Place de la Concorde**, built by Jacques Ange Gabriel for Louis XV, is a brilliant exercise in the use of open space, with three sides open for views over the river, across the Tuileries and along the Champs-Elysées; the fourth is occupied by Gabriel's grand-colonnaded palaces, now the **Hôtel Crillon**, a favourite stopping-off point for diplomats and visiting foreign ministers, the French automobile club and Hôtel de la Marine. Foreigners might quibble at André Malraux's description of it as 'the most beautiful architectural complex on this planet', but it's impossible not to recognise the grandeur of this most imposing of Paris squares, especially when lit up at night. Its tiered wedding cake fountains represent river and maritime navigation, while the obelisk in the centre comes from Luxor and, like Cleopatra's Needle in London, was a present from the Viceroy of Egypt in the 1830s.

On the flanks of the Tuileries stand the **Orangerie**, now a small gallery of Impressionist and post-Impressionist art, noted for its series of Monet waterlilies, and the **Jeu de Paume**, originally built for the game of real tennis and now used for temporary shows of contemporary art.

This is definitely high-class Paris. Fashion boutiques, china and silverware shops and luxury hotels fill the area. Leading to the Madeleine is the smart rue Royale with stuffy tea shop **Ladurée** and the legendary but now disappointing **Maxim**'s restaurant which features in the Lehár's opera *The Merry Widow*. There are more smart shops in the rue Boissy d'Anglas and along the rue du Faubourg-St-Honoré where the ultimate sporting luxuries are found at **Hermès** (note the horseman on its parapet), alongside fashion names like Guy Laroche, Karl Lagerfeld, Lanvin and Lolita Lempicka.

## Palais-Royal

Across the rue de Rivoli from the Louvre, past the giant antiques superstore the **Louvre des Antiquaires**, stands the **Palais-Royal**, originally Cardinal Richelieu's private mansion, and then used by offshoots of the royal family as a secondary residence. It now houses two major government departments, the Ministry of Culture and the Conseil d'Etat. Within the main courtyard are Daniel Buren's black-and-white-striped column stumps, commissioned in 1986 by then culture minister Jack Lang to complement the view from his office window, which provide some amusing places to sit. On the southwest corner of the palace, at place André-Malraux, is the attractive theatre housing France's oldest national theatre company, the **Comédie Française**. The company was created by Louis XIV in 1680, and given sole right to perform in the capital. The brass-fronted Café Nemours is popular with thespians.

If today the Palais-Royal gardens are cherished for their tranquility, in the 1780s this was one of the most rumbustious centres of Parisian life. In a clever entrepreneurial venture, the Duc d'Orléans (Philippe-Egalité), who inherited the palace in 1776, added the arcades around the gardens, letting out the buildings to theatres, coffee houses, shops and the like. It became an extraordinary, bawdy combination of early shopping mall, intellectual meeting point and pleasure palace, where aristocrats and the grubby inhabitants of the *faubourgs* rubbed shoulders in subversive abandon. The coffee houses in its arcades became major centres for radical debate. It was here that Camille Desmoulins called the city to arms on the eve of Bastille Day (*see* chapter **Empires & Revolutions**).

Of the great era of the Palais-Royal only the sumptuously panelled **Grand Véfour** survives, as one of Paris' best haute cuisine restaurants, although there are simpler places to eat, like the **Restaurant du Palais-Royal** and the Muscade tea room, both of which have tables outside under the arcades in summer, as well as an assortment of little shops. After the Napoleonic Wars, the Duke of Wellington and Field Marshal von Blücher supposedly lost so much money at the Palais' gam-

The **rue du Faubourg-St-Honoré** *is a favourite with fashion's big-spenders.*

bling dens that Parisians claimed they had won back their entire dues for war reparations. You can go through the arcades to rue de Montpensier to the west, and explore the narrow, stepped passages between this road and rue de Richelieu.

Behind the Palais Royal stretches Paris' traditional business district, with narrow streets, office blocks and restaurants, where perfectly coiffed women and men in button-down shirts commune at lunch time over a few glasses of wine. Most interesting for the visitor are the covered passages (*see p102*, **Visions of Arcadia**) and the **Bibliothèque Nationale Richelieu** on rue de Richelieu, with its exhibition spaces in what had been the mansion of Cardinal Richelieu, and huge nineteenth-century, iron-vaulted reading room.

## Opéra & Les Grands Boulevards

*Mainly in the 2nd, 8th and 9th arrondissements.*

Not far from place Vendôme is the wedding cake of Charles Garnier's **Palais Garnier** opera house, constructed between 1862 and 1875. One of Napoléon III's architectural extravaganzas, it perfectly illustrates the excesses of its reactionary patron and evokes the mood of opera at its very grandest. Outside, it's covered in sculptures depicting dance and music, right up to its copper dome topped by a gaudy Apollo. Garnier's interior is a treasure trove of frescoes, sculptures, grand stairways, marble, gold leaf and precious stones. It's not hard to see why the legend of the Phantom of the Opera started here.

The **Café de la Paix** overlooking place de l'Opéra was also designed by Garnier. Although expensive and full of tourists, its interior still gives a sense of stepping back into the nineteenth century. Behind, in rue Scribe, is the Hôtel Scribe where, in what was then the Jockey Club, you'll pass the venue for the Lumière brothers' first cinema show in 1895 (at No 14). The **Olympia** concert hall, at 28 boulevard des Capucines, is the legendary venue where Edith Piaf and other great French singers of the last hundred years have performed. Declared a national monument, it is nevertheless to be knocked down and rebuilt down the street.

The classical temple at the end of the boulevard is the **Madeleine**, a vaguely religious monument to the glory of Napoléon. Its massive Corinthian columns mirror the **Assemblée Nationale** across the Seine, while the interior is a riot of marble, cluttered with side altars to saints who look as if they ought to be Roman generals. But many come here to ogle the gaudy shop windows of **Fauchon**, Paris' most extravagant delicatessen, **Hédiard**, **La Maison de la Truffe** (with record-breaking giant truffle in the window), and the other luxury foodstores that dominate the square.

Just behind the Opéra, the *grands magasins*, or big department stores, which opened at the end of the nineteenth century, line up along boulevard Haussmann. Visit **Au Printemps** and **Galeries Lafayette**, with vast floors of fashion and perfumes, the adjacent Lafayette Gourmet foodhalls and a branch of Marks & Spencer.

# Visions of Arcadia

A little of the atmosphere of the Romantic era still lingers in the picturesque glass-roofed *galeries* that thread their way between Paris' boulevards. Most were built by speculators in the early nineteenth century, when properties confiscated from the church or nobility under the Revolution brought vast new tracts of land onto the market. Perhaps inspired by Arabian souks, the *galeries* or *passages* were a forerunner of the department store, where strollers could inspect the latest novelties safe from rain, mud and horses. Astute pedestrians can still make their way via *galeries* entirely undercover all the way from the Grands Boulevards to the Palais-Royal. Over 100 *galeries* existed in 1840; fewer than 20 remain today, mostly in the 1st, 2nd and 9th *arrondissements*. Several have now been renovated and once again house fashionable shops, while in the 8th *arrondissement* the tradition has been revived with the upmarket Galerie Royale. It's best to visit during the day, as most are locked at night and on Sundays.

**Galerie Véro Dodat**: *today very chic.*

## Galerie Véro-Dodat

*between 2 rue Bouloi and 19 rue Jean-Jacques-Rousseau, 1st. Mº Louvre or Palais-Royal.*
A pair of prosperous *charcutiers* – M Véro and M Dodat – built this arcade during the Restoration, equipping it with gaslights and more than recouping their investment by charging their tenants astronomical rents. The *galerie*'s wooden shop fronts, decorated with crisp Corinthian colums and arcaded arched windows, and the tiled floor are beautifully preserved, among them the vintage **Café de l'Epoque** and an eccentric selection of shops selling antique dolls, architectural salvage and leather goods.

## Passage de Choiseul

*Between rue des Petits-Champs and rue St-Augustin, 2nd. Mº Pyramides or Quatre-Septembre.*
Famed for its colourful depiction (under the name of Passage des Bérésinas) in Céline's *Mort à Crédit*, this is the *passage* where the writer grew up. More proletarian than Véro-Dodat or Vivienne (as the name '*passage*' indicates) its charm lies in the very ordinariness of its cheap clothing stores and discount shops. Like its produce, here the glass roof is functional rather than decorative.

## Galerie Vivienne & Galerie Colbert

*between rue 6 Vivienne, 4 rue des Petits-Champs and 5 rue de la Banque, 2nd. Mº Bourse.*
The most elegant and most fashionable of the *galeries* opened in 1826 and is still distinctly upmarket. Bright and spacious, Vivienne is decorated in Neo-Classical style with stucco bas-reliefs and a beautifully crafted mosaic pavement. Jean-Paul Gaultier's couture, the coveted fabrics of Wolff et Descourtis, the fine vintages of venerable wine merchant **Legrand** and pretty tea-room, A Priori Thé, make it the ideal place for an afternoon browse. Running in a parallel L-shape, is Vivienne's rival in luxury: Galerie Colbert with its huge glass dome and an exhibition space that is part of the **Bibliothèque Nationale**.

## Passage du Grand-Cerf

*between 10 rue Dussoubs and 145 rue St-Denis, 2nd. Mº Etienne-Marcel.*
A more disreputable looking and less-ornate passageway near the rue Montorgueil street market, the Passage built in 1835 is notable for its height – originally giving access to a form of hostel above the shops, wrought iron work and hanging lanterns. It has recently been restored but has yet to regain much of a sense of animation.

## Passage des Panoramas

*between 10 rue St-Marc and 11 bd Montmartre, 2nd. Mº Richelieu-Drouot.*
The earliest of the surviving galeries, built 1799-1800, takes its name from the 'panoramas' – giant circular illuminated paintings of Rome, Jerusalem, London, Athens and other celebrated capitals – that were created by Robert Fulton, the American inventor, and landscape painter Pierre Prévost and exhibited here when the passage opened in 1800, drawing large crowds. Enticing new shops and restaurants intermixed with its many unusual traditional businesses have recently given the place a new lease of life. Take in the superb premises of Stern (No 47), engraver to the *haute-bourgeoisie* since 1830, and the pleasant tea room L'Arbre à Cannelle in a decorative former *chocolatier*.

## Passage Jouffroy & Passage Verdeau

*between 10-12 bd Montmartre and 9 rue de la Grange-Batelière, 9th. Mº Richelieu-Drouot.*
Across the boulevard from the **Passage des Panoramas**, is Passage Jouffroy, built in 1845-46, with grand barrel-vaulted glass and iron roof. Past the **Musée Grévin** and pleasant **Café Zephyr** to either side of the entrance, it contains a hotchpotch of a old-fashioned printsellers, antiquarian bookshops and old-fashioned toy shops, with the characterful **Hôtel Chopin** halfway down the passage. Across the rue de la Grange-Batelière, the route continues in the quiet **Passage Verdeau**, mainly home to second-hand booksellers.

## Passage Brady

*between 46 rue du Fbg-St-Denis and 43 rue du Fbg-St-Martin, 10th. Mº Château d'Eau.*
Certainly not gentrified, rather, a slice of little India, Passage Brady is packed with South Asian grocers crammed with spices and exotic vegetables, barbers and inexpensive Indian cafés and restaurants.

## The Grands Boulevards

Contrary to popular belief, the string of *Grands Boulevards* (des Italiens, Montmartre, Poissonnière, Bonne-Nouvelle, St-Denis, St-Martin) were not a creation of Haussmann but of Louis XIV in 1670, replacing the line of fortifications of Charles II's city wall. This explains the strange changes of level, especially in the eastern section, as steps lead up to side streets or down to the road on former traces of the ramparts. The boulevards burgeoned at the end of eighteenth century and early nineteenth century, witnessed in the fine Neo-classical detail of some facades and the network of covered galleries (*see p102,* **Visions of Arcadia**). They still have something of a gaudy character today, with theatres, chain restaurants and, further east, sleazy discount stores, although the area is the next to come up for renovation on the municipal agenda.

Tucked between boulevard des Italiens and rue de Richelieu is the pretty place Boïeldieu with the **Opéra Comique**. Originally built in 1781-83 as the Comédie Italienne, the theatre caught fire in 1840 and again in 1887, and was rebuilt in 1894-98 as a fancy Neo-Classical confection adorned with caryatids and ornate lampposts. Alexandre Dumas *fils* was born across the square at No 1 in 1824.

On the other side of boulevard Montmartre is the spiky modern construction of the **Drouot** auction house. Around it are the offices of numerous specialist *commissaires-priseurs*, antique shops and rather decrepit *hôtels particuliers*. The Caves Drouot café and restaurant (8 rue Drouot, 9th/ 01.47.70.83.38) doesn't look much from the outside but has a pretty vintage interior, classic French cooking and excellent wines. Here the boulevards are crossed by the **Passage des Panoramas** and **Passage Jouffroy**, just at the colourful carved entrance of the **Musée Grévin** waxworks museum. Further along rue du Fbg-Montmartre is the legendary budget eat **Chartier**. This area is home to numerous kosher restaurants, the recently closed **Palace** nightclub and the famous Folies-Bergère, which is currently serving up musicals rather than cabaret. Dominating boulevard Poissonnière, the palatial Art Deco cinema **Le Grand Rex** is one of the largest in Europe and offers an interesting backstage tour. Beyond here are Louis XIV's crumbling triumphal arches, the Portes St-Martin and St-Denis, both being renovated, and a cacophony of levels, as narrow rue de Cléry and rue d'Aboukir lead towards Les Halles.

## Les Halles & Sentier

*In the 1st and 2nd arrondissements.*

Away from the crowded, hamburger-filled malls of the Forum des Halles itself, this area is about as close as Paris gets to a backwater. For years the district was full of crumbling houses, run-down shops and downmarket strip-joints along the rue St-Denis. In recent years, the prostitutes and neon peep-shows have been partly pushed back by an energetic pedestrianisation scheme. At the same time this remains Paris as Parisians experience it. There are few conventional cultural attractions as such, but sit in a bar with the Sentier cloth wholesalers or the traders from the rue Montorgueil market, and you'll get a taste of old tight-knit Paris.

Few places epitomise the transformation of the entire area more than Les Halles, for centuries the wholesale fruit and vegetable market for the city and now a miserably designed, semi-sunken shopping mall. This was what Zola called the 'belly of Paris', the nerve centre of life in the capital, a giant covered market graced with Baltard's green iron pavilions. In 1969 the whole lot was moved out to a new wholesale market in the southern suburb of Rungis, leaving a giant hole that was only filled in the early 1980s, after numerous political and architectural disputes about what should take its place.

The **Forum des Halles** was intended to become the new commercial heart of Paris; instead the giant multi-level complex has become seedier by the year. People still flock here, for cheap jeans, the **Vidéothèque de Paris** or the multiplex cinema, or simply because the Châtelet-Les Halles interchange beneath is the unavoidable hub of both the Métro and the RER. As 'social exclusion' has risen up as one of France's major problems, the Forum has also become a mecca for the homeless, punks and junkies, the epitome of the kind of Paris seen in Luc Besson's 1985 movie *Subway*.

On the eastern side of the garden, and now somewhat dwarfed, there is also the place des Innocents, a time-honoured meeting-point, with the Renaissance **Fontaine des Innocents** in the centre. The four-sided roofed structure was designed by Pierre Lescot who also worked on the Louvre for François 1er (the original reliefs by Jean Goujon are now in the Louvre). The decline of the area was reflected in the closure in 1994 of the high-profile Philippe Starck-designed Café Costes on place des Innocents, although towards boulevard Sébastopol, the pedestrianised rue des Lombards is another centre for nightlife, with bars, restaurants and the Baiser Salé, Sunset and Duc des Lombards jazz clubs (*see chapter* **Music: Rock, Roots & Jazz**), while the rue de la Ferronnerie is thriving with the **Banana Café** and other gay bars.

The Les Halles gardens alongside the Forum similarly seem to be largely inhabited by the homeless. Looming over them is the sixteenth-century church of **St-Eustache**, one of Paris' largest, with barnlike interior and Classical Renaissance motifs inside, and chunky flying buttresses on the outside.

At the western end of the Les Halles gardens is the **Bourse du Commerce**, an attractive circular building in yellow stone which was once the main corn exchange. Now it is a busy commodity market for coffee and sugar, and houses a world trade centre and an office of the Paris Chamber of Commerce.

This area is packed with smart clothes shops – **Agnès B**'s empire extends along most of rue du Jour, while rue Coquillière still has the 24-hour brasserie **Au Pied de Cochon**, now more geared towards tourists than market traders – although some of the old restaurant supply shops like the **Comptoir de la Gastronomie, A Simon** and **E Dehillerin** still exist. Their windows are packed with huge cauldrons and tureens, but they also sell more normal volumes to the general public.

East of here, you will come to rue Montorgueil, with its wonderful food market (*see chapter* **Food & Drink**). Often brightly decorated with pennants hanging from the lamp-posts, the street, with its cheap wine bars and restaurants like the excellent bistro **Le Brin de Zinc... et Madame**, is an irresistible place to while away a couple of hours.

At 20 rue Etienne-Marcel is the **Tower of Jean Sans Peur**, a strange medieval relic of the fortified townhouse (1409-11) of Jean Duc de Bourgogne, although over-restoration now rather hides its age. West on Etienne-Marcel you come to one of the prettiest squares in town, the **place des Victoires**. Built like the place Vendôme by Hardouin-Mansart in 1685 to commemorate Louis XIV's victories against the Dutch, it forms an intimate circle of buildings today seriously dedicated to fashion, with stores like Kenzo, Victoire and Esprit. Standing on the corner of the rue d'Aboukir, you get the best view of the smart, classical Bank of France building across the square. A mix of worlds perfectly typified by the clientele of the bistro **Chez Georges**, where bankers and fashion moguls rub shoulders.

South of Les Halles, just by the Pont-Neuf, is the giant department store **La Samaritaine**, which retains much of its original Art Nouveau interior, its grand staircase and glass roof. The café at the top is worth a visit for the spectacular view it grants across the Seine, glimpsed from behind the giant neon letters proclaiming the store's name. The quai de Mégisserie along the Seine contains a strange menagerie of animals and birds in cages.

For something altogether weirder, go to the pest extermination shop in rue des Halles, where dead rats hang in the window. It's a surreal reminder that this was the site of the city's main burial ground, the Cimetière des Innocents, which was demolished in 1786 after flesh-eating rats started gnawing their way into people's living rooms.

## Rue & Faubourg St-Denis

The tackiness is pretty unremitting up and down the traditional red-light district of rue St-Denis (and its northern continuation, the rue du Faubourg St-Denis), which snakes northward from the Forum. Kerb-crawlers gawp at the neon signs advertising *l'amour sur scène*, and size up the sorry-looking array of prostitutes in the doorways.

At the point where the street crosses boulevard St-Denis, the delapidated **Porte St-Denis**, erected in 1672 to celebrate Louis XIV's victories on the Rhine, and once one of the main entries into Paris, is being renovated. North of it, towards Gare du Nord, amid the seediness there is also the brasserie **Julien**, on rue du Faubourg St-Denis, which boasts one of the finest Art Nouveau interiors in Paris, with stunning painted panels, and eternally fashionable status. On either side of the street there are narrow passageways and slightly sinister cobbled courtyards. **Passage Brady** is a surprising piece of India, home to a small but thriving community which mainly originates from France's former Indian colony of Pondicherry.

## Sentier & the Bourse

Between rue des Petits Carreaux and rue St-Denis is the site of what was once the Cour des Miracles, so called because the paupers who came back there after a day's begging would 'miraculously' regain the use of their eyes or limbs. An abandoned aristocratic estate, it was a refuge for beggars and the underworld for decades until it was cleared out in 1667 by Louis XIV's chief of police, La Reynie. Nowadays, the surrounding area, the Sentier, is the centre of the rag trade, and the streets are filled with porters carrying long linen bundles over their shoulders. The streets around rue du Caire, built during a fit of Egyptomania after Napoléon's Egyptian campaign, are connected by a maze of passages lined with wholesale merchants.

The area attracts hundreds of illegal and semi-legal foreign workers, who line up in place du Caire every morning for work in the sweatshops. It's an inglorious modern-day slave market that highlights the hypocrisy of official anti-immigration drives, as the garment industry could not survive without this stream of cheap and desperate labour.

Rue Réaumur, cutting across the Sentier, was once the Fleet Street of Paris, and has some remarkable Art Nouveau buildings, particularly at Nos 116, 118 and 124. As in other capitals, the newspapers have nearly all moved out of the city centre, although *Le Figaro* and Agence France-Presse are still based near the **Bourse**, Paris' stock exchange, commissioned by Napoléon in 1808.

## Beaubourg & the Marais

*In the 3rd and 4th arrondissements.*

Between boulevard Sébastopol and the Bastille lies Beaubourg – the historic area in which the Centre Pompidou landed in 1977 – and the Marais, built up between the sixteenth and eighteenth centuries and now a magnet for unusual boutiques, interesting museums and trendy bars.

*Take a passage to India along* **Passage Brady**.

## Beaubourg

Contemporary Parisian architecture started with the **Centre Pompidou**, designed by the Italo-British team Renzo Piano and Richard Rogers. Before the Centre was built, the site, known by its medieval name Beaubourg, was a pitiful empty space surrounded by dilapidated tenements. Now it teems with tourists, fire-eaters and buskers, not to mention the trendy **Café Beaubourg** and busy restaurants. The **Centre Pompidou** itself, an international benchmark of high-tech, was always intended to be as much of an attraction as its contents. Inside, a giant public library, an arthouse cinema, the national museum of modern art and many exhibition spaces all work to maintain the impression of a kaleidoscopic modern cultural emporium. Although much of the centre will be closed between late 1997 and the end of 1999, the celebrated ride up the escalators (offering one of the best views in Paris) will stay open.

The other side of the piazza, peer down rue Quincampoix for its mix of art galleries, bars and the curious passage Molière. Beside the Centre Pompidou is the place Igor Stravinsky, with the IRCAM contemporary music institute on one side, and the playful **Stravinsky Fountain**, designed by Nikki de Saint Phalle and Jean Tinguely, in the centre. It's full of whirring machines and multi-coloured gadgets including a *Nana* and a snake that move and squirt water. On the south side of the square, a great spot for al fresco eating in the summertime, is the more sober church of **St-Merri**, with a Flamboyant Gothic facade complete with

an androgynous demon leering over the doorway. Inside, there is some fine vaulting, as well as the original carved wooden organ area, the oldest bell in Paris (1331), and some sixteenth-century stained glass. It is used for free concerts most weekends.

The area between Beaubourg and the **rue de Rivoli** is a maze of narrow pedestrianised streets. Among the many restaurants, the charming bistro **Le Grizzli** stands out. On the river side of the rue de Rivoli stands the **Tour St-Jacques**, alive with Gothic gargoyles, and the **place du Châtelet**, site of a prison in the Middle Ages and today home to the twin theatres **Châtelet Théâtre Musical de Paris**, a classical music and opera venue, and the **Théâtre de la Ville**, Paris' leading contemporary dance venue. East of here looms the Neo-Gothic **Hôtel de Ville**, Paris' city hall, in which the Mayor's own apartment occupies an entire floor. It overlooks a square of the same name, once known as the place de Grève, where disgruntled workers used to gather – hence the French word for strike (*grève*). Many Protestant heretics were burnt in the place during the sixteenth-century Wars of Religion, and this was where the guillotine first stood during the Terror. The building itself was gutted by fire in the 1871 Commune, and rebuilt, considerably enlarged, thereafter.

## The Marais

East of the Hôtel de Ville is the Marais, a truly magical area whose narrow streets are dotted with seventeenth-century *hôtels particuliers* (aristocratic residences), art galleries, fashion boutiques and smart cafés. The big city slows down here to a gentle strolling pace, giving you time to notice the beautifully carved doorways and turrets and the early street signs carved into the stone buildings.

The Marais (or marsh) hasn't always been fashionable. It started life as an uninhabited piece of swampy ground used for market gardening. Its rise as an aristocratic residential area came in the seventeenth century, but its prestige faded a century later. The current renaissance dates from 1962, when Culture Minister André Malraux slapped a preservation order on its dilapidated mansions, safeguarding many endangered buildings for use as museums. Today the city's yuppies have taken over, pushing the area into the luxury bracket.

Among its idiosyncracies are a thriving gay scene, particularly at night when the bars and clubs come into their own, and Paris' oldest Jewish community, centred on the rue des Rosiers and rue des Ecouffes. Originally mainly made up of Eastern European Jews who arrived in the last century, the community expanded greatly in the 1950s and '60s with a new wave of Sephardic Jewish immigration following French withdrawal from North Africa. Consequently there are now many felafel shops alongside the kosher delicatessens, as well as several, fast-encroaching, designer clothes shops.

Running through the centre of the Marais is the **rue des Francs-Bourgeois**. The street soon forgets its Les Halles legacy in the food shops of rue Rambuteau to become a street packed with elegant mansions and original boutiques, from designer clothes to unusual gifts and kitsch. Branches of **Et Vous**, **Bleu Blanc** and **Plein Sud**, the New Age partywear of **Nina Jacob**, flower arrangements and garden gadgets of Millefeuilles, the delectable bathroom accessories of **Bains Plus**, funky knickknacks of **La Chaise Longue** or quirky tea rooms **Les Enfants Gâtés** and Marais Plus, make this street irrestible to the shopper. If you're in need of culture, take a look at two of the most elegant early eighteenth-century residences in Paris, full of rococo lightness: the **Musée de l'Histoire de France** at No 60 and **Hôtel d'Albret** at No 31.

At the heart of the Marais is the **place des Vosges**, a magnificently symmetrical square of red-brick palaces and graceful arcades. Henri IV's decision in 1605 to build what was then called the place Royale sparked off the building boom in the surrounding area. Nowadays it's a perfect place to linger among the linden trees that surround the central statue (of Henri's successor Louis XIII), or in the arcades, displaying antique furniture, modern art and fashionable clothes. At one corner is the **Maison de Victor Hugo**, once occupied by the author. Luxurious **Ambroisie** restaurant is for special treats; much simpler is the touristy but undeniably charming **Ma Bourgogne**.

An archway leads from the south-western corner of the square to the **Hôtel de Sully**, built by one of Henri IV's ministers and one of the most elegant of all the Marais mansions, housing the bookshop of the Caisse Nationale des Monuments Historiques and photo-exhibition space. From its ivy-rimmed garden you can walk through into the main courtyard, adorned with stone carvings representing the elements and the seasons, and then out onto the rue St-Antoine.

There are fine relics of *Ancien Régime* Paris all around the Marais. The 1705-09 Hôtel de Soubise

*The sumptuous **Hôtel de Soubise** is a monument to Marais style at its most gracious.*

on the corner of rue des Archives and rue des Francs-Bourgeois, now home to the national archives, is a grand rococo mansion with gracious *cour d'honneur* and beautiful gardens. Some of the interiors, decorated by artists, such as Boucher and Lemoine, are open to the public as part of the **Musée de l'Histoire de France**. The adjoining Hôtel de Rohan (used for temporary exhibitions) has a fine sculpture by Robert Le Lorrain, *The Horses of Apollo*, in the first courtyard on the right.

Nearby, at 60 rue des Archives, is the Hôtel Guénégaud, built in 1654 as a residence of Louis XIV's Secretary of State by François Mansart, and now housing the **Musée de la Chasse et de la Nature**. The district's two most important museums also occupy former *hôtels*. The **Musée Carnavalet** on rue de Sévigné, dedicated to Paris history, runs across two; the Hôtel Carnavalet (1548), remodelled in 1660 by Mansart and home to the famous seventeenth-century letter-writer Mme de Sévigné, and the later Hôtel le Peletier de St-Fargeau. Curiosities among the collection include faithful reproductions of Marcel Proust's bedroom and the original Fouquet jewellery shop.

The Hôtel Salé on rue de Thorigny, built in 1656 for a salt tax collector (hence the name), has housed the **Musée National Picasso** since 1985. The mansion, which had been considerably damaged and altered during use as a school, has been finely restored with a sensitive modern extension. The original elaborate staircase remains, as do two fine sphinxes in the entrance courtyard.

Equally worth seeking out is the austere **Hôtel de Lamoignon**, on the corner of rue Pavée and rue des Francs-Bourgeois. Built in 1585 for Diane de France, illegitimate daughter of Henri II, the monumental building is now home to the **Bibliothèque Historique de la Ville de Paris**.

If you are in Paris during the *Journées Portes Ouvertes* (*see chapter* **Paris by Season**), one normally out-of-bounds address to aim for is the Hôtel des Ambassadeurs de Hollande, at 47 rue Vieille-du-Temple. Two huge oak doors are decorated with Medusas. Inside are two sundials and stone figures of Romulus and Remus. Beaumarchais wrote *The Marriage of Figaro* here, in 1778.

Even the fire station at 7 rue de Sévigné was originally designed by François Mansart for one of Louis XIII's ministers. It hides an elegant facade around its inner courtyard. If you want to see some of these more private or official buildings during the rest of the year, your best bet is to join a walking tour of the district (*see chapter* **Sightseeing**).

The lower ends of the rue des Archives and rue Vieille-du-Temple are the places to go for café life and, after dark, for happening bars like the pretty **Petit Fer à Cheval**, cocktail bar Chez Richard and **La Chaise au Plafond** in the neighbouring impasse du Trésor. This area, especially along rue Ste-Croix-de-la-Bretonnerie, is also the hub of the

Paris gay scene. Which venues are mainly gay-oriented is usually fairly obvious, whether you want to find them or avoid them. Another good street for a drink is the rue du Bourg-Tibourg, with the quirky American-style **Lizard Lounge**, the more traditional Gallic pleasures of the bistro-cum-wine bar **Le Coude Fou**, or the charming place du Marché-Ste-Catherine with the rustic **Bar de Jarente** and Jewish restaurant Pitchi-Poi.

The northern half of the Marais, stretching up towards place de la République, is only now becoming gentrified, and is home to tiny local bars, costume-jewellery and rag-trade wholesalers and industrial workshops, alongside recently arrived fashion designers. On rue de Bretagne are food shops and fashionable couscous restaurant **Chez Omar**, while behind secretive courtyard entrances along rue Vieille-du-Temple and rue Debelloyme you can find many of Paris' most avant-garde art galleries (*see chapter* **Art Galleries**).

Returning back towards Beaubourg is the historic area around Arts et Métiers, once home to one of Paris' most powerful monasteries, the Abbey of St-Martin-des-Champs, transformed into the Musée des Arts et Métiers. Some ancient houses include the Auberge Nicolas Flamel (51 rue de Montmorency, 3rd/01.42.71.77.78), today a pleasant bistro, which was built in 1407 for Nicolas Flamel, later accused of alchemy. No 3 rue Volta was long thought to be the oldest house in the city but recent analysis has decided that its half-timbered structure in fact dates from the sixteenth century.

## The St-Paul District

South of the rue St-Antoine is a quieter, more sedate residential area of the Marais known as St-Paul, but here too there are many fine historic buildings, including one of Paris' oldest domestic mansions. You might also want to pay a visit to the **Village St-Paul**, a colony of antiques and junk sellers spread across a series of small courtyards off the rue St-Paul. On the parallel rue des Jardins-St-Paul is the largest surviving section of the **wall of Philippe-Auguste**, built around Paris by the king in the twelfth century. The domed Jesuit church of **St-Paul-St-Louis** (1627) nearby on rue St-Antoine, while visible from far off in most directions, is a rather disappointing imitation of the Gesù church in Rome. Inside, there is a major religious painting by Delacroix, *Christ in the Garden of Olives*. Opened in 1996 in a restored mansion that was a dairy and then rundown tenements, the **Maison Européenne de la Photographie** has a new extension, and puts on interesting shows of historical and contemporary photography. Just across from the tip of the Ile St-Louis, the **Pavillon de l'Arsenal**, built by a rich timber merchant to put on his own private art shows in rivalry with the offical *salons*, is it today used for interesting shows about Paris architecture. It stands on what was once an island in the Seine until the boulevard Morland was filled in.

Also near the riverbank, the **Hôtel de Sens** on rue du Figuier, is one of the oldest private residences in Paris, built in 1475 for the Archbishops of Sens. It's a fanciful ensemble of turrets decorated with stone wolves and monsters. During the Wars of Religion the Guise brothers hatched many an anti-royalist plot within its walls. Today it houses the **Bibliothèque Forney**, used for temporary exhibitions associated with the graphic arts.

## The Bastille & Eastern Paris

*Mainly in the 11th and 12th arrondissements.*
Ever since the famous prison-storming that inaugurated the Revolution, the **place de la Bastille**

has remained a potent symbol of popular revolt and is still a favoured spot for left-wing demonstrations and popular gatherings. Since the 1980s, it has also become a magnet for new cafés, designer bars, restaurants, art galleries and late-night bars that have transformed the area from one of craft workshops to one of the liveliest parts of the city, now drawing a young international crowd.

Nothing remains of the Bastille fortress which served as a high-security prison and a defence for what was then the Porte St-Antoine along the city walls, although there are a few vestiges of the foundations and tiled pictures of it in the Métro station. The site of the prison itself is now taken by a Banque de France office. The gap left by the demolished castle ramparts forms the present-day square, a popular meeting point lined with cafés. The July Column at its centre commemorates a dif-

# Village Paris: Ménilmontant

A small group of houses on a hill neighbouring the village of Belleville, Mesnil-Montant (uphill farm), where vines and fruit trees were cultivated, later expanded with bistros, workers' housing, balls and bordellos. Ménilmontant, incorporated within Paris at the same time as Belleville in 1860, has always been associated with its neighbour because of its similar history of workers' agitation, resistance during the Commune, and in the early twentieth century, its large immigrant population. Today it is becoming a thriving centre of alternative Paris.

This area is a curious mix of modern monster housing projects mainly put up in the '60s and '70s and little dwellings that are the remnants of the Ménilmontant of another age, now a mix of *soignée* gentrification and near dereliction. Below the rue des Pyrénées (even the names suggest this is a hilly area), poke your nose down the Cité Leroy or Villa l'Ermitage – calm houses with gardens and an old-fashioned carpenter's workshop – not missing the odd, red-brick Neo-Gothic house at 19 rue de l'Ermitage, and the almost rustic Cité de l'Ermitage. At its junction with rue de

Ménilmontant there is an extraordinary bird's-eye view straight into the centre of town, where you can see both the Tour St-Jacques and the Centre Pompidou. Just further down below rue Henri-Chevreau you get a glimpse of the old railway tracks and bridge which led to Ménilmontant's train station. Follow the rue Julien-Lacroix to the place Maurice-Chevallier, a little square in front of the nineteenth-century Notre-Dame-de-la-Croix church. Rue des Cascades also offers points of interest: at No 119 is a Neo-classical house built in 1770; No 145 was home to the St-Simonien community.

If you need a rest, the Lou Pascalou (14 rue des Panoyaux/01.46.36.78.10) attracts an arty crowd for a day-time coffee, a night-time beer, or a game of pool. La Buvette on the same street, and Le Soleil on the boulevard (No. 136) around the corner are also filled with young people. The cool set has found a good haunt lower down the hill on rue Oberkampf in the **Café Charbon**, a restored turn-of-the-century dance hall, and at the lively club and music venue **La Cithéa** across the road, all part of the neighbourhood's new pulse.

ferent revolution, that of 1830, when Charles X was toppled after three days of fighting.

The massive **Opéra Bastille** now dominates the eastern side of the square. Opened on the bicentennial of Bastille Day in 1989, it competes with the new Bibliothèque Nationale for the honour of being the most controversial of all Mitterrand's *Grands Projets*, both for its cumbersome megalithic form and shoddy construction (some of the tiles recently started falling off, necessitating protective netting along rue de Charenton) and for the soap-operatic goings on among artistic directors and enormous running costs within, although needless to say many productions sell out.

Rue de Lappe and rue de Charonne are the focus for bars, restaurants and nightlife in the area. Rue de Lappe typifies the area's tranformation, where you'll find side by side contemporary galleries, furniture workshops, vintage nightclubs, ruggedly authentic Auvergnat bistros, an array of pseudo-Cuban and pseudo-American bars and – an ominous sign – a gift shop. **Le Balajo** is a nightclub during the week, but reverts to its traditional dance hall past on Sunday afternoons.

You can still catch a flavour of the old working-class district at the Sunday morning market on **boulevard Richard Lenoir**, or along the rue du Faubourg-St-Antoine, with its furniture-makers' ateliers and many, sometimes gloriously tacky, furniture stores. On rue de Charonne there are trendy bars and bistros like **La Fontaine, Chez Paul,** the **Pause Café**, and turn-of-the-century **Bistro du Peintre**, with pavement tables ideal for watching the world go by, as well as art galleries and shops selling strange 1960s furniture. But these main thoroughfares tell only half the story. The area developed its own distinctive style of architecture: behind narrow street frontages are quaintly named cobbled alleys, dating back to the eighteenth century, such as the Cour du Cheval Blanc, Cour du Bel Air, Cour de la Maison Brûlée or Passage de l'Homme, lined with craftsmen's shops and workshops, or quirky bistros. This land originally lay outside the city walls on the lands of the Convent of St-Antoine, where skilled furniture makers were granted privileges, free from the city's restrictive guilds. Many of the courtyard workshops are now the studios of artists, architects or designers rather than furniture makers.

There's not much in the way of standard tourist sites in this area, but bags of atmosphere. Just past Ledru-Rollin Métro station is the bustling North African-flavoured market of the **place d'Aligre**. Further east is **place de la Nation**, now a traffic junction and red light district, that's interesting for its two square pavilions and accompanying Doric columns, remnants of the tax-collectors' wall built around Paris just before the Revolution. Originally, it was called place du Trône to commemorate the arrival here of Louis XIV and his wife Marie-

*Medusa at the **47 rue Vieille-du-Temple**.*

Thérèse in 1660. During the Terror the guillotine was set up here for a while and the place was renamed Place du Trône Renversé (square of the overturned throne). In the centre is a grandiose allegorical statue by Dalou titled *Triomphe de la République*, commissioned for the centenary of the Revolution in 1889 and inaugurated ten years later.

A new attraction near the Bastille is the **Viaduc des Arts**, a railway viaduct closed since 1969, that stretches along avenue Daumesnil. Another project designed to raise the tone of the area, its 60 renovated arches contain workshops, although rather more chic designers and craftspeople than the district's more traditional artisans. Along the top, the **Promenade Plantée** is the start of a footpath going east to the **Bois de Vincennes**.

South of the Bastille, by the edge of the Seine, is the new Bercy development, with the Ministère de l'Economie et du Budget, the **Palais Omnisports de Paris-Bercy**, a pyramid-shaped modern sports stadium and concert venue, and the dramatic, now closed, American Center.

Another unexpected thoroughfare is the **Canal St-Martin**, which begins at the Seine at pont Morland, disappears underground at place de la Bastille to re-emerge north at rue du Faubourg-du-Temple east of the vast place de la République. It is this stretch that has the most charm, lined with large shady trees and occasional small gardens, and crossed by iron footbridges. Most of the old warehouses have closed, but the area is still semi-industrial and a bit shabby, with a few, plain canal-side cafés. You may even still see the odd barge puttering down the canal. Between the fifth and sixth locks is the **Hôtel du Nord** (101 quai de Jemmapes, 10th /01.40.40.78.78) which inspired

Marcel Carné's classic 1938 film set in the canal district, even though most of the locations (including the footbridges) were recreated in a studio. Threatened with demolition in the early 1980s, the hotel was saved as a piece of French cinematic heritage and has now been reopened as a lively bistro. Just east of the canal from here is the **Hôpital St-Louis**, founded in 1607 to house plague victims, and built in the form of a series of isolated pavilions to stop disease spreading between its patients.

**Champs-Elysées & the West**

*In the 8th, 16th and 17th arrondissements.*
On the western side of the city centre, the atmosphere is very different from that found in the eastern *faubourgs*. This is smart, well-brushed Paris, home to business and preferred home of the city's BCBG (*bon chic, bon genre,* or in other words old money and impeccably affluent tastes) community.

## The Champs-Elsyées

The traffic-laden **avenue des Champs-Elysées** is still described by many Parisians – who don't often go there – as 'the most beautiful avenue in the world'. The great spine of western Paris started life as an extension to the Tuileries gardens laid out by Le Nôtre as far as the Rond-Point in the seventeenth century. By the time of the Revolution, the avenue had been laid along its full stretch, but was more a place for a Sunday walk than a street.

# Village Paris: Belleville

Until the eighteenth century, Belleville was still largely agricultural. Enormous growth in the early nineteenth century increased its population to 60,000. Incorporated into the rapidly expanding city in 1860, Belleville became a work and leisure place for the lower classes, while many bourgeois still had their country houses in the area. Despite attempts to dissipate workers' agitation by splitting the former village between the 11th, 19th and 20th *arrondissements*, it became famous as the centre of opposition to the Second Empire and as the last *quartier* to surrender during the Commune.

Cabarets, music halls, artisans, organs, cinemas and workers' housing all came to signify life in Belleville at the turn of the century. During the 1930s and '40s, Belleville was the place to dance to the music of Piaf (born at 72 rue de Belleville), Chevalier, Yves Montand or Odette Laure. Today, the **Java** night club, with its original *bal-musette* décor, has traces of this history.

A promenade in the *hauts de Belleville* could begin at the top of the parc de Belleville, with the panoramic view offered from rue Piat. Below, along boulevard de Belleville, the variety of commerce attests to the mixture of people who

make up the *Bellevillois* of today. Always animated with groups in deep discussion, the boulevard has Muslim and Kosher groceries, butchers and bakers; couscous and falafel eateries; and Chinese and Vietnamese restaurants and shops.

Every Tuesday and Friday morning, one of the largest and cheapest of Paris' outdoor markets makes Belleville livelier.

On the small streets off the rue de Belleville, the old buildings hide many courtyards and gardens. At No 13 rue Jouye-Rouve is an interesting new building which hides a garden, while rue Ramponneau mixes new housing and relics of old worker's Belleville. At No 23, down a crumbling alley, an old iron smithy has become **La Forge**, a squat for artists, many of whom are ardent members of La Bellevilloise association which is trying to preserve the area from redevelopment. But as many of the buildings are falling apart, they may still suffer the same fate as countless corners of Belleville which have made way for new buildings. Hopefully the *Bellevillois* will always put up the fight necessary to preserve their village as a home and community distinct from the Paris down the hill.

Things began to change at the turn of the nineteenth century when the creation of the Faubourg St-Honoré on the avenue's northern side brought fine houses, cafés and high-class prostitutes. With the industrial revolution came street lights, pavements, sideshows, concert halls, theatres and exhibition centres, plus military parades and royal processions, and the avenue of world repute was born. The completion of the Arc de Triomphe in 1836 also played its part. Bismarck was so impressed by the Champs-Elysées when he arrived with the conquering Prussian army in 1871 that he had a replica, the Kurfürstendamm, built in Berlin.

Now dominated by fast-food joints, airline offices, car showrooms and multiplex cinemas, the best time to get some sense of its former exuberance is for the military parade on 14 July or the annual New Year's street party, or at night when crowds queue to get into the **Queen** nightclub or glitzy **Lido** cabaret. Only a few buildings hint at a once-glorious past: Guerlain's perfume house at No 68, its windows displaying vast bottles of eau de Cologne, has fine cast-iron decoration. Nearby at No 25, although marred by a foreign exchange bureau at the front, is the grand house built for the Marquise de Païva, one of the most celebrated courtesans of the nineteenth century, and now the smart Travellers' Club, while towards the Arc de Triomphe, the vast CCF bank was once a hotel. Its interior has been gutted and reconstructed but the elaborate *Beaux-Arts* exterior survives.

The best parts of the Champs-Elysées are at its two ends. At the entrance to the avenue at place de la Concorde are the winged Marly horses, copies of the eighteenth-century originals by Guillaume Coustou, now displayed in the Louvre. To the left, leading from place Clemenceau down to the Seine are the glass-domed **Grand Palais** and **Petit Palais**, both built for the 1900 World Exhibition, and still used for major shows today. The wing of the Grand Palais opening onto avenue Franklin D Roosevelt contains the **Palais de la Découverte**, a fun science museum that's a real hit with children.

The eighteenth-century **Palais de l'Elysée**, the official presidential residence, lurks on rue du Fbg-St-Honoré, although its large gardens extend right to the northern side of the Champs-Elysées.

At the **Rond-Point des Champs-Elysées**, Nos 7 and 9 give some idea of the splendid fine mansions, hiding large gardens, that once lined the avenue. From here you can also stroll down the avenue Montaigne with its array of fashion houses such as Ungaro at No 2, Thierry Mugler at No 49, Christian Dior at No 30 and Chanel at 42.

At the western end of the avenue, the **Arc de Triomphe** towers above place Charles de Gaulle, still better known as Etoile. Begun to glorify Napoléon, the giant Neo-Classical arch was modified after his disgrace to celebrate the armies of the Revolution, although the Emperor could scarcely

*An affordable seat at the **Opéra Bastille**.*

feel himself under-represented. The surrounding place was commissioned later by Baron Haussmann and most of its harmonious facades designed by Hittorff are well preserved. From the top, there is a splendid view of the twelve boulevards radiating outwards in all directions.

From here you can also see a good many prize swathes of Paris real estate: the swanky mansions along the grassy verges of the avenue Foch – the widest street in the city – or the luxury hotels and prestige office buildings of avenue Hoche and avenue Wagram. At the other end of avenue Hoche is the intimate **Parc Monceau** (main entrance on boulevard de Courcelles), with its Antique follies and large, lily-covered pond. The park is usually full of neatly dressed children and nannies from this elegant, rather stuffy residential district. The park is surrounded by some of the most expensive apartments in Paris, part of the planned expansion of the city over the plaine Monceau in the late nineteenth century. The newly renovated **Musée Jacquemart-André** (on the upper reaches of boulevard Haussmann) gives some idea of the extravagant lifestyle when this area was newly developed and newly fashionable. There are two other worthwhile museums just by the park: the **Musée Camondo**, with its superb eighteenth-century decorative arts, which looks over the park, and the **Musée Cernuschi**, a collection of Chinese art. There are some surprising exotic touches, too, such as the unlikely red lacquer Galerie Ching Tsai Too (48 rue des Courcelles, 8th) built in 1926 for a Chinese art dealer, by the fancy wrought-iron gates of Parc Monceau, or the onion domes of the Russian Orthodox cathedral **Alexandre Nevsky** on rue Daru at the heart of a little Russia.

*The* **avenue des Champs-Elysées** *– subject of a facelift in the early 1990s.*

## The 16th Arrondissement

South of the Arc de Triomphe, avenue Kléber leads to the monumental buildings and gardens of the Trocadéro, from where there are spectacular views over the river to the Eiffel Tower. This is another museum-filled area: the main building, the **Palais de Chaillot**, its 1930s classicism typical of the vaguely fascist architecture of the time, houses museums devoted to anthropology, marine and naval life, the cinema and French national monuments (*see chapter* **Museums**). There's also the **Cinémathèque** and the **Théâtre National de Chaillot**. Along avenue du Président-Wilson are the **Musée Guimet**, with its remarkable collection of Asian art (currently closed for renovation), and the **Musée d'Art Moderne de la Ville de Paris** in the Palais de Tokyo, whose collection includes works by Matisse, Rouault and Dufy.

Most of the 16th *arrondissement*, stretching south-west from Etoile and the Champs-Elysées, is as dull as it is prim and pretty. This is pearls-and-poodle country, where business executives and ambassadors make their homes in smart *belle époque* apartment blocks. Yet it's worth visiting, for a few important curiosities, some graceful and original architecture and the classy shops of Passy.

Just next to the Pont de Grenelle is the circular **Maison de Radio-France**, the giant Orwellian home to the state broadcasting bureaucracy built in the 1960s. You can attend concerts or take guided tours round its endless corridors to learn about the history of broadcasting; employees nickname the place 'Alphaville' after the Godard film.

The southern half of the 16th, the district of Autueil, boasts some fine Art Nouveau houses by Hector Guimard (better known for his Métro stations), particularly on the rue La Fontaine, where you can enjoy the fluid fantasy of the Castel Béranger at No 14 and less ambitious works at Nos 17, 19, 21 and 60, including the facade of the tiny **Café Antoine**. Marcel Proust, archetypal resident of the 16th, lived in the same street. The area's other prominent architect is Le Corbusier. The **Fondation Le Corbusier** is located in two of his houses, the Villa La Roche and Villa Jeanneret (*see also chapter* **Architecture**) and nearby in rue Mallet-Stevens are the superbly elegant houses of Robert Mallet-Stevens. At the far western end of Auteuil, right on the *Périphérique*, is Paris' most important sports stadium, the Parc des Princes.

Among the museums in the area is the **Maison de Balzac** in Passy, then still a country village outside Paris. More worthwhile is the **Musée Marmottan**, off the Parc Ranelagh on rue Louis Boilly, which features some of Monet's best work.

To the west of the 16th, across the *Périphérique* ring road, is the sprawling **Bois de Boulogne**. Once a royal hunting reserve, the Bois was made into a park by Napoléon III, although much of it is still just woodland cut by paths and roads. For all its size, it's usually packed at weekends with Parisians walking their dogs. Within there are still plenty of pretty wooded spots, plus the Lac Inférieur, where you can hire rowing boats, the Longchamp and Auteuil race-courses and the rose gardens of the Parc de Bagatelle.

## Montmartre & Pigalle

*Mainly in the 9th and 18th arrondissements.*

Montmartre, away to the north of the city centre, on the tallest hill in the city, is the most unabashedly romantic district of Paris. Yet, despite the onslaught of tourists who throng the **Sacré Coeur** and place du Tertre, it's surprisingly easy to get away from the main tourist drag. Climb and descend quiet stairways, peer into little alleys, steep stairways and deserted squares, or find the ivy-clad houses with gardens, and you'll catch some of its old village atmosphere. Also, explore surrounding streets like rue des Abbesses, where an arty young community continues to live today.

Its winding streets and cosy squares have seduced generations of artists. Toulouse-Lautrec patronised its raucous bars and clubs in the 1880s and '90s, immortalising its cabarets in his posters; later it was frequented by artists of the Ecole de Paris, such as Utrillo. The *vie de bohème* of Montmartre is no longer a byword for tuberculosis and freezing winters, romanticised by Robert Doisneau photos, but Montmartre hasn't entirely surrendered to modern chic; there's still the lurid sight of the rock venues and strip joints on the boulevards at the bottom of the hill, and, on its eastern edge, the street life of the Goutte d'Or, home to thousands of immigrant families.

For centuries, Montmartre was a quiet village packed with windmills. Then, as Haussmann sliced through the city centre, working-class families began to move outwards from the old city in search of accommodation and peasant migrants poured into rapidly industrialising Paris from across France. The hill was absorbed into Paris in 1860, but remained fiercely independent. In 1871, following the capitulation to the Prussians, the new right-wing French government sought to disarm the local National Guard by trying to take away its cannons installed on Montmartre. An angry crowd led by schoolteacher and radical heroine Louise Michel succeeded in driving off the government troops and taking over the guns, thus starting the short-lived Paris Commune (*see chapter* **The Third Republic**). In the 1880s and '90s artists moved in, and stayed until after World War I, when rising rents pushed them south to Montparnasse (*see chapter* **The Left Bank**).

The best starting point is **Abbesses** Métro station, one of only two in the city to retain its original Art Nouveau glass awning designed by Hector Guimard. Facing you across place des Abbesses as you emerge from the station is the Art Nouveau church of **St-Jean de Montmartre**, with its fake brick façade, disguising a reinforced-concrete structure, and turquoise mosaics around the door.

Along the rue des Abbesses and adjoining rue Lepic, which winds its way up the *butte*, are numerous excellent little food shops, wine merchants, busy cafés, including the constantly heaving **Le Sancerre**, and some quirky boutiques devoted to offbeat designers, such as **Bonnie Cox**, where alongside recycled fashions you can buy a moped, or the crazy hat designs of **Têtes en l'Air**. Off to the right in rue Tholozé is a famous cinema, **Studio 28**, named after the year of its opening. Buñuel's *L'Age d'Or* had a riotous première here in 1930, and you can still see the footprints made by Buñuel and Cocteau in the foyer.

In the other direction from Abbesses, at 11 rue Yvonne-Le-Tac, is the **Chapelle du Martyre**, the place where, according to legend, St Denis picked up his head after his execution by the Romans in the third century and started walking north out of the city (*see chapter* **Roman Paris & the Dark Ages**). Montmartre probably means 'hill of the martyr' in memory of him, although it could be derived from the temples to Mars and Mercury that stood here in Roman times. The present convent dates from 1887, but on the same site in 1534, the Spanish soldiers Saints Ignatius Loyola and François Xavier founded the Jesuit Order.

Around the corner, the cafés of rue des Trois Frères are a popular place to go for an evening drink. The street leads into the place Emile Goudeau, whose staircases, wrought-iron streetlights and old houses are particularly evocative, as is the unspoiled bar Chez Camille. At No 13 stood the Bateau Lavoir, named after the medieval washing stands along the Seine. Once a piano factory, it was divided in the 1890s into a warren of studios where artists lived in total penury, among them Braque, Picasso and Juan Gris. Among the ground-breaking works of twentieth-century art created here was Picasso's *Desmoiselles d'Avignon*.

**Parc Monceau**: *playground for smart Paris.*

Sadly, the original building burned down in 1970, but its replacement still rents out space to artists.

Further up the hill, back on rue Lepic, are the village's two surviving windmills, or *moulins*. The **Moulin de Radet** was moved here in the seventeenth century from its original hillock in rue des Moulins near the Palais-Royal. The **Moulin de la Galette** was made famous by Renoir's famous picture of an evening's revelry there, and is now a restaurant. Another legendary meeting point for Montmartre artists was the cabaret **Au Lapin Agile**, further up the hill on rue des Saules, which is still functioning today.

At the top of the hill, place du Tertre and the surrounding streets epitomise all that is worst about present-day Montmartre. The narrow streets are packed with souvenir shops, and soulless bars. The place du Tertre itself is the worst offender of all, with dozens of so-called artists competing to sketch your portrait or trying to flog lurid sunset views of Paris. Yet it was in this square that, according to legend, one of the best-known French words originated: the occupying Russian soldiers who came to the taverns here in 1814 demanded to be served quickly or, as they said in their native tongue, bistro. In the same square you will find the large café A la Bonne Franquette, a billiard hall in the last century.

Just off the square is the oldest church in the district, **St-Pierre-de-Montmartre**, whose medieval columns have grown bent with age. Founded by Louis VI in 1133, it is a fine example of early Gothic, and makes a striking, sombre contrast to its extravagant neighbour, the **Sacré Coeur**.

You come to Montmartre's most prominent landmark by following the tourist trail around the corner. It's the one church you can't help seeing wherever you are in Paris, since it stands on the highest point in the city. Close up it's rather vulgar, and inside is full of gaudy Neo-Byzantine mosaics, the product of a nervous Catholic establishment wanting 'to expiate the sins' of France following defeat in the Franco-Prussian war and the godless Commune that followed it. If you're climbing up to the church from square Willette, avoid the main steps and try the less crowded steps of rue Foyalter or rue Maurice-Utrillo on either side.

Back beyond the place du Tertre, on the north side, in rue Cortot is the quiet seventeenth-century manor housing the **Musée de Montmartre**, which tells the history of the area, and has some original Toulouse-Lautrec posters. Renoir, Dufy and Utrillo all had studios here. Nearby in rue des Saules, is the Montmartre vineyard, planted in 1933 in memory of the scores of vineyards that used to cover this hillside ever since the Gallo-Roman period.The grape-picking each autumn is an annual ritual (*see chapter* **Paris by Season**). Don't hold your breath for the wine itself, however. A local ditty proclaims that for every glass you drink, you pee twice as much out. And that's a polite way of putting it.

From here, a series of pretty squares leads to the rue Caulaincourt and a winding walk towards **Montmartre Cemetery**, a curiously romantic place with high stone walls and ancient trees. It has an eminent list of residents: Stendhal, Berlioz, Théophile Gautier, Alexandre Dumas the younger, Degas, Nijinsky and François Truffaut.

Winding down the back of the hill, the wide avenue Junot is lined with exclusive houses, among them the one built by Adolf Loos for Dadaist poet Tristan Tzara at No 15, a monument of modernist architecture.

## Pigalle & the New Athens

Straddling the 9th and 18th *arrondissements* from busy place de Clichy with its multiplex cinema and glitzy **Brasserie Wepler**, along boulevards de Clichy and de Rochechouart, the tone suddenly changes as you enter Pigalle, which has long been the most important sleaze centre of Paris. By the end of the nineteenth century, of the 58 houses on the rue des Martyrs, 25 were cabaret venues. Today, flashing neon signs still offer live shows, and coachloads of tourists file along the rubbish-strewn pavements to inspect the sex shops. The **Moulin Rouge**, beloved of Toulouse-Lautrec, has become a provincial tourist draw, and its befeathered dancers are no substitute for the can-can girls, La Goulue and Joseph Pujol – the *pétomane* who could fart in time to any tune – of earlier times.

But this brash area has recently become a trendy night-time spot too, and designers and advertising people are gradually moving in. The **Folies Pigalle** cabaret is a hip club, what was once the Divan Japonais, depicted by Toulouse Lautrec, has been transformed into **Le Divan du Monde**, a streetwise nightclub and music venue, while the old **Elysée Montmartre** music hall puts on an eclectic array of bands and one-nighters.

To the south of boulevard Clichy, large bourgeois *hôtels particuliers* remain, although many are now offices. Here, in an area dubbed the 'New Athens' in the early nineteenth century because of the number of writers, artists and composers living there, is the **Musée de la Vie Romantique** on rue Chaptal, devoted to George Sand and her circle. Behind the Trinité church further down the hill on rue de La Rochefoucauld is the extraordinary **Musée Gustave Moreau**, crammed with the Symbolist painter's works. Don't miss the beautiful place St-Georges, with the Hôtel Thiers and neo-Renaissance Hôtel de la Païva. Further east towards Gare du Nord are the twin towers and pedimented frontage of the early nineteeth-century St-Vincent-de-Paul; the terraced gardens in front of the church are about as close as Paris gets to Rome's Spanish steps.

## La Goutte d'Or

For an altogether different experience, head for
Barbès-Rochechouart Métro station and the area
behind it, known as the Goutte d'Or. In Zola's day
this was (and still is) one of the poorest working-
class districts in the city. Zola used it as a backdrop for *L'Assommoir*, his novel set among the
district's laundries and absinthe bars, and his
Nana grew up in the rue de la Goutte d'Or itself.

Now it's primarily an African and Arab neighbourhood, with plenty of colour to make up for the
modesty of the housing. Here you'll reputedly find
37 different nationalities, speaking innumerable
dialects. Cheap clothes, Oriental sweets and spicy
food are on offer on every street corner. There's a
lively street market under the Métro tracks on
Wednesdays and Saturdays, while people flock to
the boulevard to rummage through the boxes of
bargain clothing store **Tati**. From here rue Orsel
leads back to Montmartre via the **Marché St-
Pierre**, the covered market hall is now used for
exhibitions of naive art, but in the street, outlets
like Dreyfus and Moline vie with discount fabrics.

## North-East Paris

*Mainly in the 19th and 20th arrondissements.*

The old working-class north east of Paris is an area
in transformation. The main attraction, a few
streets north of Nation, is **Père Lachaise cemetery**. Laid out in 1804 like an English garden, it
rapidly became the society cemetery of choice.
Nowadays it is so full it looks like some kind of
eccentric city of the dead, with mausoleums for

monuments and tombstones for dwellings beneath
its arching willow trees. Ménilmontant, the area
around it, and its neighbour Belleville *(see p108
and 113,* **Village Paris: Ménilmontant** *and*
**Belleville**) both started life as pretty villages
where Parisians could escape at weekends. Today
struggling to preserve its identity, the area has
always undergone change, thanks to a constant
influx of immigrants: Russian Jews, Spanish,
Armenians, Greeks, North Africans and, most
recently, Asians, creating Paris' newest Chinatown.

Up the avenue Simon Bolivar is the eccentric
**Parc des Buttes-Chaumont** (main entrance rue
Botzaris), one of the most attractive and least-
known landscaping feats of Baron Haussmann's
designers. From the small classical temple in the
middle of the park lake there is a splendid view.
Tucked away east of the park, between place des
Fêtes and place de Rhin et Danube, are a number
of tiny hilly streets lined with small houses and
gardens that still look positively provincial.

North of here, place de Stalingrad was re-land-
scaped in 1989 to reveal to full advantage the
**Rotonde de la Villette**, one of Ledoux's
grandiose toll houses. It's used today to house
exhibitions and a display of archeological finds
from the Paris area. From here you can follow
either the Bassin de la Villette canal or avenue
Jean-Jaurès, among some of Paris' newest housing
developments, to the **Parc de la Villette**, with
the ultra-modern **Cité des Sciences et de
l'Industrie** science museum, imaginatively
designed park and playgrounds and the **Cité de
la Musique** concert hall and music museum.

**Sacré Coeur** *is at the sugary centre of Montmartre.*

# The Left Bank

*The Rive Gauche may have outlived its arty, bohemian and intellectual heyday, but its spirit still lives on.*

## The Latin Quarter

*Mainly in the 5th arrondissement.*

The section of the Left Bank east of boulevard St-Michel is known as the Latin Quarter because Latin was the language used by the students here until the Revolution. The name, though, could equally allude to the vestiges of Roman Lutétia, of which it was the heart. The first two streets laid by the Romans were on the site of the present rue St-Jacques and rue Cujas. The area remains one of the most historic *quartiers* of Paris, still boasting many medieval streets and the city's best two Roman remains: the Cluny baths, now part of the **Musée du Moyen Age-Thermes de Cluny**, and the **Arènes de Lutèce** amphitheatre.

### Quartier de la Huchette

The area is highly popular with tourists, who stream down the boulevard St-Michel and its adjoining streets during the summer. The boulevard itself has largely been taken over by the fast-food giants and downmarket shoe and clothes chains, and is mostly worth avoiding, although giant book emporium **Gibert Joseph** has been selling books to students here for over a century and the fountain with its statue of St Michael slaying the dragon in place St-Michel is an ever-popular meeting point. Down the pedestrianised rue de la Huchette or rue de la Harpe you'll find more Greek restaurants and café tables than evidence of medieval learning, although the narrow streets still ooze with charm, as well as cooking oil. Look out for the rue du Chat-Qui-Pêche, supposedly the narrowest street in Paris, rue de la Parcheminerie, named after the parchment sellers and copyists who once lived here, rue Galande which still has several overhanging medieval buildings, the **Studio Galande** cinema, famed for weekly screenings of *The Rocky Horror Picture Show*, and the venerable **Caveau des Oubliettes**, where those who visit the cabaret are graced with a tour of the torture instruments in the cellars, and the **Théâtre de la Huchette**, in rue de la Huchette, which has been playing Ionesco's *The Bald Soprano* since 1957.

There are also two outstanding churches. **St-Séverin** was built over 450 years, ending up with an exuberant Flamboyant-Gothic vaulted interior. In its garden are the curious remains of a Gothic charnel house, where bodies dug up in the commu-nal pits were stored before burial in the adjacent cemetery. **St-Julien-le-Pauvre**, off rue Galande, was built as a resting place for pilgrims in the late twelfth century, at the same time as the initial building of Notre Dame, making it one of the oldest churches in Paris. In the later Middle Ages it was used for student assemblies that became so raucous the whole church was closed in 1524. Its simple Early Gothic interior is relatively intact, and is often used for classical concerts.

Across the boulevard St-Germain lies the biggest 'sight' in the Latin Quarter, the **Musée du Moyen Age – Thermes de Cluny**, a magnificent collection of medieval art, notably the *Lady and the Unicorn* tapestries, housed in the Gothic mansion of the Abbots of Cluny, which was built at the end of the fifteenth century on top of ruined third-century Roman baths.

Down by the river, set back from the book and print sellers that line the *quais* and with a fine view of Notre Dame, is the illustrious second-hand English bookshop **Shakespeare & Co**, although no longer on the site in the rue de l'Odéon that was a daily port of call for expatriate literati in the 1920s. At 13 rue de la Bûcherie is the circular Old Faculty of Medicine, where medieval students secretly examined corpses stolen from graveyards.

Place Maubert, now a morning marketplace, was used in the sixteenth century to burn books and hang heretics, particularly Protestants. The little streets between here and the traffic-flooded *quais* are some of the oldest in the city. The rue de Bièvre charts the course of the river Bièvre, which flowed here in the Middle Ages. On the quai de la Tournelle, look for the elegant seventeenth-century Hôtel Miramion at No 53, now the **Musée de l'Assistance Publique**, telling the history of Paris hospitals.

### The Sorbonne & the Montagne Ste-Geneviève

The Montagne Ste-Geneviève still contains a remarkable concentration of academic institutions, from the Sorbonne to research centres and *Grandes Ecoles* such as the Ecole Normale Supérieure, and so is still a studenty area. However, its web of nar-

*All it needs is a little sunshine to get* **rue Mouffetard** *swinging.*

row medieval streets has also proved irresistible to the well-heeled, pushing accommodation prices out of most students' reach. The intellectual tradition persists, though, in the many specialist book stores and art cinemas around rue Champollion and rue des Ecoles (*see chapter* **Film**).

The district began its long association with scholarship and learning in about 1100, when a number of scholars, among them Pierre Abélard (*see chapter* **Middle Ages & Renaissance**), came to live and teach on the Montagne Ste-Geneviève, independently of the established Canon school of Notre Dame. They began to be referred to as a University, then understood as a loose association of scholars who regulated themselves and issued licenses to teach. The schools of Paris soon attracted scholars from all over Europe, and the number of 'colleges' – student residences – multiplied, until the University of Paris was given official recognition with a charter from Pope Innocent III in 1215.

By the sixteenth century, however, the university – by now known as the **Sorbonne**, after the most famous of its colleges – had been co-opted by the Catholic establishment. A century later, Cardinal Richelieu rebuilt the Sorbonne, but the place was past its heyday and slowly dwindled and slid into decay. After the Revolution, when the whole university was forced to close and large chunks of the Latin Quarter were destroyed, Napoléon resuscitated the Sorbonne as the cornerstone of his new, centralised, exclusively French-language education system. The university rediscovered its dissident side, and participated enthusiastically in the uprisings of the nineteenth century. The Sorbonne was also one of the seedbeds of the 1968 revolt; students battling with police ripped up the cobbles of the boulevard St-Michel (since paved over). Nowadays the university is much quieter, not least because the Sorbonne is now only one of 18 faculties of the University of Paris dotted around the city and its suburbs. The present buildings (entrance on rue de la Sorbonne) are mostly late nineteenth-century; only the domed Baroque **Chapelle de la Sorbonne**, designed by Lemercier in 1635-42 with a double-order facade opening onto place de la Sorbonne and a pedimented facade onto the courtyard still survives from the rebuilding under Richelieu, and contains his tomb. It is open sometimes for exhibitions. The courtyard is open to the public and it's occasionally possible (unless Umberto Eco or the President is speaking) to sneak into lectures in the main amphitheatre.

On the rue des Ecoles stand the late eighteenth-century buildings of the eminent, independent **Collège de France**, founded in 1530 under the patronage of François 1er by a group of humanists led by Guillaume Budé to revive the study of classical authors. Lectures are open to the public (11 pl Marcelin-Berthelot; 01.44.27.12.11). For intel-

lectual fodder, neighbouring **Brasserie Balzar** remains the fashionable place to eat.

Climb up rue St-Jacques to the south, and to your left is the huge, domed **Panthéon**, originally commissioned by Louis XV as a church for the city's patron Ste-Geneviève, but converted during the Revolution into a secular temple for the 'great men of France'. Among the notables interred in the crypt are Voltaire, Rousseau, Hugo, Zola and the most recent arrivals Resistance leader Jean Moulin, Marie Curie and De Gaulle's arts minister André Malraux. There's a superb view (after a steep climb) from the top. In the impressive place du Panthéon, conceived by the Panthéon's architect Soufflot, is the elegant classical *mairie* (town hall) of the 5th *arrondissement*, mirrored by the law faculty. On the north side, on the site of a college where Calvin, Erasmus and Ignatius Loyola all studied is the **Bibliothèque Ste-Geneviève**, which has a fine collection of medieval manuscripts and a magnificent nineteenth-century iron-framed reading room.

Behind the Panthéon stands the more intimate and altogether prettier church of **St-Etienne-du-Mont**, with its remarkable Renaissance rood screen and Baroque pulpit. Pascal and Racine are both buried here, as are the remains of the city's patron Sainte-Geneviève. Parisians still come here to ask her for favours. Jutting up behind, within the grounds of the Lycée Henri IV, is the Gothic-Romanesque **Tour de Clovis**, a tower that is the only remaining part of the once-giant abbey of Ste-Geneviève, although parts of a cloister have recently been excavated in the grounds. The Lycée is one of the most prestigious schools in the city, and is closed to the public, although you can admire its gardens from the swimming pool, **Piscine Jean Taris**. Further along rue Clovis is a chunk of Philippe-Auguste's twelfth-century city wall, of which the other main surviving section is in the Marais. It's worth exploring several of the other medieval streets, such as rue du Cardinal-Lemoine and rue Descartes, both once inhabited by Ernest Hemingway. Numerous cheap eats abound here, but **L'Ecurie**, opposite the Ecole-Polytechnique, is intriguingly housed in an underground network of medieval stables.

Nearby is **place de la Contrescarpe** (its name taken from the embankments of Philippe-Auguste's fortifications) where there are several lively cafés. To the south winds **rue Mouffetard**, known since Roman times and one of the oldest and most characterful streets in the city. Today it's lined with cheap student-filled restaurants and neighbourhood bars, and has a busy market in its lower half, towards the late Gothic church of St-Médard (*see chapter* **Food & Drink**). This area was once famously seedy, a mixture of plain poverty and penniless bohemia. One of the narrow cross-streets off rue Mouffetard is rue du Pot-de-Fer (named after the seventeenth-century 'Iron Pot'

*The wonderful Renaissance rood screen at* **St-Etienne-du-Mont**.

fountain on the corner), site of the hotel (No 6) where George Orwell stayed during his time as a *plongeur* in Paris during 1928-29, and vividly described in *Down and Out in Paris and London* as 'rue du Coq d'Or'. Nowadays the district is far more picturesque than dingy.

To the west of this knot of narrow streets, the broad rue Gay-Lussac, a hot spot in the **May '68** riots, leads to the Jardin du Luxembourg. Further down rue St-Jacques, is an altogether more eminent landmark, the **Val-de-Grâce**, the least-altered, most luxurious and most ornate of all the Baroque churches in Paris, designed by François Mansart for Louis XIII's queen, Anne of Austria, and its surrounding Benedictine monastery, which now houses a military hospital.

## The Jardin des Plantes District

East of rue Monge and rue des Fossés St-Bernard you leave the Quartier Latin proper behind to move into a quieter area that still contains several major academic institutions, and is also an important focus for Paris' Moslem community. Nestling between the Seine and the vile tower blocks of Paris university's campuses VI and VII (known as Jussieu), which is due to close at least temporarily to remove asbestos, is the **Institut du Monde Arabe**, built in 1987, one of the best modern buildings in the city. Its window panels are fashioned like ancient Islamic screens, and its exhibitions focusing on different aspects of the Arab world are regularly interesting. There are fine views and a nice café up on the roof, too.

The Paris mosque is not far away, although you may want to stop off on the way at the **Arènes de Lutèce**, the Roman amphitheatre, off the rue Monge. Rediscovered in the nineteenth century during the building of rue Monge, the central arena and many tiers of stone seating remain. The greenroofed **Mosquée de Paris** (2 place du Puits de l'Ermite) was built in 1922, and is now the centre of the largely Algerian-dominated Moslem community in France. Partly modelled on the Alhambra in Granada, it has a beautiful interior patio and a series of flamboyant domes. At the entrance on rue Geoffroy St-Hilaire there is a splendid Turkish hammam and a very enjoyable Moorish tea room.

The mosque looks out onto the **Jardin des Plantes**, Paris' botanical garden. First established in 1626 as a garden for medicinal plants, it has an eminent history as a centre for botany, and features a charming eighteenth-century maze, a winter garden brimming with rare plant species and the assorted buildings of the **Muséum National d'Histoire Naturelle**, which has been given a new lease of life with the restoration and reopening of the Galerie de l'Evolution, previously closed for 25 years. There's also a zoo called the Ménagerie, with vultures, big cats, bears and reptiles.

## St-Germain & Odéon

*Mainly in the 6th arrondissement.*
St-Germain-des-Prés is where the great myths of intellectual Paris were born. It was in its cafés that Verlaine and Rimbaud went drinking and, a few

generations later, Sartre, Camus and de Beauvoir scribbled their first masterpieces. For the visitor the area is irresistible. Often voted as the city's most liveable neighbourhood, it is ideal for an afternoon among the art galleries of the rue des Beaux-Arts, rue de Seine and rue Bonaparte (*see chapter* **Art Galleries**), the fine clothes shops around St-Sulpice, the jazz clubs along rue St-Benoît and fur Jacob, the classy street market on rue de Buci, or the elegant lawns and fountains of the Luxembourg gardens.

But St-Germain is changing. No longer do romantically impoverished students and budding geniuses sit hunched over their manuscripts in café windows. Earnest types do still stride along clutching weighty tomes, but so prestigious and therefore expensive has the district become that Gucci loafers and fur coats now outnumber cord jackets and blue berets, and any writers who inhabit the area tend to be either well-established or rich ex-pat Americans pretending to be Ernest Hemingway. Recently, luxury fashion groups long associated with the Right Bank and 'commerce' have moved in, often taking over venerable bookshops. Armani has taken over the old Drugstore, Cartier a classical record shop and Louis Vuitton has unpacked its bags at 6 place St-Germain.

## From the Boulevard to the Seine

Nerve centre of the district is the boulevard St-Germain, with the famous cafés, **Les Deux Magots** and the **Café de Flore**, which likes to think of itself as the birthplace of existentialism, and the late-night bookshop **La Hune**. The main attraction of the Flore to Sartre et al was its wood-fired stoves, which saved them an absolute bundle in heating bills. Nowadays you can spend more on a few coffees there than you would on a week's central heating.

Earlier in the century, it was also frequented by Picasso and Apollinaire, and even today remains a writer's hang-out, especially the quiet room upstairs. The Deux Magots, named after the two statues of Chinese mandarins inside, now provides an interesting sociological cross-section of US tourists in Paris, thanks to its large pavement terrace, but can no longer boast with any conviction to be a hotbed of intellectual life.

Across from its terrace is the oldest church in the city, **St-Germain-des-Prés**. Its history dates back to the sixth century, and by the eighth century it was one of the most important Benedictine monasteries in France. What you see today is merely a shadow of its former glory, as it was severely damaged by a Revolutionary mob in 1792, and was scarcely better served by some of the nineteenth-century efforts at restoration. What remains mostly dates from the eleventh and twelfth centuries; inside the simple, somewhat truncated interi-

or are some of the original Romanesque carved capitals (others are in the **Musée du Moyen Age**, *see above*) and some interesting tombs, including the remains of the founder of modern philosophy, René Descartes, who died in 1650. A few traces of the cloister can be seen in the garden adjoining the church on rue de l'Abbaye.

Behind the church is the charming place Furstenberg, once the courtyard of the Abbot's palace, now shading upmarket furnishing fabric shops and the house, now **Musée Delacroix**, where the painter Delacroix lived at the end of his life. Rue de l'Echaudé shows a typical St-Germain mix: cutting-edge fashion at **L'Eclaireur** (No 24) and died-in-the-wool bistro cooking at the ancient L'Echaudé-St-Germain (No 21). It's also worth wandering along **rue Jacob** which runs parallel to the boulevard with its specialist book and design shops and several pleasant hotels.

Further east along the boulevard at Odéon, the **rue de Buci** contains a top-class food market, running into rue de Seine with a lively scene centred around the Bar du Marché and Chai de l'Abbaye cafés.

On rue de l'Ancienne Comédie is the famous Café Procope, the oldest coffee house in Paris, where coffee was first brought to the Parisian public in 1686, following its introduction to the royal court by the Turkish ambassador. Once a favourite haunt of Voltaire, Rousseau, Benjamin Franklin and even Napoléon, it was rather over-restored in 1989, and is now an undistinguished restaurant aimed squarely at tourists. It opens at the back onto the cobbled **passage du Commerce St-André** and its adjoining courtyards. Delightful today, but with a more sinister past. Here, in the eighteenth century, Dr Joseph-Ignace Guillotin first tested out his notorious execution device, supposedly in the cellars of what is now the **Pub St-Germain**. From here towards the Seine is a charming web of narrow ancient streets, centring on winding rue St-André-des-Arts, akin in spirit to the Latin Quarter rather than St-Germain with old houses, cheap clothes shops and an arts cinema. The evocatively named rue Gît-le-Coeur ('lay down your heart') is so called because one of Henri IV's mistresses lived here. This same street also contains the hotel where William Burroughs and his Beat cohorts revised *The Naked Lunch*.

Rue Bonaparte, rue de Seine and the rue des Beaux-Arts are still packed with small art galleries. **La Palette** and **Bistro Mazarin** on rue de Seine are good stopping-off points with enviable pavement terraces on rue Jacques-Callot. At the top end of rue Bonaparte is the entrance to the seventeenth-century building (once a monastery) of the **Ecole Nationale Supérieure des Beaux-Arts**, Paris' main fine arts school, which is sometimes open for exhibitions. Complementing it on the quai de Conti is the giant **Institut de France**, with its distinctive Baroque dome and two curved wings designed 1683-84 by Louis Le Vau, recently cleaned to reveal its crisp classical decoration. Built with money bequeathed by Louis XIV's minister Cardinal Mazarin, it now houses a number of eminent academies including that finicky institution the **Académie Française**, which polices the French language like a jealous father trying to keep his offspring free of bad influences. Occasional guide tours show you Mazarin's ornate tomb built by Hardouin-Mansart, and the fusty Bibliothèque Mazarine, France's first public library. Next door is the quirky **Hôtel de la Monnaie**, the country's mint (1777-1973), and now an engrossing coin museum. In front of the Institut the iron footbridge of the **Pont des Arts** crosses the Seine to the Louvre.

## St-Sulpice & the Luxembourg

South of boulevard St-Germain lies the old covered market of St-Germain, once the site of the important St-Germain Fair. Following redevelopment it now houses a concert hall, an underground swimming pool, a few surviving food stalls hidden in the centre and a rather soulless shopping arcade dominated by a large branch of Gap, although the Irish pub **Coolín** is a pleasant stopping-off point. The little streets around are still a beguiling mix of inexpensive bistros where *plats du jour* are cooked up for students and some well-hidden late-night haunts including the **Birdland** bar and the notoriously elitist **Castel's Princess** nightclub.

Dawdle past the fashion boutiques, antiquarian book and print shops and high-class *pâtisseries* south of here and you come to **St-Sulpice**, a surprising eighteenth-century exercise in classical form with two uneven turrets propping up its colonnaded facade. The church is redeemed by Delacroix's Biblical frescoes, in the first chapel on the right, and by the lovely square containing the **Fontaine des Quatre Points Cardinaux** in front. On the place, which is used for an antiques fair every summer, the innocuous-looking **Café de la Mairie** remains a favourite with local intellectuals and students, a classic example of essential non-designer anti-chic, while the chic boutiques along the place and rue St-Sulpice include branches of Yves Saint-Laurent, Christian Lacroix and Agnès B, perfumer Annick Goutal, the sophisticated furnishings of Catherine Memmi and milliner Marie Mercié (*see chapters* **Fashion** *and* **Specialist Shops**).

To the west, prime shopping territory continues as at the carrefour de la Croix-Rouge, the clothes shops of rue du Four meet the leather and accessory shops of rue du Dragon, rue du Cherche-Midi and rue de Grenelle, including such fashion victim essentials as Prada, Patrick Cox and Stéphane Kélian (*see chapter* **Fashion**).

To the south, the wide rue de Tournon, lined by some very grand eighteenth-century residences – such as the elegant Hôtel de Brancas (now the **Institut Français de l'Architecture**) with allegorical figures of Justice and Prudence over the

Built for Marie de Médicis, the **Palais de Luxembourg** now serves as the French Senate.

doorway – opens up to the **Parc** and **Palais du Luxembourg**. Built for Marie de Médicis in the early seventeenth century and given a few Tuscan touches (its ringed columns and rough-surfaced stone) to remind her of the Pitti Palace back home in Florence, the palace now serves as the French Senate and is closed to the public, although it is possible to visit it as part of a walking tour on Sundays. The **Jardin du Luxembourg** is one of the most popular spots in a city generally starved of greenery, its formally laid paths attracting joggers galore. The wilder western side has tennis courts, and a children's puppet theatre (see chapter **Children**); leading away from the southern side of the gardens there is a long, thin extension, the Jardins de l'Observatoire, containing one of Paris' most elaborate fountains, the **Fontaine de l'Observatoire**, with figures of the continents sculpted by Carpeaux.

Heading back up towards the boulevard St-Germain, you'll pass the Neo-classical **Théâtre de l'Odéon** built in 1779, where Beaumarchais' *Marriage of Figaro* was first performed in 1784. It is now one of the leading subsidised theatres in Paris (see chapter **Theatre**). The attractive semi-circular place de l'Odéon was once home (at No 2) to revolutionary hero Camille Desmoulins; the same building today houses the fish restaurant, La Mediterranée, that was decorated by Jean Cocteau.

A more seedy, studenty hangout is **Le Bar Dix** among the antiquarian bookshops on rue de l'Odéon, the first street in Paris to have guttered pavements on either side. James Joyce's *Ulysses* was first published in 1922 at No 12 by Sylvia Beach (see above **Shakespeare & Co** in the **Latin Quarter**).

Back on the boulevard St-Germain is a statue of Danton, who lived on the site when it was just a backstreet. Now it is a popular meeting point, thanks to the Odéon Métro stop and numerous cinemas. Just up the street on rue de l'Ecole de Médecine is the colonnaded Neo-classical facade of the **Université René Descartes** (Paris V) medical school (No 12), designed during the late eighteenth century by Jacques Gondoin. Across the road, the refectory remains from the **Couvent des Cordeliers** (No 15), an important medieval priory and later hotbed of Revolutionary plotting by the Club des Cordeliers, now also part of the medical faculty. Look out for the magnificent doorway of neighbouring *hôtel*. You can climb the stairs of rue André-Dubois, for the popular budget eat **Polidor** on rue Monsieur-le-Prince. Heading towards boulevard St-Michel, and marked by sinuous Art Nouveau woodwork, is the **Bouillon Racine** on rue Racine. Once a popular working-class dining hall, later a student canteen and recently restored as a Belgian restaurant, it maintains the tradition of *bouillon* (soup) for those who wish to eat at the counter.

## The Monumental 7th & West

*Mainly in the 7th arrondissement.*

Smart townhouses spread westwards from St-Germain into the 7th *arrondissement*, but the vibrant street and café life gradually subsides in favour of calm residential blocks and government offices. In fact the *arrondissement* divides roughly into two. The more intimate eastern section known as the Faubourg St-Germain, which became part of the city with the creation of the *'boulevards du Midi'* in 1704, still contains many beautiful mansions and fine upmarket shops. To the west the windswept expanses of wide avenues nonetheless number the most famous sight of all, the Eiffel Tower.

## The Faubourg St-Germain

Often written off by Proust as a symbol of staid, *haute*-bourgeois and aristocratic society, this area remains home to some of Paris' oldest and grandest families, although most of its eighteenth-century *hôtels particuliers* have now been taken over by embassies and government ministries. You can still admire their stone gateways and elegant courtyards, especially on rue de Grenelle, rue St-Dominique, rue de l'Université and rue de Varenne, among them the 1721 **Hôtel Matignon** (57 rue de Varenne), residence of the Prime Minister. To see the decorative interiors and surprising private gardens of others like the Ministry of Agriculture (78 rue de Varenne) or the Italian Embassy (47 rue de Varenne) you'll have to wait for the Journées Portes Ouvertes (see chapter **Paris by Season**). Two *hôtels* that can by visited are the **Musée Rodin**, in rue de Varenne, and the Hôtel Bouchardon, now the **Musée Maillol** (59-61 rue de Grenelle), which retains some of its wonderful wooden panelling and its elegant curved entrance built around Bouchardon's fanciful Fountain of the Four Seasons.

This area is also another stretch of prime shopping territory with the famous **Bon Marché** department store on rue de Sèvres, the smart food and design shops of rue du Bac, including a branch of **Hédiard**, *chocolatier* **Christian Constant**, the **Conran Shop**, the colourful tablewares of Dîners en Ville, and stuffed animal emporium **Deyrolle**. The area near Bon Marché is also fast becoming a good place to eat with two of the best recently opened bistros in town, **La Bamboche** and **Au Bon Acceuil**. Along the rue du Cherche-Midi are agreeable shops and tea rooms. There are further smart fashion and design outlets on boulevard Raspail, along with Paris' most successful **Marché biologique** on Sunday mornings, where people cross town for organic food and wines.

You may be surprised to see coaches lined up beside the Bon Marché; these come not to shop but to pay pilgrimage at the shrine of Sainte Catherine

**Pont Alexandre III**: *one of Paris' most exuberant bridges.*

Labouré at the Couvent des Soeurs de St-Vincent-de-Paul (140 rue du Bac, 7th/01.45.48.43.61. open 7.30am-1pm, 2.30-7pm daily). In 1830, Catherine had a visit from the Virgin, who gave her a miraculous medal which performed many miracles. Usually full of people praying, the **Chapelle de la Médaille Miraculeuse** is one of the most visited pilgrimage sites in France, an extraordinary concoction of marble statues of the Virgin, mosaics and murals, where the bodies of Catherine and her mother superior lie embalmed. You can buy your own miraculous medal for a few francs.

Towards the Seine, antiques dealers abound in the '**Carré Rive Gauche**', concentrated within the quadrangle enclosed by the quai Voltaire and rues des Sts-Pères, du Bac and de l'Université (*see also chapter* **Paris by Season**). This area also contains one of Paris' most important cultural sights, the **Musée d'Orsay**, a giant converted railway station and now home to the national collection of Impressonist and nineteenth-century art. An expression of late nineteenth-century dreams of grandeur, the station was a lavish affair built for the 1900 World Exhibition, but went out of use because its platforms eventually proved too short. The edifice narrowly escaped demolition in the 1970s, and the idea of turning it into a museum only came to final fruition in 1986, although the facade still lists the towns once served.

Across rue de Bellechasse, is the unusual semi-circular Palais de la Légion d'Honneur, now a museum devoted to France's honours system; grim classical facade on one side and a quirky semi-circular pavilion along the Seine.

Continuing westwards along the Seine, facing the **Pont de la Concorde** and the place de la Concorde across the river, is the **Assemblée Nationale**, the lower house of the French parliament. Originally the Palais Bourbon, its pedimented Neo-classical facade was added in the early nineteenth century to mirror that of the Madeleine, then being constructed on the other side of the river, but the entrance on the place du Palais-Bourbon, through which you can see its grand *cour d'honneur* shows its softer, more domestic origins. Visitors can attend debates. Nearby, the spindly church of **Ste-Clotilde** (rue des Las-Cases) was one of the earliest examples of nineteenth-century Gothic Revival, much decried at the time.

Right alongside the Assemblée is the Foreign Ministry, often referred to by its address, the quai d'Orsay. Beyond it, stretches the long grassy esplanade leading up to the golden-domed **Invalides**, the vast military hospital complex which now houses the **Musée de l'Armée** and Napoléon's tomb. Cannons line the grand pavilions of the 196-metre (650-foot) long facade, decorated with allegorical tributes to the building's patron, Louis XIV. The two churches inside – St-Louis-des-Invalides and the Eglise du Dôme – glorify the various French monarchs and their armies. Inside the Eglise du Dôme, beneath a circular balustrade, is Napoléon's tomb. The museum, meanwhile, is chock-a-block with paintings, tapestries, banners, armour and weaponry illustrating France's wartime career from Charlemagne to the present. The esplandade gives a perspective across ornate **Pont Alexandre III** to the Grand and Petit Palais, all three constructed for the 1900 World Exhibition.

A far cosier place to visit is the **Musée Rodin**, housed in the Hôtel Biron, one of the most charming *hôtels* on rue de Varenne. Rodin was invited to move here in 1908 on the understanding that he would bequeath his work to the state. As a result, you can now see most of his great sculptures, including *The Thinker* and *The Burghers of Calais*, in a beautiful eighteenth-century setting. Many stand in the palatial, rose-filled gardens.

Not far from here along rue de Babylone, an interesting architectural oddity is **La Pagode** cinema. A genuine Japanese pagoda constructed in 1895, it became a cinema in the 1930s and also has a pleasant tea room. Film buffs will also appreciate the shop almost opposite in rue de Babylone, specialising in vintage film posters.

## West of Les Invalides

To the west of the Invalides is the **Ecole Militaire**, the military academy built by Louis XV and where Napoléon first graduated. Designed in 1751 by Jacques-Ange Gabriel, the architect of the place de la Concorde, it's a stern, rather unappealing building, and isn't open to the public. Opposite its south entrance, across the place de Fontenoy, is the Y-shaped **UNESCO** building, built in 1958 by a multi-national team – an American (Breuer), an Italian (Nervi) and a Frenchman (Zehrfuss) – and headquarters of the UN's Education, Science and Culture Organisation. A giant construction in concrete and glass, it's worth visiting for the sculptures by Picasso, Arp, Giacometti, Calder and others in the lobbies (open 9am-6pm Mon-Fri). Inside it buzzes with palpable post-war idealism like a multinational hive. Behind there's a Japanese garden, with contemplation space (a concrete cylinder) by Tadao Ando. Across place de Fontenoy, stands another monumental structure, the 1930s Modernist Ministry of Labour. But there's also some sense of residential life in this quarter of officialdom among the smart food shops and *traiteurs* of **rue Cler**.

From the north-western side of the Ecole Militaire begins the vast esplanade of the **Champ**

# Village Paris: The Butte aux Cailles

In striking contrast to the towering buildings of nearby Chinatown, is a neighbourhood of old houses, winding cobblestone streets, and funky bars and restaurants, which constitute the village Butte aux Cailles, just southwest of the Place d'Italie.

During the nineteenth century, the 13th *arrondissement* housed many small factories, including a tannery in the Butte aux Cailles. This worker's neighbourhood was one of the first to fight during the Paris Commune in 1848. The Butte has preserved its insurgent character and, in recent years, has resisted the aggressive forces of city planning and construction companies. The steep, cobbled rue de la Butte aux Cailles and the rue de Cinq Diamants can be considered the headquarters of the intellectual-artsy-*soixante-huitarde*

bohemian forces. For a complete village tour, saunter down the rustic rues Alphand, Buot, and Michal as well. Villa Daviel contains neat little villas, while the little cottages clustered around

a garden square at 10 rue Daviel were one of the earliest public housing schemes in Paris. Behind the small garden at the place Paul Verlaine, lies an attractive brick Arts-and-Crafts-style swimming pool, fed by an artesian well. Explore the passage Vandrezanne, as well as the square des Peupliers, and the rue Dieulafoy, whose houses and gardens offer some calm to the traveller persistent enough to go and find them.

To discuss art, music, or the most recent workers' strikes, the Butte offers a good selection of relaxed, inexpensive restaurants: Le Temps des Cérises (18 rue Butte-aux-Cailles/01.45.80.70.10) run as a cooperative; **Chez Gladine** has extremely busy lunch and dinner hours for snails or *cassoulet* (seconds as a wine bar/café off-hours) and more upmarket **Chez Paul**. Two feisty bars **La Folie en Tête** and **Le Merle Moqueur** offer music, cheap beer on tap and youthful crowds spilling outside.

**de Mars,** a former market garden converted into a military drilling ground in the eighteenth century and used after the 1789 Revolution for Bastille Day celebrations (*see chapter* **Empires & Revolutions**). Now it forms a spectacular backdrop to the most famous Parisian monument of them all, the **Eiffel Tower,** tallest building in the world from 1889 until New York's skyscrapers began sprouting in the 1930s. Although everyone rushes to climb as high up it as they dare, the best view in many ways is from the bottom, looking up at the incredibly complex patchwork of metal soaring from its four supporting legs.

## Fronts de Seine

Downstream from the Eiffel Tower, the 15th *arrondissement* has few mainstream tourist sites. The river-front has been mainly taken over by undistinguished 1970s tower block developments. Among recent additions to the west are some good modern housing and the highly sophisticated headquarters of the Canal+ TV channel at 2 rue des Cévennes, designed by American architect Richard Meier, and a brand new public park, the **Parc André Citroën,** opened in 1992. Created on the site of a former Citroën car factory, the park has been laid out as a contemporary formal garden with a geometric design, water gardens and two large glasshouses.

## Montparnasse & Beyond

*Mainly in the 6th and 14th arrondissements.*

In the first three decades of this century Montparnasse meant artists, vibrant café life and the rowdy cabarets of the rue de la Gaîté. Artists like Picasso, Léger and Soutine and the poet Apollinaire came to the city's 'Mount Parnassus' to escape the rising rents of Montmartre and brought a new cutting edge of intellectual life to the area. Between the wars they were joined by escapees from the Russian Revolution, who set up the lively restaurant **Dominique,** and American writers and artists like Man Ray, Henry Miller and Gertrude Stein. To some extent their legacy has lived on, although Montparnasse is definitely a sadder, more disparate place now. The high-rise blight of the Montparnasse Tower is only the most visible of several new building projects that have turned lively village communities into faceless residential blocks. But the area still has its attractions: the Breton crêperies of rue d'Odessa and rue Montparnasse (Gare Montparnasse is the main point of arrival from Brittany), the cinemas and legendary brasseries of boulevard Montparnasse, and some quirky landmarks, such as the cemetery and the catacombs.

Montparnasse's most eye-catching landmark today, though, is the 209-metre (688-foot) tall **Tour Montparnasse,** a steel-and-glass arrow that's Paris' tribute to Manhattan. You can use it to orientate yourself if you get lost just about anywhere in central Paris. The tower itself is best visited as a perch from which to view the rest of the city. The area around the Tower is the result of some particularly infelicitous 1970s planning. The old Montparnasse railway station, where the German army signed its surrender of Paris on 25 August 1944, has been transformed into a maze of steel and glass corridors housing a shopping complex, a sports centre, a car park and any number of fastfood joints. Behind it there is now a new small garden, the **Jardin de l'Atlantique,** built above the tracks of the TGV. To the west Ricardo Bofill's circular place de Catalogne is typical of this architect's postmodern version of Classicism.

The nearby rue de la Gaîté, once renowned for its cabarets and theatres, has also changed for the worse, becoming prey to strip joints and sex shops, although boulevard Edgar-Quinet has some pleasant cafés and a street market on Saturday mornings. The little place facing rue Jolivet gives some idea of what the area was like before redevelopment. The boulevard du Montparnasse, by contrast, has retained more of its character, and remains very lively, largely thanks to its huge number of cinemas. Such famed establishments as **Le Dôme** (today a luxurious fish restaurant, although you can still stop for a drink at the front) and the giant Art Deco brasserie **La Coupole,** La Rotonde, **Le Select** and Hemingway's favourite hangout **La Closerie des Lilas** are still in business for beer, oysters and lively chatter before or after a film. Not far from its junction with boulevard du Montparnasse, boulevard Raspail boasts Rodin's remarkable 1898 sculpture of Balzac, which caused such a furore because of its rugged, elemental rendition of the famous novelist that it wasn't displayed in public for 40 years.

There's no longer much sense of an artistic community in the area, although large windows often testify to former studios now converted into apartments, such as the strange tiled building at 31 rue Campagne-Première (once home to writer Louis Aragon and Surrealist photographer Man Ray, and featured in the *dénouement* of Godard's *A bout de Souffle*), along rue de la Grande-Chaumière, or around the hidden courtyard at 126 boulevard du Montparnasse. The former studios of sculptors Zadkine and Bourdelle are both now interesting museums open to the public (the **Musée Zadkine** and **Musée Bourdelle**). A recent addition is the gleaming glass **Fondation Cartier** on boulevard Raspail, an exhibition centre for contemporary art. The rustic-looking cité Fleurie, just into the 13th *arrondissement* at 65 boulevard Arago, is a reminder of former days as it's still occupied by artists. It isn't open to the public, but you can peer through the gateway into the gardens.

It's also worth making a detour towards the Porte de Versailles in the 15th *arrondissement* to visit La Ruche on passage de Dantzig, the 'beehive' designed by Eiffel as a pavilion for the 1900 exhibition that from the 1900s to the 1920s was one of the great laboratories of modern art. After the exhibition it was acquired by sculptor Alfred Boucher, who had it rebuilt on this site and let it as artists' studios. It had space for 140 artists, and Chagall, Soutine, Modigliani, Brancusi and many more all worked alongside each other here. Many of the studios are still in use today.

While the rest of the neighbourhood has gone a bit downhill, **Montparnasse cemetery** has grown in status as a resting place for the famous. It's a calmer, less crowded cemetery than Père Lachaise; numbered among the eminent dead here are Baudelaire, Maupassant, Franck, Sartre and Simone de Beauvoir, Jean Seberg and France's ultimate decadent crooner, Serge Gainsbourg.

## Denfert-Rochereau & Montsouris

A spookier kind of burial ground can be found at place Denfert-Rochereau (instantly recognisable from the large bronze lion, sculpted by Bartholdi of *Statue of Liberty* fame, which dominates the traffic junction), entrance to the Paris **Catacombs**. Some six million bones were transferred here from the over-crowded Paris cemeteries just before the Revolution. During World War II the Resistance had a hide-out here; more recently, in the 1980s, the catacombs became popular for illicit concerts and parties. The entrance to the catacombs is next to one of the toll gates of the *Mur des Fermiers-généraux* built by **Ledoux** in the 1780s, marking what was then the boundary of the city.

Returning towards Montparnasse along the avenue Denfert-Rochereau you will come to the **Observatoire de Paris**, France's royal observatory at 62 avenue de l'Observatoire, built by Perrault for Louis XIV's minister Colbert in 1668. This is where the moon was first mapped, where Neptune was discovered and where the speed of light first calculated. The French meridian (in use before the Greenwich meridian was adopted as an international standard) runs north-south through the building. However, it is open to the public by appointment only, and only on the first Saturday of each month.

The bulk of the 14th *arrondissement* to the south of place Denfert-Rochereau is a mainly residential but pleasantly spacious area. There's a small but lively street market and several cafés on rue Daguerre, which is a favourite local rendezvous, especially on Sunday mornings. Around rue d'Alésia there are some surprising, slightly un-Parisian-looking townhouses. At 4 rue Marie Rose (01.42.79.99.58) is the **Maison de Lénine**, where the founder of the Soviet Union lived for four years.

Once a compulsory stop for all East European dignitaries, it's now a rather forlorn place, and open by appointment only. The museum inside is unspectacular unless you want to see the great man's crockery and modest furniture.

The 14th *arrondissement* also boasts a lovely large park, the **Parc Montsouris**, which has some very beautiful trees and a lake. On the park's opening day in 1878 the man-made lake suddenly and inexplicably emptied and the engineer responsible promptly committed suicide.

Many of the artists who gave Montparnasse its reputation actually lived around here. Around the western edge of the park are several small streets such as **rue du Parc Montsouris** and **rue Georges-Braque** that were built up in the early years of this century with charming small villas and artists' studios, many by distinguished avant-garde architects (*see chapter* **Architecture**). Once mainly occupied by artists, they're now more likely to be the homes of lawyers and doctors. In the 1930s, Henry Miller and Anaïs Nin lived at **18 rue Villa Seurat**, off rue de la Tombe-Issoire, where the architect André Lurçat built several of the houses. On the southern edge of Montsouris is the **Cité Universitaire**, home to 6,000 students of different nationalities. It has 40 different pavilions, laid out in landscaped gardens, each designed in a supposedly appropriate national style. The much admired but rather dated slab architecture includes the Swiss Pavilion (1935) and the Brazilian Pavilion (1959), both designed by Le Corbusier.

## The 13th Arrondissement

Traditionally a working-class area that became one of the most industrialised parts of Paris in the nineteenth century, and with a strong history of political activism, this largely neglected corner of town has been undergoing massive upheaval with the building of the new **Bibliothèque Nationale de France François-Mitterrand** and, consequently, the whole development zone around it. Dominique Perrault's massive four-towered building, personally selected by Mitterrand, was dogged by criticism for its impracticality, wastefulness, expense and architectural quality during its construction, but the library finally opened (roughly on time) in December 1996. Mitterrand hoped the library, the last and most ambitious of his *Grands Projets*, would be the first in a series of developments to liven up this desolate part of the Left Bank formerly taken up by railway yards, as part of a plan called ZAC Rive Gauche. Other features of the plan include new housing and office developments, the covering-over of some of the remaining railway lines, the swallowing up of existing buildings in the area such as **Les Frigos**, and the construction of a new high-speed Météor Métro link to the centre of town due to open at the end of 1997. The building of a new footbridge between the library and the equally modernistic Bercy area across the river has been, at least temporarily, shelved.

The 13th *arrondissement* also has some more established sights: the **Manufacture Nationale des Gobelins** is home to the French state's main weaving companies. The tapestries and rugs produced here on commission (usually from the government) continue a long tradition dating back to the fifteenth century. On the northern edge of the *arrondissement*, next to the gare d'Austerlitz and the Jardin des Plantes (*see above*, **Latin Quarter**), is the huge **Hôpital Pitié de la Salpêtrière**, one of the oldest hospitals in Paris, founded in 1656. In the 1800s this was one of the first places in the world to undertake scientific treatment of the insane. Its chief architectural feature is the austerely beautiful chapel, dating from 1670, designed by Libéral Bruand with an octagonal dome in the centre and eight separate naves in order to be able to separate the sick from the insane, and the destitute from the debauched. The hospital is still in operation, although nowadays for more ordinary purposes, and the chapel is often used for exhibitions.

Acting as a focal point for the area, the busy intersection of place d'Italie has seen more recent developments with the Centre Commercial Italie II, a slightly bizarre high-tech confection which contains the **Gaumont Grand Ecran Italie**, the largest cinema screen in the city, the **Arapaho** music venue, as well as the usual underground banks, fast food outlets and shops. There's a good local food market along **boulevard Auguste-Blanqui** on Tuesday, Friday and Sunday mornings and the contrasting attractions of **Chinatown** and the **Butte aux Cailles**, *see p.124.*

## Chinatown

South of the rue de Tolbiac is Chinatown, the area's other main attraction, centred between the 1960s tower-blocks along avenues d'Ivry and de Choisy. The community that lives here actually comes from several Asian countries. The bleak modern architecture could make it one of the most depressing areas of Paris, but instead it's a fascinating piece of South-East Asia, with its specialist shops, *pâtisseries* laden with lurid-coloured cakes, and the large **Tang Frères** supermarket on avenue d'Ivry. Chinatown is a great place to come for excellent and cheap Oriental food in big, busy restaurants like Hawai, the Palais de Cristal and the gigantic **Chine Masséna**. Less easy to find is the **Buddhist temple**, where hidden in an underground car park under the tallest tower block is a large golden Buddha amid flowers and incense (Autel de la culte de Boudha, av d'Ivry, opposite rue Frères d'Astier-de-la-Vigerie. open 9am-6pm daily). To see the area at its busiest, come here for the traditional lion and dragon dances at colourful **Chinese New Year**.

**Chinese New Year** *celebrations in Paris' 13th* arrondissement.

# Beyond the Périphérique

**For most Parisians, crossing the frontier is more exotic than the farthest jungle, but taking the risk can be worth it.**

Even if Paris is no longer surrounded by a city wall, its borders are still clearly circumscribed by its ring road (the *Périphérique*). Since the late nineteenth-century, however, an ever-increasing number of outlying villages have effectively been swallowed up by the Parisian metropolis.

Paris' suburbs enjoy excellent transport links with the city, but nevertheless the vast majority of Parisians will do anything to keep an address within the 20 *arrondissements*. It is undeniable that the *Périphérique* ring road does create a world apart: the life in *pavillon* or tower block, *jardins ouvriers* and, for touches of a past lifestyle, riverside *guingettes* (*see chapter* **Clubs**). The *banlieue* at times seems to be used almost as a synonym for social problems, but also contain some more conventional attractions, such as the **Basilique St-Denis** and the **Château de Malmaison**, while, thanks to an official policy of cultural decentralisation, several have dynamic cultural centres.

## The West

Paris' most desirable suburbs lie to the west of the city; an east-west divide supposedly the result of prevailing winds which carried industrial grime eastwards. Between the wars, the wealthy middle classes began to build expensive properties here, and today much of the area is filled with substantial houses complete with gardens, which immediately give a quite different atmosphere from that of apartment-dominated Paris.

**Neuilly-sur-Seine** is the most sought-after residential suburb, more or less an extension of the BCBG 16th *arrondissement*. Expect to see lots of pearl chokers and Hermès scarves if you wander through its streets. **Boulogne-Billancourt**, to the south, now headquarters to numerous advertising and publishing companies, used to be dominated by its film studios (recently demolished) and massive Renault car works (awaiting redevelopment). Near the Bois de Boulogne, there are elegant villas and some fine examples of 1920s and '30s architecture by Le Corbusier, Mallet-Stevens and others, well pinpointed by plaques around the town.

The interesting Musée des Années 30, which focuses on artists and architects who lived there at that time, will reopen at the end of 1997 in a new building next to the monumental 1930s town hall.

Just across the Seine is **St-Cloud**, site of a château that burnt down in the Franco-Prussian war in 1870. There remains a marvellous park on a hillside overlooking the river (*see chapter* **Parks & Cemeteries**) and streets of often romantic villas. To the south of St-Cloud is Sèvres, site of the famous porcelain factory, now a museum (*see chapter* **Museums**). Northwest of here, the seventeenth-century château at Rueil-Malmaison is closely linked with Napoléon and Josephine, while the eccentric **Château de Monte Cristo** (01.30.61.61.35) at Port Marly was built for Alexandre Dumas with a tiled Moorish room. In the grounds, the strange Château d'If is inscribed with the titles of his numerous works.

Further west, the town of **St-Germain-en-Laye** is a smart commuter suburb, with a historic centre dominated by the rather forbidding château, upmarket shops and the **Musée Départemental du Prieuré**, former home of the Nabi painter Maurice Denis. Henri II lived in the château, with his wife Catherine de Médicis and his mistress Diane de Poitiers, and Louis XIV was born here. The château has several British connections: Mary Queen of Scots grew up here, and the dethroned James II lived here from 1689 until his death in 1701. It was restored by Napoléon III, who turned it into an archeological museum, the **Musée des Antiquités Nationales**. The château overlooks the Grande Terrasse, a popular promenade, designed by Le Nôtre, on the edge of a huge forest.

## The North & East

The suburbs around the north and east of Paris were the first to be industrialised, from the 1860s onwards, and they remain the grimmest parts of the greater Paris region. In the 1950s, huge estates full of tower blocks were built swiftly on cheap industrial land. Most famous is Sarcelles, considered a symbol of urban misery.

In amongst this suburban sprawl stands one of the treasures of Gothic architecture – the basilica at **St-Denis**, where most of France's monarchs were buried. St Denis also boasts the innovative **Musée de l'Art et et Histoire de St-Denis**, a busy covered market, some fine contemporary buildings such as Oscar Niemeyer's headquarters for Communist newspaper *L'Humanité* and a gleaming new tramway. Nearby a stadium is under construction for the 1998 World Cup. The *département* of Seine-St-Denis has one of greater Paris' highest immigrant populations, especially from North Africa, and has become another local byword for urban blight, but the area also has a lively cultural scene and hosts prestigious film, jazz and classical music festivals (*see chapter* **Paris by Season**).

Like St-Denis, **Bobigny**, still resolutely working-class, also has an excellent subsidised theatre (*see chapter* **Theatre**) and enterprising cultural programmes, as does **Créteil**, a planned new town built in the 1960s around a manmade lake. More upmarket residential districts are found near the Bois de Vincennes, such as **Vincennes**, **St Mandé** and **Joinville-le-Pont**, where there are villas and footpaths along the banks of the Marne.

## The South-West

Apart from the inner interwar suburbs like Montrouge and Vanves, much of this area was built up in the 1950s and '60s. Leafy **Sceaux** is a pleasant exception. In the seventeenth century Louis XIV's finance minister Colbert ordered the construction of a sumptuous château here. The present building housing the Musée de l'Ile de France (01.46.61.06.71) dates from 1856 but the large park with its Grand Canal and waterfalls still more or less follows Le Nôtre's original design. Concerts are often held in the Orangerie in summer. There's still something of a sense of village around the church. The writer Chateaubriand, forced to leave Paris for his criticism of Napoléon, lived nearby at **Châtenay-Malabry** in the romantically named Vallée-aux-Loups (87 rue Chateaubriand/01.47.02.08.62) .

# La Défense

La Défense is only a hop, skip and a jump from central Paris, but feels like a different world. What you find as you emerge from the RER station are the giant skyscrapers and walkways of Paris' mini-Manhattan. Even if somewhat cold and anonymous, it is nonetheless surprisingly lively, overwhelmingly businessy during the week, filled with visitors and shoppers at the weekends.

La Défense has been a showcase for French business since the mid-1950s, when the triangular **CNIT** exhibition hall was built as a space for major trade shows. It was a landmark in its day, and still has the largest concrete vaulted roof in the world (a 230-metre span), although its original open space has been divided up into shops, cafés, hotels and smaller exhibition spaces. Since then successive governments have all developed the idea of giving Paris an entirely new, separate  district for modern business, and La Défense soon proved popular with big corporations such as Elf and Fiat, who needed more space for their headquarters than a central location could offer.

Today, over 100,000 people work on this businesspersons' reservation, and another 35,000 dwell in the futuristic blocks of flats on the southern edge. None of the skyscrapers display any great architectural distinction, although, clustered together, they are an impressive sight. Jean Nouvel's plans for La Tour Sans Fin, a never-ending skyscraper destined to merge into the clouds, remains on the drawing board.

Spreckelsen's **Grande Arche de la Défense**, completed for the bicentenary of the Revolution in 1989, finally gave the district the monument it needed and is now a major tourist attraction with its superb view from the top. Outside on the giant forecourt are fountains and sculptures by artists such as Joan Miró and Alexander Calder. Even more fun are the kitsch, computer-controlled fountains and Takis' flashing light poles. A good introduction to the area is the 45-minute audio tour, in English and other languages, that can be hired from the Info-Défense kiosk in front of the CNIT (open 10am-6pm daily).

# Eating & Drinking

# A la Carte

*An ABC guide through French menus to help ensure that your dégustation is always delicious.*

**A**bats offal. **Agneau** lamb. **Aiglefin** haddock. **Aiguillettes** (de canard) thin slices of duck breast. **Ail** garlic; **aïoli** sauce made with ground garlic. **Aligot** mashed potatoes with melted cheese and garlic. **Aloyau** loin of beef. **Ananas** pineapple. **Anchoïade** spicy paste of anchovies and black olives. **Andouillette** chitterling sausage made from pig's offal. **Aneth** dill. **Anguille** eel. **Asperge** asparagus. **Assiette** plate.

**B**allotine a piece of meat or fish boned, stuffed and rolled up. **Bar** sea bass. **Barbue** brill. **Bavarois** moulded cream dessert. **Bavette** beef flank steak. **Béarnaise** rich sauce of butter and egg yolks. **Beignet** fritter or doughnut. **Belon** smooth, flat oyster. **Betterave** beetroot. **Biche** deer, venison. **Bifteak** steak. **Bisque** shellfish soup. **Blanquette** a 'white' stew (made with eggs and cream). **Blette** Swiss chard. **Boudin noir/blanc** black (blood) or white pudding. **Boeuf** beef; **boeuf bourguignon** beef cooked Burgundy style, with red wine, onions and mushrooms; **boeuf gros sel** boiled beef with vegetables, similar to *pot-au-feu*. **Bouillabaisse** Mediterranean fish soup. **Bourride** a *bouillabaisse*-like soup, without shellfish. **Brebis** sheep's milk cheese. **Brochet** pike. **Brochette** kebab. **Bulot** whelk.

**C**abillaud fresh cod. **Caille** quail. **Campagne/campagnard** country-style. **Canard** duck. **Cannelle** cinnamon. **Carbonnade** beef stew with onions and stout or beer. **Carré d'agneau** rack or loin of lamb. **Carrelet** plaice. **Cassis** blackcurrants, also blackcurrant liqueur used in *kir*. **Cassoulet** stew of haricot beans, sausage and preserved duck. **Céleri** celery. **Céleri rave** celeriac. **Cèpes** spongy, dark-brown mushrooms. **Cerise** cherry. **Cervelles** brains. **Champignon** mushroom; **champignon de Paris** button mushroom. **Charcuterie** cold meat hors d'oeuvres, such as *saucisson* or *pâté*. **Charlotte** moulded cream dessert with a biscuit edge; also baked versions with fruit. **Chasseur** cooked with mushrooms, shallots and white wine. **Chateaubriand** thick fillet steak, usually served for two with a *béarnaise* sauce. **Chaud** hot. **Chaud-froid** a sauce thickened with gelatine or aspic, used to glaze cold dishes. **Cheval** horse. **A cheval** with an egg on top. **Chèvre** goat's cheese. **Chevreuil** young roe deer. **Chou** cabbage. **Choucroute** sauerkraut, usually served *garnie* with cured ham and sausages. **Chou-fleur**

cauliflower. **Citron** lemon. **Citron vert** lime. **Citronelle** lemon grass. **Civet** game stew. **Clafoutis** thick batter filled with fruit, usually cherries. **Cochon de lait** suckling pig. **Colin** hake. **Confit de canard** preserved duck. **Contre-filet** sirloin steak. **Coquelet** baby rooster. **Coquille** shell. **Coquilles St-Jacques** scallops. **Côte** chop; **côte de boeuf** beef rib. **Cornichon** pickled gherkin. **Crème anglaise** custard sauce. **Crème brûlée** creamy custard dessert with caramel glaze. **Crème chantilly** sweetened whipped cream. **Crème fraîche** thick, slightly soured cream. **Crépinettes** small, flattish sausages, often grilled. **Cresson** watercress. **Crevettes** prawns (GB), shrimps (US). **Croque madame** sandwich of toasted cheese and ham topped with an egg; **croque monsieur** sandwich of toasted cheese and ham. **Croustade** case of bread or pastry, deep-fried. **En croûte** in a pastry case. **Cru** raw. **Crudités** assorted raw vegetables.

**D**arne (de saumon) salmon steak. **Daube** meat braised slowly in red wine or stock. **Daurade** sea bream. **Dégustation** tasting or sampling. **Désossé** boned. **Dinde** turkey. **Duxelles** mushrooms sautéed in butter with shallots.

**E**chalote shallot. **Endive** chicory (GB), Belgian endive (US). **Entrecôte** beef rib steak. **Entremets** cream or milk-based dessert. **Epices** spices. **Epinards** spinach. **Escabèche** sautéed and marinated fish, served cold. **Escargots** snails. **Espadon** swordfish. **Estouffade** dish containing meat that has been marinated, fried and braised. **Etrille** small crab.

**F**aïsan pheasant. **Farci** stuffed. **Faux-filet** sirloin steak. **Feuilleté** 'leaves' of (puff) pastry. **Fève** broad bean. **Filet mignon** beef tenderloin. **Fines de claire** crinkle-shelled oysters. **Fines herbes** mixture of herbs. **Flambé** food flamed in a pan in burning brandy or other alcohol. **Flétan** halibut. **Foie** liver; **foie gras** fattened liver of goose or duck. **Forestière** with mushrooms. **Fraise** strawberry; **fraise des bois** wild strawberry. **Framboise** raspberry. **Friandises** sweets or petits fours. **Fricadelle** meat-ball. **Fricassé** meat fried and simmered in stock, usually with creamy sauce. **Frisée** curly endive. **Frites** chips. **Froid** cold. **Fromage** cheese; **fromage blanc** smooth cream cheese. **Fruits de mer** shellfish. **Fumé** smoked. **Fumet** fish stock.

**G**alantine boned meat or fish pressed together, usually with a stuffing. **Galette** round flat cake of flaky pastry, potato pancake or buckwheat savoury *crêpe*. **Garni** garnished. **Gâteau** cake. **Gelée** aspic. **Gésiers** gizzards. **Gibier** game. **Gigot d'agneau** leg of lamb. **Gingembre** ginger. **Girolle** delicate wild mushroom. **Glace** ice cream. **Glacé** frozen or iced. **Goujon** strips of fish, coated in egg and breadcrumbs and fried. **Granité** water-ice. **Gratin dauphinois** sliced potatoes baked with milk, cheese and a bit of garlic. **Gratiné** browned with breadcrumbs or cheese. **Grèque** (*à la*) vegetables served cold in the cooking liquid including oil and lemon juice. **Grenouille** (*cuisses de*) frogs' legs. **Griotte** morello cherry. **Groseille** redcurrant. **Groseille à maquereau** gooseberry.

**H**achis parmentier shepherd's pie. **Hareng** herring. **Haricot** bean. **Homard** lobster. **Huître** oyster.

**I**le flottante poached whipped egg white floating in vanilla custard.

**J**ambon ham; **jambon cru** cured raw ham. **Jarret de porc** ham shin or knuckle. **Julienne** vegetables cut into matchsticks.

**L**angoustine Dublin Bay prawns, scampi. **Lapin** rabbit; **lapereau** young rabbit. **Lamelle** very thin slice. **Langue** tongue. **Lard** bacon; **lardon** small cube of bacon. **Lentilles** lentils. **Lièvre** hare. **Lieu** pollack. **Limande** lemon sole. **Lotte** monkfish. **Lyonnais** with onions.

**M**âche lamb's lettuce. **Magret** duck breast. **Maison** (*de la*) of the house. **Maquereau** mackerel. **Marcassin** young wild board. **Mariné** marinated. **Marmite** small cooking pot. **Marquise** light mousse-like cake. **Marron** chestnut. **Mélange** mixture. **Merguez** spicy sausage. **Merlan** whiting. **Meunière** fish seasoned, floured, sautéed in butter. **Miel** honey. **Mignon** small fillet of meat. **Mirabelle** tiny yellow plum. **Moëlle** bone marrow; **os à la moëlle** marrow bone. **Morille** wild morel mushroom. **Moules** (*à la*) *marinière* mussels cooked in a sauce of white wine, shallots, parsley, butter and lemon juice. **Morue** dried, salted cod, usually served puréed with potato. **Mousseline** mixture lightened with whipped cream or egg white. **Mousseron** delicate wild mushroom. **Moutarde** mustard. **Mûre** blackberry. **Muscade** nutmeg. **Myrtille** bilberry/blueberry.

**N**age aromatic liquid for poaching. **Navarin** lamb and vegetable stew. **Navet** turnip. **Noisette** small round portion, usually of meat; hazelnut. **Noix** walnut. **Nouilles** noodles.

**O**euf egg; **oeuf en cocotte** baked egg; **oeuf en meurette** egg poached in red-wine; **oeuf à la neige** another name for *Ile flottante*. **Oie** goose. **Onglet** cut of beef, similar to *bavette*.

**P**ain bread. **Palourde** clam. **Pamplemousse** grapefruit. **Panaché** mixture. **Pané** breaded. **Papillote** (*en*) fish cooked in paper packet. **Palourde** type of clam. **Parfait** sweet or savoury mousse-like mixture. **Parmentier** with potato. **Pâtes** pasta or noodles. **Paupiette** slice of meat, stuffed and rolled. **Pavé** thick steak. **Pêcheur** based on fish. **Perdrix** partridge. **Petit salé** salt pork. **Pied** foot (trotter). **Pignon** pine kernel. **Pintade/pintadeau** guineal fowl. **Pipérade** Basque-style scrambled egg with Bayonne ham, onion and peppers. **Pistou** pesto-like basil and garlic paste. **Plat du jour** daily special. **Pleurotte** oyster mushroom. **Poire** pear. **Poireau** leek. **Poisson** fish. **Poivre** pepper. **Poivron** sweet red or green (bell) pepper. **Pomme** apple. **Pomme de terre** potato; **pommes parisiennes** potatoes fried and tossed in a meat glaze. **Potage** soup. **Pot au feu** boiled beef with vegetables. **Poulet** chicken. **Poulpe** octopus. **Prune** plum. **Pruneau** prune.

**Q**uenelles light poached dumplings, usually made with fish, sometimes poultry. **Quetsch** damson. **Queue de boeuf** ox-tail.

**R**agoût brown meat stew. **Raie** skate. **Raifort** horseradish. **Râpé** grated. **Rascasse** scorpion fish. **Réglisse** liquorice. **Reine-claude** greengage plum. **Rillettes** potted meat, usually pork and/or goose. **Ris de veau** veal sweetbreads. **Rognons** kidneys. **Rouget** red mullet.

**S**ablé shortbread biscuit. **St Pierre** John Dory. **Sandre** pike-perch, a freshwater fish. **Sanglier** wild boar. **Saucisse** sausage. **Saucisson** small sausage. **Saucisson sec** dried sausage eaten cold. **Saumon** salmon. **Sauté** fried lightly and rapidly. **Suppion** small cuttlefish. **Suprême** (*de volaille*) fillets of chicken in a rich cream sauce.

**T**artare raw minced steak (also tuna or salmon). **Tarte aux pommes** apple tart. **Tarte Tatin** a warm, caramelised apple tart cooked upside-down. **Terrine** a rectangular earthenware dish or a pâté cooked in one. **Tête** head; **tête de veau** calf's head, cooked in a white *court-bouillon*. **Thon** tuna. **Timbale** dome-shaped mould, or food cooked in one. **Tisane** herbal tea. **Tournedos** small slices of beef fillet, sautéed or grilled. **Tourte** covered pie or tart, usually savoury. **Travers de porc** Pork spare ribs. **Tripes** tripe. **Tripoux** Auvergnat dish of sheep's tripe and feet. **Truffes** truffles. **Truite** trout.

**V**acherin cake of layered meringue, cream, fruit and ice cream; a soft, cow's milk cheese. **Veau** veal. **Velouté** stock-based white sauce; creamy soup. **Viande** meat. **Vichyssoise** cold leek and potato soup. **Volaille** poultry.

## Cooking time

**Cru** raw. **Bleu** practically raw. **Saignant** rare. **Rosé** pink (used of lamb, duck, liver, kidneys). **A point** medium rare. **Bien cuit** well done. **Très bien cuit.** Very well done.

# Restaurants

*From the quintessentially classical and daringly contemporary to the rustic regional, Paris has the cuisine to suit your mood.*

Paris looks set to end the century with a revival of the same cooking with which it greeted it – classical bourgeois dishes in its grandest restaurants and homely old favourites in its bistros. The popularity of various foreign kitchens notwithstanding, Paris stands more or less aloof from the bold culinary cross-fertilisation that has produced popular modern brasseries like the Oxo Tower in London or the Gramercy Tavern in New York. What's more, it seems as though the French are becoming as tetchy about lemon grass and blue corn tortillas as they've become about English-language music on their radio waves and Anglo-American slang in their advertising.

Battle lines were drawn not long ago when a public quarrel flared among the top chefs of France, pitting the classicists critical of foreign influences, including, surprisingly, **Alain Ducasse** – who made his Paris debut with an unexpectedly traditional menu, insisting that a lot of modern cooking lacks discipline – against innovators like Pierre Gagnaire and Marc Veyrat, both of whom recently closed three-star tables in the provinces. Nonetheless, the jury is still out: Alain Senderens continues to innovate at **Lucas Carton**

and Gagnaire has also now moved to the capital. At the same time, a whole crop of creative young chefs who trained with haute-cuisine masters like **Guy Savoy** or Christian Constant, chef at the Crillon's **Les Ambassadeurs**, have gone out on their own and are offering superb value set-price *menus* and some of the most interesting eating in Paris today, challenging many of the famous and over-priced classic restaurants. Not surprisingly, these restaurants, including **Chez Jean, Chez Michel, La Verrière, Au Camelot, L'Epi Dupin** and **La Régalade** are very popular, so you should book in advance. Typical of their eclectic, cosmopolitan style are chef François Pasteau's skirt steak of lamb stuffed with aubergine at L'Epi Dupin or Eric Frechon's scallops roasted with marrow and garlic chips at La Verrière. Such attention to detail and creative ingredients are evidence that there's still nowhere else in the world where you can eat as well on a day-in and -out basis.

The regional kitchens of France are also very popular in Paris, with outstanding newcomers like **Chantairelle** and **Au Bascou**. Happily, in spite of a continued flowering of indifferent American-style places, the foreign dining scene continues to

become ever larger and more diverse. Oriental restaurants – often a hybrid of Chinese, Thai and Vietnamese – abound all over the city as well as in the 'Chinatowns' of the 13th *arrondissement* and Belleville, and the quality of Paris' Italian tables has never been better.

Restaurants are listed by *arrondissement* within each category. For more-detailed listings and a larger selection, see the annual *Time Out Eating & Drinking in Paris Guide*.

## Average Prices

Prices listed are based on the cost of a starter (*entrée*), a main course (*plat*) and dessert chosen *à la carte*, but do not include drinks. Note that it is perfectly acceptable to order only an *entrée* and *plat* or *plat* and dessert rather than all three courses. *Prix fixe* refers to a *menu* or *formule*, which offer a more limited choice at a set price, again usually for three courses, and sometimes include wine. All restaurants and cafés in France are obliged by law to include a 15 per cent service change in the bill. Tables at haute-cuisine and *grands restaurants* often need to be **booked** well in advance, but always try your luck and you might get one for the same day.

## Bistros

### L'Absinthe
*24 pl du Marché-St-Honoré, 1st (01.49.26.90.04).*
*Mº Pyramides.* **Open** noon-2.30pm, 7.30-11pm, Mon-Fri; 7.30-11.30pm Sat. **Prix fixe** 148F. **Lunch menu** 180F. **Dinner menu** 189F. **Credit** AmEx, V.
Now part of Michel Rostang's Bistrots d'à Côté group, this bistro has a spacious terrace facing the Marché St-Honoré development; inside the buzz of fashion-trade regulars remains, complemented by snappily dressed waitresses. The menu is typified by proficiently prepared cheese-stuffed *ravioles de Royans* and veal chops with blue-cheese sauce.

### Chez la Vieille
*1 rue Bailleul, 1st (01.42.60.15.78). Mº Louvre.*
**Open** noon-2.30pm Mon-Wed, Fri; noon-2pm, 7.30-9pm, Thur. **Average** 250F. **Credit** AmEx, MC, V.
This bright little bistro specialises in satisfying *cuisine menagère*, or home-cooking pandering to a chic set of power-brokers. The 'old woman' (*la Vieille*), Adrienne Biasin, has retired and given way to a team of female cooks who work with co-owner Gérard Besson. There's no written menu: the hostess cheerfully tells you what they've cooked that day.

### La Tour de Montlhéry
*5 rue des Prouvaires, 1st (01.42.36.21.82). Mº Châtelet-Les Halles.* **Open** 24 hours, 7am- Mon-7am Sat. Closed 15 July-15 Aug. **Average** 200F. **Credit** MC, V.
Round-the-clock dining of a high standard at this famous, convivial old bistro in Les Halles, known to regulars as Chez Denise. You might have to share a table with all sorts of wide-eyed foodies, hungry for the huge portions of superb lamb or beef, including one of the best *côtes de boeuf* in town (for two), or lusher options like succulent veal kidneys.

### Willi's Wine Bar
*13 rue des Petits-Champs, 1st (01.42.61.05.09).*
*Mº Pyramides.* **Open** noon-11pm Mon-Sat.
**Lunch menu** 140F. **Dinner menu** 180F. **Credit** MC, V.
Owned by two Brits – Williamson and Johnston, the duo also behind Juveniles (*see chapter* **Cafés & Bars**) – Willi's exemplifies the trend comfortable in its mainly British waiting staff and cosmopolitan clientele. The cuisine is mainly French, and might include warm salads or seasonal wild boar with mashed potatoes and redcurrant sauce. Willi's famed Côtes du Rhône selection is priced accordingly (88F-1000F).

# Top of the toques

**La Tour de Montlhéry** (*see* **Bistros**)
The last of the all-night market bistros.
**Le Brin de Zinc... et Madame** (*see* **Bistros**) Vintage with vitality.
**Campagne et Provence** (*see* **Bistros**) Delicious Provençal food by the Seine.
**Chardenoux** (*see* **Bistros**) Beautiful old-fashioned local, outstanding bistro food.
**La Verrière** (*see* **Bistros**) Innovative modern bistro food by a young chef.
**L'Ambroisie** (*see* **Haute Cuisine**) The finest décor and service, intriguing food.
**Ledoyen** (*see* **Haute Cuisine**) The best female chef in Paris adds Northern flair.
**Le Coupe-Chou** (*see* **Classic**) Satisfying fare in a bewitching historic setting.
**Restaurant du Palais-Royal** (*see* **Contemporary**) Romance and creativity.
**Vivario** (*see* **Tour de France**) All the exoticism of Corsica.
**Brasserie de l'Isle St-Louis** (*see* **Brasseries**) Awash with atmosphere.
**Maison Prunier** (*see* **Fish**) Magnificent Art-Deco setting for superb seafood.
**Gros Minet** (*see* **Budget**) Cat-lovers' budget classics.
**L'Ebauchoir** (*see* **Budget**) Unposey conviviality.
**Bouillon Racine** (*see* **International**) The new Belgian buzz.
**Dominique** (*see* **International**) Russian emotion fuelled by vodka.

### Yvan-sur-Seine
*26 quai du Louvre, 1st (01.42.36.49.52). Mº Louvre.*
**Open** noon-2.30pm, 8pm-4am daily. **Average** 160F.
**Prix fixe** 138F (until midnight Mon-Fri). **Credit** V.
Celebrity chef Yvan has scored a big success with vintage Parisian night people with his colourful riverside bistro, done up to resemble the cabin of a barge, and accompanying disco backing. The food is pretty good and features dishes like stuffed aubergine and *onglet* with sautéed potatoes.

### Le Brin de Zinc... et Madame
*50 rue Montorgueil, 2nd (01.42.21.10.80). Mº Etienne-Marcel.* **Open** noon-2pm, 7-11.30pm, daily; 7-11.30pm Sun. **Average** 150F. **Credit** AmEx, MC, V.
The delightfully old-fashioned velveteen banquettes, marble tabletops and ivy-filigree sconces and busy market-street location only half explain the convivial atmosphere: the real story is food. The cooking is excellent, with generous salads and bistro classics like perfectly cooked steak, salmon and roast chicken. Dessert is the highlight, so make room for a superb chocolate *fondant* or damson tart.

### Chez Georges
*1 rue du Mail, 2nd (01.42.60.07.11). Mº Bourse.*
**Open** noon-2pm, 7.15-9.30pm, Mon-Sat. Closed first three weeks Aug. **Average** 250F. **Credit** AmEx, MC, V.

# Juggling with the wine list

Today, wine knowledge on offer is enormous. In more expensive restaurants, the *sommelier* (wine waiter) is generally well informed, and keen to advise. It's more tricky in less-expensive bistros, when advice is not always available and language can be a barrier. A *pichet* or *carafe* is usually cheap and cheerful and house wine reliable. Although it is now more common to drink the same wine throughout a meal, some guidelines do exist if you are drinking different wines. A light wine precedes a full-bodied wine; a dry white wine precedes a sweet wine, except when it is Sauternes with *foie gras*; a dry white wine precedes a red wine; a young wine precedes an older wine. Order red wine at the beginning of the meal, so that it can be allowed to breathe. White wine is chilled to highlight its acidity, but if it is too cold the taste of the fruit will be hidden.

## WHICH WINE?

Usually, wine from a region will go well with a food from the region: a Provençal wine with a Provençal dish, *cassoulet* with a full-bodied Southwestern red or *boeuf bourguignon* with red Burgundy. Wine behaves like an additional sauce, so it should heighten the flavour by contrasting, as in Sauternes and roquefort (sugar and salt), or complementing the dish. Burgundy and Bordeaux still head the great wine lists, but southern wines from the Lubéron, Languedoc, Rousillon and Corbières are gaining ground in modest restaurants.

## THE DIFFICULT CHOICES

**Red wine with fish?** Increasingly popular: choose a wine with good fruit, low tannin and high acidity – a red from the Beaujolais or the Loire, which can be served chilled if you wish.
**White wine with roast beef?** Choose a full-bodied white that has been fermented in the barrel – a Bordeaux white from the Graves.
**Chinese or Thai food?** Choose a slightly sweet white wine, such as the Colombard grape or a spicy Gerwurztraminer.
**Vegetarian food?** Start with a Grand Cru Riesling as an *apéritif* and have a glass of Banyuls at the end of the meal. A Côte de Provence will always go with a ratatouille.
**Couscous?** Choose a wine from the Côtes du Rhône, made from the Grenache grape.

With its traditional cooking and Corinthian capitals, this bistro is a little expensive for what it is, but as a timewarp experience, it can't fail. Clubby city types and fashion magnates come here for copious dishes such as roast pheasant on a bed of green lentils. Wines prices reach a sublime 3,900F.

## Baracane

*38 rue des Tournelles, 4th (01.42.71.43.33). Mº Bastille.* **Open** noon-2.30pm, 7pm-midnight, Mon-Fri; 7pm-midnight Sat. **Prix fixe** 78F, 125F, 190F, 200F. **Lunch menu** 49F. **Credit** MC, V.
The food served in this overlit, bare little dining room is excellent and affordable, with a limited but extremely good value *menu du marché*. On the *menu-carte* the cuisine takes a Southwestern turn with the emphasis on duck, as in a robust duck terrine, a tender *confit de canard* and *cassoulet*.

## Le Coude Fou

*12 rue Bourg-Tibourg, 4th (01.42.77.15.16). Mº Hôtel-de-Ville.* **Open** noon-2am Mon-Sat; 7.30pm-2am Sun. **Average** 200F. **Prix fixe** 130F (dinner only, not Fri). **Lunch menu** 110F. **Credit** AmEx, DC, MC, V.
This restaurant-cum-wine bar in the middle of the happening Marais packs in an eclectic bunch clearly out to have fun. A varied wine list is part of the appeal, but young and old gather here as much for ample, well-priced home cooking.

## Le Grizzli

*7 rue St-Martin, 4th (01.48.87.77.56). Mº Hôtel-de-Ville.* **Open** noon-2pm, 7.30-11pm, Mon-Sat. **Average** 220F. **Prix fixe** 155F (dinner only). **Lunch menu** 115F. **Credit** AmEx, MC, V.
This definitive Parisian bistro, with its turn-of-the-century setting, offers a menu which balances bistro favourites with Central and Southwestern dishes, exemplified by *fricot de veau*, a hearty meat and vegetable stew. Another speciality is fish or meat *sur l'ardoise*, grilled on heated pieces of slate.

## Ma Bourgogne

*19 pl des Vosges, 4th (01.42.78.44.64). Mº Bastille.* **Open** noon-1am (8am-noon breakfast and snacks) daily. Closed Feb, first week Mar. **Average** 200F. **No credit cards.**
French and foreigners alike vie for tables outdoors to enjoy the unrivalled view of the place des Vosges from this busy, if unexceptional, bistro. Pricey steaks, good profiteroles.

## Le Vieux Bistro

*14 rue du Cloître-Notre-Dame, 4th (01.43.54.18.95). Mº St-Michel.* **Open** noon-2pm, 7.30-10.30pm, daily. **Average** 250F. **Credit** MC, V.
Despite being almost next door to Notre Dame, Le Vieux Bistro still pulls Parisian powerbrokers with its highly reputed cuisine. Leeks vinaigrette and *frisée au lardons* are typical of starters, while traditional main courses, such as *coq au vin* and *boeuf bourguignon*, are so expertly prepared, you remember what it is that made them classics in the first place.

## Campagne et Provence

*25 quai de la Tournelle, 5th (01.43.54.05.17). Mº Maubert-Mutualité.* **Open** 7.30-11pm Mon; noon-3pm, 7.30-11pm, Tue-Fri; 7.30pm-1am Sat. **Average** 180F. **Lunch menu** 120F. **Credit** MC, V.
Breton chef Patrick Jeffroy, the owner of this southern-style Seine-side bistro has successfully revised the menu, which now aproaches real excellence at modest prices. New and able young chef David Faure creates Provençal-tinted dishes like marinated salmon in shellfish-seasoned oil and grilled sea bream with preserved fennel. Fashionable crowd.

## Chez Henri au Moulin à Vent

*20 rue des Fossés St-Bernard, 5th (01.43.54.99.37). Mº Jussieu.* **Open** 12.30-1.45pm, 7.30-10.15pm, Tue-Sat. Closed Aug. **Average** 250F. **Credit** MC, V.
This paragon of cheery authenticity sports checked table-

**Campagne et Provence**: *sun in the city.*

cloths, apron-clad waiters and a menu which reads like a list of bistro greatest hits. The cooking is excellent. Note the seasonal specialities of oysters (Oct-Apr) and autumn game. Unintentionally amusing English-language menu.

### La Truffière
*4 rue Blainville, 5th (01.46.33.29.82). M° Monge.*
**Open** noon-2pm, 7-10.30pm, Tue-Sun. **Lunch menu** 90F, 98F. **Dinner menu** 140F (until 8.30pm).
**Credit** AmEx, DC, MC, V.
This crisp bistro, with its ancient stone dining room, aims for excellence and largely succeeds. Young chef Alain Sainsard's cuisine is typified by langoustine tails with mushroom mousse and lamb and sweetbreads in 'olive juice', but the truffle dishes are the house speciality.

### Le Caméléon
*6 rue de Chevreuse, 6th (01.43.20.63.43). M° Raspail.*
**Open** noon-2pm, 8-10.30pm, Mon-Fri; 8-10.30pm Sat.
Closed three weeks in Aug. **Average** 180F.
**Credit** AmEx, MC, V.
With its cheap and cheerful floral wallpaper, this bistro stops just short of being a pastiche, but still attracts a mixture of locals and international foodies. Prompt, friendly service, fair prices and a well-balanced menu of traditional dishes like roast veal rib with fresh pasta casserole. Booking essential.

### L'Epi Dupin
*11 rue Dupin, 6th (01.42.22.64.56). M° Sèvres-Babylone.*
**Open** noon-2.30pm, 8-10.30pm, Mon-Fri; 8-10.30pm Sat.
**Lunch menu** 97F. **Dinner menu** 153F. **Credit** V.
François Pasteau's successful, recently opened bistro attracts a hugely diverse crowd which comes to sample fairly priced creative bistro dishes such as an apple and fennel *charlotte* to start, fennel-stuffed roasted guinea hen, or lamb with aubergine. Bread and desserts are made on the premises.

### Le Petit Zinc
*11 rue St-Benoît, 6th (01.42.61.20.60). M° St-Germain-des-Prés.* **Open** noon-1.30am daily. **Average** 230F.
**Prix fixe** 168F. **Credit** AmEx, DC, MC, V.
This touristy and ornately tiled Art Nouveau bistro occupies

the corner between two other members of the Leyrac group, and the open kitchen seems calculated to show that the cooking is done *sur place. A la carte* is a better bet than the disappointing *menu*, with a perfect *filet de boeuf* and seafood.

### Au Bon Acceuil
*14 rue de Montessuy, 7th (01.47.05.46.11).*
*M° Alma-Marceau/RER Pont de l'Alma.*
**Open** noon-2.30pm, 7.30-10pm, Mon-Fri; 7.30-10pm Sat.
**Average** 200F. **Prix fixe** 135F. **Credit** V.
This successful recently opened bistro is always packed with well-heeled people feasting on one of the best-value *menus* in the city. Cooking is an inventive take on tradition. Dishes change regularly, but the quality remains constant, with starters like skate terrine and main courses like veal *mignon* with spring vegetables. Dessert should not be missed. Book.

### Thoumieux
*79 rue St-Dominique, 7th (01.47.05.49.75).*
*M° La Tour-Maubourg.* **Open** noon-3.30pm, 7pm-midnight, Mon-Sat; noon-midnight Sun. **Average** 200F.
**Prix fixe** 72F, 150F. **Credit** MC, V.
Run by the Thoumieux family since 1923, this vast, mirrored, brasserie-like restaurant boasts barrel-chested country cooking which still draws local bourgeois families, especially for Sunday lunch. Pâtès, *cassoulet, confit de canard* and other specialities take a Southwestern and Corrèze slant.

### Savy
*23 rue Bayard, 8th (01.47.23.46.98). M° Franklin D Roosevelt.* **Open** noon-3pm, 7-11pm, Mon-Fri. **Average** 200F. **Prix fixe** 130F, 150F, 185F. **Credit** AmEx, MC, V.
Despite a sophisticated clientele of solicitors and stars from the TV station opposite, the welcome, like the Auvergnat fare, remains hearty and rustic, as does the vintage décor of brass rails, *banquettes*, mosaic floors and a gleaming bar. A comfort-food favourite with the regulars is the calf's liver in tangy onion sauce with split-pea purée.

### Bistro de Gala
*45 rue du Fbg-Montmartre, 9th (01.40.22.98.30).*
*M° Le Peletier.* **Open** noon-2.15pm, 7pm-12.30am, Mon-Fri; 7pm-12.30am Sat. **Average** 175F. **Prix fixe** 150F.
**Credit** AmEx, DC, MC, V.
This friendly, attractive bistro has a new chef, Courdé (previously at La Tour d'Argent), who serves up traditional dishes like house-smoked salmon with horseradish sauce, oxtail-stuffed ravioli and lamb medallions in garlic sauce. There's an interesting tray of cheeses from Northern France.

### Chez Jean
*52 rue Lamartine, 9th (01.48.78.62.73). M° Notre-Dame-de-Lorette.* **Open** noon-2.30pm, 7.30-10.30pm, Mon-Fri; 7.30-11pm Sat. Closed one week May, three weeks Aug.
**Prix fixe** 165F. **Credit** MC, V.
A surprisingly chic crowd of well-dressed professionals, arty types and gay couples has quickly discovered this restaurant, which rings with the satisfied buzz of people eating well. Outstanding-value food shows a luxury touch with ingredients. Desserts range from the mundane to the intriguing.

### La Cloche d'Or
*3 rue Mansart, 9th (01.48.74.48.88). M° Blanche.*
**Open** 7pm-4am Mon-Sat. Closed Aug. **Average** 185F.
**Credit** AmEx, DC, MC, V.
Though a culinary magnet in the 1920s, its chief virtue today is late-night dining, making it a fusty favourite for night owls and working actors. Despite the slightly perfunctory cooking, the restaurant has an extremely loyal clientele.

### Au Gigot Fin
*56 rue de Lancry, 10th (01.42.08.38.81).*
*M° Jacques Bonsergent.* **Open** 11.30am-2.30pm, 7-11pm, Mon-Fri; 7-11pm Sat. **Average** 170F. **Prix fixe** 110F,

175F. **Lunch menu** 60F. **Credit** AmEx, MC, V.
Lace curtains, zinc bar and the vine-patterned staircase make this 1920s bistro near the Canal St-Martin the perfect introduction to another era. This family business now offers even better French cuisine for the same or slimmer prices, and specialises in the *gigot d'agneau* (leg of lamb) of its name.

## Les Amognes
*243 rue du Fbg-St-Antoine, 11th (01.43.72.73.05).*
*M° Faidherbe-Chaligny.* **Open** 7.30-11pm Mon; noon-2pm, 7.30-11pm, Tue-Sat. **Prix fixe** 180F. **Credit** V.
The rustic décor is in stark contrast to the sophisticated cuisine of chef Thierry Coué, whose seasonal *menu* adds an inspired spin to bistro staples. Meat courses are clever and impressively served, but Coué is at his most imaginative when it comes to fish dishes. There are perfectly aged cheeses, innovative desserts, and a good list of French wines.

## Astier
*44 rue Jean-Pierre Timbaud, 11th (01.43.57.16.35).*
*M° Parmentier.* **Open** noon-2pm, 8-11pm, Mon-Fri. Closed Aug, 24 Dec-2 Jan, Easter. **Prix fixe** 135F. **Credit** V.
This busy, simply decorated dining room is crammed with tables and an unselfconscious mix of avant-garde, old guard and everything in between. Chef Jean-Luc Clerc's four-course *formule* offers traditional cuisine that scores high on the price-quality scale. Wine prices leap to the stratosphere.

## Au Camelot
*50 rue Amelot, 11th (01.43.55.54.04).*
*M° Chemin-Vert.* **Open** noon-2pm, 8-10.30pm, Mon-Fri. **Prix fixe** 140F. **No credit cards.**
This miniscule new bistro puts many 'budget' restaurants to shame; the no-choice, five-course, daily *formule* served here would be available at twice the price, and the service is exceptionally friendly, if sometimes slow. Talented young chef Anne Desplanques, trained by Christian Constant, delights with high-quality ingredients and cooking demonstrated in dishes like crab lasagne and duckling *pot-au-feu*.

## Chardenoux
*1 rue Jules-Vallès, 11th (01.43.71.49.52).*
*M° Charonne.* **Open** noon-2pm, 8-10pm, Mon-Fri; 8-10pm Sat. **Average** 250F. **Prix fixe** 165F (Sat dinner only). **Credit** AmEx, MC, V.
This out-of-the-way bistro's generous and excellent cooking, jovial crowd and beautiful, listed turn-of-the-century décor safely register it as a Parisian landmark. The confidently regional menu offers dishes like tender *daube de joues de boeuf à la provençale*, beef cheeks slow cooked in red wine. Game and wild mushrooms are specialities in season.

## Chez Paul
*13 rue de Charonne, 11th (01.47.00.34.57). M° Bastille.*
**Open** noon-2.30pm, 7pm-12.30am, daily. **Average** 170F. **Credit** AmEx, V.
Late evening brings an unposey mix of ages and types (and a few famous faces) to this well-loved Bastille bistro for traditional fare like bacon-wrapped *chèvre*, *steak au poivre* and *châteaubriand* with a ramekin of thick *béarnaise* sauce.

## St Amarante
*4 rue Biscornet, 12th (01.43.43.00.08). M° Bastille.* **Open** noon-2.30pm Mon, Tue; noon-2.30pm, 8-10.30pm, Wed-Fri. Closed 14 July-15 Aug. **Average** 150F. **Credit** MC, V.
Popular at lunch with folk from the nearby Opéra Bastille. Yves and Christiane Avrillaud share a commitment to quality and freshness: earthy terrines arrive in the dish for you to help yourself; meat dishes come well garnished.

## Le Square Trousseau
*1 rue Antoine-Vollon, 12th (01.43.43.06.00). M° Ledru-Rollin.* **Open** noon-2.30pm, 8-11.15pm, daily. **Average** 200F. **Lunch menu** 100F, 135F. **Credit** AmEx, DC, MC, V.

This atmospheric *belle époque* bistro in the trendy Bastille quarter is forever being used for films and commercials and has become a favourite with the moths of fashion. Unusually, it remains pleasant and easygoing and the food is good. The menu changes every month and may include dishes like delicious lamb *noisettes* in vermouth sauce. There's an interesting array of wines from lesser-known French vineyards.

## Anacréon
*53 bd St-Marcel, 13th (01.43.31.71.18). M° Les Gobelins.*
**Open** noon-2pm, 8-10.30pm, Tue-Sat. Closed one week in winter and Aug. **Lunch menu** 125F, 180F. **Dinner menu** 180F. **Credit** AmEx, DC, MC, V.
Thanks to the warm welcome and excellent contemporary food, the innocuous setting soon becomes insignificant. Talented chef André Le Letty blends hearty and elegant, creating dishes like snails in watercress cream sauce with white beans, and delicious breaded baby pork with sliced turnips.

## Chez Paul
*22 rue Butte-aux-Cailles, 13th (01.45.89.22.11).*
*M° Place d'Italie.* **Open** noon-2pm, 6pm-midnight, daily. Closed 24 Dec-2 Jan. **Average** 200F. **Credit** MC, V.
Chez Paul, a new generation bistro, with subtly modernised, chic décor, has the pleasant buzz of a place where people come knowing they'll eat well. Paul takes pride in preparing traditional seasonal dishes such as *agneau aux lingots* – thick slices of lamb and beans in a tomatoey sauce, and rediscovered cuts like *cochonnailles* – pig's tail, ears, cheek and snout.

## Contre-Allée
*83 av Denfert-Rochereau, 14th (01.43.54.99.86).*
*M° Denfert-Rochereau.* **Open** noon-2.30pm, 8-11pm, Mon-Fri; 8-11pm Sat. **Prix fixe** 160F, 190F. **Credit** AmEx, V.
The tables outside in summer on the spacious, tree-shaded *contre-allée*, or parking lane, and sleek, postmodern interior are what make this pleasant bistro so popular with well-dressed media types. The *carte* offers a clever mix of traditional and contemporary, seen in a skate terrine, and main courses like calf's liver, steak with truffles or crispy sea bass.

## La Mère Agitée
*21 rue Campagne-Première, 14th (01.43.35.56.64).*
*M° Raspail.* **Open** noon-3pm, 7.30pm-midnight, Mon-Sat. **Average** 120F. **Credit** V.
This simple bistro, frequented by a boisterous local crowd, provides a welcome escape from the chain restaurants along boulevard du Montparnasse. There's no menu; chatty Valérie Delahaye, who has a knack for creating enticing soups and simmered dishes, describes the day's offering.

## La Régalade
*49 av Jean-Moulin, 14th (01.45.45.68.58). M° Alésia.*
**Open** noon-2pm, 7pm-midnight, Tue-Fri; 7pm-midnight Sat. Closed 14 Jul-30 Aug. **Prix fixe** 170F. **Credit** MC, V.
An eclectic crowd comes here to eat well at very affordable prices. Chef Yves Camberlorde's style is *cuisine du terroir*, with earthy regional ingredients, a modern flair for lightness, and prices kept down by using offal and unusual meat cuts. Characteristic dishes might include veal with mini ravioli and steamed vegetables, or a casserole of duck hearts with *pleurotte* mushrooms. Book two weeks in advance.

## L'Os à Moëlle
*3 rue Vasco de Gama, 15th (01.45.57.27.27).*
*M° Lourmel.* **Open** noon-2pm, 7.30-11.30pm, Tue-Sat. **Lunch menu** 145F. **Dinner menu** 190F. **Credit** AmEx, DC, MC, V.
This remote but popular bistro offers a lavish, single, no-choice six-course dinner *menu* (at lunch time, there's a daily choice from four *entrées*, *plats* and desserts). Be prepared for a generous feed from a creative, yet resolutely French selection, with lots of offal and speciality meat cuts that demand a little courage, like pork cheeks with split-pea purée.

## Le Petit Rétro

*5 rue Mesnil, 16th (01.44.05.06.05). M° Victor-Hugo.*
**Open** noon-2.30pm, 8-11pm, Tue-Fri; 8-11pm Sat.
**Average** 160F. **Credit** MC, V.
With its friendly waitresses and beautiful Art Nouveau tiles, this snug little bistro offers home-style, traditional cooking in an expensive and usually rather haughty part of Paris. Starters are generally simple, while main courses include good-quality meat dishes like *pavé de boeuf.*

## Bistrot de l'Etoile

*13 rue Troyon, 17th (01.42.67.25.95). M° Charles de Gaulle-Etoile.* **Open** 10.30am-3pm, 7.30-midnight Mon-Fri; 7.30-11.30pm Sat, Sun. **Average** 200F. **Credit** AmEx, MC, V.
Guy Savoy's tiny, stylish bistro offshoot sticks more to tradition than his own haute-cuisine establishment across the street and his other more contemporary bistro annexes, but stands out for its quality of ingredients and preparation, and lower prices. Favourites include roast free-range chicken in tarragon-sprigged *jus* surrounded by tiny potatoes.
**Branches:** 19 rue Lauriston, 16th (01.40.67.11.16); 75 av Niel, 17th (01.42.27.88.44).

## L'Etrier

*154 rue Lamarck, 18th (01.42.29.14.01).
M° Guy-Môquet.* **Open** noon-2.30pm, 7.30-10.30pm, Tue-Sat. **Average** 220F. **Prix fixe** 160F (dinner only).
**Lunch menu** 55F, 65F, 76F, 110F. **Credit** MC, V.
L'Etrier is a modern bistro full of warmth and Montmartre locals who gather for innovative meals and real value. The cooking varies from good to excellent but you can count on ideas that surprise without shocking, such as cockle *timbale* brightened with Indian spices. The *filet de boeuf* is excellent.

## Le Restaurant

*32 rue Véron, 18th (01.42.23.06.22). M° Blanche.*
**Open** noon-2.30pm, 8-11pm, Tue-Fri; 8-11pm Mon, Sat.
**Lunch menu** 70F. **Dinner menu** 120F. **Credit** AmEx, DC, MC, V.

Although it is rather cramped, service is erratic and the cooking not as precise as it once was, this is still one of the better bets around Pigalle. Chef Yves Pelardeau continues to innovate, brightening his *cuisine du marché* with North African and Asian spices in dishes like *confit de tomates,* lightly dressed half-dried tomatoes served with toast, tasty tapenade and flaky Moroccan pastry.

## La Verrière

*10 rue du Général-Brunet, 19th (01.40.40.03.30).
M° Botzaris.* **Open** noon-2.30pm, 7.15-11pm, Tue-Sat. Closed Aug. **Prix fixe** 190F. **Credit** V.
It's worth the expedition here to catch the beginning of what is likely to be a brilliant career for chef Eric Frechon, who trained at the Crillon and has braved new territory at this shrewdly dressed up former café in north-east Paris. A surprisingly chic crowd gathers to witness his flair for mixing flavours like garlicky rabbit with cumin-spiked carrots.

## Les Allobroges

*71 rue des Grands-Champs, 20th (01.43.73.40.00).
M° Maraichers.* **Open** noon-2pm, 8-10pm, Tue-Sat.
**Average** 220F. **Prix fixe** 89F, 159F. **Credit** MC, V.
It may be out of the way, but this is one of the few places you might feel the need to dress up for. Chef Olivier Pateyron aims high, with an emphasis on fine ingredients. The *pièce de resistance* is a starter of langoustines and ratatouille.

# Haute Cuisine

## Gérard Besson

*5 rue du Coq-Heron, 1st (01.42.33.14.74). M° Louvre.*
**Open** noon-2.30pm, 7-10.30pm, Mon-Fri; 7-10.30pm Sat.
**Average** 500F. **Prix fixe** 520F (dinner only), 1200F (truffle menu, mid Dec-mid Mar). **Lunch menu** 280F.
**Credit** AmEx, DC, MC, V.
Peach fabric walls and blonde wood trim make this pretty space a soothing *tour-de-force* of high bourgeois French elegance. The same might be said of Besson's cuisine, which is

**Chez Paul**, *a bistro that has moved with the times in the trendy Bastille.*

# WooLLooMooLoo

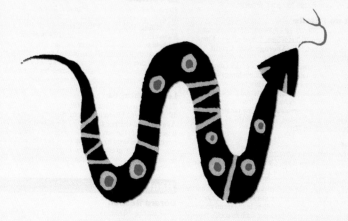

## AUSTRALIAN
## RESTAURANT & WINE BAR

JUST A KANGAROO'S HOP FROM THE BASTILLE,
AT THE CROSSROADS OF ORIENTAL AND WESTERN
GASTRONOMY, THE ECLECTIC HARMONY
OF MODERN AUSTRALIAN CUISINE.

| LUNCH | BRUNCH | DINNER |
|-------|--------|--------|
| TUES-FRI | SUNDAY | TUES-SUN |
| 12-3 | 12-3 | 7.30-11.30 |

36 BD HENRI IV, PARIS 4TH.
Mº BASTILLE.
TEL: 01.42.72.32.11

consistently pleasing without provoking much radical comment. Sample such dishes as cod on a bed of spinach with *aïoli* on the good-value lunch *menu*. Outstanding service.

## Carré des Feuillants

*14 rue de Castiglione, 1st (01.42.86.82.82). M° Tuileries.*
**Open** noon-2.30pm, 7.30-10.30pm, Mon-Fri; 7.30-10.30pm Sat. Closed Aug. **Average** 550F. **Prix fixe** 600F. **Lunch menu** 285F. **Credit** AmEx, DC, MC, V.
Set in an enclosed courtyard not far from the place Vendôme, the restaurant is decorated with light wood-panelling and outsized still-life paintings of vegetables. Southwestern chef Alain Dutournier can, at his best, give distinction to the most ordinary of ingredients, and he is particularly adept with fish and seafood, although there is an uncharacteristic abundance of bland stews and *cassoulets*. Desserts can be a delight. Make the most of the lunch-time *menu*, as at the elevated *à la carte* prices you could do better elsewhere.

## Le Grand Véfour

*17 rue de Beaujolais, 1st (01.42.96.56.27).*
*M° Palais-Royal.* **Open** 12.30-2.15pm, 7.30-10.15pm, Mon-Fri. Closed Aug. **Average** 750F. **Prix fixe** (*dégustation*) 750F. **Lunch menu** 335F. **Credit** AmEx, DC, MC, V.
Founded in 1760 as the Café de Chartres, the Grand Véfour has witnessed centuries of Parisian high society: looking out onto the tranquil gardens of the Palais Royal, this ornate panelled dining room has not only a sophisticated charm, but a tangible sense of history. Dishes like baked red mullet and an excellent, tender Bresse chicken in sweet and sour sauce are beautifully presented. The well-ripened French mountain cheeses and desserts are sublime.

## L'Ambroisie

*9 pl des Vosges, 4th (01.42.78.51.45). M° Bastille.*
**Open** noon-2.30pm, 8-10.15pm, Tue-Sat. Closed two weeks Feb, first three weeks Aug. **Average** 900F. **Credit** AmEx, MC, V.
L'Ambroisie has two exquisite dining rooms, with perfect lighting, stone floor and handsome tapestry, off the western arcade of the place des Vosges. Chef Bernard Pacaud is a perfectionist, which explains the short menu and the intense pleasure offered by each dish. A starter of plump langoustines sandwiched between sesame wafers in a delicate curried sauce is superb, as are simpler main courses with fillet of beef with airy *pommes soufflées*.

## Jacques Cagna

*14 rue des Grands-Augustins, 6th (01.43.26.49.39).*
*M° Odéon.* **Open** noon-2pm, 7.30-10.30pm, Mon-Fri; 7.30-10.30pm Sat. Closed three weeks Aug, last week Dec. **Average** 500F. **Prix fixe** 490F. **Lunch menu** 270F. **Credit** AmEx, DC, MC, V.
This is one of the handsomest, most comfortable haute cuisine restaurants in Paris, with its beamed first-floor dining room and elegant Flemish Old Master paintings. Jacques Cagna's pricey cuisine might include a veal chop in ginger and lime zest sauce, and a superb roast John Dory with chorizo sausage and spicy red pepper stuffed with langoustines.

## L'Arpège

*84 rue de Varenne, 7th (01.45.51.47.33). M° Varenne.*
**Open** 12.30-2.30pm, 7.30-10.30pm Mon-Fri; 7.30-10pm Sun. **Average** 1000F. **Prix fixe** 690F. **Lunch menu** 320F. **Credit** AmEx, DC, MC, V.
There's a buzz in the dining room at chef Alan Passard's restaurant since it was awarded its third star. Passard's obvious talent – he's a very intellectual cook – is evident in the first courses like grilled langoustines with deliciously smoky tomato jam. Main courses, such as *aiguillettes* of lobster in its shell with baby artichokes in a complex mead-based sauce, demonstrate his provocative, minimalist style, although desserts, like an intriguing sugar-and-spice-stuffed tomato, are rather gimmicky. Inconsistent service.

## Jules Verne

*Tour Eiffel, Champ de Mars, 7th (01.45.55.61.44).*
*M° Bir-Hakeim/RER Champ de Mars.* **Open** 12.30-3.45pm, 7.30-9.30pm, daily. **Average** 800F. **Prix fixe** 680F (dinner only). **Lunch menu** 290F (Mon-Fri).
**Credit** AmEx, DC, MC, V.
Two levels up the Eiffel Tower, the setting alone creates a memorable start to a meal in this expensive restaurant, which falls firmly in the *nouvelle* camp: pretty arrangements, light confections, show-off ingredients and unexpected marriages. Chef Alan Reix creates dishes like truffled pigeon with prawns and langoustine salad with *cèpes* and chestnuts.

## Les Ambassadeurs

*Hôtel de Crillon, 10 pl de la Concorde, 8th (01.44.71.16.16).*
*M° Concorde.* **Open** noon-2.30pm, 7-10.30pm, daily. **Average** 340F. **Prix fixe** 640F (dinner only). **Lunch menu** 340F (Mon-Fri). **Credit** AmEx, DC, MC, V.
Chef Christian Constant presides over what is not only the best hotel dining room in Paris but surely the most beautiful, with its checkerboard marble floor, cherubim-filled frescoes, and sublime view of the place de la Concorde. Catering to a diverse assortment of palates, the menu allows you to dine as simply or as elaborately as you choose, with inspired creations like a *suprême* of sea bass in a crust of roasted almonds with caper sauce and a dribble of maple syrup.

## Lucas Carton

*9 pl de la Madeleine, 8th (01.42.65.22.90). M° Madeleine.*
**Open** noon-2.30pm, 8-10.30pm Mon-Fri; 8-10.30pm, Sat. Closed Aug. **Average** 1200F. **Lunch menu** 395F.
**Credit** AmEx, DC, MC, V.
Alain Senderens took over this landmark Art Nouveau interior over a decade ago, where sumptuous quality and service match the grandiose surroundings. Senderens' cooking is uncluttered while deeply rich in every detail, and is typified by dishes like *foie gras* steamed in a packet of green cabbage and buttery monkfish threaded with bits of bacon. No more expensive than a meal in any number of lesser restaurants, this is the ultimate in gastronomic eroticism.

## Laurent

*41 av Gabriel, 8th (01.42.25.00.39). M° Champs-Elysées Clemenceau.* **Open** 12.30-2.30pm, 7.30pm-1am, Mon-Fri; 7.30pm-1am Sat. **Average** 600F. **Prix fixe** 390F.
**Credit** AmEx, DC, MC, V.
From the red satin-decked Napoleon III boudoir to the spacious dining hall looking on to fountains (outdoor tables in summer), Laurent offers the chance to relive the splendour that was once the Champs-Elysées. Chef Philippe Braun is a protégé of Joël Robuchon and his master's voice shows in the magic of perfect matches and distinctive flavours, like wafer-thin ravioli of fresh cod sprinkled with pungent black truffles. The set-price *menu* is worth every centime and one that, for once, is composed of dishes also offered *à la carte*.

## Ledoyen

*1 av Dutuit, 8th (01.47.42.35.98). M° Champs-Elysées-Clemenceau.* **Open** noon-2pm, 7-10.30pm, Mon-Fri. Closed Aug. **Average** 850F. **Prix fixe** 520F, 590F (both dinner only). **Lunch menu** 290F. **Credit** AmEx, DC, MC, V.
Ledoyen has become one of the most pleasant and provocative of Paris' grand tables. France's top woman chef Ghislaine Arabian's menu showcases the northern kitchens of Flanders and Picardy, and her unorthodox creations have become locally revered classics, with dishes like a terrine of eels in green sauce, and turbot in beer sauce with fried onions. Sample her cooking at lower prices in the **Cercle Ledoyen** downstairs (average 350F with wine).

## Taillevent

*15 rue Lamennais, 8th (01.45.61.12.90). M° George V.*
**Open** 12.30-2pm, 7.30-10pm, Mon-Fri. Closed Aug.
**Average** 1000F. **Credit** AmEx, DC, MC, V.

If you succeed in reserving a table at this elegant wood-panelled tabernacle, the excellent and jovial staff will helpfully guide you in to making the right gastronomic choices. Typical starters include a plump sausage of lobster tail with flawless *beurre blanc* and an intensely flavoured watercress soup dotted with cream and Sevruga caviar. A popular dish is the *ris de veau*, pure and tender in a clean, flavourful sauce.

## Le Pré Catelan

*Bois de Boulogne, route de Suresnes, 16th*
*(01.45.24.55.58). No Métro access.* **Open** noon-2pm, 7pm-1am, Tue-Sat; noon-2pm Sun. Closed two weeks Feb. **Average** 700F. **Prix fixe** 550F, 750F. **Lunch menu** 350F with wine Tue-Fri. **Credit** AmEx, DC, MC, V.
This flower-filled bower is one of the most romantic places in Paris, and while the *belle époque* dining room is a splendid riot of ormolu, the terrace is the real luxury here. Chef Roland Durand sends out a register of flirtatious classics such as a delicious spit-roast Bresse chicken with a *gratin* of macaroni and *foie gras* and baby pork ribs in aromatic spices. Desserts range from the sublime to the decorous. Staff are as well-drilled as a troop of palace guards.

## Alain Ducasse

*59 av Raymond-Poincaré, 16th (01.47.27.12.27).*
*Mº Victor Hugo.* **Open** 12.30-2pm, 7.30-9.30pm, Mon-Fri. **Average** 1200F. **Prix fixe** 1400F. **Lunch menu** 480F. **Credit** AmEx DC, MC, V.
Owner of the famed Louis XV in Monte Carlo, Alain Ducasse, the uncontested maestro of Mediterranean cooking, has assumed the reins at retired chef Joël Robuchon's eponymous *belle époque* restaurant in Paris. Ducasse's seasonal cuisine here is almost totally classic to the point of a first course as old-fashioned as a *vol au vent* filled with baby frog's legs. This is not what a worldly big-city gourmand might be hoping for from an *haute cuisine* meal, although an *à la carte* duckling in fig leaves offers a teasing idea of how interesting Ducasse can be. Indifferent and perfunctory service.

## Guy Savoy

*18 rue Troyon, 17th (01.43.80.40.61). Mº Charles de Gaulle-Etoile.* **Open** 12.30-2pm, 7.30-10.30pm, Mon-Fri; 7.30-10.30pm Sat. **Average** 700F. **Prix fixe** 880F *(dégustation).* **Credit** AmEx, MC, V.
What fascinates about this elegant, intimate restaurant, with its flirty little low-voltage lights and bold contemporary art, is the continual effort of a very talented chef to keep your attention fixed on your plate. Savoy creates vibrant dishes that consistently but subtly prove their worth, such as sumptuous scallops in oyster cream with Sevruga caviar, and a superb cream of lentils soup with two plump langoustines. Savoy is an extraordinary *pâtissier*, so be tempted.

# Classic

## Chez Pauline

*5 rue Villedo, 1st (01.42.96.20.70). Mº Pyramides.*
**Open** 12.15-2.30pm, 7.30-10.30pm, Mon-Fri; 7.30-10.30pm Sat (Sept-mid Apr). **Average** 375F. **Prix fixe** 220F. **Credit** AmEx, DC, MC, V.
This luxury bistro's menu brims with truffles – scrambled into eggs, baked whole and stuffed with *foie gras*, shaved over new potato salad and in many other guises – but strikes a balance between lush modern dishes and bistro classics.

## Pierre à la Fontaine Gaillon

*pl Gaillon, 2nd (01.47.42.63.22). Mº Quatre Septembre.*
**Open** noon-2.30pm, 7pm-12.30am, Mon-Fri; 7pm-12.30am Sat. **Average** 350F. **Prix fixe** 165F. **Credit** AmEx, DC, MC, V.
Built in 1672 by Mansard, and once the *hôtel particulier* of the Duc de Lorgues, this establishment's dining room takes you into period elegance. Typical of the well-prepared, clas-

sic bourgeois cuisine are a whole tiny *coquelet* in beer and tarragon sauce and tender *boeuf strogonoff*, while the quality of fish and shellfish is excellent. Tables outside in summer. Courteous service with a touch of swagger.

## Le Coupe-Chou

*9 rue Lanneau, 5th (01.46.33.68.69). Mº Maubert-Mutualité.* **Open** noon-2pm, 7pm-1am, daily. **Average** 200F, 250F. **Prix fixe** 150F, 200F. **Credit** AmEx, MC, V
The firelit, fourteenth-century stone walls are a bewitching spot for dining, especially since the cuisine is now even less expensive and better: the *menu* usually includes a copper pot of tender *boeuf bourguignon* and *confit de canard*. Ask for your coffee to be served among the overstuffed armchairs and *chaises-longues* in the comfortable *salon*.

## Dodin-Bouffant

*25 rue Frédéric-Sauton, 5th (01.43.25.25.14).*
*Mº Maubert-Mutualité.* **Open** noon-2pm, 7.30-11pm, Mon-Fri; 7.30-11pm Sat. **Average** 300F. **Prix fixe** 180F, 245F. **Credit** AmEx, DC, MC, V.
No longer as fashionable as in its '70s heyday, this spacious Left Bank establishment has revised its *menus* to offer exceptional value. The cooking remains within the classic register, enlivened by a distinctive house style of lightened sauces, occasional spices and particularly good fish, although meat-lovers will also like the tender *souris d'agneau*.

## La Tour d'Argent

*15-17 quai de la Tournelle, 5th (01.43.54.23.31).*
*Mº Pont Marie.* **Open** noon-1.30pm, 8-9.30pm, Tue-Sun. **Average** 1000F. **Lunch menu** 395F. **Credit** AmEx, DC, MC, V.
Founded in 1582, customers today, mostly the internationally rich, come here less for the food than for the stunning view of Notre Dame, the unctuous gallantry of the service, and the numbered postcard commemorating the world-famous duck they probably consumed. Although a new chef Bernard Guilhaudin arrived last year, he continues the duck based tradition. The *caneton Marco Polo aux quatre poivres*, a plump, golden bird on a silver tray, is served in two stages.

## Récamier

*4 rue Récamier, 7th (01.45.48.86.58).*
*Mº Sèvres-Babylone.* **Open** noon-2pm, 7-10.30pm, Mon-Sat. **Average** 375F. **Credit** AmEx, DC, MC, V.
Once the *grande dame* of Burgundian restaurants, Récamier is not what it once was, and portions remain stingy. Typical dishes include scallops *meunière* served in lemon sauce and *boeuf bourguignon* with tagliatelle. On the boldly expensive wine list, the cheapest bottle is 180F.
*Wheelchair access.*

## Chez Edgard

*4 rue Marbeuf, 8th (01.47.20.51.15). Mº Alma-Marceau.*
**Open** noon-2pm, 7-11.30pm, Mon-Sat. **Average** 280F. **Prix fixe** 195F. **Credit** AmEx, DC, MC, V.
This revered haunt of politicians and media tycoons boasts discreet banquettes separated by etched glass and four private dining rooms. The 195F *menu* features dishes like *entrecôte* and *onglet de veau* with vegetable *gratin*.

## La Fermette Marbeuf 1900

*5 rue Marbeuf, 8th (01.53.23.08.00). Mº Alma-Marceau.*
**Open** noon-2pm, 7-11.30pm, daily. **Average** 250F. **Prix fixe** 169F. **Credit** AmEx, DC, MC, V.
Now owned by the Frères Blanc, this restaurant's main, Art Nouveau dining room is a listed monument and a point of neighbourhood pride, demonstrated by the numerous French business people out to impress foreign colleagues. With such décor, the food could easily be more expensive and needn't be as good as it is. Expect dishes like *faux filet* served with flavoursome sautéed shallots, and roast salmon in a crispy crust. The staff is patient, efficient and friendly.

*Influential restaurateur* **Guy Savoy**.

## Maxim's

*3 rue Royale, 8th (01.42.65.27.94). M° Concorde.*
**Open** 12.30-2pm, 7.30-10.15pm, Tue-Sat. **Average** 900F,
1000F. **Credit** AmEx, DC, MC, V.
Once synonymous with Paris glamour and elegance, the cuisine at this once legendary address has drifted into oblivion
and the atmosphere in the ornate Art Nouveau dining room
is now more reminiscent of an upmarket Bratislavan supper
club. Although new chef Michel Kerever is attempting a
revival, dining here sadly has more to do with cash than cuisine: morels with asparagus tips might be pleasant but hardly worth 300F, and staff are surprisingly inattentive.

## Au Petit Marguery

*9 bd du Port-Royal, 13th (01.43.31.58.59). M° Gobelins.*
**Open** 12.15-2.15pm, 7.30-10.15pm, Tue-Sat. **Prix fixe**
205F, 450F (Oct-Dec). **Lunch menu** 165F. **Credit**
AmEx, DC, MC, V.
The Cousin brothers' old-fashioned outpost is cheerful and
oh-so-French. The regular menu changes seasonally, but
snails and homemade *andouillette* are on offer all year round.
Look out for the fabulous, crispy ravioli of *pétoncles* (queen
scallops), appearing only when there are adequate supplies
of this mollusc. It is especially busy from Oct to Dec, when
the 450F '*spécial gibier*' (game) *menu* is on offer.

## Contemporary

### Restaurant du Palais-Royal

*43 rue de Valois, 1st (01.40.20.00.82). M° Palais-Royal.*
**Open** 12.30-2.30pm, 7.30-10.30pm Mon-Fri; 7.30-10.30pm
Sat. **Average** 250F. **Credit** AmEx, MC, V.
Come here for the superb modern bistro food in a chic but
romantic setting, with crackle-finished egg shell walls, red
velvet *banquettes* and wrought-iron sconces. Typical of the

cuisine is the grilled sole with a crunchy Languedoc-style
garnish of baby cuttlefish, red peppers, carrots, onions and
parsley. There are tables outside in the summer overlooking
the Palais Royal gardens. Service is friendly and attentive.

### Les Bookinistes

*53 quai des Grands Augustins, 6th (01.43.25.45.94).*
*M° St-Michel.* **Open** noon-2pm Mon-Fri; 7.15pm-midnight,
daily. **Average** 200F. **Prix fixe** 130F. **Lunch menu**
160F. **Credit** AmEx, V.
Guy Savoy's attractive Left Bank bistro offshoot draws a
diverse clientele, although success means it risks being over-
run with tourists. Chef William Ledeuil reinvents classics
with a modern twist, borrowing from the best international
cuisines to create dishes like salmon and ginger in a tangy
vinaigrette, velvet crab soup and steak with shallots, rosemary and macaroni *gratin*. Friendly, young service.

### Le Chat Grippé

*87 rue d'Assas, 6th (01.43.54.70.00). M° Vavin/ RER*
*Port-Royal.* **Open** noon-2pm, 7.30-10.30pm, Tue-Fri, Sun;
dinner only Sat. **Average** 300F. **Prix fixe** 200F. **Lunch
menu** 160F. **Credit** AmEx, MC, V.
This dressy grey and pink bistro near the Luxembourg gardens is expensive *à la carte*, but the five-course *menu* gives
a good idea of chef Michel Galichon's elaborate style. He
dares unusual combinations like rabbit stuffed with snails
in a marjoram sauce, and *lieu jaune* (yellow pollack) spiked
with an eye-watering chorizo chip and white bean purée.

### Le Bamboche

*15 rue de Babylone, 7th (01.45.49.14.40). M° Sèvres-*
*Babylone.* **Open** noon-2pm, 8-11pm, Mon-Fri. Closed
three weeks Aug. **Average** 375F. **Prix fixe** 190F.
**Credit** AmEx, MC, V.
Young chef David Van Laer has scored a big success with
his high-design restaurant which draws a diverse clientele
of 30-somethings upwards for the refined and inventive
bistro cooking. Favourites include the open tart of oysters
and finely grated celeriac, and squid and sweet pepper salad.

### Les Elysées

*Hôtel Vernet, 25 rue Vernet, 8th (01.44.31.98.00).*
*M° George V.* **Open** noon-2pm, 7.30-9.45pm Mon-Fri.
Closed Aug. **Average** 600F. **Prix fixe** 390F, 530F.
**Lunch menu** 340F. **Credit** AmEx, DC, MC, V.
Reigning over a pretty dining room inside an old-fashioned
hotel, chef Alain Solivères does a brilliant take on Provençal
cuisine, adding ingredients from across southern France. Try
the sardines sautéed with red peppers with rocket salad, and
stuffed baby squid in a sauce of their own ink.

### Le Grenadin

*44-46 rue de Naples, 8th (01.45.63.28.92). M° Villiers.*
**Open** noon-2.30pm, 7-10.30pm, Mon-Fri; 7-10.30pm Sat.
Closed one week July, one week Aug. **Average** 260F.
**Prix fixe** 200F, 298F, 330F. **Credit** AmEx, MC, V.
The rather stiff interior doesn't do justice to the imaginative
cooking of pony-tailed Patrick Cirotte, whose style involves
courageous combinations and fashionable lightness, as seen
in a trademark, wafer-thin *carpaccio* of raw *foie gras*, and
sliced *magret de canard* with fennel and puréed pumpkin.

### La Maison Blanche

*15 av Montaigne, 8th (01.47.23.55.99). M° Alma-*
*Marceau.* **Open** noon-2pm, 8-10pm, Mon-Fri; 8-11pm Sat.
Closed Aug. **Average** 450F. **Credit** AmEx, MC, V.
The dome of Les Invalides and Eiffel Tower glowing gold-
en on the skyline dominate the view from this glamorous
restaurant on top of the Théâtre des Champs-Elysées. Apart
from the erratic and indifferent service, food is exemplary,
with dishes like ravioli stuffed with tomato *confit*, and succulent tuna steak with cracked pepper and bone marrow.
Attracts a stylish international crowd.

ALL AMERICAN FOOD
AND DRINKS

# MUSTANG CAFE

## Discover
## América
## Coast
## to Coast

*Seafood*
*Spécialities*

*Gospel brunch*
*every week-end.*

20, RUE DE LA ROQUETTE 75011 PARIS-TÉL. : 01 49 23 41 41
84, BOULEVARD DU MONTPARNASSE 75014 PARIS-TÉL. : 01 43 35 36 12

### L'Oulette

*15 pl La Chambeaudie, 12th (01.40.02.02.12).*
*M° Daumesnil.* **Open** noon-2.15pm, 8-10.15pm, Mon-Fri;
8-10.15pm Sat. **Average** 350F. **Prix fixe** 160F, 240F.
**Credit** AmEx, DC, MC, V.
It might be next to the Ministry of Finance, but this restaurant's contemporary feel and décor attract an agreeably varied crowd. From the Southwest, chef Marcel Baudis adds an
inventive twist and subtle use of spices to classic preparations and refined *cuisine du terroir*. Professional service.

### La Butte Chaillot

*110bis av Kléber, 16th (01.47.27.88.88). M° Trocadéro.*
**Open** noon-2.30pm, 7pm-midnight daily. **Average** 275F.
**Prix fixe** 150F, 210F. **Credit** AmEx, MC, V.
Star-chef Guy Savoy's modern bistro has been a great success with its dramatic interior design and good, simple, con-
temporary-bistro cooking. Fashionable food such as *ravioles
de Royans*, tiny cheese-stuffed pillows, a superb steak with
potato purée, and delicious *millefeuille* with red berry sauce.
Wines are pricey but well chosen.

## Brasseries

### Au Pied de Cochon

*6 rue Coquillière, 1st (01.40.13.77.00). M° Châtelet-Les
Halles.* **Open** 24 hours daily. **Average** 300F. **Prix fixe**
178F. **Credit** AmEx, DC, MC, V.
Come here if a long night has left you sufficiently sozzled to
sample the pig's trotter the restaurant is named after. For
the more squeamish, there's seafood, steaks and other trad
dishes. Marvellously gaudy glass-fruit lamps focus bleary
eyes, and synthesised muzak helps you keep awake in this
all-night institution within the Frères Blanc's brasserie chain.
*Wheelchair access.*

### Le Vaudeville

*29 rue Vivienne, 2nd (01.40.20.04.62). M° Bourse.*
**Open** noon-3pm, 7pm-2am daily. **Average** 250F. **Prix
fixe** 169F. **Lunch menu** 119F. **Credit** AmEx, DC, MC, V.
With its sleek Art Deco interior of mirrors and marble, and
its small, peaceful outdoor terrace, this is one of the more
popular and intimate Groupe Flo restaurants. Typical dishes include oysters and other shellfish, and sturdier offerings
like pork shank with lentils and *cassoulet*.

### Bofinger

*5 rue de la Bastille, 4th (01.42.72.87.82). M° Bastille.*
**Open** noon-3pm, 6.30pm-1am, Mon-Fri; noon-1am Sat,
Sun. **Average** 250F. **Prix fixe** 169F. **Credit** AmEx, DC,
MC, V.
Founded in 1864, Bofinger is the classic, Art Nouveau Paris
brasserie, and although recently purchased by the Flo chain,
has maintained its identity. The spectacular main dining
room with its glazed dome is now the non-smoking reserve
of the high-tipping Americans; the street-side and upstairs
rooms are the reserve of chic Parisians. Oysters are an eternal favourite here, as are *choucroute*, pigs' trotters and sole.

### Brasserie de l'Isle St-Louis

*55 quai de Bourbon, 4th (01.43.54.02.59).*
*M° Pont-Marie.* **Open** 11.30am-1am Mon, Tue, Fri-Sun;
6pm-1am Thur. **Average** 150F. **Credit** MC, V.
The atmosphere here is lively and irresistible, the clientele
eclectic, and this, along with low prices and an ideal location,
only a stone's throw from Notre Dame, explains its popularity. The fare is reliable, hearty Alsatian food, so expect
Mützig beer in *steins* and pork dishes like *choucroute garnie*.

### Balzar

*49 rue des Ecoles, 5th (01.43.54.13.67).*
*M° Cluny-La Sorbonne.* **Open** noon-1am daily.
**Average** 250F. **Credit** AmEx, MC, V.

*Fuel up on wine at* **Chez Edgard**.

Balzar's demure exterior belies its vibrant atmosphere,
which is especially frenetic during catwalk seasons, and
which plays host to a regular media and intellectual clientele, and an array of celebrities. Food is the very model of
good, substantial fare, and skate, roast chicken and leg of
lamb are all favourites with regulars. Book.

### Vagenende 1900

*142 bd St-Germain, 6th (01.43.26.68.18). M° Odéon.*
**Open** noon-1am daily. **Average** 200F. **Prix fixe** 138F.
**Credit** AmEx, MC, V.
Sit inside to appreciate the sinuous woodwork of the Art
Nouveau interior, originally an inexpensive workers' *bouillon* dubbed 'the poor man's Maxim's'. Cooking is classic and
perfectly acceptable, with the usual array of oysters and
*aiguillettes de boeuf*. The 138F *menu* is a good deal for the
area. It's highly touristy in the evenings and at weekends.

### La Maison d'Alsace

*39 av des Champs-Elysées, 8th (01.53.93.97.00).*
*M° Franklin D Roosevelt.* **Open** daily 24 hours. **Average**
220F. **Prix fixe** 198F. **Credit** AmEx, DC, MC, V.
Thanks to its location, this flashy 24-hour brasserie is busy
at all hours of day and night. Like its Frère-Blanc siblings,
it features oysters and a late-night *menu*, but its offerings
are tilted towards Alsatian specialities, such as the incredibly copious *choucroute garnie* and *charcuteries*.

### La Taverne Kronenbourg

*24 bd des Italiens, 9th (01.47.70.16.64). M° Opéra.*
**Open** 11am-1am daily. **Average** 200F. **Prix fixe** 140F.
**Credit** AmEx, DC, MC, V.
Recent redecoration now offers up pale wood, clocks and old
bells in place of the rustic decor of yesteryear. The classic
brasserie fare remains the same with good oysters, splendid
shellfish platters, *foie gras* and several Alsatian specialities.

### Brasserie Flo

*7 cour des Petites-Ecuries, 10th (01.47.70.13.59).*
*M° Château d'Eau.* **Open** noon-3pm, 7pm-1.30am. daily.
**Average** 220F. **Prix fixe** 121F (after 10pm), 189F

# Tour de France

## Alsace: Chez Jenny

*39 bd du Temple, 3rd (01.42.74.75.75).*
*M° République.* **Open** 11.30am-1am daily. **Average**
170F. **Credit** AmEx, DC, MC, V.
This vast brasserie, with its magnificent turn-of-the-
century inlaid wood-panelling by the *ébéniste* Spindler,
specialises in classic Alsatian *choucroute garnie* and has
two tons of it delivered weekly. Served in copper dishes,
it is piled high with first-rate *charcuterie*. Try also the
münster cheese and bilberry tart.

## Auvergne: Chantairelle

*17 rue Laplace, 5th (01.46.33.18.59). M° Maubert-*
*Mutualité.* **Open** noon-2pm, 7-30-10pm Sun-Fri.
**Average** 130F. **Lunch menu** 79F, 95F. **Credit** MC, V.
This charming restaurant is dedicated to the robust, cuisine of the Auvergne, but with a New Age twist. The
friendly young team offers a total experience of the region,
adding a local well and birdsong soundtrack to the typical stuffed cabbage and *potée*, pork and veg casserole.

## Basque Country: Au Bascou

*38 rue Réaumur, 3rd (01.42.72.69.25). M° Arts et*
*Métiers.* **Open** noon-2.30pm, 8-11pm Mon-Fri; 8-11pm
Sat. Closed first three weeks Aug. **Average** 180F.
**Lunch menu** 90F. **Credit** AmEx, MC, V.
Since this bustling little restaurant was taken over by
jovial Jean-Guy Loustau, it has attracted a fashionable
crowd with its excellent Basque cooking. Dishes include
a raw version of the classic Basque *pipérade* and roast
baby lamb. Try the *fromage de brebis*, sheep's milk cheese.

## Brittany: Chez Michel

*10 rue de Belzunce, 10th (01.44.53.06.20).*
*M° Gare du Nord/RER Gare du Nord.* **Open** noon-
2pm, 7.30-11.30pm, Tue-Sat; 7-11.30pm Sat. Closed
Aug. **Prix fixe** 150F. **Credit** MC, V.
Ever since young chef Thierry Breton opened this snug
little place, it's been packed by an affluent Parisian crowd,
drawn by the inventive and excellent-value bistro cooking, with its contemporary flair and flavour of Brittany.
Highlights include cèpes stuffed with oxtail, and *kig ha*
*farz*, a Breton *pot-au-feu* with pigs' cheeks and stuffing.

## Corsica: Vivario

*6 rue Cochin, 5th (01.43.25.08.19). M° Maubert-*
*Mutualité.* **Open** noon-2.30pm Tue-Fri; 8-11pm Mon-
Sat. **Average** 200F. **Credit** AmEx, MC, V.
This may be the most exotic restaurant you come across
in Paris, offering a young lively scene and real wild mountain fare. The waiter is happy to translate – into French
– such unfamiliar Corsican specialities as roast *cabri*, tender, strong-flavoured baby goat shanks, and *tianu d'agneau aux olives*, aromatic stewed neck of lamb with herbs
and tomatoes. Soft white brocciu cheese features heavily.

## Franche-Comté: Chez Maître Paul

*12 rue Monsieur-le-Prince, 6th (01.43.54.74.59). M°*
*Odéon.* **Open** noon-2.30pm, 7-10.30pm daily. **Average**
220F. **Prix fixe** 155F, 190F. **Credit** AmEx, DC, MC, V.
This small, slightly dressy bistro is the best place to try
the comforting cooking of the forested Jura/Franche-
Comté region near the Swiss border. Robust main courses run to free-range chicken roasted, then *gratinéed* in
cream and grated cheese or calf's liver in a sauce based
on Sauternes-like *vin de paille*.

*Ham is big time at **Au Bascou**.*

## Lyon: Cartet

*62 rue de Malte, 11th (01.48.05.17.65). M° République.*
**Open** noon-2.30pm, 7.30-9.30pm, Mon-Fri. Closed one
week Mar, Aug. **Average** 300F. **No credit cards.**
The tiny Lyonnais bistro has leapt into the 1990s with its
décor, but the menu remains blessedly unchanged.
Madame Nouailles trots out clay terrines of delicious homemade pâté, parsleyed ham and headcheese, while the veal
chop with morels and *gratin dauphinois* is a reliable classic.

## Normandy: Les Fernandises

*17 rue de la Fontaine-au-Roi, 11th (01.48.06.16.96).*
*M° Goncourt.* **Open** noon-2.30pm, 7.30-11.30pm, Tue-
Sat. Closed Aug. **Average** 190F. **Prix fixe** 130F.
**Lunch menu** 100F. **Credit** MC, V.
Les Fernandises boasts authentic, classic Normandy cuisine. Everything is homemade (even the butter) and generously served. Typical of the cuisine are starters like the
salad of sautéed cabbage and fresh duck *foie gras*, and
interesting main courses like skate in camembert sauce
and sliced duck breast with apples in cider.

## Provence: La Bastide Odéon

*7 rue Corneille, 6th (01.43.26.03.65). RER Luxembourg.*
**Open** 12.30-2.30pm, 7.30-11pm Tue-Sat. Closed Aug.
**Prix fixe** 139F, 180F. **Credit** MC, V.
This simple yet stylish beamed dining room is one of the
best Provençal restaurants in Paris, attracting folk from
the St-Germain art galleries and well-fed French senators.
Chef Gilles Ajuelos, formerly at Michel Rostang, is at his
best with fish dishes like peppered tuna steak with sun-
dried red peppers and tomatoes, and cod with capers,
although rabbit stuffed with aubergines is also notable.

## Southwest: Lous Landès

*157 av du Maine, 14th (01.45.43.08.04). M° Mouton-*
*Duvernet.* **Open** noon-2.30pm, 8-10.30pm, Mon-Fri;
8-10.30pm Sat. Closed Aug. **Average** 250F. **Prix fixe**
195F, 310F. **Credit** AmEx, DC, MC, V.
Chef Hervé Rumen has added his own sophisticated, creative touches to classic Southwestern cuisine. Duck rules
the roost, but the seasonal game and seafood are also
good, as are the *foie gras*, the Pyrenean milk-fed lamb and
the award-winning *cassoulet*. Brebis cheese is served
Basque-style with jam, before dessert.

(dinner only). **Lunch menu** 119F. **Credit** AmEx, DC, MC, V.

From the seedy, cobbled alleyway, this looks one of the city's more disreputable brasseries but, inside Flo's flagship, the long wood-panelled dining hall is convivial and the mood as close as you'll get to an Alsatian tavern in Paris. *Choucroute* is lavishly garnished, *steak tartare* prepared freshly before you and oysters shucked outside by the *écailleurs*.

### Julien
*16 rue du Fbg-St-Denis, 10th (01.47.70.12.06).*
*M° Strasbourg-St-Denis.* **Open** noon-3pm, 7pm-1.30am, daily. **Average** 220F. **Prix fixe** 121F (after 10pm). **Lunch menu** 119F. **Credit** AmEx, DC, MC, V.
Although part of the Flo chain, this classic brasserie, with its unrivalled Art Nouveau decor of curvaceous, polished wood, stained glass and bar designed by Louis Majorelle, seems to inspire its staff to cheerful antics. Food (no oysters) includes *foie gras, moules marinières, cassoulet* and profiteroles dripping with hot chocolate sauce.

### Terminus Nord
*23 rue de Dunkerque, 10th (01.42.85.05.15).*
*M° Gare du Nord.* **Open** 11am-12.30am daily. **Average** 220F. **Prix fixe** 121F (after 10pm), 189F (dinner only). **Lunch menu** 119F. **Credit** AmEx, DC, MC, V.
This handsome, low-key 1920s brasserie, another link in the Brasserie Flo chain, retains an appealingly relaxed atmosphere, and, since the inauguration of Eurostar, is an ideal place for a first or last meal in Paris. Oysters are the classic opener, to follow with signature *choucroute garnie*.

### Le Train Bleu
*Inside Gare de Lyon, pl Louis-Armand, 12th*
*(01.43.43.09.08). M° Gare de Lyon.* **Open** 11.30am-3pm, 7-11pm daily. **Average** 300F. **Prix fixe** 250F. **Credit** AmEx, DC, MC, V.
This spectacular, restored station restaurant, originally decorated to celebrate the 1900 World's Fair, invokes *belle époque* charm. Food is typical in style, but better quality than in most brasseries, with dishes like lobster salad with green beans and lettuce and salmon steak with *béarnaise* sauce.

### La Coupole
*102 bd du Montparnasse, 14th (01.43.20.14.20). M°*
*Vavin.* **Open** noon-2am daily. **Average** 185F. **Prix fixe** 119F (until 6pm, after 10pm). **Credit** AmEx, DC, MC, V.
Locals may complain that this renowned Art Deco brasserie, rather heavy-handedly renovated by brasserie king Jean-Paul Bucher, is now a food factory, but it still remains an irresistible classic for visitors and the people watching is superb. Dishes like smoked salmon, *foie gras*, steak with *béarnaise* sauce and grilled salmon are seldom bad, although the best bet is a late-night tray of fresh shellfish.

### Brasserie Stella
*133 av Victor-Hugo, 16th (01.47.27.60.54).*
*M° Victor-Hugo.* **Open** noon-1.30am daily. **Average** 230F. **Credit** AmEx, MC, V.
This lively brasserie, deep in the heart of the wealthy 16th is popular with tweed-clad locals for big trays of fresh oysters and other shellfish, and the excellent *steak tartare*. The daily specials tend to be well-simmered dishes.

### Brasserie Wepler
*14 pl de Clichy, 18th (01.45.22.53.29). M° Place de*
*Clichy.* **Open** noon-1am daily. **Average** 250F. **Prix fixe** 150F. **Lunch menu** 92F. **Credit** AmEx, DC, MC, V.
Big, flashy, animated Wepler has presided over the night-time throng of Place de Clichy for over a century and today, its 1970s chrome and mirrors somehow suit the glitz and bustle of Pigalle. Come here for impressively fresh oysters and other shellfish, or the standard range of meat (*faux filet*, roast lamb, sautéed rabbit) and fish dishes.

## Fish & Seafood

### L'Ostréa
*4 rue Sauval, 1st (01.40.26.08.07). M° Châtelet-Les*
*Halles.* **Open** noon-2.30pm, 7.30-11.30pm, Mon-Fri; 7.30-11.30pm Sat. **Average** 150F. **Credit** MC, V.
Among the many, often dubious, restaurants near Les Halles, is this tiny, pocket-friendly spot. Chef Jean-Pierre Delvaux deftly presents a limited number of ingredients with variety. Expect the usual seasonal starters – oysters, clams, mussels and herring, or salads topped with a choice of seafood. The main fish courses offer limited choice but no disappointment.

### Vancouver
*4 rue Arsène-Houssaye, 8th (01.42.72.67.63).*
*M° Charles de Gaulle-Etoile.* **Open** noon-2pm, 7-10pm, Mon-Fri. Closed Aug. **Average** 350F. **Prix fixe** 380F (*dégustation*). **No credit cards.**
Come to this intimate, elegant restaurant near the Arc de Triomphe not only for superb seafood, but also for the festive, extravagant atmosphere. Chef Jean-Louis Decout takes a worldly approach to seafood, creating dishes like his unusual 'dim sum' of Dublin Bay prawns with pleurotte mushrooms seasoned with aromatic spices or a delicious *bouillabaisse parisienne*. Appropriately light desserts.

### Le Dôme
*108 bd du Montparnasse, 14th (01.43.35.25.81).*
*M° Vavin.* **Open** noon-3pm, 7.30pm-12.30am, Tue-Sun. **Average** 350F. **Credit** AmEx, DC, MC, V.
The chrome and wood décor is sleek, service metronomic and prices astronomic, but the fish is first-rate and impeccably fresh at this Montparnasse institution. Across the road the Bistrot du Dôme, the first of the Dôme's two annexes, offers fresh seafood in convivial surroundings at lower prices. **Le Bistrot du Dôme**: 1 rue Delambre, 14th (01.43.35.32.00); 2 rue de la Bastille, 4th (01.48.04.88.44).

### Maison Prunier
*16 av Victor-Hugo, 16th (01.44.17.35.85).*
*M° Charles de Gaulle-Etoile.* **Open** noon-3pm, 7-11pm, Tue-Sat; 7-11pm Mon. Closed Aug. **Average** 500F. **Credit** AmEx, DC, MC, V.
If you're yearning for superb seafood and a glamorous night out, Prunier is ideal. The listed, renovated Art Deco mosaics are magnificent, and the menu has been brilliantly revised by Jean-Claude Vrinat, director of Taillevent (*see above* **Haute Cuisine**). The seafood cooking here remains reassuringly classic, with suberb turbot, perfect sole or the intriguingly successful, old-fashioned Saintongeaise plate – raw oysters served with grilled chipolatas, probably one of the most refined marriages of earth and sea.

### Paul Minchelli
*54 bd La Tour-Maubourg, 7th (01.47.05.89.86).*
*M° La Tour-Maubourg.* **Open** noon-3pm, 7-11pm, Tue-Sat. **Average** 500F. **Credit** MC, V.
Paul Minchelli, a gifted fish cook, is a minimalist, and this Zen outlook makes for superb if expensive eating. Using only the freshest fish and seafood, and adding only the subtlest of seasonings, he offers dishes like a silken *tartare* of scallops and a lobster split open and lightly dressed with honey and pepper. The sleek dining room is accented by a bubbling aquarium, *trompe l'oeil* views, and the showbiz clientele.

### Port Alma
*10 av de New-York, 16th (01.40.70.19.28). M° Alma-*
*Marceau.* **Open** 12.30-2pm, 7.30-10pm, Mon-Sat. **Average** 350F. **Lunch menu** 200F. **Credit** AmEx, DC, MC, V.
Enjoy the view of the Eiffel Tower across the river before you enter. Once inside and seated, Madame Canal will bring a tray of the day's catch. Many preparations have a distinctly modern and Provençal slant, with dishes like perfectly grilled red mullet accompanied by *pistou*.

# Budget

## Chez Max

*47 rue St-Honoré, 1st (01.40.13.06.82). Mº Châtelet-Les Halles.* **Open** noon-2pm, 7.30-11.45pm, Mon-Fri; 7.30-11.45pm Sat. Closed last two weeks Aug. **Prix fixe** 85F, 135F. **Lunch menu** 65F. **Credit** AmEx, MC, V.

Max will tell the indecisive what to order, scold those who let their food get cold and feign offence at anything left uneaten – as well he should, since the food is obviously made from scratch and very tasty, including dishes like homely vegetable soup and hearty *boeuf bourguignon.*

## Gros Minet

*1 rue des Prouvaires, 1st (01.42.33.02.62). Mº Châtelet-Les Halles.* **Open** 11am-2pm, 7pm-midnight, Tue-Fri; 7pm-midnight Mon, Sat. **Average** 150F. **Prix fixe** 95F. **Lunch menu** 78F. **Credit** AmEx, DC, MC, V.

This is the kind of restaurant you dream of stumbling upon as you wander the streets of Paris and, judging by its popularity, many a hungry bargain seeker has done just that. You'll be tempted in by pleasing classics like duck in bilberry sauce and red mullet with basil. Desserts are homely, and cat murals grin down from the walls.

## Chez Madame de ....

*5 rue de Sévigné, 4th (01.42.74.75.90). Mº St-Paul.* **Open** noon-2am Mon-Sat. Closed three weeks Aug, last week Dec. **Average** 100F. **Prix fixe** 66F, 91F. **No credit cards.**

A cross-section of people are drawn to this tiny bare-stone Marais restaurant, which hasn't yet suffered gentrification but has its own quirky style all the same, perhaps something to do with the cheerful young staff. The 66F *menu* provides reliable bargain standards like pâté, *steak frites* and mousse. Carafes of cheap plonk are dispensed from the bar.

**Julien**: *a belle époque legend.*

## Le Petit Gavroche

*15 Ste-Croix-de-la-Bretonnerie, 4th (01.48.87.74.26). Mº Hôtel-de-Ville.* **Open** noon-3pm, 7-11.30pm, Mon-Fri; 7-11.30pm Sat. Aug dinner only. **Average** 100F. **Prix fixe** 48F. **Lunch menu** 45F. **Credit** AmEx, DC, MC, V.

This tiny, unsophisticated old bistro is cheery proof that it is still possible to eat a three-course meal in Paris for under 50F. There is a mood of friendly eccentricity, and the eclectic lunch-time crowd makes dining here a heartwarming experience. Dishes smack of homespun authenticity, like mussels and chips, soused mackerel and goulash with pasta.

## Au P'tit Rémouleur

*2 rue de la Coutellerie, 4th (01.48.04.79.24). Mº Hôtel-de-Ville.* **Open** noon-3pm, 7-10.30pm, Mon-Fri; 7-10.30pm Sat. Closed Aug. **Average** 110F. **Prix fixe** 65F. **Credit** MC, V.

For excellent value in a typically French atmosphere look no further than this cosy little upstairs dining room, run by the friendly Corsican proprietor. Locals and tourists from the provinces come for the laid-back mood and the good-value *formule,* which offers many dishes featured *à la carte.* Typical dishes include the Corsican *pâté de sansonnets* (starling pâté) and *entrecôte grillée aux herbes* with potatoes.

## Les Philosophes

*28 rue Vieille-du-Temple, 4th (01.48.87.49.64). Mº Hôtel-de-Ville.* **Open** noon-2.30pm, 7.30-11pm, Mon-Fri; 7.30-11pm Sat. **Average** 150F. **Prix fixe** 82F, 95F, 128F. **Credit** AmEx, DC, MC, V.

This down-to-earth restaurant in the trendy Marais specialises in all things French, and its menu delivers thoughtfully prepared classics, with a philosophical twist. There's an endless assortment of starter salads, prepared in honour of Plato, Aristotle and other illustrious minds, and main courses such as *cotelette* Spinoza, steak stewed with onions.

## Le Trumilou

*84 quai de l'Hôtel de Ville, 4th (01.42.77.63.98). Mº Hôtel-de-Ville.* **Open** noon-3pm, 7.30-11pm, daily. **Average** 120F. **Prix fixe** 65F, 80F. **Credit** MC, V.

Typically Parisian, this much-loved, 140-year-old institution enables you to dine with a view of Notre Dame and the Panthéon, while the moustachioed *patron,* trophies of wild boar, deer and a lone duck strangely form part of the décor. Dishes include good game dishes in season; duck with prunes is a year-long favourite. A well-considered wine selection.

## L'Ecurie

*2 rue Laplace, 5th (01.46.33.68.49). Mº Maubert-Mutualité.* **Open** noon-3pm, 7pm-midnight, daily. **Average** 130F. **Prix fixe** 98F. **Lunch menu** 75F. **No credit cards.**

This ancient, picturesque Latin Quarter coal and wine depot, with its wood-burning grill at the entrance, medieval floor-plan and vast underground warren used for dining, attracts loyal regulars, tourists and locals for humble bistro fare – mostly steaks in sauces served with *frites.*

## La Petite Hostellerie

*35 rue de la Harpe, 5th (01.43.54.47.12). Mº Cluny-La Sorbonne.* **Open** noon-2pm, 6.30-11pm, Tue-Sat; 6.30-11pm Mon. Closed three weeks Aug. **Average** 120F. **Prix fixe** 59F, 89F. **Lunch menu** 47F, 55F, 70F. **Credit** AmEx, DC, MC, V.

One of the few French restaurants left in the ancient quarter of La Huchette, La Petite Hostellerie, with its French rustic look, is a good place to come for simple food at cheap prices. Typical dishes run to roast or Basque-style chicken or a simple *steak au poivre* and, in season, wild boar stew.

## Bistrot Mazarin

*42 rue Mazarin, 6th (01.43.29.99.01). Mº Odéon.* **Open** 8am-2am daily. **Average** 120F. **Credit** AmEx, MC, V.

Students and gallery owners crowd into this simple, popular Left Bank bistro for its convivial atmosphere, spacious

# WE LOVE ROCK 'N' ROLL !

Lee Rocker

terrace and low prices. Typical of the well-intentioned cooking are baked eggs with cream, lentil salad with Morteau sausage and main courses like *boeuf bourguignon*.

## Polidor

*41 rue Monsieur-Le-Prince, 6th (01.43.26.95.34).*
*M° Odéon.* **Open** noon-2.30pm, 7pm-12.30am, Mon-Sat; 7-11pm Sun. **Average** 90F. **Prix fixe** 100F. **Lunch menu** 55F. **No credit cards**.
A varied crowd of students, locals and tourists squeezes on to long tables in this vintage tobacco-stained dining room in the Left Bank, ordering huge portions of basic and variable French favourites and red *vin ordinaire*, although it's the lively atmosphere that draws rather than the food.

## Restaurant des Beaux-Arts

*11 rue Bonaparte, 6th (01.43.26.92.64).*
*M° St-Germain-des-Prés.* **Open** noon-2.15pm, 7-10.45pm, daily. **Average** 120F. **Prix fixe** 75F. **Lunch menu** 55F. **No credit cards**.
Join the crowds of students from the Fine Arts academy across the street in this modest turn-of-the-century bistro. Dining here is a bit like eating in a college dining hall, but the menu is authentic and honest in its offerings, with dishes like herring with warm potatoes, and *boeuf bourguignon*.

## Café Max

*7 av de la Motte-Picquet, 7th (01.47.05.57.66).*
*M° Latour-Maubourg.* **Open** noon-3pm, 7.30-11pm, Tue-Sat; 7.30pm-midnight Mon. Closed Aug. **Lunch menu** 89F. **Dinner menu** 85F, 115F. **No credit cards**.
It's difficult to get into this little café as media folk tend to book all the tables. The crimson interior soon calms the nerves, and the mix of bric-à-brac on the walls will help distract you from any failings of the cuisine, typified by dishes like piping hot Lyonnais sausage with potatoes and apples.

## Au Pied du Fouet

*45 rue de Babylone, 7th (01.47.05.12.27).*
*M° Vaneau.* **Open** noon-2.30pm, 7-9.45pm, Mon-Fri; noon-2.30pm Sat. Closed Aug, last week Dec. **Average** 75F. **No credit cards**.
This place pulls a clubby crowd of regulars which comes for the friendliness of the patron and his wife and for the simple, sincere food served in this tiny dining room. The short menu runs to classics like *oeuf mayonnaise*, sautéed chicken livers and *confit de canard*. Homemade desserts.

## La Rivaldière

*1 rue St-Simon, 7th (01.45.48.53.96). M° Solférino.*
**Open** 12.15-2.30pm, 7-10.30pm, Mon-Fri; 7-10.30pm Sat. **Average** 150F. **Prix fixe** 100F. **Credit** V.
This charming, cosy bistro, with its creaky wood floors, cushy *banquettes* and high ceilings, is the place to sample French nursery favourites. The menu changes daily, but runs to starters like cream of tomato soup and main courses like curried beef with rice or scallops with lentils.

## Chartier

*7 rue du Fbg-Montmartre, 9th (01.47.70.86.29).*
*M° Rue Montmartre.* **Open** 11am-3pm, 6-10pm, daily. **Average** 80F. **Credit** MC, V.
Don't come to this vast old *bouillon* – a sort of turn-of-the-century soup kitchen – for top-notch food, but for the experience of traditional canteen eating in beautiful period decor. Expect simple French classics like roast quail or *steak frites* and don't be surprised that the *dessert de fruits* is simply a banana, apple or orange plonked on a plate.

## A l'Ami Pierre

*5 rue de la Main-d'Or, 11th (01.47.00.17.35).*
*M° Ledru-Rollin.* **Open** noon-midnight Tue-Sat. **Average** 100F. **Credit** MC, V.
The initiated come for the well-prepared, inexpensive food

served at this simple wine bar-cum-bistro well hidden down a cobbled alleyway. Service is amiable; this is a place to linger rather than hurry. The *boeuf bourguignon* beats most and wine is by the *compteur* – you pay for what you drink.

## L'Ebauchoir

*43-45 rue de Cîteaux, 12th (01.43.42.49.31). M° Faidherbe-Chaligny.* **Open** noon-2.30pm, 8-11pm, Mon-Sat. **Average** 150F. **Lunch menu** 66F, 75F. **Credit** MC, V.
Packed with simple wooden tables and bentwood chairs, this extremely popular local favourite has the mood of a busy, unpretentious dining hall with none of the posey 'scene' of the nearby Bastille. The cooking has recently improved and offers exceptional value, although with only a limited choice on the *menu*, you may sometimes be forced *à la carte*.

## Chez Gladine

*30 rue des Cinq Diamants, 13th (01.45.80.70.10).*
*M° Corvisart.* **Open** noon-3pm, 7pm-2am, daily. Closed Aug, last week Dec. **Average** 90F. **Lunch menu** 60F. **No credit cards**.
Located in the villagey Butte-aux-Cailles, Gladine's has become an institution in just four years. Young people crowd its two tiny rooms every night for a communal party with a Basque flavour, reflected by the regional memorabila and the mainly Basque cuisine, typified by a *pipérade Basquaise*.

## Café du Commerce

*51 rue du Commerce, 15th (01.45.75.03.27). M° Emile Zola.* **Open** noon-midnight daily. **Average** 140F. **Prix fixe** 85F, 115F. **Credit** AmEx, DC, MC, V.
Set around a plant-hung atrium (the glass roof retracts in summer), this spacious three-level 1920s dining hall was originally a *bouillon* for the hungry working classes. Now a little more upmarket, the home cooking is ample and proficient, with dishes like *steak tartare, confit de canard, entrecôte* or sticky honeyed pork ribs, and wines are pleasantly affordable. A good place to come with a group of friends.

## Ty Breiz

*52 bd de Vaugirard, 15th (01.43.20.83.72).*
*M° Montparnasse-Bienvenüe.* **Open** 11.45am-3pm, 7-11pm, Mon-Sat. Closed first three weeks Aug. **Average** 100F. **Credit** MC, V.
This cheerful, bustling Breton *crêperie* is no place to linger, but provides quick, friendly service and satisfying light meals. Savoury buckwheat *galettes* are the speciality here, and include the classic *complète*, with ham, egg and gruyère. Dessert crêpe fillings range from the simple to the exotic. Breton cider is served in earthenware mugs.

## L'Etoile Verte

*13 rue Brey, 17th (01.43.80.69.34). M° Charles de Gaulle-Etoile.* **Open** 11.30am-3pm, 6.30-10.45pm, daily. **Average** 100F. **Prix fixe** 100F, 145F. **Credit** AmEx, DC, MC, V.
This deliberately anonymous restaurant feels like a throwback to the 1970s, right down to the pine panelling and mirrors. But the kitchen tries harder than most at this price, with well-presented classics such as snails, oysters, hare and even dogfish (or 'hound-shark' as the menu translates it).

## Au Rendez-vous des Chauffeurs

*11 rue des Portes-Blanches, 18th (01.42.64.04.17).*
*M° Marcadet-Poissonniers.* **Open** noon-2.30pm, 7-10.30pm, Mon, Tue, Thur, Fri; noon-3pm, 7-10.30pm, Sat, Sun. **Average** 100F. **Prix fixe** 63F (until 8.30pm, not Sun). **Credit** MC, V.
Down an unpromising street behind Montmartre, the checked tablecloths, zinc counter, wholesome posters of the French regions and warm crowd are a relief. The numerous English regulars here are attracted both by the patron's mastery of English and the simple but appealing dishes, including generous helpings of delicious pâté and *andouillette*.

# See and be scene

### Café Marly
*93 rue de Rivoli, Cour Napoléon du Louvre, 1st
(01.49.26.06.60). M° Palais-Royal.* **Open** 8am-2am
daily. **Credit** AmEx, DC, MC, V.
The Costes brothers (of Café Beaubourg fame) opened
Café Marly in 1994 and it's been one of the chicest rendezvous in Paris ever since, but then it is in the Louvre.
Deep red walls and a witty chandelier cleverly combine
historic and contemporary. Salads and steaks are pass-
able, if pricey, but décor, crowd and view are wonderful.

### Hôtel Costes
*239 rue St-Honoré, 1st (01.42.44.50.25). M° Concorde.*
**Open** noon-midnight daily. **Average** 250F.
The Costes brothers did it again with this trendy hotel
restaurant. Big guns of fashion, advertising and media –
Christophe Lambert and Antoine de Caunes – hang out
here. Modish food caters to cigar-smoking men and calo-
rie-obsessed ladies. *See also chapter* **Accommodation**.

### Le 404
*69 rue des Gravilliers, 3rd (01.42.74.57.81). M° Arts
et Métiers.* **Open** noon-3pm, 8pm-midnight, Mon-Sat;
noon-4pm Sun. Closed Aug. **Average** 220F. **Lunch
menu** 59F, 79F, 119F. **Credit** AmEx, DC, MC, V.
A showbiz set comes to comedian Smain's restaurant with
its Moorish interior and Algerian music. The North
African menu specialises in couscous and *tagines*. Book.

### Le Buddha Bar
*8 rue Boissy d'Anglas, 8th (01.53.05.90.00).
M° Concorde.* **Open** 12.30-2.30pm, 7.30pm-12.15am,
Mon-Sat. **Average** 275F.

The cavernous, new subterranean rendezvous for *le tout
Paris.* A giant buddha dominates the interior, as does the
clientele of actors, models and designers (Isabelle Adjani,
Naomi Campbell). Cooking is Pacific Rim and a bit uneven.

### Thai Elephant
*43-45 rue de la Roquette, 11th (01.47.00.42.00). M°
Bastille.* **Open** noon-2.30pm, 7pm-midnight, Mon-Fri,
Sun; 7pm-midnight Sat. **Average** 250F. **Prix fixe**
275F. **Lunch menu** 150F. **Credit** AmEx, DC, MC, V.
This beautiful Thai place near the Bastille is a magnet for
celebrities (Catherine Deneuve, Prince Albert of Monaco).
Portions are small, and seasonings tempered to protect
delicate palates. Dress up and book ahead.

### Natacha
*17bis rue Campagne-Première, 14th (01.43.20.79.27).
M° Raspail.* **Open** 8pm-1am Mon-Sat. Closed Aug.
**Average** 200F. **Credit** AmEx, MC, V.
People (Mick Jagger, Mickey Rourke) come here late and
stay till very late for the buzz of going where others go,
and for the flattering attention bestowed by dynamic hostess Natacha. Cooking is more than decent, with dishes like
chèvre-filled ravioli and sautéed rabbit.

### Zebra Square
*3 pl Clément-Ader, 16th (01.44.14.91.91). RER
Kennedy-Radio France.* **Open** 8am-2am daily. **Average**
225F. **Lunch menu** 100F. **Credit** AmEx, DC, MC, V.
This has become the 1990s canteen for TV and radio people, given its position next to the Maison de la Radio and
its slick interior, with ebony parquet and subdued lighting. Food is an exemplary rundown of currently fashionable French *terroir* with a few international excursions.

*Spot the models from the galleried bar at New Age rendezvous* **Le Buddha Bar**.

# U.S.A FOOD & BAR

EST 1981

CACTUS CHARLY

PARIS

# TEX MEX STYLE

**Brunch on Saturdays and Sundays,
noon till 4p.m.**

**Happy Hour everyday 5.30p.m till 7.00p.m.**

**Home Delivery Service Phone : 01.45.67.64.99.**

# REGULAR PARTY NIGHTS
# WITH LIVE MUSIC

**68 rue de Ponthieu, Paris 8th. Tel : 01.45.62.01.77**

**Open from noon till 2a.m, 7 days a week.**

## International

# The Americas

### Joe Allen

*30 rue Pierre-Lescot, 1st (01.42.36.70.13). M° Etienne-Marcel.* **Open** noon-2am daily. **Average** 150F. **Credit** AmEx, MC, V.

Located in the once-trendy Les Halles area, this Paris outpost of the New York theatre haunt has improved its neo-American cuisine. The Caesar salad, ribs and famous burger are still there, but dishes like grilled 'jerk' chicken marinated in lime juice, garlic and cinammon are a far cry from hackneyed Yankee stereotypes. Interesting American wine list.

### Le Studio

*41 rue du Temple, 4th (01.42.74.10.38). M° Hôtel-de-Ville.* **Open** 7.30pm-midnight daily; 12.30-3pm Sat, Sun. **Average** 140F. **Prix fixe** 100F. **Credit** AmEx, MC, V.

The popularity of this Marais restaurant set in a magnificent seventeenth-century courtyard has little to do with its food. The predictable Tex-Mex fare is okay, if uninspired, but the atmosphere is often electric, thanks to the international fashion crowd who come here. Stick with Mexican beer, or the very good and admirably strong Margaritas.

### Haynes Restaurant

*3 rue Clauzel, 9th (01.48.78.40.63). M° St-Georges.* **Open** 7pm-12.30am Tue-Sat. Closed Aug. **Average** 150F. **Credit** MC, V.

Opened by GI LeRoy Haynes in 1949, this cosy restaurant specialises in African-American soul-food, typified by a tasty New Orleans gumbo, a colourful, spicy stew with shrimps, chicken, okra and rice. This place fills up at weekends for live jazz (from 9pm) – book for groups of more than four.

# Italian

### Il Ristorantino

*9 rue d'Argenteuil, 1st (01.42.60.56.22). M° Pyramides or Palais Royal.* **Open** noon-2pm, 8-10.25pm, Mon-Fri; 8-10.25pm Sat. **Average** 250F. **Prix fixe** 140F. **Credit** AmEx, DC, MC, V.

Ciro Polge, the new chef at the former Paolo Petrini, is very good, and in a gesture to the reality of the times, he's introduced a three-course menu at 140F, although the most tempting dishes like *fettucine* with a generous mound of fish and shellfish in a deeply marine tomato sauce are found *à la carte*. The wine list, though excellent, remains very pricey.

### L'Enoteca

*25 rue Charles V, 4th (01.42.78.91.44). M° St-Paul.* **Open** noon-2.30pm daily; 7.30-11.30pm Mon-Thur; 3pm-midnight Fri-Sun. Closed one week Aug. **Average** 150F. **Lunch menu** 95F. **Credit** MC, V.

Italian wines may have inspired the name, but one look at the *antipasti* table explains its success. The unfailingly authentic northern Italian cooking usually includes dishes like *insalata misti*, sprinkled with fresh herbs and shaved parmesan. Meat dishes are invariably good.

### Da Mimmo

*39 bd Magenta, 10th (01.42.06.44.47). M° Gare de l'Est.* **Open** noon-2.30pm, 7-11.30pm, Mon-Sat. Closed Aug. **Average** 180F. **Lunch menu** 95F. **Credit** MC, V.

A brightly lit, banal dining room disguises the most bubbling Italian *trattoria* in town, and draws a talkative, fashionable crowd of Italians, French and other nationalities. Although there is a menu, dishes are just as likely to be described and specially concocted for you by a squadron of waiters and chefs. The real Italian pizzas are excellent.

# Japanese

### Higuma

*32 rue Ste-Anne, 1st (01.47.03.38.59). M° Pyramides.* **Open** 11.30am-10pm daily. Closed two weeks Jan, July or Aug. **Average** 70F. **Prix fixe** 63F, 65F, 70F. **No credit cards.**

This is the most popular Japanese ramen noodle bar in town, attracting a lively mix of Asian and French customers, as well as visiting Japanese celebrities. The enormous servings, flexible hours, excellent value and relaxed atmosphere are the main draw here. Smoking and non-smoking rooms.

### Jipangue

*96 rue La Boétie, 8th (01.45.63.77.00). M° St-Philippe-du-Roule.* **Open** noon-2pm, 7-11pm, Mon-Fri; 7-11pm Sat. Closed two weeks end July/early Aug.

*The proprietor of **La Rivaldière** is justifiably proud of his wines.*

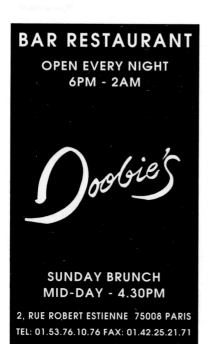

**Average** 200F. **Prix fixe** 120F, 125F, 175F, 245F.
**Lunch menu** 85F. **Credit** AmEx, MC, V.
This airy restaurant, on a busy corner in a smart business district, offers authentic Japanese favourites. The satisfying *menus* include soup, salad, a choice of stir-fried meat or sushi. Upstairs is a Korean-inflected 'barbecue', while downstairs is devoted to raw fish. Service can be rushed.

### Kifuné
*44 rue St-Ferdinand, 17th (01.45.72.11.19).*
*M° Argentine.* **Open** noon-2pm, 7-10pm, Tue-Sat; 7-10pm Mon. Closed two weeks Aug, two weeks in winter.
**Average** 400F. **Lunch menu** 135F. **Credit** MC, V.
Good sushi is almost never a bargain in Paris, but Kifuné is a glorious exception, and compares favourably to restaurants in Tokyo – it even signposts itself in Japanese only. Here you'll find the usual salmon, halibut, mackerel, sea bream and more esoteric eel, abalone and octopus, all of an impeccable freshness. The lunch menu is fairly affordable but the evening *à la carte* bill can be nearly twice as high.

## Jewish

### Chez Marianne
*2 rue des Hospitalières-St-Gervais, 4th (01.42.72.18.86).*
*M° St-Paul.* **Open** 11.30am-midnight daily. **Average** 55F-95F. **Credit** MC, V.
Marianne runs a simple corner restaurant, packing a bubbling crowd into her delicatessen shop and next-door dining room. The menu offers a wide choice of the delicatessen's cold Central European-Jewish food like felafel, aubergine purée, hummous and tzatziki. Wines are good value.

### Jo Goldenberg
*7 rue des Rosiers, 4th (01.48.87.20.16/01.48.87.70.39).*
*M° St-Paul.* **Open** noon-midnight daily. **Average** 150F.
**Credit** AmEx, DC, MC, V.
Jo Goldenberg's is an institution, and like many institutions its pull has as much to do with history and sentiment as with food. Take a look at the photos outside to get an idea: JG with Mitterrand after the 1982 terrorist bomb, with politicians and film stars. The usual assortment of cold deli fare is available (chopped chicken liver, chopped egg, taramasalata, herring, stuffed vine leaves, caviar, etc), while hot dishes take in most of Central and Eastern Europe.

## Oriental

### Chez Rosine
*12 rue du Mont-Thabor, 1st (01.49.27.09.23). M° Tuileries.*
**Open** noon-2.30pm, 7.30-11pm Tue-Sat; 7.30-11pm, Mon.
Closed Aug. **Average** 200F. **Prix fixe** 98F, 148F, 198F, 298F. **Lunch menu** 76F. **Credit** AmEx, MC, V.
Chez Rosine's setting among a cluster of ultra-luxury hotels seems at odds with the owner Rosine's gregarious character. From her native Cambodia, she has brought not so much a cuisine but a style of cooking and is quick to adapt to new ingredients: the *côtes d'agneau* is an East-meets-West triumph of marinated, grilled lamb with peanut sauce. There are also traditional Khmer dishes like steamed dumplings, chicken with ginger and giant crayfish in coral sauce.

### Le Moï
*5 rue Daunou, 2nd (01.47.03.92.05). M° Opéra.*
**Open** noon-3pm, 7-10.30pm Mon-Fri. **Average** 150F.
**Lunch menu** 80F. **Credit** AmEx, DC, MC, V.
This family-run restaurant founded in 1966 moved next to Harry's Bar in 1994. Le Moï delivers the traditional village recipes of Vietnam, beautifully executed with top ingredients, typified by dishes like *bi-cuôn*, five-flavoured pork rolls, and grilled chicken drumstick with lemon grass. Pith helmets and bamboo mats add a neo-colonial cool.

### Mirama
*17 rue St-Jacques, 5th (01.43.54.71.77). M° St-Michel.*
**Open** noon-10.45pm daily. **Average** 100F. **Credit** , V.
This teeming Chinese duplex provides a striking visual experience, as diners peer through a window at the back into a bright kitchen where shining ducks are strung up against the back wall, and frisky staff wield chopper and wok. Duck, reputed to be a speciality here, is nothing special, and there is no Peking duck, but the noodle soups are excellent.

### La Chine Masséna
*Centre Commercial Masséna, 13 pl de Vénétie, 13th (01.45.83.98.88). M° Porte de Choisy.* **Open** 9am-11.30pm Mon-Thur; 9am-1am Fri-Sun. **Average** 90F. **Lunch menu** 52F, 78F, 88F. **Credit** MC, V.
This huge, 400-seat dim sum restaurant, wedged in a canyon of high-rise apartments, is a fun place to eat, with food that is delicious, diverse and well-priced, and décor that has gone beyond the limits of taste. The epic menu (including English translations) covers some 280 dishes, including Cantonese, Szechuan, Hunan, Peking and Thai specialities. There's dancing and a pan-Asian variety show on weekend evenings. *Wheelchair access.*

### Lao Siam
*49 rue de Belleville, 19th (01.40.40.09.68). M° Belleville.*
**Open** noon-11.15pm daily. **Average** 100F. **Credit** V.
Serving a hybrid of Chinese, Laotian and Thai cooking, this is one of Belleville's most reliable and fairly priced restaurants. Unfortunately the vast menu gives little description of what's on offer, so point or ask the helpful staff. Specify if you want your order spicy-hot ('*très bien pimenté*').

### Tricotin
*15 av de Choisy, 13th (01.45.84.74.44). M° Port d'Italie.*
**Open** 9am-11.30pm daily. **Average** 100F. **Credit** V.
Most of the regulars at this extremely popular, rough-and-tumble place among the tower blocks of the 13th *arrondissement* Chinatown eat *phô*, or Vietnamese-style noodles in soup, a meal in itself at 35F, to start, followed by the *canard aux cinq parfums* and the delicious sautéed prawns.

*Ducks on display at* **Mirama**.

# The Maghreb

With the large immigrant population, North African food is perhaps the most typical foreign cuisine in Paris. As well as homely couscous, look out for refined *tagines* and *pastille*.

### Chez Omar

*47 rue de Bretagne, 3rd (01.42.72.36.26). M° Arts et Métiers.* **Open** noon-3pm, 7-11.30pm, Mon-Sat; 7-11.30pm Sun. **Average** 110F. **No credit cards.**
Equally adored by artists, gallery-folk and media types, this lovely vintage bistro always hums with a friendly buzz, carefully stoked by the genial Omar himself. Splendid meat-laden *couscous royal* or *méchoui*, and a feast of sticky North African sweets.

### Atlas

*12 bd St-Germain, 5th (01.46.33.86.98). M° Maubert-Mutualité.* **Open** noon-2.30pm, 7.15-11pm, daily. **Average** 180F. **Credit** AmEx, MC, V.

This purveyor of '*nouvelle cuisine marocaine*' is class through and through. Homely dishes like mint and barley broth share space on the menu with fanciful *tagines* involving duck, pigeon and veal sweetbreads.

### Chez Hamedi

*12 rue Boutebrie, 5th (01.43.54.03.30). M° Cluny-La Sorbonne.* **Open** noon-3pm, 6pm-midnight, daily. **Average** 80F. **Prix fixe** 112F. **No credit cards.**
In a prime Latin Quarter location, this reliable, tiny family-fun restaurant, decorated with old travel posters and souvenirs of Tunisia, serves up ample bowls of fine, very affordable couscous.

### Le Mansouria

*11 rue Faidherbe, 11th (01.43.71.00.16). M° Faidherbe-Chaligny.* **Open** noon-2.30pm Tue-Sat; 7.30-11pm Mon-Thur; 7.30-11.30pm Fri, Sat. **Average** 200F. **Prix fixe** 168F, 280F. **Lunch menu** 105F. **Credit** MC, V.
With its sleek mix of modern and Moorish, fashionable Mansouria is by far the most upmarket place on this street, appreciated for its refined, classical North African cuisine and the welcome of owner and author Fatima Hal. The cooking, mainly *pastilla* and *tagines*, recalls the grander restaurants of Marrakesh, and uses typical Moroccan sweet and savoury combinations.

# Other

### African: Le Petit Chartier

*103 av Parmentier, 11th (01.43.57.72.35). M° Parmentier.* **Open** 8pm-1.30am Tue-Sat. **Average** 130F. **Credit** MC, V.
The Petit Chartier has moved to smarter premises which seem to make the old crowd of world music fans and African taxi drivers slightly awkward. The female clan members turn out excellent Malian *yassa*, *thieb'oudjen* (fish with seasoned rice) and chicken smothered in peanut-based *maffé* sauce. The ginger drink – when loaded with rum – is a head-spinning organic pick-me-up. Live ensemble at weekends.

### Belgian: Bouillon Racine

*3 rue Racine, 6th (01.44.32.15.60). M° Odéon.* **Open** 10am-2am Mon-Sat. **Average** 160F. **Prix fixe** 78F, 108F. **Credit** MC, V.
Originally founded by Camille Chartier, this *belle époque* '*bouillon*' on the Left Bank has been splendidly renovated by a young Belgian entrepreneur and reopened in autumn 1996. Young chef Olivier Simon has concocted a very good, gently priced Flemish menu, with traditional dishes like *waterzooi*, a savoury Belgian chicken and vegetable stew. Beer is the house quaff with a great choice of on-tap and bottled abbey beers. Booking essential.

### British: Bertie's

*Hôtel Baltimore, 1 rue Léo-Delibes, 16th (01.44.34.54.34). M° Boissière.* **Open** 12.30-2pm, 7.30-10.30pm daily. Closed two weeks in Aug. **Average** 250F. **Prix fixe** 195F. **Lunch menu** 160F. **Credit** AmEx, DC, MC, V.
Bertie's is devoted to much-derided British cuisine and won the 1995 Marco Polo award for best foreign restaurant in Paris. Brittany-born Albert Roux supervises the menu, and Londoner Simon Gayle runs the kitchens, ensuring the use of British ingredients. Kentish lamb is served with mint sauce (unheard of in France), cheese is served English style at the end, while the wine list remains reassuringly French.

### Caribbean: La Table D'Erica

*6 rue Mabillon, 6th (01.43.54.87.61). M° Mabillon.* **Open** 7.30pm-midnight Mon-Sat. Closed Aug. **Average** 220F. **Prix fixe** 140F. **Credit** AmEx, MC, V.
Search out this small restaurant next to the reopened St-Germain market, for its gracious sophisticated atmosphere and excellent food. Serving some of the best West Indian food in Paris, typical dishes may include a classic *boudin créole* and *crabe farci*, and more unusual delights like *coquelet du Pirate*, smoked roast cockerel with a very spicy sauce.

### Greek: Mavrommatis

*42 rue Daubenton, 5th (01.43.31.17.17). M° Censier-Daubenton.* **Open** 7.30-11pm Tue-Sun; noon-2pm Sat, Sun. **Average** 200F. **Prix fixe** 140F, 165F (groups of 4 or more). **Credit** MC, V.
This elegant corner restaurant is worlds away in terms of refinement from the plate-smashing, bouzouki-strumming rue Mouffetard Greeks. The chef is interested in creative combos of the region's ingredients, like quail roasted in grape leaves with honey and thyme. Mavrommatis' original taverna Les Délices d'Aphrodite (4 rue de Candolle, 5th/01.43.31.40.39) offers good, but less elaborate cuisine.

### Indian: Shalamar

*59 passage Brady, rue du Fbg St-Denis, 10th (01.45.23.31.61). M° Strasbourg-St-Denis.* **Open** noon-3pm, 6pm-3.30am daily. **Average** 100F. **Prix fixe** 75F, 95F. **Credit** MC, V.
In a low-lit arcade off rue du Fbg-St-Denis, the Shalamar nestles amid a cluster of Indian cafés, shops and gaudy restaurants, where well-dressed French customers drink wine rather than lager and gingerly dig into the spicy food. Dishes are cooked to your specifications, although 'medium' is closer to 'very mild' by British Indian restaurant standards.

### Indian: Shah Jahan

*4 rue Gauthey, 17th (01.42.63.44.06). M° Brochant.* **Open** noon-2.30pm, 7-11.30pm, daily. **Average** 100F. **Prix fixe** 115F, 130F. **Lunch menu** 49F. **Credit** AmEx, MC, V.
This reliable and popular Pakistani restaurant serves up generous, authentic fare amid flashy Moghul paintings and traditional muzak. Sample the *dhal*, five vegetable curries, or *biryani* prepared with 25 different spices and the home-made pistachio *kulfi* is outstanding. Prompt, polite service. **Branches:** Les Jardins de Shah Jahan, 179 rue de Vaugirard, 15th (01.47.34.09.62); Le Palais Shah Jahan, 16 rue des Quatres-Frères-Peignot, 15th (01.45.78.21.07).

### Portuguese: Saudade

*34 rue des Bourdonnais, 1st (01.42.36.30.71). M° Châtelet-Les Halles.* **Open** noon-2pm Mon-Sat; Sat 7.30-10.30pm Mon-Thur; 7.30-11pm Fri. **Average** 200F. **Lunch menu** 129F. **Credit** AmEx, MC, V.
This charming Portuguese restaurant, with its blue and white *azuelos* tiles, recorded *fado* music and proud courtly service, offers rustic Portuguese dishes like *caldo verde*, a robust soup of stock, potatoes, kale, chorizo and olive oil. The Portuguese have 365 different ways of preparing cod: the menu dedicates a whole page to it. The wine list is a treat.

### Russian: Dominique

*19 rue Bréa, 6th (01.43.27.08.80). M° Vavin.* **Open** 12.30-2.30pm Tue-Sat; 7.15-11.30pm, Mon-Sat. Closed mid-July-mid-Aug. **Average** 180F. Prix fixe 170F. **Lunch menu** 150F (at bar only). **Credit** AmEx, DC, MC, V.
This institution has enlivened the Montparnasse landscape since the 1920s flood of post-revolution Russian refugees. Caviar, the speciality here, is currently astronomical at 135F for 35g. Other than borscht, hot dishes mainly run to grilled kebabs, but the best bet are the various *zakousky* (cold assortments). There are more than 40 vodkas (35F a shot).

## Vegetarian

### Country Life

*6 rue Daunou, 2nd (01.42.97.48.51). M° Opéra.* **Open** 11.30am-2.30pm, 6.30-10pm, Mon-Fri. **Prix fixe** 65F. **Credit** MC, V.
Close to the opulent Opéra, this austere self-service restaurant offers a sustaining daily *menu* of as much wholefood as you can eat. Desserts and soft drinks are extra. No alcohol.

### Piccolo Teatro

*6 rue des Ecouffes, 4th (01.42.72.17.79). M° St-Paul.* **Open** noon-3pm, 7-11pm, Tue-Sun. **Average** 90F. **Prix fixe** 90F, 115. **Lunch menu** 45F (Tue-Fri), 55F. **Credit** AmEx, MC, V.
Tiny, ill-lit and prone to blackouts, this cellar-like restaurant has a calm, unhurried atmosphere, and offers *gratins*, Greek-influenced dishes and English- and French-style desserts.

### La Truffe

*31 rue Vieille-du-Temple, 4th (01.42.71.08.39). M° Hôtel-de-Ville.* Open noon-3pm, 6-11pm, daily. **Average** 100F. **Lunch menu** 59F. **Credit** MC, V.
This innovative place in the Marais is arguably the most expensive and refined veggie (no meat or fish) restaurant in Paris. Mushrooms are a speciality. Stunning desserts contain no refined sugar, but dairy products and eggs are used.

### La Petite Légume

*36 rue des Boulangers, 5th (01.40.46.06.85). M° Jussieu.* **Open** noon-2.30pm, 7.30-10pm, Mon-Sat. **Average** 70F. **Lunch menu** 50F, 68F, 75F. **Credit** AmEx, MC, V.
Tucked in a corner of the Latin Quarter, this rustic, family-run restaurant uses dairy products and the occasional non-organic ingredient for exceptionally varied *assiettes complètes*, homemade *tourtes*, and a vegetarian *pot-au-feu*.

### Les Quatre et Une Saveurs

*72 rue du Cardinal-Lemoine, 5th (01.43.26.88.80). M° Cardinal-Lemoine.* **Open** noon-2pm, 7-10.30pm, Tue-Sun. **Average** 100F. **Prix fixe** 105F-115F. **Credit** AmEx, MC, V.
This splendid, Japanese-inspired place (miso and vegetable soups), just off place de la Contrescarpe, is rigorously macrobiotic: no dairy, no eggs, no sugar, 100 per cent organic.

### Le Bol en Bois

*35 rue Pascal, 13th (01.47.07.27.24). M° Gobelins.* **Open** noon-2.30pm, 7-10pm, Mon-Sat. **Dinner menu** 125F. **Lunch menu** 62F (Mon-Fri). **Credit** MC, V.
Paris' oldest hard-core macrobiotic restaurant favours Japanese accents in its cuisine, and virtually everything is organic. It uses no dairy products, sugar or eggs, and serves dishes like miso soup and *wakame* salad of seaweed.

### Aquarius

*40 rue de Gergovie, 14th (01.45.41.36.88). M° Pernéty.* **Open** noon-2.15pm, 7-10.30pm, Mon-Sat. **Average** 85F. **Lunch menu** 60F. **Credit** MC, V.
Only meat is excluded at this cheerful Paris institution, resulting in the broadest vegetarian menu in town. Dishes include lasagne, omelettes, vegetarian chili and aubergine-filled ravioli and the desserts are smashing. **Branch:** 54 rue Ste-Croix-de-la-Bretonnerie, 4th (01.48.87.48.71).

**Bouillon Racine**, *a Belgian renaissance.*

**CAFÉ CHARBON**

'Le plus parisien des cafés parisiens'
Open 7 days a week, 9am-2am Lunch every day,
noon-5pm. Brunch Saturday and Sunday
109 rue Oberkampf 11th Tel:01 43 57 55 1

# Cafés & Bars

**Paris' cafés and bars are still the best place to sit, browse through the papers and chat over a drink.**

If images of St-Germain café society at the **Café de Flore** are surprisingly enduring, wily entrepreneurs are adapting to the demands of the 1990s, as new areas and styles take off. The most evident trend is for bars with DJs, while Irish pubs continue to spring up all over town, and Latino and tapas bars also becoming popular. Destroy décor and recuperation are *à la mode*, joining Art Nouveau, Art Deco, 1950s plastic as distinctive café style.

Many cafés change function over the course of a day – '*café-tabac-brasserie-bar à vins-salon de thé*' – as customers whizz by for a quick coffee and croissant at the counter for breakfast, pile in at noon for a three-course lunch *menu*, relax over a newspaper in the mid-afternoon, or philosophise over a beer by night. Some of the hippest recent arrivals like **Café Charbon** or **Café de la Musique** have mastered this cameleon-like skill.

Every few months in *Le Monde* or one of the other French dailies, there's an article about the café crisis as they succumb to high drinks prices, the shorter lunch hour, the TV dinner and the onslaught of fast-food chains. But crisis, if there is one, is far more evident in the dead villages of the Ile de France, than in Paris intra-muros, where there are still almost 10,000 cafés and bars, beating any other European city.

Here we've chosen a selection of classic cafés, hip new bars and the best locals, but you're also sure to discover the pleasant local corner café or the tiny bar which can squeeze only a handful of people round the zinc. Note that prices are generally lowest standing at the bar, slightly higher seated inside and highest on the terrace outside. Prices often go up by about 2F after 10pm. Happy hours still tend to be most common in Anglo and Irish-style pubs. As well as beers, most cafés offer wines, spirits, coffee, light snacks and often economical meals, especially at lunch. Except in various Irish/Anglo bars, beers on tap (*pression*) are usually served as a *demi* (25cl).

## Cafés

### Bar de l'Entr'acte
*47 rue Montpensier, 1st (01.42.97.57.76). M° Pyramides.* **Open** 11am-2am Mon-Sat. **No credit cards.**
Hidden away in a sidestreet next to the Palais-Royal, this café has been around for centuries. Actors and spectators throng the bar for a nightcap after a performance at the nearby Comédie Française and Théâtre du Palais-Royal.

### Café de l'Epoque
*2 rue du Bouloi, 1st (01.42.33.40.70). M° Palais-Royal.* **Open** 7am-9pm Mon-Sat. Closed Sun. **Credit** MC, V.
Forget the glazed front that overlooks the main road, for the facade opening on to historic Galerie Véro Dodat is an attractive series of wooden-framed arches and the high-ceiling interior displays all the classic Parisian hallmarks of tall mirrors, plush upholstery and *pâtisserie* display cabinets.

### L'Apparement Café
*18 rue des Coutures-St-Gervais, 3rd (01.48.87.12.22). M° St-Sébastien-Froissart.* **Open** noon-2am Mon-Fri; 4pm-2am Sat; 12.30pm-midnight Sun. **Credit** DC, MC, V.
There's no better place to laze away an afternoon than in this dimly lit, laid-back café which is trendy without trying too hard. The name is a play on the French words for 'apparently' and 'apartment'; its various homely rooms, furnished with portraits and fleamarket bric-à-brac, are named after rooms in an apartment, like 'salon' and 'library'.

### Le Baromètre
*17 rue Charlot, 3rd (01.48.87.04.54). M° St-Sébastien-Froissart.* **Open** 7am-9.30pm Mon-Fri. Closed Aug. **Credit** MC, V.
This local café proudly boasts the 1993 Bouteille d'Or award, the wine equivalent of the Oscars. Bunches of plastic grapes decorate the bar, with fresh flowers here and there adding more colour. The choice of regional wines is impressive.

### Web Bar
*32 rue de Picardie, 3rd (01.42.72.65.55). M° République.* **Open** 11.30am-2am daily. **Credit** MC, V.

## Critics' choice

**Café Beaubourg** Sleek style, still. *See p162.*
**Café Oz** Down-under beers and conviviality with Aboriginal murals to boot. *See p167.*
**La Chaise au Plafond** Classic café revisited with funky loos. *See p162.*
**China Club** Sleek setting for sophisticated cocktails. *See p170.*
**Flèche d'Or** Art chic and ents. *See p170.*
**Jip's** Latino psychedelia. *See p166.*
**Mosquée de Paris** Oriental calm. *See p172.*
**Moulin à Vin** Great wines, bistro food and friendly Montmartre crowd. *See p171.*
**La Palette** Beautiful artists' café. *See p163.*
**Pause Café** Hipsters' lunch spot. *See p165.*
**Le Rouquet** A galaxy of genuine 1950s plastic and neon. *See p163.*
**Le Select** Relic of Montparnasse. *See p163.*

The net *plus ultra* of internet bars is more than just a cyberspace. The trendy galleried venue was once a goldsmith's workshop and today funky furniture, cool music, a neat menu, art and videos give it that touch of Marais art chic. Weekend brunch is followed by world groove concerts.

## Bar de Jarente

*5 rue de Jarente, 4th (01.48.87.60.93). Mº St-Paul.* **Open** 6.45am-10pm Mon-Sat. Closed Aug. **No credit cards.**
The delightful *patronne* has been running this tiny stone bar on place du Marché-Ste-Catherine almost as long as she's been running her husband, who obediently tends bar. Places like these make it possible to get away from Paris without going too far – a young, unpretentious crowd comes here to relax and to sample the simple food and cheap beer.

## Café Beaubourg

*100 rue St-Martin, 4th (01.48.87.63.96). Mº Hôtel-de-Ville/RER Châtelet-Les Halles.* **Open** 8am-1am daily. **Credit** AmEx, DC, MC, V.
Sleek, civilised and sophisticated, in prime position opposite the Centre Pompidou, the Costes brothers' stylish two-level contemporary reinvention of the classic café was designed by Christian de Portzamparc with a post-modernity that has aged well. Members of the art world and other fashionable types come to sit, browse through the papers and chat. The food includes very good salads and excellent desserts.

## La Perla

*26 rue François-Miron, 4th (01.42.77.59.40). Mº St-Paul.* **Open** noon-2am daily; happy hour 6-8pm Mon-Fri. **Credit** AmEx, DC, MC, V.
Connoisseurs of tequila and killer margaritas pack this popular Mexican spot. Weaker constitutions can settle for a bottle of Mexican beer and an array of Mexican snacks.

## Café du Trésor

*5-7 rue du Trésor, 4th (01.44.78.06.60). Mº Hôtel-de-Ville.* **Open** 8am-2am daily. **Credit** V.
Situated in a picturesque cul-de-sac in the most lively corner of the Marais, the Trésor's pavement terrace offers perfect summer posing, attracting young hipsters, gay and straight, in hordes. The interior is reminiscent of a Rio bar – bright, comfy chairs and wacky, hand-painted tables. Surprisingly restrained drink prices, but the food is mediocre.

## Café Martini

*11 rue du Pas de la Mule, 4th (01.42.77.05.04). Mº Bastille.* **Open** 8.30am-2am daily. **No credit cards.**
Almost on the place des Vosges itself, drop by to stay mellow in this endearingly laid-back little hang out. Dimly lit, crumbling orange walls and heavy wooden beams strike a rustic contrast to the low acid-jazz tunes in the background. Particularly popular as a lunch spot.

## La Chaise au Plafond

*10 rue Trésor, 4th (01.42.76.03.22). Mº Hôtel-de-Ville.* **Open** 9.30am-2am daily. **No credit cards.**
A cosily trendy little haunt opened by the crew from the Petit Fer à Cheval (*see below*), with a roof painted with black and white blotches like a Friesian cow. Park-bench-style seating puts you in a relaxed, summery mood at any time of year, even when not on the fight-for-space terrace. Even the toilet has a certain cool. Light snacks are nicely presented.

## Le Petit Fer à Cheval

*30 rue Vieille-du-Temple, 4th (01.42.72.47.47). Mº St-Paul.* **Open** 9am-2am Mon-Fri; 11am-2am Sat, Sun. **No credit cards.**
Around the corner from its younger sister La Chaise au Plafond, this quirky vintage café is so popular that it's often hard to squeeze inside. Dominating the front is a horseshoe-shaped zinc bar, with a large mirror on each side creating that infinity effect; behind is a seating area.

## Café de la Nouvelle Mairie

*19-21 rue des Fossés-St-Jacques, 5th (01.44.07.04.41). RER Luxembourg.* **Open** 9am-8pm Mon, Fri; 9am-10pm Tue-Thur. **No credit cards.**
Overlooking a quiet *place* near the Panthéon, this smart, attractive café attracts a bourgeois set, mixed in with a backpackful of foreign students to give it that essential bohemian touch. One of its best selling points is the selection of wines by the glass and the *plats du jour*. A very pleasant spot to while away an afternoon.

## Café Mouffetard

*116 rue Mouffetard, 5th (01.43.31.42.50). Mº Censier-Daubenton.* **Open** 6.45am-10pm Tue-Sat; 6.45am-8pm Sun. Closed July. **Credit** AmEx, MC, V.
Rue Mouffetard, with its busy open-air market, creates an easygoing, village mood around this pleasant café, which featured in Krystof Kieslowski's film *Trois Couleurs: Bleu*. Noisy students and bohemian types join tourists and locals for croissants and bread made on the premises and comfortingly traditional *plats du jour*.

## Le Reflet

*6 rue Champollion, 5th (01.43.29.97.27). Mº Cluny-La Sorbonne.* **Open** 10am-2am daily. **Credit** MC, V.
Opposite the Reflet Médicis Logos cinema, it's a short step from screen to caffeine in this relaxed café, full of students and film buffs, here for a chat and cheap, reliable food. The mock movie-studio lighting-rig throws some light on the conversations below, while jazz CDs play in the background.

## Le Balto

*15 rue Mazarine, 6th (01.43.26.02.29). Mº Odéon.* **Open** 7am-1am Mon-Fri; 9am-8pm Sat. **Credit** MC, V.
This is where the art students, rather than the tourists, come as the artworks and snapshot collages of drunken Balto nights with brass bands testify. Well-prepared bistro fare at lunch time.

## Café de Cluny

*20 bd St-Michel, 6th (01.43.26.98.40). Mº Cluny-La Sorbonne.* **Open** 6.30am-2am daily. **Credit** AmEx, MC, V.
Théophile Gauthier, Colette and Verlaine all hung out here, as did Sartre before heading up the street to Les Deux Magots. Today the Cluny is a clean, Deco-style café, with marvellous, old-fashioned hot chocolate, reasonable food served non-stop, a quiet upstairs room and spotless, modern loos. Stake out a terrace table for prime people-watching.

## Café de Flore

*172 bd St-Germain, 6th (01.45.48.55.26). Mº St-Germain-des-Prés.* **Open** 7am-2am daily. **Credit** AmEx, DC, V.
The existentialist Mecca once frequented by Sartre and de Beauvoir is still abuzz with fervent intellectual prattle in numerous tongues. The 1930s décor hasn't changed, neither has the waiter service, only the prices have risen (a lot). Eric Rohmer has discovered many an actress here; Karl Lagerfeld and Bernard-Henri Lévy are other famous regulars.

## Café de la Mairie

*8 pl St-Sulpice, 6th (01.43.26.67.82). Mº St-Sulpice.* **Open** 7am-midnight Mon-Sat. **No credit cards.**
With the summer sun beating down on St-Sulpice church and the magnificent fountain, it is no wonder the terrace is full of students and arty intellectual types, here for the quintessential Left Bank experience.

## Le Chai de l'Abbaye

*26 rue de Buci, 6th (01.43.26.68.26). Mº St-Germain-des-Prés.* **Open** 8am-2am Mon-Sat; 8am-11pm Sun. **Credit** MC, V.
This café-wine bar retains a local feel even in St-Germain, drawing a rather sodden late-night clientele. The wine selection is excellent as is the food, with an Auvergnat bent.

## Les Deux Magots

*6 pl St-Germain-des-Prés, 6th (01.45.48.55.25).*
*M° St-Germain-des-Prés.* **Open** 7.30am-1.30am daily.
Closed 3rd week in Jan. **Credit** AmEx, V.
It's easy to sit back and be inspired by the great intellectual
heritage of this famous café, which still symbolises so much
of the arty myth of St-Germain, along with its neighbour Café
de Flore (*see above*). Founded in 1875, the Deux Magots
(named after the two wise Chinamen inside the entrance) has
played host to countless writers, artists and thinkers escaping from the cold of their garrets: Picasso supposedly created cubism here, and Hemingway, Mallarmé and Sartre were
all regulars. Although at 22F for a coffee, cerebral inspiration no longer comes cheap.

## La Palette

*43 rue de Seine, 6th (01.43.26.68.15). M° Mabillon.*
**Open** 8am-2am Mon-Sat. Closed Aug, one week in
winter. **No credit cards.**
The classic artists' turn-of-the-century café, with faded paintings and palettes blending into a pub-like darkness, has plenty of tables inside and out, although those in the know prefer
the secluded back room. The crowd is a colourful mix of local
art dealers, students and glam shoppers. Some hot dishes at
lunch (noon-3pm), wines and good *tartines* all day.

## Au Petit Suisse

*16 rue de Vaugirard, 6th (01.43.26.03.81). M° Odéon.*
**Open** 7am-8.30pm Mon-Fri. Closed Aug. **No credit cards.**
Across the road from the Luxembourg Gardens, this charming, bordeaux-coloured, vintage *café-tabac* is a quirky hotchpotch of steps and levels, and has a terrace at street level.

## Le Select

*99 bd du Montparnasse, 6th (01.42.22.65.27). M° Vavin.*
**Open** 7am-3am daily; until 4am Sat. **Credit** MC, V.
It is entirely possible to lose a day in this café. Unlike other
cafés in the *quartier*, Le Select, which opened as an 'American
Bar' in 1924, manages to hold on to the image of its arty
Montparnasse heyday with dignity, thanks to its décor and
bohemian intellectual clientele. Good beers, cocktails and an
extensive list of malt whiskies.

## Le Rouquet

*188 bd St-Germain, 7th (01.45.48.06.93). M° St-Germain-
des-Prés.* **Open** 7am-10pm Mon-Sat. **Credit** MC, V.
St-Germain locals prefer to patronise this café, rather than
be patronised by the existential waiters of Les Deux Magots.
A perfectly preserved 1950s interior, plus a terrace, make this
charming café an ideal spot for idling away an afternoon.

## Le Fouquet's

*99 av des Champs-Elysées, 8th (01.47.23.70.60). M° George
V.* **Open** 9am-2am daily. **Credit** AmEx, DC, MC, V.
One of the most prestigious cafés along the Champs-Elysées,
Fouquet's (pronounce the 't' at the end) has become a land-
mark in its own right, drawing wealthy Arabs and showbizz
wannabes prepared to pay 48F for a *demi.*

## Café de la Paix

*12 bd des Capucines, 9th (01.40.07.30.20). M° Opéra.*
**Open** 10am-1.30am daily. **Credit** AmEx, DC, MC, V.
A huge showcase Parisian café complete with famous liter-
ary patronage (Oscar Wilde) in the past and packed with
wealthy tourists today. The sumptuous interior is by Charles
Garnier, best known for his Opéra Garnier across the road.
Extortionate snacks are served on the terrace outside.

## Café Zéphyr

*12 bd Montmartre, 9th (01.47.70.80.14). M° Rue
Montmartre.* **Open** 8am-2am Mon-Sat; 8am-10pm Sun.
**Credit** MC, V.
In a part of town gazumped by fast food chains and retro-
kitsch Americana it's a great relief to find such a *très parisien*
café with its quiet, elegant décor and neo-colonial feel. *Plats
du jour* and sandwiches are served all day.

## Bar la Fontaine

*1 rue de Charonne, 11th (01.47.00.58.36). M° Bastille.*
**Open** 8am-2am Mon-Sat; noon-10pm Sun. **No credit
cards.**
Less chic but no less lively than other hip tips in the area, La
Fontaine attracts a casual clientele. The boisterous, grungy
goings-on fit in with the peeling paint and beaten-up décor.
The pavement terrace fills up from early morning.

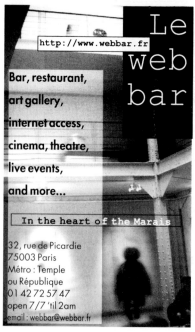

### Bistrot du Peintre
*116 av Ledru-Rollin, 11th (01.47.00.34.39). M° Ledru-Rollin.* **Open** 7am-2am Mon-Sat; 10am-9pm Sun. **Credit** MC, V.
This is a sophisticated, well-restored Art Nouveau café, with carved and highly polished wood, frosted-glass partitions, tall mirrors and an ideal corner view from the terrace. The kitchen's offerings range from snappy open sandwiches to omelettes and *plats du jour*.

### Café Charbon
*109 rue Oberkampf, 11th (01.43.57.55.13). M° Ménilmontant.* **Open** 9am-2am daily. **Credit** MC, V.
A lovingly restored *fin-de-siècle* dance hall in up-and-coming Ménilmontant has come back to life as a highly successful café-brasserie, with its gas lamps casting a gloomy half light over the bar, and a steel girder-and-pulley system which arranges the beer kegs. Local trendsters, would-be intellectuals, media types and artists sit back and read the papers or play backgammon among the plants and mirrors. At weekends, DJs plays a mix of up-tempo funk and house. Beware the Turkish loos.

### Café de l'Industrie
*16 rue St-Sabin, 11th (01.47.00.13.53). M° Bastille.* **Open** 11am-2am Mon-Fri, Sun. **Credit** V.
One of the hippest and happiest cafés in Paris, with a bric-à-brac assortment of archaic, gilt-framed oval portraits, crocodile skins and African masks, as well as photos of famous French actors. All three dimly lit rooms are graced with palmy plants, canvases and wooden Venetian blinds, creating a mellow, neo-colonial feel. Internationally spun meals.

### La Dame Pipi
*9 rue de Charonne, 11th (01.48.05.05.83). M° Bastille.* **Open** 7am-2am Mon-Sat; noon-2am Sun.
Strange meteorite-like lamps hang over the bar at this irresistibly named place (a Dame Pipi is the old lady who guards public lavatories). At noon, both rooms and pavement tables pack out as lunchers down mixed salads and hot dishes such as *steak-frites*. There's a quieter drinking crowd at night time, when the rock paradoxically pumps up.

### Pause Café
*41 rue de Charonnne, 11th (01.48.06.80.33). M° Ledru-Rollin.* **Open** 8.30am-2am Mon-Sat.
A hip, light-hearted Bastille hang-out *obligé*, beautified by temporary art exhibits, cheerful 1950s-style red and yellow formica tables, leafy neo-baroque light fittings and chic *parisiens*. The busy, chrome terrace is well placed for people who need to see and be seen. Good savoury *tourtes* and chili, cheap Météor beer and decent Beaujolais.

### Au Père Tranquille
*75 av Daumesnil, 12th (01.43.43.64.58). M° Gare de Lyon.* **Open** 7.30am-2am Mon-Sat. **Credit** MC, V.
Joining the craftsmen's workshops and designer showrooms underneath the arches of the stylishly renovated Bastille-Vincennes viaduct, this airy café-brasserie appeals with its young, laidback staff, and wide selection of beers, *grillades* and salads. The terrace outside is popular in summer.

### Au Passage des Artistes
*23 rue des Cinq-Diamants, 13th (01.45.89.58.87). M° Corvisart.* **Open** 9am-2am daily. **No credit cards.**
The electric-red neon of the jukebox looks positively futuristic in this villagey Butte-aux-Cailles café, populated mostly by local *lycéens*. Jumbled bits and bobs and maritime tableclothes lend an incoherent look.

### Café de la Place
*23 rue d'Odessa, 14th (01.42.18.01.55). M° Edgar-Quinet.* **Open** 7am-2am Mon-Fri; 9.30am-10pm Sat; 9.30am-9.30pm Sun. **Credit** V.

*Getting into the groove at* **Café Charbon**.

Adorned with pastis jugs and old advertising plaques, this tastefully revamped vintage café has become the new gathering place in the area, attracting a youthful, laidback crowd. There's a good choice of wines and tempting *charcuterie* served on hefty wooden chopping boards. The sunny terrace is busy in summer.

### Au Roi du Café
*59 rue Lecourbe, 15th (01.47.34.48.50). M° Sèvres-Lecourbe.* **Open** 7am-10.30pm daily. **Credit** MC, V.
This pretty, wood-fronted corner café is a welcome find in a once downmarket part of town that has now turned rather more boring and bourgeois. A kitsch pink neon sign encircles the top of the bar, original paintings are exhibited and the staff are into multiple body piercing, which makes up just about all the ingredients for a trendy spot.

### Café Antoine
*17 rue La Fontaine, 16th (01.46.47.86.31). RER Kennedy-Radio France.* **Open** 9am-6.30pm Mon-Sat. Closed Aug. **No credit cards.**
Hector Guimard, creator of the Art Nouveau Métro entrances, designed the facade of this charming elderly café at the turn of the century. In an area as wealthy as the 16th, it's a joy to get a glass of wine for 3F (and manage to drink it).

### Le Dôme de Villiers
*4 av de Villiers, 17th (01.43.87.28.68). M° Villiers.* **Open** 6.30am-1am daily. **Credit** AmEx, MC, V.
A highly polished café-brasserie whose bar has a popular feel, leaving the green leather seating and large terrace for the well-dressed bourgeoisie. The menu goes *moules* crazy at times, but has a few interesting additions, notably *Le Cockney Brunch* of sausage, eggs and bacon.

### L'Eté en Pente Douce
*23 rue Muller, 18th (01.42.64.02.67). M° Château-Rouge.* **Open** noon-11.15pm daily. **Credit** MC, V.
Few tourists stumble down the eastern stairs of Sacré Coeur, leaving this lovely spot to the locals. On sunny days the terrace steals the glory, as a young, unposey set lingers over the striking views of basilica and park.

## Le Sancerre

*35 rue des Abbesses, 18th (01.42.58.08.20). M° Abbesses.*
**Open** 8am-2am daily. **Credit** MC, V.
This is the place to cool your boots after climbing up out of
the colourful Métro Abbesses station. In the evening, this
laidback hangout bursts at the seams with hip youth, and
rock takes precedence. There's a long list of wines, whiskies
and beers, and food is served until late.

## Café de la Musique

*pl de la Fontaine-aux-Lions, 213 av Jean-Jaurès, 19th
(01.48.03.15.91). M° Porte-de-Pantin.* **Open** 9am-2am
daily. **Credit** AmEx, DC, MC, V.
This graceful, sumptuosly elegant café in the tip of the Cité
de la Musique is another of the Costes brothers' success stories. Decked out with heavy curtains, dark wood, velour tub
chairs and gentle lighting, the café is ideal for lunch or tranquil in the afternoon for relaxing with a view over the Parc
de la Villette. At night, it becomes a DJ-led party place.

## Bar aux Folies

*8 rue de Belleville, 20th (01.46.36.65.98). M° Belleville.* **Open**
7am-11pm daily. **No credit cards.**
A spiralling neon ceiling highlights the cosmopolitan mix of
artists that crowds in here. As proven by a grandmother clad
in hip-hugging leopard skin, it's impossible to stick out in here,
and impossible not to enjoy the sense of neighbourly love.

# Bars & Pubs

## Le Comptoir

*37 rue Berger, 1st (01.40.26.26.66). M° Châtelet-Les
Halles.* **Open** noon-2am Mon-Thur, Sun; noon-4am Fri,
Sat. **Credit** MC, V.
This postmodern designer café-bar on the less-touristy side
of Les Halles turns into a lively mini-club at the weekend.
Daytime sees a comfortable tourist trade, lunchers and
Sunday brunchers. For your francs, you get a nightly DJ,
plus good views of passers-by and the Les Halles gardens.

## Flann O'Brien's

*6 rue Bailleul, 1st (01.42.60.13.58). M° Louvre.*
**Open** 4pm-2am daily. **No credit cards.**
Tucked away in a backstreet off the rue de Rivoli, this is one
of the best Irish pubs in town. Serving arguably the creami-
est pint of Guinness in Paris as well as excellent live music
most nights, it's no surprise that this bar buzzes constantly.

## Jip's

*41 rue St-Denis, 1st (01.42.33.00.11). M° Châtelet-Les
Halles.* **Open** 11am-2am Mon-Sun. **Credit** V.
This funky Afro-Cuban bar is hard to miss: awash outside
with day-glo murals, alive inside with the psychedelic wood
carvings by Swedish artist Pablo. At lunch, owner Christine
serves exotic fruit and fish dishes to a mix of professionals.
At night the pounding Cuban salsa and jazz fusion pull in a
hardcore African following. There's an extensive cocktail list.

## Le Café Noir

*65 rue Montmartre, 2nd (01.40.39.07.36). M° Sentier.*
**Open** 7.30am-2am Mon-Fri; 4.30pm-2am Sat. **No credit
cards.**
Cheerful staff and whimsical details like bunches of dried
flowers and a worn tiled floor give this laid-back, unpretentious old corner café an inviting atmosphere. The young
crowd is a healthy mix of French and Anglophones, and the
nightly live music (jazz, blues) is usually excellent. With its
budget prices, this can be a good place to live it up.

## The Frog & Rosbif

*116 rue St-Denis, 2nd (01.42.36.34.73). M° Etienne-
Marcel.* **Open** noon-2am daily; happy hour 6-7pm Mon-
Fri. **Credit** MC, V.

With its lively, authentic pub atmosphere and all the trimmings from lunch-time doses of hearty pub grub and the
English papers to a variety of wackily named home-brews
(Inseine, Parislytic), this is the retreat of the Englishman
abroad. Live broadcasts of football and rugby bring in the
biggest crowds, and good bands liven up the evenings.
**Branch:** The Frog & Princess, 9 rue Princesse, 6th
(01.40.51.77.38).

## Harry's New York Bar

*5 rue Daunou, 2nd (01.42.61.71.14). M° Opéra.* **Open**
10.45am-4am daily. **Credit** AmEx, DC, MC, V.
A favourite with sozzled expats since 1911, this legendary
cocktail bar is lined with American college banners, polished
wood and decades of nostalgic nicotine. The birthplace of
the Bloody Mary, they still mix a mean cocktail.

## The Kildare

*6bis rue du Quatre Septembre, 2nd (01.47.03.91.91). M°
Bourse.* **Open** 11.30am-2am. **Credit** AmEx, V.
Bright downstairs with a cosy lounge upstairs, the Kildare
attracts a largely Anglophone crowd as well as the neighbouring Bourse brokers. There's live traditional Irish music
on Fridays, and lunch runs to hearty beef stew with Guinness.

## Kitty O'Shea's

*10 rue des Capucines, 2nd (01.40.15.00.30). M° Opéra.*
**Open** noon-1.30am daily. **Credit** AmEx, MC, V.
Clean-cut and traditional with wood booths, embossed wall-
paper and stained glass, this Irish pub is famous for its
Dublin counterpart, and serves Guinness, Kilkenny and pub
grub. It's generally sane and relaxed, with a civilised mix of
Irish, English and French, except on riotous rugby Five
Nations Cup days.
**Branch:** James Joyce, 71 bd Gouvion-St-Cyr, 17th
(01.44.09.70.32).

## Le Port d'Amsterdam

*20 rue du Croissant, 2nd (01.40.39.02.63). M° Bourse.*
**Open** 5pm-2am daily. **No credit cards.**
Dutch *au-pairs*, Scandinavian students and dubious French-
men keep this dark, smoky bar hopping. Most weekends,
shiny happy people dance on tables and improvise karaoke
to Dutch pop hits and 1970s classics. The staff join in, mer-
rily throwing out the Amstel.
**Branch:** Café Klein Holland, 36 rue du Roi-de-Sicile, 4th
(01.42.71.43.13).

## Tigh Johnny's

*55 rue Montmartre, 2nd (01.42.33.91.33). M° Sentier.*
**Open** 4pm-1.15pm daily. **No credit cards.**
The second-oldest Irish pub in Paris serves as an informal
Gaelic cultural centre under owner-publisher Johnny. Poets
perform in monthly Sunday afternoon readings, and tradi-
tional Irish sets or modern rock on Wed and Sun nights.

## L'Aréa

*10 rue des Tournelles, 4th (01.42.72.96.50). M° Bastille.*
**Open** 7pm-2am Tue, Thur-Sun; 7pm-4am Wed; happy
hour 7-10pm. **Credit** AmEx, MC, V.
This buzzing Bastille bar attracts a friendly crowd. On
Wednesday nights, owners Edouard and Lydie keep the festivities going, with the help of a Brazilian band and mind-
numbing cocktails. The menu has Brazilian and Lebanese
dishes. L'Area often displays work by up-and-coming artists.

## The Lizard Lounge

*18 rue du Bourg-Tibourg, 4th (01.42.72.81.34).
M° Hôtel-de-Ville.* **Open** 11am-2am daily. **Credit** V.
A stylish, split-level bar/restaurant designed and built by its
American owners with a heavy steel mezzanine, art on the
walls and a long flowing bar. Good beers, fancy drinks and
NY-style deli food. The Underground cellar bar runs diverse
themed evenings and film screenings.

## L'Oiseau Bariolé

*16 rue Ste-Croix de la Bretonnerie, 4th (01.42.72.37.12). Mº Hôtel-de-Ville.* **Open** 10am-dawn daily. **Credit** MC, V.
A miniscule, kitsch-ugly café that takes on surreal dimensions once everything else in the chic Marais closes down, acting as *quartier* sump for the trendy waste products and hip stragglers from late nights out.

## Le Pick-Clops

*16 rue Vieille-du-Temple, 4th (01.40.29.02.18). Mº Hôtel-de-Ville.* **Open** 8am-2am Mon-Sat; 2pm-2am Sun; happy hour 8-9pm daily. **Credit** MC, V.
Bright lights and fresh paint have revamped the Pick-Clops' once seedy image, but have not deterred the young, grungy rock crowd which descends upon this corner of the Marais. The terrace is perfectly positioned for people-watching.

## Stolly's

*16 rue Cloche-Perce, 4th (01.42.76.06.76). Mº Hôtel-de-Ville.* **Open** 4.30pm-1.30am daily; happy hour 4.30-8pm daily. **No credit cards.**
This hole-in-the-wall Marais bar entertains a beer-loving Anglophone crowd with quality cocktails, inexpensive house lager, dubbed *Cheap Blonde*, homespun art on the walls and a manic mix of music. Happy hour is for the serious drinker, while the sunny terrace is a favourite spot on summer nights.

## Café Oz

*184 rue St-Jacques, 5th (01.43.54.30.48). RER Luxembourg.* **Open** 11am-1.30am daily; happy hour 6.30-9.30pm Mon-Sat; 3-8.30pm Sun. **Credit** MC, V.
Wisecracking staff, a fabulous, if pricey, Australian wine list and a healthy range of draught and bottled beers (Fosters, VA, etc) make this place a popular hideout. Mock Aboriginal cave paintings cover the walls, quaint Aussie mementoes fill corners and a baby croc takes pride of place above the bar. **Branch:** 18 rue St-Denis, 1st (01.40.39.00.18).

## Connolly's Corner

*12 rue Mirabel, 5th (01.43.31.94.22). Mº Censier-Daubenton.* **Open** 4pm-1am daily; happy hour 6-8pm Mon-Fri. **No credit cards.**
This good old spit-and-sawdust Irish village pub in Paris is stunning in its simple authenticity. The Guinness and Murphy's are a dream, and occasional live music attracts a foot-stomping, shabbily arty crowd. Tie wearers beware.

## The Hideout

*11 rue du Pot de Fer, 5th (01.45.35.13.17). Mº Place Monge.* **Open** 3pm-1am Mon-Thur; 4pm-2am Fri, Sat; happy hour 3-10pm daily. **Credit** MC, V.
Just off rue Mouffetard, this oak-panelled Irish pub is dark, grungy and drunken. It's very popular with a thirsty, young, mainly Anglo student crowd, presumably because of its exceptionally long happy hour.

## Le Piano Vache

*8 rue Laplace, 5th (01.46.33.75.03). Mº Maubert-Mutualité.* **Open** noon-2am Mon-Fri; 9pm-2am Sat, Sun; happy hour 6-9pm Mon-Fri. **Credit** MC, V.
A reliable Latin Quarter student haunt, with an intimate candlelit front room, and a large, pleasantly seedy, poster-lined back bar. Markedly more French than its neighbours, smoke-stained walls and heavy wood beams give it a cosy feel. Music is mainly indie, with a live DJ on Tue and Fri.

## Le Bar Dix

*10 rue de l'Odéon, 6th (01.43.26.66.83). Mº Odéon.* **Open** 6pm-2am daily; happy hour 6-7pm daily. **No credit cards.**
This genuine Sorbonne sanctuary, attracting an international student crowd, has fuelled heated discussions for over 30 years. Small groups huddle over candles in the cramped upstairs bar, while the cellar caters to the loud debaucheries of those overindulging on jugs of inexpensive sangria.

## Birdland

*20 rue Princesse, 6th (01.43.26.97.59). Mº Mabillon.* **Open** 10pm-dawn Mon-Thur, Sun; 8.30pm-dawn Fri, Sat. **Credit** AmEx, DC, MC, V.
Birdland's dimly lit, red velvet lounge bar provides a bit of St-Germain warmth to the cool jazz tunes in the background. The prices favour the older, wealthier jazz lovers who take up the bar, but slip upstairs with a beer, and relax to the sounds of a golden age. You'll need to knock on the door to get in.

*Open-door policy at charming, vintage* **Café Antoine**.

## Coolín

*Marché St-Germain, 15 rue Clement, 6th (01.44.07.00.92).*
*M° Mabillon.* **Open** 10am-2am Mon-Sat; noon-2am Sun.
**Credit** AmEx, MC, V. Wheelchair access.
With burnt-orange paintwork, blue blinds and rustic furniture, this Irish addition installed within the revamped St-Germain covered market is an attractive synthesis of pub and Parisian café and has become one of the buzzing points of the area. Decent food is largely based around smoked salmon. Eclectic live music some evenings.

## La Closerie des Lilas

*171 bd du Montparnasse, 6th (01.43.26.70.50).*
*M° Vavin/RER Port-Royal.* **Open** 11.30am-2am daily.
**Credit** AmEx, DC, MC, V.
Founded in 1847, this bar has attracted famous clients, including Appollinaire, Picasso and Hemingway, as little brass plaques on the tables testify. The bar still attracts the political world today while mere mortals are almost ignored. Come here to sip an expertly mixed but pricey cocktail, while a pianist plays in the background. In the restaurant a creative new chef has brought the food back on track.

## Pub St Germain des Prés

*17 rue de l'Ancienne-Comédie, 6th (01.43.29.38.70). M°*
*Odéon.* **Open** 24 hours daily. **Credit** AmEx, DC, MC, V.
Monsieur Guillotin, legend has it, used the cellar to practise with his gruesome invention. Fortunately, the atmosphere today is more sanguine, with a pirate theme running through this vast drinking complex on five floors. It comes into its own for a burger, *tartare* or salad in the dead of night when everything else around here is closed. There's a huge variety of beers. Ring the doorbell to get in late at night.

## Barfly

*49-51 av George V, 8th (01.53.67.84.60). M° George V.*
**Open** noon-3pm, 7.30pm-2am, Mon-Fri, Sun; 7.30pm-2am
Sat. **Credit** AmEx, MC, V.
This determinedly fashionable, high-design modern bar aims at New York style *à la* Bukowski (from whose book hails the name) only is not nearly drunken enough. Beautiful people eat from an international menu or from the sushi bar, while wealthy, older businessmen and their 20-something women sip cocktails at the long turquoise mosaic bar. The door policy is stringent but has lightened up a little with the arrival of brother Buddha Bar (*see chapter* **Restaurants**).

## The Cricketer Pub

*41 rue des Mathurins, 8th (01.40.07.01.45).*
*M° St-Augustin.* **Open** 11am-2am daily. **Credit** MC, V.
This place is a fairly good representation of an English Home Counties pub, complete with the guffaws of RAF/rugby chaps at the bar and cricket paraphernalia. With Adnams, dollops of pub grub, live test match coverage, darts and quizzes, Brits can quickly quell those homesick blues.
**Branch**: The Bowler, 13 rue d'Artois, 8th (01.45.61.16.60).

## Montecristo Café

*68 av des Champs-Elysées, 8th (01.45.62.30.86).*
*M° Franklin D Roosevelt.* **Open** 24 hours daily. **Credit**
AmEx, DC, MC, V.
After numerous reincarnations, this Champs-Elysées bar seems to have got it right with Cuba, packing in the punters with a Latino restaurant on the ground floor and Cuban music, dancers, cocktails, beers and tapas in the basement.

## Le Dépanneur

*27 rue Fontaine, 9th (01.40.16.40.20). M° Blanche.*
**Open** 24 hours daily; happy hour 6-8pm. **Credit** AmEx,
DC, MC, V.
Masquerading as an American retro diner, this 24-hour retreat for the thirsty or hungry may lack its neighbours' street-cred, but compensates with a consumer-friendly door policy and techno DJs one or two nights a week.

*Propping up the bar at* **Le Piano Vache**.

## Au Général Lafayette

*52 rue Lafayette, 9th (01.47.70.59.08). M° Le Peletier.*
**Open** 8am-4am daily. **Credit** AmEx, MC, V.
A brightly lit bar for relaxed professionals, with its turn-of-the-century *trompe l'oeil* ceilings, mirrors and mellow, jazz-imbued atmosphere. Serious drinkers can sample the wide choice of mostly draught and bottled Belgian beers. Pleasant for a cheap early evening drink or late-night snack.

## Lili La Tigresse

*98 rue Blanche, 9th (01.48.74.08.25). M° Blanche.*
**Open** 10pm-2am Mon-Tue; 10pm-3am Thur; 10pm-5am
Fri, Sat. **Credit** MC, V.
This is a classically cool go-go bar, with a door policy favouring the clean-cut and chic. Despite the scantily clad girls along the bar, it attracts young businessmen and wad-weary tourists. The upstairs bar is more discreet; hip music compensates for this glimpse of upmarket Pigalle sleaze.

## Ministry

*1 rue Mansart, 9th (01.42.82.08.88). M° Blanche.*
**Open** 6pm-2am Mon-Thur; 6pm-2am, 4-8am, Fri, Sat;
happy hour 6-8pm. **No credit cards.**
With a mock dungeon interior reminiscent of a fairground house of horrors (gargoyles, skeletons, etc) and thrash metal music to match, this Goth bar may not be everyone's cup of tea. Prices vary wildly, but the staff are a pleasure.

## Pandora Station

*24 rue Fontaine, 9th (01.42.26.24.11). M° Pigalle.*
**Open** 6pm-2am Mon; 6pm-4am, Tue, Wed,
Sun; 6pm-9am Thur-Sat. **No credit cards.**
Ignore the tacky Tarzan-style décor, and this is the best late night bar in Pigalle. Lido dancers stop in after work, as do post-theatregoers and pre-clubbers, while celebs such as Jean-Paul Belmondo have been spotted. Groove to French *chanson* and world music on the tiny dancefloor downstairs.

## Bar des Ferailleurs

*18 rue de Lappe, 11th (01.48.07.89.12). M° Bastille.* **Open**
5pm-2am Mon-Fri; 3pm-2am Sat, Sun. **Credit** MC, V.
This hip and regularly heaving rue de Lappe dive seems to be able to do no wrong. Fashion victims and those in the know squeeze on to uncomfortably high chairs to be amiably abused by the barmen, or group around tables to gossip. As the name suggests, all the fittings from the bar stools to the beer taps are made from scrap metal.

## L'Entrepôt

*14 rue de Charonne, 11th (01.48.06.57.04). M° Bastille.*
**Open** noon-2am Mon-Fri; 4pm-2am Sat, Sun; happy hour
5-8.30pm (second drink free). **Credit** DC, MC, V.

One of the longer-running of the dimly lit Bastille nooks has an artfully 'distressed' interior – half the plaster has fallen from the ceiling, spiral stairs lead to doors on an internal courtyard that can only have come from a film set and the cellar is tiled like a Métro station.

## Le Lèche-Vin

*13 rue Daval, 11th (01.43.55.98.91). M° Bastille.*
**Open** 8pm-2am daily. **No credit cards.**
At first glance this bar appears to be a shrine to the Virgin Mary, but it soon becomes clear that it is more a tribute to the work of queens of kitsch Pierre et Gilles. Gnomes and Buddhas hidden among the religious paraphernalia shimmer in fairy lights, while a trip to the porn-packed toilet quickly dispels any thoughts of sanctified purity.

## Le Réservoir

*16 rue de la Forge-Royale, 11th (01.43.56.39.60).*
*M° Faidherbe-Chaligny.* **Open** 9.30pm-2am Mon-Sat.
**Credit** AmEx, MC, V.
This dark, cavernous new bar-cum-restaurant bang next door to La Casbah (*see* **Nightlife**) has that buzz of the place that has arrived. Carefully distressed walls, hip crowd, with-it soundtrack and live musical showcases on Friday and Saturday nights.

## Le Sanz Sans

*49 rue du Fbg-St-Antoine, 11th (01.44.75.78.78). M°*
*Bastille.* **Open** 8.30am-2am daily. **Credit** AmEx, MC, V.
Every night a cool Bastille crowd and less desirable suburban boys pack Sanz Sans to the gills for the cheap beer. Earlier on, the atmosphere is calmer, as trendsters sprawl in an amusing array of chairs from Louis XV to 1950s retro for Franco-International lunch or an early-evening drink. DJs spin acid jazz, funk and rare groove every night.

## China Club

*50 rue de Charenton, 12th (01.43.43.82.02). M° Ledru-*
*Rollin.* **Open** 7pm-2am Mon-Thur; 7pm-3am Fri, Sat; happy hour 7-9pm. **Credit** AmEx, MC, V.
From an inconspicuous street behind the Bastille opera, this beautiful people's hangout is a cool but sophisticated haven, decorated to resemble a colonial Hong Kong gentleman's club, with an eternally long bar on the ground floor and Chesterfield sofas. Many swear by the atmospheric, lacquered first-floor '*fumoir chinois*', where the barman shakes up some of the best cocktails in Paris. Dim sum bar snacks.

## Le Merle Moqueur

*11 rue de la Butte-aux-Cailles, 13th (01.45.65.12.43).*
*M° Corvisart.* **Open** 5pm-1.45am daily; happy hour 6-8pm. **Credit** MC, V.
The dark, studenty, disco-style interior is a great place to see live French indie bands on Sunday nights. Scruffy youths sweat it out at the bar, while older locals sneak into corners to soak up the atmosphere and cheap pints of draught lager.

## Les Mousquetaires

*77 av du Maine, 14th (01.43.22.50.46). M° Gaîté.*
**Open** 7am-3am Sun-Thur; 7am-5am Fri, Sat. **Credit** AmEx, MC, V.
Take the things you like most in an American bar (tasty bar snacks, friendly and efficient non-stop service, no French music), combine them with the food and cigarette smog of a French café, stick an eleven-table pool room in the back and you get Les Mousquetaires. Crowded at night with teenagers.

## Le Mustang Café

*84 bd du Montparnasse, 14th (01.43.35.36.12).*
*M° Montparnasse-Bienvenüe.* **Open** 9am-5am daily; happy hour 4-7pm Mon-Fri. **Credit** MC, V.
A thriving Tex-Mex bar-restaurant with ranch-style décor, a late-night licence and an indulgent happy hour which attract hordes of well-behaved local *lycéens*. The usual grub is dished out until late and washed down with Bud or pitchers of margaritas. Theme discos of varying degrees of amusing tackiness on Thursday nights.
**Branch:** 20 rue de la Roquette, 11th (01.49.23.81.81).

## Le Cristal

*163 av de Suffren, 15th (01.47.34.47.92).*
*M° Sèvres-Lecourbe.* **Open** 7.30pm-2am Mon-Thur; 7.30am-2am Fri; 6pm-2am Sat; happy hour 6-8pm daily.
Closed Aug. **No credit cards.**
This halfway house between pub and trad corner café, with Kilkenny and Guinness signs on the walls and Guinness on tap, throbs with French students and a handful of other nationalities most nights of the week. Friendly staff, dartboard, pinball and amusing loo murals entertain, while low prices bring in the masses. Lunch-time snacks are available.

## La Flèche d'Or

*102bis rue de Bagnolet, 20th (01.43.72.04.23). M°*
*Alexandre-Dumas.* **Open** 10am-2am daily. **Credit** MC, V.
Once a train station on the *Petite Ceinture* line that circled

Paris, this café-bar with its derelict, psychedelic mix of graffiti, photo exhibitions and railway odds and ends attracts a trendy, arty crowd. A sunny verandah overlooks the tracks and the central bar is built from railway sleepers. Most nights offer cutting-edge music, ranging from acid jazz to ambient, the DJ's booth hiding behind a bizzare train sculpture. On other occasions there are short sketches on the stage, or short films. The weekend brunch isn't bad, either.

## Wine Bars

### La Cloche des Halles

*28 rue Coquillière, 1st (01.42.36.93.89). M° Châtelet-Les Halles.* **Open** 8am-10pm Mon-Fri; 10am-5pm Sat. Closed two weeks in Aug. **No credit cards.**
Named after the bell that once tolled the opening and closing of the market at Les Halles, this is the place to go if you like wines from Beaujolais and food from the Lyon area.

### Juvéniles

*47 rue de Richelieu, 1st (01.42.97.46.49). M° Palais-Royal.* **Open** noon-11pm Mon-Sat. **Credit** MC, V.
This is one of the best wine bars in town, serving tapas, standard French dishes and enlightened English pub food. Kid brother to Willi's Wine Bar (*see chapter* **Restaurants**), Juveniles thrives on the enthusiasm of British expat owners Tim Johnston and Mark Williamson and on its wine list.

### Le Rubis

*10 rue du Marché-St Honoré, 1st (01.42.61.03.34). M° Pyramides.* **Open** 7am-10pm Mon-Fri; 9am-4pm Sat. **No credit cards.**
Even if the wines are nothing special, there is plenty of atmosphere in this cramped wine bar, notorious for November Beaujolais Nouveau celebrations that spill out onto the street. The food is simple and well-prepared.

### Les Fous d'en Face

*3 rue du Bourg-Tibourg, 4th (01.48.87.03.75). M° Hôtel-de-Ville.* **Open** noon-3pm, 7.30pm-midnight, daily (June-Aug, noon-midnight). **Credit** AmEx, MC, V.
Regular customers frequent this rustic Marais retreat for its wide variety of wines by the glass and the delicious *charcuterie* from Corsica and Spain. The best atmosphere is to be had in the evening, when booking is essential. In the summer, book a table outside on the small, attractive terrace.

### La Tartine

*24 rue de Rivoli, 4th (01.42.72.76.85). M° Hôtel-de-Ville or St-Paul.* **Open** 8.30am-10pm Mon, Thur-Sun; noon-10pm Wed. Closed Aug. **No credit cards.**
With its vintage booths and globe lights, this perennially fashionable Marais bar is a favourite with the top fashion designers who live nearby, and was once a haunt of Trotsky. Today, Beaujolais is the speciality in a wide selection of wines by the glass or bottle from a cellar of over 3,000 bottles, accompanied by a delicious range of *tartines*.

### Le Café du Passage

*12 rue de Charonne, 11th (01.49.29.97.64). M° Bastille.* **Open** 6pm-2am Mon-Fri; noon-2am Sat. **Credit** MC, V.
This sleek, sophisticated place is Soizik de Lorgeril's second attempt at launching a true wine bar: his first establishment, Le Passage, is a highly successful bistro where people come as much for the food as for the wine. There's a small, basic menu and an unusually good selection of international wines.

### Jacques Mélac

*42 rue Léon-Frot, 11th (01.43.70.59.27). M° Charonne.* **Open** 9am-5pm Mon; 9am-midnight Tue-Fri. **Credit** MC, V.
This new-generation wine bar has known better days, but people are still enjoying one of Paris' most original wine lists, with a good selection of Côtes du Rhône.

### Le Baron Rouge

*1 rue Théophile-Roussel, 12th (01.43.43.14.32). M° Lédru-Rollin.* **Open** 10am-2pm, 5-9.30pm, Tue-Fri; 10am-9.30pm Sat; 10am-3pm Sun. **Credit** MC, V.
Half wine shop, half wine bar, this is probably the cheapest and friendliest place in Paris to drink wine. Recently the trendies have started to move in, and local artists, office workers and journalists fill the tables at lunch time, accompanying their tipples with a plate of *charcuterie* or *chèvre*.

### Le Moulin à Vin

*6 rue Burq, 18th (01.42.52.81.27). M° Abbesses.* **Open** 6pm-2am Tue; noon-3pm, 6pm-2am Wed, Thur; 6pm-2am Fri, Sat. Closed Aug. **Credit** MC, V.
Late at night, groups of students and a relaxed crowd hang out in this Montmartre wine bar, which owner Danielle has

*Less wise now at the* **Les Deux Magots**.

managed to recreate, in an authentic 1950s Parisian style. It is the sort of place where the occasional accordion player will strike up a tune. Snacks and traditional bistro dishes.

### Le Baratin
*3 rue Jouye-Rouve, 20th (01.43.49.39.70). M° Pyrénées.*
**Open** noon-1am Tue-Fri; 6pm-1.30am Sat. Closed first week of Jan, one week in Aug. **Credit** MC, V.
It's well worth the climb up through the Chinese restaurants of Belleville to find wine-enthusiast Olivier Camus' modest, unassuming *bar à vins*. The clientele tends to be studenty, the wines good and cheap, and the bistro-style dishes earthy.

## Salons de Thé

### Angelina's
*226 rue de Rivoli, 1st (01.42.60.82.00). M° Tuileries.*
**Open** 9am-7pm Mon-Fri; 9am-7.30pm Sat, Sun. Closed two weeks in Aug. **Credit** AmEx, MC, V.
This is the ultimate in Parisian tea rooms, with its rococo murals, ornate gilt plasterwork and ceiling-high mirrors. Despite the bustle, it remains a must for visitors to watch well-to-do ladies taking a break from a day's shopping, seated amidst the tourists. The hot chocolate is heavenly.

### Les Enfants Gâtés
*43 rue des Francs-Bourgeois, 4th (01.42.77.07.63). M° St-Paul.* **Open** noon-8pm Mon-Fri; 11am-8pm Sat, Sun. **Credit** MC, V.
A neo-1930s décor with decrepit leather club chairs, low tables and movie posters makes this one of the coolest of the city's tea salons, complete with its own art gallery downstairs. The hip Marais clientele stops in between shopping

# Bar speak

**Créme de Menthe** A bright green drink. Inexplicably popular, unless you like drinking toothpaste.

**Demi** 25cl beer, *pression* on tap.

**Grand** 50cl beer (roughly a pint), a giveaway that you're a tourist.

**Hemingway** American writer who drank at almost every bar or café in the Latin Quarter, St-Germain and at the Ritz.

**Kir** Apéritif of blackcurrant liqueur and white wine, usually Burgundy; *kir royale* is made with Champagne.

**Sandwich** Ham or Camembert squeezed between a vast length of baguette – don't expect variety in French cafés. You may be allowed to adorn your ham with *cornichons*, or go for a *mixte*: ham and gruyère. Sandwiches on *pain Poîlane* are chicer and pricier.

**Terrasse** chairs on the pavement, allowing you to drink in vast quantities of lead as well as Parisian atmosphere. *Terrasse chauffée* has winter heating.

**Zinc** another name for the bar counter, traditionally made of zinc. Prices are often much lower here than at tables.

bouts in the area's chic boutiques. Teas come from Mariage Frères, but for a change, try the cinnamon-infused milk. The limited menu features some of the best quiche around.

### Au Lys d'Argent
*90 rue St-Louis-en-l'Ile, 4th (01.46.33.56.13). M° Pont-Marie.* **Open** 8.30pm Mon-Thur; noon-10.30pm Fri-Sun. **Credit** MC, V.
Bright yellow walls with gold stars on the ceiling, green rush chairs and marble-topped tables complement the warm welcome in this tea room-crêperie. Choose from 29 varieties of tea to accompany the tempting desserts.

### Mariage Frères
*30-32 rue du Bourg-Tibourg, 4th (01.42.72.28.11). M° Hôtel-de-Ville.* **Open** noon-7pm daily. **Credit** AmEx, MC, V.
Founded in 1854 as wholesaler to upmarket Parisian establishments, today it is open to the public and offers 350 teas in stock (a 95-page book, *L'Art du Thé*, describes each variety), along with a selection of light meals or pastries.
**Branch**: 13 rue des Grands-Augustins, 6th (01.40.51.82.50).

### La Fourmi Ailée
*8 rue du Fourrare, 5th (01.43.29.40.99). M° Maubert-Mutualité.* **Open** noon-7pm Mon, Wed-Sun. **Credit** AmEx, MC, V.
Tucked behind its own bookstore specialising in women's issues and women writers, this is just the place to come for a cup of tea and a scone on a chilly day. Curl up by the fire with a book or a friend, lulled by the classical music playing in the background. There's a good choice of *gratins* and pies.

### La Mosquée de Paris
*39 rue Geoffroy St-Hillaire, 5th (01.43.31.38.20). M° Censier-Daubenton.* **Open** 10am-midnight daily. **Credit** AmEx, MC, V.
The exotic tea room of the Paris mosque is fitted out with magnificent Moorish carved wood, tiled ceiling and brass-topped tables. The only tea on the menu is hot, sweet Middle Eastern mint tea, served with honey-laden, flaky pastries.

### L'Heure Gourmande
*22 passage Dauphine, 6th (01.46.34.00.40). M° Odéon.* **Open** 11am-7pm Mon-Sat; 1-7pm Sun. Closed three weeks in Aug. **Credit** MC, V.
L'Heure Gourmande is a haven of gentle quiet. There are 39 teas from Betjeman & Barton and Palais du Thé, eight coffees, a selection of *'eaux de fruits'*, infusions based on rosehips, hibiscus and dried fruits, as well as homemade desserts.

### Marie Thé
*102 rue du Cherche-Midi, 7th (01.42.22.50.40). M° Vaneau.* **Open** 9am-7pm daily. **Credit** AmEx, MC, V.
The real reason to come here is for dessert: chef Bruno Neveu was the former *chef de pâtisserie* at the Ritz cooking school. Choose from a selection of 30 teas from Betjeman & Barton. Light meals are also available.

### Bernardaud Galerie Royale
*8bis rue Boissy d'Anglas, 8th (01.42.66.22.55). M° Madeleine.* **Open** 8.30am-7pm Mon-Sat. **Credit** MC, V.
Situated in an upmarket business and shopping district, this chic, modern *salon de thé* was designed by Olivier Gagnère, who also designed Café Marly, attracts a well-dressed clientele for power breakfasts, light lunches and afternoon tea.

### Le Damier
*29 rue St-Blaise, 20th (01.43.72.16.95). M° Porte de Montreuil.* **Open** 9.30am-7.30pm Mon-Sat. Closed two weeks in Aug. **Credit** AmEx, MC, V.
There is something very English about this cheerfully prim tea room-cum-bistro, with its old-fashioned cocoa adverts and window full of meringues and homemade cakes.

# Shopping & Services

# Fashion

**Finding your way round the capital of world fashion, from high-design trendsetters to cool clubwear.**

In many ways, the world of fashion as it exists today, from theatrical showings to spin-off lines, couture houses to designers-cum-tastemakers, almost all took shape over the past century in the French capital. While American designers have a keen understanding of sportswear and the needs of working women, and London has contributed a vivid spark of imagination to the fashion avant-garde, it is in Paris where fashion as both a business and one of the minor arts realises its full artistic and economic potential.

Paris is home to the largest, most prestigious showcase of designer presentations in the world: the twice yearly *prêt-à-porter* showings. From Valentino to Vivienne Westwood, designers from around the globe present their collections in Paris, and it's easy to see why: nowhere else accords the creativity and artistry of fashion such deep appreciation. If the fun boy of fashion Jean-Paul Gaultier heralds a return to longer hemlines – or skull tattoos – in his autumn show, that will be carried on the 8 o'clock news, alongside reports of economic developments and crises abroad.

## HAUTE COUTURE

Paris is also the only true home of haute couture. Though most couture houses – where handfitted designs cost 50,000F and more – today lose money, the received wisdom holds that couture is both a necessary laboratory of ideas, and a turbo engine driving sales of the house's *prêt-à-porter* ranges, accessory spin-offs and perfume lines. Most couture houses, staid marble affairs whose numbers include Dior, Givenchy and Ungaro, are grouped around avenue Montaigne and Faubourg-St-Honoré, in the 8th *arrondissement*.

To the city's great credit, French fashion is truly international, and the creativity of British designers has been keenly supported. Irish designer Peter O'Brien has been designing the Rochas collection for many years, and Vivienne Westwood holds her international showings here, often as a guest of her French colleague Azzedine Alaïa. More recently, the baroque talents of John Galliano have taken the city by storm. Hired first to replace Hubert de Givenchy at the helm of one of the most venerated couture houses, Galliano has now been tapped to head the larger Christian Dior couture and ready to wear house. Meanwhile, newcomer Alexander McQueen has been recruited to take over the reins of Givenchy.

## FRENCH STYLE

Day to day, French women are rarely recognisable in the cliché of the tidy secretary in a Chanel suit. While style is certainly an unmistakable component of the national make-up, designer fashions, here as everywhere, are merely part of the *parisienne*'s wardrobe. Easily overlooked is the fact that French women have a real understanding of well-designed medium-priced sportswear, and their core look for the day is composed of casual separates that are both citified and marked by a remarkable play of subtle colours. It is worth remembering when shopping here that, for better or worse, France is a profoundly bourgeois country where people are not aiming to look enormously different from each other; in Paris, even the young don't dress in a way that's vastly different from an older generation.

## WHERE TO SHOP

Individual boutiques are the backbone of retailing in Paris, alongside French chains like Naf Naf, Chipie and **Kookaï**, and international groups such as Benetton and Esprit. Fashion junkies should make straight for the area to the north of Les Halles, along rue Etienne-Marcel to place des Victoires, and along rue du Jour and rue Jean-Jacques Rousseau (1st and 2nd). **Absinthe**, **Kashiyama** and **Maria Luisa** are good places to catch up on the latest designers. The trendy Marais is bursting with small one-off shops, especially along rue des Francs-Bourgeois and rue des Rosiers, where cutting-edge boutiques and American-style jeaneries are incongruously sandwiched between Jewish delis and religious artifact shops. There's a growing number of shops too in the Bastille area. On the Left Bank, the area between boulevard St-Germain and place St-Sulpice (6th *arrondissement*) is particularly good for clothes, while the rue du Cherche-Midi and rue de Grenelle (6th and 7th) are famed for top-quality shoes and leather goods. For cheaper clothing and shoe chains try the Forum des Halles and boulevard St-Michel. Seasonal sales in July and just after Christmas can often make that designer label accessible.

### DETAXE (TAX REFUNDS)

Non-EU residents can reclaim value-added tax (usually 20.6% of the purchase price) if they have spent more than 1,200F in any one shop, and if they've been in the country less than three months. At the shop ask for a *détaxe* form, and when you leave France have it stamped by customs. Then send a stamped copy back to the shop, who will refund the tax, either by bank transfer or by crediting your credit card. *Détaxe* does not cover food, drink, antiques and works of art.

## Designer Boutiques

### Absinthe
*74-76 rue Jean-Jacques-Rousseau, 1st (01.42.33.54.44).*
*M° Châtelet-Les Halles or Etienne-Marcel.* **Open** 11am-7.30pm Mon-Sat. **Credit** MC, V.
Owner Marthe Desmoulins tracks down and nurtures fresh international talent, and clothes by Dries Van Noten, Humbert, Julie Skarland and Union pour le Vêtement can all be found here. Also stocked are clever bags by Jamin Puech and made-to-measure shoes by Andres Hombach.

### Agnès B
*2, 3, 6, 10, 19 rue du Jour, 1st (women 01.45.08.56.56/ men 01.42.33.04.13). M° Châtelet-Les Halles.* **Open** 10am-7pm Mon-Sat. **Credit** AmEx, MC, V.
In France, Agnès B is shorthand for the French take on basic dressing. There's an Agnès B boutique for everyone on rue du Jour: women's wear and make-up at No 6, men's wear at No 3, Lolita for teens at No 10, children's wear at No 2 and at 'La Maison sur l'eau' at No 19 she offers her own bags, sunglasses and watches, along with knick-knacks picked up during her exotic travels. There's even a contemporary art gallery at No 6 (*see chapter* **Art Galleries**). The emphasis is on neutral colours, natural fabrics and durability: her white cotton button-down shirt is indestructible. Staple leggings and snap-front cardigans are carried season after season, underlining the designer's real-life approach to fashion. Cotton shirts cost around 500F, and soft knitted cotton tops run around 300F.
**Branches:** 83 rue d'Assas (women/Lolita), 6th (01.43.54.69.21); 13 rue Michelet (women), 6th (01.46.33.70.20); 22 rue St-Sulpice (men), 6th (01.40.51.70.69); 6 rue du Vieux-Colombier, (women, beauty, children), 6th (01.44.39.02.60); 17 av Pierre 1er de Serbie (women), 16th (01.47.20.22.44); 25 av Pierre 1er de Serbie (men), 16th (01.47.23.36.69).

### Azzedine Alaïa
*7 rue de Moussy, 4th (01.42.72.19.19). M° Hôtel-de-Ville.* **Open** 10am-7pm Mon-Sat. **Credit** AmEx, DC, MC, V.

Alaïa's address was passed hand to hand by women in the know years ago, when he worked out of a tiny one-room flat. Now the designer is based in a cavernous, high-tech warehouse not far from his shop. A master tailor, Alaïa cuts the sexiest suits in the world and his groupies, including Grace Jones, Tina Turner and all the supermodels, swear by his curve-hugging stretch dresses that start at around 4,000F.

### APC
*3 (men) and 4 (women) rue de Fleurus, 6th (01.42.22.12.77). M° St-Placide.* **Open** 10.30am-7pm Mon-Sat. **Credit** AmEx, MC, V.
A hip collection of jackets, A-line minis, drainpipe trousers and skinny rib knits inspired by French new wave films, in a colour palette running the gamut from black to tan. The prices are reasonable for clothes that are stylish without being over the top. APC is a favourite with design students and young fashion editors.
**Branch:** 25bis rue Benjamin Franklin, 16th (01.45.53.28.28).

### Chachnil
*68 rue Jean-Jacques-Rousseau, 1st (01.42.21.19.93). M° Châtelet-Les Halles or Etienne-Marcel.* **Open** 11am-7pm Mon-Sat. **Credit** MC, V.
Entering this boutique, tucked at the back of a courtyard, is like stepping into one of the Pierre & Gilles photos that adorn the walls. Owner-designer Chachnil creates colourful fairytale clothes, and dresses stars such as Marc Almond, Nina Hagen and famous French transvestite Marie-France.

### Christian Lacroix
*2-4 pl St-Sulpice, 6th (01.46.33.48.95). M° St-Sulpice.* **Open** 10am-7pm Mon-Sat. **Credit** AmEx, DC, MC, V.
The ebullient couturier from sunny Arles' colourful boutique houses his *prêt-à-porter* line, his signature-hammered gold jewellery and accessories, the casual lines, Bazar and Jeans, and a brightly patterned collection of sheets and towels.
**Branches:** 73 rue du Fbg-St-Honoré, 8th (01.42.65.79.08); 26 av Montaigne, 8th (01.47.20.68.95).

*Paparazzi flock to **51 Montaigne**.*

## 51 Montaigne

*51 av Montaigne, 8th (01.43.59.05.32). M° Champs-Elysées-Clemenceau.* **Open** 10am-7.30pm Mon-Sat.
**Credit** AmEx, DC, MC, V.
Rub shoulders with Jerry Hall, or even the Princess of Wales, in this high design, *très à la mode* new store. The mega-trendy clothing is mainly Italian, at mega-prices, including moon boots and underwear by Dolce e Gabbana, and a good selection of Byblos and Iceberg.

## Comme des Garçons

*40 (men) and 42 (women) rue Etienne-Marcel, 2nd (women 01.42.33.05.21/men 01.42.36.91.54). M° Etienne-Marcel.* **Open** 11am-7pm Mon-Sat.
**Credit** AmEx, DC, MC, V.
Rei Kawakubo, known for her state-of-the-art fabrics, post-apocalyptic vision of fashion, and androgynous styles, isn't for everyone, but the fashion intelligentsia swear by her. The two stores have an art-brut design of glass and bare concrete to match. Prices start at around 7,000F for men's suits, 2,000F for women's dresses. Also stocked is the quirky, colourful collection of her protégé Junya Watanabe.

## Bonnie Cox

*38 rue des Abbesses, 18th (01.42.54.95.68). M° Abbesses.* **Open** 10.30am-8pm Mon-Sat; 11am-7pm Sun. **Credit** AmEx, MC, V.
Owner and hairdresser Ludovic Lainé was first to discover Xuly Bet a few years ago, and is currently nurturing futuristic Belgian designer W&LT. The average price for a dress is 500F, and there is a nice if small collection of inexpensive, one-off jewellery, hair accessories and lava lamps.

## L'Eclaireur

*3ter rue des Rosiers, 4th (01.48.87.10.22). M° St-Paul.* **Open** 2-7pm Mon; 10.30am-7pm Tue-Sat. **Credit** AmEx, DC, MC, V.
Cutting-edge fashion and furnishings cleverly displayed in a lofty, skylit boutique. Fornasetti's playful ceramics and fabrics printed with neo-classical designs form a backdrop for clothing by Dolce e Gabbana, Ann Demeulemeester, Vivienne Westwood, Dries Van Noten, Trussardi and Véronique Leroy among other fashion renegades. This is one of the few stores in Paris stocking John Galliano.
**Branches:** 24 rue de L'Echaudé, 6th (01.43.29.58.01); 26 av des Champs-Elysées, 8th (01.45.62.12.32).

## Equipment

*46 rue Etienne-Marcel, 2nd (01.40.26.17.84). M° Etienne-Marcel or Quatre Septembre.* **Open** 11am-7pm Mon; 10.30am-7pm Tue-Sat. **Credit** AmEx, DC, MC, V.
Nothing but shirts are sold here, including the famous patch-pocketed 1501, a silk shirt that comes in over 30 colours. Only a small part of the vast choice is folded on the shelves, but the assistant will willingly pull out drawers to reveal much more, available in both fitted ladies' and a larger unisex cut.
**Branches:** 203 bd St-Germain, 7th (01.45.48.86.82); 5 av Victor Hugo, 16th (01.45.01.20.29).

## Et Vous

*25 rue Royale, 8th (01.47.42.31.00). M° Madeleine.* **Open** 10.30am-7.30pm Mon-Sat. **Credit** AmEx, DC, MC, V.
To update its image, Et Vous commissioned Andrée Putman to design this 1,200-square metre flagship store. Own-label stretch wool suits are rounded out by some great bouclé knit twin sets, and bright silk blouses. Jackets cost around 1,500F, and you can usually find minimalist dresses for around 1000F. The equally stylish Et Vous Stock at 17 rue de Turbigo, 2nd (01.40.13.04.12) sells discontinued items and collection prototypes at around half the price.
**Branches include:** 6 rue des Francs-Bourgeois (women), 3rd (01.44.58.87.15); 62 (men) and 64 (women) rue de Rennes, 6th (01.45.44.23.75); 72 rue de Passy (women), 16th (01.45.20.47.15).

## Franck et Fils

*80 rue de Passy, 16th (01.44.14.38.00). M° La Muette or Passy.* **Open** 10am-7pm Mon-Sat. **Credit** AmEx, DC, MC, V.
Opened in 1897, Franck et Fils used to be a seriously dusty old shop for bourgeois shoppers in chic western Paris; recently, it gave itself a thorough overhaul and is now one of the top designer boutiques in Paris, evident from the majestically gleaming wood and wrought iron *escalier* and the elegant second-floor tea salon to the racks laden with the likes of Chanel, Givenchy, Christian Lacroix, Ralph Lauren, Vivienne Westwood and Giorgio Armani. It also stocks hats by Marie Mercier, as well as hats made in-house, and lingerie by Capucine Puerari, Guillermina Baeza and La Perla.

## Inès de la Fressange

*14 av Montaigne, 8th (01.47.23.08.94). M° Alma-Marceau.* **Open** 10am-7pm Mon-Sat. **Credit** AmEx, DC, MC, V.
Former Chanel star model Inès de la Fressange proved life can have a second act when she set up shop here and instantly won herself a place in the Paris fashion landscape. Though there is a bit of everything here – from her own handpainted ashtrays, to sheets, dancing slippers and leaf-decorated handbags, what she does best is dressy weekend wear: velvet jeans, sporty men's style shirts and casual jackets. Suits start at around 4,000F, dresses 1,800F-2,000F.

## Galerie Gaultier

*30 rue de Fbg-St-Antoine, 12th (01.44.68.84.84). M° Bastille.* **Open** 11am-7.30pm Mon; 10.30am-7.30pm Tue-Sat. **Credit** AmEx, DC, MC, V.
Lovable Euro-pixie Jean-Paul Gaultier's witty, irreverent clothes have become icons for the stylish, with a recent emphasis on luxurious mariner-style jackets with open backs, and the omnipresent psychedelic swirls. His higher-priced line, where jackets run around 6,000F, are cleverly displayed alongside the clubby JPG diffusion line, Gaultier Jeans and perfumes. Check out his latest fashion show on the video screens set in the blue mosaic floor, the changing celestial signs on the fibre-optic ceiling and the fun-fair mirrors.
**Branch:** Boutique Jean-Paul Gaultier, 6 rue Vivienne, 2nd (01.42.86.05.05).

## Martin Grant @ Jacob

*32 rue des Rosiers, 4th (01.42.71.39.49). M° St-Paul.* **Open** 1-7.30pm Tue-Sun. **Credit** AmEx, V.
The first Australian couture outlet in Paris has set up shop in an old hairdresser in the Jewish quarter. New World-born, Grant's clean lines are classically inspired – flattering little black dresses, dashing jackets and tailored coats – and he has dressed Claudia Schiffer and Helena Christensen. Prices range from 1,000F a frock to much more for a wedding dress.

## Irié

*8 and 10 rue du Pré-aux-Clercs, 7th (01.42.61.18.28). M° Rue du Bac.* **Open** 10.15am-7pm Mon-Sat; closed first three weeks Aug. **Credit** MC, V.
Fashion editors and chic Parisians make a bee-line for this Japanese designer's twin boutiques – possibly because, in an era when fabrics are fashion's new message, Irié boldly gambles on the newest of the new: plastic coatings, stretch wools, chenille and fake-fur, sequins and hologram prints are scattered over suits, minidresses, cropped blousons and leggings – all definately aimed at a sassy young clientele.

## Kashiyama

*147 bd St-Germain, 6th (01.46.34.11.50). M° St-Germain-des-Prés.* **Open** 11am-7pm Mon; 10am-7pm Tue-Sat. **Credit** AmEx, DC, MC, V.
The Japanese firm that has made a career out of betting on – and backing – many a young French talent, is always scouting hot fashion blood, having scooped up Martin Margiela's first collection and adding Ann Demeulemeester, Rifat Ozbek, Jean-Paul Gaultier, Dries Van Noten and Véronique Leroy into the mix. Everything here is crammed

**Martin Grant:** *classically inspired clothes.*

on to the racks, like a designer thrift shop, but the prices run from high to astronomical. Downstairs is devoted to brides, as well as fabulous lingerie by La Perla, shoes by Sara Navarro, Ann Demeulemeester and Dries Van Noten and hats by Jacques Lecorré.
**Branch**: 80 rue Jean-Jacques Rousseau, 1st (01.40.26.46.46).

## Kenzo
*3 pl des Victoires, 1st (01.40.39.72.03). M° Palais-Royal.*
**Open** 11am-7pm Mon; 10am-7pm Tue-Sat. **Credit** AmEx, DC, MC, V.
An ebullient lover of colour and pattern, Kenzo is one designer who never stumbles into any worrying self-examination. The folkloric prints here stay the brightest, the pattern and fabric mixes are the wildest, and, as his many supporters attest, Kenzo cuts some of the best fitting skirts and tailored jackets in the fashion capital. Kenzo Jungle and Kenzo Jeans are the less-expensive line. A rainbow range of shirts and extravagant ties are the highlights for men.
**Branches include**: Les 3 Quartiers, 23 bd de la Madeleine (men), 1st (01.42.61.04.51); 16 (women/home) and 17 (men) bd Raspail, 7th (women 01.42.22.09.38/men 01.45.49.33.75); 18 av George V, 8th (01.47.23.33.49); 27 bd de la Madeleine (women), 8th (01.42.61.04.14).

## Maria Luisa
*2 rue Cambon, 1st (01.47.03.96.15). M° Concorde.*
**Open** 10.30am-7pm Mon-Sat. **Credit** AmEx, DC, MC, V.
Venezuelan Maria Luisa Poumaillou is the godmother to talented young designers, and was one of Paris' original stockists for Helmut Lang, Ann Demeulemeester, John Galliano and Martine Sitbon. New labels to discover here are Hannoh, Andrew Gn and Dirk Bikkembergs. A small but well chosen selection of shoes, handbags and jewellery rounds out the collection. While the top designers here are expensive, there are always a few new fashion finds – especially stretch tops and the like – for 1,000F or less.

## Mosaïque
*17 rue de Sèvres, 6th (01.45.48.53.06). M° Sèvres-Babylone.* **Open** 11am-7pm Mon; 10am-7pm Tue-Sat. **Credit** AmEx, DC, MC, V.
A recent shake-up has made this shop into a haven for women looking for cutting-edge designers, such as Michel Klein, Enrica Massei, D&G, Martine Sitbon, G Gigli, Barbara Bui and Sportmax, which are edited into stylish, easy looks.

## Plein Sud
*17 rue du Cygne, 1st (01.42.33.49.95). M° Etienne-Marcel.* **Open** 11am-7pm Tue-Sat. **Credit** AmEx, V.
Plein Sud is the unabashedly sexy, slightly costumey collection signed by Fayçal Amor. Styles range from the dandy look of long-waisted riding jackets and ankle-length *décolleté* velvet dresses, to born-again hotpants for girls who think cellulite is a mobile phone. Very 1970s-influenced: think Cher in bell sleeved synthetic dresses and tattoos on black leather.
**Branches**: 21 rue de Sévigné, 4th (01.42.72.10.60); 70bis rue de Bonaparte, 6th (01.43.54.43.06).

## Prada
*10 av Montaigne, 8th (01.53.23.99.40). M° Franklin D Roosevelt.* **Open** 10am-7pm Mon-Sat. **Credit** AmEx, DC, MC, V.
Just opened, this spacious store showcases one of the most influential names in fashion today. Soft beige carpeting and pale green walls set off 674 square metres of the universe according to Miuccia Prada: menswear, womenswear, accessories and shoes. From psychedelic prints to 1960s wallpaper patterns, black nylon luggage and handbags, everything that made Prada one of the best-recognised labels in the world can be found here. Buying a Prada bag could mean you skip paying the rent, but the quality, and status of owning one just may skew your priorities.
**Branch**: 5 rue de Grenelle, 6th (01.45.48.53.14).

## Sonia Rykiel
*175 bd St-Germain, 6th (01.49.54.60.60). M° St-Germain-des-Prés.* **Open** 10am-7pm Mon-Sat. **Credit** AmEx, DC, V.
The major return of velour as a fashion essential has put this long-running ready-to-wear house back in the fashion limelight, and Rykiel's signature loose-legged knit velour trousers and tops have become staples in many a wardrobe around the world. This boutique shows off the entire Rykiel universe, including berets, scarves, shoes, bags, luggage, and cosmetics, in an elegant wood-panelled setting.
**Branch**: 70 rue du Fbg-St-Honoré, 8th (01.49.54.61.95).

## Jil Sander
*52 av Montaigne, 8th (01.44.95.06.70). M° Franklin D Roosevelt.* **Open** 10am-6.30pm Mon-Sat. **Credit** AmEx, DC, MC, V.
There was a time Sander stood for something safe and just a tad dull – but no more; today the German designer is one of the most influential fashion forces in the world, with a legion of (rich) fans who swear by her cashmere camel coats, exquisitely cut trousers, suits, jackets and other staples of the successful career woman. Her vast Paris outpost opened in 1992, carved out of an 1890s mansion.

## Tiki Tirawa
*61 rue Bonaparte, 6th (01.43.25.80.28). M° St-Sulplice.*
**Open** 1.30-7.30pm Mon; 10.30am-7.30pm Tue-Sat. **Credit** AmEx, MC, V.
This store specialises in knitted tops, especially cropped pullovers and twin sets. The emphasis is on wool and cashmere. Many of the sweaters are decorated with novelty trimmings, including velvet collars, buttons and belts.

## Victoire
*12 pl des Victoires, 2nd (01.42.61.09.02). M° Bourse or Palais-Royal.* **Open** 9.30am-7pm Mon-Sat. **Credit** AmEx, DC, V.

A coolly elegant shop that is one of the city's more dependable pit stops for designer fashions. The well-edited mix here spotlights all of the hot designer fashions, including Marni, Donna Karan, Ozbek and Paule Ka. Next door is a branch of the shop that carries younger lines, such as DKNY, at much cheaper prices, where there is an especially good collection of nightclub dresses, cotton tops and weekend separates. **Branches**: 1 rue Madame, 6th (01.45.44.28.14); 16 rue de Passy, 16th (01.42.98.20.84).

### Y's

*59 rue des Sts-Pères, 6th (01.45.48.22.56).*
*M° St-Germain-des-Prés.* **Open** 10.30am-7pm Mon-Sat. **Credit** AmEx, DC, MC, V.
Yohji Yamamoto, whose starting point for his garments is the kimono, stocks his simpler, less expensive second line at this shop, for men and women. The fashion crowd make much of his zipped black leather wallets in three sizes. **Branches**: **Yohji Yamamoto** 47 rue Etienne-Marcel (men), 1st (01.45.08.82.52); 25 rue du Louvre (women), 1st (01.42.21.42.81); 3 rue de Grenelle, 7th (01.42.84.28.87).

## Cheap & Cheerful

### Aridza Bross

*224 rue St-Denis, 2nd (01.42.21.35.06).*
*M° Strasbourg St-Denis.* **Open** 10am-7pm Mon-Sat. **Credit** AmEx, V.
A clever, sexy *pas cher* young collection (300F-500F) that is strongest in sweaters and cropped tops, in varied new fabrics, mostly synthetics, including chenille and stretch wools. **Branches**: 53 rue Boucle, 1st (01.40.09.03.77); 88 bd de Sébastopol, 3rd (01.44.54.35.55); 15 rue de Passy, 16th (01.42.30.76.76).

### Au Vrai Chic Parisien

*8-10 rue Montmartre, 1st (01.42.33.15.52). M° Châtelet-Les Halles.* **Open** 10am-7pm Mon-Sat. **Credit** AmEx, V.
Smart, retro-looking clothes that look like they could have been worn by Brigitte Bardot in one of those films where she scootered around Paris with a chiffon scarf on her head. Women's clothes have a smart, girlish charm: chunky-knit little cardigans are paired with skimpy gingham frocks or pedal-pushers. There's also a smattering of men's casual pieces, and a small collection for children. **Branch**: 47 rue du Four, 6th (01.45.44.77.00).

### La Boutique de Lisaa

*5 rue Dupin, 6th (01.42.22.36.39). M° Sèvres-Babylone.* **Open** 10.30am-7pm Tue-Sat. **Credit** DC, MC, V.
Lisaa is the abbreviation for L'Institut Supérieur des Arts Appliqués, which celebrated its tenth anniversary in 1996 by opening a showcase for young design talents in fashion, accessories and home furnishings in the former atelier of Le Corbusier. Handkerchief dresses by Madeline Heuwagen, techno T-shirts, and sturdy workgear by Tomoko Soda are set off by ceramic jewellery by Delphine-Charlotte Parmentier and cardboard furniture by Quart de Poil.

### Kookaï

*2 rue Gustave-Courbet, 16th (01.47.55.18.00).*
*M° Victor-Hugo.* **Open** 10.30am-7.30pm Mon-Sat. **Credit** AmEx, DC, MC, V.
Kookaï, Etam and Morgan are cheap junior lines with myriad sales points throughout the city; of all of them, Kookaï has the broadest appeal. This is the chain's flagship boutique, a colourful space with ruffled ceilings and mobile furniture designed by Kristian Gavoille. Short, shiny straight neoprene skirts, tweed kilts, glazed cotton trenches and skinny see-through blouses are typical of the finds; though stock changes frequently. Look for coats at under 1,000F and skirts, dresses and sweaters in the 200F range. There are wearable finds here at prices that can't be beat.

**Branches include:** pl St-Eustache, Forum des Halles, 1st (01.40.26.55.62); 155 rue de Rennes, 6th (01.45.48.26.36).

### Patricia Louisor

*16 rue Houdon, 18th (01.42.62.10.42). M° Abbesses or Pigalle.* **Open** 11am-8pm daily. **Credit** MC, V.
Walk in as a customer and leave as a friend of this energetic, talented designer and her two sisters. The tiny boutique, between Pigalle and the Butte Montmartre, has a party atmosphere and none of the original designs cost over 600F.

### Tati: La Rue est à Nous

*28 rue Rochechouart, 18th (01.42.55.13.09 ext 242).*
*M° Barbes-Rochechouart.* **Open** 10am-7pm Mon; 9.30am-7pm Tue-Fri; 9.15am-7pm Sat. **Credit** V.
The super-cheap youthful basics (T-shirts 30F, a jersey dress 90F) of the Tati stores (*see chapter* **Specialist Shops**) are designed by Gilles Rosier and Claude Sabbah, whose own line, GR816, is urban and edgy. **Branches**: 13 pl de la République, 3rd (01.48.87.72.81); 140 reu de Rennes, 6th (01.45.48.68.31).

### Mon Ami Pierlot

*3 rue Montmartre, 1st (01.40.28.45.55). M° Châtelet-Les Halles.* **Open** 10am-7.30pm Mon-Sat. Closed Aug. **Credit** AmEx, MC, V.
Claudie Pierlot's less expensive, mostly natural fabrics basics for women, men and children. In the women's line, Pierlot's signature, school-girl silhouettes currently sport a determinedly British look, with many a tweed and heather knit.

### Toi du Monde

*7 rue du Jour, 1st (01.40.13.09.32). M° Châtelet-Les Halles.* **Open** 1-7pm Mon; 10.30am-7pm Tue-Sat. **Credit** AmEx, DC, MC, V.
Recuperated wood and suspended mini-lights set off youthful female garb. Bright colours, lots of stretch. **Branches**: 24 rue de Sévigné, 4th (01.42.72.24.23); 3 rue Montfaucon, 6th (01.46.32.01.19).

### Zara

*2 rue Halévy, 9th (01.44.71.90.90). M° Opéra.*
**Open** 10am-7.30pm Mon-Sat. **Credit** AmEx, MC, V.
Well-known in Spain for *à la mode* bargains, this chain has taken Paris by storm; it's a Gap for women who work. Women's jackets go from around 600F, dresses around 400F. Accessories, men's and children's wear are also available. **Branch**: 128 rue de Rivoli, 1st (01.44.82.64.00).

## Jeans & Casual Wear

### Autour du Monde

*8 and 12 rue des Francs-Bourgeois, 3rd (01.42.77.16.18).*
*M° St-Paul.* **Open** 2-7pm Mon; 10.30am-7pm Tue-Sat; 2-7pm Sun. **Credit** AmEx, MC, V.
Serge Bensimon began in the surplus clothing business, and soon created a traveller's outfitters which stocks timeless, authentic casual wear at good prices and for all ages. The look is wholesome and pastoral, with lots of plain colours and natural fabrics, good jumpers and chino jeans. No 8, the American colonial household shop, is full of patchwork quilts, painted folk furniture, and a line of white cotton nightgowns. **Branch**: 54 rue de Seine, 6th (01.43.54.64.47).

### Chevignon Trading Post

*49 rue Etienne-Marcel, 1st (01.40.28.05.77).*
*M° Etienne-Marcel.* **Open** 10.15am-7pm Mon-Sat. **Credit** AmEx, DC, MC, V.
Guy Azoulay, the alter-ego of his fictional hero Charles Chevignon, has created his own little piece of the American West, stocking those Parisian must-haves, Chevignon jeans and leather bomber jackets.

### Blanc Bleu
*14 pl des Victoires, 2nd (01.42.96.05.40). M° Bourse.*
**Open** 10am-7pm Mon-Sat. **Credit** AmEx, V.
Patrick Khayat, the founder of Blanc Bleu, is a seafarer at heart; recently he bought and refurbished a 1929 yacht, the *Karenita*, once owned by Errol Flynn. The same sort of 'gentleman skipper' chic infuses this line of classic sportswear, including superb cotton sweaters, often in navy and white.
**Branches:** 4 rue Vide-Gousset, 2nd (01.42.96.30.30); 62 bd de Sébastopol, 3rd (01.42.77.51.68); 5 bd Malesherbes, 8th (01.47.42.02.18).

## Clubgoers & Surfers

### Hagen + Ratz
*5 rue de Turbigo, 1st (01.40.26.07.00). M° Châtelet-Les Halles.* **Open** 10.30am-7.30pm Mon-Sat. **Credit** MC, V.
Streetwise clothes by Soochi, Velvet Monkees and Onyx and shoes by Caterpillar, Adidas and Puma, lined up with acid-jazz, funk and techno music. Also stock kids' clothes.

### Nina Jacob
*23 rue des Francs-Bourgeois, 4th (01.42.77.41.20). M° St-Paul.* **Open** 2-7pm Mon, Sun; 11am-7pm Tue-Sat. **Credit** AmEx, MC, V.
Quirky Marais shop bursts with original designer clothes for party girls: crushed velvet and floaty silk dominate; offbeat costume jewellery, trashy watches and other accessories, too.

### Le Shop
*3 rue d'Argout, 2nd (01.40.28.95.94). M° Etienne-Marcel.* **Open** 1-7pm Mon; 11am-7pm Tue-Sat.
**Credit** AmEx, MC, V.
A huge, market-like collection of individual outlets, where you might run into Tank Girl sampling the second-skin sport fashion of Daniel Poole, Lady Soul and Sexy Space Girl. For surfers (waves, concrete or Internet), there's the critical Stüssy line, Urban Outfitters, Trigger Happy, Dosse Posse and Carhartt industrial wear. The café downstairs is a good place for a break, if you can make yourself heard over the pounding techno music making waves in your beer.

### Terrain Vogue
*13 rue Keller, 11th (01.43.14.03.23). M° Ledru-Rollin.*
**Open** 11am-8pm Mon-Sat. **Credit** AmEx, MC, V.
The most streetwise of second-hand shops is strong on the 1970s psychedelic retro boots and skinny ribs, but is also

increasingly producing its own line of fun clubwear – pop T-shirts, Felix the Cat trousers, kinky vinyl skirts – and the work of young designers. Not for the timid.

### Thanx God I'm A V.I.P.
*60 rue Greneta, 2nd (01.40.28.43.14). M° Réamur-Sébastopol.* **Open** 11am-8pm Mon-Fri; 2-8pm Sat.
**No credit cards.**
The name of nightbird Sylvie Chateigner's shop, and the bright, multi-ethnic and second-hand clothes from the 1940s-'70s are irresistible to kitschophiles and nightclubbers.

## Lingerie

### Capucine Puerari
*63 rue des Sts-Pères, 6th (01.42.22.14.09). M° St-Germain-des-Prés.* **Open** 10am-7pm Mon-Sat.
**Credit** AmEx, DC, MC, V.
Capucine Puerari has graduated from modern, sexy and fashionable lingerie and swimwear to a ready-to-wear, trendy collection in the same spirit.

### Chantal Thomass
*1 rue Vivienne, 1st (01.40.15.02.36). M° Palais-Royal.*
**Open** 11am-7pm Mon; 10am-7pm Tue-Sat.
**Credit** AmEx, MC, V.
Thomass lost her company in an ouster by her Japanese investors a short while ago, but the three-storey shop, reminiscent of an over-the-top boudoir, still sells the frilly clothes and accessories under her name. The highlights remain the luxurious, sexy lingerie – think thigh-high, seams, fishnet and crochet embroidery – all fancifully displayed.

### Ci-Dessous
*48 rue du Four, 6th (01.42.84.25.31). M° St-Sulpice.*
**Open** 12.30pm-7pm Mon; 10am-1.30pm, 2.30-7pm, Tue-Sat. **Credit** AmEx, MC, V.
Mostly cotton, softly coloured, comfortable underwear which appeals to young women. Recycled packaging reinforces the natural image.

### Laurence Tavernier
*7 rue du Pré-aux-Clercs, 7th (01.49.27.03.95). M° Rue du Bac.* **Open** 10am-7pm Mon-Sat. **Credit** MC, V.
The last word in comfortable pyjamas (around 800F), wool and cashmere bathrobes (1,800F) and slippers (900F), all designed by the sister of film director Bertrand Tavernier.

*Get kitted out in Stüssy and Dosse Posse at **Le Shop**.*

# Designer bargains

The economic crisis has resulted in a flourish of discount stores opening all over the city and a new mini-industry in designer outlets. Second-hand clothes often aren't cheap, but almost every neighbourhood has a storefront marked *dépôt-vente*, sometimes with very good deals. The rue d'Alésia, in the 14th, is packed with discount factory outlets (look for 'Stock' in the name), including Chipie Stock, Cacharel and Diapositive Stock. For flea markets *see chapter* **Specialist Shops.**

### Alternatives

*18 rue du Roi-de-Sicile, 4th (01.42.78.31.50).*
*Mᵒ St-Paul.* **Open** 11am-1pm, 2.30-7pm, Tue-Sat.
**Credit** MC, V.
Owner Martine Bergossi accepts only the most trendy labels in top condition, such as Jean-Paul Gaultier, Hermès, Dries Van Noten and Comme des Garçons, in her second-hand clothing shop. Prices average 400F-3,000F.

### L'Annexe des Créateurs

*19 rue Godot-Mauroy, 9th (01.42.65.46.40).*
*Mᵒ Havre-Caumartin.* **Open** 11am-7pm Mon-Sat.
**Credit** AmEx, MC, V.
This store sells discounted designer clothing from past seasons. The 'Folies En Sous-Sol' basement sells designer duds at radically slashed prices that are 40 to 70% off.

### Azzedine Alaïa

*18 rue de la Verrerie, 4th (01.42.72.19.19).*
*Mᵒ Hôtel-de-Ville.* **Open** 10am-7pm Mon-Sat.
**Credit** AmEx, DC, MC, V.
At the back of the courtyard is a small boutique where the designer sells his body-sculpting designs from past seasons at half-price. Dresses around 2,000F, shoes 600F.

### La Clef des Marques

*20 pl du Marché St-Honoré, 1st (01.47.03.90.40).*
*Mᵒ Pyramides.* **Open** 12.30-7pm Mon; 10.30am-2.45pm, 3.30-7pm, Tue-Fri; 10.30am-7pm Sat. **Credit** MC, V.
A glossy new two-storey space designed by mega-trendy architect Ricardo Bofill, this chain carries clothes for men, women and children, with new merchandise arriving on a regular basis. There's a good supply of designer clothing, though often more than one season old, and it can look shopworn. Still, you might find a good pair of Ferre or Gaultier trousers in the 300F range or a pair of Doc Martens for 250F.
**Branches**: 126 bd Raspail, 6th (01.45.49.31.00); 86 rue du Fbg-St-Antoine, 11th (01.40.01.95.15).

### L'Habilleur

*44 rue de Poitou, 3rd (01.48.87.77.12). Mᵒ St-Sébastien-Froissart.* **Open** 11am-8pm Mon-Sat. **Credit** MC, V.
From the smartly attired mannequins in the window, you wouldn't guess that the clothes here are *dégriffés* – end of line and off the catwalk clothes and accessories bought direct from designers like Martine Sitbon, Patrick Cox, Olivier Strelli and Romeo Gigli, and sold half the price.

### Le Mouton à Cinq Pattes

*19 rue Grégoire de Tours, 6th (01.43.29.73.56).*
*Mᵒ Odéon.* **Open** 10.30am-7.30pm Mon-Fri; 10.30am-8pm Sat. **Credit** AmEx, MC, V.

*Designer* dégriffées *at* **L'Habilleur.**

Most clothes in these jumble sale-like stores are *dégriffées* (have had their label cut out), so you need to know what you're looking for to recognise the Gaultier, Helmut Lang, Claude Montana, Sybilla, Mugler and Martine Sitbon pieces that can be found here. Avoid Saturdays.
**Branches**: 15 rue Vieille-du-Temple, 4th (01.42.71.86.30); 138 bd St-Germain, 6th (01.43.26.49.25); 8, 10, 14-18 (men, women, children) and 48 rue St-Placide, 6th (01.45.48.86.26).

### Quai des Marques

*8 quai du Châtelier, 93450 L'Ile St-Denis (01.42.43.54.73/recorded info 01.48.09.04.05).*
*Mᵒ Mairie de St-Ouen, then bus 137N or 138.*
**Open** 11am-8pm Wed-Fri; 10am-8pm Sat, Sun.
**Credit** AmEx, MC, V.
Opened in February 1995, this equivalent to an out-of-town discount shopping mall is the first of its kind in the Paris region. Some 35 different factory outlets offer recent- or current-season models at 30% or more off normal retail prices. Though the designer selection is slim, there's a good variety of merchandise offered. The men's, women's and children's wear lines here include Apostrophe, Miss Maud and Karl Lagerfeld. There are also shoes by Kenzo and Montana, as well as household goods.

### Réciproque

*89, 92, 95, 97, 101 and 123 rue de la Pompe, 16th (01.47.04.82.24/01.47.04.30.28). Mᵒ Rue de la Pompe.*
**Open** 11am-7pm Tue-Fri; 10.30am-7.30pm Sat. Closed last week July, all Aug. **Credit** MC, V.
Réciproque's side-by-side second-hand boutiques are the answer for those with couture taste and limited bank accounts. Alaïa, Thierry Mugler, YSL and many other designers' wares all turn up here, though prices are not as cheap (3,000F for a Dior suit) as you would expect. Items are usually in good condition.

### Studio Lolita

*2bis rue des Rosiers 4th (01.42.84.42.94). Mᵒ St-Paul.*
**Open** 11am-1.30pm, 2.30-7pm Mon-Sat. **Credit** AmEx, MC, V.
Lolita Lempicka's sexy suits and famous décolleté dresses are snapped up by daring members of the smart young French bourgeoisie. The shop here sells collections from past seasons at half-price, with the best bargains on pieces from her lower-priced line, Lolita bis. Dresses start at 850F, trousers around 500F.

## Sabbia Rosa

*73 rue des Sts-Pères, 6th. (01.45.48.88.37).*
*M° St-Germain-des-Prés.* **Open** 10am-7pm Mon-Sat.
**Credit** AmEx, MC, V.
Moana Moati has been steering pampered wives, rich executives (50% of the clientele here is men), models and the most
beautifully dressed kept-women in Paris to the right silk pastel undies in various degrees of naughtiness for the past 18
years. This is sexy underwear at top-of-the-line prices: 800F
for a string bikini, and babydoll nighties for around 6,000F.
Moati designs the collection herself, and will be happy to
advise you on your choice of silk suspenders, satin bras, lace
slips and backless, sideless and crotchless underpants.

# Mainly Men

## Anthony Peto

*12 rue Jean-Jacques-Rousseau, 1st (01.42.21.47.15).*
*M° Palais-Royal.* **Open** 11am-7pm Mon-Sat.
**Credit** AmEx, DC, MC, V.
Going to the Prix de Diane, Longchamps or Ascot? Stop here
first for that top hat or boater and all the accoutrements you'll
need to look like a gentleman at the races.

## Façonnable

*9 rue du Fbg-St-Honoré, 8th (01.47.42.72.60).*
*M° Concorde.* **Open** 10am-7pm Mon-Sat. **Credit** AmEx,
DC, MC, V.
A male BCBG haven where new suits smell like old money.
Upstairs you'll find urbanely executive suits averaging
4,500F, as well as shoes and luggage. The ground floor
stocks traditional hunting jackets, jeans, an impressive range
of silk ties (325F) and a whole showcase of Liberty-print
boxer shorts (200F).
**Branch:** 174 bd St-Germain, 6th (01.40.49.02.47).

## Flower

*7 rue Chomel, 7th (01.42.22.11.78). M° Sèvres-Babylone.*
**Open** 11am-12.30pm, 1.30-7pm, Tue-Sat. **Credit** MC, V.
This brand new men's store is one of the rare Paris addresses showcasing young men's designers and the latest trends,
including clothes by Marc Le Bihan, Jean Colonna and Julie
Skarland and new American labels such as MMSM Work
Wear and Rockmount. Accessories include leather sunglasses by Histoire de Voir and handmade ties in 1950s
inspired fabrics by young French designer Erik Halley. A
collaboration with Savile Row tailors Denman & Coddard
allows clients to order semi-made-to-measure suits, coats and
jackets. Many of the items are deliberately unisex.

## Le Garage

*23 rue des Francs-Bourgeois, 4th (01.42.71.96.94).*
*M° St-Paul.* **Open** 2-7pm Mon, Sun; 11am-7pm Tue-Sat.
**Credit** AmEx, DC, MC, V.
Hip and expensive shirts for pale night owls have replaced
the cakes in this former Marais *pâtisserie*. Black and white
rule, although a lot of 1960s wallpaper prints *à la* Prada made
their way into the collection last season. The plainest designs
start at around 600F – more elaborate ones with zips and a
variety of silver detailing go up to around 1,500F.

## Loft Design By

*12 rue du Fbg-St-Honoré, 8th (01.42.65.59.65).*
*M° Concorde or Madeleine.* **Open** 10am-7pm Mon-Sat.
**Credit** AmEx, DC, MC, V.
Before Gap invaded Paris, this is where the French went
for grandad shirts and khaki trousers. The prices are still
higher than you would expect for casual wear (around 400F
for a pair of cotton trousers), but the cut is undeniably French
and the quality of the white cotton shirts is good.
**Branches:** 12 rue de Sévigné, 4th (01.48.87.13.07); 56 rue
de Rennes, 6th (01.45.44.88.99); 175 bd Pereire, 17th
(01.46.22.44.20).

## Paul Smith

*22 bd Raspail, 7th (01.42.84.15.75). M° Rue du Bac.*
**Open** 11.30am-7pm Mon; 10am-7.30pm Tue, Thur-Sat;
10.30am-9pm Wed. **Credit** AmEx, DC, MC, V.
*Le style anglais* in a wood-panelled interior. Smith's great
range of suits and classic shoes are on the upper floor, while
women's wear gets a funkier, more irreverent space below.

## Victoire Hommes

*15 rue de Vieux-Columbier, 6th (01.45.44.28.02). M° St-
Sulpice.* **Open** 9.30am-7pm Mon-Sat. **Credit** AmEx, DC, V.
The menswear annexe of the famed Victoire women's bou-
tiques specialises in casual sportswear, although there are
some suits; fabrics are gorgeous. Labels include Hartford,
Brine, Brando and shoes by Guagleanone.
**Branches:** 10-12 rue du Colonel-Driant, 1st
(01.42.97.44.87); 38 rue François 1er, 8th (01.47.23.89.91).

# Jewellery & Accessories

## Alexis Lahellec

*14-16 rue Jean-Jacques-Rousseau, 1st (01.42.33.40.33).*
*M° Palais-Royal.* **Open** 11am-7pm Mon-Fri; noon-7pm
Sat. **Credit** AmEx, DC, MC,V.
Extrovert jewellery and objects for the house, made by the
young lawyer-turned-designer Lahellec. Pedro Almodóvar
used his fun teapot-motif jewellery in the movie *Women on
the Verge of a Nervous Breakdown*. Chunky gilt bangles and
novelty earrings are made from lightweight resin. You'll also
find patent bags, lava lamps and *papier mâché* chairs.
**Branches:** 14-16 rue Bernard-Palissy, 6th
(01.45.48.71.98); 17 rue St-Florentin, 8th (01.42.61.07.17).

## Cartier

*13 rue de la Paix, 2nd (01.42.18.53.70). M° Opéra.*
**Open** 10.30am-7pm Mon; 10am-7pm Tue-Fri; 10.30am-
1pm, 2-7pm, Sat. **Credit** AmEx, DC, MC, V.
Cartier has done such a good job of marketing its lower
priced lines (the watch, the Panther handbag, the burgundy
keychain, etc) that it's easy to forget that serious money
comes here for tiaras. Cartier is celebrating its 150th anniversary in 1997 with a line of limited-edition gold pens, watches, cigarette lighters and elegant little bags and purses.
**Branches include:** 7 pl Vendôme, 1st (01.44.55.32.50);
23 rue du Fbg-St-Honoré, 8th (01.44.94.87.70).

## Folli Folie

*49 rue Bonaparte, 6th (01.44.07.36.49).*
*M° St-Germain-des-Prés.* **Open** 10am-7pm Mon-Sat.
**Credit** AmEx, MC, V.
Reasonable prices for jewellery that uses real 18k gold and
silver. Rings start at 150F, bracelets at 400F, pendants run
from 200F to 400F. There are also some very nice crystal
chokers, men's watches and retro-style silver lighters.

## Hermès

*24 rue du Fbg-St-Honoré, 8th (01.40.17.47.17).*
*M° Concorde.* **Open** 10am-6.30pm Mon-Fri. Hours vary
during July and Aug, and at sale times. **Credit** AmEx,
DC, MC, V.
The department store to end all department stores, at least
if you are seriously rich and the idea of dropping 10,000F on
a Kelly handbag doesn't faze you in the slightest. Hermès
sells everything from saddles to ready-to-wear, jewellery,
housewares and shoes. Hermès' trademark silk scarves come
in hundreds of bordered prints for about 1,200F. For men,
there are John Lobb custom-made shoes and riding boots.

## Jamin Puech

*61 rue d'Hauteville, 10th (01.40.22.08.32). M° Bonne-
Nouvelle.* **Open** 9.30am-6.30pm Mon-Fri. **Credit** MC, V.
Trendy handbag designers Isabelle Puech and Benoît Jamin
recently opened their first store in a former papergoods shop,

just around the corner from the china stores lining the rue de Paradis. Their unpretentious, yet wildly inventive, handbags and carry-alls use a mad mix of materials from crocheted twine, serigraphed satin to printed plaid canvas. Prices range from 50F to 1,500F.

### Joyce & Co
*1 pl Alphonse-Deville, 6th (01.42.22.05.69). M° Sèvres-Babylone.* **Open** 2-7pm Mon; 10.30am-7pm Tue-Sat. **Credit** AmEx, MC, V.
Originally conceived as a store to sell handbags and everything that comes in them, from compacts to keychains, the actual product range here is much broader, including bright leather belts, cashmere and silk shawls, stoles, diaries, gloves and more. Joyce, a former fashion editor, selects her merchandise with impeccable care, and this shiny blond wood boutique is a real treasure mine. Look for the chic and streamlined handbags by the hottest accessories designer of the moment, Peggy Hyunh-Kinh, as well as the mad, panther- or zebra-striped concoctions of Renaud Pellegrino.

### William Airman Camus
*25 rue du Dragon, 6th (01.45.48.32.16). M° St-Germain-des-Prés.* **Open** Mon, Wed-Sat 10.30am-7pm. **Credit** AmEx, MC, V.
In an area famed for its classy shoe and accessory boutiques is this handbag heaven. Beautifully made handbags in classic leather, superbly soft suede or amusing neo-Chanel fabric. Lots of sizes; designs change each season.

### D Lavilla
*47 rue du Fbg-St-Antoine, 11th (01.53.33.85.55). M° Bastille.* **Open** 11am-7pm Mon-Sat. **Credit** DC, MC, V.
From big shoulder sacks to dainty handbags, Lavilla's suede, leather and patent creations are young in mood and come in a rainbow of colours.
**Branches:** 38 rue de Sévigné, 3rd (01.42.74.76.60); 15 rue du Cherche-Midi, 6th (01.45.48.35.90).

### Lunettes Beausoleil
*28 rue du Roi-de-Sicile, 4th (01.42.77.28.29). M° St-Paul.* **Open** 9am-12.30pm, 2-6.30pm, Mon-Fri; preferably by appointment. **No credit cards.**
Frederic Beausoleil designs glasses on a grand scale. His client list reads like an all-star team: Stevie Wonder, Ray Charles, Tania Marie and true fashion cognoscenti. His special series of tortoiseshell and antique frames (from 450F to over 1,000F for customised orders), make other specs seem to be of the Thunderbirds-Brains variety.

### Madeleine Gély
*218 bd St-Germain, 7th (01.42.22.63.35). M° Rue du Bac.* **Open** 10am-7pm Tue-Sat. **Credit** MC, V.
It's probably safe to say that this shop, spilling over with umbrellas and canes, hasn't changed much since it first opened in 1834. Short or long, plain or fancy, there's an umbrella or cane here for everyone.

### Les Montres
*58 rue Bonaparte, 6th (01.46.34.71.38). M° Mabillon or St Germain-des-Prés.* **Open** 10am-7pm Mon-Sat. **Credit** AmEx, DC, MC, V.
Status-symbol watches for any occasion, among Swiss and American models for men and women. There are also collectors' watches, such as vintage Rolexes from the 1920s.
**Branches:** 7 rue Castiglione, 1st (01.42.60.65.88); 6 rue Gustave Courbet, 16th (01.47.04.85.06).

### Miu Miu
*10 rue du Cherche-Midi, 6th (01.45.48.63.33). M° Sèvres-Babylone.* **Open** 10.30am-7pm Mon-Sat. **Credit** AmEx, DC, MC, V.
As fashion insiders will rush to tell you, Miu-Miu is the nickname of Miuccia Prada, owner-designer of Italy's hottest

fashion house. This is her less expensive line, which is young and sweet, but still pricey. Patent or tanned leather bags cost 1,500F-2,500F. 'Baby' shoes and featherweight linen slip dresses are bought by flower children with a hefty allowance.

### Naïla de Monbrison
*6 rue de Bourgogne, 7th (01.47.05.11.15). M° Solférino.* **Open** 11.30am-1.30pm, 2.30-7pm, Tue-Sat. **Credit** MC, V.
Naïla de Monbrison showcases the top in contemporary international jewellery design by world-famous names, including Juliette Polac, Geraldine Grinda and Marcial Berro. Wares are exhibited in glass cases, but ask to see the one-of-a-kind pieces tucked away in the drawers, at prices to match.

### Optique Josette Poux
*40 rue du Four, 6th (01.45.48.61.33). M° St-Germain-des-Prés.* **Open** 2-7pm Mon; 9.30am-7pm Tue-Sat. **Credit** AmEx, MC, V.
A small shop packed with one of the best selections of spectacle frames in Paris. For 35 years, this father-daughter business has drawn in discriminating customers; among their designers are Gaultier, Beausoleil, Persol, Armani, Calvin Klein, Dior and Ray Ban.

### Marie Streichenberger
*23 rue du Cherche-Midi, 6th (01.45.44.93.02). M° Sèvres-Babylone.* **Open** 10am-7pm Mon-Sat. **Credit** AmEx, DC, MC, V.
Marie Streichenberger began designing jewellery in 1985; since then she has created designs for dozens of Paris fashion houses, including Dior, Kenzo and Montana, as well as bags, belts and jewellery for Thierry Mugler and Donna Karan. This shop showcases her own reasonably priced lines, including her Art Deco lace-work silver bracelets.

### 31 Fèvrier
*2 rue du Pélican, 2nd (01.42.33.48.27). M° Palais-Royal.* **Open** 10am-7pm Mon-Fri. **Credit** AmEx, MC, V.
Wonderfully witty bags, belts and gloves designed by Hélène Népomiatzi and Marc Gourmelen. Their shopping trolleys, covered in funky sequins or fuschia fake fur, have graced fashion pages around the world (around 1,000F).

## Hats

### Divine
*39 rue Daguerre, 14th (01.43.22.28.10). M° Denfert-Rochereau.* **Open** 10.30am-1pm, 3-7.30pm, Tue-Sat. **Credit** MC, V.
An unexpected treasure trove of new and vintage hats for men and women to suit all sartorial styles, pockets and occasions – including traditional straw boaters, floppy velvet, genuine Basque berets and never-worn 1920s lacy cloches.

### Elvis Pompilio
*62 rue des Sts-Pères, 7th (01.45 44.82.02). M° St-Gemain-des-Prés.* **Open** 2-7pm Mon; 11am-7pm Tue-Sat. **Credit** AmEx, MC, V.
This young Belgian hat designer is a good source for creative headgear at reasonable prices (400F-1,500F). Think multicoloured feathers soaring from a satin stovepipe, dalmation spots or crushable mesh walking-hats stuffed with spongy yellow stars or pompoms.

### Marie Mercié
*56 rue Tiquetonne, 2nd (01.40.26.60.68). M° Etienne-Marcel.* **Open** 11am-7pm Mon-Sat. **Credit** AmEx, DC, MC, V.
Paris' mad-hatter, Marie Mercier is the hat designer who put everyone in big-crowned skypieces, revolutionising the hat industry in our times. She hand-makes around 160 hats a year, and sells them from this boutique in charming striped hat boxes. There are colourful felt hats in winter, straw and

**Elvis Pompilio** *has fun with hats.*

silks in summer, in styles that go from classic to theatrical. One-offs cost from 2,000F, the season's lines 500F-1,200F.
**Branch:** 23 rue St-Sulpice, 6th (01.43.26.45.83).

### Philippe Model
*33 pl du Marché-St-Honoré, 1st (01.42.96.89.02).*
*M° Pyramides or Tuileries.* **Open** 10am-7pm Tue-Fri; 1-7pm Sat. **Credit** AmEx, MC, V.
Model's fantasy hats – cutting edge and colourful – get the most double-takes at Paris race meetings. His black stretch flat shoes in grosgrain fabrics are almost as popular by now as his hats. Also men's and children's shoes.
**Branch:** 25 rue de Varenne, 7th (01.45.44.76.79).

### Têtes en l'Air
*65 rue des Abbesses, 18th (01.46.06.71.19).*
*M° Abbesses.* **Open** 2-7pm Mon; 10.30am-7.30pm Tue-Sat. **No credit cards.**
One of several wacky design shops to have opened up along this Montmartre street, the hats here are perfect for attention seekers. Hats can be made to measure or dig the lemon-yellow and lime-green head contraption with a canary in a cage on top, an electric blue shooting star topper or floppy transparent plastic, painted rainhats.

## Shoes

### Accessoire Diffusion
*6 rue du Cherche-Midi, 6th (01.45.48.36.08). M° Sèvres-Babylone or St-Sulpice.* **Open** 10am-7pm Mon-Sat. **Credit** AmEx, V.
A French chain selling well-made fashionable styles at reasonable prices, including assorted sleek square-capped ankle boots. The Détente range, with canvas uppers and rubber soles, is more casual and less expensive.
**Branches:** 8 rue du Jour, 1st (01.40.26.19.84); 36 rue Vieille-du-Temple 4th (01.40.29.99.49); 9 rue Guichard 16th (01.45.27.80.27).

### Charles Jourdan
*86 av des Champs-Elysées, 8th (01.45.62.29.28).*
*M° Franklin D Roosevelt or George V.* **Open** 10am-8pm Mon-Sat. **Credit** AmEx, DC, MC, V.
Charles Jourdan strikes a soothing balance between fashion fads and classic styling. The Bis line has cheaper, younger lines; the Jourdan-designed Karl Lagerfeld collection, with spike or fan-shaped heels, is an engineering feat for the foot.
**Branch:** 5 bd de la Madeleine, 1st (01.42.61.15.89).

### Walter Steiger
*83 rue du Fbg-St-Honoré, 8th (01.42.66.65.08).*
*M° Miromesnil.* **Open** 10am-7pm Mon-Sat.
**Credit** AmEx, DC, MC, V.
Luxurious, beautifully crafted footwear for men and women.
**Branch:** 5 rue du Tournon, 6th (01.46.33.01.45).

### Christian Louboutin
*19 rue Jean-Jacques-Rousseau, 1st (01.42.36.05.31).*
*M° Palais-Royal or Louvre.* **Open** 11am-7.30pm Mon-Sat.
**Credit** AmEx, MC, V.
Louboutin's clientèle includes *le tout Paris* with a cash flow: Caroline of Monaco among them. 18k gold-plated heels and velvet uppers are some of the signature details. Years ago, Louboutin assisted shoe designer Roger Vivier, and his knowledge of shoe construction shows. Prices 1,400F-2,500F.

### Kabuki
*13 rue de Turbigo, 2nd (01.42.36.44.34).*
*M° Etienne-Marcel.* **Open** 1-7.30pm Mon; 10.30am-7.30pm Tue-Sat. **Credit** AmEx, DC, MC, V.
One of the few multi-mark stores in Paris, they stock designer footwear from Dolce e Gabbana, Michel Perry, Vivienne Westwood, Prada and Cesare Paciotti. There's a small assortment of designer clothing for women upstairs.

### Stephen
*42 rue de Grenelle, 7th (01.42.84.12.45).*
*M° Sèvres-Babylone.* **Open** 11am-7pm Mon-Sat.
**Credit** AmEx, MC, V.
Shoes designed by Michel Perry that cost less than his eponymous line. Strappy high-heeled sandals and chunky-heeled slippers in patent leathers, in colours such as lime-blossom, mauve and ruby. Prices run from 900F to 1,500F.

### Patrick Cox
*62 rue Tiquetonne, 2nd (01.40.26.66.55). M° Etienne-Marcel.* **Open** 10am-7pm Mon-Sat. **Credit** AmEx, V.
Cox's coveted, much-photographed shoes, especially his staple baby dolls, are snapped up by trendy Parisian couples. Prices start at under 1,000F. You can also find the cheaper 'Wannabe by Patrick Cox' line with its bestselling moccasin. Cox has added leather goods, separates and coats to his range.
**Branch:** 21 rue de Grenelle, 7th (01.45.49.24.28).

### Roger Vivier
*24 rue de Grenelle, 7th (01.45.49.95.83). M° Sèvres-Babylone or Rue du Bac.* **Open** 10.30am-7pm Mon-Sat. **Credit** AmEx, MC, V.
This octogenarian shoe master began his career fashioning exquisite footwear to accompany Christian Dior's New Look. Re-editions of Vivier's couture shoes and new styles are available to the few: prices start at 1,500F and go up to 8,900F.

### Shoe Bizz
*42 rue du Dragon, 6th (01.45.44.91.70). M° St-Germain-des-Prés.* **Open** 2-7.30pm Mon; 10.30am-7.30pm Tue-Sat. **Credit** AmEx, V.
Their bizz is to zero in on the most fashionable shoe shapes of the season, and recreate them at around 30% cheaper than their competitors. There are also tried and true classic court shoes for women and English-style brogues for men.
**Branch:** 48 rue Beaubourg, 3rd (01.48.87.12.73).

### Stéphane Kélian
*13bis rue de Grenelle, 7th (01.42.22.93.03).*
*M° Sèvres-Babylone.* **Open** 10am-7pm Mon-Sat.
**Credit** AmEx, MC, V.
High-fashion women's shoes with prices to match (1,000F upwards). Kélian also designs for Gaultier, Claude Montana and Martine Sitbon.
**Branches:** 6 pl des Victoires, 2nd (01.42.61.60.74); 36 rue de Sévigné, 3rd (01.42.77.87.91); 26 av des Champs-Elysées, 8th (01.42.56.42.26).

# Specialist Shops

**From fake fur cushions to kitsch kitchenware, Paris has everything for the shopping fanatic.**

Shopping in Paris makes one of the best excuses to explore the city on foot and revel in the charm and originality of French boutiques. Fabulous designer wares and perfumeries abound all over the city, but there are also specialist clutches, so home in on the luxury porcelain and glass shops of rue Royale, fabrics on rue Jacob, old-fashioned restaurant equipment stores around Les Halles or the bookshops of the Left Bank intellectual heartland. Most shops open until at least 7pm, but some close for lunch and on Mondays, and many close for all or part of August. For information on the *détaxe* tax refund scheme, *see chapter* **Fashion**.

## Department Stores

### BHV (Bazar de l'Hôtel de Ville)
*52-64 rue de Rivoli, 4th (01.42.74.90.00); tile shop 14 rue du Temple (01.42.74.92.12); DIY hire annexe 40 rue de la Verrerie (01.42.74.97.23). M° Hôtel-de-Ville.* **Open** 9.30am-6.30pm Mon, Tue, Thur, Fri; 9.30am-9pm Wed; 9.30am-6pm Sat. **Credit** AmEx, MC, V.
A haven for DIY-ers, BHV is the central Paris alternative to the warehouse superstores ringing the edge of town, with a vast range of plumbing, hardware, paints, electrical goods, furnishings, tools and car parts. Most of this is located in the basement. It also stocks classic clothes and accessories on the ground floor, and perfunctory health and beauty aids. *See also chapter* **Services**.
*Café. Carpet and kitchen installation. Photo developing. Printing. Tool hire. Watch repairs.*

### Le Bon Marché
*38 rue de Sèvres, 7th (01.44.39.80.00). M° Sèvres-Babylone.* **Open** 9.30am-7pm Mon-Sat. **Credit** AmEx, DC, MC, V.
The 'good bargain' was the first department store in Paris, and Gustave Eiffel is said to have had a say in the design of its iron-framed structure. The Harvey Nichols of Paris, its speciality departments range from Oriental rugs to stationery and books. Less touristy than its boulevard Haussmann rivals, Le Bon Marché is also a bit younger and more upmarket in its house fashion collections and furnishing departments. The excellent window displays provide a real margin of seasonal trends. Shop 2 contains a food hall (*see chapter* **Food & Drink**) and antiques arcade.
*Gift vouchers. One-hour photo service. Restaurants. Watch & shoe repair. Travel agency. Wedding lists.*

### Galeries Lafayette
*40 bd Haussmann, 9th (01.42.82.34.56/fashion show reservations 42.82.30.25). M° Chaussée d'Antin/RER Auber.* **Open** 9.30am-7pm Mon-Wed, Fri, Sat; 9.30am-9pm Thur. **Credit** AmEx, DC, MC, V.
The Louvre of department stores carries over 75,000 brand names, and welcomes the equivalent of the entire population of Paris each month. Numerous designer concessions include Christian Lacroix's diffusion line Bazar, Yohji Yamamoto,

Claude Montana and Vivienne Westwood. Cheaper alternatives include Agnès B, The Gap and Galeries Lafayette's own women's labels Jodhpur (classic styles), Avant Première (quick translations of catwalk looks) and Briefing (career separates). To celebrate its centenary in 1996, Lafayette Maison, a home-furnishings section, was opened on the fifth floor. As well as an entire floor devoted to lingerie, this is the largest perfume and beauty store in the world, and also features enormous departments dedicated to kitchenwares, books and records, not to mention souvenirs of Paris. There are two restaurants with panoramic views on the 6th floor, as well as a new Café Sushi adjoining Lafayette Maison.
*Baby and wedding lists. Bureau de change. One-hour photo service. Restaurants. Travel & theatre ticket agency. Watch & shoe repair.*
**Branch**: 22 rue du Départ, 14th (01.45.38.52.87).

### Marks & Spencer
*35 bd Haussmann, 9th (01.47.42.42.91). M° Havre-Caumartin/RER Auber.* **Open** 9am-8pm Mon-Sun. **Credit** MC, V.
A branch of the British chain that's every bit as good for underwear and jumpers as you'd expect, but priced about 50 per cent higher than in the UK. The food hall is a great hit with French shoppers – cox's apples, scones and chicken tikka masala are best-sellers.
**Branch**: 88 rue de Rivoli, 4th (01.44.61.08.00).

### Monoprix/Uniprix
*Branches all over Paris.* **Open** generally 9.30am-7.30pm Mon-Sat; some branches open till 10pm. **Credit** MC, V.
Sooner or later you're bound to come into a branch of dependable Monoprix, whether for food, shampoo, a notepad, a teeshirt or a pair of socks. Bigger branches have cheese and *charcuterie* counters and even wet fish counters, and the largest have entire fashion floors. The branch at 21 av de l'Opéra stocks cheap junior clothing and a wide selection of cosmetics. *See also chapter* **Services**.
*Deliveries. Photobooths. Photocopying.*

### Au Printemps
*64 bd Haussmann, 9th (01.42.82.50.00). M° Havre-Caumartin/RER Auber.* **Open** 9am-7pm Mon-Wed, Fri, Sat; 9.30am-10pm Thur. **Credit** AmEx, DC, MC, V.
Along with Galeries Lafayette, this is the other behemoth of Parisian department stores. It comprises three stores: one devoted to the home, one to menswear, and one to women's fashions, which is in the process of getting a face-lift. Established designers – Dolce e Gabbana, Martine Sitbon, Anna Sui – and rising stars such as Alexander McQueen, Hussein Chalayan and Véronique Leroy are on the second floor. The third floor carries trendy looks and sportier labels, while the fourth floor is dedicated to a more traditional approach. A huge new accessories department is planned for the ground and first floors. Housewares from kitchen basics to Lalique glass, Christofle cutlery and Limoges porcelain, and stationery are also worth a look.
*Baby and wedding lists. Bureau de change. 24-hour shopping pick-up. Gift vouchers. Repair to own goods. Restaurants. Travel & theatre ticket agency. Watch repair.*
**Branches**: 30 av d'Italie, 13th (01.40.78.17.17); 25 cours de Vincennes, 20th (01.43.71.12.41).

**Galeries Lafayette** *Art Nouveau finery.*

## La Samaritaine

*19 rue de la Monnaie, 1st (01.40.41.20.20). M° Pont
Neuf.* **Open** 9.30am-7pm Mon-Wed, Fri, Sat; 9.30am-
10pm Thur. **Credit** AmEx, DC, MC, V.
La Samaritaine has never acquired the status of Galeries
Lafayette or Printemps, but you can find just about anything
in the five-store complex, from fashion and sporting goods
to household goods and nuts'n'bolts hardware, as well as the
biggest toy department in Paris. Building two has a faded
charm, a superb location on the Seine and one of the best
views over Paris from the rooftop terrace. The view is also
excellent from the fifth-floor restaurant Le Toupary.
*Baby and wedding lists. Bureau de Change. Gift vouchers.
Restaurants. Watch repairs.*

## Tati

*4 bd Rochechouart, 18th (01.42.55.13.09). M° Barbès-
Rochechouart.* **Open** 10am-7pm Mon; 9.30am-7pm Tue-
Fri; 9.15am-7pm Sat. **Credit** V.
As much a Paris institution at the bottom end of the scale as
Galeries Lafayette at the top, the shops are a chaos of crowd-
ed racks and cheaper goods piled into boxes, and the crowd
uses rugby scrum tactics. Tati has a 'designed' range La Rue
est à Nous, aimed at younger buyers (*see chapter* **Fashion**).
**Branches:** 13 pl de la République, 3rd (01.48.87.72.81);
140 rue de Rennes, 6th (01.45.48.68.31).

# Books

See also Fnac and Virgin Megastore in **Records,
CDs, Cassettes & Hi-Fi** below.

## Abbey Bookshop

*29 rue de la Parcheminerie, 5th (01.46.33.16.24). M° St-
Michel.* **Open** 10am-7pm Mon-Sat. **Credit** AmEx, MC, V.

This small Canadian-run bookshop has an extensive section
of Canadian writers (including *Québecois*), as well as English
and American titles. They will take special and mail orders
for books, and happily serve coffee to browsers.

## Artcurial

*9 av Matignon, 8th (01.42.99.16.16). M° Franklin D
Roosevelt.* **Open** 10.30am-7.15pm Tue-Sat. **Credit**
AmEx, DC, MC, V.
A definitive art bookshop for glossy, coffee-table books on
twentieth-century art, photography and design. There is a
contemporary jewellery and gift shop, and a gallery.

## Brentano's

*37 av de l'Opéra, 2nd (01.42.61.52.50). M° Opéra.* **Open**
10am-7.30pm Mon-Sat. **Credit** AmEx, MC, V.
A good address for American classics, modern fiction and
best-sellers, plus an excellent array of business titles. English
language books are at the front; magazines in the far corner;
children's books are in the basement.

## Entrée des Artistes

*161 rue St-Martin, 3rd (01.48.87.78.58). M° Rambuteau.*
**Open** 11am-9.30pm Mon-Sat. **Credit** MC, V.
This shrine to celluloid, from the most obscure movies to
box-office blockbusters, is packed with film posters, photo
stills and film books in French and English.

## Galignani

*224 rue de Rivoli, 1st (01.42.60.76.07). M° Tuileries.*
**Open** 10am-7pm Mon-Sat. **Credit** MC, V.
Opened in 1802, Galignani was reputedly the first English-
language bookshop in Europe. Today it stocks fine and decorative arts books and literature in French and English.

## Gibert Joseph

*26 bd St-Michel, 6th (01.44.41.88.88). M° St Michel.*
**Open** 9.30am-7.30pm Mon-Sat. **Credit** AmEx, MC, V.
Best-known as a bookshop serving the Left Bank learning
institutions, with some titles in English, as well as a place to
flog your old text books, it's also useful for basic stationery,
graphic and office supplies.

## Institut Géographique National

*107 rue La Boétie, 8th (01.43.98.85.00). M° Franklin
D Roosevelt.* **Open** 9.30am-7pm Mon-Fri; 10am-12.30pm,
2-5.30pm, Sat. **Credit** AmEx, MC, V.
Paris' best cartographic shop has a range of international
maps, as well as detailed walking and cycling maps of
France, wine maps and maps of historic Paris. It also stocks
guidebooks to all regions of France, and globes.

## La Hune

*170 bd St-Germain, 6th (01.45.48.35.85).
M° St-Germain-des-Près.* **Open** 10am-11.45pm Mon-Sat.
**Credit** AmEx, DC, MC, V.
A Left Bank institution that has so far survived the luxury
fashion invasion of St-Germain, La Hune boasts a superb collection of literature and art books in French. Open until very
late, it's always busy with intellectual and arty types.

## Librairie Gourmande

*4 rue Dante, 5th (01.43.54.37.27). M° St-Michel.*
**Open** 10am-7pm. **Credit** MC, V.
Chefs from the world over hunt out Geneviève Baudon's
bookstore dedicated to old and newly published books on
cooking, gastronomy and table arts, with a good selection of
books on wine for oenophiles. Many non-French titles.

## La Maison Rustique

*26 rue Jacob, 6th (01.43.25.67.00). M° St-Germain-des-
Près.* **Open** 10am-7pm Mon-Sat. **Credit** AmEx, MC, V.
Paris' best selection of gardening, botanical and interior
design books, with some titles in English.

# Only in Paris

Despite the increasing worldwide uniformity of both shops and their products, Paris continues to entice visitors with its one-off, out of the ordinary boutiques and gifts. Whether you're after a pair of hand-made kinky boots or that custom-made bustier, somewhere one of Paris' boutiques is sure to have that sought-after item.

## Berluti

*26 rue Marbeuf, 8th (01.43.59.51.10). M° Franklin D Roosevelt.* **Open** 10am-7pm Mon-Sat. **Credit** AmEx, DC, MC, V.
Over 100 years old and still the finest purveyors of hand-made shoes for men in France. Made to measure shoes start at around 5,000F and the wait is several months, but the quality of the leather – suede, ponyskin and reptile among them – and the workmanship would be hard to better elsewhere.

## Parfums Caron

*34 av Montaigne, 8th (01.47.23.40.82). M° Franklin D Roosevelt.* **Open** 10am-6.30pm Mon-Sat. **Credit** AmEx, DC, V.
A number of French perfume houses – Guerlain and Chanel among them – sell perfumes in their Parisian flagships that aren't sold anywhere else in the world. In its elegant Art Deco boutique, Caron sells re-editions of its classic favourites from 1911-54, including the spicy, eastern rose scent *Or et Noir*. There's also a great collection of compact and loose powders, and swan's down puffs.

## Alice Cadolle

*14 rue Cambon, 1st (01.42.60.94.94). M° Concorde.*
**Open** 9.30am-1pm, 2pm-6.30pm Mon-Sat. **Credit** AmEx, MC, V.
Madame Cadolle's shop is a temple to the undergarment. Madonna and other celebrities come to the queen of the corset for superb custom-made bras, and couture houses have long turned here for their bodices and bustiers. Good-quality ready-made lingerie is on sale as well.

## L'Herboristerie du Palais-Royal

*11 rue des Petits-Champs, 1st (01.42.97.54.68).
M° Bourse.* **Open** 9am-7pm Mon-Fri; 10.30am-6.30pm Sat. **Credit** MC, V.
This boutique of herbal products is filled with sturdy, no-nonsense open shelving and mounds of dried herbs wrapped and tied in paper bags spilling out of openwork baskets. For those into aromatherapy, there are plant shampoos, herbal beauty products and essential oils.

## Catherine Memmi

*32-34 rue Saint Sulpice, 6th (01.44.07.22.28).
M° Odéon.* **Open** 12.30-7.30pm Mon; 10.30am-7.30pm Tue-Sun. **Credit** AmEx, MC, V.
The pinnacle of good taste in linens for the home, this boutique is a sea of white, cream and ecru with just a touch of taupe. The hand-embroidered table linens and sheets are meticulously folded and stored in slim little drawers at the back of the shop. There are cream lightweight wool bathrobes, a selection of cotton nightshirts for men and women, soaps, candles, metal lamps and some furniture.

## Sic Amor

*20 rue du Pont-Louis-Philippe, 4th (01.42.76.02.37).
M° Pont-Marie.* **Open** 10am-7.30pm Mon-Sat; 2pm-7.30pm Sun. **Credit** AmEx, MC, V.
A small gem of a boutique offering a window onto contemporary jewellery design and fashion accessory creations in Paris by such rising talents as Stefano Poletti, Hervé van der Straeten or Zazou. You can order jewellery, including wedding rings, to your specifications, as well as porcelain dinnerware in the colour of your choice.

## La Tuile à Loup

*35 rue Daubenton, 5th (01.47.07.28.90). M° Censier Daubenton.* **Open** 10.30am-7.30pm Mon-Sat. **Credit** V.
A unique, delightfully outfitted shop specialising in French regional crafts, from Provençal *boutis*, or quilted bedcovers, to glazed pottery from Alsace, handsome striped Basque linens and original basket work.

**Sic Amor**, *source of the very latest designer baubles.*

### Shakespeare & Co
*37 rue de la Bûcherie, 5th (01.43.26.96.50). Mº Maubert-Mutualité/RER St-Michel.* **Open** noon-midnight daily.
**No credit cards.**
A Parisian legend, if no longer on the same site as Sylvia Beach's famous shop. New, used and antique books in English are idiosyncratically arranged – mainly on the floor – and it's still packed with would-be Hemingways.

### Tea & Tattered Pages
*24 rue Mayet, 6th (01.40.65.94.35). Mº Duroc.* **Open** 11am-7pm daily. **No credit cards.**
A gentle and friendly American-style tea salon cum bookshop where you can browse through new editions and over 10,000 second-hand, mainly paperback, books in English.

### Village Voice
*6 rue Princesse, 6th (01.46.33.36.47). Mº Mabillon.*
**Open** 2-8pm Mon; 10am-8pm Tue-Sat; Mon 2pm-8 pm. *June, July* 12.15pm-6pm Sun. **Credit** AmEx, DC, MC, V.
The ever-charming Odile Hellier supports alternative literature by stocking the city's best selection of new and hard-to-get fiction and non-fiction in English, and literary magazines. She also holds literary events and play and poetry readings.

### WH Smith
*248 rue de Rivoli, 1st (01.44.77.88.99). Mº Concorde.*
**Open** 9.30am-7pm Mon-Sat. **Credit** AmEx, MC, V.
This long-established branch of the British chain carries over 70,000 titles, including paperback bestsellers, classics, travel guides, cookery books and videos. There are good reference and English-language teaching sections and a perpetual mob around the UK and US magazine and newspaper racks, which carry London *Time Out*, among many others.

## Design & Furniture

### Avant-Scène
*4 pl de l'Odéon, 6th (01.46.33.12.40). Mº Odéon.* **Open** 10.30am-1pm, 2-7pm, Tue-Sat. **Credit** AmEx, MC, V.
The more baroque side of contemporary design is gathered together by owner Elisabeth Delacarte who stocks a good mix of French and European designers, including furniture and lighting for the home from such rising talents as Tom Dixon, André Dubreuil and Hervé Van der Straeten.

### Catastrophe
*Forum des Halles, Level -2,13 Balcon St-Eustache, 1st (01.45.23.28.94). Mº Châtelet-Les Halles.* **Open** 11.30am-7pm Tue-Sat. **No credit cards.**
The four young women behind Catastrophe began as design squatters, holding shows of their recycled bottle-cap frames whenever and wherever the spirit hit them. Since they opened this space in 1995, their work has matured but remains edgy, as seen in their designs using resin, metal or wood. Also some jewellery and handbags.

### Conran Shop
*117 rue du Bac, 7th (01.42.84.10.01). Mº Sèvres-Babylone.* **Open** noon-7pm Mon; 10am-7pm Tue-Sat.
**Credit** AmEx, MC, V.
Sir Terence Conran opened this branch of the London furniture and accessories shop at the end of 1992 in an elegant building just next to the Bon Marché. Sleek furniture, wonderful kitchen gadgets, handmade wrought-iron candles, sophisticated lighting and natural linens for the home.

### Edition Limitée
*7 rue Bréguet, 11th (01.48.06.52.11). Mº Bréguet-Sabin.* **Open** 10.30am-8pm Mon-Sat. **Credit** V.
Opened in 1995 by Frédérique Caillet and Vincent Collin, this boutique puts together the minimalist sculptural works of Collin with the lamps, furniture and lighting fixtures of fel-

*La Hune is a Left Bank late-night favourite.*

low designers Olivier Gagnère (who designed the interior of Café Marly) and Memphis-originator Ettore Sottsass.

### En Attendant Les Barbares
*35 rue de Grenelle, 6th (01.42.22.65.25). Mº Sèvres-Babylone.* **Open** 2.30-6.30pm Mon; 11am-7pm Tue-Fri; 11am-6.30pm Sat. **Credit** AmEx, V.
The mightiest name among Paris' many avant-garde design boutiques shows off the leaders in spiked wrought iron, baroque flourishes and paste glass furnishings, including Garouste et Bonetti, Eric Schmitt and Migeon & Migeon.

### Galerie Frédéric de Luca
*3 rue Visconti, 6th (01.43.25.16.10). Mº St-Germain-des-Prés.* **Open** 10.30am-1pm, 2-6pm Tue-Sat. **Credit** AmEx, V.
Frédéric de Luca opened this new space in late 1996 to show off not only his own designs, but also a selection of pieces by assorted designers, such as furniture by Garouste et Bonetti and the ceramic lamps of Véronique Rivemale.

### Sentou Galerie
*26 bd Raspail, 7th (01.45.49.00.05). Mº Sèvres-Babylone.* **Open** 11am-7pm Tue-Sat. **Credit** DC, MC, V.
Sentou carries a varied selection of contemporary designs, from minimalist Japanese wood and paper lamps by Osamu Noguchi and classic Aalto chairs to the fun resin candlesticks and sculptural tableware by Tsé & Tsé Associés.
**Branch:** 18, 24 rue du Pont Louis Philippe, 4th (01.42.77.44.79).

### Volt et Watt
*29 bd Raspail, 7th(01.45.48.29.62). Mº Sèvres-Babylone.* **Open** 10am-7pm Mon-Sat. **Credit** MC, V.
A small but well-selected collection of contemporary light fixtures includes pieces by Jean-Michel Wilmotte, Gae Aulenti and Philippe Starck. It's all a question of lighting.

## Fabrics & Trimmings

### La Droguerie
*9 rue du Jour, 1st (01.45.08.93.27). M° Châtelet-Les Halles or Etienne-Marcel.* **Open** 10-6.45pm Mon-Sat; Aug1-6.45pm Tue-Sat. **Credit** AmEx, MC, V.
Baubles, beads and buttons in all conceivable colours and shapes can be selected individually or by the scoopful. Also, ribbons, feather boas and knitting yarns galore.

### Maison de la Fausse Fourrure
*34 bd Beaumarchais, 11th (01.43.55.24.21). M° Bastille.* **Open** 2-7pm Mon; 11am-7pm Tue-Sat. **Credit** AmEx, DC, MC, V.
The 'House of Fake Fur' pays tribute to our furry friends, but no need to worry about animal rights as everything here is fake and fun. There are synthetic teddy-bear coats, animal-print bags and hats in your choice of chic 'leopard' or cheeky 'monkey', as well as bolts of fake fur fabric, lampshades and furniture covered with the stuff to decorate your lair.

### Marché St Pierre
**Dreyfus** *2 rue Charles Nodier, 18th (01.46.06.92.25);* **Tissus Reine** *5 pl St-Pierre, 18th (01.46.06.02.31);* **Moline** *1 pl St-Pierre, 18th (01.46.06.14.66). M° Anvers or Barbès-Rochechourt.* **Open** 1.30-6.30pm Mon; 9.30am-6.30pm Tue-Fri; 9.30am-6.45pm Sat. **Credit** V.
The three shops listed above have the best selections of fabrics, though you'll also find stores all around and off the place St-Pierre. Reine and Moline often have good selections of discounted silks and other luxury fabrics. Dreyfus is a crowded, five-floor store. Upstairs floors carry linens, silks, woollens and home furnishing fabrics; the ground floor is a cross-section of mostly discounted bolts. Get your fabric priced from a salesperson – whatever you do, don't lose that slip – then go to the cash register to pay.

### Souleiado
*78 rue de Seine, 6th (01.43.54.62.25). M° Mabillon.* **Open** 10am-7pm Mon-Sat. **Credit** AmEx, DC, MC, V.
Specialises in bright Provençal prints. You can buy ready-made tablecloths, placemats and linens, or do like the French and buy it by the bolt and make your own.
Branches: 7 rue Lobineau (professional showroom), 6th (01.44.07.33.81); 83 av Paul Doumer, 16th (01.42.24.99.34).

### Wolff et Descourtis
*18 galerie Vivienne, 2nd (01.42.61.80.84). M° Bourse.* **Open** 11am-7pm Mon-Fri; 1-7pm Sat. **Credit** AmEx, DC, MC, V.
This shop has supplied couturiers with exotic and sumptuous materials and fabrics since 1875.

## Florists & Garden Fittings

### Jardins Imaginaires
*9 bis rue d'Assas, 6th (01.42.22.90.03). M° Sèvres-Babylone.* **Open** 10.30am-1pm, 2-7pm Tue-Sat. **Credit** AmEx, MC, V.
Pots in terracotta or blue Oriental ceramic in all shapes, and prices are just some of the elegant gifts for serious gardeners. You'll also find garden aprons and gloves reproduced from original eighteenth-century designs, luxury garden tools and a good selection of hand-woven baskets.

### Au Nom de la Rose
*4 rue de Tournon, 6th (01.46.34.10.64). M° Odéon.* **Open** 9am-9pm Mon-Sat; 9am-2pm, 3-6pm Sun. **Credit** V.
Roses and nothing but – from long-stemmed and elegant to cabbage roses and the hard-to-find black roses. Its sister shop (46 rue du Bac) sells rose-decorated items for the home, including rose jam and rose-scented candles.

### Christian Tortu
*6 carrefour de l'Odéon, 6th (01.43.26.02.56). M° Odéon.* **Open** 9am-8pm Mon-Sat. **Credit** MC, V.
Paris' most celebrated florist is famous for his buoyant natural bouquets, combining flowers, foliage, twigs and moss and sometimes bark, shells or moss into still-lifes.

## Gifts & Oddities

### Deyrolle
*46 rue du Bac, 7th (01.42.22.30.07). M° Rue du Bac.* **Open** 9am-12.30pm, 2-6pm, Mon-Fri; 9am-12.30, 2-5.30pm, Sat. **Credit** MC, V.
A taxidermist's dream, this dusty shop, established 1831, overflows with stuffed animals, ranging from a polar bear and a horse to exotic birds. You can also have your own household pets lovingly stuffed here for 3,000F and upwards or hire a beast for a few days to complete your film set.

### Diptyque
*34 bd St-Germain, 5th (01.43.26.45.27). M° St-Germain-des-Prés.* **Open** 10am-7pm Tue-Sat. **Credit** V.
Dyptique is and remains the standard by which all other scent manufacturers are measured. Beautiful fat perfumed candles in musk, heliotrope and more scents for the home.

### Estéban
*49 rue de Rennes, 6th (01.45.49.09.39). M° St-Germain-des-Prés.* **Open** noon-7pm Mon; 11am-7pm Tue-Fri; 10am-7pm Sat. **Credit** AmEx, V.
Catherine and Jean-Max Estéban, who opened this shop in 1996, have created an olfactory tour around the world with scented stones, ceramics, Japanese incense and candles.

### Kitsch
*3 rue Bonaparte, 6th (01.43.29.76.23). M° St-Germain-des-Prés.* **Open** 2-7pm Mon-Sat. **Credit** AmEx, MC, V.
What else could they have called this shop with the loudest ever ceramic fish lamps, floral-shaded sconces and curlicue vases? There are also ceramics from sought-after manufacturers from the 1930s to'50s, including Vallauris.

### Magasin Général A.P.C.
*45 rue Madame, 6th (01.45.48.72.42). M° St-Sulpice.* **Open** noon-7pm Mon-Sat. **Credit** AmEx, MC, V.
Designer Jean Toitou has collected objects from his travels around the world and housed them in his New Age general store, which includes a collection of his favourite CDs, a hi-fi set, a high-tech Japanese motorcycle helmet and even New York firemen's T-shirts. A very odd, but intriguing selection. *See* **Fashion** for his A.P.C. clothing stores.

### Paris Accordéon
*80 rue Daguerre, 14th (01.43.22.133.48). M° Denfert-Rochereau or Gaîté.* **Open** 9am-noon, 1-7pm, Tue-Fri; 9am-6pm Sat. **Credit** MC, V.
'Come share our passion,' welcomes this little yellow-painted shop, its shelves lined with all makes and colours of accordion from simplest squeeze-box to the most beautiful tortoiseshell (from 3,500F up). The French national instrument is back in fashion and here they can also restore or tune your old beat-up version, sell sheet music and advise on courses.

### Paris-Musées
*29bis rue des Francs-Bourgeois, 4th (01.42.74.13.02). M° Bastille.* **Open** 10.30am-7.30pm Tue-Sat; 2.30-7.30pm Mon. **Credit** AmEx, MC, V.
A shop run by the museums of the Ville de Paris with a collection of funky items, including lamps and ceramics, created especially for them by some of Paris' top young designers, including Mathieu & Ray and Robert Le Héros.
**Branch**: Forum des Halles, 1 rue Pierre-Lescot, 1st (01.48.06.79.10).

## Robin des Bois

*15 rue Ferdinand Duval, 4th (01.48.04.09.36).*
*M° St-Paul.* **Open** 10.30am-7.30pm Mon-Sat; 2-7.30pm
Sun. **Credit** MC, V.
The Robin Hood of the environment is linked to an ecological organisation of the same name. Everything is made with recycled or ecologically sound products, including bottle-top jewellery and buttons, ear-rings made from vegetal ivory, natural toiletries, slippers and attractive recycled notepaper.

# Home Accessories

## Axis

*Marché St-Germain, 14 rue Lobineau, 6th*
*(01.48.04.36.37). M° Mabillon.* **Open** 10am-8pm Tue-Sat.
**Credit** AmEx, MC, V.
Graves' Mickey Mouse sugar bowls (with ears), Alessi kettles and cutlery, Starck lemon squeezers, Pesce resin chairs, fab high-tech trolleys and, of course, lots of plastic, are a mix of laughable and loveable, designer and gadget.
**Branch**: 13 rue de Charonne, 11th (01.48.06.79.10).

## Bains Plus

*51 rue des Francs-Bourgeois, 4th (01.48.87.83.07).*
*M° Hôtel-de-Ville.* **Open** 11am-7.30pm Tue-Sat; 2.30-7pm
Sun. **Credit** AmEx, MC, V.
One of the many treasure troves on the main thoroughfare in the Marais. All your bathroom needs are served with the ultimate gentleman's shaving gear, duck-shaped loofahs and seductive dressing-gowns.

## La Chaise Longue

*20 rue des Francs-Bourgeois, 3rd (01.48.04.36.37).*
*M° St-Paul.* **Open** 11am-7pm Mon-Sat; 2-7pm Sun.
**Credit** AmEx, MC, V.
Accessories for the kitchen and bath, in glass, ceramic and metal, include colourful enamelled toleware, intricate Mexican-style chrome wire soap dishes and saucepan stands fashioned into horses, fish or cats, painted tumblers, plus re-editions of gadgets from the 1930s to '50s, such as whirring black electric fans. Great for gifts.
**Branches**: 30 rue Croix des Petits-Champs, 1st
(01.42.96.32.14); 8 rue Princesse, 6th (01.43.29.62.39).

## Compagnie Française de l'Orient et de la Chine (CFOC)

*170 bd Haussmann, 8th (01.45.62.12.53).*
*M° St-Philippe-du-Roule.* **Open** 10am-7pm Mon-Sat.
**Credit** AmEx, MC, V.
The newest and most impressive of several branches of this store, known to Parisians as the CFOC. The company sells high quality imported goods from the Far East, such as bamboo chairs, Mongolian pottery, eighteenth-century consoles, silks from India and blown glass from Iran. Downstairs, where traditional basketry and jars are sold, is a rare example of an interior designed by Art Deco maestro Ruhlmann.
**Branches**: 24 rue St-Roch, 1st (01.42.60.65.32); 163 & 167 bd St-Germain, 6th (01.45.48.00.18 & 01.45.48.10.31); 260 bd St-Germain, 7th (01.47.05.92.82); 65 av Victor-Hugo, 16th (01.45.00.55.46); 113 av Mozart, 16th (01.42.88.36.08).

## E Dehillerin

*18 rue Coquillière, 1st (01.42.36.53.13). M° Châtelet-Les*
*Halles.* **Open** 8am-noon, 2-6pm, Mon; 8am-6pm Tue-Sat.
**Credit** MC, V.
Dehillerin has supplied many of the great European chefs since 1820, and the shop is packed with every kind of cooking utensil you could think of, including huge and unusual cooking vessels and equipment – gargantuan casseroles and ladles big enough to serve 50.

## L'Entrepôt

*50 rue de Passy, 16th (01.45.25.64.17). M° La Muette.*
**Open** 10.30am-7pm Mon-Thur; 10am-7pm Fri, Sat.
**Credit** AmEx, V.
Gifts for everyone: party supplies, home accessories, kitsch kitchenware, tools for the serious gourmet and clothing.

## Kitchen Bazaar

*11 av du Maine, 15th (01.42.22.91.17) M°*
*Montparnasse-Bienvenüe.* **Open** 10am-7pm Mon-Sat.
**Credit** AmEx, MC, V.
High design and high-tech kitchen equipment and accessories, from traditional French kitchen linens, superb chef's knives to state-of-the-art storage components, glazed potteries and Alessi retro toasters. Across the street, a sister shop, Kitchen Bazaar Autrement (6 av du Maine, 15th/ 01.45.48.89.00), shows off exotic kitchen utensils and cooking accoutrements from around the world.

*Designers from Gaultier on have rummaged through the bins at the* **Marché St Pierre***.*

# In Remembrance of times past

The colourful reminders of France's past – from hand-embroidered linens to Art Deco cabinetry, Limoges china to turn-of-the-century sleigh beds – don't disappear in Paris, they just get regorged in the city's many and varied purveyors of antiquities. From second-hand *brocantes* and *dépot-ventes* that are just a notch above thrift shops, to the narrow, crowded stands of old wares in the flea market at Clignancourt, and the city's refined and astronomically priced antique shops, Paris has something for almost anyone in search of treasure with a provenance.

Fine antique shops tend to be clustered along the quai Voltaire (the '*quai des Antiquaires*') and in the neighbouring streets known as the *Carré Rive Gauche* – rues de Lille, de Beaune, des Saints-Pères and de l'Université (all in the 7th). It's particularly fun during the annual Cinq Jours de l'Objet Extraordinaire (*see chapter* **Paris by Season**). Other top-quality antique dealers are gathered along the rue du Fbg-St-Honoré in the 1st, and in the streets around the Drouot auction house (*see below*), while there are several dealers in top-class Art Deco and tribal art in the 6th around rue Bonaparte. If you're after one of a kind retro treasures from the 1940s to '60s, try rue de Charonne in the Bastille.

Look out, too, for the city's upmarket Biennale des Antiquaires (next in autumn 1998), or the open-air antiques and collectors fairs, known as *brocante*, held frequently during the summer, when many dealers bring in goods from the provinces. These are usually advertised by posters and banners in the street, or you can contact SADEMA (86 rue de Lille, 7th/01.40.62.95.95), for a complete calendar.

*After loot at the **Puces de St-Ouen**.*

## Antique Markets

### La Galerie des Antiquaires du Bon Marché
*rue du Bac/rue de Sèvres, 5th (01.44.39.80.00). Mº Sèvres-Babylone.* **Open** 10am-7pm Mon-Sat.
A floor of shop 2 at Bon Marché department store is set aside for 15 eclectic antiques stalls spilling over with everything from seventeenth-century furniture and tapestries to antique dolls, jewellery and old coins.

### Louvre des Antiquaires
*2 pl du Palais-Royal, 1st (01.42.97.27.00). Mº Palais Royal.* **Open** 11am-7pm Tue-Sun.
An upmarket, purpose-built antiques centre behind an old façade, home to 250 dealers. Louis XV furniture, tapestries, Chinese porcelain, silver and jewellery, scientific instruments or tin soldiers can all be found here, at a price.

### Village St-Paul
*between quai des Célestins, rue St-Paul and rue Charlemagne. Mº St-Paul.* **Open** Mon, Thur-Sun.
A maze of courtyards holds a cluster of antique shops known collectively as the Village St-Paul. As well as dealers in Art Deco, retro and rustic furniture, look out for Histoires de Table (01.40.27.95.53), crammed with vintage tableware, from dinner services to doggy knife rests.

### Village Suisse
*38-78 av de Suffren, 15th (01.47.34.06.76). Mº La Motte-Picquet-Grenelle.* **Open** 10.30am-7pm Thur-Mon.
Formerly the site of the Swiss Village erected for the 1900 World Fair, this conglomeration of roughly 150 boutiques offers a selection of antiques and second-hand collectibles ranging from Asian and African art to engravings, furniture, bric-a-brac, fine and costume jewellery and more. Sundays tend to be busy, as the village with its small landscaped gardens is an pleasant site for a walk.

## Specialised Markets

### Marché aux Livres
*Parc Georges Brassens, rue Brancion and rue des Morillons, 15th. Mº Porte de Vanves or Convention.* **Open** 9am-6pm Sat, Sun.
Arrive early to haggle over antiquarian books under the shelter of a former meat market. For more books, prints and postcards, take a look at the *Bouquinistes* – the green boxes lining the Seine, and the covered passages.

### Marché aux Timbres
*corner of av Marigny and av Gabriel, 8th. Mº Champs-Elysées-Clemenceau.* **Open** 10am-sunset Thur, Sat, Sun, public holidays.
Vintage stamps and postcards from around world, as well as the curiously tradeable modern phone cards.

## Flea Markets

Occupying sites next to the noisy *Périphérique*, or ringroad, Paris' three main flea markets originally developed outside the *portes* (gateways) to Paris so that rag-and-bone men from outside the town could avoid paying duty.

*Fine art comes under the hammer at* **Hôtel Drouot**

### Marché aux Puces de Montreuil

*Outside M° Porte de Montreuil, 20th.* **Open** 7.30am-7pm Mon, Sat, Sun.

Expect second-hand clothing, contraband videos, broken chairs and loads of miscellaneous junk. Sprawling and more anarchic than Clignancourt, with the occasional junk-aficionado's find. Little if anything here is pre-1900, but you may find fun collectables like *pastis* jugs.

### Marché aux Puces de St-Ouen (Clignancourt)

*outside M° Porte de Clignancourt, 18th.* **Open** 5am-6pm Mon, Sat, Sun.

This enormous market, reputedly the largest flea market in Europe – with over 2,000 stands and ten miles of walk-ways – is made up of arcades of semi-permanent shops. There are rare and high-quality pieces to be found here, but at a price. The whole complex is divided into ten different '*Marchés*', most of which run off the rue des Rosiers in St-Ouen, such as the Marché Serpette specialising in Art Nouveau, Art Deco, 1940s furniture and decorative objects. Earthier Marché Paul Bert has everything from garden sculpture to '50s Americana, not to mention a wonderful stand of vintage kitchenware. Marché Biron is still the place for an ormolu candelabra or Louis XV chairs – many of the dealers here also have their own shops in the 7th or 8th *arrondissements*. Smaller Marché des Rosiers has less pricey goods like antique baby clothes.

Among the specialists, check out the Marché Serpette, where Jean-Paul Costey (stand 2,3,4 allée 3/01.40.12.26.38) and Jacques Lacoste (stand 16, allée 6/ 01.40.12.34.28) feed the burgeoning market for 1940s French furniture. Olwen Forest carries costume jewellery from the 1930s to '50s, including some show-stoppers worn by Rita Hayworth (stand 7, allée 3/ 01.40.11.96.38). Madame Schwartz spe-cialises in luxurious antique bed and table linens and retro clothing – her clients include John Galliano and other designers hooked on retro-glamour (Marché Dauphine, allée Ste-Sophie, stand 24/01.49.45.14.36). Most merchants help organise delivery for large items and take Visa or MC.

### Marché aux Puces de Vanves

*av Georges Lafenestre (on bridge after Périphérique) and av Marc Sangrier, 14th. M° Porte de Vanves.* **Open** 7.30am-7pm Sat, Sun.

Smaller than St-Ouen or Montreuil, and perhaps the friend-liest. You probably won't find great treasures, but it can be a good source of small decorative or household items.

## Auctions

The secondary art market in Paris is undergoing radical changes. After a four-century monopoly wherein only a small number of authorised *com-missaires priseurs* (expert valuers who have both legal and art expertise and French nationality) – the big three of whom are Etude Tajan, Binoche and Maître Loudmer, who mainly hold their sales at Drouot (*see below*) – have been authorised to hold auctions in France, European Union laws are now insisting the French auction market be opened up. Though laws are being finalised, both Sotheby's and Christie's are gearing up to hold auctions as early as 1998, and Sotheby's is ready-ing for entry into the market with the restoration of a listed *hôtel particulier*.

In the meantime, the traditional arena for auc-tions in Paris, Drouot, a spiky aluminium and marble-clad concoction designed in the early 1980s, makes for a pleasant outing. Pieces of varying quality and all genres from Oriental paintings to jewellery to furniture usually go on public view the day before a sale. If you can't attend an auction, you can leave a sealed bid: the experts at Drouot are happy to steer newcomers through the process. Details of forthcoming sales are published in the weekly magazine *La Gazette de L'Hôtel Drouot* sold at news stands.

### Hôtel Drouot

**Drouot-Richelieu** *9 rue Drouot, 9th (01.48.00.20.20/ recorded information 01.48.00.20.17). M° Richelieu-Drouot.* **Open** 11am-6pm Mon-Sat.
**Branches: Drouot-Montaigne** *15 av Montaigne, 8th (01.48.00.20.80);* **Drouot Nord** *64 rue Doudeauville, 18th (01.28.00.20.90).*
**Sotheby's** *Galerie Charpentier, 76 rue du Fbg-St-Honoré, 8th (01.53.05.53.05). M° Champs-Elysées Clemenceau.*
**Christie's France** *6 rue Paul-Baudry, 8th (01.42.56.17.66). M° St-Philippe-du-Roule.*

**Bains Plus** *is the perfect choice for bathing beauties.*

### Geneviève Lethu
*95 rue de Rennes, 6th (01.45.44.40.35). M° St-Placide.*
**Open** 10.15am-7pm Mon-Sat. **Credit** AmEx, V.
A high-class tableware shop with china, glass and silverware all in the best possible taste, both in the plain 'pop' range and more decorative styles. It's a good place to look for classy gifts, and popular for wedding lists.
**Branches:** 91 rue de Rivoli, 1st (01.42.60.14.90); 28 rue St-Antoine, 4th (01.42.74.21.25); 1 av Niel, 17th (01.45.72.03.47); 317 rue Vaugirard, 15th (01.45.31.77.84).

### Maison de Famille
*29 rue St Sulpice, 6th (01.40.46.97.47). M° Odéon.* **Open** 10.30am-7pm Mon-Sat. **Credit** AmEx, MC, V.
A large, busy three-storey boutique that is filled with unusual French finds, from heavy brass garden scissors to rope-soled bedroom slippers. Home accessories are on the second floor, while women's and men's clothing are on the top floor.
**Branch:** 10 pl de la Madeleine (01.53.45.82.00).

### La Maison Ivre
*38 rue Jacob, 6th (01.42.60.01.85). M° St-Germain-des-Prés.* **Open** 10.30am-7pm Tue-Sat. **Credit** MC, V.
Paris became a suburb of St Rémy-de-Provence in the late 1980s, and this store is one of the many outgrowths of that phenomenon. Traditional hand-made pottery from all over France with a decided emphasis on yellow and green glazed Provençal styles. Also table cloths, wicker bread dishes, hand-woven baskets and a good selection of gifts for under 100F, including eggcups, salt dishes and candle holders.

### Rooming
*Carrousel du Louvre, 99 rue de Rivoli, 1st (01.42.60.10.85). M° Palais-Royal.* **Open** 11am-8pm Mon-Sun. **Credit** AmEx, DC, MC, V.
A shop entirely dedicated to how to put stuff away: CD racks, stacking bookcases, hanging shoe pouches and tuckaway wine racks. Lots of colourful plastic – for the truly obsessive.

### A Simon
*36 rue Etienne-Marcel, 2nd (01.42.33.71.65). M° Etienne-Marcel.* **Open** 8.30am-6.30pm Mon-Sat.
**Credit** AmEx, MC, V.
This professional kitchen supplier has gigantic tureens and saucepans for feeding from two to two hundred; plates, sundae dishes and all the trappings of blackboards and wine pitchers you could possibly want for your own bistro.

## Perfumes & Make Up

### Détaille
*10 rue St Lazare, 9th (01.48.78.68.50). M° Notre-Dame de Lorette.* **Open** 10am-1.30pm, 2-7pm, Mon-Fri; 10am-2pm Sat. **Credit** AmEx, MC, V.
Invented in 1905 by the Comtesse de Presle to protect her skin from the pollution of the new automobiles, this firm's famous 'Baume Automobile' is still on sale. The natural (no alcohol or perfume) range is now rather sophisticated, and Comme des Garçons designer Rei Kawakuba distributes it worldwide. Both the boutique and bottles – including superb rice-flour powders – retain a turn-of-the-century charm.

### Annick Goutal
*14 rue de Castiglione, 1st (01.42.60.52.82). M° Concorde.* **Open** 10am-7pm Mon-Sat. **Credit** AmEx, DC, MC, V.
Annick Goutal is a talented 'nose' and one of few women in the perfume business, yet ultimately hers is more of a merchandising story than anything. The boutique and delicately packaged scents practically flutter in ivory and gold-leaf.
**Branches:** 12 pl St-Sulpice, 6th (01.46.33.03.15); 16 rue de Bellechasse, 7th (01.45.51.36.13).

### Guerlain
*68 av des Champs-Elysées, 8th (01.45.62.52.57). M° Franklin D Roosevelt.* **Open** 9.45am-7pm Mon-Sat. **Credit** AmEx, MC, V.
The boutique, which includes a treatment centre (*see chapter* **Services**), is one of the last vestiges of the golden age of the Champs-Elysées. Many of the Guerlain fragrances for women and men were created with royal or Proustian inspirations, and today some of the scents are sold only in the Guerlain boutiques.
**Branches:** 2 pl Vendôme, 1st (01.42.60.68.61); 47 rue Bonaparte, 6th (01.43.26.71.19); 29 rue de Sèvres, 6th (01.42.22.46.60); 35 rue Tronchet, 8th (01.47.42.53.23); Centre Maine-Montparnasse, 15th (01.43.20.95.40); 93 rue de Passy, 16th (01.42.88.41.62).

### L'Occitane
*55 rue St-Louis-en-l'Ile, 4th (01.40.46.81.71). M° Pont-Marie.* **Open** 2.30-7.30pm Mon; 10.30am-7.30pm Tue-Sun. **Credit** MC, V.
Top-quality natural treatments for the body and hair made from essential oils in Provence.

### Les Salons du Palais Royal Shiseido

*142 galerie de Valois, 1st (01.49.27.09.09). M° Palais-Royal.* **Open** 9am-7pm Mon-Sat. **Credit** AmEx, DC, MC, V.
An oriental treasure trove tucked under the arcades of the Palais Royal where you can find the make-up and perfumes of the Japanese beauty line Shiseido. The interior, created by Shiseido artistic director Serge Lutens, is a sybaritic nest of East-meets-West opulence, in painted *boiseries* and mosaics.

## Records, CDs, Cassettes & Hi-Fi

### Crocodisc

*40-42 rue des Ecoles, 5th (01.43.54.47.95). M° Maubert-Mutualité/RER Luxembourg.* **Open** 11am-7pm Tue-Sat. **Credit** AmEx, MC, V.
Good value new, second-hand and off-beat records: pop, rock, funk, Oriental, African and country music; everything except classical. Crocojazz specialises in jazz, blues and gospel.
**Branch:** Crocojazz 64 rue de la Montagne-Ste-Geneviève, 5th (01.46.34.78.38).

### Fnac

*Forum des Halles, Level -3, 1-7 rue Pierre Lescot, 1st (01.40.41.40.00). M° Châtelet-Les Halles.* **Open** 10am-7.30pm Mon-Sat. **Credit** AmEx, MC, V.
The giant Fnac emporia are one-stop shops for books, music, electronics and computers, stereo, videos and photography gear, including a disposable 3D camera (99F). They also develop film and sell tickets. Most branches are stiflingly busy on Saturdays. *See also chapters* **Services.**
**Branches:** 136 rue de Rennes, 6th (01.49.54.30.00); 26-30 av des Ternes, 17th (01.44.09.18.00); 24 bd des Italiens, 9th (open till midnight, music only) (01.48.01.02.03); 4 pl de la Bastille, 12th (music only) (01.43.42.04.04).

### Gilda

*36 rue des Bourdonnais, 1st (01.42.33.60.00). M° Châtelet-Les Halles.* **Open** 10am-7pm Mon-Sat. **Credit** MC, V.

*Drunk as houses at the* **Maison Ivre.**

Buys and sells records, cassettes, CDs and books. This shop specialises in ethnic, jazz, funk, gospel, pop and classical in new and old CDs, 33s, 45s and mini CDs, and also sells used CD-Roms. Parallèles, the rue St-Honoré branch (47 rue St-Honoré, 1st/01.42.33.62.70) stocks pop, rock, jazz and classical CDs, as well as postcards, comic books and fanzines.

### Mister Disc

*36 rue de Turbigo, 3rd (01.42.78.83.84). M° Réaumur-Sébastopol.* **Open** 11am-2pm, 3.15-7.15pm, Tue-Sat. **Credit** MC, V.
The best collection of jungle and trip hop in Paris is found in this shop which also stocks techno and almost everything else that isn't classic. The friendly owner specialises in used CDs that start at 9F, and carries a good collection of jazz on vinyl. Flyers.

### Rough Trade

*30 rue de Charonne, 11th (01.40.21.61.62). M° Ledru-Rollin.* **Open** noon-7pm Mon-Wed; 11am-8pm Thur-Sat. **Credit** MC, V.
Opened in 1993, this offshoot of the famed London shop stocks plenty of indie labels, with lots of noise, techno, jungle and ambient, plus more dance music in the basement. Vinyl and CD. A good place to pick up fanzines and flyers.

### Virgin Megastore

*52-60 av des Champs-Elysées, 8th (01.49.53.50.00). M° Franklin D Roosevelt.* **Open** 10am-midnight daily. **Credit** AmEx, DC, MC, V.
The huge flagship of the Virgin empire in France creates the occasional roadblock when a headline band turns up for a record signing. The video department on the top floor has a selection of non-dubbed English films. There's a trendy café, bookstore and ticket sales kiosk. The Carrousel du Louvre branch is less hectic and includes a large international press and magazine stand.
**Branch:** Carrousel du Louvre, 99 rue de Rivoli, 1st (01.47.03.91.17).

## Stationery & Art Supplies

### Beauvais

*14 rue du Bac, 7th (01.42.61.27.61). M° Rue du Bac.* **Open** 9.30am-12.30pm, 1-6.30pm, Mon-Fri. **Credit** AmEx, MC, V.
An atmospheric old-fashioned stationery shop and printer where ink comes in several hundred shades and cabinets open up to reveal a treasure trove of different coloured papers, notebooks, envelopes and more.

### Comptoir des Ecritures

*82 rue Quincampoix, 3rd (01.42.78.95.10). M° Rambuteau.* **Open** 11am-1.30pm, 3-7pm Tue-Sat. **Credit** V.
A tiny shop specialising in calligraphy with inks, pens and an incredible range of hand-made papers from Asia.

### Graphigro

*157 rue Lecourbe, 15th (01.42.50.45.49). M° Vaugirard.* **Open** 9.30am-7pm Mon-Sat. **Credit** MC, V.
The largest and cheapest chain of stores provides a wide range of art and graphic supplies, from the essential paints and brushes to the more obscure, as well as art books.
**Branches:** 133 rue Rennes, 6th, (01.42.22.51.80); 207 bd Voltaire, 11th (01.43.48.23.57); 120 rue Damrémont, 18th (01.42.58.93.40).

### Papier +

*9 rue du Pont-Louis-Philippe, 4th (01.42.77.70.49). M° St-Paul or Pont-Marie.* **Open** noon-7pm Mon-Sat. **Credit** V.
Crayons in an infinite array of shades come in attractive boxes alongside stacks of hand-cut paper. One of the most attractive selections of blank and lined notebooks in Paris.

# Food & Drink

**Visit Paris' fashionable fromageries, star traiteurs and thriving street markets and gain a true insight into local life.**

Food remains at the heart of French culture: bakers can become superstars, *foie gras* leads Christmas celebrations and oysters can make the news headlines. Luckily, Parisians are sticklers for quality, eagerly seeking out the best *fromagers* or the freshest fish. Paris offers a comforting blend of city chic and rural authenticity as products from all over *l'hexagone* arrive in town – melons and tomatoes from the Midi, artichokes from Brittany, chickens from Bresse, hams from Bayonne, *saucisson* from the Auvergne, even such rareties as chestnut flour from Corsica.

## Bakeries & Pâtisseries

There are nearly as many types of bread as cheese in France and if daily consumption has gone down from 900g per day in 1900 to 160g today, hurried lunches mean that sandwich eating is on the rise. Although the *écoles boulangères* try to maintain standards, beware the soggy, additive-filled supermarket *baguette* and look for bakers displaying the *'pain de tradition française'* sticker.

### Boissier
*184 av Victor-Hugo, 16th (01.45.04.87.88). M° Victor-Hugo.* **Open** 9am-7pm Mon-Fri. **Credit** V.
With boxes of *boules cerises* and *froufrou* in the window beckoning you into this upmarket *pâtisserie*, you may be surprised to see children dressed in tiger outfits as Boissier puts on a tea party. At the end of the shop, chic *Parisiennes* take tea, and somehow remain slim and elegant.
**Branch:** 46 av Marceau, 8th (01.47.04.87.88).

### Carton
*6 rue de Buci, 6th (01.43.26.04.13). M° Odéon.* **Open** 7am-9pm daily. **Credit** MC, V.
The *baguettes* and *pain de campagne* are the best in the area, while the small *tarte de campagne*, individual blackcurrant mousses, mouth-watering florentines and mixed red fruit tarts will satisfy all your dessert or tea time desires.

### A la Flûte Gana
*226 rue des Pyrénées, 20th (0143.58.42.62). M° Gambetta.* **Open** 7.30am-6pm Tue-Sat. **No credit cards.**
Famed baker Bernard Ganachaud has retired (although the shop still exists), but his daughters Isabelle and Valerie have moved down the hill and trademarked his traditional bread-making method (*see also* rue Mouffetard market).

### Jean-Luc Poujauran
*20 rue Jean Nicot, 7th (01.47.05.80.88). M° Invalides or Latour-Maubourg.* **Open** 8am-8.30pm Tue-Sat. Closed Aug. **No credit cards.**
Jean-Luc Poujauran was one of the pioneers of the fashion for organic bread with his chewy *baguette biologique*. Others

to try are the sensuous fig bread (best eaten with *foie gras*) and the apricot bread, delicious with cheese.

### Lionel Poilâne
*8 rue du Cherche-Midi, 6th (01.45.48.42.59). M° Sèvres-Babylone or St-Sulpice.* **Open** 7.15am-8pm Mon-Sat. **No credit cards.**
The queue outside lets you know that Lionel Poilâne is a foodie superstar. The famous *pain Poilâne* (also available in other speciality shops around town) is made by hand each morning from stone-ground flour in a wood oven. Each giant round loaf (ask for a half or quarter) is still made to the original recipe with pungent sourdough yeast and sea salt. No two batches are ever the same.
**Branch:** 49 bd de Grenelle, 15th (01.45.79.11.49).

### Millet
*103 rue St-Dominique, 7th (01.45.51.49.80). M° Ecole Militaire/RER Pont d'Alma.* **Open** 8.30am-7.30pm Tue-Sat; 8am-1pm Sun. **Credit** V.
*Pâtisserie* Jean Millet displays mouth-watering chocolate-covered meringues with coffee filling, *tuile d'amande* biscuits, apricot *bavarois* – the choice is endless.

### Le Moule à Gâteaux
*17 rue Daguerre, 14th (01.43.22.61.25). M° Denfert-Rochereau.* **Open** 8am-7.30pm daily. **Credit** V.
The name translates as 'the cake tin', and these shops make reasonably priced fruit tarts, savoury flans and cakes.
**Branches:** 111 rue Mouffetard, 5th (01.43.31.80.47); 243 rue des Pyrénées, 20th (01.46.36.70.01).

### Pâtisserie Stohrer
*51 rue Montorgueil, 2nd (01.42.33.38.20). M° Châtelet-Les Halles.* **Open** 7.30am-8.30pm daily. **Credit** V.
When the Polish Princess Marie Leszczynska married Louis XV in 1725 she brought along her personal chef, M. Stohrer. In 1730 he opened his own *pâtisserie*, which to this day makes its romantically named *puits d'amour* (well of love) cream-filled pastry and feather-light vegetable *feuilletés*.

### René-Gérard St-Ouen
*111 bd Haussmann, 8th (01.42.65.06.25). M° Miromesnil.* **Open** 7am-7.30pm Mon-Sat. **No credit cards.**
Parisians call M. St-Ouen 'the Michelangelo of bakers'. Using flour from Chartres and olive oil from Provence, he fashions Eiffel Towers, Dali-esque suns, vintage cars and a Noah's Ark of animals (from 50F). For keeping rather than eating.

## Cheese

There is no better city in which to discover new cheeses than Paris. Every *quartier* has *fromageries*, each offering a superb seasonal selection. The sign *maître fromager affineur* identifies master cheese merchants who buy young cheeses from farmers and then age them on their premises. *Fromage fermier* and *fromage au lait cru* signify farm-produced and raw (unpasteurised) milk cheeses.

*Feast your eyes on **Marché St-Quentin**'s food halls.*

### Alain Dubois
*80 rue de Tocqueville, 17th (01.42.27.11.38).*
*Mº Malesherbes or Villiers.* **Open** 1.30-7.30pm Mon;
7.30am-1pm, 3.45-7.45pm, Tue-Thur; 7.30am-7.45pm Fri,
Sat; 8.30am-1pm Sun. **Credit** V.
Difficult to choose from the bewildering display, including
some 70 different varieties of goats' cheese. M. Dubois, who
has built a separate cellar to age his prize St-Marcellin and
St-Félicien, is the darling of the super-chefs, his cheeses
appearing on the menus of many Paris restaurants. He also
holds frequent cheese tastings, and happily ships orders.

### Alléosse
*13 rue Poncelet, 17th (01.46.22.50.45). Mº Ternes.*
**Open** 9am-1pm, 4-7.15pm Tue-Sat; 9am-1pm Sun.
**Credit** V.
People cross town to this large shop for the range of cheeses
ripened in its cellars. They include wonderful farmhouse
camemberts, delicate St-Marcellins, a very good choice of
*chèvres,* and rareties you've never seen before.

### Androuët
*41 rue d'Amsterdam, 8th (01.48.74.26.90). Mº Liège.*
**Open** 10.30am-7.30pm Mon-Sat. **Credit** AmEx, DC, MC, V.
This celebrated *fromagerie* claims to stock over 200 varieties, and even has a cheese restaurant upstairs. Pungent
époisses, munsters and maroilles mature in a warren of cellars beneath the shop, and display cases overflow with farmhouse brie and triple-cream lucullus.

### Barthélemy
*51 rue de Grenelle, 7th (01.45.48.56.75). Mº Rue du Bac.*
**Open** 8.30am-7.30pm Tue-Sat. **Credit** V.
Roland Barthélémy has been in this tiny, charming shop for
over a quarter of a century. The selection is outstanding and
creamy Mont d'Or from the Jura and brie de Malesherbes are
particularly tempting. Take-away 'cheese boards', appropriate wines and cheese-related porcelain are also available.
Try also the jars of goat's cheese preserved in olive oil.

### Fermé St-Hubert
*21 rue Vignon, 8th (01.47.42.79.20). Mº Madeleine.*
**Open** 9am-7.30pm Mon-Sat. **Credit** AmEx, DC, MC, V.
Pop in here on the way home from the Fauchon and sample
the delicious, well-aged cheese in this compact shop. The
selection is lovingly aged in owner Henry Voy's own cellars.
As well as a good choice of *chèvre,* look for the hard cow's
cheeses like cantal and tomme or the house speciality 'coro-
na' with cumin, paprika and vanilla to taste.

### Jean-Claude Lillo
*35 rue des Belles-Feuilles, 16th (01.47.27.69.08).*
*Mº Victor-Hugo.* **Open** 8am-1pm, 4-7.30pm, Tue-Sat.
**Credit** MC, V.
A busy person's dream with over 200 cheeses and cooked
cheese preparations like tarts, gnocchi and *croustades,* interesting pasta concoctions such as spinach rolled in pasta
*(daube aux epinards),* apple tarts, bottles of wine, not to
mention the huge sacks of dried mushrooms lurking on the
shelf overhead.

# Chocolate & Confectionery

Paris is a chocoholic's heaven and as well as
specialist *chocolatiers,* patisseries all over town
often make their own. Look out for Le Marché aux
Chocolats (01.42.85.18.20) fair in October.

### Christian Constant
*26 rue du Bac, 7th (01.47.03.30.00). Mº Rue du Bac.*
**Open** 8am-8pm daily. **Credit** MC, V.
For chocolates or tea, prepared *plats* and salads, Constant is
a name among *le tout Paris.* With a training in both *patisserie*
and chocolate he goes as far as the Far East for his unusual
ideas. The ultimate is the 75 per cent cocoa, dark chocolate
from the Andes (32F a bar). There's a small tea room.
**Branch:** 37 rue d'Assas, 6th (01.45.48.45.51).

# Market values

Every part of Paris has its food market, a vital local rende-vous and place to pick up gossip as well as produce. With some 70 on offer, the range of price and produce is wide.

Market streets and covered markets open Tuesday to Saturday, 8am-1pm and 4-7pm, and Sunday morning, except where stated. Late risers should beware the lengthy lunch hours.

## Market Streets

### Rue Montorgeuil
*1st. M° Châtelet-Les Halles.*
A relic of the original Les Halles market. Sniff at deliciously pungent cheese stalls and flower shops and be tempted by quaint **Pâtisserie Stohrer** at No 51.

### Rue Mouffetard
*5th. M° Monge.*
Wind your way up from medieval St-Médard to peek into *charcuteries*, sample the *flûte Gana* at Steff le Boulanger at No 123 or succumb to cakes at **Moule à Gateaux** at No 111 and pasta at Italian deli Facchetti at No 134.

### Rue de Buci
*rue de Seine and rue de Buci, 6th. M° Mabillon or Odéon.*
Locals and tourists mingle among good but pricey fruit and cheese stalls. Spend your *sous* at pâtisseries or go for *choucroute* and sausages at the Charcuterie Alsacienne.

### Rue Cler
*7th. M° Ecole-Militaire.*
Upmarket like its area. Check out *traiteur* J Ragut at No 40, **Davoli** at No 34 and *fromageries*. Le Lutin Gourmand at No 47 tempts with chocolate animals and marzipan fruit.

### Marché d'Aligre
*12th. M° Ledru-Rollin.* **Open** Mornings only.
One of the cheapest markets in Paris. North African and Caribbean products, herbs, fruit and pricey junk. A more expensive covered market next door is better quality.

### Rue Poncelet
*rue Poncelet and rue Bayen, 17th. M° Ternes.*
Take in the aroma of the Brûlerie des Ternes on this classy street which also boasts bakeries Paul and Fournil de Pierre, cheese shop **Alléosse** and German deli Le Stübli.

## Covered Markets

### Marché St-Germain
*6th. M° Mabillon.*
A shadow of its former self, the relic of the medieval fair has a cluster of cheese, *charcuterie* and other food stalls.

### Marché St-Quentin
*85 bd Magenta, 10th. M° Gare de l'Est.*
Built in the 1880s, the most elegant and authentic of Paris' few remaining cast-iron market halls is well-located for a pre-Eurostar shop. A variety of food stalls.

### Marché Passy
*rues Bois-le-Vent and Duban, 16th. M° La Muette.*
Among the chic shops of Passy, each pricey stall has its own kitsch hut. Perfect designer veg, seafood, bread and fresh pasta are extra-appetising.

## Roving Markets

### Boulevard du Port-Royal
*5th. RER Port-Royal.* **Open** Tue, Thur, Sat.
Lined up before the Val de Grâce hospital: goat's cheeses, mountain ham and specialists in onions and potatoes.

### Marché Bastille
*bd Richard-Lenoir, 11th. M° Bastille.* **Open** Thur, Sun.
A big daddy which seems to go on for miles, with huge variety, low prices and better quality at the north end of Bastille: onions, game, cheese, fish and wild mushrooms.

### Marché Biologique
*bd Raspail, 6th. M° Rennes.* **Open** Sun.
The *très chic* organic market draws elegant foodies and environmentalists from across the capital. From grass-fed Charolais beef, farm cheeses and crusty country loaves to organic wines, the produce comes at high prices. Other organic markets: bd des Batignolles, 17th (Sat); rue St-Charles, 15th (Tue, Fri).

### Boulevard de Belleville
*11th/20th. M° Belleville or Couronnes.* **Open** Tue, Fri.
Over 200 stalls: fair prices in a multi-ethnic district.

### Cour de Vincennes
*12th. M° Nation.* **Open** Wed, Sat.
Highly reputed for fruit and veg and free-range poultry.

### Boulevard Auguste Blanqui
*betw pl d'Italie and rue Baurrault, 13th. M° Place d'Italie or Corvisart.* **Open** Tue, Fri, Sun.
Long on veg, but also tempting *rôtisseried* free-range chickens, hot ham, steaming *choucroute* and Alpine cheeses.

### Boulevard de la Chapelle
*18th. M° Barbès-Rochechouart.* **Open** Wed, Sat.
At the heart of the Goutte d'Or, particularly good for Arab and African produce, alongside fabrics and hardware.

### Jadis et Gourmande
*88 bd Port-Royal, 5th (01.43.26.17.75). RER Port-Royal.*
**Open** 1-7pm Mon; 9.30am-7pm Tue-Sat. **Credit** MC, V.
The best place for novelty chocolates. The Chocolate Arcs
de Triomphe, Santas and letters of the alphabet make fun
presents. For inscriptions in white chocolate, order ahead.
**Branches:** 39 rue des Archives, 4th (01.48.04.08.03); 27
rue Boissy d'Anglas, 8th (01.42.65.23.23); 49bis av
Franklin D Roosevelt, 8th (01.42.25.06.04).

### La Maison du Chocolat
*289 av Raymond-Poincaré, 16th (01.40.67.77.83).*
*M° Victor-Hugo.* **Open** 9.30am-7pm Mon-Sat. **Credit**
AmEx, V.
Robert Linxe has just opened his latest temple to chocolate.
Besides rich chocolates in all shapes and sizes and a chocolate tart, the Maison sells drinking chocolate in half-litre
glass jars. In summer, there's a version for drinking cold.
**Branches:** 19 rue de Sèvres, 7th (01.45.44.20.40); 225 rue
du Fbg-St-Honoré, 8th (01.42.47.39.44); 56 rue François
1er, 8th (01.47.23.38.25); 8 bd de la Madeleine, 8th
(01.47.42.86.52).

### La Marquise de Sévigné
*1 pl Victor-Hugo, 16th (01.45.00.89.68). M° Victor-Hugo.*
**Open** 9.30am-7pm Mon-Sat. **Credit** AmEx, MC, V.
Known for its declicious breakfast drinking chocolate gran-
ules, chocolate truffles and bags of sugared almonds. In addition to the classic blue packets adorned with the Marquise
(an advocate of the health-giving properties of chocolate),
Jean-Charles de Castelbajac has added a cheerful modern
touch with a box in red, yellow, green and blue filled with
chocolate squares.
**Branch:** 32 pl de la Madeleine, 8th (01.42.65.19.47).

### A la Petite Fabrique
*12 rue St-Sabin, 11th (01.48.05.82.02). M° Bastille.*
**Open** 10.30am-7.30pm Mon-Sat; 10.30am-7pm Sun.
**Credit** MC, V.
Chez Rourmand is truly artisanal chocolate-making – you
can see the cauldron being stirred at the back. Little hazle-
nut or almond-studded drops are fresh and inexpensive.

### Richart
*258 bd St-Germain, 7th (01.45.55.66.00). M° Solférino.*
**Open** 11am-7pm Mon, Sat; 10am-7pm Tue-Fri. **Credit**
MC, V.
The byline here is *Richart Design et Chocolat*, and each
chocolate is a contemporary work of art. Nine beautifully
designed chocolates, 16 intensely flavoured, four-gramme
mini-chocolates or three drawers of black and white sculptures covered in nuts and sultanas taste absolutely dreamy.
**Branch:** 36 av de Wagram, 8th (01.45.74.94.00).

## Traiteurs

### Flo Prestige
*42 pl du Marché St-Honoré, 1st (01.42.61.45.46).*
*M° Pyramides.* **Open** 8am-11pm daily. **Credit** AmEx,
DC, MC, V.
This pricey but pristine *traiteur* has all you might need for
a luxury picnic or when feeling too lazy to cook: prepared
salads, smoked salmon, cold meats, cheeses, cakes and
desserts or hot dishes of the day, such as a fish stew or a
guinea fowl fricassée (at 49F). They have their own house
wines and a delivery service (*see chapter* **Services**).
**Branches:** 10 rue St Antoine, 4th (01.53.01.91.91); 36 av
de la Motte-Picquet, 7th (01.45.55.71.25); 211 av
Daumesnil, 12th (01.43.44.86.36); 22 av de la Porte de
Vincennes, 12th (01.43.754.54.32); 352 rue Lecourbe, 15th
(01.45.54.76.94); 61 av de la Grande-Armée, 16th
(01.45.00.12.10); 102 av du Président-Kennedy, 16th
(01.42.88.38.00).

### Lenôtre
*44 rue du Bac, 7th (01.42.22.39.39). M° Rue du Bac.*
**Open** 9am-7.30pm Mon-Sat; 9am-1pm Sun. Closed Aug.
**Credit** AmEx, DC, V.
The Lenôtre shops are known for their cakes and catering
service, and the chocolate truffles should not be missed. The
*plats gourmets* change regularly. Roland Durant, Meilleur
Ouvrier de France 1982, and *chef de cuisine* also creates
unusual jams of roses, violets and tilleul.
**Branches:** 15 bd de Courcelles, 8th (01.45.63.87.63); 61
rue Lecourbe, 15th (01.43.73.20.97); 48 av Victor Hugo,
750016 (01.45.02.21.21); 44 rue d'Auteuil, 16th
(01.45.24.52.52); 193 av de Versailles, 16th
(01.45.25.55.88).

## Gourmet Goodies

### Berthillon
*31 rue St-Louis-en-l'Ile, 4th (01.43.54.31.61).*
*M° Pont-Marie.* **Open** 10am-8pm Wed-Sun. Closed school
holidays. **No credit cards.**
Do not be put off by the long, winding queue outside the tiny
window where exotic ice creams and sorbets are sold, starting at around 9F a cornet or little tub. There are over 70
scoops to choose from such as wild strawberry, whisky or
chestnut. Berthillon also supplies numerous cafés and restaurants all over Paris.

### Caviar Kaspia
*17 pl de la Madeleine, 8th (01.42.65.33.52).*
*M° Madeleine.* **Open** 9am-1am Mon-Sat. **Credit** AmEx,
DC, MC, V.
The solution for the person with everything is a mini suit-
case containing a miniature of vodka and two tins of caviar.
They also have top quality smoked eel and smoked salmon.

### La Comtesse du Barry
*13 rue Taitbout, 9th (01.47.70.21.01). M° Chaussée-
d'Antin.* **Open** 9am-7pm Mon-Sat; 10am-6pm Sun.
**Credit** AmEx, DC, MC, V.
Staff will package French delicacies, like *foie gras*, terrines
and pâtés, in hampers or gift wrap. The lazy can buy high-
quality, ready-made tinned stews, soups and sauces.
**Branches:** 93 rue St-Antoine, 4th (01.40.29.07.14); 1 rue
de Sèvres, 6th (01.45.48.32.04); 317 rue de Vaugirard, 15th
(01.42.50.90.13); 88bis av Mozart, 16th (01.42.27.74.49).

### Le Comptoir de Foie Gras
*6 rue des Prouvaires, 1st (01.42.36.26.27). M° Châtelet-
Les Halles.* **Open** 8am-1pm Mon-Sat. **Credit** MC, V.
In a street running off Les Halles, Mme Antoine Pujol opens
her shop early to supply the restaurant trade. Red tins contain *foie gras* from goose liver, black tins contain duck *foie
gras* (a *bloc de foie gras* is made up from many small pieces)
and whole fresh *foie-gras* is available in vacuum packs.

### Comptoir de la Gastronomie
*34 rue Montmartre, 1st (01.42.33.31.32). M° Etienne-
Marcel.* **Open** 6am-1pm, 2.30-7pm, Tue-Sat. **Credit** V.
*Foie gras* from southwest France in all its forms, both duck
and goose, both *cru*, delivered daily and *mi-cuit*, plus snails,
caviar, *confit de canard* and dried mushrooms.

### Davoli – La Maison du Jambon
*34 rue Cler, 7th (01.45.51.23.41). M° Ecole-Militaire.*
**Open** 8am-1pm, 4-7.15pm, Tue, Thur-Sun; 8am-1pm
Wed, Sun. **Credit** V.
The elegant ladies from the Champ de Mars can be seen in
the busy rue Cler market and the temptations of Davioli are
irresistible. The counters and walls are lined with Italian
hams and salamis, as well as French *jambon de Bayonne*,
*jambon cru* and Spanish *jambon de Serrano*. Outside a board
announces the takeaway menu of the day.

### L'Epicerie
*51 rue St-Louis-en-l'Ile (01.43.25.20.14). M° Pont-Marie.*
**Open** 10.30am-8pm daily. **Credit** MC, V.
On the main street running through the Ile St-Louis, this must be the perfect present shop with its pretty bottles of blackcurrant vinegar, five-spice mustard, orange sauce, tiny pots of jam, honey with figs, tins of tea or a dozen chocolate snails. Everything is small enough to go in a suitcase.

### Fauchon
*24-30 pl de la Madeleine 8th (01.47.62.60.11).*
*M° Madeleine.* **Open** shop 9.40am-7pm, traiteur 9.40am-8.30pm Mon-Sat. **Credit** AmEx, DC, MC, V.
The most famous food store in Paris is a bit like every specialist deli rolled into one. The prepared food section resembles a museum as much as a food shop with its window displays of intricately prepared dishes, and deserve to be taken just as seriously. There are superb fruit, cheese and fish counters, and an Italian deli upstairs; quality wines in the *cave* and cakes and chocolates around the corner.

### La Grande Epicerie de Paris
*Le Bon Marché (shop 2), 38 rue de Sèvres, 7th*
*(01.44.39.81.00). M° Sèvres-Babylone.* **Open** 9.30am-9pm Mon-Sat. **Credit** (minimum 200F) MC, V.
The vast gourmet supermarket of Le Bon Marché department store (*see chapter* **Specialist Shops**) was completely redesigned recently. It carries Alsatian *charcuterie*, fish, *foie gras*, and a real depth of luxury brands from Hédiard and Fauchon to lesser-known imports. The bakery is excellent.

### Hédiard
*21 pl de la Madeleine, 8th (01.43.12.88.88). M° Madeleine.*
**Open** 10am-9pm Mon-Sat. **Credit** AmEx, DC, MC, V.
Across the place from Fauchon (*see above*) lies Paris' second most famous foodstore. Each fruit and vegetable is more

*It's oil or nothing at* **L'Olivier.**

perfect than the last and staff will explain the unknown. Excellent jams and spices make good gifts. Wine-wise, Petrus and Château Haut-Brion catch the eye as do the refrigeration panels and the discreet padlocks. Basketfuls of wines offer affordable alternatives.
**Branches:** 126 rue du Bac, 7th (01.45.44.01.98); 70 av Paul-Doumer, 16th (01.45.04.51.92); 6 rue Donizetti, 16th (01.40.50.71.94).

### Maison de l'Escargot
*79 rue Fondary, 15th (01.45.77.93.82). M° Emile-Zola.*
**Open** 9am-7.30pm Tue-Sat; 9am-1pm Sun. Closed 13 Jul-1 Sept. **Credit** V.
Only for devotees of these slimy creatures. Two women set stuffing garlic butter into the *petits gris* and Burgundy snails: these are the limit of delicacies on offer, apart from special snail plates, holders and forks. *Espace dégustation* opposite.

### La Maison du Miel
*24 rue Vignon, 8th (01.47.42.26.70). M° Madeleine.*
**Open** 9am-7pm Mon-Sat. **Credit** MC, V.
Founded in 1898, this shop stocks 28 different French honeys with flavours such as *châtaigne* (chestnut), *aubépine* (hawthorn), *tilleul* (lime tree), *rhododendron, lavande* and *thym*. Honey is at 16F for a jar, and you are expected to taste before you buy. Honey- and bee-based products, too.

### Maison de la Truffe
*19 pl de la Madeleine, 8th (01.45.65.53.22).*
*M° Madeleine.* **Open** 9am-9pm Mon-Sat.
**Credit** AmEx, DC, MC, V.
Fresh Périgord black truffles (November to March) at 5,500F/kg (depending on the year) are a snip against the rarer white truffles from Italy (22,000F/kg). Even if you don't go for the 750g monster, a few truffle shavings will do wonders for a scrambled egg. The staff will also suggest more affordable truffle oil to brighten up boiled potatoes and truffle sauce with breast of chicken. There's a tiny restaurant.

### A L'Olivier
*23 rue de Rivoli, 4th (01.48.04.86.59). M° St-Paul or Hôtel-de-Ville.* **Open** 9.30am-1pm, 2-7pm, Tue-Sat.
**Credit** MC, V.
L'Olivier's walls are lined with the company's own attractively bottled olive oils (in various strengths of fruitiness), together with other exotic oils and wine vinegars. There's also a good range of olives.

## Regional Specialities

### A la Campagne
*111 bd de Grenelle, 15th (01.47.34.77.05). M° Bir-Hakeim.*
**Open** 8.30am-1pm, 4-8pm, Tue-Sat. **Credit** MC, V.
The warm Basque welcome as well as the food in this shop will have you coming back for more. Try sheep cheese from the Pyrenees, Bayonne ham, espelette peppers (end July to November), gâteau basque and Irouléguy wines.

### Charcuterie Lyonnaise
*58 rue des Martyrs, 9th (01.48.78.96.45).*
*M° Notre-Dame de Lorette.* **Open** 8.30am-1.30pm, 4-7.30pm, Tue-Sat; 8.30am-1.30pm Sun. **Credit** MC, V.
Marmite d'Or prize-winning chef Jacques Chrétienne prepares truffled sausage, *jambon persillé, quenelles de brochet* and *hure* (pistachio-seasoned tongue), all from the Lyon area.

### A la Cigogne
*61 rue de l'Arcade, 8th (01.43.87.39.16). M° St-Lazare.*
**Open** 9am-6.30pm Mon-Fri; 8am-7pm Sat. **Credit** MC, V.
With the robust Germanic influence of a region that has switched nationality many times in its history, the array of Alsatian fare here includes sweet and savoury tarts, strüdel and beravecka fruit bread alongside Alsatian sausages.

*Come to* **Izraël** *for a taste of the exotic.*

**Branches**: 17 rue Tronchet, 8th (01.42.66.04.78); 2 quai de Grenelle, 15th (01.45.75.94.51); 48 rue de Flandre, 19th (01.40.36.87.46).

### Chez Teil

*6 rue de Lappe, 11th (01.47.00.41.28). Mº Bastille.* **Open** 9am-1pm, 3-8pm, Tue-Sat. Closed Aug. **No credit cards.**
A dusty haven of Auvergnat goodies includes country hams, sausages and bleu d'Auvergne, fourme d'Ambert and cantal cheeses, gentian liqueur and even authentic country clogs.

### A la Ville de Rodez

*22 rue Vieille du Temple, 4th (01.48.87.79.36). Mº Hôtel-de-Ville.* **Open** 8am-1pm, 3-8pm, Tue-Sat. **Credit** MC, V.
With its hams and sausages hanging from the ceiling, this pretty Marais *charcuterie* draws you in to sample produce of the Aveyron in central France, including pâtés, hams, *tripoux*, dried sausages, *boudin noir* and cheese. The friendly *patronne* will willingly create gift baskets.

## International

### The General Store

*82 rue de Grenelle, 7th (01.45.48.63.16). Mº Rue du Bac.* **Open** 10am-7.30pm Mon-Sat. **Credit** AmEx, MC, V.
Jean-Pierre Bourbeillon's shop is full of the Yankee ingredients missing for that traditional recipe. Cookies and brownies are made on the premises. English spoken.
**Branch**: 30 rue de Longchamp, 16th (01.47.55.41.14).

### Izraël

*30 rue François-Miron, 4th (01.42.72.66.23).*
*Mº Hôtel-de-Ville.* **Open** 9.30am-4pmTue-Sat. Closed Aug. **Credit** MC, V.
Stuffed full of exotic spices and other delights from as far afield as Mexico, Turkey, India and the Middle East, this *épicerie* is only the start of a trip around the world. Try the juicy dates, feta cheese, tapenades and the comprehensive selection of spirits to bring authentic kick to your cuisine.

### Korcarz

*29 rue des Rosiers, 4th (01.42.46.83.33). Mº St-Paul.* **Open** 8am-8pm daily. **Credit** MC, V.
It is difficult to pass by Korcarz' window which is stacked high with loaves of plaited bread, apple or hazelnut strüdel, onion bread and brioche. On Sunday mornings, it buzzes as people stop for quick breakfast at the bar, while they soak in the atmosphere.
**Branch**: 25 rue de Trévise, 9th (01.42.77.39.47).

### Pickwick's

*8 rue Mandar, 2nd (01.40.26.06.58). Mº Châtelet-Les Halles.* **Open** noon-8pm Tue-Sat; 11am-2pm Sun; 4-8pm Mon. **No credit cards.**
This Liverpudlian grocer started by supplying British and Irish pubs with the likes of Walkers crisps, quickly seeing the gap in the market created by homesick Brits. Tickle your tastebuds with Ambrosia rice pudding, baked beans, hob nobs and Marmite, while catching up on home news in Viz.

### Sacha Finkelsztajn

*27 rue des Rosiers, 4th (01.42.72.78.91). Mº St-Paul.* **Open** 10am-1pm, 3-7pm, Wed-Sun. **No credit cards.**
The best of Russian and central European Jewish specialities, in the heart of the Marais' traditional Jewish quarter. The cheesecake and chocolate *sachertorte* melt in your mouth, and also on offer are deli favourites such as tarama, potato *latkes*, aubergine caviar, *blinis* and *pirojkes*, rye and *challah* breads.
**Branch**: 24 rue des Ecouffes, 4th (01.48.87.92.85).

### Sarl Velan Stores

*83 passage Brady, 10th (01.42.46.06.06). Mº Strasbourg-St-Denis.* **Open** 9am-9pm Mon-Sat. **Credit** V.
This alley of Indian cafés and stores in the red light district has a surreal feel. Velan's is crammed with spices, and otherwise elusive vegetables imported from Kenya and India.

### Tang Frères

*48 av d'Ivry, 13th (01.45.70.80.00). Mº Porte d'Ivry.* **Open** 9am-7.30pm Tue-Sun. **Credit** MC, V.
Chinatown's biggest Asian supermarket is a delight for flat wind-dried duck, and unidentifiable fruits and vegetables.

### Thanksgiving

*20 rue St-Paul, 4th (01.42.77.68.29). Mº St-Paul.* **Open** 10am-7.30pm Tue-Sat; 10am-6pm Sun. **Credit** MC, V.
This store-cum-restaurant brims with Stateside delicacies from Oreos to takeaway BBQ wings or carrot cake.

## Wines & Spirits

The wine knowledge of *'cavistes'* in France is very high and most are willing to guide their clients, regardless of the price level. Look also for the burgundy-painted Nicolas chain with 130 branches in and around Paris. To buy direct from the producers, visit the Salon des Caves Particulières at the Espace Champerret in December and March.

### Les Caves Augé
*116 bd Haussmann, 8th (01.45.22.16.97).*
*M° St-Augustin or Miromesnil.* **Open** 1-7.30pm Mon; 9am-7.30pm Tue-Sat. **Credit** AmEx, MC, V.
Marcel Proust was a regular customer at this venerable establishment. Today the store is serious and professional with *sommelier* Marc Sibard on hand to give advice. There are whiskies, *eaux de vie* and cognacs for the serious buyer to taste and good buys on weekly and monthly specials.

### Caves De Georges Duboeuf
*9 rue Marbeuf, 8th (01.47.20.71.23).*
*M° Alma-Marceau.* **Open** 9am-1pm, 3-7pm, Tue-Sat. Closed Aug. **Credit** MC, V.
George Duboeuf is the dynamic King of Beaujolais, responsible for encouraging the Beaujolais Nouveau celebrations in November (*see chapter* **Paris by Season**).

### Les Caves Taillevent
*199 rue du Fbg-St-Honoré, 8th (01.45.61.14.19).*
*M° Charles de Gaulle-Etoile or Ternes.* **Open** 2-8pm Mon; 9am-7.30pm Tue-Fri, Sat. **Credit** AmEx, DC, MC, V.
On Saturday, Bruno Galmard and his young team of *sommeliers* give tastings in the *'cave du jour'* of wines starting at 24F a bottle. It is also possible to visit the idyllic cellars for spiritual temptation by 1914 Hine cognac or 1951 chartreuse.

### Les Grands Caves de Clichy
*76 bd Jean-Jaures, 92110 Clichy (01.47.37.87.13).*
*M° Mairie de Clichy.* **Open** 9am-1pm, 3-8pm, Tue-Sat; 9am-1pm Sun. Closed Mon.
When young, enthusiastic Jérôme Huard took over this place, he kept on the original, friendly staff. As well as serving a happy local clientele, most of this shop's business comes from farther afield. There's a wide and good selection of foreign wines, as well as a faithful collection from the Côte de Languedoc, Burgundy and of course, Bordeaux. They have a delivery service, and English is spoken.

### Legrand Filles et Fils
*1 rue de la Banque, 2nd (01.42.60.07.12). M° Bourse.*
**Open** 8.30am-7.30pm Tue-Fri; 8.30am-1pm, 3-7pm Sat. **Credit** AmEx, MC, V.
This old-fashioned wine shop is a must for the winelover, offering fine wines, brandies and wine gadgets under the kindly care from the Legrand family.

### Le Repaire de Bacchus
*12 village Royale, 8th (01.42.66.34.12). M° Madeleine.*
**Open** 10.30am-8pm Tue-Sat. **Credit** AmEx, MC, V.
Bacchus' lair brims with bottles from country wines to grand Burgundies. This branch has an English *sommelier* able to advise or to search out the unattainable.
**24 branches** include: 88 rue Montorgueil, 2nd (01.42.36.17.49); 112 rue Mouffetard, 5th (01.47.07.39.40); 40 rue Damrémont, 18th (01.42.52.27.78).

### Le Savour Club
*125bis bd Montparnasse, 14th (01.43.27.12.06).*
*M° Vavin.* **Open** 10am-8pm Tue-Sat; 10am-12.30pm Sun. **Credit** AmEx, DC, MC, V.
Oddly situated within an underground car park (Parking Montparnasse-Raspail), this is an ideal place to buy wine by the case and pop it straight into your car. The selection is wide and a professional staff are ready to give you advice if needed. With Georges Lepré, former head *sommelier* at the Ritz, tasting the wines, quality control is very strict. They also offer courses.

### Vignobles Passion
*130 bd Haussmann, 8th (01.45.22.25.22).*
*M° St-Augustin.* **Open** 9am-8pm Mon-Sat; 10am-1pm Sun. **Credit** MC, V.
The young enthusiastic bi-lingual team is grouping together French wine producers to sell and show their wines. Tutored tastings are given by Fernand Klee and Loïck Ducrey (possible in English for groups), as well as deliveries and advice on which wine to drink with which food.

### La Maison du Whisky
*20 rue d'Anjou, 8th (01.42.65.03.16). M° Madeleine.*
**Open** 9am-8pm Mon-Fri; 9am-1pm, 2-6.30pm Sat. **Credit** AmEx, V.
Whisky is taken seriously here and Jean-Marc Bellier is fascinating as he explains which whisky would taste good with which food or tastes such as honey and tobacco.

## Night Bites

Most areas have a local shop that stays open until around 10pm. At other times, 24-hour garages and the shops listed below help placate those insuppressible midnight munchies.

### L'An 2000
*82 bd des Batignolles, 17th (01.43.87.24.67). M° Rome.*
**Open** 7pm-midnight Mon-Sat; 11am-midnight Sun, public holidays. **Credit** V.
A traiteur where päella is always on the menu, as well as a daily *plat du jour*, cheese, *charcuterie*, salads and fruit.

### Boulangerie de l'Ancienne Comédie
*10 rue de l'Ancienne-Comédie, 6th (01.43.26.89.72).*
*M° Odéon.* **Open** 24 hours daily. **Credit** AmEx, MC, V.
Bread, *pâtisseries* and sandwiches help deal with that empty feeling before dawn, and there's a variety of hot and cold snacks in the café-bar.

### Butard
*29 rue de Buci, 6th (01.43.25.17.72). M° Odéon.*
**Open** 10am-11pm daily. **Credit** AmEx, MC, V.
This high-quality but high-priced *traiteur* has all the cheeses, salads, *charcuterie* and wines for a full-scale midnight feast.

### Noura
*27 av Marceau, 16th (01.47.23.02.20).*
*M° Iéna or Alma-Marceau.* **Open** 7am-midnight daily. **Credit** AmEx, DC, MC, V.
This up-market Lebanese *traiteur* claims to stock 'all that is refined in life' – prepared *mezze*, cheeses, *charcuterie*, sticky baklava, bread, wines and cognacs.

### Prisunic
*109 rue La Boétie, 8th (01.42.25.27.46).*
*M° Franklin D Roosevelt.* **Open** 9am-midnight Mon-Sat. **Credit** AmEx, MC, V.
Full-scale supermarket fills all your clothes, makeup, grocery and liquid needs. With deli counter, fruit and veg, it is packed nightly with foreigners.

### Select
*Shell Garage, 6 bd Raspail, 7th (01.45.48.43.12). M° Rue du Bac.* **Open** 24 hours daily. **Credit** AmEx, MC, V.
A gift for late-nighters with a large if pricey array of supermarket standards. Alcohol isn't sold between 10pm and 6am.

# Services

**Find out where to get seaweed treatment without the sea, how to hire a bike, or where to get that tattoo.**

Visitors to Paris might well get the impression that Parisians are obsessed with services. As well as the small, traditional specialist service shops that are so oddly abundant in Paris, department stores often offer everything from watch repairs to tool hire, under one roof. Yet nothing can beat the attentive customer care of smaller boutiques. Dry-cleaners, hairdressers, shoe repairers, opticians and photo developers can be found around almost every corner. As for food and drink delivery, it may not be up to American standards yet, but it is improving. As well as the services below, there are numerous help numbers starting with *SOS* or *Allô*, listed in the *Pages Jaunes*, that may be commercial enterprises or may be non-profit-making agencies. For babysitting services, *see chapter* **Children**.

## All-Purpose Services & Repairs

Many branches of the Monoprix/Uniprix supermarkets contain a range of useful services such as

**BHV** *is the plumber's gift.*

photocopiers, clothes repairers and photo booths (*see chapter* **Specialist Shops**). Dry-cleaners (*nettoyage à sec, pressing, teinturerie*) and laundrettes (*laverie libre service*), can be found in every neighbourhood. Many dry cleaners will also do alterations and repairs (*retouches*), and most clothes boutiques also offer an alterations service. For on-the-spot shoe repairs and key-cutting, try **Topy** or **Talons Minute** counters, found on high streets and in some major Métro stations.

### BHV (Bazar de l'Hôtel de Ville)
*Shop: 52-64 rue de Rivoli, 4th/DIY hire annexe: 40 rue de la Verrerie, 4th (01.42.74.97.23). M° Hôtel-de-Ville.* **Open** 9.30am-6.30pm Mon, Tue, Thur, Fri; 9.30am-9pm Wed; 9.30am-6pm Sat. **Credit** AmEx, MC, V.
The leading department store for camera cleaning and repair, photo-developing, photocopying, shoe repair, watch repair, car parts and tool hire. A fix-it-your-selfer's dream.

### Horloger Artisan/Jean-Claude Soulage
*32 rue St-Paul, 4th (01.48.87.24.75). M° St-Paul.* **Open** 9.30am-noon, 3-7pm, Tue-Fri; 9.30am-noon Sat. **No credit cards**.
Meticulous repairs and restoration for expensive or antique watches, clocks and fine jewellery.

### Madame est Servie
*(01.48.84.78.98).*
Madame est Servie will iron your clean laundry within 24 hours. They also dry clean leather and suede, as well as clean your carpets (between 48F and 135F per square metre).

### Nestor Pressing
*6bis rue Jonquoy, 14th (01.45.41.55.55). M° Plaisance.* **Open** 9am-9pm Mon-Fri. **No credit cards**.
Full-service cleaning, ironing, shoe repair and even film developing for those in western Paris and Neuilly, Levallois and Boulogne. Home pick-up from 3pm until 10.30pm.

### Rainbow International
*(01.60.60.18.16).* **Open** 7am-8pm daily. **No credit cards**.
Rainbow will clean your carpets (around 250F for 15 sq metres), sofas, and the like. Also clean leather.

## Car & Bike Hire

To hire a car you must be aged 21 or over and have held a licence for at least a year. Take your licence and passport with you. Most places prefer that you pay by credit card; otherwise, they may demand a huge cash deposit. If you're coming from the US, it's cheaper to arrange car hire before you leave.

### Hire Companies
**Ada** 01.46.58.01.52. **Avis** 01.46.10.60.60. **Budget** 0800.10.00.01. **Eurodollar** 01.49.58.44.44. **Europcar**

01.30.43.82.82. **Hertz** 01.47.88.51.51. **Rent-a-Car**
01.40.56.32.32. **Valem** 01.43.55.81.83.

Most of the companies listed here offer special reduced-rate deals at weekends (usually Friday to 9am Monday) – Ada, Rent-a-Car and Valem generally have the best offers. Prices for a basic group A-type car (Peugeot 106, Ford Fiesta, Renault Clio) with insurance range from about 210F-995F a day to 1,795F-3,650F for a week.

## Chauffeur-driven Cars

### Les Berlines de Paris
*159 rue Blomet, 15th (01.45.33.14.14). M° Convention.*
**Open** 8am-7pm daily. **Credit** AmEx, DC, MC, V.
Chauffeur driven car service and multi-lingual guided tours.

### International Limousines
*182 bd Péreire, 17th (01.53.81.14.14). M° Porte Maillot or Ternes.* **Open** 24 hours daily. **Credit** AmEx, DC, MC, V.
Luxury limousines (from 393F an hour) or something more modest. All come with an English-speaking driver.

### Ser'Gent Fox-Trot
*15-17 rue Fournier, 92110 Clichy (01.41.06.92.22).*
**Open** 24 hours daily. **Credit** AmEx, MC, V.
Their 25 cars are equipped with CD player, phone and newspapers, and have bilingual chauffeurs.

# Being pampered

### Alexandre de Paris
*3 av Matignon, 8th (01.42.25.57.90). M° Franklin D Roosevelt.* **Open** 9am-7pm Mon-Sat. **Credit** AmEx, MC, V.
Mr Glamour himself tends to your locks and those of stars like Catherine Deneuve, Jodie Foster and Vanessa Paradis: *coupe création*, a unique hairdo (from 570F); *chignon création*, an artfully knotted plait (350F-600F); or *balayage*, added highlights (600F-980F).

### Guerlain Institut de Beauté
*68 av des Champs-Elysées, 8th (01.45.62.11.21).*
*M° Franklin D Roosevelt.* **Open** 9am-6.45pm Mon-Sat (last appointment 5pm). **Credit** AmEx, MC, V.
Art Deco touches by Cocteau and Giacometti surround the 15 cabins where miracles occur – skin purification, exfoliation or massage from 380F. Treat yourself to a facial (from 570F), a manicure (210F) and a pedicure (290F) for that million-dollar look.

### Institut Payot
*10 rue de Castiglione, 1st (01.42.60.32.87). M° Concorde or Tuileries.* **Open** 9.30am-6.30pm Mon-Sat. **Credit** AmEx, DC, MC, V.
Separate salons provide facials (about 450F), make-up application (165F-245F), eyelash and brow tinting (from 150F) and body massage (390F/45 minutes).

### Villa Thalgo
*218-220 rue du Fbg St-Honoré, 8th (01.45.62.00.20).*
*M° Ternes.* **Open** 9am-8.30pm Mon; 8.30am-8.30pm Tue-Thur; 9am-7pm Fri-Sat. **Credit** AmEx, MC, V.
Discover the restorative properties of thalassotherapy, whether it's *balnéothérapie*, an hour's bath (350F), or *enveloppement*, a seaweed wrap (270F; 3,700F for 12 sessions). Join for a month and enjoy water gymnastics in a pool of reconstituted sea water (700F, includes bathrobe and slippers).

## Cycles, Scooters & Motorbikes

Note that bike insurance may not cover theft. For more on bikes, *see also chapter* **Sport & Fitness**.

### Agence Contact Location
*10bis av de la Grande Armée, 17th (01.47.66.19.19). M° Charles de Gaulle-Etoile.* **Open** 9.30am-1pm, 2-6.30pm, Mon-Fri; 9.30am-1pm Sat. **Credit** AmEx, DC, MC, V.
Rent a scooter for 230F a day or 850F a week; motorbike, 320-950F per day or 1,350-3,900F per week (including accessories). Weekend rates (Fri-Mon) work out best. A 7,000F-30,000F refundable deposit is required (credit card preferred). A car driver's licence suffices for all engines under 1,000cc.

### Bicloune93
*93 bd Beaumarchais, 3rd (01.42.77.58.06). M° Chemin Vert.* **Open** 10.30am-7.30pm daily. **Credit** AmEx, V.
Cycle rentals from 80F per day, as well as a large selection of new and vintage bicycles and hard-to-find parts.

### Maison du Vélo
*11 rue Fénélon, 10th (01.42.81.24.72). M° Gare du Nord or Poissonnière.* **Open** 10am-7pm Tue-Sat. **Credit** MC, V.
Bikes for hire, new and used cycles on sale, as well as repairs and accessories. *The* rendezvous for English-speaking cyclists.

### Paris-Vélo
*2 rue du Fer-à-Moulin, 5th (01.43.37.59.22). M° Censier-Daubenton.* **Open** 10am-12.30pm, 2-6pm, Mon-Sat; *summer only* 10am-2pm, 5-7pm, Sun. **Credit** MC, V.
Mountain bikes and 21-speed models for hire by day, month or weekend (baby-carrying seats also available).

## Costume & Formal Wear

### L'Affaire d'un Soir
*147 rue de la Pompe, 16th (01.47.27.37.50). M° Rue de la Pompe.* **Open** 10.30am-7pm Tue-Sat. **Credit** AmEx, MC, V.
Rents out fashionable gowns, specially created by designer Sophie de Mestier. 48-hour rental of outfits for women (700F-1,000F) and men (400F-800F). Also glass, linen, cutlery and china rental to a specific theme (Renaissance, Moroccan).

### La Femme Ecarlate
*42 av Bosquet, 7th (01.45.51.08.44). M° Ecole Militaire.*
**Open** 11am-7pm Tue-Sat. **No credit cards.**
Chi-chi women's evening glitz; meringue or cocktail dresses abound from 600F to 1,600F for a few days. For something borrowed, wedding dresses by the week cost from 1,000F to 3,000F. Attentive service; personalised designs available.

### Latreille
*62 rue St-André-des-Arts, 6th (01.43.29.44.10).*
*M° Odéon or St-Michel.* **Open** 2-7pm Mon; 9.45am-7pm Tue-Sat. **Credit** AmEx, DC, MC, V.
Its staff will suit any gent up *en penguin*, preferably eight days before the occasion. Rental is 395F-695F (Fri-Tue).

### Mucha Costumes
*17 rue La Bruyère, 9th (01.49.95.04.42). M° St-Georges.*
**Open** 11am-7pm, 2.30-7pm, Mon-Thur; 11am-8pm Fri; 11am-5pm Sat. **No credit cards.**
Eccentric Monika Mucha has a huge choice of affordable fancy-dress costumes, with a strong theatrical and film bent (200F-400F), as well as haute couture and wedding dresses (750F-1250F), and items of appeal to the nouveau-raver. The shop will move to larger premises up the road in mid-1997.

### A la Poupée Merveilleuse
*9 rue du Temple, 4th (01.42.72.63.46). M° Hôtel-de-Ville.*
**Open** 10am-7pm Mon-Sat. **Credit** MC, V.

A friendly shop with an outlandish collection of high-quality fancy- dress costumes, mad masks, wigs, decorations and practical jokes. Slip into disguise for 150F-800F, not including deposit (48-hour rental).

# Party Essentials

### Alfa Juke Box
*21-23 rue du Dr-Bauer, 93400 St-Ouen (01.40.11.87.87). Mº Marie de St-Ouen.* **Open** 9am-12.30pm, 2-6pm Mon-Fri. **No credit cards.**
Nostalgic notes of 1950s and 1960s Americana to hire: juke box (avg 1,800F) and neon signs (avg 600F). To buy a brand new juke box prices range from 3,000F to 45,000F.

### Allô-Glaçons
*12 rue d'Orléans, 92200 Neuilly-sur-Seine. (01.40.88.39.65). Mº Sablons.* **Open** 4am-7pm daily. **No credit cards.**
This ice-cube seller delivers (55F) ice to Paris and the provinces at bargain basement prices: 75F for 20kg of ice. For the fanatic ice sculptor.

### Montmartre Production
*76 rue Marcadet, 18th (01.42.57.38.79). Mº Marcadet-Poissonniers.* **Open** 9am-5.15pm Mon-Fri. **No credit cards.**
Professional magicians for an unmagical 4,000F. Plus jugglers, puppets, clowns.

### Nicolas
*31 pl de la Madeleine, 8th (01.42.68.00.16). Mº Madeleine.* **Open** 9am-8pm Mon-Sat. **Credit** AmEx, MC, V
Wine merchant offers free glass rental, but each broken glass costs 15F. Branches all over Paris.

# Flowers

### Interflora
*(freephone 0800.20.32.04 credit card orders).* **Open** 8am-8pm Mon-Sat. **Credit** AmEx, DC, MC, V.
The head office of Interflora. Prices start at 270F for a standard bouquet delivered in Paris; order by phone only.

### Lachaume
*10 rue Royale, 8th (01.42.60.57.26). Mº Concorde or Madeleine.* **Open** 9am-7pm Mon-Fri; 9am-6pm Sat. **Credit** AmEx, MC, V.
Probably Paris' most regal flower shop, founded 1845, with staff as grand as their exquisite arrangements. Call before 2pm for same-day delivery in Paris or the nearby suburbs.

# Food & Drink Delivery

With take-away and home delivery establishments on the increase, it's handy to know who to call when you get those irrepressible munchies, *see also* **Flo Prestige** and **Hédiard** *in chapter* **Food & Drink**.

### Allô Champagne
*11 rue Ambroise Paré, 10th (01.44.53.93.33).* **Open** 10am-10pm daily (order evening before on Fri and Sat). **No credit cards.**
M Foucher stocks some 50 champagne labels, from Mumm Cordon Rouge (149F) to Dom Perignon at 499F. Delivery 75F.

### Allô Couscous
*70 rue Alexandre Dumas, 11th (01.43.70.53.82). Mº Alexandre Dumas.* **Open** 6-10pm Mon; 11am-2pm, 6-10pm, Tue-Sun. **No credit cards.**

The Halimi family will deliver this North African – but now quintessentially French – dish piping hot in a *couscoussier.* A pot for four is enough for six hungry people. Lamb, beef, chicken, meatballs, mutton and spicy merguez sausage cost 75F per person. Delivery is 20F-50F, depending on the area.

### Cuisine du Monde
*62 rue de Rome, 8th (01.43.87.20.27).* **Open** 11.30am-2pm, 7pm-midnight Mon-Fri; 7pm-midnight Sat, Sun. **Credit** AmEx, MC, V.
Deliveries from several reputed restaurants: Kambodgia (Cambodian), Fakh El Dine (Lebanese), Sushi-Cho Yakitori (Japanese), Finzi (Italian), Indra (Indian), Coco d'Ile (Creole), Amazigh (Moroccan) and Olssen's (Scandinavian smoked fish). You can order across restaurant menus. Delivery is 50F.

### Domino's Pizza
*(central phone 01.36.57.21.21).* **Open** 11am-2.30pm, 6-11.30pm daily. **No credit cards.**
In 30 minutes these American pizza tossers will deliver you vegetarian and meat creations with a variety of toppings.

### Le Lotus Bleu
*17 rue de la Pierre-Levée, 11th (01.43.55.57.75).* **Open** 11.30am-2.30pm, 6.30-10.30pm, Mon-Fri; 6.30pm-10.30pm Sat, Sun. **Minimum** order 60F. **No credit cards.**
This Chinese delivery service offers standards plus excellent steamed dim sum and spicier Thai specialities.
**Branches:** 26 rue Lakanal, 15th (01.45.32.24.20); 6 rue Anatole-France, 15th (01.42.71.99.91).

### Pizza Hut
*(freephone 0800.30.30.30).* **Deliveries** 11am-2.30pm, 6-11pm daily. **No credit cards.**
The international leader in delivered American-style pizzas offers 'classic' thin crust and doughier 'pan' crust. They also deliver ice cream, brownies, beer and wine.

### Intermagnum
*(freephone 0800.00.50.20).* **Open** 9am-1pm, 2.30-7pm, Mon-Sat. **Credit** AmEx, MC, V.
Instead of saying it with flowers, why not a liquid alternative. Ring this number, or visit any branch of wine merchant Nicolas (*see chapter* **Food & Drink**) for gift-boxed bottles, with a personal message if wanted. Delivery within 48 hours.

### Matsuri Sushi Service
*(01.40.26.12.13).* **Open** noon-2.30pm, 7-10.30pm Mon-Fri; 7-10.30pm Sat. **No credit cards** MC, V.
The excellent sushi and sashimi of this successful Japanese home delivery service are made to order. It takes an hour to reach you, but the wait is worth the expense (250F minimum).

# Beauty Parlours

### Espace Epilation
*3 rue Etienne-Marcel, 1st (01.53.40.72.20). Mº Etienne-Marcel.* **Open** 2.30-9pm Mon; 10am-9pm Tue-Fri. **Credit** AmEx, DC, MC, V.
Leg, armpit and bikini-line hair removal at friendly prices (each at 20F for both legs, or 50F for a month).

### Institut Yves Saint-Laurent
*32 rue du Fbg-St-Honoré, 8th (01.49.24.99.66). Mº Concorde.* **Open** 8.30am-8.30pm Mon-Fri; 8.30am-7.30pm Sat. **Credit** AmEx, DC, MC, V.
Among the myriad treatments on offer are *soin régénération* – a two-hour facial with gravity defying results – or you can be made up for the evening (*maquillage du soir*, 420F).

### Oréna Beauté
*9 rue du Fbg-St-Honoré, 8th (01.42.65.62.37). Mº Concorde.* **Open** 11am-7pm Mon-Fri. **No credit cards.**

Oréna Beauté will give you an hour-long massage for 400F in the comfort of your own home. They also perform make-up miracles (400F for semi-permanent eyelashes), manicures (120F), facials (250F), hair extensions and the like.

The lads at this tattoo parlour provide a relaxed mood for the work of art to be created. Choose from generic cherubs, hearts and Celtic bracelets, surprisingly tasteful intricate black-toned designs, or bring your own design with you.

## Hairdressers

### Jacques Dessange
*43 av Franklin D Roosevelt, 8th (01.43.59.31.31). M°
Franklin D Roosevelt.* **Open** 9.30am-7pm Mon-Sat (last appointment 5.45pm). **Credit** AmEx, MC, V.
Women's cuts 350F; men's 250F; 210F for under-25s, or on Tuesday to Thursday. Women can brave a 40F haircut by student snippers at Dessange's Ecole de Coiffure (51 rue du Rocher, 01.44.70.08.08), but only if at least 3-4cm is to be cut. **Branches** include: 52 bd Sébastopol, 3rd (01.42.71.45.23); 2 rue de la Bastille, 4th (01.40.29.98.50); 7 rue de l'Odéon, 6th (01.43.26.39.93).

### Jean-Claude Biguine
*15 rue des Halles, 1st (01.44.76.88.10). M° Châtelet-Les
Halles.* **Open** 10am-7pm Mon-Thur; 10am-8.30pm Fri.
**Credit** V.
With 47 branches, you're never far from one of Paris' largest (and cheapest) salons. Trendy young clippers will shampoo, cut and style your hair at low prices: 150F (women), 110F (men).

### Ecole Jean-Louis David
*5 rue Cambon, 1st (01.42.97.51.71). M° Concorde.* **Open** 9.30am-1.30pm, 2.30-6pm Mon-Fri. **No credit cards.**
Free snip or curl by fledgling hairdressers practising new techniques from this ubiquitous chain. First-timers must show up to get on the client list (hair type permitting).

### Salon Vendôme
*5 rue Rouget-de-Lisle, 1st (01.42.60.48.44). M° Concorde.*
**Open** 9.30am-6.30pm Tue-Sat. **Credit** MC, V.
Women are now admitted to this clubby salon, but it remains a predominantly male preserve. Distinguished gents can have a haircut (270F), a shave (120F) or their ears plucked (60F).

## Solariums & Spas

### Les Bains du Marais
*31-33 rue des Blancs-Manteaux, 4th (01.44.61.02.02).
M° Rambuteau.* **Open** 10am-7pm Mon, Wed, Fri, Sat;
10am-10.30pm Tue, Thur. *Steam bath/sauna women*
Mon-Wed; *men* Thur-Sat; *mixed* Sun; 180F (includes towel rental). **Credit** MC, V.
Morrocan décor for a steam bath or massage *à l'arabe* (180F).

### Espace Bronzage
*65 rue St-Honoré, 1st (01.42.36.26.22). M° Châtelet-Les
Halles.* **Open** 10am-9pm Mon-Sat. **Credit** AmEx, MC, V.
Sessions last between five and thirty minutes. Bargain prices range from 10F for 15 minutes to 100F per month.

### Hammam de la Mosquée de Paris
*39 rue Geoffroy St-Hilaire, 5th (01.43.31.18.14).
M° Censier-Daubenton.* **Open** *Women* 10-am-8pm Mon,
Wed-Sat. *Men* 10-am-8pm Tue, Sun. **Admission** 65F.
**Credit** AmEx, DC, MC, V.
The *hammam* (Turkish baths) is a perfect place to unwind. Languish in steam rooms, take an invigorating massage, or lounge on mattresses in the Mosque's Arab bath.

## Tattooists

### All Tattoo
*16 rue St-Sabin, 11th (01.43.38.64.64). M° Bastille.*
**Open** 10am-7pm Mon-Sat. **No credit cards.**

## Opticians

### Alain Afflelou
*43-45 av des Ternes, 17th (01.42.27.10.14). M° Ternes.*
**Open** 9.30am-7pm Mon-Sat. **Credit** AmEx, DC, MC, V.
The largest of 30 Parisian branches: over 1,000 different styles. Prescription glasses can be ready within one hour.

### SOS Optique
*(01.48.07.22.00).* **Open** *Shop* 10am-7.30pm daily.
24-hour repair service. **Credit** AmEx, MC, V.
Glasses repaired at your home by a certified optician. The mobile repair shop will correct your vision within 30 minutes.

## Packing & Shipping

For courier services, *see chapter* **Business**.

### Hedley's Humpers
*(UK contact 0181 9658733); 6 bd de la Libération,
93284 St-Denis (01.48.13.01.02). M° Carrefour-Pleyel.*
**Open** 8am-7pm Mon-Fri. **Credit** MC, V.
An English company specialising in transporting goods between France and the UK (and the US).
**Branch:** stand 412, allée 7, Marché Palbert, 102 rue des Rosiers, 93400 St-Ouen. Variable hours.

### Logistic Air/Sea France
*14 rue Morand, 11th (01.48.62.80.42). M° Couronnes.*
**Open** 8.30am-7.30pm Mon-Fri; 9am-noon Sat. **Credit**
MC, V.
Shipping worldwide for roughly 12F per kg (45kg minimum), plus a 500F pick-up charge for packages up to 100kg.

## Photographic

**Photo Station** has over 20 branches in Paris and offers a cheap reliable developing service (around 29F for 24 prints).

### Fnac Service
*136 rue de Rennes, 6th (01.49.54.30.00). M°
Montparnasse-Bienvenüe.* **Open** 10am-7.30pm Mon-Sat.
**Credit** AmEx, MC, V.
High-quality same-day service by the Fnac chain.

## Ticket Agencies

### Chéque Théâtre
*33 rue Le Peletier, 9th (01.42.46.72.40). M° Richelieu-
Drouot.* **Open** 10am-7pm Mon-Sat. **Credit** AmEx, DC,
MC, V.

### Fnac
*Forum des Halles, 1-5 rue Pierre Lescot, level –3, 1st
(01.40.41.40.00). M° Châtelet-Les Halles.* **Open** 10am-
7.30pm Mon-Sat. **Credit** MC, V. Booking in person only.
**Branches:** 136 rue de Rennes, 6th; 24 bd des Italiens, 9th;
4 pl de la Bastille, 12th; 26 av des Ternes, 17th.

### Kiosque Théâtre
*across from 15 pl de la Madeleine, 9th. M° Madeleine.*
**Open** 12.30-8pm Tue-Sat. **Credit** V. *square in front of
Gare Montparnasse, 14th. M° Montparnasse-Bienvenüe.*

*Even the French will queue for the theatre ticket bargains at **Kiosque Théâtre**.*

**Open** 12.30-8pm Tue-Sat. **Credit** V. Half-price, same day tickets, plus 16F commission per seat.

### Specta Plus

*(01.43.59.39.39/fax 01.45.63.56.26).* **Open** 9.15am-7pm Mon-Fri; 10am-6pm Sat. **Credit** AmEx, DC, MC, V.

### Virgin Megastore

*52 av des Champs-Elysées, 8th (01.49.53.50.00).* M° *Franklin D Roosevelt.* **Open** 10am-midnight Mon-Sat (by telephone from 11am); noon-midnight Sun. **Credit** AmEx, DC, MC, V.
**Branches:** Carrousel du Louvre, 1st (01.44.68.44.08).

## Travel

## Hitch-hiking

### Allô Stop

*8 rue Rochambeau, 9th (01.53.20.42.42).* M° *Cadet or Poissonnière.* **Open** 9am-7.30pm Mon-Fri; 9am-1pm, 2-6pm, Sat. **Credit** MC, V.
This company puts passengers in touch with drivers. There's an initial fee (30F-70F depending on distance), plus petrol costs (max 20 centimes per km). Call a week ahead.

## Hot Air Balloons

### France Montgolfières

*76 rue Balard, 15th (01.40.60.11.23).* M° *Balard.* **Open** 9am-6pm Mon-Sat. **Credit** AmEx, DC, MC, V.
Weather permitting, flights daily from the countryside. The trip lasts three to four hours, with 1-1½ hours in the air.

## Travel Agencies

### Cash & Go

*34 av des Champs-Elysées, 8th (01.53.93.63.63/Minitel 3615 CashGo).* M° *Champs Elysées-Clemenceau.* **Open** 9am-7pm Mon-Fri; 10am-6pm Sat. **Credit** MC, V.
Broker offering well-priced flights around the world.

### Maison de Grande Bretagne

*19 rue des Mathurins, 9th (01.44.51.56.20).* M° *Havre-Caumartin/RER Auber.* **Open** 9.30am-6pm Mon-Fri; 10am-5pm Sat.
The British Tourist Office and other help if going to the UK.

British Rail (01.44.51.06.00/Minitel 3615 BR). **Credit** MC, V. **Brittany Ferries** (01.44.94.89.00). **Credit** MC, V. **Edwards & Edwards** (01.42.65.39.21). For theatre tickets in the UK. **Credit** AmEx, MC, V. **Sealink** (01.44.94.40.40). **Credit** AmEx, DC, MC, V. **Le Shuttle** (01.44.05.62.00). **Credit** MC, V.

### Nouvelles Frontières

*5 av de l'Opéra, 1st (01.42.60.36.37/fax 01.40.15.03.75/ Minitel 3615 NL).* M° *Pyrénées.* **Open** 9am-8pm Mon, Wed-Fri; 9am-8pm Tue; 9am-7pm Sat. **Credit** DC, MC, V. Branches throughout Paris. Phone 01.41.41.58.58 for details.

### USIT

*6 rue de Vaugirard, 6th (01.42.34.56.90/telephone bookings only 01.30.75.30.00).* M° *Cluny-La Sorbonne.* **Open** 9.30am-6pm Mon-Fri; 1-4.30pm Sat. **Credit** MC.
Coach, air and train tickets for the under-26s.
**Branches:** 12 rue Vivienne, 2nd (01.42.96.06.03); 31bis rue Linné, 5th (01.44.08.71.20).

## Video & Cassette Rental

### Reels on Wheels

*12 villa Croix- Nivert, 15th (01.45.67.64.99).* M° *Cambronne.* **Open** 11.30am-10.30pm daily. **Rates** 70F for three nights (22F-35F, members). **Credit** AmEx, MC, V.
Ian, a Scot, can deliver over 3,500 films (in English or with subtitles, if in a foreign language). Membership is 500F a year, 250F three months. Unless your VCR and TV are Pal-Secam you'll have to view in black and white, or he can rent you a Pal-Secam VCR. Tex Mex or Indian food deliveries.

### V.O. Only

*25 bd de la Somme, 17th (01.43.80.70.60).* M° *Porte de Champerret.* **Open** 11am-8pm Mon-Sat. **Rates** 35F per day. **Credit** AmEx, MC, V.
Their rental library includes 1,000 PAL videos and laserdiscs in non-subtitled English – new releases plus a fair share of classics and concert videos. Also laser discs for sale.

### Perfect Video Duplication

*9 rue Louis-Rouquier, 92300 Levallois-Perret (01.47.48.91.32/fax 47.48.93.14).* M° *Porte de Champerret.* **Open** 9am-7pm Mon-Fri. **No credit cards**.
This video lab converts American and British videos to the French Secam standard. 570F to convert a 90-minute tape.

## Visit Claude Monet's House, Gardens and Studio,

The foundation is open daily from 10am - 6pm
from March 28th to November 2nd.
closed Mon. except March 31st, May 19th, July 14th 1997.

Train 1 hr to Vernon from Paris Gare St. Lazare

**GIVERNY, 27620 TEL: 02.32.51.28.21 Fax: 02.32.51.54.18**

# Museums & Galleries

# Museums

*The ultimate museum city has something to suit all interests, from first-rate fine art collections to esoteric specialists.*

More than two centuries after it first opened to the public, the **Louvre**, granddaddy of all Paris museums, still makes the headlines. If the vast projects within the Louvre itself are coming to an end with the reopening of the Egyptian galleries in June 1997, outlying parts of the *Grand Louvre* project are also worth attention as the triumvirate of the **Musée des Arts Décoratifs**, **Musée de la Publicité** and the **Musée de la Mode et du Textile** reach the culmination of renovation and expansion works. Other projects at fruition include the reopened **Musée Jacquemart-André** and the innovative new **Musée de la Musique**, while photography flourishes with the successful new **Maison Européenne de la Photographie**.

Change is also in prospect at the rather neglected museums of the Palais de Chaillot. President Chirac may have said that the time for *Grands Projets* is over, but he has put forward a proposal for a Musée des Arts Premiers, to be formed essentially by merging the collections at the **Musée des Arts d'Afrique et d'Océanie** and the **Musée de l'Homme**, which means the **Musée de la Marine** is seeking a new home.

Note that most museums are closed on Monday or Tuesday. To avoid queues, try to visit major museums and exhibitions during the week, especially at lunch time or evening; reduced rates on Sundays often generate big crowds. Guided tours in English tend to be available only in the larger museums (*see chapter* **Sightseeing** for guided tours in English, that sometimes include museums). There are reduced admission charges for certain categories of people (pensioners, students), but make sure you have an identity card or a passport proving your status. Most ticket counters close 30-45 minutes before closing time. Note that prebooking is now often possible – and sometimes essential – for major shows at the **Grand Palais**. It's also possible to prebook tickets for the Louvre.

## A dozen to discover

**Maison de Victor Hugo** The multifarious talents of the author of *Les Mis*. *See p223.*

**Musée de l'Air et de l'Espace** Fun for budding pilots of all ages. *See p225.*

**Musée des Arts Forains** All the fun of the fair. *See p220.*

**Musée de la Chasse et de la Nature** The luxury pastime of hunting. *See p217.*

**Musée Dapper** African masks and statues beautifully displayed. *See p220.*

**Musée d'Ennery** Oriental arts in a time-capsule setting. *See p221.*

**Musée Jacquemart-André** Mansion of Italian primitives and Old Masters. *See p212.*

**Musée Marmottan** Unrivalled Monets and First Empire chandeliers. *See p212.*

**Musée Gustave Moreau** Paris' most eccentric one-man show. *See p213.*

**Musée National du Moyen Age** The Lady & the Unicorn and other intimate marvels of the Middle Ages. *See p218.*

**Musée de la Mode et du Textile** The haute-couture tradition on show. *See p217.*

**Musée Zadkine** Modern sculpture in the artist's house and garden. *See p215.*

### Paris Carte-Musées et Monuments (CM)

**Price** one day 70F, three days 140F, five days 200F. This card gives free entry into 65 museums and monuments around Paris, and also allows you to jump queues. Very good value if you're in Paris for a few days and plan to do some intensive museum visiting, although you have to pay extra for special exhibitions. It can be bought at museums, monuments, tourist offices (*see chapter* **Essential Information**), branches of Fnac and principal Métro and RER stations.

## Fine Art

### Centre Pompidou – Musée National d'Art Moderne

*rue Beaubourg, 4th (01.44.78.12.33). M° Châtelet-Les Halles, Hôtel-de-Ville or Rambuteau.* **Open** noon-10pm Mon, Wed-Fri; 10am-10pm Sat, Sun, holidays. Closed Tue, 1 May. **Admission** *Musée National d'Art Moderne* 24F; free under-16s, unemployed, CM. *Grande Galerie* 45F; 30F 18-25s. *Galeries Contemporaines & CCI* 27F; 20F 18-25s; free under-13s. *Day-pass* to museum and all exhibitions 70F; 45F 16-25s, over-60s; free under-16s. **Credit** (over 100F) MC, V.
Celebrating its twentieth anniversary in 1997, the radical high-tech building designed by Renzo Piano and Richard Rogers in a way set the trend for all the later *Grands Projets*. A truly polyvalent cultural space, the Pompidou hosts dance, cinema and contemporary music, as well as art shows, but will close for large-scale rearrangement of the building's inte-

*French Romantic painting, inspiring the crowds at the **Louvre** ever since the Revolution.*

rior from October 1997 until late 1999, to enlarge the museum space and provide a separate entrance for the public library. With a collection of modern and contemporary art rivalled only by the Museum of Modern Art in New York, the Musée National d'Art Moderne has over 30,000 works from 1905 to the present, with major holdings from Matisse, Picasso and the Surrealists to *nouvelles réalistes*, Pop Art, Minimalist art and Arte Povera. While the museum is closed, some of its works will be loaned to other Paris collections and to exhibitions in France and abroad. Until 29 September 1997, the museum collection on the third and fourth floors have been rehung for a show 'Made in France 1947-1997', reevaluating postwar creation in France from late Matisse via Balthus, Klein and Viallat to contemporary artists like Buren, Raysse and Absalon and including foreigners who've worked here, like Chagall, Ernst, Jorn and Francis. The fifth floor is used for blockbuster exhibitions, with smaller contemporary art, design and architecture shows on the mezzanines and in the central forum, while Brancusi's studio has been reopened on the piazza (*see below* **One-Man Shows**). During the works, part of the building will stay open, allowing the celebrated ride up the escalators to catch the view, and a temporary exhibition space. *See also chapters* **Sightseeing, Architecture, Dance, Children** *and* **Study.**
*Bookshop & design shop. Café-restaurant. Cinema. Reference library. Slide, video and record libraries; specialist design library. Wheelchair access.*

### Musée d'Art Moderne de la Ville de Paris/ARC

*Palais de Tokyo, 11 av du Président Wilson, 16th (01.53.67.40.00/recorded information 01.40.70.11.10). M° Iéna or Alma-Marceau.* **Open** 10am-5.30pm Tue-Fri; 10am-6.45pm Sat, Sun. *Temporary exhibitions* 10am-6.45pm Tue-Sun. Closed Mon. **Admission** 27F; 14.50F students; free under-7s, CM. *Temporary exhibitions* 40F; 30F students; free under-7s. *Combined ticket* 45F; 35F students; free under-7s. **Credit** (bookshop only) AmEx, DC, MC, V.
This monumental museum was built as the Electricity

Pavilion for the 1937 Exposition Universelle, and Dufy's vast mural *Electricité* can still be seen in a curved room. Today the building holds the municipal collection of modern art, which is strong on the Cubists, the Fauves, Rouault, the Delaunays, Gromaire, Soutine, Modigliani and the Ecole de Paris. Contemporary artists such as Boltanski, Lavier, Ange Leccia, Sarkis and Buren are also represented, and there are some recently discovered panels from an early version of Matisse's *La Danse*, alongside his later reworking (1932-33). The contemporary department, ARC (Animation, Recherche, Confrontation), puts on some of the most adventurous contemporary art exhibitions in Paris, ranging from established names to the first museum shows of young artists.
*Bookshop. Café-restaurant (tables outdoors). Concerts. Wheelchair access.*

### Musée Cognacq-Jay

*Hôtel Denon, 8 rue Elzévir, 3rd (01.40.27.07.21). M° St-Paul.* **Open** 10am-5.40pm Tue-Sun. Closed Mon. **Admission** 17.50F; 9F students, over-60s; free under-18s, CM. **No credit cards.**
Put together by Ernest Cognacq and his wife Louise Jay, founders of the Samaritaine department store, this collection concentrates on paintings, furniture and ceramics of the eighteenth century. They are displayed in different panelled interiors from the period, some of which already belonged to the Hôtel Denon, and others which were collected by Cognacq himself. There are paintings by Boucher, Chardin, Canaletto, Fragonard and Greuze, and pastels by Quentin de la Tour. *Bookshop.*

### Musée Départmental du Prieuré

*2bis rue Maurice Denis, 78100 St-Germain-en-Laye (01.39.73.77.87). RER St-Germain-en-Laye.* **Open** 10am-12.30pm, 2-5.30pm, Wed-Fri; 10am-12.30pm, 2-6.30pm, Sat, Sun. **Admission** 35F; 25F students. **No credit cards.**
Out in the elegant commuterland of St-Germain-en-Laye, this former royal hospital became home and studio to Nabi painter Maurice Denis in 1915. The remarkable collection, housed in ancient wards and attics, comprises paintings,

# Musée National du Louvre

entrance through Pyramid, Cour Napoléon, 1st,
or via Carrousel du Louvre (01.40.20.50.50/
recorded information 01.40.20.51.51/advance booking
01.49.87.54.54). M° Palais Royal. **Open** 9am-9.45pm
Mon, Wed; 9am-6pm Thur-Sun. *Temporary exhibitions*
10am-9.30pm Mon, Wed-Sun. *Medieval Louvre &*
*bookshop* 9.30am-9.45pm Mon, Wed-Sun. Closed Tue,
some public holidays. **Admission** 45F (until 3pm)/26F
(after 3pm & Sun); free under-18s, CM, first Sun of the
month. *Temporary exhibitions* admission varies.
**Credit** (shop only) AmEx, MC, V.
*Book and gift shop. Bureau de change. Café-restaurant.*
*Concerts. Films. Guided tours in English. Lectures.*
*Nursery. Post office. Wheelchair access.*
Although the Louvre first opened to the public in 1793, when
the Richelieu wing wasn't even built, President Mitterrand's
*Grand Louvre* project, beginning in 1987 with I M Pei's glass
pyramid, has transformed this venerable museum into one
of the world's most modern museums, with almost double
its former exhibition space. The Egyptian and Classical
Antiquities galleries should take their final form at the end
of 1997, as will a secondary entrance, the Porte des Lions.
One unexpected feature of the new Louvre is that a section
of the massive fortified stone ramparts of Philippe-
Auguste's first keep built in 1190 can now be seen beneath
the Cour Carrée.

The collections are based around the original royal collections, augmented by revolutionary seizures and later
acquisitions. It's important to be selective, for the museum
is truly huge, and you could easily spend days or even
weeks just gazing at French or Italian painting, not to mention the rich reserves of stunning Classical sculpture,
Ancient Egyptian, Islamic and Medieval works of art.

The museum is organised into different wings – Richelieu
(along the rue de Rivoli), Sully (around the Cour Carrée) and
Denon (along the Seine) – which lead off on three sides from
beneath the entrance pyramid. They are further subdivided
into *arrondissements*, and each section is colour coded and
labelled, but it is almost impossible not to get lost at some
point while exploring this treasure trove. Always pick up
one of the free orientation leaflets at the entrance.

## French Sculpture

*Richelieu, ground floor.*
The most dramatic features of the Richelieu wing, opened
in November 1993, are its two magnificent sculpture courts.
A high-tech glazing system lets light flood into these covered courtyards, casting warm shadows around the monumental pieces here. The Cour Marly gives pride of place to
Guillaume Coustou's two giant horses the *Chevaux de Marly*
of 1745, being restrained by grooms in a freeze-frame of rear-
ing struggle. Coustou used live models to achieve this degree
of naturalism, which contrasts with the courtly correctness
of the two winged horses opposite, *Fame* and *Mercury*, created by Coysevox, Coustou's uncle, for Louis XIV in 1706.
In the Cour Puget, admire the four bronze captives that originally adorned a statue in place des Victoires and Clodion's
rococo frieze. Spacious side rooms are devoted to French
sculpture from medieval tombs and the original
Renaissance reliefs by Jean Goujon for the Fontaine des
Innocents in Les Halles to the pompous official sculptures
of eighteenth-century heroes and Neo-Classical mythological subjects and wild animals studies of Barye. A truly
remarkable piece is the fifteenth-century Tomb of Philippe
Pot, with an effigy of this Burgundian aristocrat supported
by eight ominous black-cowled figures.

## Northern Painting

*Richelieu, second floor.*
The Dutch, Flemish and German schools have been given
new breathing space. The 24 typically bravura canvases
painted by Rubens for Marie de Médicis are displayed together in the Galerie Médicis. Since she commissioned the
work for the Luxembourg palace to celebrate her own virtues, you'd hardly expect an objective view. Despite all the
re-hanging, there are still some major works tucked away
in small rooms or 'cabinets' – look out for masterpieces such
as Bosch's *Ship of Fools*, a Durer self-portrait, Holbein's
*Anne of Cleves*, penetrating self-portraits by Rembrandt and
Vermeer's exquisite *Lacemaker* and *The Astronomer*.

## French Painting

*Richelieu, Sully, second floor, Denon, first floor.*
For a quick survey of French art, head to the Richelieu and
Sully wings, starting with late Medieval and Renaissance
work, including the striking *Diana the Huntress* by an
unknown artist, thought to be an idealised portrait of Diane
de Poitiers, Henri II's mistress. There are fine portraits by
Clouet and landscapes by Claude Lorraine, as well as *The*
*Four Seasons* and other Biblical and mythological canvases by Poussin. The peasant scenes of Le Nain and strikingly lit religious works of Georges de la Tour from the 1640s
give way to the eighteenth-century frivolity of Watteau,
Fragonard and Boucher, and the stern Neo-Classical portraits of David. In the Denon wing are stirring, monumental
Romantic works of the early nineteenth century, including

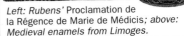

*Left: Rubens'* Proclamation de la Régence de Marie de Médicis; *above: Medieval enamels from Limoges.*

Géricault's *Raft of the Medusa*, inspired by a shipwreck that was a cause célèbre at the time, as the survivors resorted to cannibalism, David's monumental representation of the coronation of Napoléon and Delacroix's *Liberty Leading the People*, celebrating the Revolution of 1830.

### French Objets d'Art
*Richelieu, first floor.*
Highlight among the Medieval jewels, gold and ivories is the Treasure of St-Denis. There are also Renaissance enamels, furniture and early clocks.

### Italian Painting
*Denon, first floor.*
The Grande Galerie of Italian paintings is closed until mid-1997, but the major works are temporarily displayed elsewhere. The Louvre's most famous sole work *Mona Lisa* (*La Joconde*) tends to draw all attention, but don't overlook Leonardo's *Virgin on the Rocks* and *The Virgin, The Child and St-Anne* and Early Renaissance paintings by Fra Angelico, Giotto and Uccello or masterpieces of the Venetian

school, with works by Titian and Tintoretto and Veronese's magisterial *The Marriage at Cana*. Recent acquisitions include works by Parmigianino and Jacopo Bassano.

### Spanish Painting
*Denon, Pavillon de Flore.*
The Spanish collection includes paintings by El Greco, Zurbarán, Velazquez and Goya.

### Non-French European Sculpture
*Denon, basement, ground floor.*
Michelangelo's *Dying Slave* and the *Rebel Slave*, created for the tomb of Pope Julius II in 1513-15, are perhaps the best known works in the Louvre's post-Classical sculpture collection, but there also pieces by Donatello, Giambologna, Cellini, Della Robbia terracottas, Neo-Classical works by Canova and some Spanish and northern European works.

### Greek, Etruscan & Roman Antiquities
*Denon, Sully, ground and first floors.*
Reorganisation of the department of Classical Antiquities should be completed by the end of 1997. As well as Greek painted vases, the treasures include the magnificent *Winged Victory of Samothrace*, the *Borghèse Gladiator* and the *Venus de Milo*. The unusual Etruscan Sarcophagus of a *Married Couple* in terracotta depicts a couple happily reclining together at a banquet. There are also mosaics from Carthage, Pompeii and Antioch.

### Egyptian Antiquities
*Sully, ground and first floors; Denon.*
This extensive collection had its beginnings in Napoléon's Egyptian adventure of 1798. The department will reopen at the end of 1997 arranged thematically. The Coptic department, including textiles and the church from Baouit monastery, will open in the Denon wing.

### Oriental Antiquities
*Richelieu, ground floor.*
Pieces from Anatolia, Iran and Mesopotamia are now grouped around a magnificent reconstruction of the courtyard of Khorsabad, with breathtaking Assyrian winged bulls. The remarkable Law Code of Hammurabi (circa 1750 BC) could be the original tablet of stone, although not laws but royal pronouncements are carved on the basalt stele.

### Islamic Art
*Richelieu, basement.*
The Islamic collections include early glass, ceramics, inlaid metalwork, carpets and funerary stele and an introductory section, about Islamic architecture, decorated with pierced wooden screens.

### Nineteenth-Century Louvre
*Richelieu, second floor.*
The opulent apartments of Napoléon III (used until 1989 by the Ministry of Finance for receptions) have been preserved with their chandeliers and crimson upholstery intact.

prints and decorative objects by the Nabis (a group that includes Sérusier, Bonnard, Vuillard, Roussel and Valloton). There are also paintings by their forerunners Gauguin and the Pont-Aven school, and by Toulouse-Lautrec. The collection is rich in works by Denis, who also painted the frescoes and designed the stained glass in the small chapel. *Wheelchair access.*

## Musée Jacquemart-André

*158 bd Haussmann, 8th (01.42.89.04.91). M° St-Philippe-du-Roule.* **Open** 10am-6pm daily. **Admission** 45F; 35F under-25s, students, unemployed; free under-7s. **Credit** (over 100F) MC, V.

Reopened after renovation, the magnificent collection gathered by Edouard André and his wife Nélie Jacquemart is as worth visiting for its illustration of the life of the nineteenth-century *haute bourgeoisie*, as for the paintings and other treasures they unearthed in the salerooms or as they scoured Europe. André had the magnificent Hôtel André constructed in the 1870s in the newly desirable neighbourhood outlined by Baron Haussmann. On the ground floor lies the circular Grand Salon, rooms of tapestries and French furniture, Boucher mythological fantasies, the library with its Dutch paintings, including Rembrandt's *The Pilgrims of Emmaus*, smoking room with Moorish stools and English portraits and the magnificent polychrome marble winter garden with its double spiral staircase. Upstairs, what was to have been Nélie's studio (she gave up her brushes on marriage) became their 'Italian museum': a small, exceptional, Early Renaissance collection that includes Uccello's exquisite *St George and the Dragon*, virgins by Perugino, Botticelli and Bellini, Mantegna's *Ecce Homo*, a superb Schiavone portrait, a Carpaccio panel and Della Robbia terracottas. The audio-guide (in English), is extremely informative. *Audio guide. Bookshop. Café. Wheelchair access.*

## Musée Marmottan

*2 rue Louis-Boilly, 16th (01.42.24.07.02 ). M° La Muette.* **Open** 10am-5.30pm Tue-Sun. Closed Mon. **Admission** 40F; 25F 8-25s, over-60s; free under-8s. **No credit cards.**

Fragonard and the Winter Garden at the **Musée Jacquemart-André**.

This museum achieved fame with Michel Monet's bequest of 165 works by his father, including a breathtaking series of late water-lily canvases, displayed in a special basement room. Sit and absorb the intensity of viridian green and electric blue: these exercises in pure colour show Monet at his most original and closest to abstraction. The collection also contains Monet's *Impression Soleil Levant* – which gave the Impressionist movement its name – and Impressionist canvases by Sisley, Renoir, Pissarro, Caillebotte and Berthe Morisot as well as some by the nineteenth-century Realists. The rest of the collection should not be ignored. As well as a room containing the Wildenstein collection of medieval illuminated manuscripts, the recently restored ground- and first-floor salons house smaller Monets, early nineteenth-century gouaches and a superb array of First Empire furnishings, much of it adorned with pharaoh's busts, eagles and sphinxes under the influence of Napoléon's Egyptian campaigns. *Shop.*

## Musée de l'Orangerie

*Jardin des Tuileries, 1st (01.42.97.48.16). M° Concorde.* **Open** 9.45am-5.15pm Mon, Wed-Sun. Closed Tue. **Admission** 30F; 20F 18-25s, over-60s, all visitors Sun; free under-18s; CM. **Credit** (shop only) MC, V.

Across the Tuileries Gardens from the Jeu de Paume is the Orangerie, home of Monet's Water Lilies *(see also above* Musée Marmottan*).* The eight huge panels of were conceived for these oval rooms, and left as a 'spiritual testimony' by Monet. Presented to the public in 1927, a year after his death, they still have an extraordinary freshness and depth. The Jean Walter and Paul Guillaume collection on the floor above has some big names of Impressionism and the Ecole de Paris, such as Soutine, Renoir, Cézanne, Sisley, Picasso, Derain, Matisse, Rousseau and Modigliani. *Shop. Wheelchair access.*

## Musée du Petit Palais

*av Winston Churchill, 8th (01.42.65.12.73). M° Champs Elysées-Clemenceau.* **Open** 10am-5.40pm Tue-Sun. Closed Mon, public holidays. **Admission** 27F; 14.50F 7-18s, students, over-60s; free under-7s, CM. *Temporary exhibitions* 40F; 30F students, over-60s. **Credit** (bookshop only) V.

Standing sedately across the road from the Grand Palais *(see below* Exhibition Centres*)* and similarly constructed for the 1900 Great Exhibition, the Petit Palais contains a hotchpotch of collections belonging to the city, including Greek painted vases and Antique sculpture, Chinese porcelain, Beauvais tapestries, French furniture and paintings by Millet, Delacroix, Géricault, Daumier, Courbet, Redon and a good selection of Impressionists and works by Vuillard and Bonnard, plus numerous maquettes for public sculpture around Paris. It's most often visited, however, for temporary exhibitions, often devoted to Oriental or decorative arts. *Bookshop. Guided tours 12.30pm, 2.30pm Tue, Fri. Library. Wheelchair access.*

# One-Man Shows

## Atelier Brancusi

*piazza Beaubourg, 4th (01.44.78.12.33). M° Châtelet-Les Halles or Hôtel-de-Ville.* **Open** noon-10pm Mon, Wed-Fri; 10am-10pm Sat, Sun. Closed Tue. **Admission** 27F. **No credit cards.**

When Constantin Brancusi died in 1956 he left his studio in the 15th *arrondissement* and all its contents, including sculptures, maquettes, tools, photos, his bed and his wardrobe, to the state. Rebuilt first within the Palais de Tokyo and then in 1977 outside the Centre Pompidou, the studio has since been completely reconstructed again to faithfully reproduce the artist's living and working spaces. Fragile works in wood and plaster, including his celebrated endless columns, show how Brancusi revolutionised sculpture early this century.

### Atelier-Musée Henri Bouchard

*25 rue de l'Yvette, 16th (01.46.47.63.46). M° Jasmin.*
**Open** 2-7pm Wed, Sat. Closed last two weeks of Mar,
June, Sept and Dec. **Admission** 25F; 15F students,
under-25s; free under-7s, over-60s. **No credit cards**.
This small, rather dusty studio museum displays the work
of sculptor Henri Bouchard (1875-1960). He undertook many
official commissions including the tomb of Cardinal Dubois
in Notre Dame and the neo-Romanesque reliefs on St-Pierre
de Chaillot in the 1930s.

### Espace Dalí Montmartre

*11 rue Poulbot, 18th (01.42.64.40.10). M° Anvers or
Abbesses.* **Open** 10am-6pm daily. **Admission** 35F; 25F
students, 8-25s, over-60s; free under-8s. **No credit cards**.
The black-walled interior, artistically programmed lighting
and specially composed soundtrack make it clear that this
is a high-marketing presentation of an artist's work. The collection runs to over 300 works, but don't come expecting to
see Dalí's celebrated Surrealist paintings: the museum concentrates on sculptures (mainly bronzes) from the 1970s, at
the tacky end of his over-long career. There are also reproductions of his book illustrations – La Fontaine's fables,
Freud, de Sade, Dante and *Alice in Wonderland* – where he
fully exploited his taste for the fantastic and the sexual.
*Bookshop.*

### Fondation Jean Dubuffet

*137 rue de Sèvres, 6th (01.47.34.12.63). M° Duroc.*
**Open** 2-6pm Mon-Fri. Closed Aug, public holidays.
**Admission** 20F. **No credit cards**.
Changing display of drawings and sculptures by the French
artist (1901-85), plus maquettes of the monumental archi-
tectural sculptures from his *L'Hourloupe* cycle.
*Archives (by appointment).*

### Musée Bourdelle

*16 rue Antoine-Bourdelle, 15th (01.49.54.73.73).
M° Montparnasse-Bienvenüe or Falguière.*
**Open** 10am-5.40pm Tue-Sun. Closed Mon, public
holidays. **Admission** 17F (27F during exhibitions); 9F
(19F during exhibitions) students, over-60s; free under-7s,
CM. **No credit cards**.
An interesting museum devoted to the sculptor Antoine
Bourdelle, a pupil of Rodin, who produced several monumental works including the Modernist relief friezes at the
Théâtre des Champs-Elysées *(see chapter* **Music: Classical
& Opera**). Housed in a mix of buildings around a small garden, the museum includes the artist's studio and apartments,
a 1950s extension revealing the evolution of Bourdelle's monument to a General Alvear in Buenos Aires, and an impressive
new wing added by Christian de Portzamparc, with smaller
bronzes and maquettes.
*Reference library (by appointment only). Wheelchair access.*

### Musée Delacroix

*6 pl Furstenberg, 6th (01.44.41.86.50). M° St-Germain-
des-Prés.* **Open** 9.45am-5pm Mon, Wed-Sun. Closed Tue,
public holidays. **Admission** 23F; 18F 18-25s, over-60s;
free under-18s, CM. **No credit cards**.
Delacroix moved to the pretty place Furstenberg in 1857 to
be nearer the church of St-Sulpice where he was painting
the murals which can still be seen there, and lived here until
his death in 1863. The Louvre and the Musée d'Orsay house
his major paintings, but the collection displayed in the three
rooms of his apartment and the cube-shaped studio in the
garden includes several small oil paintings (including a self-
portrait as Hamlet and a portrait of his housekeeper), some
wonderfully free pastel studies of skies and sketches for larger works, and still conserves some of the atmosphere of the
studio as it must have been. Other displays relate to his
friendships with Baudelaire and George Sand. Recent extension has added a new documentation room. Works may be
rehung during temporary exhibitions.

**Musée Bourdelle** *extension
by Christian de Portzamparc.*

### Musée Maillol

*59-61 rue de Grenelle, 7th. (01.42.22.59.58). M° Rue du
Bac.* **Open** 11am-6pm Mon, Wed-Sun (last tickets at
5.15pm). Closed Tue. **Admission** 40F; 26F students,
over-60s; free under-18s. **No credit cards**.
Dina Vierny met the sculptor Aristide Maillol (1861-1944) at
the age of 15, and for the next ten years was his principal
model, idealised in such sculptures as *Spring* and *Air*. In 1995
she opened this museum in a carefully restored eighteenth-
century *hôtel*, displaying his drawings, pastels, ceramics,
engravings and paintings, as well as sculpture. The collection also contains works by his contemporaries (Vierny also
sat for Matisse, Dufy and Bonnard) including Picasso, Rodin,
Gauguin, Bonnard, Degas, Cézanne, Matisse and Dufy, some
rare Surrealist documents and multiples by Marcel Duchamp
and Villon, naive art, and works by the Russian artists
Vierny has championed from Kandinsky to Ilya Kabakov,
whose installation *The Communal Kitchen*, recreates the
atmosphere and sounds of a shared Russian kitchen.
*Bookshop. Café (11am-5.30pm). Wheelchair access.*

### Musée Gustave Moreau

*14 rue de la Rochefoucauld, 9th (01.48.74.38.50). M°
Trinité.* **Open** 11am-5.15pm Mon, Wed; 10am-12.45pm,
2-5.15pm, Thur-Sun. Closed Tue. **Admission** 22F; 15F
students, over-60s; free under-18s, CM. **No credit cards**.
The most eccentric of all the one-man museums in Paris. The
enormous double-height studio, with a further storey above
reached by an impressive spiral staircase, is crammed wall
to wall with Moreau's paintings – many unfinished – and
there are thousands more of his drawings and watercolours
to pull out from shutters on the walls. Here the Symbolist
painter Gustave Moreau (1825-98) lived, worked and taught
his art to the likes of Matisse, Rouault and Puy. The museum will transport any visitor back into the mystical and
dreamily abstract artistic movement that peaked in the late

# The Musée d'Orsay

*1 rue de Bellechasse, 7th (01.40.49.48.14/recorded information 01.45.49.11.11). Mº Solférino/RER Musée d'Orsay.* **Open** *10am-6pm Tue, Wed, Fri, Sat; 10am-9.45pm Thur; 9am-6pm Sun. Closed Mon.* **Admission** *36F; 24F 18-25s, over-60s, all visitors Sun; free under-18s, CM.* **Credit** *(bookshop only) AmEx, MC, V. Audioguide. Bookshop. Café-restaurant. Concerts. Guided tours. Library. Wheelchair access.*

Opened in 1986, the Musée d'Orsay occupies a Beaux-Arts train station built for the Grand Exposition of 1900, which was saved from demolition to become Paris' museum of the nineteenth century, devoted to the pivotal years 1848-1914. Milanese architect/designer Gae Aulenti remodelled the interior, inserting postmodern partitions and lift shafts, keeping the iron-framed coffered roof and creating galleries running either side of a light-filled central canyon. Most visitors come to see the impressive array of works by the Impressionists and post-Impressionists, but the collection actually covers all the main movements of the period, including late Romantics, Realists, Symbolists, Pointillistes and Nabis, as well as decorative arts, architectural drawings and photography.

The museum is planned so that visitors follow a more-or-less chronological route, starting on the ground floor, whizzing up to the upper level and finishing on the middle floor. The drawback of the design is that it gives too much space and prestige to the *artistes pompiers* of the nineteenth century – the languidly gasping nudes of Cabanel and Couture or the grandiose history subjects of Meissonier and Chassereau – while the famous Impressionists are crammed together, knee deep in tourists, upstairs. Even so, this does mean that the museum gives an authentic impression of the art of the period, for these artists were highly regarded in their lifetimes, and allows you to see the continuities between the Impressionists and their forerunners, the Realists and the Barbizon School, as well as to appreciate the true revolutionary effect of their use of light and colour.

The first rooms to the right (Lille side) of the central aisle are dedicated to the Romantics and history painters. Some typically classical portraits by Ingres contrast with the Romantic passion of Delacroix's North African period. Further on, there are examples of the early output of Degas, as well as melancholically mystical works by the Symbolists Gustave Moreau and Puvis de Chavannes.

The first rooms to the left (Seine side) of the central aisle are given over to the Barbizon landscape painters, such as Corot and Daubigny and Millet's idealised depictions of rural virtue, including *Angelus*. Don't miss the set of clay busts by Daumier caricaturing notables of his time. There is a room dedicated to Gustave Courbet, with *The Artist and his Studio* and his monumental *Burial at Ornans*, which seem the bridge with the Impressionists. A recent

acquisition, Courbet's sexually explicit *Le Fin du Monde* – still has incredible power to shock today.

This floor also covers pre-1870 works by the Impressionists, several of whom are depicted in Fantin-Latour's *Un atelier aux Batignolles*. There are early Monets, fine Pissarros, Van Gogh's *The Potato Eaters*, Boudin seascapes and Manet's once-scandalous *Olympia*, which although based on the classic nudes of Titian and Velasquez refused to idealise or prettify the model, who to contemporaries clearly appeared to be a prostitute.

The most interesting element of the central aisle is the work of sculptor Jean-Baptiste Carpeaux, whose faces have an almost rococo sensiblity including his controversial *La Danse*, from the Palais Garnier facade, which shocked nineteenth-century moralists with its abandoned naked dancers. A fascinating model of the Palais Garnier reveals just how much of the building is taken up by reception rooms and the lavish stairway, how little by the auditorium.

Escalators whisk you straight up to the upper level, where you can take in major masterpieces by Pissarro, Renoir and Caillebotte, Manet's controversial *Déjeuner sur l'Herbe*, possibly the most famous picnic in history, several of Monet's paintings of Rouen cathedral, by which he explored the changing qualities of light at different times of the day and depictions of his garden at Giverny (*see chapter* **Trips Out of Town**), and paintings and sculptures by Degas whose backstage at the ballet scenes, influenced by Japanese prints, broke all previous rules of composition. The riches continue with the Post-Impressionists. Among the boiling colours and wriggling brushwork of Van Gogh are his *Church at Auvers* and his last painting *Crows*. There are Cézanne still lifes, Gauguin from both Breton and Tahitian periods, recently augmented by the *Self-Portrait with Yellow Christ*, Toulouse-Lautrec's depictions of Montmartre lowlife and the Moulin Rouge, works by the

*Recent acquisitions by Gauguin (above) and Monet (below).*

Pointillistes Seurat and Signac, the mystical works of Redon and the primitivist jungle of Douanier Rousseau.

You have to go downstairs for the Nabis painters, Vallotton, Denis, Roussel, Bonnard and Vuillard, treating both religious and domestic scenes in a wonderful, flat , decorative style. Several rooms are given over to the decorative arts, with a mouth-watering collection of Art Nouveau and Jugendstil furniture, along with fine paintings by Munch and Klimt. The sculpture terraces include a typically melting face by Medardo Rosso, powerful busts by Rodin and his *Gates of Hell* and *Balzac* (also in the Musée Rodin) and bronzes by Bourdelle and Maillol. Finally, it is worth taking a look at the ornate reception room, formerly part of the vast 370-room station hotel. Equally impressive is the museum's Café des Hauteurs. *See also chapter* **Sightseeing**.

nineteenth century. Moreau developed a personal mythology, filling his fantastically detailed canvases with images of *St John the Baptist*, *St George*, *Salomé*, griffins and unicorns, using jewel-like colours that, like those of his near contemporaries the English Pre-Raphaelites, owed much to the rediscovery of the early Italian masters. Don't miss the small private apartment, crammed with furniture and ornaments, where Moreau lived with his parents.
*Bookshop. Library (by appointment only).*

## Musée National Hébert

*85 rue du Cherche-Midi, 6th (01.42.22.23.82).*
*M° Sèvres-Babylone.* **Open** 12.30-5.30pm Mon, Wed-Fri; 2-5.30pm Sat, Sun and public holidays. Closed Tue, 1 May. **Admission** 16F; 12F students, over-60s; free under-18s, CM. **No credit cards.**
Now largely forgotten, Ernest Hébert (1817-1908) painted landscapes of Italy and figurative subjects, bending to the fashion of the time with pious portraits and sentimental shepherdesses during the mid-century, or brightly-coloured, Symbolist-influenced muses, Ophelias and Impressionist-tinged ladies towards the end of his career. The endless watercolours and oils are mostly unremarkable, if an interesting testament to nineteenth-century taste. The run-down house is strangely appealing, though: a curious mix of marble additions, and some fine rooms on the second floor, which still have their original early eighteenth-century panelling.
*Shop.*

## Musée National Jean-Jacques Henner

*43 av de Villiers, 17th (01.47.63.42.73). M° Malesherbes or Monceau.* **Open** 10am-noon, 2-5pm, Tue-Sun. Closed Mon. **Admission** 20F; 15F students, over-60s; free under-15s, CM. **No credit cards.**
A surprising one-man museum north of the Parc Monceau, with more than 700 paintings, sketches and drawings by the prolific Henner (1829-1905), a rather modest, solitary character. The collection is interesting not so much for the quality of the works, but as an illustration of how obsessively he reworked and transformed the same subjects. Look out for the Islamic balcony in the first-floor drawing room.

## Musée National Picasso

*Hôtel Salé, 5 rue de Thorigny, 3rd (01.42.71.25.21). M° Chemin-Vert or St-Paul.* **Open** 9.30am-5.30pm Mon, Wed-Sun. Closed Tue. **Admission** 30F (38F during exhibitions); 20F (28F during exhibitions) 18-25s, students, over-60s, all visitors Sun; free under-18s, CM. **Credit** (bookshop only) MC, V.
The *grand siècle* mansion, lushly decorated with stone carvings, is alone worth the trip here. Opened in 1985 in a renovated Marais *hôtel particulier*, the Musée Picasso possesses an unparalleled collection of paintings representing all phases of the master's long and varied career, acquired by the French state in lieu of inheritance taxes. Many of the paintings Picasso could not bring himself to part with are on display here. The result is a collection spanning six decades of creativity, including not only his famous gaunt blue figures and harlequins, his Cubist and classical phases, but also the boldly drawn and unabashedly ribald pictures he produced in his later years, wonderful beach pictures and portraits of his favourite models Marie-Thérèse and Dora Maar. The drawings for the pivotal *Demoiselles d'Avignon* are on display, as well as prints and ceramics that demonstrate the versatile nature of Picasso's genius. What stands out above all is the sculpture: from the vast head on the staircase to a girl skipping. Look closely at the sculpture of an ape – you'll see that its face is made out of a 2CV. Picasso stands out for his continual inventiveness, and surprisingly rare in great art, his wonderful sense of humour. Also there is Picasso's collection of tribal art – interestingly juxtaposed with the 'primitive' wood figures he carved himself – and of paintings, including works by Matisse and Douanier Rousseau.
*Bookshop. Wheelchair access.*

## Musée Rodin

*Hôtel Biron, 77 rue de Varenne, 7th (01.47.05.01.34). M° Varenne.* **Open** 9.30am-6.45pm Tue-Sun. Closed Mon. **Admission** 28F; 18F 18-25s, over-60s, all visitors Sun and public holidays; free under-18s, art students, CM. *Gardens only* 5F. **Credit** (bookshop only) AmEx, MC, V.
One of Paris' most pleasant museums, the Rodin occupies the stately *hôtel particulier* where Rodin actually lived and sculpted at the end of his life. The famous *Kiss*, the moving *Cathedral*, Rodin's studies of *Balzac* and other pieces of note occupy the rooms indoors, accompanied by several works by Rodin's mistress and pupil Camille Claudel, and paintings by Van Gogh, Monet, Renoir and Rodin himself. In the recently replanted gardens there is the tragically moving *Burghers of Calais*, the elaborate *Gates of Hell*, the final proud portrait of *Balzac*, and the eternally absorbed – and absorbing – *Thinker*, *Orpheus* under a shady stretch of trees, as well as several unfinished nymphs seemingly emerging from the marble. Rodin fans can also visit the Villa des Brillants at Meudon (01.45.34.13.09), where he worked from 1895. On display are sculptures, as well as plaster casts and sketches for his major works (Apr-Oct only: 1.30-6pm Fri-Sun).
*Bookshop. Café (in garden). Wheelchair access.*

## Musée Zadkine

*100bis rue d'Assas, 6th (01.43.26.91.90). M° Notre Dame des Champs/RER Port Royal.* **Open** 10am-5.30pm Tue-Sun. Closed Mon, public holidays. **Admission** 17.50F (27F during exhibitions); 9F students (19F during exhibitions); free under-18s, CM. **No credit cards.**
Arresting works by the Russian-born Cubist sculptor Ossip Zadkine are displayed around the garden and over the tiny

*Mythic* **Musée Gustave Moreau**.

house he inhabited from 1928 – when Montparnasse was centre of the artistic world – until his death in 1967. Zadkine's compositions include musical, mythological and religious subjects and his style varies with his materials: bronzes tend to be geometrical, wood more sensuous, flowing with the grain. Numerous sculptures and preparatory studies are cleverly displayed on ledges around the rooms at eye-level, along with drawings by Zadkine and some paintings by his wife Valentine Prax. In the garden are his largest sculptures, and the studio has been converted for temporary exhibitions. *Bookshop. Library (by appointment). Certain works accessible and captioned for the visually handicapped.*

## Photography

### Caisse des Dépôts et Consignations
*13 quai Voltaire, 7th (01.40.49.41.66). M° Rue du Bac.* **Open** noon-6.30pm Tue-Sat. **Admission** free. **No credit cards.**
Enormously wealthy quango has substantial collections of contemporary photography. Month-long displays are supplemented by three-day solo shows by contemporary artists, photographers and video-makers that have so far included Bill Viola, Claude Closky and Marie-Ange Guilleminot.

### Centre National de la Photographie
*Hôtel Salomon de Rothschild, 11 rue Berryer, 8th (01.53.76.12.31). M° Charles de Gaulle-Etoile.* **Open** noon-7pm Mon, Wed-Sun. Closed Tue. **Admission** 30F; 15F 10-25s, over-60s; free under-10s. **No credit cards.**
The national photography centre will eventually move (yet) again to the Hôtel de Sully. New director Régis Durand is taking a more contemporary line with, in addition to major monographic exhibitions such as Hannah Collins and Thomas Ruff, or winners of the Niepce photojournalism prize, two rooms destined for short shows by new talents and an international biennial planned from 1998.

### Espace Photographique de Paris
*Nouveau Forum des Halles/4 pl Carrée, 8 Grande Galerie, 1st (01.40.26.87.12). M° Châtelet-Les Halles.* **Open** 1-6pm Tue-Fri; 1-7pm Sat, Sun. **Admission** 10F. **No credit cards.**

This space presents the work of both internationally known and more obscure photographers. It is due to move into the Vidéothèque next door *(see chapter* **Film***)* in late 1997. *Wheelchair access.*

### Maison Européenne de la Photographie
*5-7 rue de Fourcy, 4th (01.44.78.75.00). M° St-Paul.* **Open** 11am-7.45pm Wed-Sun. Closed Mon, Tue, public holidays. **Admission** 30F; 15F students. **Credit** AmEx, MC, V.
This new institution in a restored Marais mansion with strikingly minimalist extension by architect Yves Lion has proved hugely successful since opening in February 1996. Solo shows have included William Klein, Bettina Rheims and Pierre et Gilles. The cellars are used for experimental and multi-media works. Organises the biennial Mois de la Photo. *Auditorium. Café. Library. Wheelchair access.*

### La Mission du Patrimoine Photographique
*Hôtel de Sully, 62 rue St-Antoine, 4th (01.42.74.47.75). M° St-Paul or Bastille.* **Open** 10am-6.30pm Tue-Sun. Closed Mon. **Admission** 25F; 15F students, under-25s, over-60s. **Credit** (bookshop only) MC, V.
Classic, primarily historic, photographic shows are put on – often in association with bodies like the Royal Photographic Society – of individuals like Cecil Beaton and dandy Jacques-Henri Lartigue or themes such as the Egyptian pyramids.

## Decorative Arts

### Musée des Arts Décoratifs
*Palais du Louvre, 107 rue de Rivoli, 1st (01.44.55.57.50). M° Palais-Royal.* **Open** from June 1997: 12.30-6pm Tue, Thur, Fri; 10am-6pm Wed, Sat, Sun. Closed Mon. **Admission** 35F; 25F under-25s, over-60s; free CM. **Credit** (shop only) AmEx, MC, V.
From Medieval chests to twentieth-century avant-garde via extravagant rococo, this fascinating museum, housed in the north-west wing of the Louvre since 1985, displays the treasures of France's rich tradition of decorative arts. However, along with its neighbours, the Musée de la Mode et du Textile and the Musée de la Publicité, also run by the Union Centrale des Arts Décoratifs, the museum is currently getting a

*Robert Frank at the* **Centre Culturel Suisse** *for the Mois de la Photo, see p229.*

facelift as part of the *Grand Louvre* programme and expanding into some of the space vacated by the Ministry of Finance in 1991. The first of the newly restored displays covering the Medieval and First Empire periods will reopen in June 1997, with furniture, furnishings, ceramics, metal work and objects displayed both in cabinets and in period rooms. The seventeenth-, eighteenth- and nineteenth-century collections will reopen in autumn 1998. The twentieth-century galleries, which will include a new *galerie des créateurs* focusing on iron, glass and ceramics, will open in 1999. There will also be a space for large-scale exhibitions.
*Reference library. Shop. Wheelchair access.*

### Musée de la Chasse et de la Nature
*Hôtel Guénégaud, 60 rue des Archives, 3rd  .
(01.42.72.86.43). M° Hôtel-de-Ville.* **Open** 10am-12.30pm, 1.30-5.30pm, Mon, Wed-Sun. Closed Tue. **Admission** 25F; 12.50F students. **No credit cards**.
Housed on three floors of a beautifully proportioned (and maintained) mansion built by François Mansart in 1654, this museum brings together a group of objects ranging from Stone Age arrow heads to Persian helmets via Louis XV console tables under the common theme of hunting – nature, unless it is in the form of a rather alarming collection of stuffed animals, doesn't get much of a look-in. Although nearly all the decorative arts are represented, the highlight is the collection of wonderfully ornate weapons: crossbows inlaid with ivory and mother of pearl, guns decorated with hunting scenes and swords engraved with elaborate arabesques or masks, all reminding us that hunting was a luxury sport and its accoutrements were important status symbols. There is also a collection of French hunting pictures by artists such as Chardin, Oudry and Desportes as well as a Cranach (attributed) and a Rembrandt sketch.

### Musée du Cristal Baccarat
*30 bis rue de Paradis, 10th (01.47.70.64.30). M° Poissonnière.* **Open** 9am-6.30pm Mon-Fri; 10am-5.30pm Sat. **Admission** 15F; 7.50F students, under-25s, over 60s. **Credit** (shop only) AmEx, DC, MC, V.
The showroom of celebrated glass-maker Baccarat, with a museum attached. The main interest here is in seeing which fallen head of state or deposed monarch used to drink out of Baccarat glasses. There are also some kitsch but technically magnificent pieces produced for the great exhibitions last century. Baccarat moved its glass workshops here in 1832; and this street remains full of glassware and china outlets. *Shop.*

### Musée Christofle
*9 rue Royale, 9th (01.49.22.41.15). M° Concorde.* **Open** 2-6pm Mon-Fri. Closed Sat, Sun, Aug. **Admission** free. **Credit** (shop only) AmEx, DC, MC, V.
This small museum celebrates Christofle – the man who gave the world silver-plated cutlery – and his company, founded in 1830. The silverware constitutes a design history illustrating the trends in nineteenth- and early twentieth-century taste, from the Turkish-style *cloisonné* coffee service shown at the London Universal Exhibition in 1862, via a Japanese-style table bell of 1870, through to Art Deco bronze 'serpent' vases. There are more modern items, including pieces from the Villeroy cutlery service made for a dinner held at Versailles in 1957 when the Queen was the guest of honour. Two further rooms and two display rooms at the Christofle factory in St-Denis (01.49.22.40.00) are open to groups only. *Shop.*

### Musée de l'Eventail
*Hôtel Hoguet, 2 bd de Strasbourg, 10th (01.42.08.19 89). M° Strasbourg-St-Denis.* **Open** 2-5pm Tue. Workshop 9am-noon, 2-6pm, Mon-Fri. **Admission** 30F; 20F under-12s. **No credit cards**.
This collection, belonging to the Hoguet family of fan-makers, is housed in the former *atelier*'s neo-Renaissance

*Sculpture garden at*
**Musée Zadkine, p215.**

showroom complete with its original 1893 walnut fittings. The exhibits range from eighteenth-century painted fans with mother of pearl and ivory sticks to contemporary fans by designers such as Karl Lagerfeld. There is also an interesting display on the techniques and materials used in making these luxury items – which until the French Revolution only the nobility was allowed to use.

### Musée des Lunettes et Lorgnettes
*380 rue St-Honoré, 1st (01.40.20.06.98). M° Madeleine or Concorde.* **Open** 10am-noon, 2-6pm, Tue-Sat. **Admisssion** 20F; 10F students, over-60s. **No credit cards**.
One room above the Pierre Marly optician is crammed full of every conceivable type of sight-enhancing gadget, including eighteenth-century glasses, nineteenth-century monocles and telescopes in tooled leather cases, through to Brigitte Bardot's black and white plastic sun specs. An eyeful.

### Musée de la Mode et du Costume
*Palais Galliéra, 10 av Pierre 1er de Serbie, 16th (01.47.20.85.23). M° Iéna or Alma-Marceau.* **Open** during exhibitions only 10am-5.40pm Tue-Sun. Closed Mon. **Admission** 35F; 25F students; free under-7s. **Credit** V.
Opposite the Musée d'Art Moderne de la Ville de Paris (*see above* **Fine Art**), this fanciful 1890s mansion opens its doors to the public during its regular fashion and costume exhibitions; themes vary from historical periods to individual dress designers. The museum's own collection has a particular emphasis on nineteenth-century town clothes, but the exhibitions often include items loaned from other institutions. *Library (by appointment).*

### Musée de la Mode et du Textile
*Palais du Louvre, 107 rue de Rivoli, 1st (01.44.55.57.50). M° Palais-Royal.* **Open** 11am-6pm Tue, Thur, Fri; 11am-10pm Wed; 10am-6pm Sat, Sun. Closed Mon. **Admission** 35F; 25F under-25s, over-60s. **Credit** (shop only) AmEx, MC, V.
Reopened in January 1997 after extensive reorganisation, the new-look fashion museum has moved into a much bigger space as part of the *Grand Louvre* project, so that for the first time part of its collection is on permanent show. The display, rotated every six months, gives an overview of the history of costume from rare seventeenth-century items through to

pieces by contemporary *haute couturiers*. Highlights include Renaissance damasks and velvets, the collection of the Empress Eugénie's dressmaker as well as important donations from designers such as Madeleine Vionnet, Elsa Schiaparelli and Paul Poiret. The twentieth century is particularly well displayed, with archive film footage of the period complementing the clothes, and the poverty of war-time shoes an interesting antidote to Dior's New Look of the 1950s and fantastic beaded shoes by Roger Vivier.

*Research centre (by appointment). Wheelchair access.*

## Musée National du Moyen Age – Thermes de Cluny

*6 pl Paul-Painlevé, 5th (01.53.73.78.00). M° Cluny-La Sorbonne/RER St-Michel.* **Open** 9.15am-5.45pm Mon, Wed-Sun. Closed Tue. **Admission** 28F; 18F 18-25s, over-60s, all visitors Sun; free under-18s, CM. **No credit cards.** Occupying the fifteenth-century Hôtel de Cluny, the Paris mansion of the abbots of Cluny, which was built into the ruins of third-century Roman baths, this intriguing museum of Medieval art and artefacts retains a domestic scale suitable for the small-scale intimacy of many of its treasures. Its most famous pieces are the *Lady and the Unicorn* tapestries, depicting convoluted allegories of the five senses, beautifully displayed in a special circular room. The millefiore-style tapestry, filled with rabbits and flowers, is wrought in exquisite colour and detail. Elsewhere there are displays of enamel bowls and caskets from Limoges, carved ivories and gold reliquaries and church plate, medieval books of hours to leaf through, wooden chests and locks. There are also early fabrics, including ancient Coptic weaving from Egypt and heavily embroidered bishop's copes, Medieval sculpture with capitals from churches all over France, and heads of the kings of Judea from Notre Dame, which had been destroyed in the Revolution under the mistaken belief that they represented the kings of France, and were discovered by chance (minus their noses) in 1979. *See also chapter* **Sightseeing**.

*Bookshop. Concerts. Guided tours.*

# Musée Carnavalet

*23 rue de Sévigné, 3rd (01.42.72.21.13). M° St-Paul.* **Open** 10am-5.40pm Tue-Sun. Closed Mon, some public holidays. **Admission** 35F; 25F students; free under-18s, CM. **Credit** (bookshop only) AmEx, V.

The museum of Paris history owes its origins to Baron Haussmann who persuaded the City of Paris to buy the Hôtel Carnavalet in 1866 to house some of the interiors from buildings destroyed to make way for his new boulevards. Since then the museum has built up a huge collection which tells the history of the capital from pre-Roman Gaul to the twentieth century through archeological finds, *objets d'art*, prints, paintings and furnishings.

The museum is housed in two buildings. The Hôtel Carnavalet, started in 1548 and remodelled by Mansart in the 1660s, contains the main collection and retains much of its old atmosphere, with an attractive *cour d'honneur* and a formal garden. Carnavalet's most famous resident was Madame de Sévigné, the writer whose letters to her daughter bring alive aristocratic life under Louis XIV. A good collection of related memorabilia includes portraits of the author and her circle, her Chinese-export, lacquered desk and some of her letters, displayed in the panelled first-floor gallery and salon. The adjoining seventeenth-century Hôtel Le Peletier de St Fargeau, of which all that remains is the elegant grand staircase and one restored, panelled *cabinet*, was added in 1989.

The displays are arranged chronologically. The original sixteenth-century rooms appropriately house the Renaissance collections with portraits by Clouet, furniture and pictures relating to the Wars of Religion that dominated French politics for most of the period.

The first floor covers the period up to 1789 with furniture, applied arts and paintings displayed in recently restored, period interiors. The bold, new colours, particularly in the oval *boudoir* from the Hôtel de Breuteuil (1782),

may come as a bit of a shock to people with pre-conceived ideas about the subdued, good taste of the eighteenth century; however the use of strong royal blues and vivid greens is correct as the colours have been copied from original paint samples. Some of the most interesting interiors include the rococo cabinet painted for the engraver Demarteau by his friends, Fragonard, Boucher and Huet in 1765, the Chinoiserie rooms painted with 'exotic' landscapes and the Louis XIII-style Cabinet Colbert.

The collections from 1789 on are housed in the *hôtel* next door. The Revolutionary items are the best way of getting an understanding of the convoluted politics and bloodshed of the period from the calling of the Estates General through to the Directory. Here are portraits of all the major players, prints, objects and memorabilia including a bone model of the guillotine made by French prisoners of war in England, commemorative china and a small chunk of the Bastille prison. Those of a sentimental bent should look at the pathetic souvenirs from the Temple prison where the royal family were held: among them, the Dauphin's lead soldiers and Louis XVI's shaving kit.

The nineteenth-century collections are on the ground and first floor, and range from items belonging to Napoléon, through contemporary views of Paris depicting the effects of Haussmann's programme to the early twentieth-century ballroom from the Hôtel Wendel. Highlights include the ornate cradle given to Napoléon III on the birth of his son by the city of Paris and the Art Nouveau Boutique Fouquet designed by Alphonse Mucha in 1901 complete with a sea-horse fountain. Rooms devoted to French literature finish off the tour with portraits and room settings, including Proust's cork-lined bedroom.

*Bookshop. Guided tours. Reference section.*
*Wheelchair access.*

### Musées des Parfumeries-Fragonard
*9 rue Scribe, 9th (01.47.42.93.40) and 39 bd des Capucines, 2nd (01.42.60.37.14). M° Opéra.*
**Open** 9am-5.45pm Mon-Sat. Closed Sun.
**Admission** free. **Credit** (shop only) AmEx, MC, V.
Get on the scent at the two museums showcasing the collection of perfume house Fragonard. The five rooms at rue Scribe range from Ancient Egyptian ointment flasks to eighteenth-century vinaigrettes and Meissen porcelain scent bottles, while the second museum contains bottles designed by Lalique and Schiaparelli, among others. Both also have displays on scent manufacture and an early twentieth-century 'perfume organ' with rows of the bottled ingredients used by 'noses' when creating their valuable concoctions. *Shop.*

### Musée de la Publicité
*Palais du Louvre, 107 rue de Rivoli, 1st (01.44.55.58.50). M° Palais-Royal.* **Open** from early 1998, ring for details.
**Admission** ring for details.
This museum started life as the Poster Museum in 1978, becoming the Advertising Museum in 1982, and will re-open in early 1998 after relocation from its old 10th *arrondissement* premises to the Louvre as part of the *Grand Louvre* programme. A permanant display of posters from 1700 to 1945 will be complemented by ads and other more recent items donated by graphic artists and advertising agencies.

### Musée National de Céramique de Sèvres
*pl de la Manufacture, 92310 Sèvres (01.41.14.04.20). M° Pont de Sèvres.* **Open** 10am-5pm Mon, Wed-Sun. Closed Tue. **Admission** 22F; 15F 18-25s, over-60s; free under-18s, CM. **Credit** (showroom only) AmEx, DC, MC, V.
Founded in 1738 as a private concern, the porcelain factory moved to Sèvres from Vincennes in 1756 and was soon taken over by the state. On display are finely-painted, delicately-modelled pieces that epitomise French rococo style, together with nineteenth-century pieces, such as porcelain copies of Raphäels and Titians, that demonstrate an extraordinary technical virtuosity. The collection also includes Delftware, Italian majolica, Meissen, Della Robbia reliefs, Oriental and Hispano-Moorish pieces. Don't miss the outstanding collection of glowing Ottoman plates and tiles from Iznik and the elegantly decorated, eighteenth-century *faïence* commode. *Shop and showroom. Wheelchair access.*

### Musée National de la Renaissance
*Château d'Ecouen, 95440 Ecouen (01.34.38.38.50). SNCF from Gare du Nord to Ecouen-Ezanville, then bus 269.* **Open** 9.45am-12.30pm, 2-5.15pm, Mon, Wed-Sun. Closed Tue. **Admission** 21F; 18F students, Sun; free under-18s. CM. **No credit cards.**
Overlooking an agricultural plain, yet barely outside the Paris suburbs, the Renaissance château built for Royal Constable Anne de Montmorency and his wife Margaret de Savoie between 1538 and 1555 is the authentic setting for a wonderful collection of sixteenth-century decorative arts. The display is low-key but there are some real treasures here arranged over three floors of the château (some parts only open in the morning or afternoon). Best of all are the imposing original painted chimneypieces, not unlike those at Fontainebleau, only here the caryatids and grotesques, as well as the Biblical and mythological scenes, are painted rather than sculpted. There is also furniture, Limoges enamels, tin-glazed earthenware decorated with Classical and religious scenes, armour, embroideries, rare painted leather wall hangings with scenes of Scipio and a magnificent cycle of ten tapestries depicting the story of David and Bathsheba. *Wheelchair access.*

### Musée Nissim de Camondo
*63 rue de Monceau, 8th (01.45.63.26.32). M° Monceau or Villiers.* **Open** 10am-5pm Wed-Sun. **Admission** 27F; 18F 5-25s, over-60s; free under-5s, CM. **No credit cards.**

*Style tips at the* **Musée de la Mode et du Textile***.*

The Camondos were a rich banking family who moved to Paris from Constantinople in 1867. The collection put together by Count Moïse de Camondo exploits to the full a love for fine French furniture and ceramics, as well as loudly patterned Italian marble, and is named after his son Nissim, who died in World War I (the rest of the family died at Auschwitz). Moïse replaced the two families' houses near Parc Monceau with this palatial residence in 1911-14, and lived here in a style quite out of his time. A succession of rooms is crammed with furniture by leading craftsmen of the Louis XV and Louis XVI eras, including Oeben, Riesener and Leleu, and there are huge silver services and sets of Sèvres and Meissen porcelain. All are set off by superb carpets and tapestries (Gobelins, Aubusson, Beauvais, Savonnerie), which are mostly in extremely good condition. Most remarkable is the circular Salon de Huet, overlooking the Parc Monceau and adorned by eighteenth-century pastoral scenes.

### Musée de la Serrurerie – Musée Bricard
*1 rue de la Perle, 3rd (01.42.77.79.62). M° St-Paul.*
**Open** 2-4.45pm Mon-Fri. Closed Sat, Sun. **Admission** 30F; 15F students, over-60s, free under 18s. **No credit cards**.
This museum is housed in the cellars of the elegant mansion that architect Libéral-Bruant built for himself in 1685. The collection focuses on locks and keys from the Roman times to the end of last century, as well as other types of metalwork including window fastenings, hinges and the elaborate, seventeenth-century, gilded door handles from the state apartments at Versailles complete with Louis XIV's personal sun-burst. There is also a collection of tools on show.

## Architecture & Urbanism

### Fondation Le Corbusier
*Villa La Roche, 10 square du Docteur Blanche, 16th (01.42.88.41.53). M° Jasmin.* **Open** 10am-12.30pm, 1.30-6pm Mon-Thur; 10am-5pm Fri. Closed Sat, Sun, public holidays, Aug. **Admission** 15F; 10F students.
**No credit cards.**
In a part of Paris surprisingly rich in avant-garde architecture, this house, designed by Le Corbusier in 1923 for a Swiss banker and art collector, provides a good opportunity to see the architect's ideas in practice, and also contains a collection of his drawings, paintings, sculpture and furniture. Here are all the typical *pilotis*, roof terraces, split volumes, internal balconies and built-in furniture, although not the stereo-

type Modernist white – the interior is painted in muted pinks, maroons, greys and greens. The adjoining Villa Jeanneret – also by Le Corbusier – houses the Foundation's library (*see also chapter* **Architecture**).
*Bookshop. Library (1.30-6pm).*

### Institut Français d'Architecture
*6 rue de Tournon, 6th (01.46.33.90.36). M° Odéon.* **Open** (during exhibitions only) 12.30-7pm Tue-Sat. **Admission** free. **No credit cards.**
Exhibitions on twentieth-century architects or aspects of the built environment.
*Lectures. Library. Wheelchair access.*

### Musée des Monuments Français
*Palais de Chaillot, pl du Trocadéro, 16th (01.44.05.39.10). M° Trocadéro.* **Open** until Apr 1997: 10am-6pm Mon, Wed-Sun. Closed Tue. **Admission** 36F; 24F under-25s, over-60s; free under-13s. **Credit** (shop only) MC, V.
This museum was founded by the Gothic revivalist Viollet-de-Duc to record the architectural heritage of France, through mouldings and copies that take you from Chartres to Vézelay without leaving Paris. The museum will close in mid-April 1997 and reopen in 1999 with an enlarged collection as the Centre pour le Patrimoine Monumental and Urbain.
*Shop. Wheelchair Access.*

### Pavillon de l'Arsenal
*21 bd Morland, 4th (01.42.76.33.97). M° Sully-Morland.* **Open** 10.30am-6.30pm Tue-Sat; 11am-7pm Sun. Closed Mon. **Admission** free. **Credit** (shop only) V.
This centre presents imaginative exhibitions on urban design and architecture, in the form of drawings, plans, photographs and models. There's an illuminated 50-square metre (165ft) model of Paris, and a permanent exhibition on the historic development of the city and the *Grands Projets*.
*Bookshop. Guided tours. Lectures. Wheelchair access.*

### Villa Savoye
*82 rue Villiers, 78300 Poissy (01.39.65.01.06). RER Poissy, then 15min walk.* **Open** May-Oct 10am-noon, 1.30-5.30pm; Nov-Apr 10am-noon, 1.30-4.30pm, Mon, Wed-Sun. Closed Tue. **Admission** 25F; 15F 12-25s, students, CM. **No credit cards.**
This house built in 1929 for a family of rich industrialists is perhaps Corbusier's most successful domestic work, noted for its sculptural spiral staircase. It still has much of its original built-in furniture and fittings.

## Ethnology, Folk & Tribal Art

### Musée des Arts d'Afrique et d'Océanie
*293 av Daumesnil, 12th (01.44.74.84.80). M° Porte Dorée.* **Open** 1.30-5.30pm Mon, Wed-Fri; 1.30-6pm Sat, Sun. *Temporary exhibitions* 10am-5.30pm, 10-6pm, Sat, Sun. Closed Tue. **Admission** 36F; 26F 18-25s, over-60s, all on Sun; free under-18s, CM. **Credit** (shop only, from 100F) MC, V.
Housed in a building that reeks of colonialism, this is a wonderful collection of tribal art, often deserted except for art students and parties of schoolchildren. The museum, on the east of Paris just by the entrance to the Parc de Vincennes, was actually designed for the 1931 Exposition Coloniale, and as well as the astonishing bas-relief of the facade, there are two remarkable Art Deco rooms furnished by Ruhlman. The tribal art, especially the African masks and statues in the upper galleries, is stunning. In addition, there are fabrics and embroidery from the Maghreb and artefacts from the Pacific. Surprisingly, the basement contains an enormous aquarium – a great hit with children – full of tropical fish and crocodiles. The museum is likely to move to Trocadéro as part of the Musée des Arts Premiers by the end of the century.
*Aquarium. Bookshop. Wheelchair access.*

*Rites and magic at* **Musée Dapper**.

### Musée des Arts et Traditions Populaires
*6 av du Mahatma Gandhi, 16th (01.44.17.60.00). M° Sablons.* **Open** 9.30am-5pm Mon, Wed-Sun. Closed Tue. **Admission** 23F; 13F 18-25s, over-60s; free under-18s, CM. Temporary exhibitions 23F, 16F 18s-25s, over-60s; 10F 5-18s; free under-5s. **Credit** (shop only) AmEx, MC, V.
This important centre of French folk art, on the edge of the Bois de Boulogne, spotlights the traditions and popular culture of pre-industrial France, describing all aspects of rural life through displays of agricultural tools, household objects, furniture, reconstructions, costumes and models. The liveliest sections are those devoted to customs and beliefs, which includes a crystal ball, tarot cards, thunder stones and early medicines, and to popular entertainment, with displays on the circus, sports, puppet theatres and music.
*Auditorium. Bookshop. Library. Record collection.*

### Musée Dapper
*50 av Victor Hugo, 16th (01.45.00.01.50). M° Victor-Hugo.* **Open** during exhibitions only, 11am-7pm daily. **Admission** 20F; 10F students, schoolchildren, over-60s; free under-12s, all visitors Wed. **No credit cards.**
Changing exhibitions of African art are masterfully lit and displayed according to a chosen theme or region, such as masks, the Dogon or (until September 1997) magic and ritual. The beautifully designed space is reached through a courtyard behind a jungle-like garden that sets the tone perfectly. One or two exhibitions are arranged every year, with related performances of African tales on Wednesday afternoons.
*Library (by appointment).*

### Musée des Arts Forains
*53 av des Terroirs de France, 12th (01.43.40.16.22). M° Bercy.* **Open** ring to confirm, probably 2-7pm Sat, Sun. **Admission** 42F; 35F over-60s; 25F 3-25s; free under-3s. **No credit cards.**
Depending on when you visit this collection of fairground rides and shows, it may either seem like a museum or a kid's birthday party. It has recently moved to one of the last wine warehouses at Bercy, fortunately listed after the rest of the site had been demolished. The collection, gathered by Jean-Louis Favand who recognised the importance of a disappearing art, covers fairgrounds from 1880 to 1950, and includes several old roundabouts (painted cows and pigs as well as horses) – some of which are operational – a tincan alley, a

*Domestic items at the **Musée de l'Homme**.*

shooting range, *montagne russe* precursor of the rollercoaster, old bar, fairground organs and mechanical theatres. *Guided tours.*

### Musée de l'Homme

*Palais de Chaillot, pl du Trocadéro, 16th (01.44.05.72.72). Mº Trocadéro.* **Open** 9.45am-5.15pm Mon, Wed-Sun. Closed Tue, public holidays. **Admission** 30F; 20F 5s-25s, students, over-60s; free under-4s. **Credit** (bookshop only) MC, V.

Starting off with an exhibition on world population growth, this compendious museum goes on to consider topics such as birth control, death, disease and racial distinction before turning to tribal costumes, tools, idols and ornaments from all over the world. Displays and tableaux are arranged by continent, with Africa and Europe on the first floor and Asia and the Americas on the second. A section devoted to music provides a collection of curious instruments and recordings of the noises they make. The displays tend to be slightly dowdy and could do with some labelling in English, but the variety of the collections alone, including a shrunken head, a stuffed polar bear and a reconstruction of a Mayan temple, make this an ideal departure point for exotic escapism on a rainy day. The museum will form the core of Chirac's proposed Musée des Arts Premiers.
*Café. Cinema. Concerts. Lecture room. Library. Photo Library. Wheelchair access.*

## Oriental Arts

### Musée National des Arts Asiatiques – Guimet

*6 pl d'Iéna, 16th (01.47.23.61.65). Closed until 1999. Les Galeries du Panthéon Buddique, 19 av d'Iéna, 16th (01.40.73.88.11). Mº Iéna.* **Open** 9.45am-5.45pm Mon, Wed-Sun. **Admission** 16F; 12F students, over-60s, all visitors Sun; free under-18s, CM. **No credit cards.**

The stunning national collection of Oriental and Asian art, notably the Cambodian Khmer sculptures from the civilisation of Angkor Wat, is closed for renovation until at least 1999. Currently only the Panthéon Buddhique is open: Emile Guimet's original collection tracing the religious history of China and Japan from the fourth to nineteenth centuries displayed in a Neo-Classical *hôtel.*

### Musée Cernuschi

*7 av Velasquez, 8th (01.45.63.50.75). Mº Villiers or Monceau.* **Open** 10am-5.40pm Tue-Sun. Closed Mon; public holidays. **Admission** 17.50F (27F during exhibitions); 9F 18-25s (17F during exhibitions); free under-18s; CM. **No credit cards.**

Often nearly deserted, this collection of Chinese art near Parc Monceau ranges from neolithic terracottas from several millenia BC to Han and Wei dynasty funeral statues – in which Chinese potters displayed their inventiveness to the full by creating entire legions of animated musicians, warriors, dancers, animals and other lifestyle accessories to take to the next world. Other highlights include refined Tang celadon wares, Sung porcelain, fragile paintings on silk, bronze vessels and jade amulets. The collection was originally built up at the end of the last century by a private collector. However, it is still being expanded today, and among the recent additions there is some contemporary Chinese painting.
*Wheelchair access.*

### Musée d'Ennery

*59 av Foch, 16th (01.45.53.57.96). Mº Porte Dauphine.* **Open** 2-5.45pm Thur, Sun. **Admission** free. **No credit cards.**

This extraordinary collection of Oriental decorative arts, put together by author Adolphe d'Ennery and his wife, is as interesting for what it says about late nineteenth-century taste as for the actual objects. The 7,000 items are still in the D'Ennery's lavish Napoléon III *hôtel* and many have been kept in their original rosewood and mother of pearl showcases; early photographs show that the displays have hardly been touched since the beginning of the century. The collection, dating from the seventeenth to nineteenth centuries, includes a bit of everything: lacquer, ceramics, crystal, jade, ivories, bronzes, masks, wood carvings as well as a large collection of *netsuke.*

### Musée de l'Institut du Monde Arabe

*1 rue des Fossés St-Bernard, 5th (01.40.51.39.53). Mº Jussieu.* **Open** 10am-6pm Tue-Sun. *Temporary exhibitions* 10am-6pm Tue-Sun. Closed Mon. **Admission** 25F; 20F 18-25s, students, over-60s; free under-18s, CM; *Temporary exhibitions* 30F; 25F 18-25s, students, over-60s. **Credit** (shop only) AmEx, DC, MC, V.

Opened in 1987, the Institute of the Arab World is yet another *Grand Projet,* bringing together a library, cultural centre, exhibition spaces and museum. Since many of the objects originally displayed her have returned to the Louvre, the museum has created for itself a new role as the 'Museum of the Arab Museums'. The Institute will display items on long-term loan from museums in alternating Arab countries alongside its own permanent collection; Syria and Tunisia started the ball rolling. The objects, covering a huge geographical (India to Spain) and historical (prehistoric to contemporary) span, are set off well in the high-tech space and include examples from almost every branch of the applied arts, calligraphy, metalwork, ceramics, textiles and miniatures. The collections of early scientific instruments, nineteenth-century Tunisian costume and jewellery and contemporary fine art are particularly strong.
*Bookshop. Cinema. Guided Visits. Lectures. Library. Tea Room. Wheelchair access.*

### Musée Kwok-On

*Telephone enquiries (01.45.75.85.75). Closed until 1998.* **Open** ring for details. **Admission** ring for details. **No credit cards.**

This colourful collection, built up in Hong Kong, aims to present the myths and legends which underpin Asian culture through displays relating to theatre, religious ceremonies, ritual and oral tradition. It includes Peking opera costumes, Japanese Nô robes, Indian masks and musical instruments, and Indonesian shadow puppets. Currently closed, it is due to reopen at a new address in 1998.

# History

## Mémorial du Maréchal Leclerc de Hauteclocque et de la Libération de Paris & Musée Jean Moulin

23 allée de la DB, Jardin Atlantique (above the Grandes Lignes tracks of Gare Montparnasse), 15th (01.40.64.39.44). M° Montparnasse-Bienvenüe. **Open** 10am-5.40pm Tue-Sun. Closed Mon. **Admission** 17.50F (27F during exhibitions); 9F students, over-60s (19F during exhibitions); free under-18s, CM.

A double museum dedicated to two men who were instrumental in the Liberation of Paris, from opposing sides of the political spectrum. General Leclerc commanded the French Division that was the first Allied unit to enter Paris; Moulin was a Communist resistance martyr. Both halves are full of war memorabilia, and the Memorial has a *vidéothèque*. *Bookshop.*

## Musée de l'Armée

Hôtel des Invalides, esplanade des Invalides, 7th (01.44.42.37.67). M° Varenne or Latour-Maubourg. **Open** 10am-5pm daily. **Admission** (valid for 2 consecutive days) 37F; 27F under-18s, students, over-60s; free under-7s, CM. **No credit cards.**

Apart from housing the monolithic tomb of Napoléon, this museum is a feast for boys prone to war fantasies. Military history is explained through prints, paintings, diagrams, maps, uniforms, weapons and armour, from paleolithic times up to World War II. The museum is vast, and there are miles of exhibits devoted to the Napoléonic era alone. A cinema screens simulations and rare footage of French battles from World Wars I and II. The Musée des Plans en Relief (included in the ticket) displays large models of French fortified cities. *See also* **Les Invalides** *in chapter* **Sightseeing.** *Cinema (films on World War I at 2.15pm; World War II 4.15pm). Lectures. Shop. Wheelchair access to half the museum.*

*Eastern art at* **Musée d'Ennery**, *p221.*

## Musée de l'Art et d'Histoire de St-Denis

22bis rue Gabriel-Péri, 93200 St-Denis (01.42.43.05.10). M° St-Denis Porte de Paris. **Open** 10am-5.30pm Mon, Wed-Sat; 2-6.30pm Sun. Closed Tue, public holidays. **Admission** 20F; 10F students, under-18s. **No credit cards.**

This prizewinning museum in the suburb of St-Denis is housed in the former Carmelite convent that in the eighteenth century numbered Louise de France, daughter of Louis XV, among its incumbents. Although there are displays of local archaeology, prints and drawings about the Paris Commune (*see chapter* **History**), Modern and post-Impressionist drawings and documents relating to the poet Paul Eluard who was born in the town, the most vivid part is the first floor where the nuns' austere cells have been preserved.

## Musée de l'Assistance Publique

Hôtel de Miramon, 47 quai de la Tournelle, 5th (01.46.33.01.43). M° Maubert-Mutualité. **Open** 10am-5pm Wed-Sat. Closed Mon, Tue, Aug. **Admission** 20F; 10F students, over-60s; free CM. **No credit cards.**

The history of Paris hospitals, from the days when they were receptacles for abandoned babies to the beginnings of modern medicine with anaesthesia, is explained in a surprisingly lively fashion through paintings, prints, various grisly medical devices and a reconstructed ward and pharmacy; texts are unfortunately in French only. Recent temporary exhibitions have ranged from Daniel Spoerri's artworks using prints of skin diseases to displays on childbirth.

## Musée du Cabinet des Médailles

Bibliothèque Nationale, 58 rue de Richelieu, 2nd (01.47.03.83.30). M° Bourse. **Open** 1-5pm Mon-Sat; noon-6pm Sun. **Admission** 22F; 15F students, over-60s; free under-12s. **Credit** (shop only) MC, V.

This major collection of coins and medals is kept on the first floor of the Bibliothèque Nationale. It's a place for the initiated: there are some 400,000 specimens, including the world's largest collection of cameos and intaglios. If your eyes begin to blur after focusing on such small exhibits, there are also some works of art. Of particular interest is the Merovingian King Dagobert's throne, as well as items of silverwork and a selection of paintings, with works by Boucher and Van Loo. *Shop. Wheelchair access.*

## Musée Grévin

10 bd Montmartre, 9th (01.47.70.85.05). M° Rue Montmartre. **Open** *Term-time* 1-6pm daily. *School holidays* 10am-7pm daily. **Admission** 55F; 36F 6-14s; free under-6s. **Credit** (from 130F) MC, V.

The French version of Madame Tussaud's with an easy-to-miss entrance since it's near a hundred years old, but is smaller than its London counterpart. Realism is variable (Depardieu's nose is well done but Gainsbourg's stubble is particularly unconvincing), though the costumes are very good. There are some odd touches: spot the recurring black cats or the collection of famous revolutionaries' death masks. Although there is a fair quota of international film stars and well-known statesmen (Clinton, Kohl), the emphasis is on episodes from French history (the trial of Joan of Arc, the death of Marat) and personalities. Unfortunately the labelling is unhelpfully incomplete, and a list of all the figures is not available until you get to the souvenir stand at the end on sale for 5F).

## Musée de l'Histoire de France

Hôtel de Soubise, 60 rue des Francs-Bourgeois, 3rd (01.40.27.62.18). M° Hôtel-de-Ville or Rambuteau. **Open** noon-5.45pm Mon, Wed-Fri; 1.45-5.45pm Sat, Sun. Closed Tue. **Admission** 15F; 12F students, over-60s; free under-18s. **No credit cards.**

Housed in one of the grandest mansions in the Marais, this museum of French history is part of the National Archives. There's a permanent display of 200 historical documents relating to the social and political history of France, from King

Dagobert to the end of World War II, while other rooms are used for temporary exhibitions. All slightly dry, but the Hôtel de Soubise also contains the finest rococo interiors in Paris, the apartments of the Prince and Princess de Soubise, decorated in the early eighteenth century with superb plasterwork, panelling and paintings by prominent artists of the period including Boucher, Natoire, Restout and Van Loo. *Shop.*

### Musée de la Marine

*Palais de Chaillot, pl du Trocadéro, 16th (01.45.53.31.70). M° Trocadéro.* **Open** 10am-6pm Mon, Wed-Sun. Closed Tue. **Admission** 38F; 25F under-26s, over-60s; free under-5s, CM. **Credit** (shop only) MC, V.
A favourite among mariners craving the smell of the sea or the pull of the tides, this museum has one of the largest maritime collections in the world. Apart from Vernet's imposing series of 13 paintings of the ports of France (1754-65), the collection boasts the Emperor's barge, built when Napoléon's delusions of grandeur were reaching their zenith in 1811. There are also carved prows, numerous models of ships, old maps, antique and modern navigational instruments, underwater equipment, a model of a nuclear submarine and romantic maritime paintings. The museum will move in the next few years to an as yet undecided location.
*Lectures. Shop.*

### Musée de la Monnaie de Paris

*11 quai de Conti, 6th (01.40.46.55.28/atelier 01.40.46.55.35). M° Pont-Neuf.* **Open** 1-6pm Tue-Sun. Closed Mon. *workshop visits* 2.15pm, 2.45pm Tue; 2.15pm Fri. **Admission** 20F; 15F students, all visitors Sun; free under-16s. **No credit cards.**
The National Mint and its museum are found in this spectacular Louis XVI edifice overlooking the Seine. Coins and medals from all epochs are displayed, as are drawings, models, relevant tools and objects. The workshops themselves can be visited (15F) on Tuesday and Friday only.
*Shop. Wheelchair access.*

### Musée de Montmartre

*12 rue Cortot, 18th (01.46.06.61.11). M° Lamarck-Caulaincourt.* **Open** 11am-6pm Tue-Sun. Closed Mon. **Admission** 25F; 20F students; free under-8s. **Credit** V.
At the back of a peaceful garden, this seventeenth-century manor is a haven of calm after touristy Montmartre. Administered by the Société d'Histoire et d'Archéologie du Vieux Montmartre, which since 1886 has aimed to preserve documents and artefacts relating to Montmartre, the collection consists of a room devoted to Modigliani, who lived in rue Caulaincourt, the re-created study of composer Gustave Charpentier, paintings and Toulouse-Lautrec posters, porcelain from the short-lived manufacture at Clignancourt and a homage to the famous local bistro the Lapin Agile. The artist's studios above the entrance pavilion were occupied at various times by Renoir, Emile Bernard, Raoul Dufy and Suzanne Valadon with her son Maurice Utrillo and his friend her husband André Utter. Long rather sleepy, the arrival of a new curator promises to boost the level of temporary exhibitions in the museum.
*Archives (by appointment). Bookshop.*

### Musée de la Préfecture de Police

*1bis rue des Carmes, 5th (01.44.41.52.54). M° Maubert-Mutualité.* **Open** 9am-5pm Mon-Fri; 10am-5pm Sat. **Admission** free. **No credit cards.**
The history of crime and its prevention since the founding of the Paris police force in the sixteenth century. Among eclectic treasures here are prisoners' expenses from the Bastille, including those of dastardly jewel thief the Comtesse de la Motte, the exploding flowerpot planted by Louis-Armand Matha in 1894 in a restaurant on the rue de Tournon and the gory *Epée de Justice*, a seventeenth-century sword blunted by the quantity of noble heads chopped.

**Musée de la Musique**: *musical mystery tour.*

## Literary

### Maison de Balzac

*47 rue Raynouard, 16th (01.42.24.56.38). M° Passy.* **Open** 10am-5.40pm Tue-Sun. Closed Mon, public holidays. **Admission** 17.50F; 9F students, 18s-25s, over-60s; free under-18s, CM. **No credit cards.**
Balzac moved to an apartment at this address in 1840 to avoid his creditors and quickly established a password system to sift friends from bailiffs: *'J'apporte des dentelles de Belgique'* would open the door. The charming and slightly melancholy pavilion and its garden makes a delightful showcase for a wide range of memorabilia. On display are first editions, letters, corrected proofs and portraits of friends and Polish mistress Mme Hanska. The study houses his desk, chair and monogrammed coffee pot, an important item since coffee was to Balzac what tea was to Sam Johnson, fuelling all-night work on many of the best-known titles of *La Comédie humaine*. There's also a 'family tree' of all Balzac's characters covering several walls, and many items that, by association with the author, provide a comprehensive window on French literature of the mid-nineteenth century.
*Library (by appointment).*

### Maison de Victor Hugo

*Hôtel de Rohan-Guéménée, 6 pl des Vosges, 4th (01.42.72.10.16). M° Bastille or St-Paul.* **Open** 10am-5.45pm Tue-Sun. Closed Mon, public holidays. **Admission** 27F; 19F 18s-25s; free under-7s, over-65s, CM. **No credit cards.**
One of the most Parisian of all the great nineteenth-century novelists, Victor Hugo lived in this seventeenth-century townhouse on the place des Vosges from 1832 until he was forced to flee – first elsewhere in Paris and then to Guernsey – following the 1848 revolution. The luxurious apartment witnessed the writing of part of *Les Misérables* and a number of poems and plays. When not writing, the author kept himself busy drawing, decorating, carving – much of the furniture is his work – and engraving. The inte-

rior is much altered, but the collection includes typical period portraits of Hugo and his large family, his own drawings and some of the Oriental-influenced furniture he designed himself. One room is devoted to the then new middle-class hobby of photography.

## Musée de la Vie Romantique

*16 rue Chaptal, 9th (01.48.74.95.38). M° Blanche.* **Open** 10am-5.30pm Tue-Sun. Closed Mon, public holidays. **Admission** 17.50F (27F during exhibitions); 9F (19F during exhibitions) over-60s, students; free under-18s, CM. **No credit cards.**
When artist Ary Scheffer lived in this villa, this area south of Pigalle was known as the New Athens because of the concentration of writers, composers and artists living here. George Sand (1804-76) was a frequent guest at Scheffer's soirées, and the house is now a little museum devoted to the writer, her family and her intellectual circle, which included Chopin, Delacroix and the composer Charpentier. Quietly charming, the museum reveals little of her writing or proto-feminist ideas, nor her affairs with Chopin (represented by a marble bust) and Alfred de Musset; rather it presents a typical bourgeois portrait in the watercolours, lockets and jewels she left behind. In the courtyard is Scheffer's studio.

## Music, Cinema & Media

### Musée du Cinéma Henri Langlois

*Palais de Chaillot, pl du Trocadéro, 16th (01.45.53.74.39). M° Trocadéro.* **Open** guided tours only 10am, 11am, 2pm, 3pm, 4pm, 5pm Wed-Sun. **Admission** 30F; 20F students; free CM. **No credit cards.**
Cinema really is a religion in Paris, and this museum is testimony to the devotion of its highest priest Henri Langlois, who devoted his life to assembling the collection of the Cinémathèque (*see chapter* **Film**). The museum concentrates on the technical inventions of the early years. You pass from precursors of the silver screen, such as Chinese silhouettes, through the history of photography to the first animated cartoons, and the development of different cameras. There is a video (in French) about Démeny, who filmed simple movements before the Lumière brothers invented cinema, film posters, photos of early stars such as Lilian Gish and Mary Pickford, costumes and reconstructions of film sets, including one for the Expressionist masterpiece *The Cabinet of Doctor Caligari* and a reconstruction of Meliès' studio.

### Musée Edith Piaf

*5 rue Crespin-du-Gast, 11th (01.43.55.52.72). M° Ménilmontant.* **Open** by appointment only, 1-6pm Mon-Thur. **Admission** voluntary donation. **No credit cards.**
The tiny, private Edith Piaf museum in the working class *quartier* where she grew up is dedicated to Paris' famous 'little sparrow', who died in 1963. Piaf memorabilia accumulated by adoring devotees of the Friends of Edith Piaf includes her little black dress, tiny shoes, letters and posters, gold and platinum discs, as well as photos and paintings of the singer. Call a couple of days ahead to visit.

### Musée de la Musique

*Cité de la Musique, 221 av Jean-Jaures, 19th (01.44.84.46.00). M° Porte de Pantin.* **Open** noon-6pm Tue-Thur, Sat; noon-9.30pm Fri; 10am-6pm Sun. **Admission** 35F; 24F students, 18s-25s, over 60s; 10F under-18s; free CM. **No credit cards.**
The final element of the Cité de la Musique opened in January 1997, displaying musical instruments from the Renaissance to the present, including instruments from India and across the globe, with the chance to hear some of them in action at concerts in the museum's amphitheatre. The collection originated shortly after the Revolution with the creation of the Conservatoire de Musique in 1795, quickly helped along by 316 works seized in 1796 from foreigners. The collections, ranging from important violins by Amati and Stradivarius, inlaid lutes, French piano-fortes by Erard and Pleyel to Adolphe Sax's brass instruments and Frank Zappa's E-Mu synthesiser, are arranged within their historical context, augmented by musical paintings, sculptures and prints, and an

*Space, life, matter and communication at the* **Cité des Sciences et de l'Industrie.**

audioguide that allows you hear relevant musical snippets. *See also chapter* **Music: Classical & Opera**. *Library. Restoration laboratory. Wheelchair access.*

## Musée de l'Opéra

*1 pl de l'Opéra, 9th (01.40.01.24.93). M° Opéra.* **Open** 10am-4.30pm daily. **Admission** 30F; 20F students; free under 10s. **No credit cards.**
Squeezed in next to the huge Opéra library, which contains the scores of all operas and ballets performed at the Opéra, as well as drawings and photos of costumes and sets, this little museum displays nineteenth-century scale models of opera sets and other opera-related memorabilia such as Debussy's desk, Nijinsky's sandals, Pavlova's tiara and portraits of other less eminent patrons. *See also chapters* **Sightseeing, Dance** *and* **Music: Classical & Opera**.

# Religion

## Musée d'Art Juif

*42 rue des Saules, 18th (01.42.57.84.15). M° Lamarck-Caulaincourt.* **Open** 3-6pm Mon-Thur, Sun. Closed Aug, Jewish holidays. **Admission** 30F; 20F students, under-16s. **No credit cards.**
Founded in 1948, this slightly ramshackle sanctuary of Jewish art and artefacts above a Jewish social centre is due to move to the Marais in the next few years when the collection will be extended. Rare pieces include a beautiful wooden eighteenth century tabernacle from Italy, ornamental plaques, incense burners, candlesticks and a display of model Central European synagogues, while the art collection includes works by Chagall, Benn, Mane-Katz and Lipschitz. *Library.*

## Musée de la Franc-Maçonnerie

*16 rue Cadet, 9th (01.45.23.20.92). M° Cadet.* **Open** 2.30-6pm Mon-Sat. Closed Sun, public holidays. **Admission** free. **No credit cards.**
Situated at the back of the Masonic Temple, this museum displays insignia, paintings glorifying the brotherhood, objects used in ceremonies and documents relevant to the Society's past. While trying to fathom what all this esotericism is about, beware the six-fingered handshake.

# Science, Medicine & Technology

## Centre International de l'Automobile

*25 rue Honoré d'Estienne d'Orves, 93502 Pantin Cedex (01.48.10.80.00). M° Hoche.* **Open** 11am-6pm Sat, Sun and public holidays. **Admission** 45F; 35F 5-15 years; free under-5s. **No credit cards.**
Opened in 1990, around 100 cars, mainly lent by enthusiasts, are spaciously arranged by theme in a pristine new warehouse. This a far from comprehensive selection, but nonetheless includes a 1901 Renault, Ford Ts and other early cars, luxury Bentleys and Delahayes, a basement of sports cars, and changing exhibitions that recently included an amusing display of taxis from around the world.

## La Cité des Sciences et de l'Industrie

*Parc de la Villette, 30 av Corentin-Cariou, 19th (01.40.05.12.12/recorded information 08.36.68.29.30). M° Porte de la Villette.* **Open** 10am-6pm Tue-Sat; 10am-7pm Sun. Closed Mon. **Admission** Cité Pass 50F; 35F students, schoolchildren; free under-7s; Cité/Géode Pass 90F; 75F children; not valid weekends or holidays. **Credit** MC, V.
Set within the Parc de la Villette (*see chapter* **Sightseeing**), this ultra-modern science museum has been riding high since its opening in 1986 and pulls in over five million visitors a year. The Cité started out as a modern abattoir, a huge poured-concrete structure designed to replace the old La Villette stockyards. In mid-construction, the expensive project was wrecked by the realisation that stockyards in Paris *intra muros* were an antiquated concept. To save face, the government transformed the structure into a gigantic, state-of-the-art science museum. With clever design, and plenty of money, the Cité's architect Adrian Fainsilber and directors managed to pull off the transformation with great bravado. Explora, the permanent show, occupies the upper two floors, whisking visitors through 30,000 square metres of 'space, life, matter and communication', where scale models of satellites including the Ariane space shuttle, planes and robots make for an exciting journey. There's an impressive array of interactive exhibits on language and communication enabling you to learn about sound waves, try out different smells, and see what you'd look like wearing different styles of clothing. The Espace section, devoted to man's conquest of space, lets you experience the sensation of weightlessness. Other sections feature climate, ecology and the environment, health, energy, agriculture, the ocean and volcanoes. The new Automobile gallery looks at the car both as myth and technological object, including driving simulator and displays on safety, pollution and designs of the future. The lower floors house temporary exhibitions, a documentation centre and special children's sections. The Louis Lumière cinema shows films in 3-D, and there's a restored submarine moored next to the Géode. *See also chapters* **Film** *and* **Children**. *Bookshop. Café. Cinema. Conference centre. Library (multimedia). Wheelchair access & hire.*

## Musée de l'Air et de l'Espace

*Aéroport de Paris-Le Bourget, 93352 Le Bourget Cedex (01.49.92.71.99/recorded information 01.49.92.71.71). M° La Courneuve then bus 152/RER Le Bourget plus bus 152.* **Open** *May-Oct* 10am-6pm; *Nov-Apr* 10am-5pm Tue-Sun. Closed Mon, 1 Jan, 25 Dec. **Admission** 30F; 22F students, 8-16s; free under-8s. **Credit** V.
The air and space museum is a potent reminder that France is a technical and military as well as cultural power. Housed in the Modernist former passenger terminal at Le Bourget airport, the collection begins with the pioneers, including fragile-looking early biplanes and the contraption with which the Romanian Vivia succeeded in flying 12 metres on 12 March 1906. Outside on the runway are several Mirage fighter planes, a Boeing 707, the American Thunderchief with shark-tooth painted grimace and Ariane launchers 1 and 5. Within a vast hangar, walk through the prototype Concorde 001 and view wartime survivors including a German Heinkel bomber and Spitfire. There are further hangars full of military planes, helicopters, commercially exploited jets and some prototypes like the Leduc, designed to be launched off the back of another plane, sporting and acrobatic planes and a hall devoted to space missiles and satellites. A recently added section is devoted to hot air balloons, invented in 1783 by the Montgolfier brothers and soon in use for military reconnaissance. Dramatic displays make this museum great fun and most captions are summarised in English. *Café. Shop.*

## Musée d'Histoire de la Médecine de Paris

*Université René Descartes, 12 rue de l'Ecole de Médecine, 6th (01.40.46.16.93). M° Odéon.* **Open** 2-6.30pm Mon-Sat. **Admission** 20F; 10F students, under-12s. **No credit cards.**
The collection of the René Descartes medical faculty covers the history of medicine from ancient Egyptian instruments used in embalming through to a 1960s electrocardiograph. There is a particularly gruesome array of serrated-edged saws and curved knives used for amputations in the seventeenth and eighteenth centuries as well as a variety of stethoscopes, endoscopes and syringes. You can also see the case containing the surgical instruments belonging to Dr Antommarchi, who performed the autopsy on Napoléon, and the scalpel of Dr Félix, who operated on Louis XIV.

## Musée National des Techniques

*292 rue St-Martin, 3rd (01.40.27.22.20/recorded information 01.40.27.23.31). Mº Arts et Métiers.* **Open** Closed until end 1988.

Occupying the medieval church and abbey of St-Martin-les-Champs, this historic science museum has a wealth of objects relating to great inventions from the sixteenth century onwards. When the museum re-opens in 1998 it will be rearranged into seven sections covering different aspects of science and technology, with visits ending in the twelfth-century chapel.

## Muséum National d'Histoire Naturelle

*57 rue Cuvier, 5th (01.40.79.30.00). Mº Jussieu or Gare d'Austerlitz.* **Open** 10am-6pm Mon, Wed, Fri-Sun; 10am-10pm Thur. Closed Tue. **Admission** *Grande Galerie* 40F; 30F students, under-16s, over-60s. *Other pavilions, each* 30F; 20F students, 4-16s, over-60s. **No credit cards**.

Within the Jardin des Plantes botanical garden, the brilliantly renovated Grande Galerie d'Evolution has taken Paris' Natural History Museum out of the dinosaur age. Skeletons and stuffed animals were restored and architect Paul Chemetov successfully integrated modern lifts, stairways and the latest lighting and audio-visual techniques into the nineteenth-century iron-framed structure. As you enter, you will be confronted with the 13.66 metre-long skeleton of a whale: the rest of the ground floor is dedicated to other sea creatures. Don't miss the unpleasant-looking swordfish, or the narwhal with its two metre-long tusk. On the first floor are the big mammals, organised by habitat (savannah, jungle, etc) mostly in the open – with the exception of Louis XVI's rhinoceros, stuffed on a wooden chair frame shortly after its demise (and that of monarchy) in 1793. Video screens and interactive computer screens give information on life in the wild. Glass-sided lifts take you up through suspended birds to the second floor, which deals with man's impact on nature and considers demographic problems and pollution.

**Museum National d'Histoire Naturelle.**

The third floor traces the evolution of species, while a gallery at the side, deliberately retaining old-fashiond glass cases, displays endangered and extinct species. Striking a very neat balance between fun and education, the museum is popular with kids, with a 'discovery' room for the under-12s and laboratories for teenagers. The departments of geology, fossils, skeletons and insects are housed in separate pavilions over the park, the Jardin des Plantes (*see also chapters* **Parks & Cemeteries, Children**).

*Auditorium. Bookshop. Café. Library. Wheelchair access.*

## Musée Pasteur

*Institut Pasteur, 25 rue du Docteur-Roux, 15th (01.45.68.82.82). Mº Pasteur.* **Open** 2-5.30pm Mon-Fri. **Admission** 15F; 8F students. **No credit cards**.

The apartment where the famous chemist and his wife lived for the last seven years of his life (1888-95) has hardly been touched since his death; you can still see their furniture and possessions as well as family photographs, memorabilia and objects such as Pasteur's ceremonial Academy of Science coat; there is also a room full of scientific instruments. Particularly fascinating is the extravagant, Byzantine-style funerary chapel built to house Pasteur's tomb on the ground floor of the Institute; the brightly coloured mosaics illustrate some of his most important scientific achievements, including the discovery of a vaccine against rabies.

*Shop.*

## Musée de Radio-France

*116 av du Président-Kennedy, 16th (01.42.30.21.80). Mº Ranelagh/RER Kennedy-Radio France.* **Open** guided tours only 10.30am, 11.30am, 2.30pm, 3.30pm, 4.30pm, Mon-Sat. **Admission** 18F; 12F students. **No credit cards.**

On the second floor of the giant headquarters of France's national radio is a museum of communications. Starting a fair way back with Roman fire beacons (clumsy but cost-effective), it takes you through Chappe's telegraph, a number of Marconi originals, crystal receivers from the 1920s, imposing 1930s Art Deco radios, early television sets and the latest colour models. *See also chapters* **Right Bank**, **Media** *and* **Music: Classical & Opera**.

## Palais de la Découverte

*Grand Palais, av Franklin D Roosevelt, 8th (01.40.74.80.00/recorded information 01.43.59.18.21). Mº Franklin D Roosevelt.* **Open** 9.30am-6pm Tue-Sat; 10am-7pm Sun. Closed Mon, 1 Jan, 1 May, 14 July, 15 Aug, 25 Dec. **Admission** 27F; 17F under-18s, over-60s. *With Planetarium* 40F; 30F under-18s, over-60s. **No credit cards.**

Paris' original science museum, housing works and designs from Leonardo da Vinci's extraordinary inventions onwards. Replicas, models, audiovisual material and real apparatus are used to bring the displays to life. Permanent displays cover man and his biology, light and the thrills of thermo-dynamism. One of the latest additions is a room dedicated to all you could ever possibly want to know about the sun, including the reassuring information that it has enough energy to shine for a few billion years yet. The panels are written in French, but if you go behind the model of the sun, there is recorded information in English. There is also a theatre, where demonstrations of electrostatics are presented at 11am, 1pm, 3pm and 5pm. Members of the audience are electrocised so that their hair stands on end, or so that they can create long sparks. Housed at the back of the Grand Palais, it is far more conveniently located than the Cité des Sciences, if a bit old-fashioned by comparison, and teems with young children. The Planetarium has shows up to six times a day, depending on the time of year, and films are screened in the cinema at 2pm and 4pm. Scientific experiments are conducted at 11am and 3pm.

*Bookshop. Cinema. Guided tours.*

*Climb to the contemporary at the* **Jeu de Paume** *with Barcelo's* Ex Voto *(detail).*

# Eccentricities

## Musée de la Contrefaçon
*16 rue de la Faisanderie, 16th (01.45.01.51.11).*
*M° Porte Dauphine.* **Open** 2-5pm Mon-Thur; 9.30am-
noon Fri; 2-6pm Sun. **Admission** 10F. **No credit cards**.
The counterfeit industry is big business and French luxury
brands are prime targets. Paris' 'museum of forgery' shows
how this lucrative business dates back to 200 BC – with fake
wine from Narbonne – and continues in Portugal with Audak
(Kodak) cameras and in Italy with countless handbags (Louis
Vuitton is ever-popular). The museum takes care to under-
line the penalties awaiting you in case you're tempted.

## Musée de la Curiosité
*11 rue St-Paul, 4th (01.42.72.13.26). M° St-Paul or Sully*
*Morland.* **Open** 2pm-7pm Wed, Sat, Sun. **Admission**
45F, 30F under-14s. **No credit cards**.
A museum of magic at the heart of the Marais, with a show
of card tricks, a talk (in French) on the history of magic going
back to Egyptian times and displays of a whole range of
objects such as magic wands, a cabinet for cutting people in
half, optical illusions and posters. The welcome is warm and
enthusiastic, and you'll be guided through the collection by
specialists whose passion for their art is absolutely conta-
gious. They might even teach you a magic trick or two.

## Musée de la Poste
*34 bd de Vaugirard, 15th (01.42.79.23.45).*
*M° Montparnasse-Bienvenüe.* **Open** from late 1997,
10am-6pm Mon-Sat. **Admission** 28F; 14F 18-25s, over-
60s; free under-18s. **No credit cards**.
Closed for refurbishment, the museum of postal history is
expected to open during the second half of 1997. The extensive collection includes artists' designs for stamps, examples
of different methods of communication including pigeons
and metal balls floated down the Seine during the Prussian
seige in 1870, transport, postmen's uniforms, letter boxes and
tools. The ground floor is open for temporary exhibitions.
*Shop.*

## Musée de la Poupée
*impasse Berthaud, 3rd (01.42.72.55.90). M° Rambuteau.*
**Open** 10am-6pm Tue-Sun. Closed Mon. **Admission** 35F;
25F students; 20F 3-18s. **No credit cards**.
A private collection of French dolls from 1860 to 1960, with
an strong emphasis on the late nineteenth century, which
includes items by the manufacturers Jumeau, Steiner and
Gaultier. Most of the dolls have ringlets, large eyes, rose-bud
lips, arching eyebrows and peaches-and-cream complexions,
giving a good idea of the period's concepts of delicate female
beauty. The dolls' elaborate costumes (mostly original) and
the selection of period toys, such as dolls houses, tea-sets and
teddies, also give an insight into nineteenth-century middle-
class life.
*Shop.*

## Musée de la SEITA
*12 rue Surcouf, 7th (01.45.56.60.17). M° Invalides or*
*Latour-Maubourg.* **Open** 11am-7pm Mon-Sat.
**Admission** *Museum* free. *Temporary exhibitions* 25F;
15F students, over-60s. **No credit cards**.
The official museum of the French state-run tobacco company SEITA traces the development of the lowly weed that
came from relative obscurity to become a household name.
In France, it's all thanks to Jean Nicot (of nicotine fame), who
in 1561 first introduced tobacco to the country in his diplo-
matic bag. Smoking paraphernalia from around the world,
some with literary connotations, such as George Sand's
favourite pipe, or astrological links, such as a model pipe
engraved with Zodiac signs, are featured. The museum also
has an adventurous programme of temporary art exhibitions
seemingly unrelated to smoking, with subjects as varied as
Nijinsky, Otto Dix and Jean-Michel Basquiat.

## Musée du Vin
*5 square Charles Dickens, 16th. M° Passy*
*(01.45.25.63.26).* **Open** 2-6pm Tue-Sun. Closed Mon.
**Admission** 35F; 29F students, over-60s. **Credit** AmEx,
DC, MC, V.
Of the many small specialist museums in Paris, this has to
be one of the most convivial. Housed in Medieval cellars, it

has scenes showing the wine-making process, as well as corkscrews, bottles, and other wine-related objects. A free glass of wine ends the visit. *Shop.*

# Exhibition Centres

## Bibliothèque Forney
*Hôtel de Sens, 1 rue du Figuier, 4th (01.42.78.14.60). Mᵒ Pont-Marie.* **Open** 1.30-8pm Tue-Sat. **Admission** 20F; 10F under-12s, students, over-60s. **No credit cards.**
Set in the turrets and Gothic vaulting of this medieval mansion – the oldest in the Marais – the library specialises in the applied and graphic arts, and has a wing given over to temporary displays. *See also chapter* **Sightseeing.**

## Bibliothèque Nationale de France Richelieu
*Galeries Mansart and Mazarine, 58 rue de Richelieu, 2nd (01.47.03.81.26). Galerie Colbert, 6 rue Vivienne, 2nd (01.47.03.81.26). Mᵒ Bourse.* **Open** 9am-8pm Mon-Fri; 9am-5.30pm Sat. **Admission** *Galeries Mansart and Mazarine:* both galleries 35F; 24F students, over-60s, under-26s; one gallery 22F; 15F students. *Galerie Colbert* free. **No credit cards.**
Within the old Bibliothèque Nationale, the Galeries Mansart and Mazarine, once Cardinal Mazarin's art gallery and library, have regular exhibitions ranging from Indian miniatures to contemporary etchings, while the Galerie Colbert, situated in the library annexe, hosts contemporary photography and print displays. *See also chapter* **Sightseeing.**

## Bibliothèque Nationale de France François Mitterrand
*quai François-Mauriac, 13th (01.53.79.59.59). Mᵒ Quai de la Gare.* **Open** 10am-7pm Tue-Sat; noon-6pm Sun. Closed Mon. **Admission** varies. **No credit cards.**
The gigantic new library could not be more different from its historic parent, but shares a similarly erudite programme, that began with a show at both sites on the encyclopedic task of compiling dictionaries and encyclopedias across continents and centuries. *See also chapter* **Sightseeing.**

## Chapelle de la Salpêtrière
*47 bd de l'Hôpital, 13th (01.42.16.04.24). Mᵒ Gare d'Austerlitz.* **Open** 11am-5.30pm daily. **Admission** free. **No credit cards.**
Louis Le Vau's austere seventeenth-century chapel provides a fantastic setting for contemporary art. Recent exhibitions have included a group show of artists who work with light and projected images and a superb video installation by Bill Viola for the Festival d'Automne. *See chapter* **Left Bank.**

## Couvent des Cordeliers
*15 rue de l'Ecole de Médicine, 6th (01.40.46.05.47). Mᵒ Odéon.* **Open** hours vary, usually 11am-7pm Tue-Sat. **Admission** free. **No credit cards.**
Under the joint administration of the Ville de Paris and the medical school, this barn-like hall, once the refectory of a Franciscan convent, is used for varied shows of contemporary and decorative art. It is one of the spaces likely to be used by the Centre Pompidou during closure.

## Ecole Nationale des Beaux-Arts
*13 quai Malaquais, 6th (01.47.03.50.00). Mᵒ St-Germain-des-Prés.* **Open** 1-7pm Mon, Wed-Sun. **Admission** 20F; 10F students, over-60s. **Credit** (bookshop only) AmEx, MC, V.
The exhibition halls of France's central art college are used regularly for exhibitions which vary from the pick of recent graduates to a group show of artists working with plastic. *See also chapter* **Sightseeing.** *Bookshop.*

## Espace Electra
*6 rue Récamier, 7th (01.45.44.10.03). Mᵒ Sèvres-Babylone.* **Open** 11am-6.30pm Mon, Wed-Sun. **Admission** varies. **No credit cards.**
Space owned by the French electricity board used for varied fine-art, graphic and design exhibitions, sometimes with a light-based theme, as in an interesting show of artists' projects for illuminating Paris.

## Fondation Cartier pour l'art contemporain
*261 bd Raspail, 14th (01.42.18.56.72/recorded information 01.42.18.56.51). Mᵒ Raspail.* **Open** noon-8pm Tue, Wed, Fri-Sun; noon-10pm Thur. **Admission** 30F; 20F students, over-60s, under-25s; free under 10s, unemployed. **Credit** AmEx, MC, V.
Jean Nouvel's glass and steel building for the Fondation Cartier, which moved here in 1994, is as much a work of art as the exhibitions presented inside, which have ranged from solo shows and installations by contemporary artists like Jean-Pierre Raynaud and Raymond Hains to themes as wide-ranging as 'Birds' or 'Love', which have taken a multi-cultural approach adding art from other civilisations to historical and contemporary pieces. There are 1,200 square metres of exhibition space on the ground floor, although its total transparency means that artists often seem happier with the white basement space. Concerts, contemporary dance and video are presented in the Soirées Nomades at 8pm every Thursday between September and June. *Wheelchair access.*

## Fondation Coprim pour l'art contemporain
*112 av Kléber, 16th (01.47.55.61.64). Mᵒ Trocadéro.* **Open** 10.30am-6.30pm Mon-Fri. **Admission** free. **No credit cards.**
Reached through a complex of modern offices, exhibitions tend to feature accessible figurative artists like Combas, but the Fondation, which belongs to a property group, also laudably aims to support young artists with an annual prize.

## Fondation Mona Bismarck
*34 av de New York, 16th (01.47.23.38.88). Mᵒ Alma-Marceau.* **Open** 10.30am-6.15pm Tue-Sat. Closed Mon, Sun, public holidays. **Admission** free. **No credit cards.**
Very chic setting for widely varied exhibitions of everything from Etruscan antiquities to Haitian painters, often lent by prestigious foreign collections.

## Galéries Nationales du Grand Palais
*av du Général Eisenhower, 8th (01.44.13.17.17). Mᵒ Champs-Elysées-Clemenceau.* **Open** 10am-8pm Mon, Thur-Sun; 10am-10pm Wed. Prebooking compulsory before 1pm. Closed Tue, 1 May, 25 Dec. **Admission** 50F; 35F students, all visitors Mon. *Two exhibitions* 63F; 43F students, all visitors Mon. **Credit** (shop) V.
A striking leftover from the 1900 Exhibition, the Grand Palais is Paris' premiere venue for blockbuster exhibitions. Important monographic shows – Poussin, Cézanne, Picasso – are complemented by grandiose theme exhibitions, such as Venetian painting, Cambodia or Japanese Buddhist art. The central glass-domed hall, however, is currently closed for restoration, but two other exhibition spaces remain. Prebooking is obligatory for certain shows at peak hours. *See also chapter* **Sightseeing.**
*Audioguides. Bookshop. Café. Wheelchair access.*

## Jeu de Paume
*pl de la Concorde, 1st (01.42.60.69.69). Mᵒ Concorde.* **Open** noon-9.30pm Tue, noon-7pm Wed-Fri; 10am-7pm Sat, Sun. **Admission** 38F; 25F students, over-60s. **No credit cards.**
When the Impressionist museum moved from here to the Musée d'Orsay, the former real tennis court of the Tuileries

*Easter Island bird meets sixteenth-century Mannerism in the **Fondation Cartier**'s 'Comme un oiseau'.*

Palace was redesigned by Antoine Stinco as a space for contemporary and modern art exhibitions. Its record has been mixed, with a recent emphasis that seems to have switched to the 1950s and '60s. Some good respectives have included Broodthaers, Martial Raysse, Jeff Wall and Miguel Barcélo. A basement cinema mounts artists' film and video series. *Bookshop. Café. Cinema. Wheelchair access.*

### Passage de Retz

*9 rue Charlot, 3rd (01.48.04.37.99). M° Filles du Calvaire.* **Open** 10am-7pm daily. **Admission** 30F; 15F under-26s, students. **No credit cards**.
A Marais mansion which became a toy factory and has now been resurrected as a gallery. Varied shows have included contemporary design as well as fine art and the fun summer offerings of Hurrah for the Bra and the ever-so-hip techno-music led Global Techno.
*Café.*

### Pavillon des Arts

*101 rue Rambuteau, 1st (01.42.33.82.50). M° Châtelet-Les Halles.* **Open** 11.30am-6.30pm Tue-Sun. **Admission** 30F; 20F students, over-60s, 6s-25s; free under-6s. **No credit cards**.
Next to the Forum des Halles, this first-floor gallery hosts varied exhibitions from contemporary photography to Surrealism to the history of Paris.
*Wheelchair access.*

### Renn Espace d'Art Contemporain

*7 rue de Lille, 7th (01.42.60.22.99). M° Rue du Bac.* **Open** during exhibitions only 3-7pm Tue-Sat. **Admission** usually free. **No credit cards**.
This well-designed space owned by film director Claude Berri mainly hosts retrospective-style exhibitions, lasting six to nine months, devoted to modern abstract or conceptual masters such as Yves Klein, Sol LeWitt and Daniel Buren.

## Cultural Centres

The following regularly host interesting temporary exhibitions, often but not exclusively related to the art of the countries they represent.

### Centre Culturel Calouste Gulbenkian (Portugal)

*51 av d'Iéna, 16th (01.53.23.93.93). M° Iéna.* **Open** 9am-6pm, Mon-Fri.

### Centre Culturel Suisse

*38 rue des Francs-Bourgeois, 3rd (01.42.71.44.50). M° St-Paul.* **Open** 2-7pm Wed-Sun.

### Centre Wallonie-Bruxelles

*127 rue St-Martin, 4th (01.53.01.96.96). M° Rambuteau.* **Open** 11am-6pm Tue-Sun.

### Goëthe Institut (Germany)

*31 rue de Condé, 6th (01.40.46.69.60). M° Odéon/ RER Luxembourg.* **Open** noon-6pm Wed, Fri; noon-8pm Mon, Tue, Thur.

### Institut Néerlandais

*121 rue de Lille, 7th (01.53.59.12.40). M° Assemblée Nationale.* **Open** 1-7pm Tue-Sun.

### Maison de l'Amérique Latine

*217 bd St-Germain, 7th (01.49.54.75.00). M° Rue du Bac.* **Open** 10am-7pm Mon-Fri.

# Art Galleries

**The Paris art world may often seem like a hermetically sealed intellectual bubble but some galleries are taking new directions.**

Installation, photography and the often-troubled world of video remain at the forefront of contemporary creation, as the relation between gallery and studio, gallery and life, and issues like AIDS, identity and gender are up for constant appraisal. The '70s revival of Britpop and fashion is also evident in art, as lifestyles come under scrutiny.

Long supported by generous public purchase budgets and weighed down by memories of a grander past, the Paris art scene lacks the ostensible solidarity (or shared interest) of the reinvigorated London scene, with no publicity-attracting crowdpuller like the Turner Prize to widen, for good reason or bad, the art audience. Paris galleries have retrenched with the recession – indeed, a cull may be just what is needed – but it is still on the commercial gallery circuit that you'll discover adventurous new work long before it reaches the museum. A good gallery will support and nurture an artist over the years, seeking out new talents and developing projects with their existing ones.

## FIAC & THE SALONS

Things looked up in 1996 when a smaller, leaner FIAC (Foire Internationale de l'Art Contemporain, *see chapter* **Paris by Season**) at last remembered the contemporary in its name, after several years when the focus had seemed to be fossilising on modern museum classics. Le Cirque, a personal initiative by gallery owner François Mitaine at the same dates in the exotic Cirque d'Hiver added a bit of festive party spirit and was a rare success at crossing boundaries in attracting the gay nightclub set to the cognoscenti's artists.

Salons, such as the Salon de Mai, Salon des Indépendants and Nouvelles Réalités, currently held like FIAC at the Espace Eiffel Branly, no longer have the influence of last century and standards are extremely variable, although the art world still likes to look at the Salon de Montrouge in the suburbs every May and head south for the Biennale de Lyon, while new technology and virtual reality get a look-in at the biennial Artifices in St-Denis.

## THE ART CIRCUIT

For new and innovative work head for the northern part of the Marais, on rues Vieille-du-Temple and Debelleyme, where galleries often occupy former industrial spaces hidden at the back of historic courtyards, or the growing cluster on rue St-Gilles.

Several galleries around the Bastille mainly present young artists, while the galleries around St-Germain-des-Prés, home of the avant-garde in the 1950s and '60s, and near the Champs-Elysées, the centre before that, now largely confine themselves to traditional sculpture and painting. Keep an eye, too, on the previously uncharted territory of the 13th *arrondissement*, where six young galleries have set up shop together (*see p234*, **Heading East**).

## KITCHEN SHOWS

The circuit of alternative spaces is less developed in Paris these days than in some cities, but shows are occasionally put on in disused garages, empty blocks of flats, shops or cafés. A discreet sign of new activity is the trend for exhibitions in people's private apartments. Although clearly partly to cut costs, its motivation goes beyond that in seeking a new relation with artist and art work, as when Hans-Ulrich Olbrist invited 70 artists into his (small) hotel bedroom in 1995. Or take the 'micro-expositions' curated by Eriko Momotani in her tiny oneroom Marais flat: here Mathieu Mercier built his white melamine shelving unit directly around the sofa-bed: a case of art truly intruding on daily life. It's a risky business, where bed, kitchen, even what breakfast cereal you eat is open to public scrutiny.

## FROM SQUATS TO STUDIOS

Artists still flock to Paris from across the globe, aided by subsidised studios, such as the Cité des Arts near Hôtel de Ville and Cité Fleurie near Montparnasse. There are also some more alternative studio complexes, often originally art squats. The best known, the Hôpital Ephémère (2 rue Carpeaux, 18th/01.46.27.82.82), occupying a former hospital, has been partly demolished but 20 artists remain; a new Ephémère is planned in Pantin. Les Frigos (91 quai de la Gare, 13th/ 01.44.24.96.96), artists' and musicians' studios in imposing disused refrigerated railway warehouses, has been engulfed by the development zone around the new Bibliothèque Nationale. A public enquiry will decide whether the whole or only two-thirds of the complex will be saved. Other 'squats' include La Forge at 23 rue Ramponneau in Belleville.

The Génie de la Bastille (*see chapter* **Paris by Season**) and the 13ème Art are the best known-opportunities to visit artists' studios, but there are also '*portes ouvertes*' in Belleville, Ménilmontant,

*Hirschhorn's installation at* **Chantal Crousel** *takes in issues of art history and viruses.*

St-Germain, the 18th *arrondissement* and the suburbs of Montrouge, Montreuil and Ivry-sur-Seine. Many take place over a weekend in May or early October. Check listings magazines for details.

### INFORMATION & MAGAZINES

Principal local publications include *Beaux Arts*, which focuses on the historical and the art market, and the bilingual *Art Press*, which covers contemporary art. For a more alternative approach look out for trendy young mags *Block Notes* and *Purple Prose*, which take a multi-disciplinary look, including design, philosophy, literature, fashion, music and film in a break from white-cube orthodoxy rarely evident in the galleries themselves.

Only some of the most active of the hundreds of galleries can be listed here. For information on shows, look for the leaflet *Galeries Mode d'Emploi* (for the Marais/Bastille), the foldout published by the Association des Galeries (Left and Right Bank) and the review-based *Journal des Expositions* which carries ads for some of the more alternative spaces, available at many galleries. Virtually all galleries close from late July to early September.

## Beaubourg & the Marais

### Galerie des Archives

*4 impasse Beaubourg, 3rd (01.42.78.05.77). M° Rambuteau.* **Open** 2-7pm Tue-Sat.
An interesting mix of mainly young artists is shown in all media, including the installations of Thomas Shannon, paintings by Lydia Dona, the photos/videos of Florence Paradeis, video artist Gary Hill and duo Art Orienté Objet.

### Galerie Aréa

*10 rue de Picardie, 3rd (01.42.72.68.66). M° Filles du Calvaire.* **Open** 2-7pm Wed-Sat; 3-7pm Sun.
A small, two-level gallery bravely committed wholly to French painters, usually with a figurative/expressionist bent.

### Gilbert Brownstone & Cie

*26 rue St-Gilles, 3rd (01.42.78.43.21). M° Chemin-Vert.* **Open** 11am-1pm, 2-7pm, Tue-Sat.
Elegant artists, often with a minimalist aesthetic, including John Armleder, photographers Seton Smith and Bettina Rheims, and German painter Imi Knoebbel, are shown in this glass-roofed space, but it is shopping and fashion addict Sylvie Fleury who most consistently shows new directions.

### Farideh Cadot

*77 rue des Archives, 3rd (01.42.78.08.36). M° Arts-et-Métiers.* **Open** 10.30am-1pm, 2.30-7pm, Tue-Fri; 11am-7pm, Sat.
20 years after she founded her gallery, then in the 13th, shows continue to reflect Farideh Cadot's personal taste and long-term loyalty to a particular set of artists, including Connie Beckley, Meret Oppenheim, Georges Rousse, Joël Fisher, Jorge Molder and Markus Raetz.

### Chantal Crousel

*40 rue Quincampoix, 4th (01.42.77.38.87). M° Châtelet-les-Halles.* **Open** 11am-1pm, 2-7pm, Tue-Sat.
One of the longest-standing Beaubourg galleries hosts a cohesive programme of internationally known artists, including Sigmar Polke, Tony Cragg, Annette Messager, Sophie Calle and Mona Hatoum, reinforced by younger figures such as German artist Thomas Hirschhorn and Marie-Ange Guilleminot, whose fabric dolls are based on the body.

### Jean Fournier

*44 rue Quincampoix, 4th (01.42.77.32.31). M° Châtelet-Les-Halles.* **Open** 10am-1pm, 2-7pm, Tue-Sat.
A spacious gallery committed to painting with the French '70s *support-surface* artists Claude Viallat and Pierre

Buraglio, independent Hantaï and US West Coast abstract painters Sam Francis and Jean Mitchell all represented.

## Galerie de France

*54 rue de la Verrerie, 4th (01.42.74.38.00).*
*Mº Hôtel-de-Ville.* **Open** 10am-7pm Tue-Sat.
Shows here mix all generations and aspects of twentieth-century art from Rosso and Dubuffet to contemporary names Rebecca Horn, Jean-Pierre Bertrand and Suzanne Laffont.

## Galerie Karsten Greve

*5 rue Debelleyme, 3rd (01.42.77.19.37). Mº St-Sébastien-Froissart.* **Open** 11am-7pm Tue-Sat.
Three floors of an historic Marais building were converted by Karsten Greve in 1992, as a Parisian outpost of his Cologne gallery. Since then he has held impressive retrospectives of major international artists such as Cy Twombly, Louise Bourgeois, John Chamberlain and Lucio Fontana.

## Galerie Ghislaine Hussenot

*5bis rue des Haudriettes, 3rd (01.48.87.60.81).*
*Mº Rambuteau.* **Open** 11am-7pm Tue-Sat.
Hussenot has a strong stable of high-profile, intellectually stimulating names, usually well-presented in a two-level warehouse space. You might find the conceptual date paintings of On Kawara or knitted toys of Mike Kelley. Younger-generation artists include the sexually ambivalent sculptures of Jean-Marc Othoniel and Vanessa Beecroft's interventions which explore fashion and the artistic context.

## Galerie du Jour Agnès B

*6 rue du Jour, 1st (01.42.33.43.40). Mº Châtelet-Les Halles.* **Open** 10am-7pm Tue-Sat.
A former butcher's shop amid Agnès B's clothing empire (*see* chapter **Fashion**) is used for nicely presented if safe shows by artists who share the fashion designer's interests in the Third World, the environment, society and AIDS, be it social commentary by British photographer Martin Parr or African artist Felix Brouly Bouabré.

## Galerie Laage-Salomon

*57 rue du Temple, 4th (01.42.78.11.71). Mº Rambuteau.*
**Open** 2-7pm Tue-Sat.
This gallery has close links with several German galleries and represents German neo-Expressionists such as Georg Baselitz, but has recently made a conscious move to include newer trends, with photographers Axel Hütte and Hannah Collins and Belgian installation artist Mark Luyten.

## Yvon Lambert

*108 rue Vieille-du-Temple, 3rd (01.42.71.09.33).*
*Mº Filles du Calvaire.* **Open** 10am-1pm, 2.30-7pm, Tue-Fri; 10am-7pm Sat.
A virtually non-stop succession of major names makes this warehouse-like gallery an essential stop on the circuit. Lambert has recently come back in force with shows by Anselm Kiefer (his first in Paris for seven years), Joseph Kosuth and Christian Boltanski, as well as adding undoubted photographer of the '90s Nan Goldin.

## Galerie Nikki Diana Marquardt

*9 pl des Vosges, 4th (01.42.78.21.00). Mº St-Paul or Bastille.* **Open** 1-7pm Tue-Sat.
This surprising former industrial space is reached through a courtyard from the place des Vosges. The American gallery owner has long worked with artists like Dan Flavin, but many of her shows have a political content. Sarajevo and Northern Ireland (in a project with the Orchard Gallery, Derry) have naturally figured as topics for group shows.

## Galerie Gabrielle Maubrie

*24 rue Ste-Croix-de-la-Bretonnerie, 4th (01.42.78.03.97).*
*Mº Hôtel-de-Ville.* **Open** 2-7pm Tue-Sat.
In a Marais apartment, Maubrie consistently shows social-

ly or politically committed artists, including Dennis Adams, Alfredo Jaar, Stephen Willats and Kryzysztof Wodiczko.

## Galerie Nathalie Obadia

*5 rue du Grenier-St-Lazare, 3rd (01.42.74.67.68).*
*Mº Rambuteau.* **Open** 11am-7pm Tue-Sat.
Obadia is very supportive of young artists, many women, such as new British abstractionist Fiona Rae and French painters Pascal Pinaud and Carole Benzaken.

## Galerie Roger Pailhas

*88 rue St-Martin, 4th (01.48.04.71.31). Mº Hôtel-de-Ville.* **Open** 11am-1pm, 2-7pm, Tue-Sat.
An offshoot of a Marseilles gallery known for its influential work with Dan Graham and Jeff Wall. The Paris space has shown a lot of photo-based work, plus works on architecture and space by artists such as Langlands and Bell, and the anarcho-politico projects of Peter Fend.

## Galerie Claudine Papillon

*17 rue St-Gilles, 3rd (01.40.29.98.80). Mº Chemin-Vert.* **Open** 2-7pm Tue-Sat.
Claudine Papillon shows important contemporary European artists, usually of Conceptual bent, such as Tony Carter, Erik Dietman, Michael Craig-Martin and Sigmar Polke.

## Galerie Polaris

*8 rue St-Claude, 3rd (01.42.72.21.27). Mº St-Sébastien-Froissart.* **Open** 1-7.30pm Tue-Fri; 11am-1pm, 2-7.30pm Sat.
Bernard Utudjian works over the long term with a small number of artists, including photographer Stéphane Couturier and photographer/performance artist Nigel Rolfe.

## Galerie Putman

*33 rue Charlot, 3rd (01.42.76.03.50). Mº Filles-du-Calvaire.* **Open** 10.30am-1pm, 2-7pm, Tue-Sat.
Eclectic shows mainly of sculpture and installation, as well as some interesting video projects have included James Turrell, Richard Hamilton and Fabrice Hybert.

## Galerie Jacqueline Rabouan-Moussion

*110 rue Vieille-du-Temple, 3rd (01.48.87.75.91). Mº Filles du Calvaire.* **Open** 10am-7pm Mon-Sat.
Unusual young French artists feature here, such as Anne Ferrer, whose satin pigs touch lightly on feminism and sexuality, and Pierrick Sorin, whose videos have a rare, melancholy humour, plus some older artists, such as Jean Degottex, and Korean artists concerned with environmental art.

## Galerie Rachlin Lemarié Beaubourg

*23 rue du Renard, 4th (01.44.59.27.27). Mº Hôtel-de-Ville.* **Open** 10.30am-1pm, 2.30-7pm, Tue-Sat.
When the long-established Galerie Beaubourg moved south to a château in Vence and museum-like status, Rachlin and Lémarie took over the list that includes *nouveau réaliste* sculptors Arman and César, *nouvelle figuration* painter Combas and the role-playing Philippe Perrin, and added a few artists of their own like François Boisrond.

## Galerie Philippe Rizzo

*9 rue St-Gilles, 3rd (01.48.87.12.00). Mº Chemin-Vert.* **Open** 11am-1pm, 2-7pm, Tue-Fri; 11am-7pm Sat.
Rizzo presents artists in all media and has been active in introducing many young American and British artists to the Paris scene, like Tracey Emin, Gavin Turk or Gary Simmons.

## Galerie Thaddaeus Ropac

*7 rue Debelleyme, 3rd (01.42.72.99.00). Mº St-Sébastien-Froissart.* **Open** 10am-7pm Tue-Sat.
Established international names are stylishly presented by Austrian gallerist Ropac, including Italian transavanguardia painter Sandro Chia, British sculptors Antony Gormley and Anish Kapoor, and American Pop, neo-Pop and neo-Geo artists, like James Rosenquist and David Salle.

**Galerie Philippe Rizzo**: *first Paris showcase for the statements of Sarah Morris.*

### Galerie Samia Saouma
*16 rue des Coutures-St-Gervais, 3rd (01.42.78.40.44). Mᵒ St-Sébastien-Froissart or St-Paul.* **Open** 2-7pm Tue-Sat.
A tiny gallery that often features works on paper and photographs by high-calibre artists, including Martin Kippenberger, kitsch duo Pierre et Gilles and Jeanne Dunning, often with a provocative touch.

### Le Sous-Sol
*12 rue du Petit Musc, 4th (01.42.72.46.72). Mᵒ Sully-Morland or Bastille.* **Open** 2.30-7pm Tue-Sat.
A labyrinthine basement with exposed airducts and steel girders shows mainly young artists, as well as some site-specific interventions by known artists like Felice Varini, whose optical illusions are suited to the curious setting.

### Daniel Templon
*30 rue Beaubourg, 3rd (01.42.72.14.10). Mᵒ Rambuteau.* **Open** 10am-7pm Mon-Sat.
A favourite with the French art establishment, Templon shows big-name European painters such as German neo-Expressionist Jörg Immendorff and Italian transavanguardia artists Paladino and Cucchi. French artists include Raymond Hains, Jean-Michel Alberola and Vincent Corpet.

### Galerie Anne de Villepoix
*11 rue de Tournelles, 4th (01.42.78.32.24). Mᵒ Bastille.* **Open** 11am-7pm Tue-Sat.
Anne de Villepoix shows interesting work in varied media, alternating established figures such as veteran American photographer John Coplans and conceptual artists Vito Acconci or Thomas Locher, with talented, new wave, younger artists such as Beat Streuli and Valérie Jouve.

### Galerie Reno Xippas
*108 rue Vieille-du-Temple, 3rd (01.40.27.05.55). Mᵒ Filles du Calvaire.* **Open** 10am-1pm, 2-7pm, Tue-Sat.
In a U-shaped space around Yvon Lambert, this gallery presents artists as varied as Thomas Demand, Nancy Dwyer, Joan Hernández Pijoan and names from Xippas' native Greece.

### Claire Burrus
*14-16 rue de Lappe, 11th (01.43.55.36.90). Mᵒ Bastille.* **Open** 2-7pm Tue-Fri; 11am-7pm Sat.
Less active than in the past, this long-established Bastille gallery shows mainly British and North Americans, including Angela Bulloch, Hirschl Perlman and David Robbins.

### Durand-Dessert
*28 rue de Lappe, 11th (01.48.06.92.23). Mᵒ Bastille.* **Open** 11am-1pm, 2-7pm, Tue-Sat.
A powerhouse of the French art scene, representing movements from the 1960s to today. Long committed to artists associated with arte povera (Kounellis, Pistoletto, Penone and Merz), major French artists such as François Morellet,

Gérard Garouste and Bertrand Lavier, the quirky dog photos of William Wegman and Dijon-based Chinese painter Ming are also shown. There's an excellent art bookshop.

### Galerie J & J Donguy
*57 rue de la Roquette, 11th (01.47.00.10.94). Mᵒ Bastille.* **Open** 1-7pm Tue-Sat.
An idiosyncratic gallery that has long concentrated on the photos and documents of *art corporel* (body art) and artists of the Austrian action art scene such as Otto Mühl.

### Galerie Alain Gutharc
*47 rue de Lappe, 11th (01.47.00.32.10). Mᵒ Bastille.* **Open** 2-7pm Tue-Fri; 11am-7pm Sat.
Aside from paintings by David Medalla, Gutharc has a taste for the intimate, seen in the knick-knacks photographed by Valérie Belin and Agnès Propeck's neo-Surrealist images.

### Galerie Lavignes-Bastille
*27 rue de Charonne, 11th (01.47.00.88.18). Mᵒ Bastille or Ledru Rollin.* **Open** 2-8pm Tue-Fri; 11am-7pm Sat.
This three-tiered gallery shows approachable, often flamboyant, figurative work, for a fashionable clientele of private collectors. Among artists represented are Bedri Baykam, Libessart, Calum Fraser, Rosaz and Jean-Claude Maynard.

### Galerie Météo
*4 rue St-Nicolas, 12th (01.43.42.20.20). Mᵒ Ledru-Rollin.* **Open** 2.30-7.30pm Tue-Sat.
Look here for invidualistic French artists, such as Philippe Ramette and Jean-Luc Mylayne. Météo has been conducting a solo 'strike' and now only puts on shows on request.

### Espace d'Art Yvonamor Palix
*13 rue Keller, 11th (01.48.06.36.70). Mᵒ Bastille.* **Open** 2-7pm Tue-Sat.
A Mexican gallerist who moved to Paris from Madrid in 1993 and has quickly established a presence. Her slickly presented artists mainly use photography and/or new technology, and include Sandy Skogland, Joseph Nevchatel, Steve Miller and Paloma Navares. A little different is Paris-based, British-born Lucy Orta whose projects involve the homeless.

### Galerie Jousse Seguin
*34 rue de Charonne, 11th (01.47.00.32.35). Mᵒ Bastille or Ledru-Rollin.* **Open** 11am-1.30pm, 2.30-7pm, Mon-Sat.
Committed to progressive new art, this dynamic gallery picks up on '90s issues like gender (Chuck Nanney) or no issue at all. A hangar-like second space round the corner at 5 rue des Taillandiers is devoted to furniture and ceramics by designers of the 1930s to '50s such as Perriand and Prouvé.

### Galerie Louis Carré et Cie
*10 av de Messine, 8th (01.45.62.57.07). Mᵒ Miromesnil.* **Open** 10am-12.30pm, 2-6.30pm, Mon-Sat.
Founded in 1938. Shows today largely focus on a small sta-

# Heading East

Venturing into the previously uncharted territory of the 13th *arrondissement* – in mutation since the opening of the new Bibliothèque Nationale – six young galleries (most escaping expensive Marais rents) have set up shop together as the Association Scène Est in a new building at 20 rue Louise-Weiss, 13th/ 01.40.27.80.07 (Mᵒ Chevaleret). Attempting to reinvigorate the scene, the six plan to share openings and organise occasional joint exhibitions and multi-disciplinary events.

### Air de Paris
Named after Duchamp's famous bottle of air, this gallery gives a taste of an insouciant, ironic new generation including Paul McCarthy, Philippe Parreno, Pierre Joseph, Carsten Höller and Liam Gillick, who use varied media to play witty games with the concepts and language behind contemporary art.

### Galerie Arps
Half of former gallery Froment & Putman, Aline Froment began the project with a group show.

### Art: Concept
Moving from sunny, but isolated Nice, Art: Concept's stable includes Max Mohr and Guillaume Paris.

### Galerie Jennifer Flay
New Zealander Jennifer Flay has a talent for picking up on interesting young artists among them Americans Sean Landers and John Currin, British sculptor Cathy de Monchaux and up-and-coming French names Xavier Veilhan, Claude Closky and Dominique Gonzalez-Foerster.

### Galerie Emmanuel Perrotin
Many of Perrotin's young European artists are exploring portraiture and/or autobiography, including Maurizio Cattelan, Mark Wallinger and Alix Lambert. He has also taken up several interesting Japanese artists such as troubling photographer Noritoshi Hirakawa and glossy cyberpunkette Mariko Mori.

### Galerie Praz-Delavallade
Formerly based in the Bastille, this gallery shows mainly young artists often on paper,111 such as the cartoon-style antics of Chicago bad boy Jim Shaw.

*Cathy de Monchaux's bondage-like contraptions at **Jennifer Flay**.*

ble of contemporary French artists such as *nouvelle figuration* painter Hervé di Rosa and Haïtian-born sculptor Hervé Télémacque, although you'll also find Calder, Dufy, Delaunay and Léger among the artists in stock.

### Galerie Lelong
*13 rue de Téhéran, 8th (01.45.63.13.19). Mᵒ Miromesnil.* **Open** 10.30am-6pm Tue-Fri; 2-6.30pm Sat.
Lelong shows major twentieth-century artists such as Alechinsky, Miró, Kounellis, Tàpies, Chillida, Kirkeby and Louise Bourgeois. Branches in New York and Zurich.

## St-Germain-des-Prés

### Jeanne Bucher
*53 rue de Seine, 6th (01.44.41.69.65). Mᵒ Mabillon.* **Open** 9am-6.30pm Tue-Fri; 10am-12.30pm, 2-6pm, Sat.
Founded in 1925, the gallery now occupies a lovely, very simple, airy space hidden in a courtyard, and specialises in post-war abstract and Cobra painters such as Aguayo, Dubuffet, Bissière, Jorn and De Staël, with a few contemporary artists.

### Galerie 1900-2000
*8 rue Bonaparte, 6th (01.43.25.84.20). Mᵒ St-Germain-des-Prés.* **Open** 2-7pm Mon; 10am-12.30pm, 2-7pm, Tue-Sat.
Marcel Fleiss' eclectic range shows a strong predilection for Surrealism, Pop and the Fluxus movement.

### Galerie Claude Bernard
*7 rue des Beaux-Arts, 6th (01.43.26.97.07). Mᵒ Mabillon or St-Germain-des-Prés.* **Open** 9.30am-12.30pm, 2.30-6.30pm, Tue-Sat.
This large gallery shows mostly realist, figurative paintings from the 1960s to the present, by the likes of Peter Blake, David Hockney, Xavier Valls and Balthus.

### Galerie Dionne
*19bis rue des Sts-Pères, 6th (01.49.26.03.06). Mᵒ St-Germain-des-Prés or Rue du Bac.* **Open** 2-7pm Mon, 10am-7pm Tue-Fri; 10.30am-7pm Sat.
A huge, rather plush space with tasteful coir floors: not hot on new names but has gathered some interesting retrospective-style shows of veterans like Mattà and Mimmo Rotella.

### Galerie Jean-Jacques Dutko
*13 rue Bonaparte, 6th (01.43.26.96.13). Mᵒ St-Germain-des-Prés.* **Open** 2.30-7pm Mon; 10.30am-1pm, 2.30-7pm, Tue-Sat.
This gallery combines the preoccupations of St-Germain to effect. Exhibitions of abstract paintings or contemporary sculpture are conceived around an impressive display of superb quality Art Deco furniture and African tribal art.

### Samy Kinge
*54 rue de Verneuil, 7th (01.42.61.19.07). Mᵒ Rue du Bac.* **Open** 2.30-7pm Tue-Sat.
This tiny venue in the antiques district promotes European artists in the Surrealist tradition, with a fine collection of works by the late Victor Brauner, plus some younger names.

### Galerie Maeght
*42 rue du Bac, 7th (0145.48.45.15). Mᵒ Rue du Bac.* **Open** 9.30am-1pm, 2-7pm, Tue-Sat.
This famous gallery rests on past glories. Contemporary shows, with a few exceptions like Tàpiès, are decidedly pale compared to a past that once included Giacommetti and Miró. They continue the tradition of beautifully produced artists' books, printed in their own workshops.

### Galerie Montenay-Giroux
*31 rue Mazarine, 6th (01.43.54.85.30). Mᵒ Odéon.* **Open** 11am-1pm, 2.30-7pm, Tue-Sat.
This expansive sky-lit gallery, which started life as a garage,

*Ming ware at **Durand-Dessert**, p233.*

is now used for exhibiting a mixed selection of contemporary painters including Eric Dalbis and Jean-Pierre Pincemin.

### Galerie de Paris
*6 rue du Pont de Lodi, 6th (01.43.25.42.63). Mᵒ Odéon.*
**Open** 2.30-7pm Tue-Sat.
An adventurous gallery that shows a range of established and younger artists, and continues to plough an independent course in an increasingly staid area, often putting on interesting themed shows, including artists such as Jean-Luc Vilmouth and Bordeaux cooperative Présence Panchouette.

### Galerie Denise René
*196 bd St-Germain, 7th (01.42.22.77.57). Mᵒ St-Germain-des-Prés.* **Open** 10am-1pm, 2-7pm Tue-Sat.
Something of an institution, Denise René has remained firmly committed to kinetic art and geometrical abstraction ever since Tinguely first presented his machines here in the '50s. **Branch:** 22 rue Charlot, 3rd (01.48.87.73.94).

### Galerie Darthea Speyer
*6 rue Jacques-Callot, 6th (01.43.54.78.41). Mᵒ Odéon.*
**Open** 11am-12.45pm, 2-7pm Tue-Fri; 11am-7pm Sat.
Often colourful, representational painting and sculpture and naive artists are the speciality here. It can be fairly kitsch, but at best features the politically committed expressionism of Leon Golub or the American dreams of Ed Paschke.

### Galerie Stadler
*51 rue de Seine, 6th (01.43.26.91.10). Mᵒ Mabillon.*
**Open** 2.30-6.30pm Tue-Sat.
Stadler opened in the 1950s in what was then the heart of avant-garde Paris, and in the '60s was one of the first to present the *art corporel* (body art) of Gina Pane, Urs Lüthi, Hermann Nitsch and others. It still does, along with abstract art by painters such as Sigrid Glöerfelt and Arnulf Rainer.

### Georges-Philippe Vallois
*38 rue de Seine, 6th (01.46.34.61.07). Mᵒ Mabillon.*
**Open** 10.30am-1pm, 2-7pm, Mon-Sat.
Son of Art Deco furniture and modern sculpture specialist Galerie Vallois (at Nos 36 and 41), Georges-Philippe takes a more contemporary outlook, specialising in sculpture.

### Galerie Lara Vincy
*47 rue de Seine, 6th (01.43.26.72.51). Mᵒ Mabillon.* **Open** 2.30-7.30pm Mon; 11am-12.30pm, 2.30-7.30pm, Tue-Sat.
Lara Vincy is one of the more eccentric characters of the area and one of the few to retain a sense of the '70s Fluxus-style 'happenings', seen in interesting theme shows perhaps involving music, or the work of epigram maestro Ben.

## Photo Galleries

### Galerie Bouqueret + Lebon
*69 rue de Turenne, 3rd (01.40.27.92.21).*
*Mᵒ Chemin-Vert.* **Open** 2-7pm Tue-Sat.
Visit this small apartment for risk-taking work, from rediscovered avant-garde pioneers, to contemporary photographers like Dörte Eissfeldt and gender-bender Gerd Bonfert.

### Michèle Chomette
*24 rue Beaubourg, 3rd (01.42.78.05.62). Mᵒ Rambuteau.*
**Open** 2-7pm Tue-Sat.
More classical historical and contemporary photographic work, from Man Ray to Alain Fleischer and Lewis Baltz.

### Galerie Contrejour
*96 rue Daguerre, 14th (01.43.21.41.88). Mᵒ Gaîté.*
**Open** 10am-7.30pm daily.
Contrejour specialises mainly in French and Italian photographers, publishes catalogues and has darkroom facilities.

### Agathe Gaillard
*3 rue du Pont Louis-Philippe, 4th (01.42.77.38.24).*
*Mᵒ Pont-Marie or Hôtel-de-Ville.* **Open** 1-7pm Tue-Sat.
This long-established photography specialises in classic masters such as Gibson, Cartier-Bresson and Kertesz.

### La Laverie
*9 rue Keller, 11th (01.47.00.11.38). Mᵒ Bastille.*
**Open** 2-7pm Tue-Sat.
Association run by four French and Chinese photographers promotes exchanges between France and Asia and has an archive of photography from China, Hong Kong and Taiwan.

### Zabriskie
*37 rue Quincampoix, 4th (01.42.72.35.47). Mᵒ Châtelet-Les Halles.* **Open** 2-7pm Tue-Fri; 11am-7pm Sat.
With galleries in Paris and New York, Zabriskie shows big names of classic art photography, like Atget, Steiglitz and Klein, and some contemporary artists who use photography.

## Design & Architecture Galleries

### Galerie Néotu
*25 rue du Renard, 4th (01.42.78.96.97). Mᵒ Hôtel-de-Ville.* **Open** 10am-7pm Mon-Fri; 10am-12.30pm, 2-6pm Sat.
The contemporary furniture, ceramics and carpets by design gurus from Pesce to Szekely are as much art as function.

### Galerie Uzzan
*11 rue de Thorigny, 3rd (01.44.59.83.00). Mᵒ St-Paul.*
**Open** by appointment only.
Philippe Uzzan has carved out a niche as a specialist in architecture, exhibiting designs by big-name Americans, such as Peter Eisenman, plus some natives like Odile Decq.

### VIA
*29-37 av Daumesnil, 12th (01.46.28.11.11). Mᵒ Gare de Lyon.* **Open** 9am-7pm Mon-Sat; 11am-6pm Sun.
Moved from St-Germain to three arches in the Viaduc des Arts, VIA promotes industrial and domestic design by providing information and showcasing talent. Wilmotte, Nouvel, Garouste et Bonetti, even Gaultier, have passed through here.

# Arts & Entertainments

# Media

*The French media expresses all the contradictions of French society, from late-night porn to philosophy on the airwaves.*

As with many things in France, 'national' tends to read as 'Paris'. One in two French people reads a daily (Monday-Saturday) newspaper, but only some 20% read the heavily Paris-biased, Paris-based nationals. Important regional papers, such as *Ouest-France*, outdo these in the provinces. The biggest national seller is sports specialist *L'Equipe*, followed by *Le Monde*.

French newspapers tend to be serious, expensive (6F or 7F) and reflect an abiding passion for politics. There is no real equivalent to British or American tabloids, thanks to a combination of strict privacy laws and easy acceptance of extramarital affairs. There is also little tradition of investigative journalism; major revelations often emerge first in the satirical weekly *Le Canard Enchaîné*. Rather than an appetite for Sunday papers, more in-depth reports and analysis tend to be found in the weekly news magazines. There is also a vast choice of women's glossies, household and interior decoration titles, teen mags, cinema mags and other special interest titles, although the two top sellers – *TV Magazine* and *Télé 7 Jours* – are both TV listings magazines.

## Newspapers

### Le Figaro
A right-wing, middlebrow broadsheet founded in 1866. On Wednesdays, *Figaroscope* gives weekly listings of Paris arts, entertainment and restaurants. The Saturday edition comes with *Madame Figaro*, *Figaro Magazine* and a TV guide.

### France Soir
Broadsheet in format but tabloid in spirit, *France Soir* is graphic chaos. Owned like *Le Figaro* by Groupe Hersant, it supposedly has a social issues emphasis, although you could be forgiven for believing it is gossip. The rest of the world? Forget it, unless it's British beef or Clinton's effect on women.

### L'Humanité
The Communist Party paper has kept going despite the collapse of the Party's colleagues outside France. Publishes *Humanité Dimanche* magazine on Sunday (out on Saturday).

### Le Journal du Dimanche
This thin broadsheet is the sole Sunday news offering. Most of France waits until Monday to read about Saturday's events, but at least it tries.

### Libération
Once symbolic of the post-'68 generation, *Libé* was founded in the early 1970s as a radical left-wing paper, by a group that included Sartre and de Beauvoir. Through successive redesigns, it has rather lost its focus and has been hit by

declining circulation and financial problems, although news and arts coverage are wide ranging. It's worth reading for guest columnists, such as Baudrillard, and the caustic editorials of Serge July. Multimedia insert on Friday.

### Le Monde
Created in 1944 by Resistance leaders and owned by its journalists, *Le Monde* has retained its humanist ideology and is not afraid to criticise the current regime. It remains France's most influential newspaper, often running articles by top politicians and, despite a highbrow reputation and taste for extremely long articles, subject matter is surprisingly eclectic, although international coverage is very selective. The front page sticks to tradition and is illustrated only by a Plantù cartoon; even inside, there are very few photographs. Out in Paris at around 1pm (with the next day's date).

### Le Parisien-Aujourd'hui
Tabloid in format with colour front and back, the easy-read *Parisien* is strong on social issues, with lots of vox pop surveys. The Paris edition has an interesting central section covering Paris news, history and events. A useful map shows where you'll be blocked by the day's demonstrations.

### L'Equipe & Paris-Turf
Two for the sports fan: *L'Equipe* is an excellent, comprehensive sports daily; *Paris-Turf* is the horse-racing paper.

### La Tribune & Les Echos
Monday-Friday financial papers. *Les Echos* has ample economic information but little analysis or general news: if there's a war in the Third World don't expect to learn about it here. The more left-wing *Tribune* likes to see itself as 'a *Libé* of the economy' and is suffering similar financial problems.

### Satirical Weeklies
Despite an old-fashioned look, the venerable **Canard Enchaîné** (out on Wednesday) still regularly carries influential scoops on political, judicial and economic scandals. You're unlikely to understand much if you are not up-to-date with current national events or familiar with French politicians. **Charlie Hebdo** is mainly bought for its cartoons.

## Magazines

For more specialised magazines, see the relevant chapters.

### Fashion & Women's Magazines
**Elle**, which recently celebrated its half century, was a pioneer among liberated women's mags and has spawned editions across the globe. Here it is weekly and remains spot-on for interviews and fashion coverage. The other homegrown world success, **Marie-Claire**, is monthly and takes itself more seriously with a more feminist line and campaigning stance on women in the Third World. **Biba** treats similar fashion/sex/career topics with a younger, more urban approach. New life-style magazine **Atmosphères** does a similar juggling act but for a slightly older readership. The French edition of **Vogue**, read both for its fashion coverage and big-name guests (including the Dalai Lama),

*You're never short of something to read in Paris.*

is rivalled when it comes to fashion week by **L'Officiel de la Mode** and **Depèche Mode**.

## Gossip

**Paris Match** is a French institution: no one admits to buying but everyone seems to have read it. With lots of photostories and syrupy celebrity interviews, it stays ahead of its rivals by the occasional scoop and the quality of its photos, from Mitterrand *en famille* to the war in Chetchene. Photoled scandal sheet **Voici** is full of the usual paparazzi photos of celebrity weddings and film openings, and favours catching female stars naked on the beach. Plus some helpful little articles on losing your cellulite and keeping your man. Belonging to the German-owned Prima Press group of Axel Ganz, its sister mag **Gala** tells the same stories in *Hello!* format with happy endings. Veteran **Point de Vue** is more parochial and more downmarket. **Entrevue** favours rock and film star interviews and just loves Sharon Stone.

## News Weeklies

With **Le Nouvel Observateur**, **Le Point**, **L'Express** and **L'Evénement du Jeudi**, France has a strong tradition of heavyweight weekly news magazines, many of which come out on Thursday. **Le Nouvel Observateur** is furthest to the left, although it's rather lost the influence it held in the 1970s. All summarise the main French and international events of the week, with more limited cultural sections, but are of most interest for the varied in-depth reports, be they on political scandal, unemployment or agriculture.

## Paris Listings Magazines

Two pocket-sized publications rival for basic Wednesday to Tuesday listings information: **L'Officiel des Spectacles** (2.80F) and the slightly more detailed **Pariscope** (3F), bible of the Parisian cinema-goer, which includes the **Time Out Paris** section giving a critical selection of exhibitions, events and restaurant suggestions – in English. Linked to Radio Nova, youthful **Nova Magazine** provides an adventurous and rigorously multi-ethnic A-Z guide to the month's trendiest cultural events. Another useful source is highbrow TV magazine **Télérama**, which has good arts and entertainment features and a local listings insert in its Paris edition. *See also above* **Le Figaro**.

## Television

The audiovisual landscape is set to change with the imminent arrival of numerical technology as dozens of new channels become available through subscription on cable and satellite and as established channels attempt to regain lost viewers, finally tired of a consensual diet of game shows and dubbed sit-coms. Main news slot on both TF1 and France 2 is at 8pm.

### TF1

France's first private TV channel (and now part of the empire of construction giant Bouyges), TF1 has long been the most successful channel with its mass-market programming, quick to whisk flops off the air. The 8pm evening news has star anchors Patrick Poivre d'Arvor (PPDA) and Claire Chazal. In *Sept sur Sept* on Sunday evenings interviewer Anne Sinclair grills celebrities, usually politicians, but much of the early evening schedules is taken up with teen sitcoms.

### France 2

France's leading public service channel – funded, like France 3, by a mix of advertising and *la redevance*, the French licence fee – saw scandal in 1996 over some of the exorbitant fees awarded to the 'presenter-producers' of some of its most successful shows, several of whom (Nagui) were since lured to rival TF1; others, like Jean-Luc Delarue, have remained. The affair led to the resignation of director-general Jean-Pierre Elkabbach (*see below* Europe 1 under **Radio**). The long-running, late-night cultural chat show *Le Cercle de Minuit* and Bernard Pivot's literary *Bouillon de Culture* show that an intellectual audience does exist out there somewhere.

### FR3

France 3 is regarded as the more serious of the two state channels, although the eternally popular *Questions pour un champion* quiz show invites doubt. Its charter as the 'regional' channel ties it to a heavy itinerary of local programming. Late Sunday night *Cinéma de Minuit* offers film classics in their original language.

# Virtual Paris

Although France has been notoriously slow to get online, Parisian cyberspace boasts a burgeoning array of web sites ranging from standard billboard dreck to the truly visionary and weird. Not for nothing was France home to the world's first virtual diocese (**http://www.partenia.fr**), renegade bishop François Gaillot's divinely inspired endrun around Vatican diktat.

Paris' offerings are superbly organised and easy to navigate. Direct access to much of what's available can be found via **Paris Page's Page of Other Links** (http://www.paris.org/Links/), which provides hyperlinks to over 150 individual sites plus connections to other links/pages. (See **Tennessee Bob's French Links** (http://unix1.utn.edu/departments/french/french.html) and **Le petit coin des grenouilles** (http://web.cnam.fr/fr/)).

Many sites are bilingual, but you may want to brush up on your parly voo before visiting the rest. Among several sites catering to linguistic needs, **The dictionaries of Jouni Santara** (http://mlab-power3.uiah.fi///EnglishFrench/avenues.html0) generously provides the eponymous dictionaries, interactive courses and more.

Tourist information is plentiful and easy to come by. **Maison de France** (http://www.franceguide.com) is an exhaustive French-English guide to practically every conceivable aspect of travel in France. **L'Office de Tourisme** (http://www.paris.org/OTP/) hospitably provides French, English, German, Spanish and Italian versions of its site and a link to the **Chambre de Commerce et de l'Industrie**. **Hotels-Paris and Environs** (http://www.paris.org/Hotels/) is a listing of over 2,000 hotels, conveniently cross-referenced by neighbourhood and rating.

**Time Out**'s electronic tribute to Paris (accessible via http://timeout.co.uk) offers extensive guide information, a weekly updated selection of the city's best arts and entertainment and classified ads. **Pariscope** (//www.pariscope.fr) covers a broad range of local information in French, English and Spanish. **World Media** (http://www. worldmedia.fr/wm/) boasts six separate online magazines covering French tourism, fashion, cinema, sports and politics. **Nirvanet** (http:// www.nirvanet.fr/) combines virtuoso design with incisive local reportage on cinema, cyberculture, music and more.

Keen custodians of their culture and lavish in their devotions to the past, the French have been swift to appropriate the Internet to the task,

Tap into the life and times of Serge.

making the real glories of Parisian cyberspace seemingly better suited to the likes of Umberto Eco than the stereotypical web-head. The colossal **ARFTL Project** (http://humanities.uchicago.edu/ARTFL/) is a vast database on all aspects of French language and literature that features full-text databases of 1,880 texts. **Historical Maps of Paris** (gopher://gutentag.cc.columbia.edu/11/fun/pictures/art-history) assembles scores of street plans and urban renderings of Paris from the eighteenth and nineteenth centuries, while **The Siege and Commune of Paris** (http://www.library.nwu.edu/spec/siege/), gathers a haunting collection of photos, portraits, political caricatures and related material from one of the bloodiest episodes in the city's history.

Those in search of less sober mementos and a bit of smoky ambiance should drop in on **Serge Gainsbourg** (http://www.imaginet.fr/~relig/Gainsbourg.html). Similar offerings are on tap at **The Nights of Edith Piaf** (http://soundprint.brandywine.american.edu:80/~soundprt/more-info/piaf.html).

Underground but up to date, two of the city's odder institutions can now be found on the web. **Carrières et Catacombes** (http://www.lapoubelle.com/kta) is a fascinating, subtlely subversive site to the damp and dangerous labyrinth of bone-strewn tunnels underlying the city, providing maps, history, photos and, pro forma warning to the contrary, a tacit inducement to venture below and see for yourself. End it all at **Père Lachaise** (http://www.cemetery.org/Lachaise/lachaise.intro.html), a site dedicated to the world's most famous resting place, where you can pay your respects to the dead, Oscar Wilde and Jim Morrison among them.

## Canal +

A subscription channel – most programmes can only be viewed with a special signal *décodeur*. Popular for its sports coverage and recent movie releases. Available unscrambled to non-subscribers in the early morning, at lunchtime and in the early evening for the talk show *Nulle Part Ailleurs*.

## Arte/La Cinquième

Franco-German hybrid Arte launched in 1992. It offers some fascinating programmes, including strong world music coverage, although its taste for themed evenings can be hit and miss. Films are often in VO. The news slot at 8.30pm gives an interesting counterpoint to the French-dominated news on the main channels. Arte shares its wavelength with the French educational channel La Cinquième (5.45am-7pm).

## M6

M6 has leapt in the ratings, especially with the under-30s, with its recipe of afternoon music videos, late-night soft porn, lots of ageing British and American shows (dubbed) – and a few newer ones like cult series *The X-Files*, but there are also some excellent homegrown series, such as *Culture Pub*, about advertising, and economic magazine *Capital*.

## Cable TV & Satellite

Paris-Cable (01.44.25.89.99) began hooking up Paris homes to its network in the mid-1980s. The basic package (152F per month, plus connection fee) provides 15 channels, including **Euronews**, TF1's continuous news programme **LC1**, **MTV**, French music imitator **MCM**, **Planète** which specialises in documentaries, **Série Club**, **RTL9**, **Eurosport**, 'women's' channel **Téva** and Paris arts and fashion specialist **Paris Première**. Trendiest channel is **Canal Jimmy**, which boasts hip US and British series including *Seinfeld*, *NYPD Blue*s, *Friends*, *Absolutely Fabulous*, screened both in English with subtitles and dubbed into French. **CNN**, **BBC Prime** and other foreign-language channels including German **ZDF** and Italian **Rai Uno** are on the next package up (187F/month).

Originally a monopoly, Paris Cable has recently come up against competition from satellite TV. Better-quality reception, lower (if any) subscription prices and, potentially, a better-targeted *bouquet* of channels suggest that, despite opposition from some local authorities, satellite will soon be at the fore. At present, operators include Eutelsat (capturing channels from the rest of Europe and the Middle East), Canal Satellite (linked to Canal +), Astra, TPS and AB Sat.

# Radio

The absorption of small stations by big groups has meant a standardisation of the radio offering since the initial cacophony of deregulation in the early 1980s. Twiddle the dial, though, and specialist tastes are catered for among the pop hits and phone-ins. 1 January 1996 supposedly brought in a 40% quota for *chanson française*, since challenged in the European court, but it's far from apparent.
An FM selection:

**87.8 MHz France Inter** State-run, it broadcasts mostly MOR music and international news. Also known for Bernard Lenoir's Black Sessions of indie rock and Jean-Louis Foulquier's Pollen – live recordings of native newcomers.
**90.4 MHz Nostalgie** As it sounds.
**90.9 MHz Chante France** 100% French *chanson*.
**91.7 MHz; 92.1 MHz France Musique** The national classical music channel offers concerts, live orchestras, top jazz and too much talk (*see also* the Maison de la Radio in **Music: Classical & Opera**).
**93.5/93.9 MHz France Culture** Highbrow state culture station: literature, poetry, history, cinema and music.

**94.8MHz Radio Communauté/Radio J/Judaique FM/ Radio Shalom** Shared wavelength for Paris' local Jewish stations.
**96MHz Skyrock** Pop station goes for effect by outspoken presenters.
**96.4 MHz BFM** Business and economic station with the Wall Street results in English every evening.
**96.9 MHz Voltage FM** Dance music.
**97.4 MHz Rire et Chansons** A non-stop diet of jokes – racist, sexist or just plain lousy – and pop oldies.
**97.8 MHz Ado** Local music station: much ado(lescents) about nothing.
**98.2MHz Radio FG 98.2** Gay station. Techno music, rave announcements and very explicit lonely hearts.
**99 MHz Radio Latina** Great mix of Latin and salsa music, increasingly adding raï, Spanish and Italian pop.
**101.1 MHz Radio Classique** More classical pops than state rival France Musique, but also less pedagogical in tone. Music and business news mix at breakfast time.
**101.5 MHz Radio Nova** Hip hop, trip hop and whatever else is hopping now: refreshing or infuriating depending on your mood. The talk is very hip and sometimes incomprehensible. *Bon plans* are announced every day between 6-7pm.
**100.3 MHz NRJ** Energy: national leader with the under-30s.
**101.9 MHz Fun Radio** Pop channel was a hit with teenagers for its sexual problems phone-in with the 'Doc', but has been losing ground to imitators. Now trying to embrace techno alongside Anglo pop hits.
**102.3 MHz Ouï FM** Ouï rock you.
**103.9MHz RFM** The ultimate in easy listening.
**104.3 MHz RTL** The voice of middle France: the most popular French station nationwide mixes music and talk programmes. Grand Jury on Sunday is a debate between journalists and a top politician.
**104.7 MHz Europe 1** News bulletins, press reviews, sports, business, gardening and music. Much the best weekday breakfast news broadcast, when Jean-Pierre Elkabbach interviews politicians or businessmen on air.
**105.1 MHz FIP** Traffic bulletins, news of what's on in Paris and a musical mix of jazz, classical, world and pop.
**105.5 MHz France Info** The 24-hour diet of international news, economic updates and sports reports is useful if you want to catch up on the latest headlines, but as everything gets repeated roughly every 15 minutes, it's guaranteed to drive you mad – good though if you're learning French.
**106.7 MHz Beur FM** Aimed at Paris' North Africans.
**107.5 MHz Africa No 1** Broadcast direct from Gabon.

# English-Language Media

The Paris-based **International Herald Tribune** is on sale throughout the city; major British dailies and **USA Today** are also widely available on the day of issue at larger kiosks in the city centre. British Sunday papers are also increasingly easy to find (at a price).

On the local front, **Time Out Paris** is a six-page supplement inside the weekly *Pariscope* (*see above* **Listings Magazines***)*, available at all news stands, covering selected Paris events, exhibitions, films, concerts and restaurants. **FUSAC** (France-USA Contacts) is a fortnightly small-ads free-sheet with flat rentals, job ads and appliances for sale, available at US-and British-oriented bookshops and bars. The monthly **Paris Free Voice** is community oriented with reasonable arts coverage, available at English-language bookshops, bars and the American Church.

**BBC World Service** (648 KHz AM): Continuous English-language broadcasting, with international news, current events, pop, drama. Also on 198KHz LW, from midnight to 5.30am daily. At other times this frequency carries **BBC Radio 4** (198 KHz LW): British news, talk and The Archers directed at the home audience.

**RFI** 738 KHz AM English-language programme of news and music 3-4pm daily.

# Cabaret
# & Comedy

**Dancing girls are only the high-kicking candyfloss of Paris cabaret; a more subversive underbelly also exists.**

The good old days of *belle époque* glamour still echo down the years, as some of the world's longest-running shows continue at the legendary **Lido** and **Moulin Rouge**. Elsewhere, the capital's cabaret scene has long left behind the lavish *fin-de-siècle* scale, even if new arrival **Cabaret** tries to take on the top hat era. Traditional cabaret is typically animated by a larger-than-life character, helped by an array of inventive comics, impressionists, magicians, the obligatory Piaf, Chevalier or Brel medley, and performers with all manner of fauna from tigers to snakes. In among them all, there are also some subversive interlopers.

## COMEDY & CAFÉ-THÉÂTRE

The nearest Parisian equivalent to the fringe theatre and comedy circuit, Café-Théâtres developed out of cabaret, and it is in these venues that you'll find much sharper-edged acts than the fossilised world of chorus girls. Shows run the range from pure cabaret and comedy to political skits and small-scale plays, and quality is just as variable. Musical acts like Les Nonnes Troppos (singing drag nuns) are also popular. Look out in listings magazines for the occasional British or English-language comedian adding a Paris date to a London tour: Eddie Izzard, Jeremy Hardy and Will Durst have all appeared in the past couple of years.

## AT THE CIRCUS

Circus in France means much more than Dumbo-style performing elephants, moustache-twirling ringmasters and ball-balancing seals. Thanks to state support, circus arts have been flourishing since the 1970s, with a new generation of talent developing outside the traditional circus dynasties, such as the Bouglione (famous for their horses), Gruss (famous clowns) and Franconis. Internationally renowned Archaos combines anarchic energy with machines, videos and motorbikes. Bartabas' touring Théâtre Equestre Zingaro, famous for dashing equestrian exploits, performs in a wooden arena in Aubervilliers for a couple of months each year (176 av Jean-Jaurès, 93 Aubervilliers, 01.48.39.18.03). Look out, too, for other roving troupes such as the Besançon-based

Cirque Plume, which combines slick acrobatics, music and a socio-political slant, at venues such as the Parc de la Villette. There's also the Festival Mondial du Cirque de Demain, a showcase for innovative, new performers at the Cirque d'Hiver every January (*see chapter* **Paris by Season**).

## Cabaret

### Glitz & Dancing Girls

**Cabaret**
*68 rue Pierre-Charron, 8th (01.42.89.44.14). M° George V.* **Open** 10pm-3am daily. **Show** 1am on. **Admission** free, drinks from 70F. **Credit** AmEx, MC, V.
Quirky cabaret enlivens the already bubbling atmosphere at this new rendezvous for the night set. A wash with claret velvet and faux gilt, former businessman's haunt Le Millionaire has been transformed, as glossy groups huddle conspiratorially around nests of tables, order up the bubbly and gossip the night away, while on-stage variety acts offer bite-size sketches with an emphasis on drag.

**Crazy Horse Saloon**
*12 av George V, 8th (01.47.23.32.32). M° Alma-Marceau.* **Show** 8.30pm, 11pm Mon-Fri, Sun; 7.30pm, 9.45pm, 11.50pm Sat. **Admission** *show and champagne* 195F-650F; *with dinner* 750F. **Credit** AmEx, DC, MC, V.
The foot soldiers of fantasy at the Crazy Horse all boast uniformly naturally curvaceous bodies to titillate a high-rolling clientele. Mad names abound, as Looky Boop, Lumina Neon and Pussy Duty-Free whet the appetite nightly. The revue 'Teasing' is subtitled 'the art of the nude', but the identikit girls are kept a draconian distance from their audience and, bizarrely, are weighed twice a month.

**Le Lido**
*116 bis av des Champs-Elysées, 8th (01.40.76.56.10). M° George V.* **Show** 10pm, 12.15am daily. *show and champagne* 540F; *with dinner* 805F-900F. **Credit** AmEx, DC, MC, V.
The 60 Bluebell Girls shake their endowments in a show entitled *C'est Magique* – almost the only words in French, showing clearly at which side of the Atlantic it is aimed. Special effects include a fire-breathing dragon, an ice rink and a waterfall, but it's most notable for the sheer number of costume changes. Ever-popular with Japanese businessmen.

**Moulin Rouge**
*82 bd de Clichy, 18th (01.46.06.00.19). M° Blanche.* **Show** *dinner* 8pm, *show* 10pm, midnight, daily. **Admission** *show and champagne* 450F; *with dinner* 750F. **Credit** AmEx, DC, MC, V.
This high temple of kitsch is the only place to go for a time-

warp can-can. For two hours, the plumed Doriss Girls prance across the stage, with the energy and synchronisation necessary for so much pounding flesh in such a small space. Showstoppers include live crocodiles and Macbeth, the horse.

### Paradis Latin
*28 rue du Cardinal-Lemoine, 5th (01.43.25.28.28).*
*M° Cardinal-Lemoine.* **Show** 8pm (dinner), 9.45pm Mon, Wed-Sun. **Admission** *show and champagne* 465F; *with dinner* 680F. **Credit** AmEx, DC, MC, V.
Reputedly the oldest big show in town, in a theatre designed by Gustave Eiffel. Under new ownership, *Viva Paradis*, a glittering, new, no-expense-spared show, has just taken off.

## Cabaret & Turns

### Les Assassins
*40 rue Jacob, 6th (no telephone). M° St-Germain-des-Prés.*
**Open** 7pm-midnight Mon-Sat. **Average** 110F.
**No credit cards.**
'No reservations, no cheques, no coffee, no telephone': this bistro is a relic of a bygone age when St-Germain was far less refined. Dine on bistro classics like *lapin à la moutarde*, while singer-guitarist Maurice Dulac serenades with '*La grosse bite de Dudul*' (or Little Dulac's big dick). He's very funny, although it takes a pretty good command of French anatomical slang to keep up with the innuendos.

### Le Canotier du Pied de la Butte
*62 bd Rochechouart, 18th (01.46.06.02.86). M° Anvers.*
**Open** 10.30pm-4am daily. **Admission** 190F before midnight, 80F after. **Credit** MC,.V.
This tiny Pigalle cabaret was frequented by Piaf, Brel and Chevalier in the old days, and now welcomes modern French variety stars. Acts change frequently, but include accordionists, Piaf-style singers, impressionists and magicians.

### Caveau des Oubliettes
*11 rue St-Julien-le-Pauvre, 5th (01.43.54.94.97).*
*M° St-Michel.* **Show** 9pm Mon-Sat. **Admission** 70F.
**No credit cards.**

Wallow in renditions of traditional ballads (with the odd Piaf thrown in) in the medieval cellars of the former prison of Petit-Châtelet. It's a largely tourist crowd, but the atmosphere is fun and agreeably tongue-in-cheek.

### Caveau de la République
*1 bd St-Martin, 3rd (01.42.78.44.45). M° République.*
**Show** 9pm Tue-Sat; 3.30pm Sun. **Admission** 120F Tue-Thur; 170F Fri, Sat, Sun; 105F over-60s (Tue-Fri); 85F students, under-25s (Tue-Fri). **Credit** V.
One of the few remaining '*chansonniers*', where a team of singers and impressionists pick up the stories of the moment, and political scandal. The show changes every October.

### Chez Madame Arthur
*75 bis rue des Martyrs, 18th (01.42.64.48.27/ 01.42.54.40.21). M° Pigalle.* **Show** 9pm (dinner), 10.30pm daily. **Admission** *show with one drink* 165F; *with dinner* 295F-595F. **Credit** AmEx, DC, MC, V.
The French equivalent of Dame Edna Everage presents a non-stop show of drag artists and transsexuals, who mime to female singers or camp-up historic scenes. The make-up is as heavy as the *doubles entendres*. If you sit at the front , be prepared to be teased, tantalised and kissed.

### Au Lapin Agile
*22 rue des Saules, 18th (01.46.06.85.87). M° Lamarck-Caulaincourt.* **Show** 9pm Tue-Sun. **Admission** *show and one drink* 110F; 80F students (Tue-Fri, Sun).
**No credit cards.**
This cosy parlour whisks you back to the late nineteenth century, when the Agile Rabbit was a fave with Montmartre's bohemians. The artists have been replaced by a team of performers, such as accordionist Cassita, strident singer-songwriter Arlette Denis and songster Monsieur Yves.

### René Cousinier – La Branlette
*4 impasse Marie Blanche (off rue Lepic), 18th (01.46.06.49.46). M° Blanche.* **Open** 10pm-1.30am Tue-Sat. Closed July, Aug. **Admission** 100F.
**No credit cards.**

*For the ultimate in kitsch, there's still only one* **Moulin Rouge**.

# Michou

Eccentric cabaret owner Michou has achieved the status of a French national treasure. His trademark blue glasses, suits, smalls and Chelsea boots have helped make his nightclub a fixture on the Paris cabaret circuit. The vivacious club owner has also touched the very heart of the political establishment: Jacques Chirac has shared the stage with the kind-hearted king of drag, who works with France's First Lady on charity projects. A gallery of stars cosying up to Michou, including Juppé, Chirac and Johnny Halliday, are displayed in the entrance hall to the club.

Blue dominates Michou's home, too – from blue chandeliers, statues, tables, chairs and a giant blue sofa, to the telephone, which has the campest ring. Always at the centre of *le tout Paris*, Michou muses over a glamorous past with Jean Genet: 'During the early 1950s, we used to meet in the brasserie Cyrano at the place Blanche. I have a signed copy of *Querelle de Brest*. We were great friends.'

Nightly on the tiny stage, larger-than-life incarnations range from French torch-song *chanteuse* to wannabe Michael Jacksons and Barbra Streisands. When Shirley Bassey visited, she got up on stage with her double. Michou guides the proceedings from beside the stage, launching irrepressible salvos of whoops and laughter, and prides himself on keeping up with the times. No sooner had Madonna turned herself into a big-screen Evita than the House of Michou was premiering its larger-than-life version.
*80 rue des Martyrs, 18th (01.46.06.16.04). Mº Pigalle.* **Show** *dinner* 8.30pm (reservation essential); *show* 10.30pm, daily. **Admission** *show only* 200F; *with dinner* 550F. **Credit** V.

A grubby little cellar bar where René Cousinier, a living legend, will, if your French is up to it, keep you chuckling for a good hour and a half. If his nickname means anything to you (slang for wanking), you'll already have a good idea of his humour. Vulgar, truculent and very funny, he's full of charm.

## Café-Théâtre & Musical Comedy

### Au Bec Fin
*6 rue Thérèse, 1st (01.42.96.29.35). Mº Palais-Royal or Pyramides.* **Shows** usually 7pm, 8.15pm, 10pm, Mon-Sat. **Restaurant** open 10.30am-2.30pm, 7.30pm-2am, Mon-Sat. **Tickets** 80F; 65F student; *dinner and show* from 178F. **Credit** MC, V.
An intimate 60-seater theatre above a restaurant. Expect to see short plays (Oscar Wilde et al) and comic sketches, plus open auditions on Monday evenings.

### Aux Blancs-Manteaux
*15 rue des Blancs-Manteaux, 4th (01.48.87.15.84). Mº Hôtel-de-Ville or Rambuteau.* **Shows** 8pm, 9.15pm, 10.30pm, Mon, Sun; 8pm, 9.15pm, 10.30pm, Tue-Sat. **Bar** 5pm-midnight daily. **Tickets** *one show* 80F Mon-Fri, Sun; 90F Sat; *two shows* 130F Mon-Fri, Sun; 180F Sat; 65F students, under-25s. **No credit cards.**
Two 100-seat theatres stage lots of satires of BCBG life and one-person shows, with some quality acts, such as award-winner Remi Rosello. One of the longest-established café-théâtres, it is home to the popular 'Mad Cow' revue.

### Café Edgar
*58 bd Edgar-Quinet, 14th (01.42.79.97.97). Mº Edgar-Quinet.* **Shows** usually 8.15pm, 9.30pm, 10.30pm, Mon-Sat. **Tickets** 80F-100F; 65F-70F students, under-25s. **No credit cards.**
Good-quality small plays and one-man shows in a suitably sized venue. Some productions run for years.

### Café de la Gare
*41 rue du Temple, 4th (01.42.78.52.51/reservations 01.40.09.64.06). Mº Hôtel-de-Ville.* **Shows** 8pm, 10pm, Wed-Sat; 6.30pm Sun. **Tickets** 80F-100F; 50F-80F students. **Credit** MC, V
The former stables of a Marais mansion saw the emergence of Coluche and Depardieu and is still one of the best bets for a fun evening. A mixed diet of stand-ups and musical acts.

### La Pepinière Opéra
*7 rue Louis-le-Grand, 2nd (01.42.61.44.16). Mº Opéra.* **Shows** usually 7pm, 9pm, Mon-Sat. **Tickets** 100F-150F; 70-120F students, under-25s. **Credit** AmEx, MC, V.
Music hall and musical comedy, plus some straight *chanson*, in a pretty little theatre. Acts are usually of a high-standard. Look out for L'Ultima Récital, a talented double act of a monstrous operatic diva and her long-suffering accompanist.

### Petit Casino
*17 rue Chapon, 3rd (01.42.78.36.50). Mº Arts-et-Métiers.* **Shows** 9pm, 10.30pm, Tue-Sun. **Restaurant** 7.30pm-midnight daily. **Tickets** *two shows* 100F; *dinner and two shows* 140F Mon-Fri, Sun; 170F Sat. **Credit** V.
A trendy haunt that for a quarter of a century has been hosting one-man/woman shows, double acts and short plays.

### Point Virgule
*7 rue Ste-Croix-de-la-Bretonnerie, 4th (01.42.78.67.03). Mº Hôtel-de-Ville.* **Shows** 8pm, 9.15pm, 10.15pm, daily. **Tickets** *one show* 80F; *two shows* 130F; *three shows* 150F; 65F unemployed, students. **No credit cards.**
This tiny, kitsch, red theatre is a real star of the contemporary circuit, with a reputation as a talent-spotter. Shows consist mainly of one-person and musical acts. This is one of the few venues to stay alive during August.

# Clubs

**The dancing has never been more intense, the music never louder. Party boys and girls just want to have fun in fin-de-siècle Paris.**

Paris nightlife requires an appetite for constant change which whirlwinds through a capital determined not to relinquish its self-perceived monopoly on what is hip, stylish and *branché* (French slang for 'plugged in'). Although London and New York have overtaken Paris with what the world's club cognoscenti define as 'universal cool', the party scene in Paris at the wane of the 1990s is akin to a wildly delicious, Bacchanalian fête, trumpeting the end of a long and glorious empire. Conjure up visions of dizzy decadent 1930s Berlin, and you will find a 1990s Paris where everyone is seeking an escape. The current Parisian malaise invigorates and electrifies the club atmosphere. London and New York may attract the best DJs, but Paris still seduces the most BPs (Beautiful People).

## WHAT'S ON

Before you head out, find out if your favourite haunt is actually open (especially for one-nighters and, lately, for clubs). Clubbers often arrive to discover the club has been closed for a week of '*fermeture administrative*' which, in local club-owner speak, usually means a narcotics bust by the police, although for the famed Palace, bust really meant just that. The club is, at the time of writing,

awaiting new owners and its various nights have migrated to other venues. While party people like Cathy and David Guetta or Sylvie Chateigner are longstanding names on the Paris night scene, they may not always stay at the same venue.

The current club scene is dominated by House and its Latin, Jungle, Garage permutations. Techno can be found in a few venues and one-nighters, while several clubs have a night dedicated to retro disco. Afro, Acid-Jazz and Latin rhythms are worshipped in the smaller clubs. Hip late-night bars which put on DJs are an increasing phenomenon, as clubs price themselves out of the market (*see* La Flèche d'Or, Le Reservoir, Le Café de la Musique and Le Sanz Sans *in chapter* **Cafés & Bars**).

Tune in to Radio Nova (101.5 MHz) at around 6pm daily for last-minute club, concert and rave details, or at 7.15pm to Radio FG (98.2 MHz). Party flyers can be found at hip bars and at indie 'technopole' record stores such as BPM (1 rue Keller, 11th/01.40.21.02.88). The Minitel services 3615 Party News and 3615 Rave also have handy information. Entry prices, where applicable, usually include one *consommation* (drink). Many clubs accept credit cards for drinks only, not for entry.

### Les Bains

*7 rue du Bourg-l'Abbé, 3rd (01.48.87.01.80). Mº Etienne-Marcel.* **Open** *Club* 11.30-6.30am daily. *Restaurant* 9pm-1am daily. **Admission** *Club* 100F. **Drinks** 50F-70F. **Credit** AmEx, DC, MC, V.

Once Turkish baths, you can now roast in the disco packed with models and older men. Les Bains is set for a new lease of credibility since David and Cathy Guetta moved here after the demise of Le Palace. The new weekend after-hours (6am-2pm) are an attempt to attract the post-Queen crowd.

### Le Balajo

*9 rue de Lappe, 11th (01.47.00.07.87). Mº Bastille.* **Open** 11pm-5am Mon, Thur-Sat; 9pm-2am Wed. *Balmusette* 3-6.30pm Sun. **Admission** 50F-100F. **Credit** V.

The colourful West-Side story interior is unchanged since it opened in 1936. Rock 'n' roll on Wednesdays, and disco, Cuban and techno other nights.

### Le Bataclan

*50 bd Voltaire, 11th (01.47.00.39.12/30.12). Mº Voltaire.* **Open** 11pm-5am. **Admission** 100F-150F. **Drinks** 20F-50F. **No credit cards.**

Once mainly a live music venue (*see chapter* **Music: Rock, Roots & Jazz**), the Bataclan is now unsure of its identity. From a hip gay house following, it turned into a Gen X techno emporium. One-nighters are eclectic, so ring to check.

### Bus Palladium

*6 rue Fontaine, 9th (01.53.21.07.33/02.31). Mº Pigalle.* **Open** 11pm-6am Tue-Sat. **Admission** 100F Tue, Fri, Sat (girls free Tue); free Wed, Thur. **Credit** AmEx, MC, V.

This Pigalle venue belongs to the Queen-Les Bains power base, but draws a rockier, mainly French party crowd.

### La Casbah

*18-20 rue de la Forge-Royale, 11th (01.43.71.71.89). Mº Faidherbe-Chaligny.* **Open** *Bar* 8pm-4am Tue-Sun. *Disco* 11pm-6am Thur-Sat. **Admission** 80F-120F. **Drinks** 70F-90F. **Credit** AmEx, MC, V.

Despite the Moroccan souk décor and pricey North African restaurant/bar (8pm-midnight), the crowd (international *au pair* and *banlieue*) lacks the sheen of trendier days. Triphop, acid jazz and house midweek; disco/dance at weekends.

### Castel's Princess

*15 rue Princesse, 6th (01.40.51.52.80). Mº Mabillon.* **Open** 8.30pm-6am Mon-Sat. **Admission** 'members only'. **Drinks** members 95F; guests 145F. **Credit** AmEx, V.

This long-running haunt prides itself on being notoriously difficult to get into. If you care enough to try, inside you'll find a restaurant (9am-4am Tue-Sat), a disco and 1970s décor setting off the tacky showbiz types and jaded aristos.

### Le Cithéa

*114 rue Oberkampf, 11th (01.40.21.70.95). Mº Parmentier.* **Open** 9pm-5am Mon-Sat. **Admission** free. **Drinks** 25F-60F. **Credit** MC, V.

A small bar-club with dance floor up in with-it Ménilmontant. From Thursday to Saturday, live music (from salsa to jazz rock), is followed by DJs playing an eclectic mix of funky dance music, while the innovative 'Workshop' on Wednesday promises encounters between ethnic/experimental musicians and DJs who give an instant follow-on. As there is no entrance fee, the clientele is very mixed. Things can get very steamy. *See also chapter* **Music: Rock, Roots & Jazz**.

### Le Colonial

*port Debilly, quai de New York, 16th (01.53.23.98.98). Mº Alma-Marceau.* **Open** 11.30pm-dawn Mon-Sat. **Admission** free. **Drinks** 40F-80F. **Credit** AmEx, DC, MC, V.

# Winning the nightclub battle

• **Wear Black:** This goes for men and women. Women should always be dressed in something short, tight and sexy. The same rule could apply to men depending on the venue. Although Paris is the fashion capital of the world, there is little evidence of this inside the clubs.

• **Show Attitude:** Don't be intimidated by the door people's attitude. Any hesitation can result in automatic rejection. Be confident, act like you belong in this club. Even better, act like you own it.

• **Talk Fashion:** While waiting in line at the door drop a few fashion names, preferably British and American designers. Door people are always seduced by the superficiality of the fashion world.

• **Bring a Model:** If all fails, bring a model (of either sex) with you. An attractive companion is your automatic visa to the inside.

• **Use the Same Bartender:** Always go back to the same bartender and tip generously at first. The drinks will acquire a higher alcohol content

with each visit. This can save a lot of money in the long run as drinks prices are extortionate.

• **Order Champagne:** The fastest ticket to a VIP area is to order champagne. This will allow you and your friends to actually sit down and sneer at lesser mortals milling about upright. At least 800F a bottle, try splitting the cost.

• **Use Your Foreign Charm:** Mistakenly labelled the City of Love, Paris is the City of Sex. Don't be put off by the cold attitude of Parisian nocturnals, they can easily be disarmed by a few words of English or French with a charming accent.

• **Getting Home:** If you're part of the mass exodus at 5am, be prepared to wait for a taxi with scores of revellers. The driver will ask where you're going before he even opens the door. If you're only going a short way, mutter something about the airport, then say you've changed your mind half way to your destination.

**Le Queen**, *guarded by its 'physiognomists', remains the happening nightspot in Paris.*

Moored opposite the Eiffel Tower, this 70m yacht has a restaurant (8pm-1am), romantic bar in the former first-class cabins and a club on the lower decks. Eclectic music.

### Les Coulisses

*5 rue du Mont-Cenis (pl du Tertre), 18th (01.42.62.89.99). M° Abbesses.* **Open** 11.30pm-4am Tue-Sun. **Admission** free Tue-Thur, Sun; 100F Fri, Sat. **Drinks** from 50F. **Credit** AmEx, DC, MC, V.

The theatrical La Comédie has a new restaurant (8pm-2am) and a new name, but, perched so close to the tourist heart of Montmartre, it's unlikely to get the clientele it seeks. The basement décor is fun, though – gilt chairs and Italian Baroque-inspired stage sets – and less mainstream than the music.

### Elysée Montmartre

*72 bd Rochechouart, 18th (01.44.92.45.42). M° Anvers.* **Open** 11pm-5am Sat, some other nights. **Admission** 80F-100F. **Drinks** from 30F. **No credit cards.**

The fortnightly *Bal* is perhaps the best, least-pretentious fun in town where all types and ages rock 'n' roll, yé yé and java to a big band. Sylvie Chateigner's Thanx God I'm a VIP draws fashion people, gay muscle boys and drag queens to big-name guest DJs from London's Ministry of Sound or New York's Tunnel. Monthly salsa parties. *See also chapter* **Music: Rock, Roots & Jazz**.

### Folies Pigalle

*11 pl Pigalle, 9th (01.40.36.71.58). M° Pigalle.* **Open** 11pm-7am Thur-Sat. **Admission** 100F. **Drinks** 50F. **Credit** AmEx, DC, MC, V.

A great club for people-watching as the dance floor is overlooked by a balcony furnished with red velvet cinema seats. The weekends are sacrificed to House and Garage and attract friendly BP; 50:50 gay and straight all willing to shake their stuff. Look out for the *Bal des Folies* on Sundays (3-8pm) when the 'physiognomist' is given the day off and young, old (and tourists) dance to accordion *musette*, disco and rock.

### Le Gibus

*18 rue du Fbg-du-Temple, 11th (01.47.00.78.88). M° République.* **Open** 11.30pm-7am Tue-Sun. **Admission** 50F-80F. **Drinks** 30F-50F. **Credit** AmEx, DC, MC, V.

Long a grungy rock club, the Gibus (French for folding opera hat) now makes an ideal location for trance, techno and jungle nights. Once you get past the huge gates and bouncers, the club is small and cave-like with an ample dance floor and a chill-out area. A very mixed, relaxed crowd goes for it on the dance floor. Dress casual for a hot and sweaty night out.

### La Locomotive

*90 bd de Clichy, 18th (01.53.41.88.88). M° Blanche.* **Open** 11pm-6am daily. **Admission** 70F-105F. **Credit** AmEx, DC, MC, V.

This mammoth three-storey venue next to the Moulin Rouge draws a teenage crowd but is aiming to get the punters back with Max of Fun Radio on Friday nights and the Gay Tea Dance, a refugee from Le Palace, on Sunday, 5-11pm.

### Le Néo

*21 rue Montorgueil, 1st (01.42.33.39.33). M° Châtelet-Les Halles.* **Open** 11pm-6am Wed-Sun. **Admission** 60F-80F. **Drinks** 25F-45F. **Credit** MC, V.

A tightly packed labyrinth of cellars with cooler chill-out area, a bar and smallish dance floor draws different types to its mix of evenings. Firmly in a soul, funk groove Fridays and Saturdays; hip hop, Gothic, disco or ambient other nights.

### Le Queen

*102 av des Champs-Elysées, 8th (01.53.89.08.90). M° George V.* **Open** midnight-dawn daily. **Admission** 50F Mon; free Tue-Thur, Sun; 80F Fri, Sat. **Drinks** 50F. **Credit** AmEx, DC, V.

Now firmly reigning as hippest nightspot. Though certain events are male-only, such as the summer Mousse parties (foam parties, don't ask), it appeals across the board. The most hetero is Wednesday's Respect, when door staff are less hostile to women. 1970s disco on Monday; otherwise it's House all the way. Look out for big-name guests and the monthly Boy parties. *See also chapter* **Gay & Lesbian**.

### Rex Club

*5 bd Poissonnière, 2nd (01.42.36.83.98). M° Bonne-Nouvelle.* **Open** 11.30pm-6am Mon-Sun. **Admission** 60F-80F. **Drinks** 60F-80F. **Credit** MC, V.

Now firmly anchored in the House-Techno orbit, with star DJ Laurent Garnier more or less resident on Thursdays. Look out also for guests like London's Carl Cox or New York's Damon Wild and Josh Wink. A young, stylish crowd can seem a little snobbish, but once you've made it down the long cat-walk to the slippery dance floor, anything goes.

### Le Saint

*7 rue St-Séverin, 5th (01.43.25.50.04). M° St-Michel.* **Open** 11pm-5am Tue-Sun. **Admission** 60F-90F. **Drinks** 15F-50F. **Credit** MC, V.

Three communicating thirteenth-century cellars in which well-bred students and *au pairs* dance the night away to an eclectic mix from French pop oldies and disco to house numbers and techno. Very studenty, thanks to the cheap drinks.

### Shéhérazade

*3 rue de Liège 9th (01.42 85 53 78). M° Place de Clichy.* **Open** 11pm-6am Fri, Sat. **Admission** around 80F-100F. **Credit** MC, V.

The red and gold columns of this Arabian Nights style grotto alone make this venue worth a visit, although it's been suffering noise complaints from the neighbours. Friday's Planet Rock with DJ Grebo is a pop and indie favourite with Brits and young BCBGs; other events vary (dance, salsa, Latin...).

### Villa Barclay

*3 av Matignon, 8th (01.53.89.18.91). M° Franklin D Roosevelt.* **Open** *Bar* 11pm-2.30am Mon-Wed, Sun; 11pm-4am Thur-Sat. *Club* 11pm-5am Thur-Sat. **Admission** 100F. **Drinks** 40F-70F **Credit** AmEx, DC, MC, V.

The former Safari has undergone the full BCBG treatment.

Decorated by the Hôtel Costes designer Jacques Garcia, the place buzzes with the young, moneyed of Neuilly. There's a bar, restaurant and piano bar, but best is the downstairs disco. The DJ spins groovy rather than crucial cuts.

### Le Village
*40 rue Fontaine, 9th (01.40.16.40.24). M° Pigalle.* **Open** midnight-5am Fri, Sat. **Admission** 100F. **Drinks** 25F-50F **Credit** AmEx, DC, MC, V.
Another mini-club to sprout up in Pigalle, the Village (after Village People) prides itself on being stuck in a '70s and '80s timewarp. The door policy ensures only over-25s get in.

### What's Up Bar
*15 rue Daval, 11th (01.48.05.88.33). M° Bastille.* **Open** 8pm-2am Mon-Thur, Sun; 8pm-4am Fri, Sat. **Drinks** 15F-40F. **Admission** free Mon-Thur, Sun; 50F after midnight Fri, Sat. **Credit** MC, V.
Designer music bar, What's Up resembles a sparse concrete bunker. Features hip DJs every night with the latest sounds. A selective door policy make it a halfway-point between bar and club, but finding enough space to dance is a challenge.

## Afro/Latin

### La Chapelle des Lombards
*19 rue de Lappe, 11th (01.43.57.24.24). M° Bastille.* **Open** 8pm-dawn Thur; 10.30pm-dawn Fri, Sat. **Admission** 100F Thur (with concert), 70F after; 120F Fri, Sat. **Drinks** 30F-70F. **Credit** AmEx, MC, V.
Like the Balajo on rue de Lappe, this club has been pumping out hot dance sounds of 'all that is tropical' for over 15 years, but then pick-up joints just never die. Unaccompanied gents may run into trouble at the door – don't wear trainers. There's a live concert (chiefly Latin) at 8pm on Thursday.

*Party to a variety of sounds at **Le Tango**.*

### Dancing de la Coupole
*102 bd du Montparnasse, 14th (01.43.20.14.20). M° Montparnasse-Bienvenüe or Vavin.* **Open** ring to check. **Admission** 90F. **Drinks** 45F-60F. **Credit** AmEx, DC, MC, V.
The glitzy basement of the famous Art Deco brasserie (*see chapter* **Restaurants**) mainly spins retro and disco, but look out for the Latin/salsa seasons.

### Divan du Monde
*75 rue des Martyrs, 18th (01.44.92.77.66). M° Pigalle.* **Open** 7.30pm-4am daily. **Admission** 40F-80F. **Drinks** from 20F. **Credit** MC, V.
Once a cabaret depicted by Toulouse-Lautrec, this is a happening place for DJs and MCs with the accent on street (break-dancers at weekends). Pibamos crew presents bands, art, DJs and cabaret; Black Sugar (two Sundays a month) puts on fashion shows by Afro-Caribbean designers and plays soul, reggae and funk. *See chapter* **Music: Rock, Roots & Jazz**.

### Les Etoiles
*61 rue du Château d'Eau, 10th (01.47.70.60.56). M° Château d'Eau.* **Open** 9pm-4am Thur-Sat. **Admission** 100F at 9pm food and concert; 60F at 11pm for concert. **Drinks** 40F-70F. **No credit cards**.
This rundown music hall claims to be the oldest venue to have continuously presented live music in Paris, and one of the first in the world to have exhibited talking motion pictures. Top-quality live *salseros* are the staple of the menu.

### La Java
*105 rue du Fbg-du-Temple, 11th (01.42.02.20.52). M° Belleville.* **Open** 9pm-5am Tue, Thur-Sat. **Drinks** 30F. **Admission** 60F-90F. **Credit** MC, V.
La Java has perfectly preserved its old-world atmosphere down to the Morocco leather booths from 1928, the year it opened. There's a top salsa band (Thur-Sat) followed by DJs playing Latin American music for an enthusiastic older crowd. Java regulars may even give you a free dance lesson. A superbly relaxed atmosphere. World music bands Tue.

### Le Tango
*13 rue au Maire, 3rd (01.42.72.17.78). M° Arts et Métiers.* **Open** 11pm-5am Fri, Sat. **Admission** 60F. **Drinks** from 25F. **No credit cards**.
The funky Afro-Caribbean evenings at this old dance hall are now only on Saturdays. Friday (and some Thursdays) varies with anything from gay *musette* to techno.

## Guinguettes

Clustered along the Marne river south-east of Paris, the *guinguette* dance halls are a tribute to France's rustic past of red wine and the accordion.

### Chez Gégène
*162 quai de Polangis, Joinville-le-Pont (01.48.83.29.43). RER Joinville-le-Pont.* **Open** Apr-mid Oct 9pm-2am Fri, Sat, 3-7pm Sun. **Admission** 90F; 210F with meal. **Credit** AmEx, MC, V.
The classic *guinguette*, unaltered for years. Elderly French dance fiends, families and young Parisians pack the place.

### Le Martin-Pêcheur
*41 quai Victor-Hugo, Champigny-sur-Marne (01.49.83.03.02). RER Champigny.* **Open** Mar-May, Sept-Nov 8pm-2am Tue-Sat; noon-8pm Sun. June-Aug 8pm-2am Mon-Sat; noon-midnight Sun. **Admission** from 30F. **No credit cards**.
The youngest and hippest of the *guinguettes* on tiny island in the Marne. Great music, cute young trendies trying to look like Jean Gabin and Edith Piaf, and a live band on Fri-Sat.

# Dance

**From the highly stylised and contemporary to the more traditional and romantic, dance forms are flourishing in Paris.**

In spite of complaints in cultural circles that the no-longer young 'young' contemporary dance scene in France has reached a dead-end, indulging in nihilism, violence and simulated sexual abuse, Paris has become over the past decade the dance capital of the world. No city can boast more performance spaces devoted to choreography, festivals and dance centres, and audiences are growing as, with multi-media the name of the game, dance, theatre and the visual arts are merging into a distinct form of entertainment.

Big-time funded national choreographic centres abound in the provinces, directed by the nation's leading choreographers, such as Angelin Preljocaj, Karine Saporta and Mathile Monnier, but the pressure to produce often results in an expensive and confused letdown. The **Théâtre de la Ville** remains the indisputable (but sold-out) showcase for these avant-garde artists, as well as for visiting foreign companies like Sankai Juko and Merce Cunningham. Meanwhile, the **Ballet de l'Opéra National de Paris** maintains its role as guardian of the classical ballet tradition, yet increasingly dares to present ultra-modern works like the surprise addition to the repertory of a way-out Pina Bausch piece in 1997. The most exciting dance is being created in the independent spaces around Paris like **Danse, Théâtre & Musique** and its affiliated company Tendanse, the **Regard du Cygne** and a few well-established theatres, including **Théâtre de la Bastille** and **Théâtre Dunois**.

## Dance Venues

### Ballet de l'Opéra National de Paris

*Palais Garnier, pl de l'Opéra, 9th (01.44.73.13.00). M° Opéra.* **Box office** 11am-6.30pm Mon-Sat: telephone bookings 11am-6pm Mon-Sat. **Tickets** 30F-380F (reductions for some matinées). **Credit** AmEx, MC, V. *Opéra de Paris Bastille, pl de la Bastille, 12th (01.44.73.13.00). M° Bastille.* **Box office** 11am-6pm Mon-Sat. **Tickets** 45F-380F. **Credit** AmEx, V.
After renovation, the sumptuous Palais Garnier is now host to an even richer selection of classical works, keeping die-hard ballet fans happy with standard and revised hits such as the *Nutcracker*, besides giving its versatile stars like Marie-Claude Pietragalla, Nicolas Le Riche and Fanny Gaïda a chance to show off their modern dance prowess in mixed programmes of works by Jiri Kylian, Angelin Preljocaj, Carolyn Carlson and Pina Bausch. The Bastille highlights opera, with the occasional big-scale, crowd-pulling dance production. *See also chapter* **Sightseeing**. *Wheelchair access at Bastille, notify when booking.*

*A **Tendanse** for the avant-garde.*

### Théâtre de la Ville

*2 pl du Châtelet, 4th (01.42.74.22.77). M° Châtelet-Les Halles.* **Box office** 11am-6pm Mon; 11am-8pm Tue-Sat; telephone bookings 9am-6pm Mon; 9am-8pm Tue-Sat. **Tickets** 80F-190F; 60F-120F under-25s. **Credit** DC, MC, V.
Paris' leading contemporary dance forum and gathering spot for the cultural elite's Who's Who, founded by the nineteenth-century actress Sarah Bernhardt. This 1,000-seat modern auditorium has excellent sight lines and a strong policy of co-productions to aid the creation of challenging new pieces. Wim Wandeykebus, Anne Teresa de Keersmaeker, Mathilde Monnier, Jan Fabre, Pina Bausch and Carolyn Carlson make regular appearances. *See also chapters* **Music: Classical & Opera, Music: Rock, Roots & Jazz,** *and* **Theatre.** *Wheelchair access.*

### Centre Pompidou

*19 rue Beaubourg, 4th (box office 01.44.78.13.15). M° Rambuteau.* **Box office** from noon on day of performance. **Tickets** 70F-90F. **No credit cards.**
The Grande Salle features dance works by contemporary dance companies and hosts the annual Video Dance festival. Like the rest of the Centre, it will close from late 1997 to 1999. *Wheelchair access.*

### Châtelet – Théâtre Musical de Paris

*1 pl du Châtelet, 1st (01.40.28.28.40). M° Châtelet-Les Halles.* **Box office** 11am-7pm daily; telephone bookings 10am-7pm. **Tickets** concerts 70F-200F; operas 70F-570F. **Credit** AmEx, MC, V.
Used for opera and classical concerts, Châtelet-TMP also plays host to visiting ballet companies. William Forsythe and

Ballet Frankfurt will continue their annual residency until the end of 1997. *See also chapter* **Music: Classical & Opera.**

## Théâtre de la Bastille
*76 rue de la Roquette, 11th (01.43.57.42.14).*
*M° Bastille.* **Box office** 10am-6.45pm Mon-Fri; 2.30-6.45pm Sat. **Tickets** 100F; over-60s, students, unemployed 70F. **Credit** AmEx, DC, MC, V.
High-quality experimental dance works alternate with theatre productions in two different spaces. Besides crowd-pleasers such as a video-dance creation by Meredith Monk, the theatre searches out experimental young choreographers for new productions. *See also chapter* **Theatre.** *Wheelchair access.*

## Théâtre des Champs-Elysées
*15 av Montaigne, 8th (01.49.52.50.00).*
*M° Alma-Marceau.* **Box office** 11am-7pm Mon-Sat; telephone bookings 10am-noon, 2-6pm, Mon-Sat. **Tickets** 40F-500F. **Credit** V.
This elegant, 1,900-seat theatre, made famous by modern dance pioneer Isadora Duncan before World War I, attracts a well-heeled crowd. Mainly a classical music venue, it also holds regular tango and flamenco programmes and the Paris International Dance Competition. *See also chapter* **Music: Classical & Opera.**

# Independent Dance Spaces

## Centre Mandapa
*6 rue Wurtz, 13th (01.45.89.01.60). M° Glacière.* **Box office** open 30min before performance Mon-Sat. **Tickets** 80F-100F. Reductions 60F-70F. **No credit cards.**
Dedicated to traditional dance forms. Companies from India, China, the Middle East, North Africa and Eastern Europe visit regularly. It also houses a school of Indian dance. *Wheelchair access.*

## Danse, Théâtre & Musique
*6 rue de la Folie Méricourt, 11th (01.47.00.19.60).*
*M° St-Ambroise.* **Box office** 10am-7pm. **Tickets** 35F (lectures); 80F. Group rates and reductions 60F.
**No credit cards.**
DTM is one of the friendliest, and most dynamic spaces (60-seat) in town, offering classes in dance, theatre and music, and presenting festivals, children's events and performances by the centre's affiliated company **Tendanse**, as well as by international companies. Tea and discussion after events.

## Dix-Huit Théâtre
*16 rue Georgette Agutte, 18th (01.42.26.47.47).*
*M° Guy-Môquet.* **Box office** 10am-6pm Mon-Fri; telephone bookings 11am-7pm Mon-Fri. **Tickets** 50F-120F. Reductions 59F, 80F. **Credit** (over 100F) V.
The Dix-Huit is off the beaten track, but the quality of programmes attracts a faithful crowd. Dance productions alternate year-round with theatre works; three or four different dance companies, such as Cécile Proust's and Philippe Jamet's, usually inaugurate the autumn season over a month-long period (Sept/Oct), start off the post-holiday period (Jan/Feb), and close the season in July. *Wheelchair access.*

## Le Regard du Cygne
*210 rue de Belleville, 20th (Bookings answerphone 01.43.58.55.93). M° Place des Fêtes.* **Tickets** 70F.
**No credit cards.**
Tucked away off the beaten track at the back of a courtyard, this converted seventeenth-century wood-beamed, stone barn has played an important part over the past decade in promoting new choreographic talent through its eclectic Worksweek festivals. Events guarantee at least one surprise discovery. It also hopes to put on theatre and music in future.

## Théâtre Dunois
*108 rue du Chevaleret, 13th (01.45.84.72.00).*
*M° Chevaleret.* **Box office** 10am-6pm Mon-Fri. **Tickets** 50F-100F. **No credit cards.**
After renovation, the Dunois' new, eclectic policy favours contemporary dance and dance-theatre. Jean Guizerix, Maïte Fossen and Elsa Wolliaston have all performed here.

# Dance Centres

## Centre de Ressources Musique et Danse
*Cité de la Musique, 221 av Jean-Jaurès, 19th (01.44.84.45.00). M° Porte de Pantin.* **Open** noon-6pm Tue-Sat; 10am-6pm Sun.
A great new state-of-the art documentation centre for dance and music, the Centre boasts over 20,000 videos, CDs, books, scores, magazines, archival material and databases.

## Fédération Française de Danse
*12 rue St-Germain l'Auxerrois, 1st (01.42.36.12.61).*
*M° Châtelet-Les Halles.* **Open** 9am-5pm Mon-Fri.
Paris' main clearing house for information on the current dance scene if you're seeking facts and figures, names of teachers or upcoming auditions and job offers.

## Théâtre Contemporain de la Danse (TCD)
*9 rue Geoffroy l'Asnier, 4th (01.42.74.44.22).*
*M° Pont Marie.* **Open** 9.30am-6.30pm Tue-Fri.
The main hang-out for the professional modern dance crowd, TDC promotes dance programmes in association with Théâtre de la Ville and several suburban performance spaces. It organises public studio performances, publishes studies through its documentation centre and hosts professional workshops with renowned choreographers such as Carolyn Carlson and Betty Jones.

## Centre de Danse du Marais
*41 rue du Temple, 4th (01.42.72.15.42). M° Hôtel-de-Ville.*
**Open** 9am-9pm Mon-Sat; 9am-7pm Sun. **Classes** average price 85F; 12 lessons for 700F.
You name the technique, this Mecca for aspiring dancers of all ages has got it. With multiple studios and packed classes, this is the ultimate hypermarket for the dance consumer.

## Académie des Arts Chorégraphiques
*4bis Cité Véron, 18th (01.42.52.07.29).*
*M° Blanche.* **Open** 9am-9pm Mon-Sat; 11am-7pm Sun.
**Classes** average price 70F; 10 classes 600F.
This three-studio triplex space is one of Paris' friendliest dance centres. It is home for several dance schools, including the Tchaika Ballet School.

## Studio Harmonic
*5 passage des Taillandiers, 11th (01.48.07.13.39).*
*M° Bastille.* **Open** 9.30am-10pm Mon-Fri; 9.30am-7pm Sat.
**Classes** 79F; 20 classes for 1180F. **No credit cards.**
This trendy dance school draws a young, high-adrenalin crowd. Professional dance training in contemporary and modern jazz, as well as a wide range of amateur classes.

## Ménagerie de Verre
*12-14 rue Lechevin, 11th (01.43.38.33.44). M° Parmentier.*
**Open** 10am-6pm Mon-Fri. Classes in the morning, 65F.
Home to France's new National Dance Centre, it offers daily morning workshop classes or masters' classes with Europe's leading contemporary choreographers.

## Salle Pleyel
*252 rue du Fbg-St-Honoré, 8th (01.45.61.53.00).*
*M° Ternes.* **Open** 9am-6pm Mon-Fri.
Various, mostly ballet-oriented, dance schools, such as the Stanlowa and Goubé Schools, are housed in the spaces located above and below the posh Salle Pleyel concert hall.

# Film

**Long symbolised by the romantically shabby Left Bank picture house, the world capital of serious cinema is getting a facelift.**

Big money is now being thrown at Paris screens. Following the global trend, a number of key cinemas have undergone transformation into stylish multiplexes. **UGC Ciné Cité** is a subterranean ciné-sprawl below Les Halles. Place de Clichy is now dominated by the towering facade of **Pathé Wepler**, while **Gaumont** has an eleven-screen flagship in Montparnasse. At Bercy a brand new multiplex will bring celluloid life to this eastern *quartier*, while directly across the Seine a different venue hopes to draw on the intelligentsia using the new national library. 'This area of the 13th *arrondissement* will be the Latin Quarter of the year 2000,' claims MK2 boss Marin Karmitz.

However, cinephiles with a taste for the endearingly dog-eared need not despair. Cash-strapped independent repertory cinemas live on. Together the old and new manage to present weekly over 300 films, from blockbusters to Buñuel.

The avant garde MK2 group has invested heavily in its 14 Juillet chain which now has a 10 per cent share of the Paris audience, and offers ciné events, director talks and film promotions. The shape of things to come for the group is the **14 Juillet sur Seine**, a welcome arrival which has helped transform an area before famed only for crack dealing.

Meanwhile the French filmmakers of ARP are flying the flag for French cinema in Pigalle. Known as the **Cinéma des Cinéastes**, such a grandly named establishment could only call Paris home.

## PRACTICAL INFORMATION

Details of current programmes can be found in *Pariscope* and *l'Officiel des Spectacles*. Programmes change on Wednesdays. Films shown in their original language, with French subtitles, are identified as VO (*version originale*). VF (*version française*) films are dubbed into French. The occasional VA (*version anglaise*) signifies a film made by a French director in English, such as Luc Besson's *Léon*.

The Latin Quarter remains home to the golden oldie and obscure exotica; the Champs-Elysées, St-Germain and Montparnasse score for first runs. Expect screenings at around 2pm, 4pm, 6pm, 8pm and 10pm, often with late shows on Saturday. Tickets cost about 45F, but many cinemas offer 20-30 per cent off on Mondays and/or Wednesdays. Student discounts (*réduction étudiante/tarif réduit*) are available at early shows during the week but rarely on Friday nights, at weekends or

*Le Champo champions celluloid classics.*

on public holidays. Many of the independents and mini-chains offer their own *carte de fidelité*: after a number of screenings, you're entitled to another film free of charge. The Gaumont and UGC chains each issue discount cards valid at all their cinemas.

### Allô Ciné
*(01.47.47.74.85).*
A free, 24-hour film information service (in French only) details films by category or area.

## In the Wings

### Les Etoiles du Rex
*Le Grand Rex, 1 bd Poissonnière, 2nd (08.36.68.70.23).* *M° Bonne Nouvelle.* **Visit** every 10 mins 10am-7.30pm Wed, Sat, Sun, public holidays. **Admission** 40F adults; 35F under 26, students. 69F tour and film.
The 40-minute behind the scenes tour of the huge Art Deco Rex cinema is a wacky high-tech experience. After a presentation showing the construction of the auditorium, visitors ascend behind the big screen in a unique chance to see cinema from the other side. Further surprises are in store: the inner sanctum of the projection booth mock-up, newsreel footage of Rex history highlights and an insight into film production tricks with sensurround effects to jolt the strongest nerves.

## Ciné Showcases

### Le Cinéma des Cinéastes
*7 av de Clichy, 17th (01.53.42.40.00). M° Place Clichy.*
In keeping with the right-on persuasions of French cineastes, this three-screen shrine to the cinema opened in October 1996 in a slickly converted local fleapit just off place de Clichy. Masterminds behind this showcase of the best of world cinema (with France at the forefront) are Jean-Jacques (*Betty Blue*) Beneix and Claude Lelouch, president of ARP, the association of French cinema directors and producers. Opening attractions included Cocteau's *Beauty and the Beast*, accompanied by piano, and a Muhammad Ali screen portrait.

# Paris as a film set

From *The Aristocats* cavorting on the rooftops to the Gare d'Orsay in Kafka-esque disguise in Orson Welles' *The Trial*, romance with *Forget Paris* and revolution with *Jefferson in Paris*, only New York rivals Paris as the world's most-filmed city. The Hôtel de Ville gladly accommodates film crews, and Parisians indulge the disruption they cause, which only enhances the chic of their town. Many succumb to the ultimate cliché – the view of the Eiffel Tower from the Trocadéro. But for every shot of the tower, there is an off-beat Parisian nook immortalised on celluloid that's worth discovering.

**Jules et Jim** *the classic* ménage à trois.

### Hôtel du Nord (1938)

Even though most scenes of this hotel by the Canal St-Martin were actually shot in a studio, it's now a national monument – as was leading lady Arletty in this Marcel Carné film. In front of the hotel, our shrill heroine uttered scathingly the immortal 'Atmosphere! Atmosphere!'

### Funny Face (1956)

Audrey Hepburn was in her element filming in Paris. In this *très* fashion number with Fred Astaire, she sings 'Bonjour Pareee' to a range of Paris sights, including, the ubiquitous Eiffel Tower and Champs-Elysées. A photo shoot takes Audrey and Co to the Opéra Garnier, but best is the existentialist dance in a Montmartre cellar bar.

### A Bout de Souffle (Breathless, 1959)

Godard's classic tale of girl-meets-vagabond, with a lovingly observed Jean Seberg as the cutest *Trib* vendor on the Champs-Elysées. The offices where she picked up copies have since moved to more prosaic Neuilly, but you can pitch up like Seberg at their former building at 21 rue de Berri, in the 8th. Otherwise, stand significantly in the middle of rue Campagne-Première in Montparnasse to relive a timeless image of Belmondo.

### Zazie dans le Métro (1960)

A real Paris imagefest. Louis Malle's film offers the ultimate New Wave Paris tour in the company of impish Zazie. The whole city is featured, but the star of the show is the Eiffel Tower, scene of some truly vertiginous images.

### Jules et Jim (1961)

Are they coming or going from the wrong side of the

*Narcissus rules in* **Last Tango in Paris.**

tracks? Jeanne Moreau and her two suitors in the most famous still from Truffaut's *nouvelle vague* classic are on the bridge behind Gare de l'Est, off rue de l'Aqueduc.

### What's New Pussycat? (1965)

This fabled 1960s psychedelic cult film was largely set in Paris. Woody Allen in goggles and a three-wheeled car scatters the tables and customers of the famed Closerie des Lilas in Montparnasse *(see chapter* **Cafés & Bars***)*.

### Last Tango in Paris (1972)

Bertolucci traversed the city, including the memorable crossing of the Pont Bir-Hakeim by Métro. Brando heads for a steamy rendezvous with Maria Schneider in a Passy apartment, overlooking the Passy Métro station.

### Diva (1981)

The trigger for this operatic drama is the misdirection of a cassette into the pouches of the young postman on his moped. Revisit the bloody scene at the post office at the rear entrance to Gare St-Lazare, on rue d'Amsterdam.

### Subway (1985)

*Enfant terrible* Luc Besson's notorious subterranean world of hustlers and hassle is a million miles from the cute postcard world of Paris. Christophe Lambert and Isabelle Adjani most frequently turn up at the RER in La Défense and Les Halles. Hold onto your handbag.

### Three Colours: Blue (1993)

Juliette Binoche goes to great lengths in the pretty Piscine de Pontoise *(see chapter* **Sport & Fitness***)* dressed up for the occasion for the Blue part of Kieslowski's *liberté, egalité, fraternité* trilogy, and downed many a coffee in Café Mouffetard *(see chapter* **Cafés & Bars***)*.

### Pret à Porter (1994)

Robert Altman took on the fashion world in chic locations across the capital: notably a room at the Grand Hôtel, where Tim Robbins and Julia Roberts got acrobatic under a duvet, the Bagatelle gardens and the Tout Paris Party at Ledoyen on the Champs-Elysées.

### La Haine (1995)

Matthieu Kassovitz's grainy black and white agitprop opus was mostly shot in the *banlieue* of Chanteloup-les-Vignes outside Paris, but came intra-muros for the protagonists to meet the art bourgeoisie. Our three likely lads outrage the art world at a *vernissage* at Galerie Gilbert Brownstone in the Marais.

### Gaumont Grand Ecran Italie
*30 pl d'Italie, 13th (01.45.80.77.00). M° Place d'Italie.*
In a complex designed by Japanese architect Kenzo Tange, the 24m by 10m screen and THX sound suit big-screen extravaganzas. Avoid the two small screens.
*Wheelchair access.*

### Gaumont Montparnasse
*3 rue d'Odessa, 14th (08.36.68.75.55).*
*M° Montparnasse-Bienvenüe.*
Two Montparnasse cinemas transformed into a glitzy multiplex: eleven screens, bar and the obligatory Internet.
*Air conditioning. Bar. Wheelchair access.*

### Max Linder Panorama
*24 bd Poissonnière, 9th (01.48.24.88.88/ 08.36.68.00.31). M° Rue Montmartre.*
A state-of-the-art screening facility in a house founded in 1919 by comic Max Linder. Look out for all-nighters.
*Air conditioning. Wheelchair access.*

### La Pagode
*57 bis rue de Babylone, 7th (08.36.68.75.07).*
*M° St-François-Xavier.*
A genuine pagoda built in 1896: the wooden framework came from Japan, while most of the lavish glass and ceramic detailing was created in Paris. It became a cinema in 1931.
*Salon de thé. Wheelchair access to Salle Japonaise.*

### Pathé Wepler
*140 bd de Clichy, 18th (08.36.68.20.22). M° Place Clichy.*
A brightly lit, twelve-screen edifice unusual in a city where cinemas are hideaways. Latest releases, mostly dubbed.
*Air conditioning. Wheelchair access to some screens.*

### 14 Juillet sur Seine
*14 quai de la Seine, 19th (08.36.68.47.07). M° Stalingrad.*
This stylish six-screen, waterfront complex, complete with restaurant and exhibition space offers an all-in-one night out.
*Air conditioning. Restaurant. Wheelchair access.*

### UGC Ciné Cité Les Halles
*pl de la Rotonde, Nouveau Forum des Halles, 1st (08.36.68.68.58). M° Châtelet-Les Halles.*

This ambitous 15-screen development offered Parisians their first taste of the multiplex. Seating in certain theatres is built on a fearsome angle adding that north face of the Eiger *frisson* to any good movie. The usual facilities, plus the inevitable Internet cafe.

## The Left Bank Ciné Village

The art cinemas crowded in the 5th and 6th *arrondissements* make up a truly unique collection of screens all within walking distance of each other. Quaint, even rundown, they offer the most diverse programming in the world.

### Action
**Action Christine** *4 rue Christine, 6th (01.43.29.11.30/ 08.36.65.70.62). M° Odéon.*
**Action Ecoles** *23 rue des Ecoles, 5th (01.43.25.72.07/ 08.36.65.70.64). M° Maubert-Mutualité.*
**Grand Action** *5 rue des Ecoles, 5th (01.43.29.44.40/ 08.36.65.70.63). M° Cardinal-Lemoine.*
*Wheelchair access to at least one screen.*
**Mac Mahon** *5 av Mac Mahon, 17th (01.43.29.79.89/ 08.36.65.70.48). M° Charles de Gaulle-Etoile.*
Home from home for those nostalgic for 1940s and '50s Tinseltown classics – recent series have included Cary Grant, Westerns and musicals. Showpiece is the Grand Action.

### Le Champo
*51 rue des Ecoles, 5th (01.43.54.51.60).*
*M° Cluny-La Sorbonne.*
A charming Latin Quarter veteran with a seemingly nonstop supply of Hitchcock and vintage gems. Neighbouring Quartier Latin (9 rue Champollion) and Reflet Médicis Logos (3 rue Champollion) are also worth checking for their international art-house programming.
*Wheelchair access to one screen.*

### Europa Panthéon
*13 rue Victor Cousin, 5th (01.43.54.15.04).*
*M° Cluny-La Sorbonne/RER Luxembourg.*
Founded in 1907 in the Sorbonne gymnasium, this is Paris' oldest movie house. Screenings range from Rossellini to Russian movies to new releases by young French directors.

*New port of call for cinephiles at the **14 Juillet sur Seine**.*

### St-André-des-Arts
*30 rue St-André-des-Arts, 6th (01.43.26.48.18); 12 rue Gît-le-Coeur, 6th (01.43.26.80.25). M° St-Michel.*
A two-screen renowned for its quality programming – Mike Leigh, Bergman, Kieslowski, classic retrospectives, and a range of shorts. Occasional meet-the-director sessions. *Wheelchair access to salle 2.*

### Studio Galande
*42 rue Galande, 5th (01.43.26.94.08/08.36.65.72.05). M° St-Michel.*
A hole-in-the-wall institution that holds high the tradition of *The Rocky Horror Picture Show*, every Friday and Saturday at 10.30pm and 12.10am. It also regularly shows *A Clockwork Orange*, amid a wide range of art movies.

### Studio des Ursulines
*10 rue des Ursulines, 5th (01.43.26.19.09). RER Luxembourg.*
Arthouse pioneer since 1926. It went on to screen incendiary avant-garde films, but now offers a repertory programme. *Wheelchair access.*

### Les 3 Luxembourg
*67 rue Monsieur le Prince, 6th (01.46.33.97.77/ 08.36.63.93.25). M° Odéon/RER Luxembourg.*
Not too comfortable, but a superb selection of international movies has included tributes to Cassavetes, Godard and Japanese director Yasujiro Ozu.

## Other Art Cinemas

### Le Balzac
*1 rue Balzac, 8th (01.45.61.10.60). M° George V.*
Built in 1935 with a mock ocean-liner foyer, Le Balzac scores highly for both design and programming.

### Denfert
*24 pl Denfert-Rochereau, 14th (01.43.21.41.01). M° Denfert-Rochereau.*
A valiant little place with hugely eclectic repertory selection from Ealing Comedies to Eric Rohmer and new animation. *Wheelchair access.*

### Elysées Lincoln
*14 rue Lincoln, 8th (01.43.59.36.14/08.36.68.81.07). M° George V.* **Reduced price** Mon, Wed and up to 6.30pm Tue-Fri.
Arthouse cinema shows smaller-scale and independent films, and organises frequent meet-the-director screenings.

### L'Entrepôt
*7-9 rue Francis de Pressensé, 14th (01.45.43.41.63). M° Pernéty.*
Based in a former warehouse, L'Entrepôt offers three bare screening rooms, a cinema bookshop and a restaurant and bar. New or Third World directors, shorts, gay cinema and retrospectives all get a look in. *Air-conditioning. Wheelchair access to Salle 1.*

### Le Latina
*20 rue du Temple, 4th (01.42.78.47.86). M° Hôtel-de-Ville.*
Le Latina (established 1913) screens films from Spain, Portugal and Latin America. There are also Latin-themed dances, a gallery and a lively Latin American restaurant.

### Studio 28
*10 rue Tholozé, 18th (01.46.06.36.07). M° Abbesses.*
Part of the history of avant-garde Paris, the Montmartre movie house where Buñuel premièred *L'Age d'Or* in 1930. It's decorated with souvenirs and posters, and the entrance is embedded with footprints of the great. Family-run, the Studio offers a repertory mix of classics and recent movies.

*Nature goes spherical at* **La Géode**.

## Cinema in the Round

### Dôme IMAX
*1 pl du Dôme, 92095 Paris La Défense (01.46.92.45.45). M° Grande Arche de la Défense.* **Tickets** 55F; 45F unemployed, students; 75F Sat.
A 1,114 square metre OMNIMAX screen is the ideal locale for experiencing such startling cinema-in-the-round as the 90-minute Rolling Stones show, a regular feature. *Wheelchair access.*

### La Géode
*26 av Corentin-Cariou, 19th (08.36.68.29.30/same day booking 01.42.05.50.50). M° Porte de la Villette.* **Tickets** 55F; 40F unemployed, students, disabled.
An OMNIMAX cinema housed in a glorious shiny geodesic dome at La Villette. The 386-seat auditorium is tipped at a 30° angle to the horizon, and the hemispherical screen wraps around the viewer. Most films feature dizzying 3-D plunges through dramatic natural scenery. Booking is advisable. *Wheelchair access.*

## Public Repertory Institutions

### Auditorium du Louvre
*entrance through Pyramid, Cour Napoléon, 1st (01.40.20.54.55). M° Palais Royal.* **Tickets** 25F-100F; 15F students.
Like the Louvre pyramid, this 420-seat auditorium was designed by IM Pei. Recent film themes have included Dante's *Inferno*. It's also a good venue to see silent movies with musical accompaniment, as the acoustics are splendid. *Wheelchair access.*

### La Cinémathèque Française
*Palais de Chaillot, 7 av Albert-de-Mun, 16th (01.47.04.24.24). M° Trocadéro.* **Admission** 28F; membership available.
Founded in 1936 by film fanatics Georges Franju and Henri Langlois, the Cinémathèque played a seminal role in shaping the New Wave directors at the end of the 1950s, and is still a great meeting point for devoted cinephiles with its retrospectives (Melville, Delon), series (*film noir*, crime movies, '30s musicals) and theme nights. *See also* Musée du Cinéma-Henri Langlois *in chapter* **Museums**.
**Branch:** Cinémathèque République, 18 rue du Fbg-du-Temple, 11th (01.47.04.24.24).

### Vidéothèque de Paris
*2 Grand Galerie: Porte St-Eustache, Forum des Halles, 1st (01.44.76.62.00). M° Châtelet-Les Halles.* **Open** 1-9pm Tue, Wed, Fri-Sun; 1-10pm Thur. **Admission** 30F per day; 25F students; membership available.
An addictive public archive which acts as an image-bank of

the city. No matter how brief the clip – from the Eiffel Tower scene in *Superman II* to the letter of introduction scene in *Babette's Feast* – if Paris is on film, it's here, along with ads, trailers, news reels, short films, animation and documentaries. A Star Trek-like consultation room has 40 video consoles with Minitel-style keyboards to access computerised data by theme, year or author. The two auditoria show wide-ranging urban-themed series of films and videos featuring Paris and other metropolises.

## Festivals & Special Events

Each year there are any number of movie festivals in Paris. Listed here are some regular, easily accessible events. Also of note are the women's film festival (*see chapter* **Women's Paris**) and Cinéma en Plein Air (*see chapter* **Paris by Season**).

### Cinéma du Réel
*Cinéma des Cinéastes (see above).* **Dates** March. **Admission** 27F per film; 60F per day; 250F per week. Despite its billing as an 'ethnographic and sociological' fes-

tival, this international documentary survey is a compilation of impressive, fascinating or off-putting films.

### Côté Court
*Ciné 104, 104 av Jean Lolive, 93500 Pantin (01.48.46.95.08). M° Eglise de Pantin.* **Dates** 2nd and 3rd weeks of June. **Admission** 32F per film, 160F per week; 24F, 135F, students.
A major festival of short films, running from 30 seconds to 30 minutes, serious to comic, experimental to golden oldies.

### Rencontres Internationales du Cinéma
*Vidéothèque de Paris (see above).* **Dates** last three weeks in Oct. **Admission** 30F.
A truly global section of new independent feature, documentary and short films in competition for a Grand Prix du Public, plus a programme of workshops.

### CinéMémoire
*Cinémathèque (see above) and other venues.* **Dates** late Nov-Dec. **Admission** 15F-120F.
This remarkable five-week festival shows rare, restored and recently rediscovered films as they were intended, at the right speed and often with orchestral accompaniment.

# Reality bites

Young cinema talent is finding its voice as France openly questions past verities. Mathieu Kassovitz's *La Haine* and Cyril Collard's *Les Nuits Fauves* can be credited with moving centre stage left of field. Though famously sensitive, earlier French filmmakers for the most part saw the world through bourgeois *auteur* eyes. Bertrand Blier's *Merci La Vie*, and Tavernier's hellraising *L'Appât* tell it like it is. But while taboos were happily tackled, only the white French cast got to munch the forbidden fruit. Now there has been a multicultural revolution.

A case in point is establishment pillar André Techiné swept up in the reality of contemporary French life. His recent *Les Voleurs* stationed policeman Daniel Auteuil in a grimy Lyon suburb, while screen legend Catherine Deneuve portrayed a lonely, middle-aged lesbian. Reality has bitten the French cinema. The mainstream monopoly of battling bourgeois couples is threatened.

Black and Arab actors remain sidelined but they are getting the breaks alongside a new generation of wild side actors. *A Toute Vitesse* by *Les Roseaux Sauvages* star Gaël Morel (*photo*) offers the traditional ado angst but with a gay and ethnic perspective. 'When I included Samir in my script it was not a question of tokenism, it was because that was the world I grew up in,' explains the 24-year-old debutant director.

Over the past two years the ground rules seem to have changed, as films like Karim Dridi's *Pigalle*, billed by critics as a *Mean Streets* of Paris, and Jean-François Richet's grainy *banlieue* flick *Etat des Lieux* offer a multicultural, issue-led viewpoint. Xavier Beauvois' *N'Oublie pas que tu vas mourir* portrays France's Generation X face to face with AIDS and drugs. 'There has been a distinct social bias in films recently and it is certainly true that the choice of both actors and the way subjects are treated is much closer to the street. Before there was a French school which imposed bourgeois values even on marginal people. Realism is here and probably to stay,' observes Christophe Carrière of French film magazine *Première*.

The new generation has the limelight and high-profile releases approach that will surely carry the new cinema forward. Kassovitz's *Assassins* is awaited impatiently and everyone is talking about *Dobermann*, directed by Jan Kounen. His ultra violent, cyber-short *Vibroboy* was watched by bad boy Eric Cantona in his big screen debut *Le Bonheur est dans le pré*. Kounen has cast rising star Vincent Cassell as leading man: an actor who significantly broke through in *La Haine*. Will French cinema take on board social issues and at the same time a Tarantino aesthetic, to produce the first celluloid trend of the twenty-first century?

# Music: Classical & Opera

**The flourishing Parisian musical scene is reaping the rewards of past investment.**

The Paris classical music scene is as alive and kicking as ever. The *Grands Projets* are bearing fruit and despite moans about cuts in subsidies, the state music budget is on a level unthinkable in Britain or the USA. The downside is the degree of political interference that is part and parcel of French life. The powers that be have recently decided that the **Orchestre de Paris** should have a French musical director, which is bad news for the celebrated foreign conductor who was on the point of signing a contract. All of which provides a source of musical gossip unequalled in Europe. Nowhere is this more apparent than in the comings and goings at the **Opéra National de Paris-Bastille**. Still, the fact that such a vast opera house is up and running is in many ways a miracle. The decision to split performances between **Palais Garnier** and the Opéra Bastille is to be applauded. It had always seemed a typically perverse move to perform only ballet in Garnier, where the sightlines are poor, but the acoustics excellent, and only opera in the Bastille, where the reverse is true.

There is also rejoicing at the opera for another reason, for it seems the (three) tenors' natural successor is to be the (one) French tenor, Roberto Alagna. Post-war French singing has had more downs than ups but is now beginning to produce singers of real quality like the high-flying coloratura Natalie Dessay, the Rossini mezzo Martine Dupuy and the extravagant diva Françoise Pollet, not to mention a plethora of Early Music singers, very much a speciality of the new Conservatoire.

The international success of the Early Music movement is led in France by the high priest of authenticity, American conductor and harpsichord-player, William Christie, and his ensemble **Les Arts Florissants**. Look out also for Jean-Claude Malgoire and his company and Phillipe Herreweghe's stylish **Chapelle Royale**.

Contemporary music is still dominated by the Pierre Boulez school of Modernist abstraction. However, since Pärt, Adams and Gorecki have shown that contemporary music can have a non-specialist audience, the Boulez camp is beginning to look inceasingly isolated in the **IRCAM**.

*Verdi's* Rigoletto *at the* **Opéra Bastille**.

In addition to the main concert halls, churches are regularly used for organ recitals, choral music, chamber ensembles, and even the odd symphonic concert. Watch out for recitals by top organists on the organs of Notre Dame, St-Eustache or La Trinité, for summer concerts in the Sainte-Chapelle and highstandard choral concerts in La Madeleine. **Concertsolo** (01.44.62.70.90) organises concerts at various churches, usually Eglise St-Germain-de-Prés and Eglise St-Louis-en-l'Ile.

The French are crazy about festivals, and these tend to spring up without warning and disappear as quickly. Often two or three concerts by the same composer will be grandly labelled a festival. For the main festivals, *see chapter* **Paris by Season**. The **Festival d'Art Sacré** is a celebration of religious music in Paris churches in the weeks building up to Christmas and Easter ( 01.44.70.64.10).

## BOOKING AHEAD

To find out what's on turn to *Pariscope* and *L'Officiel des Spectacles*. The monthly *Le Monde de la Musique* and *Diapason* also list classical concerts, while *Opera International* provides the best coverage of all things vocal. *Cadences* and *La Terrasse*, two free monthly publications, are distributed outside concerts. Generally there is little music in Paris from late July until mid September, but this is the time of the **Paris Quartier d'Eté** festival, when concerts are organised in gardens across the city. *See also chapter* **Paris by Season**.

Ticket prices and availability are largely governed by the artists performing. If Solti is visiting the Orchestre de Paris then it's likely the concert will be booked up ahead and the tickets fairly pricey. Most venues offer special cut-rate tickets to students (aged under-26) an hour before the performance. Beware of ticket touts who hang around the Opéra and at big name concerts. For ticket agencies, *see chapter* **Services**. If you are in Paris on the 21 June don't miss **La Fête de la Musique**, where events are free, as are some concerts at the Maison de Radio France, the Conservatoire de Paris and Paris churches.

### La Flûte de Pan

*49, 53, 59 rue de Rome, 8th (strings, woodwind 01.42.93.65.05 /sax, brass, percussion, jazz 01.43.87.01.81/vocal, keyboard 01.42.93.47.82).* **Open** 10am-6.30pm Mon-Sat. **Credit** MC, V.
This long-established music shop offers the most comprehensive selection of sheet music and scores in Paris.

### Jeunesses Musicales de France

*20 rue Géoffroy l'Asnier, 4th (01.44.61.86.86). M° Pont Marie.* **Open** 10am-1pm, 2-7pm, Mon-Thur; 10am-1pm, 2-6pm, Fri. **Membership** 150F; 100F 18-30s; 20F under-18s.
Membership gives the equivalent of student discounts at various theatres, good value if you are in Paris for some time.

## Orchestras & Ensembles

### Les Arts Florissants

It is a measure of the success of William Christie's ensemble that it is not unusual for him to be invited to replace the orchestra at the Palais Garnier for Baroque performances. Some find his highly decorated purist style a little pallid, but he has undoubtedly set a new standard for performing Lully and Rameau, one by which all others are judged.

### La Chapelle Royale

Philippe Herreweghe is one of France's most celebrated Early Music conductors, and like Frans Brüggen, is now beginning to conduct music of all periods with an eye for authenticity. This 'clean' style of performance has its fans.

### Ensemble InterContemporain

*Based at the* **Cité de la Musique**. The world-famous contemporary music ensemble is in the safe hands of American David Robertson, successor to Pierre Boulez. The repertoire remains strictly avant garde. To mention the Minimalist movement (of Glass, Reich etc) is a heresy not to risk.

### Ensemble Orchestral de Paris

*Based at the* **Salle Pleyel**. Jean-Jacques Kantorow continues to extend the repertoire of this chamber orchestra with

*Baroque perfection from* **William Christie.**

the occasional premieres of works by living composers. More traditional fare is equally carefully programmed, with occasional large-scale works not usually associated with a chamber orchestra. John Nelson will take the reins in 1998.

### Les Talens Lyriques

A spin-off from Les Arts Florissants. This opera group is run by Christophe Rousset, who is Christie's favoured harpsichordist. Mostly young singers perform Baroque opera in productions as authentic as the musical presentation.

### Orchestre Colonne

*Based at the* **Salle Pleyel**. Antonello Allemandi is trying to breathe new life into this rather tired orchestra. The programme is enlivened by the young prize-winning soloists that the orchestra is anxious to promote.

### Orchestre Lamoureux

*Based at the* **Salle Pleyel**. Yutaka Sado has turned round the fortunes of this subscription orchestra. Not only has the level of orchestral playing risen, but the programmes have a new vigour and sense of purpose.

### Orchestre National de France

*Based at the* **Maison de Radio France** *and* **Théâtre des Champs Elysées**. Canadian Charles Dutoit has the double advantage of being an expert in the French Romantic repertoire, and having a name that sounds French. This has served the orchestra well and it can now claim to be the finest in the land, as far as French music is concerned. Jeffrey Tate is the principal guest conductor, which means that Mozart and opera are well catered for.

### Orchestre de Paris

*Based at the* **Salle Pleyel** *and* **Châtelet, Théâtre Musical de Paris**. The excellent Semyon Bychkov's contract expires at the end of 1998, and already the orchestra has fallen into a hotbed of rumour and intrigue. The new administrator is revealing none of his plans for future seasons but apparently a French conductor is to be named as the Russian Bychkov's successor. The orchestra, nonetheless, is often considered the country's finest, and is still favoured by the world's great maestri such as Sawallisch and Sanderling.

### Orchestre Philharmonique de Radio France

*Based at the* **Maison de Radio France** *and* **Salle Pleyel**. Marek Janowski is considered by many to be one of the world's great Wagnerian conductors, as his recording of the *Ring* is testimony. The orchestra continues to explore new and interesting repertoire and has benefitted from its long and stable relationship with its musical director, to such an extent that some give it the number-one spot.

## Concert Halls

### Châtelet – Théâtre Musical de Paris
*1 pl du Châtelet, 1st (01.40.28.28.40/recorded information 01.42.33.00.00). M° Châtelet-Les Halles.* **Open** *box office* 11am-7pm daily; *telephone bookings* 11am-7pm Mon-Sat. **Tickets** phone for details. **Credit** AmEx, MC, V.
Converted into a concert hall and opera house twenty years ago, the old Châtelet will close in 1998-1999 for its first major facelift. Its solid reputation has been built by inviting top directors and conductors for operatic events that have often outshone the Bastille. Programming has been consistently interesting, linking concerts, operas and ballet (*see chapter* **Dance**) with a twentieth-century focus. The Philharmonia visits annually, and June 1997 sees the Orchestre de Paris in the pit for the Salzburg production of Strauss' *Salome*. *Wheelchair access.*

### Cité de la Musique
*221 av Jean Jaurès, 19th (01.44.84.45.45/recorded information 01.44.84.45.00/reservations 01.44.84.44.84). M° Porte de Pantin.* **Open** *box office* noon-6pm Tue-Sun; *telephone bookings* noon-8pm daily. **Tickets** 60F-160F; reduced prices over-60s, unemployed. **Credit** (in person only) MC, V.
The double complex up at La Villette consists of the new Conservatoire de Paris music school (01.40.40.45.45), and the Cité de la Musique concert hall and museum. The main concert hall is an impressive venue, which can be rearranged to create varying performance spaces. So far the emphasis has been on contemporary music and Early Music. Rehearsals can be watched for free. The museum holds a smaller concert space (*see chapter* **Museums**). The *conservatoire*, home to 1,250 students of classical, jazz and Baroque music and of dance, welcomes world-class performers and professors, with free concerts by the student orchestra or soloists. *Wheelchair access.*

### IRCAM
*1 pl Igor Stravinsky, 4th (01.44.78.48.34). M° Châtelet-Les Halles.* **Open** phone for details.
The Ensemble InterContemporain has poked its head up above ground and is now based at the Cité de la Musique, but there is still the odd concert given in this underground musical research centre adjoining the Centre Pompidou. Above all it is used for musical symposiums, where mem-

**Cité de la Musique** *modernity.*

bers of the Modernist world mull over avant-garde music. Officially retired, Pierre Boulez remains the spiritual head.

### Maison de Radio France
*116 av du Président Kennedy, 16th (01.42.30.22.22/ concert information 01.42.30.15.16). M° Ranelagh or Passy/RER Kennedy Radio France.* **Open** *box office* 10am-4pm daily. **Tickets** *concerts* phone for details. **No credit cards.**
The cylindrical Radio France complex is a landmark in the 16th *arrondissement* just beyond the Trocadéro. The range of classical concerts, operas, choral concerts and ethnic music is impressive, and some events are free, such as daily lunchtime piano concerts or Présences, February's contemporary music festival. The main venue is the Salle Olivier Messiaen, a rather charmless hall, but the quality of music here is a compensation. The Orchestra National de France and Orchestra Philharmonique de Radio France are based here. *See also* **France Musique** *in chapter* **Media**.

### Opéra Comique/Salle Favart
*5 rue Favart, 9th (reservations 01.42.44.45.46/recorded information 01.42.96.12.20). M° Richelieu Drouot.* **Open** *box office* 11am-7pm Mon-Sat; *telephone bookings* 11am-1pm, 2-6pm, Mon-Fri. **Tickets** 50F-490F. **Credit** (in person only) AmEx, MC, V.
The list of French operas that have had their premieres in this charming jewel box of a theatre is impressive. *Carmen* was first performed here, as were *The Damnation of Faust, The Tales of Hoffmann, Pelleas and Melisande*, Delibes' *Lakme*, Massenet's *Manon*, Ravel's *l'Heure Espagnole* and many more. The building is nowadays considered technically inadequate, which is why it is cold-shouldered by most important new productions; however, it remains a great place to hear small-scale French opera. *Wheelchair access.*

### Opéra National de Paris Bastille
*Opéra Bastille, pl de la Bastille, 12th (01.44.73.13.00/ recorded information 01.43.43.96.96). M° Bastille.* **Open** *box office* 11am-6pm Mon-Sat. **Tickets** 60F-610F. **Credit** AmEx, MC, V.
The Opéra Bastille remains something of a *bête noire* for Parisians. Expensive to build, aesthetically questionable and the home of much unmusical intrigue and scandal. However, standards are rising, the building serves its purpose and the new director Hugues Gall and his excellent new musical director James Conlon can look forward to a period of stability. If this optimism comes crashing down, as the fascia tiles of the new opera house are prone to do, then it's only par for the course. *See chapters* **Sightseeing** *and* **Dance**. *Wheelchair access (disabled reservations 01.40.01.18.08).*

## Maestro trail

When wandering around Paris watch out for the following composers' homes.

| | |
|---|---|
| **Bizet** | 26 rue de la Tour d'Auvergne, 9th. |
| **Chausson** | 22 bd de Courcelles, 8th. |
| **Chopin** | 9 square d'Orléans, 9th. |
| **Debussy** | 58 rue Cardinet, 17th. |
| **Duparc** | 7 av de Vilars, 16th. |
| **Faure** | 32 av des Vignes, 16th. |
| **d'Indy** | 7 av de Vilars, 7th. |
| **Offenbach** | 8 bd des Capucines, 9th. |
| **Poulenc** | 5 rue de Médicis, 6th. |
| **Saint-Saens** | 83 bis rue de Courcelles, 8th. |

### Opéra National de Paris Garnier

*pl de l'Opéra, 9th (01.44.73.13.00). Mᵒ Opéra.* **Open** *box office* 11am-6.30pm Mon-Sat; *telephone bookings* 11am-6pm Mon-Sat. **Tickets** 60F-610F. **Credit** AmEx, MC, V.
Restored to something like its glittering original, the Palais Garnier is now performing its original function as an opera house, sharing the task with the Bastille: smaller-scale and earlier operas such as early Mozart are put on here. The perfect acoustics and undeniable glamour make this a privilege, but the building's tiara-shape means some seats have poor visibility. *See chapters* **Sightseeing, Museums** *and* **Dance**. *Wheelchair access (disabled reservations 01.40.01.18.08).*

### Palais des Congrès

*2 pl Porte Maillot, 17th (01.40.68.00.05). Mᵒ Porte Maillot.* **Open** *box office* 12.30-7pm Mon-Sat. **Tickets** phone for details. **Credit** MC, V.
A vast conference hall where there is the occcasional large-scale recital or symphony concert.

### Salle Gaveau

*45 rue La Boétie, 8th (01.49.53.05.07). Mᵒ Miromesnil.* **Open** *box office* 11am-6pm Mon-Fri; 11am-4pm Sat; Sun when concerts on. **Tickets** phone for details. **Credit** AmEx, MC, V (three days in advance).
The Paris equivalent of London's Wigmore Hall, the charming Salle Gaveau is also due to have a facelift from April 1997 for around seven months. Frequently used for intimate recitals and chamber music, it's also the favoured venue for senior prima donnas giving that very last farewell recital. *Wheelchair access.*

### Salle Pleyel

*252 rue du Fbg-St-Honoré, 8th (01.45.61.53.00). Mᵒ Ternes.* **Open** *box office* 11am-6pm Mon-Sat. **Tickets** 75F-360F. **Credit** MC, V (15 days before).

*Divine music at the* **Sainte-Chapelle**.

The Salle Pleyel is a vast and unatmospheric hall, but one which is home to a great many orchestras and ensembles. The acoustics are good for large-scale orchestral or choral concerts, but not for hall recitals, which is a pity as the hall plays host to all the great recitalists of the world. If you have the choice, go and hear them performing with an orchestra. Many people have subscriptions for the season, rendering concerts fuller than in other venues. Watch out for the Berlin Philharmonic's visit with Abbado in October 1997. *Wheelchair access.*

### Théâtre des Champs-Elysées

*15 av Montaigne, 8th (01.49.52.50.00). Mᵒ Alma Marceau.* **Open** *box office* 11am-7pm Mon-Sat; *telephone bookings* 10am-noon, 2-6pm Mon-Fri. **Tickets** 40F-750F; cheaper *matinée* 3pm or 5pm Sun. **Credit** V.
This beautiful theatre, designed by Auguste Perret, with its bas-reliefs by Bourdelle, has won a place in history as the site of the premiere of Stravinsky's *Le Sacre du Printemps* on 29 May 1913, and the subsequent riot. The interior is well preserved, with the famous ceiling by Maurice Denis, but the seating is old-fashioned and the cheaper seats on the upper levels cramped. One of the homes of the Orchestre National de France, as well as occasional visiting opera companies, it remains a chic evening out for elegant Parisians.

### Théâtre de la Ville

*2 pl du Châtelet, 4th (01.42.74.22.77). Mᵒ Châtelet-Les Halles.* **Open** *box office* 9am-6pm Mon; 11am-8pm Tue-Sat. **Tickets** 90F-195F. **Credit** (above 100F) MC, V.
With its large, steeply raked concrete amphitheatre, the Théâtre de la Ville's occasional concerts feature hip classical outfits like the avant-garde Kronos Quartet or Fabio Biondi. *See also chapter* **Dance**.
*Wheelchair access.*

## Music in Museums

For musical memorabilia *see chapter* **Museums**.

### Musée de Cluny (Musée National du Moyen Age)

*6 pl Paul Painlevé, 5th (01.53.73.78.00). Mᵒ Cluny-La Sorbonne.* **Open** 9.15am-12.45pm Mon, Wed-Sun. **Tickets** 43F-53F (includes museum entry).
Concerts of medieval music in keeping with the collection.

### Musée du Louvre

*Auditorium du Louvre, Cour Napoléon, 1st (information 01.40.20.52.99/reservations 01.40.20.52.29). Mᵒ Palais Royal.* **Open** *box office* 9.30am-7.30pm Mon-Sat. **Tickets** 85F-130F.
Top-quality chamber music in imaginative series.

### Musée d'Orsay

*1 rue de Bellechase, 7th (01.40.49.47.17). RER Musée d'Orsay/Mᵒ Solférino.* **Times** 12.30pm, 6.45pm, 8pm. **Tickets** 60F-130F, 100F students.
Attracts international artists for varied programmes focusing, like the collection, on the high nineteenth century.

### Musée de la Vie Romantique

*16 rue Chaptal, 9th (01.48.74.95.38). Mᵒ Pigalle.* **Times** 3pm Sun. **Tickets** 50F.
Evocation in words and music of the life and times of George Sand, in a house to which Chopin and Charpentier were frequent visitors.

### Théâtre Grevin

*10 bd Montmartre, 9th (01.48.24.16.97). Mᵒ Rue Montmartre.* **Open** tickets on sale 30min before concert. **Times** 8.30pm Mon; 11am Sun. **Tickets** 90F-200F.
Small-scale vocal and chamber music recitals.

# Music: Rock, Roots & Jazz

***More than just a stop on the global circuit, Paris is also the place to discover Breton bagpipes and the comeback of accordion musette.***

Paris is a sure stop on the international tour agenda, be it rock supergroups playing the stadia, indie and metal stalwarts at the **Arapaho** or a record label's latest 18-year-old hopeful at the **Divan du Monde**. Also, the city remains a good place to catch big British bands in smallish venues. Look out for the Festival Fnac-Inrockuptibles in November (*see chapter* **Paris by Season**) for a barometer on interesting new indie bands.

There's also a more homegrown scene to discover. Other than **Johnny Hallyday** (*see box*), suave rapper MC Solaar is the nearest France has to an international star, but there's also a new generation of native singers and songwriters attempting to challenge *chanson*'s bad name (*see below*, **Chanson**). Rap, ragga, Latin and the north and south of the Sahara sounds of Paris' immigrant communities have been a big influence on new French music, which has found its soul by going back out on the street. Riotous multi-racial combos like Les Négresses Vertes have been joined by crossover groups like FFF, soul-influenced Mad in Paris or musicians who have rediscovered the French 'national instrument', the accordion.

It is not an easy time for local bands, as Parisian authorities clamp down on noise levels and so smaller bar venues suffer sudden closure periods. More ominous was hardcore rap group NTM's three-month prison sentence in November 1996 for song lyrics allegedly inciting violence against the police.

The best source of info is *Lylo*, a free booklet available from bars and ticket agencies (*see chapter* **Services**). Look out for freebie mag *Blah Blah* and specialist magazines *Les Inrockuptibles* (indie), and *L'Affiche* (rap, reggae).

## Stadium Venues

### Palais Omnisports de Paris-Bercy
*8 bd de Bercy, 12th (01.44.68.44.68). M° Bercy.*
**Box office** 11am-6pm Mon-Sat. **Admission** from 170F.
**Credit** MC, V.
With grass on the outside and 16,000 echoing seats inside, Bercy hosts some of the strangest sporting events in town and music crowdpullers (*see also chapter* **Sport & Fitness**).

### Zénith
*211 av Jean-Jaurès, 19th. M° Porte de Pantin.* **No box office. Admission** from 160F.
Lacks atmosphere, but almost everyone plays here, from rockers Pearl Jam to bagpiping Breton supergroup Tri Yann.

## Rock Venues

### Arapaho
*Centre Commercial Italie II, 30 av d'Italie, 13th (01.45.89.65.05). M° Place d'Italie.* **Concerts** 8pm daily.
**Admission** 60F-100F. **No credit cards.**
This cramped concrete basement (entry left of Printemps) has become a quality rock venue. Rock predominates, viz The Melvins, Wedding Present, but also occasional techno (Moby) and reggae-ska events. Dour door muscle.

### La Bataclan
*50 bd Voltaire, 11th (01.47.00.55.22). M° Oberkampf.*
**Box office** 11am-7pm Mon-Sat. **Admission** 100F-150F.
**No credit cards.**
Many people's favourite venue is an attractive, horseshoe-

# Johnny

When it comes to ancient monuments, forget the Arc de Triomphe and get a load of the greatest cultural relic of them all: Johnny Hallyday. Granted, he's not as old as Notre Dame, but he's a lot more weatherbeaten and he's been wooing the French with cheesy rock ballads for more than 30 years. With skin like a sun-dried tomato and hair like a 1970s footballer, Hallyday is a gristly, leathery, tattooed icon a devoted nation simply calls 'Johnny'.

Paradoxically, for a man who had more column inches dedicated to him in the French press than any other celebrity last year, Johnny is a virtual nobody everywhere else on the planet. Who outside France could name his most famous song? (answer: Tennessee). Perhaps the French secretly realise this phenomenon, with a penchant for young wives, could wreck their reputation as intellectuals and send their cultural kudos into free-fall.

Johnny was born in Belgium in 1943 as Jean-Philipe Smet. After a childhood being dragged around the music halls of Europe by a cabaret-singing aunt, he joined a Franco-American band called The Hallidays in 1959. Showing promise, he released his first solo single in 1960, complete with the new user-friendly name. The music sold, he developed a trademark and he has never looked back.

After 30 years of albums and film roles, Johnny soared to such dizzy heights of Gallic fame that he finally fled France to live in Miami, complaining he could no longer go out in public without getting mobbed by fans.

In November 1996 he fulfilled his 'last great ambition' – to perform at the same Las Vegas venue where his boyhood hero Elvis Presley gave his last concert. He shrewdly jetted in 6,000 French fans on specially chartered aircraft and played to a packed house every night.

shaped former theatre that hosts top names and rising stars from Oasis to Angélique Kidjo. *Fin-de-siècle* murals, a large dance area in front of the stage and a bar with good sightlines add to the fun. *See also chapter* **Clubs**.

## Café de la Danse

*5 passage Louis-Philippe, 11th (01.47.00.57.59).*
*M° Bastille.* **Box office** 30min before concert.
**Admission** 50F-120F. **No credit cards.**
A stone-walled former theatre space. Specialises in more left-field events, such as experimental art-music performances and world music, although mainstream rock gets a look-in.

## Chesterfield Café

*124 rue La Boétie, 8th (01.42.25.18.06).*
*M° Franklin D Roosevelt.* **Bar** 10am-5am daily. **Music** 11.30pm Tue-Sat. **Admission** free. **Credit** AmEx, MC, V.
Cavernous bare brick Tex-Mex bar-restaurant is the place to spot new American rock bands (free), plus Joe Ely and oldies making a comeback and the ominous prospect of star turns like John McEnroe and Keanu Reeves wielding a guitar.

## La Cigale

*120 bd Rochechouart, 18th (01.49.25.49.99). M° Pigalle.*
**Box office** one hour before concert. **Admission** 120F-160F. **No credit cards.**
An old horseshoe-shaped vaudeville house, La Cigale holds 2,000 to 3,000 people. It hosts many international rock bands – when Echobelly shared the bill here with Oasis a couple of years ago, singer Sonya rated it the best gig of her career – with a few excursions, such as top-rate jazz from Joshua Redman. The springy floor is a boon to pogoers, but if that gets too tiring, the balcony allows a more sedate experience.

## Le Divan du Monde

*75 rue des Martyrs, 18th (01.44.92.77.66). M° Pigalle.*
**Bar** 7pm-5am daily. **Admission** free-100F.
**No credit cards.**
This former cabaret (immortalised by Toulouse-Lautrec when Le Divan Japonais) has established itself as the best medium-small venue, with an impressive array of up-and-coming international acts like Red Snapper or Kula Shaker. Monday's Pollen is France Inter's free showcase for French bands. The interior has an intimate feel, with excellent visibility in both moshpit and balcony. *See also chapter* **Clubs**.

## Elysée Montmartre

*72 bd Rochechouart, 18th (01.44.92.45.42). M° Anvers.*
**Box office** 11am-7pm Mon-Fri. **Music** 7.30pm most nights. **Admission** about 130F. **No credit cards.**
The leader of the musical action in the Pigalle-Montmartre area, it has retained its authentic music-hall character and presents an eclectic mix of music from reggae vets and rap to Portishead. Also used for fun parties, *see chapter* **Clubs**.

## Jazz

The Cartesian need to classify means that today the city map is laid out like a battleground: good time trad and swing in the Latin Quarter, hard bop in aspic in a cocktail setting in St-Germain, serious local work-outs around Châtelet and the great post-Coltrane adventure scattered around a few well-sunk bunkers, so well camouflaged as to seem to be intended to resist occupation and nuclear attack.

In the last ten years, jazz has begun to emerge from the desert that stretched from the far edge of Motown to the near end of punk. Today there is more jazz in Paris than any one person can reasonably be expected to cope with. Not only do all the

*Cool jazz and funky sounds from* **Hot Brass**.

big names from America visit, but France has a revered grand master in pianist Martial Solal, and the younger generation of jazzmen is perhaps the finest France has ever seen.

Musicians like Louis Sclavis (reeds), Bojan Z (piano), Bruno Chevillon (bass), Yves Robert (trombone) and Michel Godard (tuba) have a subtlety and a vigorous intelligence that seem peculiarly French. And yet something is missing. Jazz in France is a socially isolated art form. The crossover with the new street music should be strong in a city that boasts so many immigrants. But – outside the **Hot Brass** or the streetwise **Cithéa** – it just doesn't happen. Nor is there much exchange with Africa. While French jazz can impress and seduce, it lacks that bad liquor, raw energy feeling. In Paris, you often come out of a club feeling more intelligent than when you went in. You rarely come out feeling so happy you should be arrested.

## The Big Three

### Hot Brass
*Parc de la Villette, 211 av Jean-Jaurès, 19th (01.42.00.14.14). M° Porte de Pantin.* **Box office** 8pm. **Music** 9.30pm Wed-Sun. **Admission** 100F-140F; reductions 60F-70F. **Credit** AmEx, MC, V.
Tucked in one of La Villette's bright red pavilions, the newest club in town is also the best. Not too big, with neat lighting and good air-conditioning, the recipe for success has been equal parts jazz, salsa and funk, with a strong post-M-Base slant to the jazz. Steve Coleman is unofficial house musician, and the October 'New York is Now' Festival sounds the key note. Look out for the homegrown Bobun Brass Band and resident Venezuelan salsa man Orlando Poleo.

### Instants Chavirés
*7 rue Richard Lenoir, 93100 Montreuil (01.42.87.25.91). M° Robespierre.* **Box office** 8.30pm Tue-Sat. **Admission** 50F-80F; reductions 30F-50F. **No credit cards**.
A leading centre for creative improvised music, there are strong links with the English and German avant-gardes, and regulars include guitarists Marc Ducret, Gil Coronado and Noel Achkoté. It also hosts Japanese rock bands, jazz-with-poetry sessions and world-folk crossover projects.

### New Morning
*7-9 rue des Petites Écuries, 10th (recorded information 01.45.23.51.41). M° Château d'Eau.* **Box office** 5-7pm Mon-Fri. **Music** 9pm. **Admission** 110F. **No credit cards**.
A historic club founded in the early 1980s. Musicians who have found a second home here include Lester Bowie, Archie Shepp, John Scofield and Betty Carter. Nowadays, the jazz is diluted with some pretty serious blues and Latin and the occasional Peter Gabriel-style 'Real World' night, notably Malian singer Oumou Sangare. In summer, salsa runs riot.

## Left Bank Clubs

### Caveau de la Huchette
*5 rue de la Huchette, 5th (01.43.26.65.05). M° St-Michel.* **Bar** 9.30pm-2.30am Mon-Fri; 9.30pm-4am Sat, Sun. **Admission** 60F Mon-Thur, Sun; 70F Fri, Sat; 55F students Mon-Thur, Sun. **Credit** DC, V.
Trumpeter Harry 'Sweets' Edison is a regular in this medieval cellar. The mix of trad, swing, boogie and rock is more for dancing and it helps if you're under twenty.

### Petit Journal Montparnasse
*13 rue du Commandant-Mouchotte, 14th (01.43.21.56.70). M° Montparnasse-Bienvenüe.* **Bar** 6pm-2am Mon-Sat. **Music** 10pm. **Admission** 110F (inc first drink); dinner and concert 280F. **Credit** DC, MC, V.
If it weren't for the neon trumpeter, it would be hard to find this large, modern club in redeveloped Montparnasse. The

# The Chanson renaissance

French *chanson* has an image problem. Memories of Piaf, Gainsbourg, and smoke-filled cabarets in Montmartre only serve to obscure the facts – which are that in the last ten years there has been a true renaissance of the vernacular song tradition in France. New and more eclectic styles have found a new and younger audience seeking out new and authentic groups long before they reach the hallowed **Olympia**. If the words are still generally more important than the music, the mix of pretension, nostalgia, incomprehensible poetry and outright melodrama once associated with the genre is now only one small part of the story. French *chanson* has made its peace both with post-punk and with the ghost of Brassens. More vital than neo-bop, more streetwise than most hip-hop, it's the happening thing. From idiosyncratic Arthur H to all-girl accordion combo Castafiore Bazooka, this is real popular music, as remote from Val Doonican as it is from REM. If you speak the lingo, smile sardonically and tap your feet, this could be one of the best nights out you can find.

Café-style venues where you can hear traditional *chanson* include Au Café Chantant (36 rue Bichat, 10th/01.42.08.83.33); La Bohème (underneath the theatre Les Déchargeurs, 3 rue des Déchargeurs, 1st/01.42.36.10.29); Le Loup du Faubourg (21 rue de la Roquette, 11th/01.40.21.90.95); Magique (42 rue de Gergovie, 14th/01.45.42.26.10); Paris' Aller-Retour (25 rue de Turenne, 4th/01.40.27.03.82).

For information on who is singing where, listen to 'Pollen' hosted by the godfather of *chanson*, Jean-Louis Foulquier, on France Inter (87.8 MHz) from 8 to 10pm on Fridays (or go to see the show recorded at the **Divan du Monde**).

**Arthur H** *is the consummate showman.*

## Café Concert Ailleurs

*13 rue Jean Beausire, 4th (01.44.59.82.82).*
*M° Bastille.* **Bar** 6.30pm-1.30am **DAYS???**. **Music** 9pm. **Admission** 30F, 50F or 80F. **Credit** V.
A small atmospheric café run by a non-profit organisation dedicated to nurturing young singer-songwriters. It's a good place to catch rising talents just before their first big break, and a pleasant way to spend an evening. Choose your ticket price according to your means.

## La Folie en tête

*33 rue de la Butte-aux-Cailles, 13th (01.45.80.65.99).* *M° Place d'Italie.* **Bar** 5pm-2am Mon-Sat. **Music** 9pm. **Admission** 40F (incl first drink). **No credit cards.**
None of the 2,572 (approximately) instruments suspended in lieu of wallpaper seem to work, but that doesn't stop the variety of music from playing on. Possibly the smallest feasible venue in Paris. Programming is anarchic (in keeping with the management's politics), but worth a try. Great for a late drink.

## Au Limonaire

*18 cité Bergère, 9th (01.45.23.33.33).*
*M° Rue Montmartre.* **Bar** 5pm-2am Tue-Sun.
**Music** 10pm. **Credit** V.
Transplanted from the 12th *arrondissement* to the Jewish quarter of the 9th, the Limonaire is alive and well. The food is simple and superb, and the artists' collective that owns the venue manages to pull in many fine performers. Quintessentially friendly and quintessentially French. Look out, too, for the Grande Klezmer de Paris.

## Olympia

*28 bd des Capucines, 9th (01.47.42.82.45/telephone bookings 01.47.42.25.49).* *M° Opéra.* **Box office** 10am-7pm Mon-Sat; 11am-7pm Sun. **Admission** 150F-240F. **No credit cards.**
A season at the temple of French *chanson* (although it also programmes international pop and rock) is the ultimate accolade of French *variété*. Despite listed status, it is due to be demolished and reconstructed a few metres down the street during 1997 (reopening November).

## Le Sentier des Halles

*50 rue d'Aboukir, 2nd (01.42.36.37.27).*
*M° Sentier.* **Music** 8.30pm **DAYS???**. **Admission** 50F-120F. **No credit cards.**
Created ten years ago by Nicole Londeix, herself a one-woman institution, this 100-seat cellar has established itself as the undisputed headquarters of everything that is most inventive and most vital in French popular music. Some of the star acts who started out here, such as Arthur H and Mauranne, are now big enough to play the Olympia and more, but still come back to remind themselves what an audience looks like at close quarters. Don't miss Les Têtes Raides, La Tordue or the magnificent Elizabeth.

## Théâtre du Tourtour

*20 rue Quincampoix, 4th (01.48.87.82.48).*
*M° Hôtel-de-Ville.* **Music** 7pm, 8.30pm, 10.15pm **DAYS???**. **Admission** varies. **No credit cards.**
Once an important centre for *chanson*, but now principally a theatre. There are still some important showcase runs, and the management also programme world music. Fine Algerian singer Djamel Allem is a regular.

programme covers an unpredictable range, so you might find Michel Petrucciani, Luther Allison and Sacha Distel on successive nights. The best gigs are often world-oriented.

### Petit Journal St-Michel
*71 bd St-Michel, 5th (01.43.26.28.59). RER Luxembourg.* **Bar** 10pm-3am Mon-Sat. **Music** 10.30pm. **Admission** 100F (inc first drink). **Credit** MC, V.
A palace to dixieland, crammed into a medieval cellar. Audiences are even less glamorous than the musicians, and both often seem to be having an inexplicably good time.

### La Villa
*29 rue Jacob, 6th (01.43.26.60.00). M° St-Germain-des-Prés.* **Bar** 10.30pm-2am Mon-Sat. **Admission** 120F Mon-Thur; 150F Fri, Sat (incl first drink). **Credit** AmEx, DC, MC, V.
This basement club is the only venue on the Left Bank that can still attract top-flight international names. American headliners play either with their own groups or the best local rhythm sections. Recent visitors include Von Freeman, Kenny Garrett and Cyrus Chestnut. Lots of great vocalists.

## Châtelet Clubs

### Au Duc des Lombards
*42 rue des Lombards, 1st (01.42.33.22.88). M° Châtelet-Les Halles.* **Bar** 6pm-4am daily.
**Music** 10pm. **Admission** 50F-100F. **Credit** MC, V.
Known as 'the bar that Bobby built' since American pianist Bobby Few introduced live music here in the 1970s; he still plays here. Regulars include pianists Kirk Lightsey, Faton Cahen and Jean-Michel Pilc and Paris's resident Italians: Aldo Romano, Paolo Fresu *e altri*. Monday is big band night.

### Petit Opportun
*15 rue des Lavandières-Ste-Opportune, 1st (01.42.36.01.36). M° Châtelet-Les Halles.* **Bar** 10pm-5am Tue-Sat. **Music** 10.45pm. **Admission** 80F (incl first drink). **No credit cards.**
More of a jazz dungeon than a jazz cellar, with a piano that should be burned at the stake. But the programming is always ingenious, matching the best local talent with the odd visitor. No house style, other than gregarious and catholic.

### Le Slow Club
*130 rue de Rivoli, 1st (01.42.33.84.30). M° Châtelet-Les Halles or Pont-Neuf.* **Bar** 10pm-3am Tue-Sat. **Admission** 60F Tue-Thur; 75F Fri, Sat. **Credit** MC, V.
They used to store bananas here to ripen for the market at Les Halles. Doorman Constantinos is the only Greek ever to play for Newcastle United (second team). Sister to the Caveau de la Huchette (*see above*), but a more mature (25+) crowd.

### Le Sunset
*60 rue des Lombards, 1st (01.40.26.46.60). M° Châtelet-Les Halles.* **Bar** 9.30pm-dawn daily. **Music** 10pm. **Admission** 60F-90F. **Credit** MC, V.
Serious programming includes Didier Lockwood, Laurent de Wilde, Steve Lacy and Steve Grossman. Vocalists on Sundays, jam sessions on Mondays. A clear acoustic.

## The North

### Cithéa
*114 rue Oberkampf, 11th (01.40.21.70.95). M° Parmentier.* **Bar** 9pm-2am Thur-Sat. **Music** 10.30pm. **Admission** free. **Credit** V.
Manu Boubli and Eric Trosset are determined to cross frontiers, programming African, funk, jazz and acid jazz – look out for Crazy Dance People or Julian Lourou – followed by a DJ session. Most recent innovation has been teaming drum 'n' bass MCs with jazz musicians. *See also* chapter **Clubs**.

### Houdon Jazz Club
*5 rue des Abbesses, 18th (01.46.06.35.91). M° Abbesses.* **Music** 10.30pm Thur-Sat. **Admission** free. **Credit** (above 100F) V .
A friendly neighbourhood café in the heart of Montmartre, which turns into a jazz club three nights a week. Talented sax player Xavier Richardeau can often be found here raising the roof with friends such as the Belmondo brothers.

### Lionel Hampton Jazz Club
*Hôtel Le Méridien-Etoile, 81 bd Gouvion-St-Cyr, 17th (01.40.68.34.34). M° Porte Maillot.* **Music** 10.30pm-2am DAYS???. **Admission** 130F. **Credit** AmEx, DC, MC, V.
In a plush hotel, the Lionel Hampton is a leading venue for soul, gospel and rhythm 'n' blues, with mainly American singers and musicians. Book a table close to the stage.

### Studio des Islettes
*10 rue des Islettes, 18th (01.42.58.63.33). M° Barbès-Rochechouart.* **Jam sessions** 7-10.30pm Mon-Fri. **Concert** 7.30pm Sat, Sun. **Admission** free Mon-Fri; 50F Sat, Sun. **No credit cards.**
Wonderfully shabby jazz cooperative. In theory, there are formal gigs at the weekend, and jam sessions during the week, though even at concerts most of the audience seem to end up taking their turn on a chorus.

## Blues

*See also* **New Morning** *and* **Lionel Hampton**.

### Quai des Blues
*17 bd Vital Bouhot, 92200 Neuilly-sur-Seine (01.46.24.22.00). M° Porte de Champerret, then bus 164 or 165.* **Music** 10.30pm, midnight Thur-Sat. **Admission** 80F Thur, students; 100F Fri, Sat. **Credit** MC, V.
A new club dedicated to black American blues, soul, gospel, boogie-woogie and r'n'b. There's also a good restaurant.

### St Louis Blues
*33 rue Blomet, 15th (01.47.34.30.97). M° Volontaires.* **Music** 8pm-2am Fri, Sat. **Admission** 45F. **Credit** MC, V.
Round the corner from UNESCO, a perfect den of iniquity openly contravenes all international conventions on pleasure limitation. Local groups play here.

### Utopia
*79 rue de l'Ouest, 14th (answerphone 01.43.22.79.66). M° Pernéty.* **Music** 10.30pm Tue-Sat. **Admission** free; 1st drink 50F. **Credit** MC, V.
A dedicated live music café, the Utopia programmes blues, folk and country most nights of the week.

## Music Bars

### L'Archipel
*50 rue Basfroi, 11th (01.43.70.37.26). M° Voltaire.* **Bar** 6pm-2am daily. **Music** 9pm. **Admission** free-60F. **Credit** MC, V.
The Archipel's *raison d'être* is live music, although it has recently been suffering from clampdowns by the authorities. When permitted, bands – French indie rock types, although other styles get a look-in – play in the dimly lit basement.

### Chez Adel
*10 rue de la Grange-aux-Belles, 10th (01.42.08.24.61). M° Gare de l'Est.* **Bar** 7pm-2am daily. **Music** 8pm. **Admission** free. **No credit cards.**
In a surprisingly groovy pocket of the 10th is this studenty hang-out. Against the backdrop of a mural of the nearby Canal St-Martin, a huge variety of bands appear, from modern

and traditional French (including sea-shanties!), via Russian and Irish, to Afro-Cuban. Reasonable drink prices.

## Horse's Mouth

*120 rue Montmartre, 2nd (01.40.39.93.66). M° Sentier.*
**Bar** 5pm-2am daily. **Music** 9.30pm Wed-Sat.
**Admission** free. **Credit** MC, V.
Basically just another rue Montmartre bar masquerading as an English pub (pronounced *'ze 'orzez mouz*). Live music is mostly French rock/*chanson* with occasional comedy, reggae and funk. Highly smoky – asthmatics steer clear.

## Molly Malone's

*21 rue Godot de Mauroy, 9th (01.47.42.07.77).*
*M° Madeleine.* **Bar** 4pm-2am daily. **Music** 9.30pm.
**Admission** free. **No credit cards.**
A classic Irish pub serving the black stuff to a crowd of older French locals and the odd Irishman in a dark, smoky atmosphere. The live music ranges wildly in style and quality from trad Irish folk to a mixed bag of rock.

## Wait & See

*9 bd Voltaire, 11th (01.48.07.29.49). M° République.*
**Bar** 6pm-2am. **Music** 9pm Tue-Sun. **Admission** free.
**Credit** MC, V.
This stalwart of the Paris live circuit is looking good after its recent face-lift. Problems with the local council can mean interruptions in the regular stream of live bands. DJs at weekends. Groovy young clientele, and a restaurant upstairs.

## Music on Board

Round Notre Dame and further upstream in front of the new Bibliothèque Nationale de France, musical barges are all the rage. The quality can vary, but the unpretentious atmosphere, eclectic music, cheap drinks and river views make them a good alternative to earthbound venues.

# Vive la différence

*Music producer Ben Rogan exchanges cross-channel lessons.*

I first came to Paris to record with Sade. For her third album *Love is Stronger than Pride*, we decided to overdub and mix in Paris, finally spending the best part of a year to complete the project. I had already worked for about ten years as an engineer and producer in all styles of music from The Damned to Sting, The Smiths to Everthing But The Girl.

My first taste of French music came when I was asked to work with French pop star Etienne Daho who, on our first meeting, decided to make me a compilation of classic French songs including some by Serge Gainsbourg, Jacques Dutronc, Françoise Hardy, Michel Polnareff and Jacques Brel. This was probably the first time I had listened seriously to something in French; these are songs you will hear if you spend any time in Paris and songs I have grown to love. I realised that although a guitar recorded in London, Paris or New York is basically the same, as a producer working in another country, one had to be aware of cultural traditions and differences in language. As anyone who has ever struggled to learn French will know, it is necessary to roll your words and phrases together in order to be understood, which tends to give French a more flowing and melodic line, whereas in English we separate words and syllables which makes the language seem more percussive. This may be why English is the adopted language of rock and roll and France is perhaps better known for

sweeping ballads. Try listening to *'Heartbreak Hotel'* by Elvis or *'La vie en rose'* by Piaf and you'll get the point. Another difference is that the song words are particularly important in France, leading to an attention to voice level and comprehension of the lyrics bordering on the obsessional. Whether this is due to French literary tradition or just a difference of language, I'm not sure, but it may not be mere coincidence that precursor of modern-day rap, Serge Gainsbourg, talked his way through at least half his songs.

Interestingly the biggest explosion of the past few years has been the rise of French rap. Although its origins are obviously American, it works surprisingly well in French. Though the music is clearly rhythmic, the constant unending stream of words gives a colour and texture altogether different to American rap. French rapper MC Solaar, for example, probably feels he is following as much in the tradition of Gainsbourg and *la culture française* as an American import.

As an English producer, I feel I'm often wanted to bring a bit of 'attitude' to the proceedings. Whether this is an inherent Anglo-Saxon trait or just a question of forty years of rock culture, who can say? Anyhow, whether it be recording an album entirely in the bar with Polnareff or living and recording in a French château or simply meeting Gainsbourg, I am happy I now have two different languages and cultures to draw from: keep an open mind and *Vive la différence*.

### La Balle au Bond
*facing 35 quai de la Tournelle, 5th (01.40.51.87.06).*
*M° Maubert-Mutualité.* **Bar** 10pm-2am. **Music** 10pm.
**Admission** 40F. **No credit cards.**
Concerts, café-théâtre and bar on a barge.

### La Guinguette Pirate
*quai de la Gare, 13th (01.44.25.89.89). M° Quai de la*
*Gare.* **Bar** 6pm-2am Mon-Sat; noon-11pm Sun. **Music**
8.30pm. **Admission** free. **No credit cards.**
A three-masted Chinese junk. Chess and food in the hold.

### Le Kiosque Flottant
*quai de Montebello, 5th (01.43.54.19.51). M° St-Michel.*
**Bar** 10am-2am. **Music** 9pm Fri, Sat. **Credit** DC, MC, V.

### Péniche Makara
*quai de la Gare, 13th (01.44.24.09.00). M° Quai de la*
*Gare.* **Bar** 6pm-2am Tue-Sun. **Music** 9pm Tue-Sat;
6pm Sun. **Admission** 30F-80F. **Credit** DC, MC, V

### Le Six-Huit
*quai Montebello, 5th Paris (01.43.80.74.54). M° Maubert-*
*Mutualité.* **Open** 7pm-2am daily. **Music** 10pm Thur-Sat.
**Admission** 30F-40F. **Credit** AmEx, DC, MC, V.

*It's not all junk on the* **Guignette Pirate**.

## World Music

Paris has established itself as a major centre on the
world music circuit. Many top African musicians
are based here and several fine venues programme
traditional artists from every conceivable corner
of the globe, although it's for a mainly elite audience: there's very little crossover between this milieu and Paris' immigrant communities. Strangely,
while classical Arab music gets serious attention
at the **Institut du Monde Arabe**, there are no
serious permanent venues for the popular music
of North Africa – Algerian urban raï, as exemplified by the hedonistic, apolitical fun of Khaled and
Cheb Mami, and the lyrical and often socially committed rural Berber songs from Kabylie. Other
stars based in Paris include Djamel Allem, Idir and
Lounes Matoub. There's no telling where they may
play next – ask your friends, scour the listings
magazines, and tune in to Beur FM (106.7MHz).

Look out also for Latin and salsa at Les Etoiles
and La Java (*see chapter* **Clubs**) and for the
Africolor Festival before Christmas (*see chapter*
**Paris by Season**). See also New Morning (*above*,
**Jazz**) and Cité de la Musique (*see chapter* **Music:
Classical & Opera**).

### Auditorium du Châtelet
*Forum des Halles, 5 porte St-Eustache, 1st*
*(01.42.36.14.09). M° Châtelet-Les Halles.* **Box office**
noon-7pm DAYS???. **Admission** 100F-150F; reductions
80F-120F. **Credit** AmEx, MC, V.
This modern auditorium has cramped, too-steeply pitched
seating but good acoustics. Wide programming includes
flamenco, *chanson française*, gospel, world and jazz.

### Centre Mandapa
*6 rue Wurtz, 13th (01.45.89.01.60). M° Glacière.*
*Telephone bookings* 11am-7pm Mon-Fri. **Music** 8.30pm.
**Admission** 80F-90F; reductions 40F-70F.
**No credit cards.**
The unpretentious 100-seater hall at this Indian dance centre

is Paris's oldest traditional music venue. Alongside rising
stars from the sub-continent, Milena Salvini programmes
fine Persian music, singers from Ireland and Bolivia, and
more. Regulars include Persian zarb virtuoso Djamchid
Chemirani, Indian sarangi star Ustad Sabri Khan and Berber
singer Houria Aïchi. *See also chapter* **Dance**.

### Institut du Monde Arabe
*1 rue des Fossés St Bernard, 5th (01.40.51.38.14).*
*M° Jussieu.* **Box office** 10am-6pm Tue-Sun.
**Admission** 100F; reductions 80F. **Credit** AmEx, MC, V.
The basement auditorium takes airport lounge seating to
new breadths and new heights. But not even the frequent
logistical cock-ups and the near-total lack of atmosphere can
detract from the riches of the classical Arab music on offer.

### Maison des Cultures du Monde
*101 bd Raspail, 6th (01.45.44.41.42). M° Notre Dame*
*des Champs.* **Music** 8.30pm Tue-Fri; 7pm Sat; 5pm Sun.
**Admission** 100F; reductions 80F. **Credit** V.
Music plays second fiddle to theatre most of the year, and
programming is uneven, but watch out for occasional gems.

### Satellit' Café
*44 rue de la Folie Méricourt, 11th (01.47.00.48.87).*
*M° Oberkampf.* **Bar** 6pm-2am Mon-Thur; 6pm-5am Fri,
Sat. **Admission** free. **No credit cards.**
Adventurous bar featuring mid-week multi-ethnic acoustic
gigs. A junior cousin on the circuit, but an excellent place to
explore Brazilian swing or Balkan free folk.

### Suds
*55 rue de Charonne, 11th (01.43.14.06.36).*
*M° Ledru-Rollin.* **Music** 9.30pm Wed; 7.30pm Sun.
**Admission** free. **Credit** V.
A colourful restaurant dedicated to food from all points south
(Mediterranean, Latin America). Concerts in the cellar bar
include some fine Latin, Portuguese *fado* and Afro-funk
musicians, so it's a pity that no one pays much attention.

### Théâtre de la Ville
*2 pl du Châtelet, 1st (01.42.74.22.77). M° Châtelet-Les*
*Halles.* **Box office** 11am-6pm Mon; 11am-8pm Tue-Sat.
*Telephone bookings* 9am-6pm. **Admission** 90F.
**Credit** DC, MC, V.
The largest world music venue in Paris now in competition
with the Cité de la Musique (*see* **Classical**). Acoustically
there are no bad seats, but up top you can feel a long way
from the action. The programme is magnificent, with very
few duds, and most concerts are sold well in advance.
Strong on India and Central Asia. *See also chapter* **Dance**.

# Sport & Fitness

**If you want to sweat it out on the field, go for a canter or wallow in a pool, Paris has an activity to suit your every mood.**

It was a Frenchman, Baron Pierre de Coubertin, who started the modern Olympic Games with that twaddle about taking part and not winning, and the sporting ethic is still alive and kicking all over Paris. As a gauge of just how important sport is to the French, the national sports daily *l'Equipe* is the best-selling newspaper in France.

Sport in France benefits greatly from government investment, and municipal sports facilities are plentiful and standards are generally good. To use them you will need a *carte* for which you must show some form of identity, bring a photo and in the case of sports perceived as risky, proof of insurance. The local Mairie has an Office Municipal des Sports which details all sports, clubs and facilities by *arrondissement* in its booklet, *Guide du Sport à Paris*. Municipal facilities are used by individual clubs which are advertised on a noticeboard in the centre. If you want to compete, affiliation to the sport's governing body is necessary as this gives you insurance cover, but this usually comes when you join a club and costs around 150F. For all kinds of sports equipment, **GoSport**'s largest branch is at Forum des Halles (01.40.26.40.52).

## Keeping Informed

**Allô-Sports**
*(01.42.76.54.54).* **Open** 10.30am-5pm Mon-Thur; 10.30am-4.30pm Fri.
Helpful municipal phoneline giving information on sports and sporting events in the Paris area. The staff speak English, but you could spend days getting through to them.

**Maison des Associations de Paris**
*14 Grande Galerie, Forum des Halles, 4th (01.42.33.74.00). M° Châtelet-Les Halles.* **Open** 10am-7pm Tue-Fri; 10am-noon, 1-6pm Sat.
General information on sports clubs and associations in Paris, though their lists are not exhaustive and a call to the relevant federation could be more fruitful.

## Activities

### American Football

American football does happen in Paris, and there are six clubs to prove it. **Les Mollosses** (01.39.76.17.05; the answering machine is for a furniture business, but it's correct) have a large squad and train at **Stade Jacques Anquetil**, rue Pierre Boudou, Asnieres. RER Les Grésillons. Turn right out of the station, continue until you cross over a motorway, turn left and the ground is on the right. Plenty of hut-huts and high-fives on a top-class pitch. Training Mon and Fri at 8pm.

### Athletics & Running

If you need a track, Paris bristles with them: the municipal sites are pretty good on the whole; find your local one in the OMS booklet. To give an idea of the scale, Paris has eight indoor running tracks and Britain has two.

For an open-air run the Bois de Boulogne and the Bois de Vincennes are beautiful, though some parts of the Bois de Boulogne are frequented by men cruising even in daylight hours – take note if not part of your training schedule. The Paris marathon in April and the Paris-Versailles (16km) in late September are the two main running events. Call **Allô-sports** (*see above* **Keeping Informed**) for details.

### Baseball & Softball

Baseball and softball clubs are predictably Americanised and many players speak English.
**Club Patriots de Paris (Baseball Club)** *(06.08.75.95.56/ recorded information 01.48.87.22.22)* has competitive and recreational sections. **Annual membership** 1,170F (plus 900F kit obligatory for competitions) and 600F (recreation). Shorter-term stays are possible. Turn up at 6.30pm on Saturdays, at **Gymnase Croix Nivert** 107 rue Croix Nivert, 15th. M° Commerce.

### Basketball

Basketball is hugely popular in Paris and almost every municipal sports centre has as least one court and clubs that play there. For something less structured, French teenagers frequent two newish courts under the Métro tracks near the Glacière stop in the 13th *arrondissement*, and there's a hoop in the Jardin du Luxembourg in the 6th. This isn't the Bronx, but respect the court hierarchy nonetheless. The **French Basketball Federation** (01.49.23.69.00) has a list of clubs.

### Bowling

The Paris region has over 25 bowling centres. The two listed below are among the most pleasant. Both rent out shoes and have restaurants and games rooms.

**Bowling-Mouffetard**
*13 rue Gracieuse, 5th (01.43.31.09.35). M° Place Monge.* **Open** 11am-2am daily. **Prices** 23F per game Mon-Fri, after 8pm 32F; 32F Sat, Sun, public holidays. Under-26s, Wed for all, get two games plus shoe hire and a drink for 59F. **Shoe hire** 10F. **Credit** V.
Eight bowling lanes and a lively atmosphere.

**Bowling de Paris**
*Jardin d'Acclimatation, Bois de Boulogne, 16th (01.40.67.94.00). M° Sablon.* **Open** 11am-2am daily.
**Prices** 5F per game 11am-1pm daily; 23F per game Mon-Fri before 8pm; 32F after 8pm; Fri after 8pm, Sat, Sun 34F (discounts for students, members of French and other bowling federations). **Shoe hire** 11F. **Credit** AmEx, DC, MC, V.
Inside the Jardin d'Acclimatation, so you have to pay a 12F entry fee to get into the complex. The centre has 24 lanes plus pool, billiards and numerous video games.

# Climbing

The French are big on sport climbing and bolt their climbs, so if trad is your thing there may be a culture gap to overcome. If you can't make it to the Alps, Paris offers five outdoor municipal *murs d'escalade*. Though usually reserved for schools and climbing clubs, facilities are open to individuals who have a one-month membership (available from any location for 17F; photo, proof of insurance and passport) and their own gear. A good climbing and general outdoor shop is **Au Vieux Camper** 48 rue des Ecoles, 5th (01.43.29.12.32).

### Centre Sportif Poissonnier
*2 rue Jean-Cocteau, 18th (01.42.51.24.68). M° Porte de Clignancourt.* **Open** to public for climbing noon-2pm Mon-Fri; noon-4pm Sat, Sun. **Prices** 17F.
A basic, 21m unlit outside wall. Has a little 'real rock' section. For details of club meetings, telephone for information.

### Mur Mur
*55 rue Cartier Bresson, 93500 Pantin (01.48.46.11.00). M° Aubervilliers Quatre Chemins.* **Open** noon-11pm Mon-Fri; 9.30am-6.30pm Sat, Sun. **Prices** 50F noon-6pm; 60F 6pm-11pm Mon-Fri; 60F 9.30am-6.30pm Sat, Sun; three month pass 900F.
Cited as the best climbing wall in Europe if not the world, with 1,400 square metres of wall and 9,000 holds. All kit for hire and tuition offered.

*Reach new heights at **C.S. Poissonnier**.*

# Cricket & Football

Yes, cricket exists in France, though the French don't understand the rules, hence clubs are run by Asians or Britons. With over 400 football clubs in Paris, it's best to pick up the OMS booklet to find out where the nearest team can be found.

### Château de Thoiry Cricket Club
*Chateau de Thoiry, 78770 Thoiry. Autoroute 13 direction Rouen; exit St-Quentin en Yvelines. (Bill Ratcliffe, president: answering machine 01.47.43.19.01).*
The top cricket club in France and seat of the French National team. With a squad of 30 they field teams of varying standards and receive teams from all over the world. The season runs from April to October with 45 matches for men and a growing 15 for women. A good social calendar and all are welcome to play. The château is also home to a zoo.

### Standard Athletic Club
*Route Forestière du Pavé de Meudon, 92360 Meudon-la-Forêt (01.46.26.16.09). By train SNCF from Gare Montparnasse to Meudon-Bellevue, then a 20-minute walk/By car N116 or D2.* **Open** 9am-9pm daily.
This private, non-profit-making club open to Britons living in Paris fields two cricket sides. The cricket season runs from May to September and includes friendlies against six local teams. The club also has eight tennis courts, two squash courts, a heated outdoor pool, men's and women's hockey, football and rugby. The club has a noticeboard at The Bowler, 13 rue d'Artois, 8th/01.45.61.16.60.

# Cycling

For cycle hire companies, *see chapter* **Services**. For cycle lanes, *see chapter* **Getting Around**.
    Paris has many cycling clubs, some competition-based, others more leisurely. Both the Bois de Boulogne and the Bois de Vincennes offer good cycling away from the urban snarl. Either find your nearest club in the OMS booklet or get out there and pick up a group.
    Mountain biking (VTT, *vélo tout terrain* in French) is limited in Paris. To get gnarly, Parisian MTBers head for Fontainebleau, Verrières-Meudon and Montmorency. There is a law against riding on paths less than 2.5m wide.
    For general bike needs, the GoSport in Les Halles is sufficient. For specialist MTB, try VTT Center, 1 place Rungis, 13th (01.45.65.49.89). A hike from Métro Corvisart, but they are the real thing. Cycles la Roue d'Or, 65 bd de Strasbourg, 10th, is for top-notch road racing. To pick up a second-hand bike, try Au Réparateur de Bicylettes, 46 bd Sébastopol, 1st.

# Diving

If you are in Paris for some time it's worth joining a club as it works out cheaper. If time is limited, a pricier, commercial outfit will get you your certificate. For a diving shop, try **Plongespace**, 80 rue Balard, 15th (01.45.57.01.01).

### ASCAN Plongée
*(01.40.63.61.82/answering machine 01.42.21.18.14).*
Well-qualified, experienced scuba instructors offer courses in English, aimed at a variety of underwater interests. Courses for beginners, including textbooks, insurance and scuba gear rental, cost 1,600F (for the French licence); courses for the PADI (International licence) cost 1,750F. Courses are held Wed evenings at the Marché St-Germain pool, 6th/M° Mabillon, and all day Sat and Sun at Piscine Alfred Sévestre, 70 bd Gallieni, Issy les Moulineaux, 92130/M° Mairie d'Issy.

### Club de Plongée du 5ème Arrondissement
*(01.47.20.26.67).* **Open** 7-9pm Wed. **Annual membership** (Sep-July) 990F; reductions of 330F in January and 660F if you join after Easter.

A friendly club with all ages represented, where you can train for the French licence (PADI is not available, *see below*). Organises trips to the Med and further afield. Meets at the Piscine Jean Taris, 16 rue Thouin, 5th/M° Monge.

# Golf

Now that tennis has been thoroughly democratised, golf has become the French status-seeker's sport of choice. There are no courses in Paris, but scores in the Paris region, many of them open to non-members. Green fees are usually much cheaper during the week. For a full list of courses, contact the **French Golf Federation** (69 av Victor-Hugo, 16th/ 01.44.17.63.00).

**Golf Clément Ader, Domaine du Château Péreire** *77220 Gretz Armainvilliers (01.64.07.80.43). SNCF from Gare de Lyon to Gretz Armainvilliers.* **Open** 8.30am-7.30pm Mon, Wed-Sun. **Fee** 200F weekdays; 450F Sat, Sun. Challenging, Japanese-designed course with plenty of water hazards.

**Golf Disneyland Paris Marne-la-Vallée** *77777 Marne-la-Vallé (01.60.45.68.04). RER Marne-la-Vallé/ Chessy then free shuttle.* **Open** 8.45am-dusk Mon-Fri; 7.45am-dusk Sat, Sun. **Fee** 120F Mon-Fri; 200F Sat, Sun. Mickey's course has the lot: 27 holes, great clubhouse, American professional, buggies and equipment for hire, even Mouse-shaped bunkers.

**Golf du Réveillon Ferme des Hyverneaux** *77150 Lesigny (01.60.02.17.33). SNCF from Gare de L'Est to Pontault-Combault.* **Open** summer 9am-5pm Mon-Fri; 8.30am-5.30pm Sat, Sun; reduced winter hours. **Fee** 100F Mon-Fri; 169F Sat, Sun. Attractive, 36-hole public course.

# Health & Fitness

Health clubs hit Paris in the late 1980s and they continue to proliferate. Clubs fill up at lunchtime and on weekday evenings, so stick to off-peak hours. Paris residents might consider joining a municipal club with a weights room (contact Allô-Sports or the Maison des Associations for information; *see above* **Keeping Informed**).

## Club Quartier Latin

*19 rue de Pontoise, 5th (01.43.54.82.45). M° Maubert-Mutualité.* **Open** 9am-midnight Mon-Fri; 9.30am-7.30pm Sat, Sun. **Membership** Join either the Fitness (weight and aerobic training) or the Squash section: one gives reductions for the other and both give access to pool. Fitness and pool: *annual* 3,100F/2,100F student; *1 month* 800F/500F; *day pass* 70F/50F. **No credit cards.** The gym has plenty of well-maintained machines, although not all new. Free weights range from the Herculean to Lilliputian, and there's one Olympic bar. A helpful instructor is sometimes present. The club also houses four squash courts, dance, Tai Chi and aerobics classes in a classy studio. Piscine Pontoise has a pool of anglophone members (*see box* **Swimming Pools**). Nice relaxed atmophere.

## Espace Vit'Halles

*48 rue Rambuteau, 3rd (01.42.77.21.71). M° Rambuteau.* **Open** 8am-10pm Mon-Fri; 10am-7pm Sat; 11am-4pm Sun. **Membership** *annual* 3,900F/student 2,900F; *1 month* 600F; *per hour* 100F. **Credit** MC, V. Friendly and professsional. The gym is good if a little cluttered with machines, free weights, knowledgeable instructors and a non-posey crowd. There's a bewildering range of fitness classes run by enthusiastic and tolerant instructors. The changing rooms are surgically clean.

## Gymnase Club

*19 locations in Paris and environs, contact 01.44.37.24.24/01.46.51.88.16 for full list. The most central are:* **Gymnase Club Palais Royal** *147bis rue St-Honoré, 1st (01.40.20.03.03/01.42.61.09.21).*

*M° Palais Royal.* **Gymnase Club Salle des Champs** *26 rue de Berri, 8th (01.43.59.04.58). M° George V.* **Gymnase Club Grenelle** (with pool) *8 rue de Frémicourt, 15th (01.45.75.34.00). M° Cambronne.* **Membership** *annual* 4,000F or 4,580F (reductions for company membership and students); *ten visits* 600F; *day pass* 140F. **Credit** AmEx, MC, V. The clubs are well-equipped and clean, and instruction standards are generally good. Usual gamut of classes plus martial arts and weight ones. Overly keen blue-coated staff.

# Horse Riding

Both the Bois de Boulogne and the Bois de Vincennes are beautiful places to ride but it must be done under the auspices of a riding club. You can join one of the following clubs: La Société d'Equitation de Paris (01.45.01.20.06); the Centre Hippique du Touring (01.45.01.20.88) and the Cercle Hippique du Bois de Vincennes (01.48.73.01.28).

## Club Bayard Equitation

*Bois de Vincennes, Centre Bayard/UCPA de Vincennes, av de Polygone, 12th (01.43.65.46.87).* Complete beginners can learn to ride in the lovely setting of this unpretentious riding club. Membership runs either on three month cycles (1,140F), or there is one month's membership (320F), or a five-day course in July and August (1,200F).

## Poney Clubs du Relais

*Bois de Boulogne, route de Suresnes, 16th (01.45.27.54.65). M° Porte Maillot, then bus 244.* Rents ponies for 80F for half an hour, 150F for an hour and requires riders to be accompanied by a monitor who will pitch the pace according to the client. Individual lessons are 200F an hour, or there's a day course for 350F.

# Ice Skating

If the temperature drops extremely low and the park's staff posts signs declaring the ice safe, there is also skating on the Lac Supérieur in the Bois de Boulogne. Otherwise, go to:

## Patinoire de Boulogne

*1 rue Victor Griffuelhes, Boulogne-Billancourt (01.46.21.04.26). M° Marcel Sembat.* **Open** 3.45-6.15pm Mon, Thur; 3.45-6.30pm, 9.15-11.30pm, Tue, Fri; 2.45-6pm Wed; 10am-12.30pm, 2.30-5.45pm, 9.15-11.30pm, Sat; 9.45-12.30pm, 3-6.30pm, Sun. **Admission** 31F; 23F under-16s; 19F skate hire. **No credit cards.**

# Rowing & Watersports

In France everyone learns to scull before doing sweep-oar and you will be marginalised if you can't scull. The two main rowing clubs in the Paris area are:

## Société d'Encouragement du Sport Nautique

*Ile des Loups, 94130 Nogent-sur-Marne (01.43.24.38.06).* Hard-core, competitive, men-only members. Nice location.

## Société Nautique de la Basse Seine

*26 quai du President Paul Doumer, 92400 Courbevoie (01.43.33.03.47). Next to La Défense.* Competition and recreational sections. Good equipment, strong history.

## Base Nautique de la Villette

*15-17 quai de la Loire, 19th (01.42.40.29.90). M° Jaures.* **Open** over-16s free, every hour from 9am to 4pm Sat (15F per month registration fee); *children* free 9am-noon, 2-5pm Wed. Children and adults can row, canoe and kayak in the 600m x 65m basin at La Villette. Equipment is provided.

# Taking the plunge

Paris has 35 swimming pools open to the public. Opening times are complicated: most open to the general public at lunch time (11.30am-1.30pm), but are largely for school use at other times, and close in summer for renovation. Admission to the municipal pools is 15F (adults) and 7F50 (children). Privately-run or -owned pools cost a bit more.

### Piscine Suzanne-Berlioux
*10 pl de la Rotonde, 1st (01.42.36.98.44). M° Châtelet-Les Halles.* **Open** till 10pm Tue, Thur, Fri; till 5pm Sat, Sun. **Admission** 24F.
This 50-metre pool in the Forum des Halles is clean and crowded. Has a tropical greenhouse. Young, hip clientele.

### Piscine de Pontoise
*19 rue de Pontoise, 5th (01.43.54.82.45). M° Maubert-Mutualité.* **Open** 7am-midnight Mon-Wed, Fri. **Admission** 23F-44F.
Vintage pool with 1930s-style glass roof and retro tiles has classes for tots and expectant mothers. Music and underwater lighting by night. *See above* **Club Quartier Latin.** *Indoor. Solarium. Pool: 33 x 15m. Café.*

### Piscine Jean Taris
*16 rue Thouin, 5th (01.43.25.54.03). M° Monge.*
Look out onto the Panthéon and the Lycée Henri IV gardens from this lovely but rather cramped pool. *Indoor. Two pools: 25 x 15m, children's pool 15 x 6m.*

### Piscine du Marché St-Germain
*7 rue Clément, 6th (01.43.29.08.15). M° Mabillon.*
An underground pool in revamped St-Germain market. *Indoor. Pool: 25 x 12.5m.*

### Piscine Reuilly
*13 rue Hénard, 12th (01.40.02.08.08). M° Montgallet.*
This bright, friendly municipal facility has the two newest pools in Paris. Three, large bay windows look on to a park. *Indoor. Solarium. Two pools: 25 x 15m; 12 x 6m.*

### Piscine Roger-LeGall
*34 bd Carnot, 12th (01.44.73.81.12). M° Porte de Vincennes.*
This calm pool is covered with a tent every winter. Mixed nude bathing takes place at 9-11pm Mon and Wed. *Outdoor. Solarium. Pool: 50 x 15m.*

*A vintage swim at **Piscine Pontoise**.*

### Piscine Butte-aux-Cailles
*5 pl Paul Verlaine, 13th (01.45.89.60.05). M° Place d'Italie.*
Built in 1910, the main indoor pool has Italian tiles and a vaulted 1930s Art Deco ceiling. Two outdoor pools are open in the summer and are fed by artesian wells. *Indoor pool: 33 x 12m. Two outdoor pools: 25 x 12.5m and 12.5 x 6m.*

### Aquaboulevard
*4 rue Louis-Armand, 15th (01.40.60.10.00). M° Balard/ RER Boulevard Victor.* **Open** 9am-11pm Mon-Sun. **Admission** Mon-Fri 59F for 4 hours; 3-12s 50F; Sat, Sun 77F; 3-12s 56F; under-3s free; 10F after every hour.
If you want a big, splashy time with your children, this is the place to come. The 70,000 square feet of indoor-outdoor water sports facilities include a tropical lagoon, wave pool, water slides and hot baths. There are also tennis courts, a gym, a bowling alley, ten bars, and restaurants.

### Piscine Armand-Massard
*66 bd du Montparnasse, 15th (01.45.38.65.19). M° Montparnasse-Bienvenüe.*
A vast underground swimming complex under the reviled Montparnasse skyscraper. The renovated complex has three pools; one for beginners and one for diving. *Indoor. Three pools: 33 x 15m, 25 x 12.5m, 12.5 x 6m.*

### Piscine Emile-Anthoine
*9 rue Jean-Rey, 15th (01.53.69.61.59). M° Bir-Hakeim.*
An ultra modern pool with an outdoor jogging track and a view of the nearby Eiffel Tower. Very crowded. *Indoor with terraced garden. Two pools: 25 x 12.5m and 12.5 x 6m.*

### Piscine Henry-de-Montherlant
*32 bd Lannes, 16th (01.45.03.03.28). M° Porte-Dauphine.* **Open** until 8.30pm on Tue.
Popular, modern pool with a chic clientele. Not oppressive. *Indoor with outdoor tanning area. Two pools: 25 x 15m, 15 x 6m.*

### Piscine Hébert
*2 rue des Fillettes, 18th (01.46.07.60.01). M° Marx-Dormoy.*
Dating from 1896 and recently renovated, this is a lovely (but crowded) pool with a retractable roof. *Indoor. Two pools: 25 x 15m, 14 x 12m.*

### Piscine Georges-Vallerey Tourelles
*148 av Gambetta, 20th (01.40.31.15.20). M° Porte des Lilas.* **Open** until 9.15pm Tue, Thur.
The first pool to hold swimming competitions as an Olympic sport (in 1924). Johnny Weismuller swam to gold and glory here before taking on the role as Tarzan. *Indoor with sliding roof. Solarium. Pool: 50 x 18m.*

### Piscine en Plein Air du Parc du Sceaux
*148bis av du Général de Gaulle, 92160 Antony (01.43.50.39.35). RER Croix de Berny.* **Open** dawn-dusk May-Sept.
Located next to a regional forest, just 10 minutes from central Paris by RER, this park has three outdoor pools: an uncluttered, 50m Olympic-size pool, separate deep-diving tank and a children's pool. There's a café and a lawn with sunbathing and picnic space.

## Rugby

Top level rugby goes on at **Racing Club de France** headquarters: 5 rue Eblé, 7th (01.45.67.55.86). Ground: Terrain Yves-du-Manoir, 12 rue François Faber, 92700 Colombes. Part of a huge multisport club, the top team is professional. For a good club standard try: **Athletic Club de Boulogne**. If you want to play on a French-speaking team, call the Comité Ile de France de Rugby 01.43.42.51.51.

### Athletic Club de Boulogne Billancourt

*Saut du Loup, route des Tribunes, 16th (01.46.51.11.91).* Fields three teams: head down at 7.30pm on Wed to check it out. It is also a multi sports club. For general information on sports activities call 01.47.31.03.95/01.41.10.25.30. For athletics call 01.47.12.78.29/01.46.99.09.56. Venues vary.

### British Rugby Club of Paris

*(01.41.37.68.80/01.42.94.29.26).* This club, run by Graham Spensley is 'convivial' rather than fanatical, and runs two Saturday sides and trains just once a week in Meudon at the Standard Athletic Club (*see above* **Cricket**). The club also has a noticeboard at The Bowler, 13 rue d'Artois, 8th (01.45.61.16.60).

## Snooker/Billiards

The French have their own brand of (pocketless) billiards, and many halls here have only French or American pool tables. The few snooker facilities include the **Bowling de Paris** (*see above* **Bowling**), which has three tables.

### Académie de Billard Clichy-Montmartre

*84 rue de Clichy, 9th (01.48.78.32.85). M° Place de Clichy.* **Open** 10am-4am daily. **Rates** 53F-68F per hour. With tile floor, high ceilings and tall mirrors, this is a beer and Gitanes establishment. Has a full-size snooker table.

### Blue-Billard

*111-113 rue St-Maur, 11th (01.43.55.87.21). M° St-Maur.* **Open** 7.30am-2am Mon-Fri; 11am-2am Sat, Sun. **Rates** 38F in the morning; 60F-65F per hour. French and American tables, relaxing atmosphere and a bar. You can play for free if you have lunch.

# World Cup

Come 1998 the Football World Cup circus comes to France, and a new stadium is being built in St-Denis to host the Paris-based matches. According to co-president Michel Platini, the aim of the organisers is to 'have full stadiums and a World Cup that is accessible to everyone'. Tickets are available from 2,500 of the 5,500 branches of Crédit Agricole; or by Minitel on 3615 France 98; or by calling 08.03.00.19.98; or in writing to France 98, BP 1998, 75201 Paris, Cedex 16. Tickets for the first and second rounds have been on sale since November 1996 on a first come first served basis. A pass (725F-2,250F) is on offer to a particular venue giving access to five or six matches. Since no team is fixed to a particular venue, a good rotation is guaranteed. Single tickets won't be on sale until 1998.

### Hôtel Concorde St-Lazare

*108 rue St-Lazare, 8th (01.40.08.44.44). M° St-Lazare.* **Open** noon-midnight daily. **Rates** 60F-70F per hour. A velveteen atmosphere with the scent of cigars and Cognac: this is the most elegant setting for playing French billiards.

### Les Mousquetaires

*77 av du Maine, 14th (01.43.22.50.46). M° Gaité.* **Open** 7am-3am Mon-Thur, Sun; 7am-5am Fri, Sat. **Rates** 30F-60F per hour. This American bar, with an eleven-table pool room in the back, is a good place to shoot French or American pool.

## Tennis: Public Courts

If you want to use any of the 170 city-operated courts, you can either show up and hope for the best or, if you are a resident, you can use Minitel 3615 Paris (*see chapter* **Survival**). To register for this service, pick up an application form from one of the city's 43 tennis centres and post it along with a copy of your identity card and two passport-size photos; you'll have to wait over a month to get a reservation number. Whether you use the Minitel or simply show up, the price is the same: 36F per hour, 52F per hour with lights.

You can also join a club and play on municipal courts. The cost depends on how long you're staying in Paris. Some clubs cost only 500F in membership fees, plus the 22F court rental fee. Compared to a private club, this is a bargain. For a list, contact **Allô-Sports** (*see above* **Keeping Informed**).

### Centre Sportif La Faluère

*Route de la Pyramide, Bois de Vincennes, 12th (01.43.74.40.93). M° Château de Vincennes.* **Open** (lights) 7am-10pm Mon-Sat; 7am-7pm Sun. Hitting wall 4.50F for 30min. **Game** 36F per hour. Symmetrical complex, with a mixture of 21 acrylic and asphalt courts in good condition.

### Centre Sportif Henry-de-Montherlant

*30-32 bd Lannes, 16th (01.45.03.03.64). M° Porte-Dauphine or La Pompe.* **Open** 7am-10pm Mon-Sat; 8am-7pm Sun (lights). **Game** 52F per hour. On the edge of the Bois de Boulogne, this complex with swimming pool and six hard courts gets a lot of use from college students and clubs. Best to make a reservation. Free hitting wall for those without a partner.

### Jardin du Luxembourg

*6th (01.43.25.79.18). M° Notre-Dame-des-Champs or RER Luxembourg.* Six asphalt courts in the romantic setting of the Jardin de Luxembourg. A great place to be seen playing, hence their popularity. There's a same-day sign-up sheet, so arrive early.

### Club Forest Hill

*Fourteen clubs in the Paris region (01.46.30.00.30). 4 rue Louis-Armand, 15th (01.40.60.10.00). M° Balard/RER Boulevard Victor.* **Membership** Annual membership 3,000F; 249F a month, plus 500F entry fee the first year. *Non-members* 155F-200F per hour. **Credit** V. An affordable alternative, even if most of its locations are beyond the *Périphérique*. Generally, there are indoor and outdoor courts, mainly acrylic, and some are of international standard. Most sites have squash, gyms, and fitness classes. A Forest Hill membership also gives access to **Gymnase Club** and **Aquaboulevard** (*see above*).

## Tennis: Private Clubs

There are some lovely private clubs in and around Paris, but they're very expensive and have very long waiting lists. Courts, though, are generally in superb condition and you don't have to figure out the Minitel to get a reservation.

*Amateurs and experts alike try out their pot luck at* **Les Mousquetaires**.

### Stade Jean Bouin

*26 av du Général-Sarrail, 16th (01.46.51.55.40). M°*
*Porte d'Auteuil.* **Open** 7.30am-10.30pm. **Membership**
*annual only* 5,300F (plus 3,000F entry fee the first year).
**No credit cards**.
The site of the men's qualifying tournament for the French
Open: 21 red clay courts (10 indoors).

### Tennis de Longchamp

*19 bd Anatole-France, 92100 Boulogne (01.46.03.84.49).*
*M° Jean-Jaurès.* **Membership** *annual* 5,750F (plus
1,800F entry fee the first year); *daily* 180F (includes gym).
No membership on shorter term basis. **Credit** MC, V.
The club has 20 well-maintained hard courts along with a
new complex that includes weights and a sauna.

## Spectator Sports

### Palais Omnisports de Paris-Bercy

*8 bd de Bercy, 12th (01.40.02.61.67). M° Bercy.* **Box**
**office** 11am-6pm Mon-Sat. **Admission** 90F-280F.
**Credit** MC, V.
A giant, futuristic sports hall that hosts major competitions
such as indoor tennis tournaments and a bizarre selection of
other events – indoor windsurfing, mountain biking and ski-
ing. *See chapter* **Music: Rock, Roots & Jazz**.

## Athletics

Every year, usually in early June, top athletes assemble in
St-Denis for the Fédération Française d'Athletisme (IAAF)
Humanité Meeting at the Stade Auguste-Delaune, 9 av Roger-
Semat (bookings from April: 01.49.22.74.10). Tickets cost
90F-120F, available by post or in person at 32 rue Jean-Jaurès,
93528 St-Denis. The IAAF (01.53.80.70.00) has information
on meetings in various stadiums, including Stade Charlety,
which is to host the 1997 meeting of the IAAF (athletics only).

## Basketball

The French professional leagues are still light years behind
the NBA, but the level is fairly high. Racing PSG and

Levallois are two of the better teams in the French Pro A
division. Matches take place from early Sept to late May.

### Levallois Sporting Club Basket

*Palais des Sports Marcel Cerdan, 141 rue Danton,*
*92300 Levallois-Perret (01.47.58.15.92/01.47.39.21.20).*
*M° Pont de Levallois.* **Tickets** 60F-80F.

### Racing PSG Basket

*Stade Pierre de Coubertin, 82 av Georges Lafont, 16th*
*(01.45.27.79.12). M° Porte de St-Cloud.* **Tickets** 40F-60F.

## Cycling

Cycling is a much greater sport in France than almost anywhere else in the world, and the Tour de France remains the
number one event for cycling and for France. The three-week
race, born as a publicity stunt in 1903, follows a different
route every July, but always finishes on the Champs-Elysées.
For cycling fans who want to avoid huge crowds, there are
four other major events that begin in Paris: Paris-Nice in
March, Paris-Roubaix in April, Paris-Brussels in September
and Paris-Tours in early October. For information call the
**Fédération Française de Cyclisme** (01.49.35.69.00) or
**Allô-Sports**.

## Football

### Paris St-Germain F.C.

*Parc des Princes, 24 rue du Commandant-Guilbaud, 16th*
*(ticket info 01.49.87.29.29). M° Porte d'Auteuil.*
**Matches** late July-early May.
Until the new stadium is built in St-Denis for the 1998 World
Cup, the 50,000-seat Parc des Princes remains the epicentre
of football attention. It's home to PSG, and a shrine for fans
who make the pilgrimage draped in the team's red, white and
blue. Tickets to a garden-variety match are not hard to get,
but for a major like PSG-Nantes it's a bit of a scramble.
Season tickets (01.40.71.10.73) are available from the stadium
(370F-3,000F). Occasional believers can get tickets for most
games a month in advance at the ground or two weeks in
advance at Fnac or Virgin (*see chapter* **Services**). Matches
draw a passionate but generally well-behaved crowd.

*Making waves at **Bercy**, p273.*

## Golf

There are three top-flight professional tournaments in the Paris region, all of which attract the first-rank European players. Tickets (50F-100F) are available in advance from the organisers or on the day of competition at the gate.
**Tournoi Perrier de Paris. Dates** October.
Information 01.47.95.18.19.
**Peugeot Open de France, Golf National de Guyancourt**, *2 av du Golf, 78280 Guyancourt. RER Guyancourt and look for shuttle buses.* **Dates** late June.
Information 01.47.72.28.10.
**Trophée Lancôme, Golf de St-Nom-la-Brétèche,** *rue Henri Frayssineau, 78860 St-Nom-la-Brétèche. Directions: A13 toward Rouen, exit at Versailles Ouest, take RN 307 and follow signs.* **Dates** mid-Sept.
Information 01.45.03.85.03.

## Rugby

Most French Rugby Union teams are concentrated in South-western France with Paris (and Grenoble) merely outposts. But to catch a good local scrum, hop on bus 164 out to Stade Yves du Manior (12 rue François Faber, 92700 Colombes) where Racing Club de France hosts its rivals a dozen or so times a year. Tickets are 30F-110F and games are well attended. For the team schedule, ring 01.45.67.55.86. Five Nations' Cup matches (Jan-Feb) and the French cup final (in mid-May) are held at the **Parc des Princes** (*see above* **Football**).

## Tennis

### Open Gaz de France
*Stade Pierre de Coubertin, 82 av Georges-Lafont, 16th (information 01.45.03.85.03/tickets 01.44.68.44.68). M° Porte de St-Cloud.* **Dates** mid-Feb. **Tickets** can be booked 3 months in advance; 92F-152F.
Big-name women players like Graf and Pierce compete for more fame and a lot more fortune in this WTA indoor event.

### Tournée Roland Garros/French Open
*Fédération Française de Tennis, Stade Roland Garros, 2 av Gordon Bennett, 16th (01.47.43.48.00). M° Porte d'Auteuil.* **Dates** end May-early June.
The second leg of the Grand Slam is always referred to by the name of the stadium Roland Garros, a French aviation pioneer and rugby player who died in World War I. The Open runs from the last week of May to the first week of June. Getting tickets (at least 150F for a decent seat) is difficult but not impossible. To reserve, write for a reservation form before the end of February. Unsold tickets go on sale at the stadium two weeks before the Open starts. *Entrée stade* and *billet* courts annexes are cheaper tickets to watch the lesser, unseeded players play away from the centre court.

### Open de Paris
*Palais Omnisport de Paris-Bercy, 8 bd de Bercy, 12th (01.40.02.61.67). M° Bercy.* **Dates** early Nov.
**Tickets** can be booked 6 months in advance.
Boris and Stefan have both won this men's indoor tournament.

## Horse Racing

For the expert or the ignorant, racing in Paris is accessible and fun. To experience the eastern passion of '*Le Trot*' – trotting races, both sulky races (pulling a light two-wheeled trap) and mounted, head for the **Hippodrome de Vincennes**, which has racing all year – the most important race being the *Prix d'Amérique* – and evening races (March-Dec).

The courses are easily accessible by public transport and, apart from the Arc de Triomphe at Longchamp, when the English flood over the Channel, are not overcrowded. Some of the best horses from the world are present. The other major event is the *Prix de Diane* at the pretty course of Chantilly, and is accessible from the Gare du Nord – the train stops next to the course. Alternatively picnic from the back of the car and watch the hats arrive, each one bigger than the next. The race track and presentation ring are very close, so you can really soak up the atmosphere.

The smaller courses are also worth a visit, the track of Maison Laffitte being surrounded by woods and beautiful houses. Training starts early in the morning and the horses take right of way on the roads as they return to their stables. Opposite the stadium there is a wonderful café, *Le Pur Sang* (meaning thoroughbred/01.39.62.03.21), used by the locals and trainers alike before the races.

The daily newspaper *Paris Turf* gives the latest racing updates. For the serious racer to have the full write-up, it is necessary to buy yesterday's newspaper for today's race, but there is also a condensed version on the day of the race.

### FRANCE GALOP
*46 place Abel Gance, 92655 Boulogne Cedex. (01.49.10.20.30/fax 01.47.61.93.37).* **Admission** 35F-40F and 15F for the Vincennes.
This organisation is responsible for racing, and any kind of racing information can be be obtained here. They also have a racing calendar (*Calendrier des Courses*). Ask for *Service Communication* and English-speaking service.

## Race Courses

**Auteuil** *Bois de Boulogne, 16th (01.40.71.47.47). M° Porte d'Auteuil.* Steeple chase season: March to last Thur in Apr, end of May to mid July, mid Oct to mid Dec.
**Chantilly** *41 km from Paris. Train from Gare du Nord. (03.44.57.16.71).* Flat racing season: June.
**Enghien** *18 km from Paris. Train from Gare du Nord.* Steeple chase and trotting season: Feb-Dec.
**Longchamp** *Bois de Boulogne, 16th (01.44.30.75.00). M° Porte d'Auteuil, then free bus to the course.* Flat racing season: Apr, May, June, Sept, Oct. Prices on the Arc day double!
**Maisons-Laffitte** *17km from Paris. RER A in the direct of Poissy and then the number 9 bus (01.39.62.90.95).* Racing season: Feb-Dec.
**Saint Cloud** *1 rue du Camp Canadien, 92210 St-Cloud. RER A to Reuil-Malmaison (01.41.12.00.30).* Flat racing season: Apr-Oct.
**Paris-Vincennes** *Bois de Vincennes, 12th (01.49.77.17.17). M° Vincennes or RER Joinville le Pont.* Trotting season: all year round. Evening racing March-Dec 8-11pm Tue, Fri ; Dec-Feb 1.30pm daily. Restaurant – **Le Sulky** *(01.43.53.68.40).* **Le Paddock** (01.43.53.68.48). Most important race – *Prix d'Amérique* – last Sun in Jan.

# Theatre

*From the contemporary marginal to the classical mainstream, Paris theatre caters to all tastes.*

Paris has always been famed for its encouragement of the avant-garde; in fact it is so encouraging that, thanks to subsidised public theatre, experimental work has ironically become part of the establishment. The capital's private theatres enjoy no such luxury and, in order to survive, are forced to satisfy a mainstream demand for often trite drawing-room and romantic comedy, preferably with a star in the cast to draw the crowds; authors **Yasmina Reza**, **Eric-Emmanuel Schmitt** and **Jean-Marie Besset**) are notable exceptions. Classics proliferate in both sectors, from the **Comédie Française** (whose actors employ a heavy, formal style) to innovative productions such as the Théâtre du Soleil's *Tartuffe* set in modern-day Algeria at the **Cartoucherie**.

Directors continue to hold both creative and financial power in French theatre (especially state-run), and people will talk of **Mnouchkine's** *Tartuffe*, for example, rather than Molière's. Only since the 1980s have playwrights become important again in the theatre; in the '70s, directors were interested in non-text-based productions. Writers are now making up for lost time, with wordy, philosophical mood pieces which have more in common with music and poetry than with Anouilh or Shakespeare. Much of contemporary theatre is 'high art' rather than storytelling or entertainment, with experimentation into language, form and subject matter, undoubtedly influenced by the Theatre of the Absurd (Beckett, Ionesco, etc), the order of the day. Be prepared for the lack of interval – a 90-minute play (or longer) without a break is the norm. Quality-wise, look for the annual Molière Awards for some idea of the best private theatre (although supposedly for both sectors, most go to private productions). Most public productions are of a reasonable standard; the Festival d'Automne (*see chapter* **Paris by Season**) is especially worth a look, perennially attracting big-name directors such as **Peter Brook** and Bob Wilson or productions which have been premiered at the Festival d'Avignon.

## BOOKING TIPS

Few theatres are open on Monday or Sunday evenings, and many close in July and August. For full details of current programmes check local listings magazines. You can book theatre tickets by Minitel, on 3615 THEA. Many private theatres offer 50 per cent reductions on previews. The agencies below specialise in theatre tickets; for general ticket agencies, *see chapter* **Services**.

**Agence Chèque Théâtre** *2nd floor, 33 rue Le Peletier, 9th (01.42.46.72.40). M° Le Peletier.* **Open** 10am-6.45pm Mon-Sat. **Credit** V.

**Kiosque Théâtre** *across from 15 pl de la Madeleine, 9th (no phone). M° Madeleine.* **Open** 12.30-8pm Mon-Sat; 12.30-4pm Sun. Same-day tickets at half-price, plus 16F commission per seat. **Credit** V.

**Branch**: In front of Gare Montparnasse, 15th.

*Chéreau and Greggory in **Koltès'** Dans la Solitude des Champs de Coton.*

## National Theatres

### Comédie Française

Salle Richelieu *2 rue de Richelieu, 1st (01.44.58.15.15). M° Palais-Royal.* Box office 11am-6pm daily. Closed Aug. Tickets 70F-185F; 30F students 1hr before play. Credit (in person only) AmEx, MC, V. *Guided tours. Wheelchair access.*
Théâtre du Vieux-Colombier *21 rue du Vieux-Colombier, 6th (01.44.39.87.00). M° St-Sulpice.* Box office 11am-7pm Tue-Sat; 1-6pm Mon, Sun. Closed Aug . Tickets 160F; 110F over-60s, unemployed; 65F under-25s, students under 27 (45mins before play). Credit AmEx, V. *Guided tours. Wheelchair access.*
Studio Théâtre *pl de la Pyramide inversée, Galerie du Carrousel (entrance at 99 rue de Rivoli), 1st (01.44.58.98.58). M° Palais-Royal.* Box office 5.30pm day of performance only. No reservations. Tickets 80F. Credit (over 150F only) AmEx, MC, V.
*Wheelchair access.*
Founded by Louis XIV, the oldest theatre company in France is based in a historic building adjoining the Palais Royal. This is the only national theatre to have its own permanent troupe, the famous *Pensionnaires*, who perform a minimum of four plays a week, ranging from Molière and Racine to modern classics by authors like Claudel, Genet or Anouilh. In 1993 the company opened a second theatre in the restored Théâtre du Vieux-Colombier offering a mix of small-scale classics and contemporary works, and in 1996 a small studio space in the Carrousel complex under the Louvre. The latter is used for a mixture of short classics and modern plays, literary salons with writers or actors (twice a month), and is home to a *théâtrothèque* showing plays on video.

### Odéon, Théâtre de l'Europe

*1 pl de l'Odéon, 6th (01.44.41.36.36). M° Odéon/RER Luxembourg.* Box office 11am-6.30pm Mon-Sat; *telephone bookings* only 11am-7pm Sun. Closed mid July-mid Sept. Tickets 50F-150F. Credit V.
Created in 1968, and based in a beautiful Neo-Classical theatre, the Odéon, under director Georges Lavaudant, stages a contrasting mix of French and international productions, classics and contemporary creations. It also welcomes famous visiting companies, including the Deutsche Schaubühne and the Royal Shakespeare Company.

# Names to watch

## Directors

**Stéphane Braunschweig** Young whizzkid noted for stunning visual productions.
**Peter Brook** Based here since the 1970s, Paris theatre's most famous British exile (*photo*) concentrates on experimental productions at the legendary Bouffes du Nord.
**Patrice Chéreau** Important contemporary director, whose history includes an acclaimed array of theatre and film, including the gory *La Reine Margot*. Collaborated with Koltès, whose work he championed in the 1980s.
**Alain Françon** Director of the Colline since November 1996, Françon's numerous large-scale productions include Marlowe's *Edward II* at the Odéon in 1996.
**Patrice Kerbrat** Directs many of Jean-Marie Besset's plays and other contemporary classics, such as *Waiting for Godot,* at well-known private and municipal theatres, such as the Hebertot, Rond-Point and Théâtre 14.
**Jorge Lavelli** Latin-American director famed for his socio-political slant. Now retired from the Colline; look out for him as a visiting director.
**Ariane Mnouchkine** Director of the Théâtre du Soleil, famous for her bold directorial stance and spectacular productions at the Cartoucherie.
**Jérôme Savary** Founder of the anarchic company the Grand Magic Circus in the 1960s. He now concentrates on large-scale, popular shows at the Théâtre de Chaillot, where he is director.

## Playwrights

**Michel Vinaver** The godfather of contemporary French playwriting has managed to fit in being managing director of Gillette France with numerous successful plays that experiment with timescale and overlapping reality. The gritty stuff of daily life features prominently.
**Bernard-Marie Koltès** Poetic, haunting works cover themes ranging from homelessness to the notion of life as a series of 'deals' in *Dans la Solitude des Champs de Coton*. Patrice Chéreau has directed his work before, and after, Koltès' death from AIDS in 1989.

**Jean-Marie Besset** Now living in New York, Besset continues to write easy, accessible plays for the French stage, satirising middle-class mores and government bungles.
**Philip Minyana** One of a new generation of 'poet' playwrights, who paints pictures with words and experiments with structure.
**Noëlle Renaude** She takes a similar approach to Minyana, but with plenty of humour and a fascination with everyday speech and its rhythms. Still no plot.
**Yasmina Reza** Popular in both public and private sectors for her well-crafted works. Her '*Art*' has had huge success in Paris and London.
**Eric-Emmanuel Schmitt** Author of the most popular production of autumn 1996, *Variations Enigmatiques*, marking the comeback of Alain Delon to the French stage.

### Théâtre National de Chaillot
*1 pl du Trocadéro, 16th (01.47.27.81.15). M° Trocadéro.*
**Box office** 11am-7pm Mon-Sat; 11am-5pm Sun.
**Tickets** 160F; 120F under-25s, over-60s. **Credit** (in person only) MC, V.
Flamboyant productions, with the emphasis on popular entertainment, are staged in a monumental 1930s theatre in the Palais de Chaillot. Jérôme Savary is artistic director. For those interested in experiencing French theatre, but unsure of their language skills, there's an innovative laptop subtitling system in various languages for some performances. *Wheelchair access (advance notice needed).*

### Théâtre National de la Colline
*15 rue Malte-Brun, 20th (01.44.62.52.52). M° Gambetta.*
**Box office** 11am-6pm Mon; 11am-8pm Tue-Sat. Closed 25 June-Sept. **Tickets** 150F; 110F over-60s, students.
**Credit** (in person only) AmEx, DC, MC, V.
Founded in 1987, this modern theatre with its main and studio spaces is devoted to international contemporary drama. Alain Françon recently replaced Jorge Lavelli as director. *Wheelchair access.*

*Pristine new* **Théâtre des Abbesses**.

## Theatres of Interest

### Bouffes du Nord
*37bis bd de la Chapelle, 10th (01.46.07.34.50). M° La Chapelle.* **Box office** 11am-6pm Mon-Sat. Closed July-Aug. **Tickets** 10F-140F. **No credit cards.**
Home to Peter Brook's experimental creations as well as to visiting companies, this nineteenth-century building is itself worth a visit. Its flaking walls and open-plan performance space provide the backdrop for everything from Beckett to medieval tales of witchcraft, wolves and fireworks.

### Cartoucherie de Vincennes
*route de Champ-de-Manœuvre, 12th. M° Château de Vincennes, then shuttle bus or bus 112.* All theatres operate independently.
Deep in the Bois de Vincennes, the warehouses of a former cartridge factory are home to a theatre complex opened by theatre pioneer Ariane Mnouchkine in 1970. The complex houses the internationally acclaimed **Théâtre du Soleil**; the **Théâtre de l'Epée de Bois** (01.48.08.39.74); Jacques Kraemer's **Théâtre de la Tempête** (01.43.28.36.36); the **Théâtre de l'Aquarium** (01.43.74.99.61) and the **Atelier du Chaudron** (01.43.28.97.04). All five produce good-quality contemporary and classic creations.

### Comédie des Champs Elysées
*15 av Montaigne, 8th (01.53.23.99.19; telephone bookings 01.47.20.08.24). M° Alma-Marceau.* **Box office** 11am-6pm Mon; 11am-7.30pm Tue-Fri; 11am-4pm Sat. **Tickets** 110F-250F. **Credit** MC, V.
Reached by lift, the baby brother of the Théâtre des Champs Elysées next door (*see* **Music: Classical & Opera**), offers an interesting diet of mainly twentieth-century plays.

### Guichet-Montparnasse
*15 rue du Maine, 14th (01.43.27.88.61). M° Montparnasse-Bienvenüe.* **Box office** reserve by telephone. **Tickets** 100F; 80F Mon. **No credit cards.**
A minuscule 50-seat theatre staging several shortish productions each night, featuring a good range of contemporary creations from young, lively companies.

### La Ménagerie de Verre
*12-14 rue Léchevin, 11th (01.43.38.33.44). M° Parmentier.* **Box office** 30mins before performance, reserve by telephone. **Tickets** 60F-80F. **Credit** V.
A converted warehouse space which promotes contemporary theatre, allowing small companies scope for some interesting experimental stagings.

### Théâtre de l'Atelier
*pl Charles Dullin, 18th (01.46.06.49.24). M° Anvers.* **Box office** 11am-7pm Mon-Sat; 11am-2.30pm, 4.30-7.15pm, Sun. **Tickets** 50F-250F; 90F students. **Credit** (over 150F) V.
A historical Montmartre theatre, which stages French and international classics, ranging from TS Eliot to Dürrenmatt. *Wheelchair access.*

### Théâtre de la Bastille
*76 rue de la Roquette, 11th (01.43.57.42.14). M° Bastille.* **Box office** 10am-6.45pm Mon-Fri. **Tickets** 100F; 70F over-60s, students. **No credit cards.**
An innovative mix of modern, often experimental, theatre and dance, sometimes at the same time (*see chapter* **Dance**). *Wheelchair access.*

### Théâtre de la Huchette
*23 rue de la Huchette, 5th (01.43.26.38.99). M° St-Michel.* **Box office** 5-9pm Mon-Sat. Closed 1-15 Jan. **Tickets** 100F; 70F students (not Sat). **No credit cards.**
The home to Nicolas Bataille's original production of Ionesco's *La Cantatrice Chauve* (*The Bald Prima Donna*) since 1957. As well as other Ionesco works, there's the occasional detour into authors such as Fassbinder.

### Théâtre du Palais-Royal
*38 rue Montpensier, 1st (01.42.97.59.81). M° Palais-Royal.* **Box office** 11am-7pm Mon-Sat; 11am-6pm Sun. Closed Aug. **Tickets** varies. **Credit** MC, V.
Light farce and satire in an ornate Rococo setting.

### Théâtre du Rond-Point
*2 bis av Franklin D Roosevelt, 8th (01.44.95.98.00). M° Franklin-D-Roosevelt.* **Box office** 10am-7pm Mon-Fri. **Tickets** 160F; 80F students, under-26. **Credit** (in person only) V.
Previously home to the famous Renaud-Barrault company, this renovated nineteenth-century circus building is now in the hands of Marcel Maréchal and his theatre company,. Classics are performed alongside a lively contemporary repertoire, poetry and play readings.

### Théâtre de la Ville/Théâtre des Abbesses
*2 pl du Châtelet, 4th (01.42.74.22.77). M° Châtelet-Les Halles.* **Box office** 11am-6pm Mon; 11am-8pm Tue-Sat; *telephone bookings* 9am-7pm Mon-Sat; 9am-8pm Tue-Sat. **Tickets** 80F-190F; 50% reduction on day of performance under-25s, students. **Credit** DC, MC, V.

Funded by the City of Paris, this major dance venue also presents some plays, varying from first rate to highly controversial. It recently opened Les Abbesses, a new theatre in Montmartre by Belgian architect Charles Vandenhove, at 31 rue des Abbesses. M° Pigalle. *See chapters* Dance, Music: Classical & Opera *and* Music: Rock, Roots & Jazz.

### Théâtre de la Villette
*211 av Jean Jaurès, 19th (01.42.02.02.68). M° Porte de la Villette.* **Box office** from 4pm. **Tickets** 135F; 65F under-26. **No credit cards.**
Part of the huge La Villette arts and science complex, this is a stylish, popular venue staging a varied programme.

## Suburban Theatres

Paris' suburbs are home to a number of significant public theatre operations, run by famous directors who include Bernard Sobel at Gennevilliers and Jean-Pierre Vincent at Nanterre, and some interesting private venues such as the Manufacture des Oeillets at Ivry-sur-Seine (01.46.58.81.81). All are easily accessible by Métro or RER.

### Aubervilliers/Théâtre de la Commune
*2 rue Edouard Poisson, 93300 Aubervilliers (01.48.34.67.67). M° Aubervilliers-Pantin-4 Chemins.* **Box office** 10.30am-1pm, 2-6pm, Mon-Fri. Closed Aug. **Tickets** 130F; 70F under-26s. **No credit cards.**

### Bobigny/MC93
*1 bd Lénine, 93000 Bobigny (01.41.60.72.72). M° Bobigny-Pablo Picasso.* **Box office** 10am-7pm Mon-Sat. Closed mid July-mid Aug. **Tickets** 140F; 90F Tue, Thur, Sun. **Credit** MC, V.

### Gennevilliers/Théâtre de Gennevilliers
*Centre Dramatique National, 41 av des Grésillons, 92230 Gennevilliers (01.41.32.26.26). M° Gabriel Péri.* **Box office** 1-7pm Tue-Sat. Closed mid July-mid Aug.

**Tickets** 140F; 90F under-25s. **Credit** (in person only) AmEx, V.
*Wheelchair access.*

### Nanterre/Théâtre des Amandiers
*7 av Pablo Picasso, 92022 Nanterre (01.46.14.70.00). RER A Nanterre Préfecture, then free shuttle bus.* **Box office** noon-7pm Tue-Sat. Closed Aug. **Tickets** 140F; 110F Thur, 80F under-25s, 100F over-60s. **Credit** AmEx, MC, V.

### St-Denis/Théâtre Gérard Philipe
*59 bd Jules Guesde, 93207 St-Denis (01.48.13.70.00). M° St-Denis Basilique.* **Box office** 1-7pm Mon-Sat. Closed Aug. **Tickets** 110F; 70F over-60s, students under-26; 60F unemployed. **Credit** (in person only) AmEx, MC, V.
*Wheelchair access.*

## Home from Home

Paris possesses a surprising number of resident English-language theatre companies. The bilingual **Dear Conjunction** was founded in 1991 by Les Clack and Barbara Bray to perform new and established plays, they also do play readings at the Village Voice bookshop (*see* **The Literary Muse**). Contemporary playwrights are also featured by the **On Stage Theatre Company** and Bob Meyer's **Gare St-Lazare Company**, all regularly found at the Théâtre de Nesle (8 rue de Nesle, 6th/01.46.34.61.04).

**ACT** (01.40.33.64.02), run by Ann and Andrew Wilson, is an educational theatre company which also performs modern classics such as Oscar Wilde at the Théâtre de Ménilmontant (15 rue du Retrait, 20th, and other venues). The Odéon, MC93 Bobigny and Bouffes du Nord occasionally host leading English-language companies on tour.

# The literary muse

For over a century, Paris has been haven and muse for aspiring anglophone writers seeking inspiration, patronage and freedom of expression. Since the times of Edith Wharton, Wilde, Joyce, Hemingway, Fitzgerald and Anaïs Nin, Paris has been the birthplace of many a great English-language novel, play or poem. Several generations have since left their mark; small press journals – the *Paris Review*, in the fifties, and *Frank, Handshake Editions, Sphinx, Paris Exiles* – bear witness to an avant-garde tradition that is constantly luring the adventurous.

The anglophone literary community can often be found mingling at the same gatherings, as it did in the 1920s, when writers flocked around Sylvia Beach and her legendary bookshop **Shakespeare & Company**. A remnant of literary bohemia, its successor of the same name and owner George Whitman welcome poor poets to sleep among obsolete Russian hardcovers and first editions of Joyce and provide a platform to share their works.

Writers and literary enthusiasts also hover around the **Village Voice** bookshop, where Odile Hellier has discovered and supported numerous young, promising authors, and hosts English-language readings and book signings, attracting a cosmopolitan crowd of intellectuals. For a more informal atmosphere, the **Live Poet's Society** puts on monthly poetry readings by young poets at Tigh Johnny's Irish pub (55 rue Montmartre, 2nd/01.42.33.91.33).

Apart from the places listed above, other English-language bookshops also invite authors for occasional readings and signings. *See chapters* **Specialist Shopping** *and* **Study**.

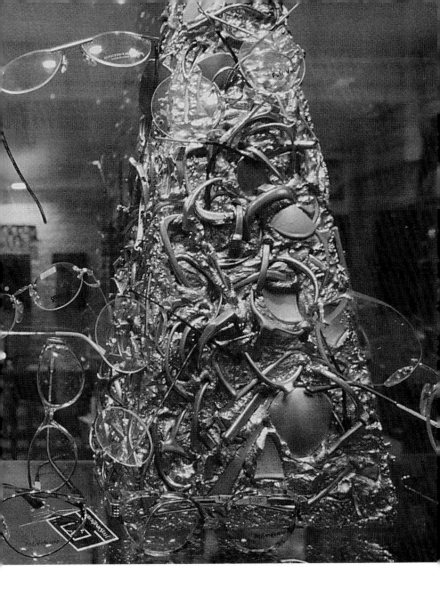

# In Focus

# Business

*Services and organisations that can open doors in Paris when you really mean business.*

France boasts the world's fourth largest economy and Paris hosts more trade shows and conventions than any other city: amazing accomplishments, considering how hard it remains to get things done here. If old stereotypes die hard, it's because it still too often takes half a dozen phone calls to reach a result that in other modern cities would require but one. Invariably, every initiative to rationalise the country's famously complex taxes, regulations and employment rules seems to make them even more baffling. Aware of these perceptions and of the underlying realities, government agencies, service providers and electronic information purveyors are all well practiced in guiding terrified foreigners through the bureaucratic maze.

Foremost advice: keep smiling. Many a minion who appears impervious to reason will cede to *le charme*. From the obligatory *'bonjour'* vital to clerks and cashiers, to the sacrosanct business lunch, the French refuse to let you divorce business from pleasure. Embrace that etiquette, and you may just find the method in their madness.

## INSTITUTIONS & INFORMATION

Paris embassies are big bureaucracies, and not the best place to get advice. The French Embassy or consulate in your own country, your own government's trade office or professional associations may be more helpful. In Paris the best first stop for anyone initiating business in France is the Bourse du Commerce. Most major banks can refer you to lawyers, accountants and tax consultants, and several US and British banks provide other expatriate services. For everyday banking, *see* chapter **Essential Information**.

For business and financial news, the French dailies *La Tribune* and *Les Echos*, and the weekly *Investir* are the tried and trusted sources. German-owned *Capital*, its sister magazine *Management* and the weightier *L'Expansion* are worthwhile monthlies. *Défis* has tips for the entrepreneur, while *Initiatives* is for the self-employed. There's also the all-news business radio station BFM 96.4 (*see chapter* **Media**). *Les Echos* gives stock quotes and the like on http://www.lesechos.com and the Minitel service 3615 CD offers real-time stock quotes. The business directories *Kompass France* and *Kompass Régional* can be consulted in the Centre Pompidou library (*see chapter* **Study**), which also has detailed French market profiles, or

by Minitel on 3617 KOMPASS. Standard English-language reference is *The French Company Handbook*, published by the *International Herald Tribune* (01.41.43.93.00). *Paris-Anglophone* (90F), lists 4,000 English-speaking companies, professionals and organisations, also on http://www.paris-anglo.com.

## American Chamber of Commerce
*21 av George V, 8th (01.40.73.89.90/fax 01.47.20.18.62). Mº George V or Alma-Marceau.* **Open** 9am-5.00pm Mon-Fri. *Library* open to non-members 10am-12.30pm Tue, Thur, 50F per day.
The American Chamber hosts social events for members, and has an active small-business committee. Its directory, listing Franco-American firms and organisations, is available to non-members for 500F; its *Guide to Doing Business in France* also costs 500F.

## Bourse du Commerce
*2 rue de Viarmes, 1st (01.45.08.37.06). Mº Châtelet-Les Halles.* **Open** 9am-6pm Mon-Fri.
This branch of the **CCIP**, which has plans to relocate in mid-1997, houses a wide range of services for new businesses, including L'Espace Création (01.45.08.39.16), which offers help in setting up in France. The Centre de Formalités des Entreprises (01.45.08.38.11), will route your application to start a business to the vast number of French authorities involved in company registration, and may stay on at this address: ring to check.

## British Embassy Commercial Library
*35 rue du Fbg-St-Honoré, 8th (01.44.51.34.56/ fax 01.44.51.34.01). Mº Concorde.* **Open** 10am-1pm, 2.30-5pm, Mon-Fri, by appointment only.
The library has trade directories, and will assist British companies who wish to develop sales in France, set up a French subsidiary or find an agent to do so. Appointment required.

## Chambre de Commerce et d'Industrie Franco-Britannique
*41 rue de Turenne, 3rd (01.44.59.25.20/fax 01.44.59.25.45). Mº Chemin Vert or St-Paul.* **Open** 2.15-5.30pm Mon-Thur; 2.15-5pm Fri.
Promotes contacts in the Franco-British business community through talks, social events and seminars. The annual trade directory costs 375F; non-members can use the library at 31 rue Boissy d'Anglas, 1st. open 2-5pm, for 50F per day.

## Chambre de Commerce et d'Industrie de Paris (CCIP)
*27 av de Friedland, 8th (01.42.89.70.00/fax 01.42.89.79.68). Mº George V.* **Open** 9am-6pm Mon-Fri.
A huge organisation providing services for businesses. At 16 rue Chateaubriand is one of the chamber's information centres, and the best business library in the city (30F per day or 300F per year). *Foreigners: Starting Up Your Company in France*, one of the Chamber's only publications in English, costs 48F. The CCIP also provides trade, market and export information on Minitel 3615 CCIP, 3617 CCIPLUS and 3617 FIRMET.

*The Paris **Bourse**, though now electronic, is still the heart of the French stock exchange.*

### Créa Conseil
*41 rue St-Augustin, 2nd (01.47.42.25.70/fax 01.42.76.34.29). M° Opéra.* **Open** 9.30am-6pm Mon-Fri.
A non-profit-making association that offers tax, legal and regulatory advice to entrepreneurs starting up their own business. A consultation is 300F an hour, or 3,000F for setting up an SARL or limited liability company.

### US Embassy Commercial Section
*4 av Gabriel, 8th (library 01.43.12.22.22). M° Champs-Elysées-Clemenceau.* **Open** 9am-noon, 2-5pm, Mon-Fri, by appointment only.
A business library that provides individual advice on contacts, research and information. Minitel 3617 USATRADE will respond to enquiries within 24 hours on weekdays.

## Trade Fairs & Conferences

The leading centre for international trade fairs, Paris hosts over 500 exhibitions a year, from the Auto Show to the major fashion collections.

### Fédération Française des Salons Spécialisés
*4 pl Valois, 1st (01.42.86.82.99/fax 01.42.86.82.97). M° Palais-Royal.* **Open** 9am-1pm, 2pm-6pm, Mon-Fri.
See the free calendar *Salons Nationaux et Internationaux en France* or consult Minitel 3616 SALONS.

### CNIT
*2 pl de la Défense, BP 200, 92053 Paris La Défense (01.46.92.28.66/fax 01.46.92.15.78). M° Grande Arche de La Défense.*

### Palais des Congrès
*2 pl de la Porte Maillot, 17th (01.40.68.22.22). M° Porte Maillot.*

### Paris-Expo
*Porte de Versailles, 15th (01.43.95.37.00/fax 01.53.68.71.71). M° Porte de Versailles.*

### Parc des Expositions Paris-Nord
*Villepinte, BP 60004, Paris Nord 2, 95970 Roissy-Charles de Gaulle. (01.48.63.30.30). RER B Parc des Expositions.*

## Business Services
### Accountants

### France Audit Expertise
*148 bd Malesherbes, 17th (01.43.80.42.98/fax 01.47.64.03.92). M° Wagram.* **Open** 9am-1pm, 2-7pm, Mon-Fri.
Handles companies of all sizes.

### Maximilien Lambert
*26 rue de la Pépinière, 8th (01.42.93.76.16/fax 01.42.93.76.09). M° St-Augustin.* **Open** 9am-6pm Mon-Fri.
This independent French-certified accountant and statutory auditor works with self-employed business people.

### Lawyers

### Levine & Okoshken
*51 av Montaigne, 8th (01.44.13.69.50/fax 01.45.63.24.96). M° Franklin D. Roosevelt.* **Open** 9am-6pm Mon-Fri.
A specialist in tax and corporate law, with many US clients.

### Shubert & Dusausoy
*190 bd Haussmann, 8th (01.40.76.01.43/fax 01.40.76.01.44). M° St-Philippe-du-Roule.* **Open** 9.30am-6pm Mon-Fri.
Helps English-speaking business people set up in France.

### Translators & Interpreters

Certain documents, from birth certificates to loan applications, must be translated by certified legal translators, listed at the **CCIP** (*see above*). For standard French-English business translations, there are dozens of reliable independents. The

Minitel offers a variety of translating services and aids. Check out 3615 MITRAD to find translators.

### Association des Anciens Elèves de L'Esit
*Centre Universitaire Dauphine, 16th. (01.44.05.41.46). M° Porte-Dauphine.* **Open** phone only 9am-6pm Mon-Fri.
A translation and interpreting cooperative whose 1,000 members are graduates of one of France's top translating schools, L'Ecole Supérieure d'Interprètes et de Traducteurs.

### International Corporate Communication
*3 rue des Batignolles, 17th (01.43.87.29.29/fax 01.45.22.49.13). M° Place de Clichy.* **Open** 9am-1pm, 2-6pm, Mon-Fri.
Translators of financial and corporate documents: annual reports, prospectuses and shareholder communications.

## Computers & Office Equipment

### Surcouf Informatique
*139 av Daumesnil, 12th (01.53.33.20.00/fax 01.53.33.21.01). M° Gare de Lyon.* **Open** 9.30am-7pm Tue-Sat. **Credit** MC, V.
An impressive superstore for all your computer wants and needs. Repair service and an English-language software stall.

### KA
*14 rue Magellan, 8th (01.44.43.16.00/fax 01.47.20.34.39). M° George V.* **Open** sales & rental 9am-7pm Mon-Fri; technical service 9am-6pm, Mon-Fri. **Credit** AmEx, MC, V.
Sale and rental of IBM, Apple and Compaq computers.

### Prorata Services
*27 rue Linné, 5th (01.45.35.94.14/fax 01.45.35.19.13). M° Jussieu.* **Open** 9am-7pm Mon-Fri; 10.30am-6pm Sat. **Credit** V.
Use top-of-the-line Macs and PCs with about every software programme imaginable. 1F a minute at the keyboard; discounts on subscription. Prorata has a graphic design studio, Studio PAO, close by at 15 rue Jussieu.

## Internet Services

### America Online
*Freephone 0800.903.910 or http://www.aol.fr.*

### Compuserve
*Freephone 0801.63.81.22 or http://www.compuserve.fr.*

### Imaginet
*01.43.38.10.24 or http://www.imaginet.fr.*

### Microsoft Network
*Freephone 0800.917.242 or http://www.msn.com.*

## Couriers

For general postal services, *see chapter* **Survival**.

### Chronopost
*9 rue Hérold, 1st (01.40.26.21.87/information freephone 08.03.801.801). M° Châtelet-Les Halles or Sentier.* **Open** 8am-8pm Mon-Fri; 8am-1pm Sat. **Credit** AmEx, MC, V.
A division of the post office, this is the most widely-used service for parcels of up to 30kg. International service.

### DHL
*59 av d'Iéna, 16th (freephone 0800.20.25.25). M° Iéna.* **Open** 9am-7.45pm Mon-Fri; 9am-4.30pm Sat. **Credit** AmEx, MC, V.

One of the big names in international courier services. **Branch:** 82 rue de Richelieu, 2nd (01.42.96.14.55).

### Flash Service
*32 rue des Blancs-Manteaux, 4th (01.42.74.26.01/fax 01.42.74.11.17). M° Rambuteau.* **Open** 9am-6.30pm Mon-Fri. **No credit cards.**
A local bike and van delivery company. Minimum charge for non-account customers for a delivery within Paris is 60F.

## Office Hire

### CNIT
*2 pl de La Défense, BP 200, 92053 Paris La Défense (01.46.92.24.24/fax 01.46.92.15.78). M° Grande Arche de La Défense.* **Open** 6.30am-midnight daily.
The World Trade Centre houses 800 firms and offers a permanent data-processing service, video-conference facilities and offices and meeting rooms to rent.

### Dernis Organisation
*23 av de Wagram, 17th (01.45.72.91.11/fax 01.45.72.91.12). M° Charles de Gaulle-Etoile.* **Open** 9am-7pm Mon-Fri.
Eight offices plus meeting rooms for hire, with multilingual secretarial services, in a central location.

### Jones Lang Wootton
*49 av Hoche, 8th (01.40.55.15.15/fax 01.46.22.28.28). M° Charles de Gaulle-Etoile.* **Open** 9am-6pm Mon-Fri.
Britain's leading office-rental firm also has branches at La Défense, and in eastern Paris.

## Removals & Relocation

The major companies Grospiron, Arthur Pierre, Interdean, Desbordes and Transpaq International are the big five of removals in France: see *Déménagement* in the local yellow pages. Relocation services will also help with finding apartments and opening bank accounts.

### Cosmopolitan Services Unlimited
*113 bd Pereire, 17th (01.55.65.11.65/fax 01.55.65.11.69). M° Pereire.* **Open** 9am-6pm Mon-Thur; 9am-5pm Fri.
One of the bigger and better specialised relocation services. Contact Joy Chevaud, who speaks English.

### Grospiron
*15 rue Danielle Casanova, 93300 Aubervilliers (01.48.11.71.71/fax 01.48.11.71.70). M° Fort d'Aubervilliers.* **Open** 9am-1pm, 2-6pm, Mon-Fri.
Contact Nancy Ravenel for English-speaking expat service.

## Secretarial Services

### ADECCO International
*4 pl de la Défense, Cedex 26, 92090 Paris La Défense (01.49.01.94.94/fax 01.46.98.00.08). M° Grande Arche de La Défense.* **Open** 8.30am-12.30pm, 2-6.30pm Mon-Fri.
This branch of the large French employment agency group specialises in bilingual secretaries and other office staff on a permanent or temporary basis.

### TM International
*36-38 rue des Mathurins, 8th (01.47.42.71.00/fax 01.47.42.18.87). M° Auber.* **Open** 9am-6pm Mon-Fri.
Recruitment consultancy known for reasonable rates and well-selected French-English bilingual secretarial staff.

# Children

***From gigantic dinosaurs and grotesque gargoyles to smelly sewers,
Paris is full of surprises that will fascinate children of all ages.***

After obvious sights like the Eiffel Tower (*see chapter* **Sightseeing**), you'll discover that Paris is also awash with parks, squares and gardens, most equipped with a play area – from modest to quite elaborate. In the warmer months, you can treat everyone to candy floss and rides at one of the city's funfairs, in the Jardin des Tuileries and at the Foire du Trône.

Paris' museums can also look like playgrounds to young children. One of the best places to take kids is the huge new wing in the Louvre dedicated to monumental outdoor sculpture, where they can stretch their legs and goggle at the size of the artwork, or, also in the Louvre, the wings dedicated to Greek and Roman antiquities, with all of their myths, warriors and sarcophagi. Children like to swoop around the colourful masterpieces in the **Musée de Picasso**, mimic the Degas dancers at the **Musée d'Orsay**, or visit the sculptures in the garden of the **Musée Rodin**. Old standbys are the horrors of the **Musée Grevin** wax museum and Marie Antoinette's cell in the **Conciergerie**, while a new attraction is the fairground museum, the **Musée des Arts Forains** (*for all the above, see chapter* **Museums**). In a creepy, underground vein, try the **Catacombs** and the **Egouts** (sewers), while **Paristoric** gives the history of Paris in a lush slideshow (*see chapter* **Sightseeing**). Most museums have special programmes (in French) for children on Wednesday afternoons.

For special shows and attractions, check out the weeklies *Pariscope* or *L'Officiel des Spectacles*. Note that many children's events take place on Wednesdays, Saturdays and school holidays.

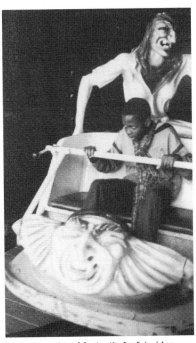

*Kids never tire of fantastic funfair rides.*

## Help & Information

### Inter-Service Parents

*(01.44.93.44.93).* **Open** 9.30am-12.30pm, 1.30-5pm, Mon, Tue, Fri; 1.30-5pm Wed; 9.30am-12.30pm Thur.

A free telephone advisory service giving details of babysitting agencies and children's activities. English-speaking mothers can meet (with their children) at La Maison Ouverte, 5 Impasse Bons Secours, 11th (2.30-6.30pm Thur, Fri).

### Message

*c/o Sallie Chaballier (01.48.04.74.61); Oona Cadorin (01.39.65.79.29); Sally Burlet (01.69.89.94.75).*

A 900-member non-profit mothers network, geared towards English-speaking ex-pat expectant women, mothers or pre-schoolers. Breastfeeding seminars, preparation for parenthood classes, toddler group activities and support groups for new mothers in Paris. Check out their quarterly magazine.

## Parks & Playgrounds

Parks are usually open daily dawn to dusk (*see chapter* **Parks and Cemeteries**). The **Tuileries** and the **Luxembourg** gardens both have playgrounds, roundabouts, sandpits, pony rides and ponds; similar attractions are found in many other public parks. There is a boating lake, gazebo and an artificial cave and waterfall at the strangely picturesque **Parc Buttes-Chaumont**, and roller-skating rinks at the **Parc Monceau**. Another fun place for kids to explore is the **Parc de Belleville**. There are outdoor mini-kingdoms for children in the Bois de Boulogne and the Bois de Vincennes, where the **Foire du Trône**, the city's most popular, sprawling funfair, is held in spring (*see chapter* **Paris by Season**).

## Jardin d'Acclimatation

*Bois de Boulogne, 16th (01.40.67.90.82). Mº Sablons, then short walk, or Mº Porte Maillot and Le Petit Train (5F, every ten minutes daily from behind L'Orée du Bois restaurant during holidays, and 1.30-6pm Wed, Sat, Sun).* **Open** 10am-6pm daily. **Admission** 12F; free under-3s. This classic funfair and amusement park has been welcoming Parisian families for 125 years. The children's zoo, a hall of mirrors, *guignol* puppet theatre and an all-wooden under-12s playground are free. Dodgems, donkey rides, remote-control speed boats or a trip down the 'enchanted river' each cost around 10F extra. New children's (3-11s) workshops in drawing, gardening, rollerblading and trampoline are offered (50F for two hours). A baby-sitting service is available at weekends (20F per hour). *See also* **Musée en Herbe** *below*.

## Le Parc Floral de Paris

*route de la Pyramide, Bois de Vincennes, 12th (01.43.43.92.95). Mº Château de Vincennes, then 112 bus to Parc Floral or 15-minute walk.* **Open** summer 9.30am-8pm daily; winter 9.30am-5pm daily. **Admission** 10F; 5F 6-18s; free under-6s, over-65s.
On schooldays, this pleasant park has a slower pace than its western counterpart the Jardin d'Acclimatation. A playground with an array of slides, climbing frames, and swings; ping-pong tables and pedal karts for four to ten year-olds and a miniature train (5F per ride), all add to the experience.

## Parc de la Villette

*Mº Porte de la Villette or Porte de Pantin.*
As well as indoor thrills at La Cité des Enfants (*see* **Museums** *below*), the park offers a surreal succession of themed gardens – all free. Best for children are the Monster Dragon slide, the Jardin des Voltiges obstacle course and the Jardin des Vents air mattresses, plus the touch and sound games, not to mention the scary noises of the Jardin des Frayeurs Enfantins and the mists and light effects of the Jardins du Brouillard and des Miroirs. Visitors can picnic on the lawns.

## Activity Museums

### Centre Pompidou – Atelier des Enfants

*Centre Pompidou, rue Beaubourg, 4th (01.44.78.12.33). Mº Châtelet-Les Halles or Rambuteau.* **Sessions** *July-Aug* 2-3.30pm; *June, Sept* 3.45-5.15pm, Mon, Wed-Sat. Closed bank holidays. Reserve a place by telephone 3 weeks in advance, or in person 30 minutes before session starts. **Admission** 30F-70F.
A top-notch, first-come-first-served workshop for kids (6-12s). Leave your child to artistic activities often linked to the exhibitions going on upstairs. The atelier may be relocated in Sept 1997; phone ahead for details (*see chapter* **Museums**).

### La Cité des Enfants & Techno Cité

*Cité des Sciences et de l'Industrie, 30 av Corentin Cariou, 19th (01.36.68.29.30). Mº Porte de la Villette.* **Open** 10am-6pm Tue-Sun (visits by session, normally 3-4 daily, more frequent Wed and weekends; phone for details or Minitel 3615 Villette). **Admission** *Day pass to Cité des Sciences* 45F; 35F under-16s. *Cité des Enfants only* 20F per session. *Techno Cité* 25F. **Credit** AmEx, MC, V.
Paris' most thoroughly entertaining museum attraction for kids and adults alike. The museum is spread over one of the largest parks in Paris, so be sure to know which part of it you are going to and what you can do there. In the **Cité des Enfants**, three-to-five year olds learn how to build a house in a mini-construction site with hard-hats, wheelbarrows and cranes; children aged six to 12 can observe how sound travels through tubes and telephones. Sessions last 90 minutes. Parents can join in, and must accompany younger children.
At **Techno Cité**, children aged over eleven can learn how to programme computer software into a video game. Three more hi-tech sections will let them discover the role of robot-ics in lifts and automatic parking. Sessions here are also 90 minutes. A visit to the Cité des Enfants or Techno Cité can be combined with a whole day out at the Cité des Sciences et de l'Industrie (*see chapter* **Museums**). Particularly good for children are the Planetarium, the Argonaute (a real submarine visitors can climb around in), and the Géode 180-degree cinema. Under-fives can participate in workshops proposed by La Folie des Petits Enfants (01.40.03.75.15).

## Halle St-Pierre

*2 rue Ronsard, 18th (01.42.58.72.89). Mº Anvers or Abbesses.* **Open** *Guignol* 3pm, 5pm Wed, Sat, Sun. *Museum* 10am-6pm daily. **Admission** 40F; 30F under-26s, over-60s.
One-hour walkway visits, *ateliers* and *guignol* are offered for children. The Halle also shows temporary art exhibitions focusing on contemporary popular and naïve art forms. Wheelchair access.

## Musée de la Curiosité

*Espace Magique du Marais, 11 rue St-Paul, 4th (01.42.72.13.26). Mº St-Paul or Sully Morland.* **Open** 2-7pm Wed, Sat, Sun. **Admission** 45F; 30F children.
Conjuring shows, optical illusions, psychic phenomena and interactive curiosities in a vaulted cellar, plus an exhibition of magic props including boxes for sawing ladies in two. English-speaking guides decline to reveal all the secrets. Children's courses in magic during school holidays.

## Musée en Herbe du Jardin d'Acclimatation

*Bois de Boulogne, 16th (01.40.67.97.66). Mº Pont de Neuilly.* **Open** 10am-6pm Mon-Fri, Sun; 2-6pm Sat. **Admission** 16F; free for under-3s (plus 10F entry to Jardin d'Acclimatation).
Recently renovated, the museum has a spacious new centre dedicated to European Art. There's an educational centre and art museum designed to introduce children to the history of art, with numerous *ateliers*, guided tours and exhibitions themed to introduce them to various artists and periods.

## Le Palais de la Découverte

*av Franklin D Roosevelt, 8th (01.40.74.80.00). Mº Franklin D Roosevelt.* **Open** 9.30am-6pm Tue-Sat; 10am-7pm Sun; closed public holidays. **Admission** 27F; 17F children; free under-7s; planetarium 13F.
This science museum offers kids the chance to see a commune of ants at work in a glass box. The planetarium seats 200.

## Meet the Animals

### Aquarium Tropical

*Musée National des Arts d'Afrique et d'Océanie, 293 av Daumesnil, 12th (01.44.74.84.80). Mº Porte Dorée.* **Open** 10am-noon, 1-5.30pm; Mon, Wed-Fri; 10am-6pm Sat, Sun. **Admission** 38F; 28F under-26s; free under-18s.
In the tropical aquarium downstairs, a vast collection of exotic fish are placed at just the right height for children to eyeball in wide-eyed fascination. Beware of the crocodiles.

### Château et Parc Zoologique de Thoiry

*78770 Thoiry en Yvelines (01.34.87.52.25). Train from Gare Montparnasse to Montfort l'Aumaury, then by taxi; phone château for taxi details and book in advance. By car Autoroute A13 west, then A12, N12 and D11 (45km/28 miles).* **Open** *Winter* 10am-5pm daily. *Summer* 10am-6pm daily. **Admission** *Park* 100F; 99F children. *Château* 25F; 20F children. **Credit** AmEx, MC, V.
Half an hour from central Paris, this safari park is home to 80 species of wild animal roaming the grounds of a château. Less ferocious beasts can be viewed from a little train that tours the gardens. There's a reptile house, tea room and a pleasant picnic area.

## Une Journée au Cirque

*Parc des Chanteraines, 115 bd Charles de Gaulle, 92390
Villeneuve-La Garenne (01.47.99.40.40). RER
Gennevilliers/SNCF St-Denis.* **Sessions** 10am-5pm Wed,
Sun, public and school holidays; closed July-end Sept.
**Tickets** *Show* 70F-155F; 45F-95F under-12s. *Day at
circus and one meal* 235F-295F; 195F-230F under-12s;
*Menagerie* 10F. **Credit** V.

Circus aficionado Francis Schoeller throws a day-long extravaganza. Children can train with circus artists in clowning,
conjuring, trapeze and tightrope, and there's also a show of
jugglers and magicians, and a visit to a funfair museum.

## Musée Océanographique – Centre de la Mer et des Eaux

*195 rue St-Jacques, 5th (01.44.32.10.90). RER
Luxembourg.* **Open** 10am-12.30pm, 1.15-5.30pm Tue-Fri;
10am-5.30pm Sat, Sun. **Admission** 30F; 18F students;
12F 4-12s; free under-4s.

Aquariums full of tropical fish, a giant diorama of undersea
life plus Jacques Cousteau films.

## Muséum National d'Histoire Naturelle

*57 rue Cuvier, in the Jardin des Plantes, 5th
(01.40.79.30.00). M° Gare d'Austerlitz.* **Open** *Main
Museum* 10am-5pm Mon, Wed-Sun. *Grande Galérie de
l'Evolution* 10am-6pm Mon, Wed, Fri-Sun; 10am-10pm
Thur. **Admission** 4F-25F. *Grande Galerie de l'Evolution*
40F; 30F 4-16s.

The impressive new Grande Galerie de l'Evolution, complete
with suspended whale, investigates the origins of life up to
man's own interventions in nature. Child-oriented films and
texts accompany exhibitions. In the Espace Découverte, kids
(5-12s) have hands-on contact with various specimens, using
microscopes. Also in the Jardin des Plantes is the Ménagerie,
a small zoo. *See also chapter* **Museums**.
*Wheelchair access.*

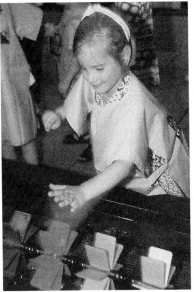

*Science fascinates at* **La Cité des Enfants**.

## Zoo de Vincennes

*53 av de St-Maurice, 12th (01.44.75.20.10/00). M° Porte
Dorée.* **Open** *Apr-Sept* 9am-6pm daily; *Oct-Mar* 9am-
5.30pm daily; *Dec-Jan* 9am-5pm. **Admission** 40F; 20F 4-
16s; free under-4s.

This well-maintained zoo tries to replicate the habitats of
animals so that lions, tigers and rhinos wander in relative
landscaped freedom. Check at entrance for the animals' feeding times. A miniature train tours the zoo and the park.

# Theme Parks

For **Disneyland Paris**, *see chapter* **Trips out of
Town**.

## France Miniature

*25 route du Mesnil, 78990 Elancourt (01.30.62.40.79).
RER to St-Quentin-en-Yvelines, then bus 420 every hour
at a quarter to the hour. By car A13 direction St Quentin-
En-Yvelines/Dreux, then Elancourt Centre.* **Open** mid
Mar to mid Nov 10am-7pm daily; summer holidays 10am-
11pm Sat. **Admission** 68F; 48F 3-13s; under-3s free.

An outdoor museum of France with over 200 models of monuments and sites reduced to a 30th of the original size. Latest
additions include the Moulin Rouge, Montmartre and Sacré
Coeur, which join Notre Dame and the Eiffel Tower.

## La Mer de Sable

*60950 Ermenonville (03.44.54.00.96/03.36.68.26.20).
RER to Roissy-Charles de Gaulle, then shuttle (10am only)
or taxi. By car A1 to exit 7 for Ermenonville.* **Open**
March 29 to Sept 28 10am-6pm Mon-Fri; 10.30am-7pm
Sat, Sun. June-Aug daily. **Admission** 80F; free under-3s.

Amid forests and a stretch of sand deposited millions of
years ago by the sea, this 33-year-old Wild West theme park
has the usual attractions, plus canoeing down rapids, animals, a village of puppets and an equestrian show.

## Parc Astérix

*60128 Plailly (03.16.44.62.31/recorded information in
English 03.44.62.34.34). RER to Roissy-Charles de Gaulle,
then shuttle 9.30am-1.30pm, 4.30pm-closing time (35F
return). By car Autoroute A1 towards Lille, exit Parc
Astérix.* **Open** *5 Apr-12 Oct* 10am-6pm daily; *July-Aug*
9.30am-3pm daily. **Admission** 160F; 110F 3-11s; free
under-3s. **Credit** MC, V.

Just 35km from Paris, this theme park dedicated to plucky
Gaul Astérix offers an enjoyable escape back to the days of
gladiators, slave auctions and feasts of wild boar. It isn't
Disneyland by a long shot, and it's best if your children are
familiar with the comic-strip character. There are rides, games,
parades, puppeteers, roving actors and bilingual staff.

## Parc de St-Vrain

*91770 St-Vrain (01.64.56.10.80). RER to Bouray, then
taxi or shuttle. By car Autoroute A6, exit at Viry onto
N445/D19 to Brétigny-sur-Orge.* **Open** *Apr-Sept*
10.30am-5.30pm daily. **Admission** 85F; 68F 3-10s; free
under-2s. **Credit** V.

A safari park 45km from Paris, with free-roaming beasts and
birds, and outdoor scenes featuring dinosaurs and prehistoric men. Take it in by riverboat or monorail.

# Theatre & Guignol Puppets

Many of Paris' smaller theatres present children's
shows on Wednesday, Saturday and Sunday afternoons, and more frequently during school holidays. The following theatres put on kids' shows:
**Au Bec Fin**, 6 rue Thérèse, 1st/01.42.96.29.35;

**Café d'Edgar**, 58 bd Edgar Quinet, 14th/ 01.42.79.97.97; **Point Virgule**, 7 rue Ste-Croix-de-la-Bretonnerie, 4th/01.43.71.43.48.
The French equivalent of Punch and Judy has no wife-battering, but the policeman comes in for a good deal of flak. There are loads of opportunities for audience participation, but the French can be mighty difficult to work out.

**ACT, the English Theatre**
*84 rue de Pixérécourt, 20th (01.40.33.64.02). M° Place des Fêtes.* **Tickets** 50F-90F.
This English-language theatre presents a regular Christmas season show, and some other productions suitable for children during the year. They reside at various theatres around Paris; call for the address of their current production.

**Marionnettes du Luxembourg**
*Jardin du Luxembourg, 6th (01.43.26.46.47/ 01.43.29.50.97). RER Luxembourg.* **Shows** (covered) 2.30pm, 3.30pm, 4.30pm Wed, Sat, Sun, public holidays; closed July, Aug. **Tickets** 22F. Shows last 45 minutes.

**Marionnettes de Montsouris**
*Parc Montsouris, entrance av Reille/rue Gazon, 14th (01.69.09.72.13). RER Cité Universitaire.* **Shows** presented in a spacious and comfortable covered theatre, at 5pm Tue; 3.30pm, 4.30pm Wed, Sun; 3.30pm, 4.30pm Sat; closed July, Aug. **Tickets** (available a week in advance) 15F.

**Marionnettes du Parc Georges Brassens**
*86 rue de Brancion, 15th (01.43.98.10.95). M° Porte de Vanves.* **Shows** 3pm, 4pm, Wed; 3.15pm, 4.15pm Sat. **Tickets** 14F adults, children.

## Supervised Activities

**Jardin des Enfants aux Halles**
*105 rue Rambuteau, 1st (01.45.08.07.18). M° Châtelet-Les Halles.* **Open** 9/10am-4/6pm daily; times can vary. **Admission** 2.50F per hour.
An open-air children's (7-11s) activity garden, including underground tunnels, rope swings, secret dens and 'swimming pools' of coloured ping-pong balls. Well-supervised by a team of *animateurs*. Adults are not allowed, except from 10am to 1pm on Saturdays, when they can bring along younger tots. Maximum stay one hour.

**Les Petits Dragons Playgroup**
*St George's Church, 7 rue Auguste-Vacquerie, 16th. (1.49.52.01.03). M° Charles de Gaulle-Etoile.* **Open** 9am-noon Mon, Wed; 9am-4pm Fri. **Rates** from 400F monthly for three days a week to 2,150F monthly for 25 hours a week, depending on attendance. Playgroup.
Friendly place for children aged 18 months to six. You can take your child in on an informal, long- or short-term, but regular, basis (book a week in advance).
**Kindergarten** *2 rue Jacquemont, 17th (01.42.28.56.17). M° La Fourche.* **Open** 8.30am-7pm Mon-Fri. Day-school for 2-6 year olds.
**Kindergarten Church of Scotland** *17 rue Bayard, 8th (Grethe Gravesen, director 01.49.52.01.03). M° Franklin D Roosevelt or Alma-Marceau.* **Open** 9am-3pm Tue, Thur.

### Summer Schools
If you are visiting Paris in the summer, you might consider putting your child into a programme that lasts a few weeks. For children between three and six, classes are usually in the morning, with an afternoon recreational activity.

**The Bilingual Montessori School of Paris**
*65 quai d'Orsay, 7th (01.45.55.13.27). M° Invalides.* **Hours** *Two sessions* 9am-noon; 9am-3pm. **Rates** Weekly and monthly rates. Field trips, art projects and music for children aged two to six.

**International School of Paris**
*96bis rue du Ranelagh, 16th (for 4-10s 01.42.24.43.40/12-18s 01.42.24.09.54). M° Ranelagh.* Three-week in July.
**The Lennen Bilingual School**
*65 quai d'Orsay, 7th (01.47.05.66.55). M° Invalides.* **Rates** 3,000F a month; 200F a day. Trips, arts, computers (for 3-8s).

## Toys & Books

**Attica 3**
*64 rue de la Folie Méricourt, 11th (01.48.06.17.00). M° Oberkampf.* **Open** 2-7pm Mon; 10am-7pm Tue-Sat. **Credit** MC, V.
Attica's slogan is 'literature for pleasure' for English speakers or those wanting to learn English. There's a large stock of TEFL literature, British children's classics, English translations of French comics and English-language videos.

**Chantelivre**
*13 rue de Sèvres, 6th (01.45.48.87.90). M° Sèvres-Babylone.* **Open** 10am-6.50pm Tue-Sat; closed one week mid-Aug. **Credit** MC, V.
Over 10,000 titles covering infants, adolescents, health and psychology. A small English language section carries primarily children's books. Also, there are cassettes, CDs, videos, toys, posters, games and party supplies. Kids' play area.

**Il Etait une Fois**
*1 rue Cassette, 6th (01.45.48.21.10). M° St-Sulpice.* **Open** 10am-7.30pm Mon-Sat. **Credit** AmEx, MC, V.
A delightful children's toy box filled with marionettes, Tintin and Babar dolls, toys, games and small wooden gadgets.

**Le Monde à Part**
*16 rue des Halles, 1st (01.42.33.68.97). M° Châtelet-Les Halles.* **Open** 10.30am-7pm Mon-Sat. **Credit** AmEx, MC, V.
Tiny, detailed dolls' houses – available in kits from 650F to 3,000F – and their furnishings, and other old-fashioned toys.

**Au Nain Bleu**
*406-410 rue St-Honoré, 8th (01.42.60.39.01). M° Concorde.* **Open** 9.45am-6.30pm Mon-Sat. **Credit** AmEx, MC, V.
The most prestigious toy shop in France, dating from 1836, and with a huge stock of toys from all around the world.

**Si Tu Veux**
*68 galerie Vivienne, 2nd (01.42.60.59.97). M° Bourse.* **Open** 10.30am-7pm Mon-Sat. **Credit** MC, V.
This old-fashioned toy store stocks skipping-ropes, wendyhouses and other traditional toys. It also has good party gear.

## Kids' Clothes

**Bonpoint**
*67 rue de l'Université, 7th (01.45.55.63.70). M° Solferino.* **Open** 10-7pm Mon-Sat. **Credit** AmEx, DC, V.
The kids shop to the French gentry, with charming children's dress-up clothes. Bonpoint has furniture and nursery accessories at 7 rue Solférino; a layette shop for newborns at 67 rue de l'Université; a shop for boys (12-16s) at 86 rue de l'Université; and lessons at 82 rue de Grenelle.
**Branch:** 15 rue Royale, 8th (01.47.42.52.63); 64 av Raymond Poincaré, 16th (01.47.27.60.81); 184 rue de Courcelles, 17th (01.47.63.87.49).

**Dipaki**
*18 rue Vignon, 8th (01.42.66.24.74). M° Madeleine.* **Open** 10am-7pm Mon-Sat. **Credit** MC, V.
One of Paris's best shops for reasonably priced, easy-to-care-for baby and kids' clothing in bold, primary colours. Cheaper still is the Dipaki old-season stock shop, at 98 rue d'Alésia.

*Gladiators with a comic-strip twist at* **Parc Astérix**.

**Branches**: 5 rue Brea, 6th (01.43.26.04.39); 22 rue Cler, 7th (01.47.05.47.62); 46 rue de l'Université, 7th (01.42.97.49.89).

### Gaspard de la Butte
*10 bis rue Yvonne Le Tac, 18th (01.42.55.99.40).*
*M° Abbesses.* **Open** 10am-7pm daily. **Credit** MC, V.
Little rompers and knits for babies and young ones are all handmade with tender loving care. Great hand-me-downs.

### Du Pareil au Même
*59 rue du Commerce, 15th (01.48.28.86.76). M° Émile Zola.* **Open** 10am-7pm Mon-Sat. **Credit** MC.
A chain selling good, sturdy but keely-priced, fashionable basics for babies and kids. The new, newborn shop at 122 rue du Fbg St-Antoine is great for gifts.
**Branches include**: 15-17 rue des Mathurins, 8th (01.42.66.93.80).

### Petit Faune
*33 rue Jacob, 6th (01. 42.60.80.72). M° St-Germain-des-Prés.* **Open** 2.30-7pm Mon; 10am-7pm Tues-Sat. **Credit** MC, V.
Chic, pricy corner boutique for children up to 8 years old. Contenders for the best-dressed-child-in-Paris award shop here.

## Eating Out

Unless trapped in a food wilderness around the great monuments, you should have no trouble finding places to fuel kids' energy. **Bistro Romain**, 30 rue St-Denis, 1st/01.40.26.82.80, has numerous branches, all with a kids' menu and an Asterix theme. **Hippopotamus**, 29 rue Berger, 1st/01.45.08.00.29, has 15 colourful steakhouses and offers every child a play pack. The Food Court, in the Carrousel du Louvre, has a self-service smorgasbord of pizzas, burgers, crêpes and the like. Listed below are places that happily welcome kids.

### Café de la Jatte
*60 bd Vital-Bouhot, 92200 Neuilly (01.47.45.04.20).*
*M° Pont de Levallois (on foot, cross pedestrian footbridge; by car, take Pont de Courbevoie).* **Open** noon-2.30pm, 8-11pm, Mon-Fri; noon-3pm, 8pm-midnight, Sat; noon-3pm, 8-11.30pm, Sun. **Average** 230F. **Credit** AmEx, DC, V.
This upmarket restaurant on the Ile de la Grande Jatte offers a children's (under-12s) Sunday lunch at 70F. There's a life-size model dinosaur skeleton to gawp at, suspended above the galleried dining-room, and a courtyard below.

### La Dame Tartine
*2 rue Brise-Miche, 4th (01.42.77.32.22). M° Hôtel-de-Ville.* **Open** 2pm-11pm daily. **Average** 100F. **Credit** V.
The much loved 'sandwich lady' has an ideal place for a light, cheap and quick snack, near the Stravinsky fountain.

### Hôtel Méridien Montparnasse
*19 rue du Commandant Mouchotte, 15th (01.44.36.44.00).*
*M° Montparnasse-Bienvenüe or Gaîté.* **Open** Sept-June noon-3pm Sun. **Average** 230F; 110F under-12s; free under-4s. **Credit** AmEx, DC, MC, V.
'Baby Brunch' is a veritable banquet of mini-pizzas, quiches, burgers, waffles and candyfloss. After the kids eat their brunch, a play supervisor gives them fun activities.

### La Patata
*25 bd des Italiens, 2nd (01.42.68.16.66). M° Opéra.*
**Open** 11.30am-midnight daily. **Prix fixe** 90F, 100F.
**Credit** MC, V.
Baked spuds with various accompaniments. Under-12s dine for 38F with gifts and balloons.

## Babysitting

English-speaking baby-sitters also advertise on the notice board at the American Church, 65 quai d'Orsay, 7th (01.40.62.05.00).

### Ababa
*8 av du Maine, 15th (01.45.49.46.46). M° Montparnasse-Bienvenüe.* **Open** 8am-8pm Mon-Fri; 11am-8pm Sat. **Rates** from 31F per hour; 62F booking fee (discounts). Two hours' notice needed.
350 English-speaking baby-sitters, both male and female.

### Contact B
*10 rue Rodier, 9th (01.45.26.81.34).* **Open** 9am-4pm Mon-Fri. **Rates** from 30F per hour; 60F booking fee.
English-speaking babysitters (mainly British *au pairs*).

### EuroBaby
*(01.60.61.81.79).* **Prices** from 100F a week; plus a refundable deposit on all rentals. Delivery available.
This English-speaking service supplies a wide range of baby equipment for short- or long- term rental in the Paris area.

### Kid's Service
*75 bd Pereire, 17th (01.47.66.00.52). M° Wagram.*
**Open** 8am-8pm Mon-Fri; 10am-8pm Sat; reduced hours Aug. **Rates** from 32F per hour; 60F booking fee.
One of the oldest baby-sitting agencies in Paris. Has a young, dependable team of qualified nannies or play supervisors.

# Gay & Lesbian

**Parisian gays have got hedonism down to a fine art, but if the bar scene is flourishing, the undercurrent is serious.**

Paris is easily the most liberal city in France simply because of the number of gays who come to live here, escaping isolation in the provinces. Although the French generally leave private lives private, gays are tolerated more than accepted. *Pédé* (pouf) is a common swear word, although some gays have ironised by using it to describe themselves. This mitigated acceptance of gays can cause serious problems. When AIDS (*le SIDA*) was brought to light in 1982 the French were slow to act and, even recently, controversy has surrounded the annual media AIDS campaign which still refuses to target gays directly. One ad showing two pairs of male feet poking out of a duvet had to be scrapped as too shocking, and replaced by two pairs of discarded male shoes, which prompted Act Up Paris to zap the press conference launch. This, in a country where the incidence of the epidemic is way ahead of any other in western Europe. It is perhaps this barely covert homophobia that has finally knocked French gays out of their apathy and, ironically, kick-started a gay scene which had become staid and depressed in the late 1980s.

A special effort is being given to the *Contrat d'union social*, a proposed law which would give any couple, gay or straight, the same legal and financial rights as married couples. The mayors of certain *arrondissements* already allow gay couples to sign a *Certificat de concubinage* which, while it has no legal significance, can give access to special fares on trains and planes.

With increased political activity inevitably comes increased visibility, but you may be disappointed by the lack of diversity. French gays tend to conform to an image, and only slowly are people learning to be more free in appearance: a dress code is very much in evidence down the rue de la Ferronerie at Châtelet, where every other shop or café is now gay. The fun continues in the cafés and restaurants of rue des Lombards which effectively links the frothy youth of the Châtelet scene with the traditional gay ghetto of the Marais.

Finding a lesbian scene is more difficult. Paris has always catered more for gay men than women, and lesbians tend to be discreet, perhaps because the main lesbian bars are not in the Marais or because lesbians are more difficult to recognise. Either way, gay men and lesbians tend not to socialise together, as few male bars are welcoming to women even if they are not strictly banned.

## THE GREAT OUTDOORS

Open-air cruising is a French favourite and, apart from the obvious looks you'll get in the street, several cruising grounds have become so institutionalised they are even listed by *arrondissement* in magazines such as *Illico* or *Double Face*. Gay bashing is rare, but caution should be exercised nonetheless; be warned that since Chirac became president, the police have been cracking down on bars and cruising areas with newfound zeal.

Next to the Canal St-Martin in the 10th and under the warehouses on quai d'Austerlitz in the 13th are busy at night, as is square Barye at the tip of the Ile St-Louis, where steps lead down to a quay-side walk popular with sunbathers. Most entertaining, day or night, is 'Tata Beach' (on the banks of the Seine between Pont Neuf and the Tuileries), where on any day with the merest hint of sun you'll find all manner of people trying to tan and scan. After dark things become more serious. Avoid place Dauphine, where rent boys congregate, and the Bois de Boulogne which can be unsafe at night.

*Hanging out at the **Centre Gai et Lesbien**.*

## Information & Associations

For information on all health services, and AIDS/HIV services *see chapter* **Survival: Health**.

### Centre Gai et Lesbien

*3 rue Keller, 11th (01.43.57.21.47). Mº Ledru-Rollin.*
**Open** noon-8pm Mon-Sat; 2-8pm Sun.
After initial finance problems, the Lesbian and Gay Centre has become a valued community resource providing information and a meeting space for all, as well as legal and other advice services. The Association des Médecins Gais (gay doctors) mans a telephone line here 6-8pm Mon and 2-4pm Sat. Noticeboards are good for flat and job hunting, and the café is a pleasant place to digest the magazines and flyers on offer. Café Positif (2-7pm Sun) allows HIV+ people and their friends to socialise in a relaxed atmosphere. Numerous contact groups that hold meetings here include ASB (transsexuals), Beit Haverim (Jewish gays and lesbians), Rando's (gay ramblers), Gais Nounous (for the cuddly overweight), Long Yang Club (Asiatic) and Gais Retraités (over-60s). The Centre publishes its own monthly magazine *3 Keller*.

### Act Up Paris

*45 rue Sedaine, 11th (answerphone 01.48.06.13.89). Mº Bréguet-Sabin.*
Very active branch of the world-wide anti-AIDS group, whose 'zaps' have included putting a flourescent pink condom over the obelisk on place de la Concorde. Weekly meeting Tuesdays at 7.30pm in amphitheatre 1 of the Ecole des Beaux-Arts (14 rue Bonaparte, 6th. Mº St-Germain-des-Prés).

### SNEG (Syndicat National des Entreprises Gaies)

*37 rue de Rivoli, 4th (01.44.59.81.01). Mº Hôtel-de-Ville.*
**Open** 10am-6.45pm Mon-Fri.
Gay and lesbian business group, of which many bars and clubs are members. Organises HIV and safe-sex awareness training for staff, and ensures free condoms are available.

## Press & Media

Check bars and shops for the free papers; some can be found at large newsstands as well. All the gay press has dozens of ads for Minitel contact services, accompanied by the obligatory naked torso.

**FG 98.2FM** The gay radio station goes from strength to strength with techno, house, news and information.
**Action** Act Up Paris' free monthly: health news and hits.
**Gai Pied** The weekly magazine may be defunct, but a slimmed-down group now organises the Bastille Day Gay Ball, and has just launched a serious new bi-monthly **Café**; they also publish the SM/fetish monthly **Projet X**.

**Illico** out at the beginning of the month puts out news, puff pieces and a useful map. They also publish **Double Face** (leisure and lifestyle monthly), lifestyle titles **Idol**, aimed at a younger market, and **Ex Aequo**, an austere politics and debate monthly.
**Lesbia** The leading lesbian journal; also organises discos.
**Têtu** Floundering monthly lifestyle mag with special HIV information section, which hoped to attract big-name advertisers with glossy design and low porn content. The troubled face of new gay media.
**3 Keller** Published by the Centre Gai et Lesbien.

## Gay Bars & Cafés

### Amnesia

*42 rue Vieille-du-Temple, 4th (01.42.72.1694). Mº Hôtel-de-Ville.* **Open** 10.30am-2am daily. **Credit** MC, V.
Rescued from naffness a few years ago by a complete change of image, Amnesia is now a warm meeting place with comfy sofas and an easy-going crowd. Calm in the afternoon, the action hots up at night. Busy at weekends for brunches (noon-4.30pm), the most luxurious of which includes salmon, scrambled eggs with prawns, and hair-of-the-dog champagne or a Bloody Mary.

### Banana Café

*13 rue de la Ferronerie, 1st (01.42.33.35.31). Mº Châtelet-Les Halles.* **Open** 4.30pm-dawn daily. **Credit** AmEx, V.
*The* place to be seen for hedonistic 30-somethings, gay and straight, the Banana Café's theme nights are legendary; camp, decadent and often downright silly, there's rarely enough room to strike a pose, although the minor celebs and good-time boys do make a valiant effort.

### Le Bar

*5 rue de la Ferronerie, 1st (01.40.41.00.10). Mº Châtelet-Les Halles.* **Open** 5.30pm-2am Mon, Tue; 5.30pm-3am Wed, Thur, Sun; 5.30pm-4am Fri, Sat. **Credit** MC, V.
Cavernous three-level bar with a usually men-only basement (*see below* **Ladies Room**) and subtle lighting conducive to strange encounters. Loud music and late opening make it perfect for a pre-club drink or three. Always packed.

### BarBi

*23 rue Ste-Croix-de-la-Bretonnerie, 4th (01.42.78.26.20). Mº Hôtel-de-Ville.* **Open** 5pm-2am daily. **No credit cards.**
There's nothing bisexual about this place, doll. Don't be surprised if the whole bar starts singing along to the music playing on the giant video screen. Conversation can be difficult.

### Le Central

*33 rue Vieille-du-Temple, 4th (01.48.87.99.33). Mº Hôtel-de-Ville.* **Open** 2pm-1am Mon-Thur, Sun; 2pm-2am Fri, Sat. **Credit** AmEx, MC, V.

One of the city's oldest gay bars and popular with tourists (Paris' only strictly gay hotel is upstairs), might seem dull compared to its spritely neighbours, but can be a welcome respite after bar-hopping in the area. Older crowd, no attitude.

### Coffee Shop
*3 rue Ste-Croix-de-la-Bretonnerie, 4th (01.42.74.46.29). M° Hôtel-de-Ville.* Open noon-midnight daily. No credit cards.
For a spot of calm in the afternoon or evening you couldn't do better than the Coffee Shop. A popular meeting place, or pick-up joint. MTV plays lightly in a corner and tables are at a premium. Decent bistro food is served until late.

### Le Cox
*15 rue de Archives, 4th (01.42.72.08.00). M° Hôtel-de-Ville.* Open 1pm-2am daily. No credit cards.
Despite a name to make most English-speakers cringe, the Cox is probably the best new Marais bar. Afternoons are calm, with two computers for gay Internet, but evenings are hot, with loud house music, dishy barmen and a good mix of body-conscious punters. Good for flyers, too.

### Le Duplex
*25 rue Michel-le-Comte, 3rd (01.42.72.80.86). M° Rambuteau.* Open 8pm-2am daily. Credit AmEx, MC, V.
Monthly exhibitions and an eclectic music policy attract all sorts to this smoky bar; but don't be fooled, cruising here is down to a fine art. A real squeeze at the weekend, it now boasts a computer with 'intranet' where you can learn new French insults, or leave a message for others to ponder.

### Mic Man
*24 rue Geoffrey l'Angevin, 4th (01.42.74.39.80). M° Rambuteau.* Open noon-2am Mon-Sat; 2pm-2am Sun. Credit V.
An entrance fetooned with flowers belies the true nature of this bar. Beards and moustaches abound, and the basement means business.

### Le Bar du Palmier
*16 rue des Lombards, 4th (01.42.78.53.53). M° Châtelet-Les Halles.* Open 6pm-5am daily. Credit AmEx, V.
Gets busy late (all the barmen from surrounding bars come here after work), but also good from 6-8pm during happy hour, where beer is served with copious nibbles. Bizarre pseudo-tropical décor, a nice terrace, this is one of the few places where women are welcome and numerous.

### Le Piano Zinc
*49 rue des Blancs-Manteaux, 4th (01.42.74.32.42). M° Hôtel-de-Ville.* Open 7pm-2am Tue-Sun. Admission free Sun-Thur; 45F (includes one free drink), 35F (without drink) Fri, Sat. Credit AmEx, MC, V.
Unique in Paris, this multi-cellared bar has a pianist, reams of sheet music, and any number of people willing to have a sing-song. Friendly, popular, and often very busy.

### Quetzal
*10 rue de la Verrerie, 4th (01.48.87.99.07). M° Hôtel-de-Ville.* Open 2pm-3am Mon-Thur; 2pm-4am Fri, Sat. No credit cards.
Still the cruisiest bar in the Marais, despite heightened competition. Quetzal attracts a beefy crowd looking for a drink and company. It's at the end of the rue des Mauvais-Garçons (Bad Boy Street), so you know what to expect.

### Le Tropic Café
*66 rue des Lombards, 11th (01.40.13.92.62). M° Châtelet-Les Halles.* Open 6pm-4am daily. Credit AmEx, MC, V.
Sister of the Amazonial restaurant opposite, this bright upbeat bar teems with pretty young things. People-watching can be addictive here, so grab a table at the edge of the terrace to experience the full horror.

## Gay Restaurants

### Au Rendezvous des Camionneurs
*72 quai des Orfèvres, 1st (01.43.54.88.74). M° Pont-Neuf.* Open noon-2.30pm, 7-11.30pm daily. Average 180F. Dinner menu 128F. Lunch menu 78F. Credit AmEx, MC, V.
Classic French favourites and a charming location by Pont Neuf make this restaurant a consistent gay success.

### L'Amazonial
*3 rue Ste-Opportune, 1st (01.42.33.53.13). M° Châtelet-Les Halles.* Open noon-3pm, 7pm-1.30am daily. Prix fixe 83F, 129F. Credit AmEx, V.
The largest gay restaurant sports a huge terrace, heated in winter, decent French cuisine with a twist of the exotic and tight T-shirted waiters. There's cabaret on Thursday nights.

### Le Loup Blanc
*42 rue Tiquetonne, 2nd (01.40.13.08.35). M° Etienne-Marcel.* Open 8pm-2am Mon-Sat; noon-5pm Sun. Average 130F. Credit MC, V.
One of a host of new gay restaurants in the area, Le Loup Blanc is reasonably priced and friendly. As well as grilled meat and fish, they, unusually, have certain dishes suitable for vegetarians and even do a vegetarian brunch on Sunday.

## Gay Clubs & Discos

Apart from the gay clubs listed below, many clubs have a large gay contingent (Folies Pigalle) or specific gay nights. Check press or flyers for one-nighters such as Thanx God I'm A VIP, and remember that nothing gets going before 1am. Admission prices usually include one drink.

### Club 18
*18 rue de Beaujolais, 1st (01.42 97.52.13). M° Palais-Royal.* Open 11pm-dawn Wed-Sun. Admission free Wed, Thur, Sun; 65F Fri, Sat. Credit MC, V.
Time travel made real: camp reigns supreme in this club. Friendly, but don't expect an adventurous music policy.

### L'Equivoque
*40 rue des Blancs-Manteaux, 4th (01.42.71.03.29). M° Rambuteau.* Open 11.30pm-dawn Tue-Sun. Admission free Tue-Thur, Sun; 50F Fri, Sat. Credit AmEx, MC, V.
Tiny cellar club in the Marais. A mixed older crowd struts its stuff to light techno, house, and gay diva Dalida.

### L'Enfer
*36 rue du Départ, 14th (01.42.79.94.94). M° Montparnasse-Bienvenüe.* Open 11.30pm-dawn Thur; 6am-noon Sat; 6am-noon, 5.30-11pm, Sun. Admission 50F-60F. Credit AmEx, MC, V.
A Brazilian review bar under the Montparnasse tower has become the surprising inheritor of the Palace's defunct Gay Tea Dance, with a happening weekend after-hours.

### Le Queen
*102 av des Champs-Elysées, 8th (01.42.89.31.32). M° George V.* Open 11.30pm-dawn daily. Admission 50F Mon; free Tue-Thur, Sun; 80F Fri, Sat. Credit AmEx, DC, V.
Still the pick of the crop and crammed every night. Going to Queen takes courage – the door staff are rude and ruthless, especially with women. Dress up and smile is our advice. You can get soaped up and hosed down at the notorious men-only foam parties in the summer, or don your gaudiest shirt and flares for Monday's disco extravaganza. Flyers found in most bars keep you updated on other nights, although it's generally house music and hedonism all the way.

*Waiting for the hordes at **Le Cox**.*

## Scorpion

*25 bd Poissonnière, 2nd (01.40.26.01.50). Mº Rue Montmartre.* **Open** midnight-6am daily. **Admission** free Mon-Thur, Sun; 70F Fri, Sat. **Credit** AmEx, MC, V.
Playing music that you thought had gone out of fashion (and it has) the Scorpion caters for those who weren't gorgeous enough to get into the Queen. The 4am drag show is popular and weekends are busy. A refreshing lack of attitude.

# Men-Only Clubs – The Dark Side

## L'Arène

*80 quai de l'Hôtel-de-Ville, 4th (unlisted telephone). Mº Hôtel-de-Ville.* **Open** noon-6am Sun-Thur; noon-8am Fri, Sat. **No credit cards.**
Don't even pretend you're here just for a drink; your first beer will come complete with condoms and lube. Two floors of dark corners and popular theme nights have made this newcomer a success, but drinks are expensive in the evening.

## Banque Club

*23 rue de Penthièvre, 8th (01.42.56.49.26). Mº Miromesnil.* **Open** 4pm-2am Mon-Sat; 2pm-2am Sun. **Admission** 30F 4-6pm, 45F after 6pm Mon-Sat; free Sun. **No credit cards.**
Cruise club with three cellars – each more sinister as you descend –, videos and private cabins.

## Docks

*150 rue St-Maur, 11th (01.43.57.33.82). Mº Goncourt.* **Open** 4pm-2am daily. **Admission** 45F. **No credit cards.**
Heavy cruise club with theme nights.

## Le Keller

*14 rue Keller, 11th (01.47.00.05.39). Mº Bastille.* **Open** 10pm-2am daily. **Admission** free. **No credit cards.**
A long-established leather bar. The customers may look a bit rough and worn, but that's part of their charm. Legend has it that the pool table is put to various unusual uses.

## La Luna

*28 rue Keller, 11th (01.40.21.09.91). Mº Bastille.* **Open** 9pm-5am daily. **Admission** free. **Credit** V.

Once the club where Laurent Garnier cut his teeth, now a cruise bar with a basement maze of corridors and cabins. Very busy at weekends and for Tuesday's 'Incorporo' (Army) night.

## QG

*12 rue Simon-le-Franc, 4th (01.48.87.74.18). Mº Rambuteau.* **Open** 5pm-6am Mon-Thur, Sun; 5pm-8am Fri, Sat. **Credit** MC, V.
No entrance fee, cheap beer, late opening and a sense of humour guarantee success for this bar. Open until 8am at weekends, you'll need the free coffee and croissants to get your strength back. Things get tough downstairs, and don't even ask what the bath on the ground floor is for.

## Le Tranfert

*3 rue de la Sourdière, 1st (01.42.60.48.42). Mº Tuileries.* **Open** 11pm-dawn daily. **Credit** AmEx, MC, V.
Leather/SM bar so small that being just a spectator is barely possible. Entertaining.

## Le Trap

*10 rue Jacob, 6th (01.46.54.53.53). Mº St-Germain-des-Prés.* **Open** 11pm-4am daily. **Admission** free Mon-Thur, Sun; 50F Fri, Sat. **No credit cards.**
One of the few gay venues left on the Left Bank, Le Trap has been packing them in for nearly 20 years. The television on the ground floor bar plays a surreal selection of clips from a stock of over 300 video cassettes, and dark rooms upstairs ensure variety. Expect naked dancing on the bar ('and more!', they say) on Mondays and Wednesdays.

# Men-Only Saunas

## IDM

*4 rue du Fbg-Montmartre, 9th (01.45.23.10.03). Mº Rue Montmartre.* **Open** noon-1am Mon-Thur; noon-2am Fri-Sun. **Admission** 95F; 60F under-26, all after 10pm. **No credit cards.**
The largest Parisian sauna has a newly refurbished gym, steam room and small jacuzzi.

## Key West

*141 rue Lafayette, 10th (01.45.26.31.74). Mº Gare du Nord.* **Open** noon-1am Mon-Thur, Sun; noon-2am Fri, Sat. **No credit cards.**
Europe's most beautiful sauna, as it modestly describes itself, has a small pool, gym, a large steam room and discreet staff who clean constantly. Upstairs the cubicles come complete with TV screens playing saucy videos.

# Gay Shops

## Body Guard

*11 rue de la Ferronerie, 1st (01.42.33.50.31). Mº Châtelet-Les Halles.* **Open** 1.30pm-1am Mon-Thur, Sun; 1.30pm-2am Fri, Sat. **Credit** AmEx, MC, V.
Located on what is now an almost exclusively gay street, Body Guard is the place to come for something with Lycra.

## D'Instinct

*25 rue Vieille-du-Temple, 4th (01.48.87.49.78). Mº Hôtel-de-Ville.* **Open** 1-8pm Mon-Sat; 3-6.30pm Sun. **Credit** AmEx, V.
Designer emporium with an original choice of glitzy club- and streetwear, with prices to match.

## DOM – Christian Koban

*21 rue Ste-Croix-de-la-Bretonnerie, 4th (01.42.71.08.00). Mº Hôtel-de-Ville.* **Open** 11.30am-9pm Mon-Thur; 11.30am-11pm Fri, Sat; 2-9pm Sun. **Credit** MC, V.
Assistants dressed in black sell essential items for the home, from tea towel holders to fluffy lamps. Chic but not *cher*.

## IEM

*208 rue St-Maur, 10th (01.42.41.21.41). M° Goncourt.*
**Open** 10am-7.30pm Mon-Sat. **Credit** AmEx, MC, V.
At the end of a long alley, this huge store has an enormous
video section (sale and rental), clothes, books, magazines and
condoms. Upstairs houses everything leather and rubber.
**Branches**: 4 rue Bailleul, 1st (01.42.97.05.74); 33 rue de
Liège, 9th (01.45.22.69.01).

## Lionel Joubin

*10 rue Filles-du-Calvaire, 3rd (01.42.74.37.51). M° Filles
du Calvaire.* **Open** 11am-9pm Tue-Sat; 10am-1.30pm Sun.
**Credit** MC, V.
Famous for its extravagant window displays, florist Joubin
has decorated entire floats for the Gay Pride march.

## Les Mots à la Bouche

*6 rue Ste-Croix-de-la-Bretonnerie, 4th (01.42.78.88.30).
M° Hôtel-de-Ville.* **Open** 11am-11pm Mon-Sat. **Credit**
MC, V.
Gay-interest literature from around the world, including an
English-language section, and a selection of travel guides
and magazines. The community noticeboard is interesting.

## TTBM

*16 rue Ste-Croix-de-la-Bretonnerie, 4th (01.48.04.80.88).
M° Hôtel-de-Ville.* **Open** 1-9pm Mon, Tue; 1-11pm Wed-
Sat; 3-11pm Sun. **Credit** AmEx, DC, MC, V.
The unpretentious name is short for 'very, very well hung'.
Rubber and leatherware is a speciality, and you can also get
pierced and tattooed on the premises. Video rental service.

# Summer in the city

The Gay Pride march has exploded in the last
few years to become a massive carnival to rival
those of its European neighbours, and with
Europride and the Euro Gay Games being held
in Paris in 1997, expect party fever to hit an all-
time high. Look out for the annual Bastille Day
gay ball on the quai de la Tournelle on 13 July.

## Gay Pride/Europride

*Lesbian & Gay Pride, 27 rue du Fbg-Montmartre, 9th
(01.47.70.01.50). M° Rue Montmartre.* **Date** 28 June
1997.
Despite record attendance, last year's Pride left the organisers heavily in the red after the *soirée* at the end attracted
not 17,000 people, but 5,000. Many criticised the organi-
sing committee after it registered itself as a company and
copyrighted all variations of the word 'Pride'. While scep-
tics question the wisdom of an unelected, unaccountable
body having this power, the Pride committee contends
that the group is open to all, but several important members including Act Up Paris and the Centre Gai et Lesbien
resigned in protest at what they see as the 'privatisation
of the major homosexual event of the year'. Despite inter-

nal squabbles the committee is hopeful that Europride '97,
with its seven million franc budget, will be the biggest
and most flamboyant yet. Over 300,000 are expected to
attend, with the march being held under the theme of better integration for lesbians and gays in society, and negotiations for a high-profile route are already in progress
(the rue de Rivoli would be perfect), although final autho-
risation is given only a few weeks beforehand. The big
day is preceded by a week-long programme of events
including debates and traditional *bals musettes*.

## EuroGames 5

*postal address Eurogames, 13 rue Pache, 11th.* **Date** 20-
24 June 1997. or CGPIF (Gay Sport Fed) (01.47.00.60.03).
Anyone male or female, and of any standard, can enter
the European Gay Games, either individually or with a
club. Sports including athletics, field and court events, and
even *pétanque*. Alas, no synchronised swimming.

## EuroSalon de l'Homosocialité

**Date**: yet to be decided. e-mail: eurosalon@gaipied.fr
A sort of Gay and Lesbian Lifestyle show, albeit with a serious side, the Salon hopes to bring together exhibitors from
all over Europe on travel, leisure, sport, health, etc. Previous
editions on the banks of the Seine drew 10,000 visitors.

**Gay Pride '96** *celebrations along boulevard St-Germain.*

# Gay Services

### Eurogay's
*23 rue du Bourg-Tibourg, 4th (01.48.87.37.77).*
*M° Hôtel-de-Ville.* **Open** 10am-1.30pm, 2.30-7pm, Mon-Fri. **Credit** MC, V.
From train tickets to world tours, this gay travel agent can book it all, and proposes 80 gay destinations around the world. Packages for Europride are also available.

### Hôtel Central Marais
*33 rue Vieille-du-Temple, 4th (01.48.87.56.08/fax 01.42.77.06.27). M° Hôtel-de-Ville.* **Rates** *single* 400F; *double* 485F; *breakfast* 35F. **Credit** MC, V.
The city's only strictly gay hotel has seven rooms (but no private bathrooms), plus a furnished apartment opposite (595F-720F). Perfectly placed for going out. Book well in advance. **Hotel services** *Ground floor bar.* **Room services** *Double glazing. Telephone.*

### Hôtel Saintonge
*16 rue de Saintonge, 3rd (01.42.77.91.13/fax 01.48.87.76.41). M° Filles du Calvaire.* **Rates** *single* 300F-410F; *double* 400F-490F; *suite* 680F. **Credit** AmEx, DC, MC, V.
Although this hotel is open to everyone, its owners want to encourage a gay clientele. All rooms have a private shower. **Room services** *Alarm clock. Hair dryer. Minibar. Safe. TV (Cable).*

### Pharmacie du Village
*26 rue du Temple, 4th (01.42.72.60.71). M° Hôtel-de-Ville.* **Open** 8.30am-l0pm Mon-Sat. **Credit** MC, V.
If the thought of having to explain intimate problems to aged men in white coats fills you with fear, this gay-staffed chemist is the answer. The pharmacists can advise on anything from wrinkle cream to dental dams without a blush.

### Phot'Express
*23 bd Poissonnière, 2nd (01.42.33.05.30). M° Rue Montmartre.* **Open** 8am-7.30pm Mon-Fri; noon-7.30pm Sat. **Credit** MC, V.
Gay-owned photo developer, with one-hour service, total discretion and a free film for gay customers.

# Lesbian Paris

Compared to the male gay scene in Paris, lesbians have a much lower profile. Over the last couple of years, though, there have been signs that this is changing. Activist group **Les Lesbiennes Se Déchaînent** has demanded higher visibility in the Gay Pride march (*see above*). Lesbians now share with gay men the Centre Gai & Lesbien (*see above*); several militant groups are based at the Maison des Femmes (*see chapter* **Women's Paris**); and DJ Sex Toy has been making a name in the male-dominated techno scene.

# Information, Groups & Media

### Les Archives, Recherches, Cultures Lesbiennes (ARCL)
*Maison des Femmes, 8 cité Prost, 11th (answerphone 01.43.56.11.49). M° Faidherbe-Chaligny.* **Open** 7-10pm Fri.
This organisation produces audio-visual documentation, a yearbook and bulletins on lesbian and women's activities, and runs an archive and library of lesbian and feminist documents, essays and novels.

### Les Lesbiennes se déchaînent
*c/o Centre Gai & Lesbien, 3 rue Keller, 11th (01.43.57.21.47). M° Ledru-Rollin.*
An active group set up to give lesbians a more visible presence in Paris. Tuesday night socials are at 8pm in the Café du Trésor (5-7 rue du Trésor, 4th/01.44.78.06.60), and meetings on Fridays at 8.30pm in the Centre Gai et Lesbien.

### MIEL
*Maison des Femmes, 8 Cité Prost, 11th (answerphone 01.43.48.24.91). M° Charonne or Faidherbe-Chaligny.* **Open** 7.30pm first and third Thursday of the month.
Created in 1981, this is a militant discussion group based at the Maison des Femmes. Their social evening – Caféteria Hydromel – is every Friday from 8pm.

### Quand les Lesbiennes se font du cinéma
*Espace Culturel André Malraux, 2 pl Victor-Hugo, 93 Kremlin-Bicêtre. M° Kremlin-Bicêtre.* **Information** Cineffable 01.48.70.77.11. **Dates** late Oct-early Nov.
Women-only film festival screens a range of mostly never-seen-before international films from documentaries and experimental videos to lesbian features, plus debates, exhibition, bar and a party at the end.

# Bars, Restaurants & Clubs

### La Champmeslé
*4 rue Chabanais, 2th (01.42.96.85.20). M° Bourse.* **Open** 5pm-2am Mon-Wed; 5pm-5am Thur-Sat. **No credit cards.**
The pillar of the Paris lesbian bar community; women-only at the back. It picks up at weekends, and on Thursdays for cabaret. Monthly exhibition and a fortune teller every Friday.

### Chez Nini Peau de Chien
*24 rue des Taillandiers, 11th (01.47.00.45.35). M° Bastille.* **Open** noon-2pm, 8-11pm, Tue-Sat. **Average** 120F. **Lunch menu** 68F. **Prix-fixe** 89F, 119F. **Credit** MC, V.
This lesbian-run restaurant has a mixed clientele during the week, but becomes more lesbian-orientated at weekends.

### L'Enfer
*36 rue du Départ, 14th (01.42.79.94.94). M° Montparnasse-Bienvenüe.* **Open** 11.30pm-5am Fri, Sat. **Admission** 50F-60F. **Credit** AmEx, MC, V.
Thriving girls'-own parties under the Montparnasse tower (*see also above* **Gay Clubs & Discos**).

### L'Entr'acte
*25 bd Poissonnière, 2nd (01.40.26.01.93). M° Rue Montmartre.* **Open** midnight-dawn Tue-Sun. **Credit** V.
Now under new management, this lesbian club has widened its musical mix with a soul, funk, reggae emphasis on Sunday, house and techno dominant Wednesday, Friday and Saturday and Latino on Thursdays. Busiest at the weekends.

### Ladies Room
*Postal address: 15 rue des Halles, 1st.*
Runs two successful nights a month, every other Thursday. A free bar session 8pm-2am at Les Piétons (8 rue des Lombards, 1st/01.48.87.82.87) – Spanish tapas and Latin house mix – and wildly successful (500 people) monthly dance club in the basement at Le Bar (*see above* **Gay Bars**) with DJ Sex Toy and guests. Boys admitted if accompanied.

### Les Scandaleuses
*8 rue des Ecouffes, 4th (01.48.87.39.26). M° Hôtel-de-Ville.* **Open** 6pm-2am daily. **Credit** MC, V.
When she transformed this former gay club, Nicole Miquel, ex of El Scandalo, kept the cellar rooms, thus inaugurating a new trend in the usually sedate lesbian scene. Lively crowd and changing exhibitions by women artists.

# Study

**A guide to understanding the French student system, courses, libraries and how to master 'the three Ps'.**

The university of Paris proper is split into 18 separate units spread around the city and suburbs, of which the renowned Sorbonne is just one. Anyone who has passed the *baccalauréat* can apply, over-crowded facilities and huge drop-out rates (up to 50 per cent at the end of the first year) are perennial problems. Lectures are huge and can be very difficult to hear, because everyone talks and shuffles continuously, and there is very little tutor-pupil contact. It is all very far from the heady militant days of May '68, although there have been student sit-ins about over-crowding, and the Ministry of Education is planning reforms.

The situation is different in the prestigious, highly selective *Grandes Ecoles*, the specialist institutes, such as the Ecole National d'Administration (ENA), Ecole Normale Supérieure or Ecole Polytechnique, which are unchallenged at the top of the French educational tree. A degree from one of these elitist institutions guarantees a golden future.

Students from EU countries can enter the French university system via the **Socrates-Erasmus** scheme. Registration takes about three weeks, as each course has to be signed up for separately, and involves queuing at a different office to obtain a reading list. Most bureaucratic information, such as essay deadlines (infrequent), is obtained through the grapevine and easily missed.

Students at French universities study either for a *License*, a three-year degree course, or a two-year *DEUG*. Many students now take vocational or business-oriented courses, and many do a *stage*, a practical traineeship in a particular job, after their main degree. Other study options are private colleges, whether to improve your French or make the most of Paris' cultural opportunities by studying photography, fashion or haute-cuisine.

Despite the dispersal of the modern university, Paris' students still crowd out of the science campus at Jussieu, the Sorbonne arts faculty and nearby medical faculty to pack the Latin Quarter cafés between lectures. Foreign students tend to hang out in this area at night, but it's the cheaper bars of the Bastille and the outer *arrondissements* that are most popular with French students. Meeting other students can be difficult as most students live with their parents and there are few organised social activities. Sport is one good way, as you can do free sports courses as part of your degree and there are very cheap organised ski trips.

## STUDENT & YOUTH DISCOUNTS

A wide range of student discounts makes budget living possible despite Paris' expensive reputation. To claim the *tarif étudiant* (around 10F off some cinema seats, up to 50 per cent off museums and standby theatre tickets, 20 per cent in some hairdressers), you must have a French student card or an International Student Identity Card (ISIC), available from **CROUS**, student travel agents and the **Cité Universitaire**. Theatre, concert and opera deals usually work by buying discounted (often top) seats at the last minute. The Opéra Bastille, Palais Garnier and Comédie Française have notable bargains. ISIC cards are only valid in France if you are under 26. Under 26s can also get up to 50 per cent off rail travel with the Carrissimo card on certain trains, or buy the Carte Jeune (120F from branches of Fnac), which gives discounts on museums, cinema, theatre, insurance and some clothes shops. Look out also for the magazine *JAP* (*Jeune à Paris*), which has useful discount vouchers.

## Information

### CIDJ (Centre d'Information et de Documentation Jeunesse)
*101 quai Branly, 15th (01.44.49.12.00). M° Bir-Hakeim/ RER Champ de Mars.* **Open** 10am-6pm Mon-Sat.
The CIDJ is mainly a library, where students seek career advice, but it also houses the main youth bureau of the ANPE (Agence Nationale Pour l'Emploi), the state employment service (*see chapter* **Survival**). It is not, though, a good place to look for jobs, as queues are long, and many employers think that foreign students are desperate to do any kind of work. It also has information on study and recreation.

### Centre de Réception des Etudiants Etrangers
*13 rue Miollis, 15th (01.53.71.51.68). M° Cambronne.* **Open** 8.30am-4pm Mon-Fri.
Friendly help for foreign students through the bureaucratic nightmare of getting the *carte de séjour*, necessary for housing benefit (*see below* **Student Accommodation**).

### CROUS (Centre Régional des Oeuvres Universitaires et Scolaires)
*39 av Georges-Bernanos, 5th (01.40.51.36.00). RER Port-Royal.* **Open** 9am-5pm Mon-Fri.
The CROUS is best known for its Resto-U student canteens, and is the best place to book a bed in the *foyers* or student residences (*see below*). It also issues the ISIC card, organises excursions, sports and cultural events, provides information on accommodation and jobs, and offers theatre and concert tickets at a substantial discount. There is a Resto-U and sports facilities in the building.

### Socrates-Erasmus Programme

In Britain: *UK Socrates-Erasmus Council, RND Building, The University, Canterbury, Kent CT2 7PD (01227-762712).*
In France: *Agence Erasmus, 10 pl de la Bourse, 33081 Bordeaux Cedex (05.56.79.44.10).*
The Socrates-Erasmus scheme aims to increase mobility in Europe and enables European Union students with a reasonable standard of written and spoken French to spend a year of their degree following appropriate courses in the French university system. The UK office publishes a brochure and helps with general enquiries, but applications must be made through the Erasmus Co-ordinator at the student's home university.

## Courses

### Cours d'Adultes

Information: *Hôtel de Ville, pl de l'Hôtel de Ville, 4th (01.42.76.40.40). M° Hôtel-de-Ville.*
An enormous range of inexpensive adult-education classes, from accountancy and computing to pottery and pâtisserie, are run by the City of Paris, in town halls and colleges around Paris. Information is available at the Mairie of each *arrondissement.* To enrol (usually in September for year-long courses) you must have a residency card, a *carte de séjour.*

### CIDD Découverte du Vin

*30 rue de la Sablière, 14th (01.45.45.44.20). M° Pernéty. Open 9am-7pm Mon-Fri. Fees soirées 200F-300F; one class 385F; three classes 950F; five classes 1,460F.*
Tickle your oenological senses at this well-reputed school. Courses (some in English) from beginner to advanced include identifying wines and wine-tasting, plus open days with producers and tours. Week-long summer courses cost 3,250F.

*Gastronomy on course at* **Ritz-Escoffier***.*

### Cordon Bleu

*8 rue Léon-Delhomme, 15th (01.48.56.06.06). M° Vaugirard. Open 9am-7pm Mon-Fri. Fees 200F-4,950F.*
Come here for three-hour sessions on classical and regional cuisine, market visits, one-week workshops and ten-week courses aimed at those embarking on a culinary career.

### Ecole du Louvre

*34 quai du Louvre, 1st (01.40.20.56.14/01.40.20.56.16).*
Within the Louvre complex, this prestigious school runs courses on art history and archaeology which are open to foreign students. Those not wanting to take a full degree can enrol (May-September) as *auditeurs* to attend lectures.

### Ritz-Escoffier
### Ecole de Gastronomie Française

*15 pl Vendôme, 1st (01.42.60.38.30). M° Opéra. Fees demonstration 230F; one-week 5,750F; diploma 79,000F.*
From afternoon-long demonstrations and week-long courses, in such subjects as regional cookery, chocolate and cake making, to twelve-week diploma courses, classes are great fun and surprisingly informal, despite the grandiose setting, with plenty of hands-on experience and spotless facilities. Lessons are in French with English translation.

### INSEAD

*bd de Constance, 77251 Fontainebleau (01.60.72.40.00).*
This highly regarded international business school, in a regal location near Napoléon's favourite château of Fontainebleau, offers a ten-month MBA programme, in English. The 450 students are drawn from all over the world.

### Parsons School of Design

*14 rue Letellier, 15th (01.45.77.39.66). M° La Motte Piquet-Grenelle. Open 9am-5pm Mon-Fri. Fees 350F registration fee plus 1,850F per non-credit course or 2,472F per credit course.*
American art and design college, with New York parent, offers full- and part-time courses in fine art, fashion, interior design, illustration, photography and computing, in English.

### Spéos – Paris Photographic Institute

*7 rue Jules-Vallès, 11th (01.40.09.18.58). M° Charonne. Open 9am-6pm Mon-Fri. Fees full-time (Jan-May, Oct-Jan) 36,500F per term; part-time 4,500F per term; one-week course 3,000F.*
Bilingual photo school affiliated to the Rhode Island School of Design offers courses and intensive workshops in photography and photojournalism, including theory, photographic skills, laboratory, studio and computer techniques.

## Language Courses

Unless you are a complete beginner, be prepared for some sort of assessment test before you start.

### Alliance Française

*101 bd Raspail, 6th (01.45.44.38.28). M° St-Placide. Open reception 9am-6pm Mon-Fri; 9am-1pm Sat. Fees enrolment 250F; extensive 1,350F per month; intensive 2,700F per month; business French 4,800F per month.*
A highly regarded, non-profitmaking French-language school. Teachers are highly trained, and courses run from complete beginners' to specialist (conversation, business, translation, literature). There's also a *médiathèque,* a film club, talks and lectures. Courses begin at the start of every month, with enrolment a few days before. Also a good place to look for small ads for accommodation or part-time work.

### Berlitz France

*38 av de l'Opéra, 2nd (01.44.94.50.00). M° Opéra. Open 9.30am-6.30pm Mon-Fri; 8am-12.30pm Sat. Fees four week intensive 8,765F; individual 60 hrs 29,735F.*

Well known and effective, but expensive, and mainly used by businesses. There are several schools around Paris, offering day and evening classes on a group or individual basis.

## British Institute

*9 rue Constantine, 7th (01.44.11.73.73). M° Invalides.* **Open** 10am-1pm, 2-7.45pm, Mon-Fri. **Fees** 2,400F-4,000F per term.

Linked to London University, the Institute has a dual role of English courses for Parisians, and French courses at various levels (not beginner) in specialities, such as professional translation, commercial French, film and literature. Enrolment in the one-term courses is on the basis of a test. It is also possible to study at the Institute for a three-year degree in French from the University of London (details from Senate House, Malet Street, London WC1/0171-636 8000). The Institute has a café and a library (*see below*).

## Eurocentres

*13 passage Dauphine, 6th (01.40.46.72.00). M° Odéon.* **Open** 8.30am-6pm Mon-Fri. **Fees** *four weeks* 6,900F.

This international group offers intensive classes (lasting two to 24 weeks) for a maximum of 15 students, with summer courses running from July to September. Courses emphasise communication rather than grammar, and include cultural activities and the use of an audio-visual *médiathèque*.

## Institut Catholique de Paris

*12 rue Cassette, 6th (01.44.39.52.68). M° Rennes.* **Open** 10am-4pm Mon-Fri. **Fees** *enrolment* 300F; *registration* 3750F; *15-week course* 3,400F.

A reputable school offering fairly traditional courses in French language and culture. The equivalent of a French *bac* is required, plus proof of residence. Students must be aged 18 or above, but don't have to be Catholic.

## Institut Parisien

*87 bd de Grenelle, 15th (01.47.83.52.76). M° La Motte Piquet-Grenelle.* **Open** 8.30am-5pm Mon-Fri. **Fees** *enrolment* 250F; *one-term extensive* from 1950F; *one week intensive* 990F-1650F; *four-week business course* 2900F.

This dynamic private school recognised by the University of Paris offers courses all year in language and in French civilisation (fashion, gastronomy, cinema), summer courses in French for business and teachers and has recently introduced evening courses, with a maximum of twelve in a class. Courses can be started any week, except for beginners, with various options from extensive to intensive-plus.

## Université de Paris/La Sorbonne – Cours de Langue et Civilisation

*47 rue des Ecoles, 5th (01.40.46.22.11, ext 2664/75). M° Cluny-La Sorbonne/RER Luxembourg.* **Open** 10am-noon, 2-4pm, Mon-Fri. **Fees** 3,100F-10,300F per half-year.

The classes for foreigners at the Sorbonne ride on the name of this eminent institution and make use of some of its facilities, but you are unlikely to brush elbows with French students. Courses are more grammar- than conversation-based, and traditionally structured. The main course includes lectures on politics, history and culture, as well as obligatory language-lab sessions. Courses are open to anyone over 18, and in great demand. Register several months in advance.

## Libraries

Each part of the University of Paris has library facilities for enrolled students, which tend to be a little old-fashioned, although some have good specialist departments. All Paris *arrondissements* have free public libraries. To obtain a library card, you will need ID and two documents proving

residency in the district, such as a recent phone bill or tenancy agreement. Book and magazine loan are free, but there are charges for CD and video loan.

## American Library

*10 rue Général-Camou, 7th (01.45.51.46.82/ 01.45.51.47.47). M° Alma-Marceau then cross Pont de l'Alma or Ecole-Militaire.* **Open** 10am-7pm Tue-Sat. **Admission** *day pass* 70F; *annual pass* 525F.

Claims to be the largest English-language lending library in mainland Europe, and also organises talks by authors (*see* chapter **Theatre**) and readings for children.

## Bibliothèque Historique de la Ville de Paris

*Hôtel Lamoignon, 24 rue Pavée, 4th (01.44.59.29.40). M° St-Paul.* **Open** 9.30am-6pm Mon-Sat. **Admission** free.

Reference books and documents on all aspects of Paris history are housed in one of the classic mansions of the Marais. There is a particularly strong theatre section. Books for use on Saturday have to be requested in advance.

## Bibliothèque Nationale de France François Mitterrand

*quai François-Mauriac, 13th (01.53.79.59.59). M° Quai de la Gare.* **Open** 10am-7pm Tue-Sat; noon-6pm Sun. **Admission** *day pass* 20F; *annual pass* 200F.

The last of the *Grands Projets* opened to general readers in December 1996 with miles of corridor and acres of wood-furnitured reading rooms, arranged by subject. Books, newspapers and periodicals, including many titles in English, are on public access to anyone over 18, while an easily addictive audio-visual room allows you to browse through photo archives, film documentaries or sound recordings. The more specialist research library will open in 1998. *See also* chapters **Sightseeing**, **Left Bank** *and* **Museums**.

## Bibliothèque Nationale de France Richelieu

*58 rue de Richelieu, 2nd (01.47.03.81.26). M° Bourse.* **Open** 9am-6pm Mon-Sat. **Admission** accredited researchers and postgraduate students only.

The old national library continues to house historic manuscripts and certain other specialist departments. *See also* chapters **Sightseeing**, **Right Bank** *and* **Museums**.

## Bibliothèque Publique d'Information

*Centre Pompidou, rue Beaubourg, 4th (01.44.78.12.33). M° Châtelet-Les Halles, Hôtel de Ville or Rambuteau.* **Open** noon-10pm Mon, Wed-Fri; 10am-10pm Sat, Sun. **Admission** free.

This vast public reference library will close along with the Pompidou Centre from October 1997 to late 1999, but will open a temporary annexe in a nearby building. Be prepared for long queues at midday, it's quieter by night. It has large English-language and press sections, and popular first-come, first-served language laboratories.

## Bibliothèque Ste-Geneviève

*10 pl du Panthéon, 5th (01.44.41.97.97). RER Luxembourg.* **Open** 10am-10pm Mon-Sat. **Admission** free.

With a spectacular iron-framed reading room, designed by Labouste, who also designed that of the original Bibliothèque Nationale, this reference library is open to anyone over 18. Bring ID and a photo to register (until 6pm).

## British Council Library

*9-11 rue Constantine, 7th (01.49.55.73.00). M° Invalides.* **Open** 11am-6pm Mon-Fri. **Admission** *day pass* 35F; *annual pass* 250F; *with EFL centre* 400F; 200F students.

A home from home for British residents, and a good place to meet French students of English, but the book selection is

*The bookish new* **Bibliothèque Nationale de France François Mitterrand**.

small and rather idiosyncratic. There are also newspapers, and a specialist TEFL resource centre.

## Documentation Française

*29 quai Voltaire, 7th (01.40.15.70.00). Mº Rue du Bac.*
**Open** 10am-6pm Mon-Wed, Fri; 10am-1pm Thur.
**Admission** free.
The official government archive and central reference library has information on just about any aspect of French life.

## Médiathèque de Paris

*Forum des Halles, 8 porte St-Eustache, 1st (01.42.33.20.50). Mº Châtelet-Les Halles.* **Open** noon-7pm Tue-Sat. **Admission** *annual pass* 200F.
Records on vinyl, CD and cassette available on loan, plus sound archives, videos and musical and choreographic literature and documents open for consultation.

## Student Accommodation

The simplest budget accommodation for medium to long stays are the **Cité Universitaire** or the *foyers*, student hostels with individual or shared rooms for about 2,000F per month, which can be booked through **CROUS** and **UCRIF**. Another option (more common for women than men) is a *chambre contre travail* – free board in exchange for childcare, housework or English lessons. Look out for ads at accommodation offices, at language schools and at the American Church (*see chapter* **Survival**). For budget hotels and youth hostels, *see chapter* **Accommodation**.

If you're looking to rent a flat yourself, be prepared for large amounts of the three 'P's: paperwork, *pognon* (cash) and patience. As students often cannot provide proof of income, a *porte-garant* (guarantor) is required, usually a parent, who must write a letter (in French) declaring that he/she guarantees payment of rent and bills. Bring this with you, or you'll waste time waiting for it to be sent. You will also probably have to pay a large initial deposit, an agency fee and the first month's rent before you can move in. Students are eligible for the *allocation de logement* (housing benefit), available through each *arrondissement*'s Caisse d'Allocations Familiales, but to qualify you must have all your official documents (birth certificate translated by an approved translator – list available from your embassy or consulate, *carte de séjour*, proof of student status, etc) and a proper

lease with the names of all people wanting to claim on it. The 700F-800F a month is worth it if you can face the bureaucracy. *See also chapter* **Survival**.

## Cité Universitaire

*19 bd Jourdan, 14th (01.42.53.51.44). RER Cité Universitaire.* **Open** *administration* 9am-3pm Mon-Fri.
Foreign students enrolled on a university-style course (Sorbonne, British Institute or similar) or *stagiaires* under 30, can apply for a place at this huge campus of halls of residence on the southern edge of Paris. Excellent facilities (extensive lawns, tennis courts, a pool, theatres, music studios and a restaurant), and a friendly atmosphere compensate for the rather basic rooms. Rooms must be booked for the entire academic year (October to June). Rents are about 1,800F per month for a single room, 1,800F per person for a double. Prices vary according to which *maison* you live in. UK citizens must apply in first instance to the *Collège Franco-Britannique*, stating which hall they wish to live in. From 1 July to 30 September rooms are available to anybody with an ISIC card, for 100F per night, minimum one week.

## UCRIF (Union des Centres de Rencontres Internationales de France)

*72 rue Rambuteau, 1st (01.40.26.57.64). Mº Châtelet-Les Halles.* **Open** 9am-6pm Mon-Fri.
Operates a language school and several cheap, short-stay hostels in France, including 14 in Paris. They also organise social events for those hostels, and there's no age limit.

## Cheap Meals

Cheapest Parisian supermarket for basics is the **Ed L'Epicier** chain, although it's advisable to check sell-by dates on their fresh produce. You can also get great bargains at street markets at the end of the day, when prices for fruit and greens are often slashed. Being on a low budget doesn't mean you'll never eat out again; you just have to be selective. Numerous cafés offer *menus* at around 60F, especially at lunch. *See also chapter* **Restaurants**.

## Resto-U

*3 rue Mabillon, 6th (01.43.25.66.23). Mº Mabillon.*
**Open** 11.30am-2pm, 6-8pm, Mon-Fri. **No credit cards**.
CROUS runs a chain of Restos-U (university restaurants), of which some are listed here. Food is not hugely appetising (seemingly eternal couscous and *merguez*), but prices are rock bottom. Buy a *carnet* of tickets at 13F per ticket. A full list of restaurants and times is available from the CROUS or the restaurants listed here. An ISIC card is required.
**Branches include:** 10 rue Jean-Calvin, 5th (01.43.31.51.66); 3 rue Censier, 5th (01.45.35.41.24); 5 rue Mazet, 6th (01.46.33.20.17).

# Women's Paris

**With women like Sainte Geneviève and astronaut André-Deshays colouring French history, today's parisienne has a lot to live up to.**

Paris has always been associated with strong women, beginning with Sainte Geneviève (420-502), the city's patron saint, who is said to have saved the capital from famine in 486 and succeeded in averting its destruction by Attila the Hun and his army in 451. She is also credited with prompting the first king of France, Clovis, to convert from paganism to Catholicism. Today, her exploits are honoured in the handsome frescoes by Puvis de Chavannes inside the **Panthéon**, while her remains are buried in the nearby church **St-Etienne-du-Mont**. Further tribute is paid on the **Pont Marie**, where you can find her ghostly looking marble statue.

Impressive and exceptional women have figured throughout the city's history, and are remembered for helping to shape its culture, fashions and social life. Not only did Catherine and Marie de Médicis leave an indelible mark on the city's architecture and gardens, but mistresses like Madame de Pompadour promoted the porcelain works at Sèvres, the Encyclopedia of Diderot and d'Alembert, and set a new standard of *savoir-vivre* at the Elysée Palace, now the official presidential palace. Even Madame de Maintenon, the mistress and later morganatic wife of Louis XIV, deserves a mention, founding the first school for young girls.

Parisian women are historically recognised as among the most intellectual: their eighteenth- and nineteenth-century salons became the most important forums for intellectual debate. The philosopher Montesquieu said of the renowned hostess, the Marquise du Deffand: 'I love this woman with all my heart. You cannot be bored a single moment with her.' While she may have been the queen of hostesses, she had to put up with other unmarried or widowed woman ready to challenge her supremacy, including Madame Geoffrin, who drew such personalities as Voltaire and Marivaux, and painters Boucher, Vernet and Van Loo. The influence of these hostesses was such that upon his arrival to the capital, Rousseau was informed that 'you can't do anything in Paris without women.'

Not all women were content to wield power behind the scenes. Many took an active part in the French Revolution, including Charlotte Corday and Germaine de Stael, daughter of Jacques Necker, Louis XVI's finance minister. Others, like the playwright Olympe de Gouges fought both on behalf of human rights and on behalf of women: not only

did she form a women's political club, she penned *The Declaration of the Rights of Woman* in 1791, a year ahead of Mary Wollstonecraft's *A Vindication of the Rights of Women*. Two years later, she was guillotined by the Montagnards.

Another woman who refused to conform to the strictures set out for her by men was Aurore Dupin, who after obtaining a legal separation from her husband, adopted the male pen name George Sand. Living on the Left Bank's rue de Seine and later in the rues Taitbout and Pigalle in the Nouvelle-Athènes, Sand became known for her utopian and rural novels, and her embracing of humanitarian causes. Her various passions and memorabilia are now on view at the **Musée de la Vie Romantique**, the former home of painter Ary Scheffer, a mutual friend of Sand and her lover Chopin. Nearby at 14 rue St-Georges is the former home of the feminist newspaper *La Fronde*, published by Marguerite Durand (1897-1903). Its all-female staff was not legally permitted to print a daily, since labour laws didn't allow women to work at night; however, Durand refused to work with male employees for fear that they would be suspected of ghostwriting the paper's articles.

While Paris has been known as a city for female renegades – and famous expatriates including Gertrude Stein, Nathalie Barney, Djuna Barnes, Josephine Baker and Mary McCarthy –, it also has a well-deserved reputation as a bastion of male chauvinism. Even though women account for 51.3 per cent of the French population (29 million inhabitants) and now represent 44.5 per cent of the labour force, they make up only 6.2 per cent of the nation's legislature, 4.3 per cent in the regional governments, and 17 per cent members of city government – a rather dismal performance. Matters took a turn for the worst in 1996, when the newly elected Chirac-Juppé government made headlines when it gave eight highly placed women, *'les jupettes'* the boot. To counter this sorry state of affairs, the Socialist opposition has vowed to make sure that 30 per cent of the candidates selected in the next election in 1998 will be women.

Women's financial status is hardly better. While women like Liliane de Bettancourt, l'Oréal's largest shareholder, and the second richest woman in Europe after Queen Elisabeth II, make good business copy, the reality demonstrates that less than 5 per cent of the ranks of upper management are filled by women, and only a handful head up or sit on the boards of major corporations. Despite the law passed in 1983 instituting equality in the workplace between men and women,women's salaries are on average 20 per cent less than those of men. Even though legislation was passed in 1992 to punish sexual harassment in the workplace, sexual harassment cases are practically unheard of in France. Flirtatious advances are commonly accepted as consistent with male machismo, and marital infidelity is openly accepted. Last year, when Mitterrand's mistress and illegitimate daughter attended his funeral, their presence was widely accepted and even condoned, much as it would have been during the reign of Louis XIV.

While the *parisienne* maintains her longstanding reputation for being a chic coquette, she is also known for being both multifaceted and talented, whether she's the Secrétaire d'Etat Anne-Marie Couderc, fashion designer Inès de la Fressange, the feminist philosopher Elisabeth Badinter, union leader Nicole Notat, anti-corruption magistrate Eva Joly, the social commentator cartoonist Claire Brétécher, film actress Jeanne Moreau or France's first woman in space, astronaut Claudie André-Deshays. Like other emancipated women, they still confront a stalwart male opposition, thus making their achievements all the more outstanding.

## MEDIA

*Paris Féministe* is the bulletin of the **Maison des Femmes**. The quarterly *Femmes Artistes* provides insight into women's contribution in the art world. *See also* chapter **Media**.

If you're interested in tuning into French TV's top female media personalities, watch Claire Chazal on the 8pm evening news on TF1, and Anne Sinclair on '*Sept sur Sept*', France's most widely watched political interview programme broadcast on Sunday evenings at 7pm on TF1. Or stay up late to see Laure Adler, former cultural adviser to Mitterrand as well as feminist author, lead her own unique blend of culture and debate in the *Cercle de Minuit* (12.30am Mon-Thur on France 2). Tune into Téva (launched in Oct 1996), France's first cable network dedicated to women's programming, which claims to reflect a female viewpoint on current social and cultural issues, from soaps to chat shows. For women-oriented radio slots, try Paris Radio Libertaire (89.4MHz) (01.48.05.34.08) at 6.30pm on Wed.

## SEXUAL HARRASSMENT

Paris is essentially unthreatening for a women, although the usual precautions of not going out alone late at night apply as they would to any other large city. Violent crime tends to be concentrated in the suburbs, although be careful in areas like Pigalle, the rue St-Denis (a mecca for peep shows and prostitutes), the Bois de Boulogne and the Bois de Vincennes. While French men refrain from whistling and bottom-pinching, many of them are not shy about picking women up anywhere. The best brushoff is a withering stare, well-practised among streetwise *parisiennes*. If you're looking to beat sexual harassment, check out the self-defense classes at Terre des Sources (01.40.59.86.52).

## Information Centres

### Maison des Femmes

*8 cité Prost, 11th (01.43.48.24.91). M° Charonne or Faidherbe-Chaligny.* **Open** 4-7pm Wed, Fri; café 8pm-midnight Fri.
Run with heartfelt enthusiasm, it hosts a feminist library, a café and assorted women's groups, such as Les Archives, in an environment that is strictly women-only. The volunteers can give you invaluable guidance on where to look for legal or employment advice, a rape crisis centre or how to become involved in one of many discussion groups.

### Bibliothèque Marguerite Durand

*79 rue Nationale, 13th (01.45.70.80.30). M° Tolbiac or Place d'Italie.* **Open** 2-6pm Tue-Sat.
A collection of 30,000 books, some in English, on the history of women and feminism, many of which were assembled by feminist pioneer Durand, founder of the women's newspaper *La Fronde*, and which she donated to the state in 1931. This public library also has a collection of posters, postcards and photographs available for consultation.

### Centre Nationale d'Information et de Documentation des Femmes et des Familles (CNIDFF)

*7 rue du Jura, 13th (01.42.17.12.34). M° Gobelins.* **Open** 1.30-5.30pm Tue-Thur; phone enquiries 9am-12.30pm Mon-Fri.
Legal, professional and health advice for women: consult its information services or order any of its useful publications.

*Sand at the* **Musée de la Vie Romantique**.

## Service des Droits des Femmes

*31 rue Le Peletier, 9th (01.47.70.41.58). M° Le Peletier.*
**Open** phone calls only 9am-5pm. Library 9am-5pm Wed,
Thur (consultation only).
Dependent on the Ministère du Travail et des Affaires
Sociales, the Women's Rights Service's mission is to oversee
the implementation of specific women's programmes aimed
at achieving equal employment opportunity and to promote
women's rights (immigration, health care or civil law).

## Alliance des Femmes pour la Démocratie et Observatoire de la misogynie (Misogyny Watch)

*5 rue de Lille, 7th (01.45.48.83.80). M° Rue du Bac.*
Both of these groups mobilise against various aspects of sexual discrimination, whether it's giving political asylum to
feminist writers or opposing international prostitution rings.

## WICE (Women's Institute for Continuing Education)

*20 bd du Montparnasse, 15th (01.45.66.75.50).*
*M° Montparnasse.* **Open** 9am-5pm Mon-Fri. Membership
350F individual; 500F joint; 250F students.
An American expatriate cultural/educational centre with a
predominantly anglophone membership. It runs courses
ranging from art, history and literature to cooking and wine
tasting. Membership benefits include discounts to certain
shops and leisure facilities, and a library.

## L'Annuaire au Feminin

*25 rue Duconédic, 14th (01.43.21.27.54).*
If you're looking for a way to network with other professional
women in Paris – from fashion designers to government rep-
resentatives –, check out this international directory which
you order through the mail or locate on the Net.
*e-mail: femmes@iway.fr.http://www.iway.fr/femmes/*

# Accommodation

## Union des Foyers des Jeunes Travailleurs

*19 rue d'Enghien, 10th (01.42.46.31.35). M° Château-
d'Eau.* **Open** 9am-noon, 2-5pm, Mon-Fri. **Rates** per
month 2,500F (demi-pension). **No credit cards.**
An organisation running several hostels throughout Paris,
many specifically for women. To be eligible, you must be a
non-resident of France, aged 18-25 and able to prove you are
either working or unemployed but looking for work.

## Union Chrétienne de Jeunes Filles

*22 rue de Naples, 8th (01.45.22.23.49). M° Villiers.*
**Open** 9am-7pm daily. **Rates** per night (minimum 3 nights)
100F-120F; per month 2,270F-2,800F. **No credit cards.**
Individual and dormitory rooms for women aged 18-24.
Breakfast and dinner are included in the monthly price.

# Bookshops

*See also chapters* **Specialist Shops** *and* **Gay &
Lesbian Paris**, and the Maison des Femmes for
its bookstore.

## La Fourmi Ailée

*8 rue du Fouarre, 5th (01.43.29.40.99). M° Maubert-
Mutualité.* **Open** noon-7pm Mon, Wed-Sun. **Credit**
AmEx, MC, V.
A bookshop specialising in feminism and works by women,
conveniently attached to an excellent tea room. There's a
good selection of books on theatre, philosophy and art, with
some English poetry collections.

## Librairie des Femmes

*74 rue de Seine, 6th (01.43.29.50.75). M° Mabillon.*
**Open** 11.30am-7pm Mon-Sat. **Credit** AmEx, MC, V.
Paris' main feminist bookshop also has a gallery area and
leaflets on cultural activities. Owned by France's main feminist publishing house, Editions des Femmes, it was created
by Antoinette Fouque, the founding head of the Mouvement
de la Libération des Femmes (MLF).

# Film

## Festival de Films des Femmes

*Maison des Arts, pl Salvador Allende 94000 Créteil
(01.49.80.38.98). M° Créteil-Préfecture.*
**Dates** March 14-23. **Admission** 35F per film; 25F
students; 250F ten film subscription. **Credit** V.
An important women's film festival with an impressive selection of retrospectives and new international films by female
directors. Held every spring in a new town just outside Paris.

# Help & Health

To obtain the Pill, a diaphragm or the morning-
after pill, you'll need a prescription (available on
appointment from the first two places below or
from a *médecin généraliste* (GP) or gynecologist).
Spermicides and condoms (*préservatifs*) are available in pharmacies, and there are condom dispens-
ing machines in Métros, club lavatories or street
corners. For sanitary products, supermarkets are
your best bet. Although abortion was legalised in
1975, it has recently come up against a Catholic
backlash, especially in the provinces; that said, violent anti-abortion campaigners have come in for
severe punishment. For more information on all
health services, *see chapter* **Survival**.

## Centre de Planification et d'Education familiale

*27 rue Curnonsky, 17th (01.48.88.07.28). M° Porte de
Champerret.* **Open** 9am-5.30pm Mon-Fri.
Free consultations in French, on family planning and abor-
tion. Phone for an appointment.

## MFPF (Mouvement Français pour le Planning familial)

*10 rue Vivienne, 2nd (01.42.60.93.20). M° Bourse.*
**Open** noon-4pm Mon; 4-6pm Tue; noon-3pm Thur.
For contraception advice and prescriptions, phone for an
appointment. For abortion advice, just turn up at the centre.
The branch at 94 bd Massena (13th/01.45.84.28.25) is open
11am-3pm on Fri.

## SOS Help

*(01.47.23.80.80).* **Open** 3-11pm daily.
English-language helpline. Listeners can refer you to
English-speaking lawyers, doctors and so on.

## Violence conjugale: Femmes Info Service

*(01.40.02.02.33).* **Open** 8am-midnight Mon-Fri;
10am-8pm Sat.
Telephone hotline for battered women, directing them
towards medical aid or shelters, if need be.

## Viols Femmes Informations

*(0800.05.95.95).* **Open** 10am-6pm Mon-Fri.
A freephone in French for dealing with rape.

# Trips Out of Town

# Getting Started

**Much as Parisians would like to think so, Paris is not France, but you don't have to go far to find La France Profonde.**

As the French get five weeks of paid holiday and tend to all depart together, avoid travelling at weekends from mid-July to the end of August. The other favourite holiday time is from mid-February to mid-March, when people head for the ski slopes.

Most of the sights we've listed in the following chapter are easy day trips, but should you wish to stay, France is well supplied with affordable hotels, often in the town centre (forget the rash of little computer-operated cubby holes by motorway exits or at the outskirts of many towns, where you never see even a receptionist). If you are travelling in the peak periods, it's advisable to reserve accommodation in advance; at other times, it's often easy to find a hotel on the day of your arrival, and most local Offices du Tourisme provide some sort of same-day booking service, as well as city maps and information on local sites and events.

### Logis de France/Gîtes de France

Fédération Nationale des Logis de France *83 av d'Italie, 13th (01.45.84.70.00/booking 01.45.84.83.84)*
Gîtes de France *35 rue Godot-de-Mauroy, 9th (01.49.70.75.75/Minitel 3615 Gîtes de France).* **Open** 10am-6.30pm Mon-Fri; 10am-1pm, 2-6.30pm, Sat.

Hotels that are members of the association **Logis de France** are judged on hospitality as well as facilities. Most are traditional, family-run hotels, often with a restaurant, and mainly in small towns and villages. An annual guide is available from bookshops or the national federation. Another option is the ever expanding number of *gîtes* or rural holiday cottages, which can be rented for anything from a weekend to several weeks. Details and regional lists are available from the umbrella organisation **Gîtes de France**, which also covers rural bed-and-breakfast places and farm campsites.

### Travelling by Train

A comprehensive rail network is the main means of public transport for getting around France, for there are few long-distance bus services. Several attractions within the Paris suburbs, notably **Versailles** and **Disneyland Paris**, are served by the **RER** (*see chapter* **Getting Around**). Most locations further from the city are served by French national railways, the **SNCF**.

The prestigious *TGV* (*Train de Grande Vitesse*, or high-speed train) has revolutionised journey times on trunk routes, and is gradually being extended to all the main regions. On the downside, travel by *TGV* requires a hefty price supplement and obligatory reservation, and can mean that there are fewer mainline trains to lesser towns.

### SNCF Reservations & Tickets

*(national 08.36.35.35.35/Ile de France 01.53.90.20.20).* **Open** *information* 7am-10pm daily; *reservations* 8am-8pm daily; *car transportation* 8.30am-7pm Mon-Fri; 9am-1pm Sat. **No credit cards.**

There are different tariff bands (Red, White and Blue periods) to encourage passengers to travel outside peak hours, and a range of discount cards such as the *Carte Vermeil* for pensioners and *Carissimo* for people aged under 26. You can make a preliminary reservation on Minitel 3615 SNCF or by phone through the central number: you must then pick up and pay for the reservation within 48 hours. **Before you board any train,** *always* **stamp your ticket in the little orange** *composteur* **machines located by the platforms.** Inspectors on trains are authorised to charge for the full price of a ticket, plus a fine, if this is not done.

### Paris Mainline Stations

Each Paris mainline station serves a different region:
**Gare Montparnasse** West France, Brittany, Bordeaux
**Gare St-Lazare** Normandy
**Gare du Nord** North-east France, most Channel ports, Belgium and the Netherlands
**Gare de l'Est** Alsace, Champagne and south Germany;
**Gare de Lyon** Burgundy, the Alps, Provence and Italy;
**Gare d'Austerlitz** central and south-west France and western Spain.

### Travelling by Car

Travelling by car is still the best way if you want to explore France at your own pace. French roads are divided into *Autoroutes* (motorways, with an 'A' in front of the number), *Routes Nationales* (national 'N' roads) *Routes Départementales* (local, 'D' roads) and tiny, rural *Routes Communales* ('C' roads). The Autoroutes are toll roads (*péages*), although some sections, including most of the area immediately around Paris, are free. Motorways have a speed limit of 130kph (80mph). On most Routes Nationales the limit is 90kph (56mph). For car hire, *see chapter* **Services**; for driving in and around Paris, *see chapter* **Survival**.

Various *portes* of the *Périphérique* give access to the main roads out of Paris. To go south (**Fontainebleau**, Lyon, the Riviera) take the Porte d'Orléans or Porte d'Italie to the A6, to go south-west (**Chartres, the Loire**, Bordeaux) join the A10 either via the A6 or via the N118 from Porte de Sèvres; to go west (**Versailles, Rouen**), take the Porte de St Cloud to the A13; to go north (**Chantilly**, Calais, Lille), take the Porte de la Chapelle to the A1. The A4 to the east (**Disneyland Paris, Reims**, Alsace), starts near Gare de Lyon on quai de la Rapée or you can access from Porte de Bercy.

# Trips Out of Town

**Magnificent châteaux, windswept beaches, champagne makers, artists' retreats, and Mickey are all just a short journey away.**

## Châteaux & Palaces

### Versailles

Until 1661 Versailles was a simple hunting lodge and boyhood refuge of Louis XIV. But in a fit of envy after seeing the château Vaux-le-Vicomte, he decided on a building to match his ego and his dreams of absolute power over an aristocracy he mistrusted. Louis Le Vau and painter Charles Le Brun began work on transforming the château, while André Le Nôtre began to lay out the gardens, turning marshland into terraces, pools and paths.

In 1678 Jules Hardouin-Mansart took over as principal architect, and dedicated the last 30 years of his life to the construction of the building, enlarging it by five times its original size. The palace could house 20,000 people, including all the courtiers and royal ministers, who reluctantly agreed to move there. Louis moved in 1682, even

though work was far from complete, and thereafter rarely set foot in Paris. In the eighteenth century, Louis XV chose his favourite architect Jacques Ange Gabriel to add the sumptuous **Opéra Royal**, still sometimes used for concerts by the Centre de Musique Baroque (01.39.20.78.10).

Voltaire described Versailles as 'a masterpiece of bad taste and magnificence'. Like a stretch limo, it impresses more by size and lavishness than anything else. Under the *Ancien Régime*, 'Versailles' was a tangible symbol of the remoteness of the monarchy from the rest of the country. Marvel at the architectural purity of the vast classical facades before being bowled over by 73m-long **Hall of Mirrors**, where 17 mirrors echo the 17 windows in a brilliant play of light and reflections; the **King's Bedroom**, with ceilings by Le Brun, where the King rose in the presence of the court; the **Apollo Salon**, an aptly named throne room for the Sun King; and the **Queen's bedroom**, domi-

*The palace and gardens of **Versailles** defy all limits of modesty.*

nated by a huge bed, where queens gave birth in full view of courtiers, there to confirm the sex of the child and to ensure no substitutes were slipped in.

Outside, the park stretches over 815 hectares, and is dominated by its grand perspectives, especially the view down the X-shaped Grand Canal. Magnificent statues are scattered throughout the formal gardens, and there's a spectacular series of ponds and fountains, served by an ingenious hydraulic system also designed by Le Nôtre. Near the château is Hardouin-Mansart's **Orangerie**, whose vaulted gallery could house over 2,000 orange trees. The **Potager du Roi**, the King's Vegetable Garden, has been recently restored and is open 2.30-5pm April-November.

The main palace being a little unhomely even for *Le Grand Louis*, in 1687 he had Hardouin-Mansart build the **Grand Trianon**, on the north side of the park, a pretty, but still scarcely tiny, palace of stone and pink marble, where Louis stayed with Mme de Maintenon. Napoléon, who made little use of Versailles, also stayed there a number of times with his second empress, Marie-

Louise, and had it redecorated in Empire style. It was extensively restored in the 1960s.

The **Petit Trianon** is a perfect example of Neo-classicism, and was built for Louis XV's mistress Mme de Pompadour, although she died before its completion. Marie-Antoinette did, however, manage to take advantage of the *Hameau de la Reine* ('Queen's Hamlet'), 12 mock farm buildings arranged around a lake, where the Queen of France could play at being a lowly milkmaid.

From May to October the great fountains in the gardens are set in motion, to music, each Sunday in the **Grandes Eaux Musicales**, and four times a year the **Grandes Fêtes de Nuit** seeks to capture something of the grandeur of the celebrations of the Sun King (*see chapter* **Paris by Season**).

### Further Information

**Getting there** Versailles is 20km from Paris. *By car* by the A13 from the Porte de St Cloud or D10 from the Porte de Sèvres. *By train* RER line C to Versailles-Rive Gauche. **Office du Tourisme** *7 rue des Réservoirs (01.39.50.36.22).* **Open** *May-Oct* 9am-7pm daily; *Nov-Apr* 9am-12.30pm, 1.30-6pm Mon-Sat.

# Disneyland Paris

Out to the east of Paris, near the new town of Marne-la-Vallée, Disneyland is still managing to pull the crowds through its pink portals. A long way from French culture, this is a world of trans-posed Americana where the bilingual staff manage to keep up cheesy grins all day long. But, it's undeniable – a trip out here can be a fun, if exhausting, day off from the city.

The theme park is divided into five parts, all grouped around Victorian **Main Street USA**. **Fantasyland**, the most suitable part for young children, has gentle rides such as Dumbo the Flying Elephant, and Alice's Curious Labyrinth, an Alice in Wonderland maze up to the top of Sleeping Beauty's castle. Big kids and adults should head for film-set adventure in tropical **Adventureland**, **Wild West Frontierland** and futuristic **Discoveryland**.

Aim to do as many as possible of the spectacular big-thrill rides: **Big Thunder Mountain** rollercoaster; the dank and dripping **Pirates of the Caribbean**; **Star Tours**, a bumpy intergalactic rocket ride with tongue-in-cheek commentary by a robot pilot; **Indiana Jones et le Temple du Péril**, a scary loop-the-loop tour in a rickety ore truck; and the most

stomach-lurching of them all, **Space Mountain**. Inspired by Jules Verne's *Voyage to the Moon*, it shoots intrepid voyagers up a 20-metre long cannon into outer space. Guaranteed to get your knees knocking.

The Festival Disney complex has restaurants, bars, souvenir shops and a multiplex cinema. If you're into country music, head for Billy Bob's Country & Western Saloon, but don't bother with the pricey Wild West show.

There are plenty of places serving snacks, and Disney even takes on French cuisine. Note that some rides can be scary for young children, and some have minimum age and height requirements. Expect queues of up to 40 minutes. Should you need to sleep-over, there are six hotels at the complex providing over 5,000 rooms (central booking 01.60.30.60.30).

### Essential Information

*Marne-la-Vallée (01.64.74.30.00; from UK 0990.030303).* **Open** *Oct-23 June* 10am-6pm Mon-Fri, 10am-8pm Sat; *24 June-Sept* 9am-11pm daily. **Admission** *Apr-Sept* 195F adults; 150F 3-11s; prices rising in Oct '95, but not confirmed at time of writing. **Credit** AmEx, DC, EC, MC, V. **Getting there:** *By car* (32km) A4 to exit 14, and follow signs. *By train* RER line A to Marne-la-Valley-Chessy.

**Château de Versailles** *(01.30.84.74.00).*
**Open** *Château May-Sept* 9am-6pm. *Oct-Apr* 9am-5pm,
Tue-Sun. *Grand Trianon and Petit Trianon May-Sept*
9am-12.30pm, 2-6pm, Tue-Sun. *Oct-Apr* 9am-12.30pm, 2-
5.30pm, Tue-Sun. *Gardens* times vary, usually dawn-
dusk Tue-Sun. **Admission** *Château* 45F; 35F 18-25s;
free under-18s; *Grand Trianon* 25F; 15F 18-25; free under-
18s; *Petit Trianon* 15F; 10F 18-25s; free under-18s.
*Gardens* free (except on Sun for **Grandes Eaux**).
**Where to eat** The elegant *Trianon Palace* (1 bd de la
Reine/01.39.50.34.12), has a luxury restaurant (average
650F), a hotel and health club. Less extravagant in fact the over-
recommended *La Cuisine Bourgeoise* (10 bd du Roi/
01.39.53.11.38) serves good contemporary bistro cooking
(average 180F, *prix-fixe* 165F, 110F).

## Chantilly

In the middle of a lake, cream-coloured Chantilly
looks like the archetypal French Renaissance
château, with its domes and turrets. But the over-
the-top main wing is a largely nineteenth-century
reconstruction, as much of the original was destroyed during the Revolution. Beside it the **Petit
Château** – what remains of the original château
built for Anne de Montmorency in the sixteenth
century – seems much humbler. But Chantilly is
notable for its artistic treasures – three paintings
by Raphael; Filippino Lippi's *Esther and Assuarus*;
a cabinet of portraits by Clouet; several mythological scenes by Poussin; and the medieval miniatures from the *Très Riches Heures du Duc de Berry*
(facsimiles only are usually on show).

Today, the park laid out by Le Nôtre is rather
dilapidated, but still contains an extensive canal
system and an artificial 'hamlet' pre-dating that of
Versailles. To one side is a nineteenth-century
'English Garden'. In summer, a ten-minute ride in
a hot-air balloon gives an aerial view of château,
park and forest.

Chantilly's other claim to fame is as the home of
French racing, for this is where the most important French racing trainers have their stables, and
the town has a major racetrack (*see chapter* **Sport
& Fitness**). The eighteenth-century Great Stables
once housed 240 horses, 500 dogs and almost 100
palfreys and hunting birds. Today they are open
as a living museum of the horse and pony.

To the south of the château is the extensive
**Forêt de Chantilly**, which has numerous footpaths and is infested with picnickers in summer.
A pleasant walk (7km) circles the four Etangs de
Commelles (small lakes) and passes the 'Château
de la Reine Blanche', a mill converted in the 1820s
by the Duc de Bourbon into a pseudo-medieval
hunting lodge.

**Senlis**, 9km east of Chantilly, has been bypas-
sed since its glory days as the royal town where
Hugh Capet was elected king in 987. Its historical
centre contains several old streets, some handsome
mansions, a fine, predominantly Gothic cathedral,
some chunks of Gallo-Roman city ramparts and
the remains of a Roman amphitheatre.

**Chambord**: *François 1er's masterpiece.*

### Further Information

**Getting there** Chantilly is 41km (25 miles) from Paris.
*By car* take the A1, exit Chantilly and then the D924, or
the N16 directly from Paris. *By train* frequent trains from
Gare du Nord, then 30 minute walk or short taxi-ride.
**Château de Chantilly (Musée Condé)**
*(03.44.57.03.62/ 03.44.57.08.00).* **Open** *Mar-Oct* 10am-
6pm Mon, Wed-Sun; *Nov-Feb* 10.30am-12.45pm, 2-5pm,
Mon, Wed-Sun. **Admission** 37F; 32F under-18s; 10F
aged 3-11. *Park only* 17F; 10F under-18s.
**Musée Vivant du Cheval et du Poney** *Grandes
Ecuries (03.44.57.13.13/03.44.57.40.40).* **Open** *Apr-Oct*
10.30am-6.30pm daily (closed Tue in Apr and Sept); *Nov-
Mar* 2-5.30pm Mon, Wed-Sat; 10.30am-6.30pm Sun.
**Admission** 50F; 45F student, over-60s; 40F 4-16s .
Dressage demonstrations at 11.30am, 3.30pm, 5.15pm, daily.
**Montgolfier** balloon (03.44.57.29.14). *Mar-Nov* 10am-7pm.
**Office Nationale des Forêts** *1 av Sylvie*
*(03.44.57.03.88).* runs guided walks from the Carrefour
de la Table de Mongrésin (on the D924A) every Sunday
(3pm), June-Sept, and has leaflets on footpaths.

## Compiègne & Pierrefonds

North of Paris on either side of the substantial hunting forest of Compiègne stand two very different
châteaux with an Imperial stamp. On the edge of
the old town of Compiègne, the **Château de
Compiègne** looks out over a huge park and the
surrounding forest, and for the French royal family's
obsession with *la chasse* brought them here every
year. Although there had been a royal residence
here since the Capetians, it was Louis XV who was
responsible for the present look of the château as
in 1751 he entrusted architect Jacques Ange Gabriel
with the reconstruction work. In the process
Gabriel created an austere, classical pleasure palace arranged around a central *cour d'honneur*.

Although some of the decoration dates from the eighteenth century (in particular an elegant, circular bathroom), most of the interior was ruthlessly remodelled by Napoléon for his second wife Marie-Louise (Josephine who detested hunting spent little time here) and is stuffed with Imperial eagles, bees, palms and busts of the great self-publicist. You can see the Empress' state apartments including fully furnished salons, boudoirs, the ballroom (used as a military hospital in World War I) and her bedroom with its wonderfully over-the-top gilded bed and crimson damask furnishings; the only eighteenth-century piece is a commode, which belonged to Marie-Antoinette, put there as Marie-Louise wanted a souvenir of her unfortunate aunt.

Napoléon III also left his mark at Compiègne, where he and the Empress Eugenie hosted lavish house parties every autumn; you can see much of their comfortable, mid-nineteenth-century furnishings as well as some of the games used to entertain their guests. However, perhaps Napoléon III's most popular bequest to Compiègne was the heating system he installed, which still works today and makes a visit to the château bearable even in the depths of winter.

In one wing of the château, the Musée de la Voiture is devoted to early transport, including Napoléon I's state coach, Napoléon III's railway car and early motorcars, including an 1899 Renault and the Jamais Contente electric car of 1899.

In a clearing in the forest 6km from Compiègne is the **Clairière de l'Armistice** (take the N31 towards Soissons, then follow signs), a sombre memorial to the site where the Germans surrendered to Maréchal Foch, ending World War I at 5.15am on November 11, 1918 (it is also where in 1940 the French surrendered to the Germans). There's the mark where the two railway lines met, a statue of Foch, and, within a shed, a reconstructed carriage.

At the other edge of the forest, a sudden dip in the land gives the view of strange turrets. At first sight, the neo-medieval castle of **Pierrefonds** is so clearly fake and so harsh it is almost grotesque; yet it merits a look. Napoléon I bought the ruins of a fourteenth-century castle for 2,950F. In 1857, Napoléon III, staying nearby at Compiègne, asked Viollet le Duc to restore one of the towers as a romantic hunting lodge. But the project grew and fervent medievalist Viollet le Duc reconstructed the whole massive edifice, in part on the remaining foundations, in part borrowing elements from other castles, or simply creating medieval as he felt it should be, putting all his Gothic fantasies into practice. Walk up in circles between the ramparts and fortifications, through a crenellated gateway and admire the wonderful crocodile waterspouts in the courtyard. Inside, there are grand baronial halls with elaborate chimneypieces carved with beasts, dragons and figures. Particularly magnificent is the Salle des Preuses, designed as a ball-

room for Napoléon III, with minstrels' gallery for the musicians. The fireplace is sculpted with figures of nine ladies (one of them bears resemblance to the Empress Eugénie). One wing has a permanent exhibition about Viollet-Le-Duc. Another fantasist Michael Jackson recently expressed interest in buying the château, but it was not for sale.

### Further Information

**Getting there** Compiègne 80km (50miles) from Paris by A1. Trains go direct from Gare du Nord. Pierrefonds is 14km from Compiègne on the D973.
**Château de Compiègne** *5 pl du Général-de-Gaulle, 62005 Compiègne (03.44.38.47.00).* **Open** 9.15am-5.15pm Mon, Wed-Sun. **Admission** 35F; 25F 18-25s; free under-18s. **No credit cards.**
**Clairière de l'Armistice** *rue de Soissons, (03.44.85.14.18).* **Open** *Museum Apr-15 Oct* 9am-12.15pm, 2-6pm; *16 Oct-Mar* 9-11.45am, 2-5pm. **Admission** 10F. **No credit cards.**
**Château de Pierrefonds** *rue Viollet-le-Duc, 60350 Pierrefonds (03.44.42.72.72).* **Open** 10am-11.45am, 2-6.15pm, daily. **Admission** 32F; 21F 12-25years; free under-12s. **No credit cards.**

# Fontainebleau

Fontainebleau would be just another sleepy provincial French town were it not for the sumptuous palace which dominates it. In 1528, François 1er brought in Italian artists and craftsmen – including Rosso and Primaticcio – to help his architect Gilles le Breton transform it from a neglected royal lodge into the finest Italian Mannerist palace in France. This style, between the Renaissance and the Baroque, is noted for its grotesqueries, contorted figures and crazy fireplaces, all of which gave sculptors an ideal chance to show off their virtuosity, still visible in the Ballroom and Long Gallery.

Other monarchs liked Fontainebleau too, adding their own touches, so that much of the palace's charm comes from its very disunity of design. Henri IV added two courtyards and a tennis court, Louis XIV and XV added further classical trimmings, and Louis XIII added the celebrated double-horseshoe staircase that dominates the principal 'farewell' courtyard; while Napoléon redecorated a suite of rooms in Empire Style.

The **Fontainebleau Forest** where François 1er liked to hunt is now used by Parisian weekenders for walking, cycling, riding and rock climbing. It covers 25,000 hectares (61,750 acres) and is a ten-minute stroll from town. A free map, available from the tourist office, marks all the paths. Bikes can be hired from Georges Mullot at the Gare de Fontainebleau (01.64.22.36.14). A good starting point is off the road N7 from **Barbizon** (*see below* **Artists' Corners**) to the Gorges d'Apremont and the Gorge de Franchard.

### Further Information

**Getting there** Fontainebleau is 65km (40 miles) from Paris. *By car* A6 to Fontainebleau exit, then N7. *By train* from Gare de Lyon to Fontainebleau-Avon (50 minutes), then bus marked Château.

**Amboise**: *where François 1er spent his childhood.*

**Office du Tourisme** *4 rue Royale, 77300 Fontainebleau (01.60.74.99.99).* **Open** *June-Sept* 9.30am-6.30pm Mon-Sat; 10am-12.30pm, 3-5.30pm Sun; *Oct-May* 9.30am-12.30pm, 1.45-6pm, Mon-Sat.
**Château de Fontainebleau** *(01.60.71.50.70).* **Open** 9.30am-5pm Mon, Wed-Sun. **Admission** 35F; 23F 18-25s, all on Sun; free under-18s.

## Vaux-Le-Vicomte

Less well-known than Versailles or Fontainebleau, and certainly less crowded, this château has a story almost as interesting as the building itself. As you round the moat, the square, sober frontage doesn't prepare you for the Baroque rear aspect.

Nicholas Fouquet (1615-1680), protégé of the ultra-powerful Cardinal Mazarin, bought the site in 1641. In 1653 he was named *Surintendant des Finances*, and set about building himself an abode to match his position. He assembled three of France's most talented men for the job: painter Charles Lebrun, architect Louis Le Vau and landscape gardener André Le Nôtre.

In 1661, Fouquet held a huge soirée to inaugurate his château and invited the King. They were entertained by jewel-encrusted elephants and spectacular imported Chinese fireworks. Lully wrote music for the occasion, and Molière a comedy. The King, who was 23 and ruling *de facto* for the first time, was outraged by this ostentatious show of wealth and by the way in which Fouquet's grandeur seemed to overshadow his own. Shortly afterwards Fouquet was arrested, and his embezzlement of state funds exposed in a show trial. His personal effects were taken by the crown and the court sentenced him to exile; Louis XIV promptly changed the sentence to solitary confinement.

The most telling symbol of the fallen magnate is the unfinished, domed ceiling in the vast, elliptical Grand Salon, where Lebrun only had time to paint the cloudy sky and one solitary eagle holding the chandelier in its beak. Fouquet's *grand projet* did live on in one way, however, for Louis XIV was so impressed by the château that it inspired him to build Versailles, to the extent that he took away Fouquet's architect and workmen to do it.

Watch out for the fountains, which spout from 3pm to 6pm on the second and last Saturday of every month. The biggest draw however is the candlelit evenings, which transform the château into a palatial jack-o-lantern with hundreds of flickering candles illuminating house and gardens.

### Further Information

**Getting there** Vaux-Le-Vicomte is 60km (37 miles) from Paris. *By car* take A6 to Fontainebleau exit; follow signs to Melun, then N36 and D215. *By train* from Gare de Lyon to Melun, (40 minutes) and then taxi (80F-100F, there are no buses). Remember to arrange for a taxi to come back for you afterwards. *By tour coach* **Paris-Vision** run half-day and day trips from Paris (*see chapter* **Sightseeing**).
**Château Vaux-Le-Vicomte** *77950 Maincy (01.64.14.41.90).* **Open** *Château* and *gardens Apr-mid Oct* 10am-1pm, 2-6pm, daily. **Admission** 56F; 46F under-16s. *Candlelit visits May-mid Oct* 8.30-11pm Sat. **Price** 75F; 65F children. **Credit** V.

## The Châteaux of the Loire

Seat of power of the Valois kings, who preferred to rule from Amboise and Blois rather than Paris, the Loire valley became the wellspring of the French Renaissance. François 1er was the main instigator, bringing architects, artists and craftsmen from Italy to build his palaces, and musicians and poets to keep him amused. Royal courtiers followed suit with their own elaborate residences. The valley is now an easy weekend trip from Paris: we've concentrated on the area between Chambord in the east, and Azay-le-Rideau in the west.

The **Château de Chambord** (02.54.50.40.00), is François 1er's huge masterpiece, and was probably designed in part by Leonardo da Vinci. It's a magnificent, but also rather playful place, from the ingenious double staircase in the centre – it was possible to go up or down without crossing someone coming the other way, although you could glimpse them through the open fretwork – to the wealth of decoration and the 400 draughty rooms. Built in the local white stone, with decorative diamonds and other shapes applied in black slate, its extraordinary forest of turrets, domes and crazy chimneys are brilliantly seen from close up as you walk around the parapet.

In total contrast of scale is the charming **Château de Beauregard** (02.54.70.40.05), nearby at Cellettes. Its main feature is the unusual panelled portrait gallery, depicting in naïve style 327 famous men and women. The precious character of the room is accentuated by its fragile, blue and white Dutch Delft tiled floor. The château also boasts the tiny panelled *Cabinet des Grelots* (bells).

From here the road to Amboise follows one of the most attractive parts of the Loire valley, under the looming towers of the **Château de Chaumont** (02.54.20.98.03), and past numerous roadside wine cellars dug into the tufa cliffs (with equally numerous opportunities to indulge). Chaumont is chiefly worth visiting for its innovative annual garden festival (mid-June-mid Oct) when over 20 designers, artists and architects create themed gardens.

The lively town of Amboise, not far from Tours, grew up at a strategic crossing point on the Loire. The **Château Royal d'Amboise** (02.47.57.00.98), was built within the walls of a medieval stronghold, although today only a (still considerable) fraction of Louis XI's and Charles VIII's complex remains. This is the château where François 1er grew up, but its interiors span several styles from vaulted Gothic hall to nineteenth-century Empire style. Across the gardens, the exquisite Gothic chapel has a richly carved portal, fine vaulted interior and, supposedly, the tomb of Leonardo da Vinci.

From the château, it's a short walk up the hill past several cave dwellings to the fascinating **Clos Lucé** (02.47.57.62.88), the Renaissance manor house where Leonardo da Vinci lived at the invitation of François 1er for the three years before his death in 1519. There's an enduring myth of a – so far undiscovered – tunnel linking the two. The museum concentrates on Leonardo as Renaissance Man: artist, engineer and inventor. It's part furnished as a manor house of the period, part filled with large models derived from Leonardo's drawings of inventions, from a helicopter to a hydraulic

drilling machine. Just outside the town is the pagoda of **Chanteloup**, an eccentric eighteenth-century pagoda built when Chinese style was the rage, in the grounds of a now-demolished château. There's a panoramic view from the top.

South of Amboise, the sixteenth-century **Château Chenonceau** (02.47.23.90.07), occupies a unique site on a bridge spanning the river Cher. Henry II gave the château to his beautiful mistress Diane de Poitiers, until she was forced to give it up to a jealous Catherine de Médicis, who commissioned Philibert Delorme to add the three-storey long gallery that extends across the river. Chenonceau is packed with tourists in summer, but its watery views, many original ceilings and fireplaces, its fine tapestries and paintings (including a portrait of Diane de Poitiers by Primaticcio) are well worth seeing. Visits are unguided.

Seeming to rise directly out of the water, **Azay-le-Rideau** (02.47.45.42.04), built on an island in the river Indre west of Tours, must be everyone's idea of a fairytale castle. Built between 1518-27 by Gilles Berthelot, the king's treasurer, it combines the turrets of a medieval fortress with the style of the Italian Renaissance.

At **Villandry** (02.47.50.02.09), it's not the château but the Renaissance gardens that are of interest. One part is a typical formal garden of geometrical shapes made with neatly cut hedges and flowers; much more unusual is the *jardin potager*, where the neat patterns are done not with flowers but with artichokes, cabbages and other vegetables in what has to be the ultimate kitchen garden.

### Further Information

**Getting There** *By car*. The best way to get around the region. Take the A10 direct to Blois (182km), or leave at Mer for Chambord. An attractive route follows the banks of the Loire from Blois to Amboise and Tours, along the D761. *By train* A much less-desirable option: TGV from Gare Montparnasse to Blois or Tours, from where it's possible to visit some châteaux by coach. *By tour coach* several tour companies in Paris run trips to the Loire (for addresses, *see chapter* **Sightseeing**).
**Where to Stay & Eat** The small town of Amboise is a pleasant, centrally placed stopping-off point with several hotels. Within the town, try the small, family-run *Hôtel Le Français* (1 pl Chaptal, 37400 Amboise/02.47.57.11.38). double 190F, or the *Lion d'Or* (17 quai Charles-Guinot/ 02.47.57.00.23). double 292F-312F, which also has a restaurant. For something a little grander, try the *Château de Pray* (02.47.57.23.67) at Chargé, 3km outside the town (double 550F-720F), which has gardens overlooking the Loire. *L'Epicerie*, 46 pl Michel-Debré (02.47.57.08.94) is a pleasant restaurant opposite the entrance to the château with *prix-fixe* menus at 110F, 130F and 185F. More hotels and a greater choice of restaurants are to be found at Tours.

## Artists' Corners

## Van Gogh at Auvers-sur-Oise

Auvers-sur-Oise, 30 km north of Paris, has become synonymous with the name of Van Gogh, even

*Wander around **Auvers-sur-Oise** and compare Van Gogh's paintings to what you see.*

though the Dutch painter only spent 70 days in what was then a small agricultural village. However, during his time there, he executed over 60 paintings, drawings and sketches, including many since-famous works. He arrived on 20 May 1890, and rented a room at the Auberge Ravoux. On 27 July, he fired a bullet into his chest, and died two days later. His grave is in the cemetery, alongside that of his beloved brother, Theo.

If you are not already familiar with Van Gogh's works, make sure you visit the **Musée d'Orsay** before you come, for this is above all an evocation of place, although there is also a well-prepared video on Van Gogh's period in the village.

The decrepitude has been perfectly preserved in the tiny attic room where he stayed (the cheapest in the Auberge at 3.50F a day) and the bedroom of another artist next to it, simply furnished as it would have been at the time: a bed, a chair and a washstand with a basin and a jug.

Equally worth visiting is the **Atelier de Daubigny** built by the successful Barbizon school artist in 1861. The house and lofty studio are decorated from top to bottom with murals painted by himself, his son and daughter and artist friends, including Corot and Daumier.

Despite being so near to Paris and industrial Pontoise, Auvers still retains a surprising degree of rustic charm. The cornfields, where Van Gogh painted his famous crow painting, the town hall, across the square from the inn, which he painted on Bastille day, and the church, have barely changed. Van Gogh and Daubigny were not the

only painters to set up easels here. Cézanne stayed for 18 months between 1872 and 1874, not far from the house of Doctor Gachet, who was the subject of portraits by both him and Van Gogh. A clever system of illustrated panels around town lets you compare the paintings to their locations today.

The recently renovated seventeenth-century **Château de Léry** offers an audio-visual experience devoted to the Impressionists, while the **Musée de l'Absinthe** is devoted to memorabilia of the Impressionists' favourite (now banned) drink, as depicted by Monet, Van Gogh and many others.

### Further Information

**Getting There** Auvers-sur-Oise is 35km (22 miles) north of Paris. *By car* A15 and then at exit 7 take the N184 towards Chantilly, exit Méry-sur-Oise for Auvers. *By train* from Gare du Nord or Gare St-Lazare direction Pontoise, change at Persan-Beaumont or Creil for Auvers-sur-Oise, change at Persan-Beaumont RER line A to Cergy-Préfecture, then bus for Butry, stopping at Auvers-sur-Oise. Paris Vision (*see chapter* **Sightseeing**) runs coach tours from Paris.
**Office de Tourisme** *Manoir des Colombières, rue de la Sansonne, 95430 Auvers-sur-Oise (01.30.36.10.06).* Open 9.30am-12.30pm, 2-5pm, daily.
**L'Atelier de Daubigny** *61 rue Daubigny (01.34.48.03.03).* Open *Easter-Oct* 2-6.30pm Tue-Sun, bank holidays. **Admission** 25F; free under-12s.
**Château d'Auvers** *rue de Léry (01.34.48.48.50).* Open *May-Oct* 10am-6.30pm. *Nov-Apr* 10am-5pm, Tue-Sun. **Admission** 50F; 40F over-60s; 35F 6-25 years; free under-6s.
**Musée de l'Absinthe** *44 rue Callé (01.30.36.83.26).* Open *June-Sept* 11am-6pm Wed-Sun. *Oct-May* 11am-6pm Sat, Sun. **Admission** 25F; 20F students, over-60s; 10F 6-15s.
**Musée Daubigny** *Manoir des Colombières, rue de la Sansonne (01.30.36.80.20).* Open *May-Oct* 2.30-6.30pm,

# Beside the seaside

Dieppe's beaches and the 'Alabaster Coast' of northern Normandy are an easy weekend trip, and can be combined with a visit to Rouen (*see p313*).

An important port since the Middle Ages, **Dieppe** is also the nearest seaside town to Paris. The charming area around the harbour along quai Henri IV is lined with little fish restaurants. The maze of old streets, between the harbour and the newer quarters along the promenade contains brick seamen's houses with wrought-iron balconies, and the Gothic church of St-Jacques, once a starting point for pilgrimage to Compostella. The shingle beach is overlooked by the gloomy Musée Municipal du Vieux Château, now the municipal museum, known for its alabaster collection.

Along the coast to the west is chic **Varengeville-sur-Mer**, celebrated for its clifftop churchyard, where Cubist painter Georges Braque and composer Albert Roussel are buried. The **Parc du Bois des Moustiers** (02.35.85.10.02; closed 15 Nov-15 March), planted by Lutyens and Gertrude Jekyll, and the unusual sixteenth-century Renaissance **Manoir d'Ango** are also here.

South of Dieppe (8km) is the **Château de Miromesnil** (02.35.85.14.80; open Apr-15 Oct) where Maupassant passed his childhood.

### Getting There & Information

Dieppe is 171km (106 miles) from Paris. *By car* take the A13 to Rouen and then the N27. *By train* frequent trains from Gare St-Lazare (2 hours 30min). **Office du Tourisme de Dieppe** *Pont Jehan Ango, 76200 Dieppe (02.35.84.11.77).* **Open** *May-Sept* 9am-1pm, 2-7pm, Mon-Sat; 10am-1pm, 3-6pm, Sun; *Oct-April* 9am-noon, 2-6pm, Mon-Sat.

*Nov-Apr* 2.30-6pm, Wed-Sun. **Admission** 20F; free under-16s.
**La Maison de Van Gogh** *Auberge Ravoux, pl de la Mairie (01.30.36.60.60).* **Open** 10am-6pm daily. **Admission** 30F; free under-12s; 60F family ticket (2 adults, 2 children).

## Monet at Giverny

In 1883, Claude Monet moved his large personal entourage (one mistress, eight children) to Giverny, a rural retreat 80km north-west of Paris. He died in 1926, having immortalised his flower garden, and the water-lilies beneath his Japanese bridge. In 1966, Michel Monet donated his father's property to the Académie des Beaux-Arts, which transformed the modest estate into the major tourist site it is today. Don't be put off by the tour buses in the car park or by the outrageously huge gift shop – the natural charm of the pink-brick house, with its cornflower-blue and yellow kitchen, and the rare glory of the gardens survive intact. A little tunnel leads (under the road) between the flower-filled Clos Normand garden in front of the house to the second, Japanese, water garden with all the pools, canals, little green bridges, the punt, willows and water lilies familiar from the paintings.

Up the road, the modern **Musée Américain Giverny** is devoted to American artists who came to France, inspired by the Impressionists.

### Further Information

**Getting There** *By car* take the A13 from Porte d'Auteuil to Bonnières, where you cross the Seine and follow D201 to Giverny. *By train* trains from Gare St-Lazare to nearby Vernon take 45 minutes; then a 5km (3 mile) taxi or bus ride from the station.
**Musée Claude Monet** *27620 Giverny (02.32.51.28.21).* **Open** *Apr-Oct* 10am-6pm Tue-Sun. **Admission** 35F; 25F students; 20F 7-12s; free under-7s.
**Musée Américain Giverny** *99 rue Claude Monet (02.32.51.94.65).* **Open** *Apr-Oct* 10am-6pm Tue-Sun. **Admission** 35F; 20F students, over-60s; 15F 7-12s; free under-7s.

## Rousseau & Millet at Barbizon

A rural hamlet straggling along a single country lane into the forest of **Fontainebleau** (*see above*), Barbizon was an ideal sanctuary for pioneers Corot, Théodore Rousseau, Daubigny (*see above* **Auvers-sur-Oise**) and Millet. From the 1830s onwards, these artists, the Barbizon school, demonstrated a new concern in painting peasant life and landscape as they really were, and paved the way for the Impressionists. The three main sights at Barbizon are all on this road, and although it's touristy, some of the atmosphere remains. Commemorative plaques point out who lived where.

Hordes of other artists soon followed them to Barbizon. Many stayed at the **Auberge du Père Ganne** inn, painting on the walls and furniture of the long-suffering (or perhaps far-sighted) Ganne, in lieu of rent. The Auberge now contains the municipal art collection as well as a near-legendary sideboard painted by some of the artist habituees. The **Office du Tourisme** is based in the former house of Théodore Rousseau. Prints and drawings by Millet and his followers can be seen in the **Maison et atelier Jean-François Millet**. Millet moved here in 1849 to escape cholera in Paris, and remained, living very simply, for the rest of his life, painting the local people and their work in the fields, to which he ascribed an almost saintly value. Millet and Rousseau are both buried in the churchyard at nearby Chailly.

### Further Information

**Getting there** Barbizon is 57km from Paris and 10km from Fontainebleau. *By car* A6 to Fontainebleau exit, then N7 and D64 to Barbizon. *By train* from Gare de Lyon to Melun, then taxi.
**Office du Tourisme** *55 rue Grande, 77630 Barbizon (01.60.66.41.87)*. **Open** 10am-12.30pm, 2-6pm, Mon, Wed-Fri; 10am-6pm Sat, Sun.
**Maison et Atelier Jean-François Millet** *27 rue Grande (01.60.66.21.55)*. **Open** 9.30am-12.30pm, 2-5.30pm, Mon, Wed-Sun. **Admission** free.
**Musée de l'Auberge du Père Ganne** *92 rue Grande, 77630 Barbizon (01.60.66.22.27)*. **Open** *Apr-Oct* 10am-12.30pm, 2-6pm, Mon, Wed-Fri; 10am-6pm Sat, Sun. *Nov-Mar* 10am-12.30pm, 2-5pm, Wed-Fri; 10am-5pm Sat, Sun. **Admission** 25F; 13F 12-25s, students; free under-12s, unemployed.

## Le Cyclope

Not far from Barbizon but coming from a quite different art perspective is an extraordinary twentieth-century monster. A shimmering, clanking 20m-high confection of mirrors and iron cogs, the Cyclope lurks down a secluded forest track, rumbling and spitting out balls. The creature was the life-work of Swiss artist Jean Tinguely, who began it in 1969, in a rare form of collaboration with several fellow artists including Nikki de Saint Phalle (with whom he also created the Stravinsky Fountain in Paris), although it was only finished after his death and opened to the public in 1994. Inside, it's as if a DIY addict had gone mad. A weird assortment of machines carry aluminium balls up through the body before ejecting them down the tongue, and a narrow passageway leads you past various art works including Spoerri's *Chambre de Bonne* and Eva Aeppli's *Holocaust* memorial. You need to reserve with the Office du Tourisme to visit the interior; the exterior can be viewed from the fence.z

### Further information

Milly-la-Forêt is, 61 km from Paris, 18km from Fontainebleau, Cyclope is 2km outside town. **Open** *Apr-Nov* 11am-5.30pm Fri-Sat; reserve on 01.64.98.83.17.

## Chartres

Looming over a flat agricultural plain, Rodin called **Chartres Cathedral** the 'French Acropolis'. Certainly, with its two uneven spires – the stub-

*Monet's much-pictured garden at **Giverny**.*

bier dates from the twelfth century, the taller second one wasn't completed until the sixteenth century – and richly sculpted doorways, the cathedral has an enormous amount of slightly wonky charm and is a pristine example of Early Gothic art. The cathedral was a pilgrimage site long before that, ever since it was built to house the *Sacra Camisia* (said to be the Virgin Mary's lying-in garment), which was donated to the city in 876 by the Carolingian King Charles I, 'the Bald', and is now displayed in the cathedral treasury. When the existing church caught fire in 1194, local burghers clubbed together to reconstruct it, taking the model of St-Denis for the new west front, 'the royal portal', with its three richly sculpted doorways. On the cusp between Romanesque and Gothic, the stylised, elongated figure columns above geometric patterns still form part of the door structure. Do walk all the way round the Cathedral. Two other interesting portals were added later: the north transept door is a curious, top-heavy concoction of lively figures and slight columns, and there's also an unusual clock.

Inside the cathedral, with its wide and harmonious nave, yet another epoque of sculpture is represented in the brilliantly lively, sixteenth-century scenes of the life of Christ that surround the choir. Note also the circular labyrinth of black and white stones in the floor; such mazes used to exist in most cathedrals but have now mostly been destroyed. But Chartres is above all famed for its stained glass, in brilliant 'Chartres blue', punctuated by rich red, depicting Biblical scenes, saints and medieval trades. To learn all about them take one of the erudite and highly entertaining tours given in English by Malcolm Miller. He specialises in deciphering medieval picture codes in order to 'read' the messages in the windows. Between Easter and mid-Nov, Mr Miller's tours are at noon and 2.45pm Mon-Sat (30F adults, 20F students). At other times phone 02.37.28.15.58.

The cathedral may dominate the town from a distance, but once in the streets, the medieval street plan is surprisingly complete, with narrow streets and overhanging gabled houses, and glimpses of the cathedral only occasional. Wander past the iron-framed market hall, down to the river Eure, crossed by a of string attractive old bridges, past the partly Romanesque Eglise St-André and along the rue des Tanneries that follows the banks. There's more fine stained glass in the thirteenth-century Eglise St-Pierre. There's a good view from the Jardin de l'Evêché at the back of the cathedral, adjoining the **Musée des Beaux-Arts** in the former Bishop's Palace. Inside, the collection includes several fine eighteenth-century French paintings, among them works by Boucher and Watteau, and a large array of medieval sculpture.

The other main tourist attraction is very much of this century and a reminder that Chartres towers over the Beauce region, known as the 'bread basket of France' for its prairie-like expanses of wheat. The **COMPA** agricultural museum in a renovated, former engine shed near to the station has a small but lively presentation of the history of agriculture, food – and consequently society – from 50,000BC to the present, with the emphasis on machinery, from vintage tractors and threshing machines to some old fridges.

For curiosity value, you can also visit (Easter-October) the **Maison Piccassiette**, just outside the centre (22 rue de Repos/02.37.34.10.78), a colourful, naïve mosaic house constructed with bits of broken pottery by a former Chartres civil servant.

### Further Information

Getting There *By car* take the A11 direction Le Mans, exit Chartres (88km). *By train* hourly from Gare Montparnasse (less than an hour).
**Office du Tourisme** *pl de la Cathédrale, 28005 Chartres (02.37.21.50.00).* **Open** *Apr-Sept* 9.30am-6.30pm Mon-Fri; 10am-6pm Sat; 10.30am-1pm Sun. *Oct-Mar* 9.30am-6pm Mon-Fri; 10am-5pm Sat; 10.30am-1pm Sun.
**Conservatoire de l'Agriculture (COMPA)**
*1 rue de la République (02.37.36.11.30).* **Open** 10am-12.30pm, 1-6pm, Tue-Fri; 10am-12.30pm, 1-7pm, Sat, Sun. **Admission** 25F; 20F over-60s; 10F 6-12s.
**Where to eat** *La Vieille Maison* (5 rue au Lait/02.37.34.10.67) is just that, but the classical cooking is excellent, and desserts are delicious; the 158F *prix-fixe* menu offers good value for cooking and service of this calibre. Simpler but with an attractive setting facing the cathedral, the *Café Serpente* (2 Cloître Notre Dame/02.37.21.68.81) triples as café, tea room and restaurant.

## Reims

Begun in the thirteenth century, the magnificent **Cathédrale Notre Dame** is of dual importance to the French, as the coronation church of most French monarchs since Clovis in 996 and for the richness of its Gothic decoration. The facade, with thousands of figures on the portals and the Kings of Judea high above the rose window, shows how sculptural style developed over the century. Heavy shelling in World War I, together with erosion, means that many of the carvings have been replaced by copies; the originals are on show next door in the **Palais de Tau**, the Bishop's palace. It's possible that some of the masons from Chartres also worked on Reims, but the figures generally show more Classical influence in their drapery and increasing expressiveness, with its winsome 'smiling angel' and St-Joseph sculpture. Inside take a look at the capitals decorated with elaborate, naturalistic foliage with birds hiding among the leaves.

A few blocks south of the cathedral, the **Musée des Beaux-Arts** (8 rue Charizy/03.26.47.28.44, closed Tue), has one of the best collections of all the provincial museums, with some great Lucas Cranach portraits of thirteenth-century German princes, 26 canvases by Corot, and the famous '*The Death of Marat*' by Jean-Louis David. From the museum, head down the rue Gambetta to visit the **Basilica of St-Rémi**, which honours the fifth-century saint who baptised Clovis. In art historical terms, the Romanesque St-Rémi (built 1007-49), is a fascinating complement to the cathedral. Subsequent alterations added Gothic elements to the original interior, allowing you to see how the Romanesque evolved into the Gothic. Don't miss the remarkable series of ten sixteenth-century tapestries depicting the life of Saint Rémi in the **Musée St-Rémi** (53 rue Simon/ 03.26.85.23.36), in a series of restored monastic buildings next to the basilica.

Reims is also, of course, at the heart of the Champagne region. Many of the leading producers of the famous bubbly are based in the town and offer visits of their cellars, generally an informative insight into the laborious and skilled champagne-making process. The fine cellars of **Champagne Pommery** (03.26.61.62.63) occupy Gallo-Roman chalk mines 30m below ground and are decorated with Art Nouveau bas-reliefs by Emile Gallé. **Champagne Taittinger** (03.26.85.45.35) doesn't look much until you descend into the cellars: on the first level are the vaulted Gothic cellars of a former monastery; below are the strangely beautiful, Gallo-Roman chalk quarries. Wear your woollies: champagne vaults are cold and clammy.

### Further Information

Getting There *By car* take the A4 to Reims (150km). *By train* from Gare de l'Est to Reims takes about 90 minutes. **Office du Tourisme de Reims** *2 rue Guillaume-de-Machault, 51100 Reims (03.26.77.45.25).* **Open** 9am-

*The cellars of Champagne Pommery in* **Reims** *occupy Gallo-Roman chalk mines.*

7.30pm Mon-Fri; 9.30am-5.30pm Sun, public holidays.
**Where to eat** The haute cuisine mecca is Gérard
Boyer's restaurant at **Château des Crayères**, 64 bd
Henri-Vanier (03.26.82.80.80), in an imposing Second
Empire château on the south-east fringe of town. Within
town there are numerous brasseries, restaurants and
cafés, grouped around the place Drouet d'Erlon. If you'd
like to sample Boyer's cooking style at gentler prices, he
has a lively bistro-annexe named **Au Petit Comptoir** at
17 rue de Mars (03.26.40.58.58). The **Hotel Univers** at 41
bd Foch (03.26.88.68.08; double 350F) is well-located
across from Reims station and offers comfortable,
recently renovated rooms at moderate prices.

## Rouen

The capital of Normandy is a cathedral town of
contrasts. The centre retains lots of drunken, half-
timbered buildings and narrow streets, while the
port areas by the Seine were almost totally destroyed by bombing during the war. Begun at the start
of the thirteenth century, the **Cathédrale Notre-
Dame**, depicted by Monet, spans the Gothic periods. Of the two towers, the north tower, Tour St
Romain, dates from the early period while the more
Flamboyant Tour de Beurre is from the late fifteenth century. Among the tombs inside is that of
Richard the Lionheart. Nearby is the famous Gros-
Horloge gateway, with its ornamental clock over
the busy medieval rue du Gros Horloge, leading to
picturesque streets of half-timbered houses.

The city has two more Gothic churches worth a
visit, the **Eglise St-Ouen** and the **Eglise St-
Maclou**, as well as an enormously fanciful
Flamboyant Gothic **Palais du Justice**. The striking contemporary **Eglise Ste-Jeanne d'Arc**,

adjoining a funky modern market hall on place du
Vieux-Marché has a boat-shaped structure with a
swooping wooden roof and stained-glass windows
recovered from a bombed-out city church.

The **Musée des Beaux Arts** (26 bis rue Jean
Le Canuet/02.35.71.28.40) has just been renovated.
It contains one of France's best regional art collec-
tions, including works by Gérard David, Velázquez,
Perugino and Caravaggio, some wonderful oil
studies by Géricault (a native of Rouen) and
Impressionist works by Monet and Sisley.

### Getting There & Information
**Getting there** Rouen is 137km from Paris. *By car* A13
from Porte d'Auteuil. *By train* from Gare St-Lazare.
**Office du Tourisme** *25 pl de la Cathédrale, 76000
Rouen (02.32.08.32.40).* **Open** *May-Sept* 9am-7pm Mon-
Sat; 9.30am-12.30pm, 2.30-6.30pm, Sun; *Oct-Apr* 9am-
12.30pm, 2-6.30pm, Mon-Sat; 10am-1pm Sun.
**Where to eat** The best-known gourmet restaurant is
fish specialist *Gill* (9 quai Bourse/02.35.71.16.14), but
there are also several pleasant cheaper bistros, especially
on place du Vieux-Marché, or the quietly formal
*L'Orangerie* (2 rue Cormeille/02.35.88.43.97).

## Troyes

A thriving market city during the Middle Ages,
Troyes, 150km south of Paris, was the seat of the
counts of Champagne. Never significantly damaged by war, the old town, shaped like a champagne
cork after a medieval expansion of its original circular walls, delights with its hundreds of remarkably preserved half-timbered houses and what
many consider to be the most magnificent concentration of original stained glass in France. Add

one of the finest modern art collections in Europe, and several other good museums, and you have a first-rate excursion, preferably overnight, although a day trip from Paris is practical.

Begin your visit with a stroll through the old town along the rue Champeaux, the main street in the quarter during the sixteenth century, and don't miss the ruelle des Chats, a narrow lane that conjures up a vivid idea of what the city was like during the Middle Ages. The ruelle des Chats also leads to the **Eglise Ste-Madeleine**, the oldest church in the city, which was completed in the twelfth century and remodelled in the sixteenth. Entering, you'll be struck by the Flamboyant Gothic rood screen, but the real draw is the superb fifteenth-century stained-glass windows in the nave. Unusually, they're mounted low enough to be examined closely, illustrating with wonderful detail the story of the Creation.

Nearby, the **Basilique St-Urbain** was built (1262-86) on the orders of Pope Urbain IV, a native of Troyes. This church represents an early apogee of Gothic architecture and its ambitions of replacing the heavy masonry of the Romanesque with lacy stone workwork and glass. As the exterior of the church, cluttered with heavy flying buttresses shows, however, it took a good century to refine the necessary building techniques. Inside, the stained glass is magnificent, and the statue of the Virgin

**Troyes'** *medieval, half-timbered houses.*

with the Grapes is a fine example of local sixteenth-century sculpture. Heading down rue Champeaux to the **Cathédrale St-Pierre St-Paul**, you'll pass through the café-lined place du Maréchal-Foch, one flank of which is occupied by the handsome seventeenth-century Hôtel de Ville, and then cross a canal into the oldest part of the city.

The cathedral impresses with the richness of its facade, part of which was done by Martin Chambiges, who also worked on the cathedrals at Sens and Beauvais. Construction took place between the thirteenth and seventeenth centuries. Inside, the elegance and lightness of the architecture are overwhelming; the arcaded triforium atop the pillars of the choir was one of the first in France to be pierced with windows instead of filled with stone. The stained glass offers a miniature art-history lesson, as the windows are a catalogue of styles from the thirteenth to sixteenth centuries. Particularly impressive are the richly coloured, thirteenth-century scenes from Virgin's life and the portraits of popes and emperors in the choir.

The **Musée d'Art Moderne** (pl St-Pierre/ 03.25.76.26.80), next to the cathedral, opened in 1976 when two important collectors, Pierre and Denise Lévy, deeded their art collection to the state as part of a tax settlement. Housed in the former bishop's palace, the collection is distinguished by its splendid Fauvist canvases, including works by Derain and Vlaminck, in addition to works by Braque, Courbet, Degas, Seurat and Vuillard, and an important collection of modern sculpture and drawings.

If you have time, the **Maison de l'Outil** (7 rue de la Trinité/03.25.73.28.26), has a fascinating array of handmade eighteenth-century tools used by blacksmiths, weavers, carpenters and other tradesmen, while the **Musée des Beaux-Arts et d'Archéologie** housed in the Abbaye St-Loup (1 rue Chrétien de Troyes/03.35.42.33.33), next to the cathedral, has some fine Gallo-Roman bronzes and an impressive haul of cloisoned arms and jewellery found in a fifth-century Merogovinian tomb.

### Further Information

**Getting there** *By car,* take the A6 south to Evry, where you pick up the A5 to Troyes. *By train,* hourly trains from the Gare de Lyon (1 hr 15 minutes).
**Office du Tourisme** 16 bd Carnot, 10014 Troyes, (03.25.82.62.70). **Open** 9am-12.30pm, 2.30-6.30pm, Mon-Sun.
**Where to stay & eat** *Le Champ des Oiseaux* (20 rue Linard Gonthier/03.25.80.58.50) is a pleasant new hotel occupying two beautifully restored, half-timbered houses right next to the cathedral and art museums (doubles 450F). The *Royal Hôtel* (22 bd Carnot/03.25.73.19.99) near the station, is reasonably priced (double 335F), friendly and comfortable with modern fittings and an excellent restaurant. *Le Bouchon Champenois* (1 cour du Mortier d'Or, 10 ruelle des Chats/03.25.73.69.24) is a delightful little restaurant overlooking a half-timbered courtyard in the heart of the city. It specialises in regional cuisine, including the famous *andouillette*, or chitterling sausage, and local chesses. Many consider *Le Clos Juillet* (22 bd du 14-Juillet/03.25.73.31.32) to be the best table in town; its young chef specialises in modernised regional dishes.

# Survival

# Survival

*Your problems solved: how to rent a flat, use the phone system, find a hospital and much more.*

## Emergencies

The following services operate 24 hours daily. In a real medical emergency, call the Sapeurs-Pompiers, who are trained paramedics, rather than the SAMU.

**In an emergency, phone:**

| | |
|---|---|
| Police | 17 |
| Fire (Sapeurs-Pompiers) | 18 |
| Ambulance (SAMU) | 15 |
| Gas leaks (GDF) | 01.43.35.40.87 |
| Electricity (EDF) | 01.43.35.40.86 |

## English-Language Helplines

### SOS Help

*(47.23.80.80).* **Open** 3-11pm daily.

A non-profit-making, English-language crisis hotline staffed by a team of trained listeners. If they can't help, they will refer you to doctors, lawyers, and so on, who can.

### FACTS-Line

*(01.44.93.16.69).* **Open** 6-10pm Mon, Wed, Fri.

English-speaking crisis line gives information and support for those touched by HIV/AIDS.

## Paperwork

Anyone from abroad coming to live in Paris should be prepared for the sheer weight of bureaucracy to which French officialdom is doggedly devoted, whether it's for acquiring a *carte de séjour* or resident's permit, opening a bank account, reclaiming medical expenses or getting married. Among documents regularly required are a *Fiche d'Etat civile* (essential details translated from your passport by the embassy/consulate) and a legally-approved translation of your birth certificate (your embassy will provide lists of legal translators; for general translators, *see chapter* **Business**). You are meant to be able to prove your identity to the police at all times; always carry your *carte de séjour* or your passport.

### Cartes de Séjour

Officially, all foreigners, both EU and non-EU citizens, who stay in France for more than three months must apply for a *carte de séjour*. Valid for one year, once you have it you can open a bank account, use various municipal facilities and the like. People who have had a *carte de séjour* for at least three years, have been paying French income tax, can show proof of income and/or are married to a French national can apply for a *carte de résident*, valid for 10 years.

### CIRA (Centre Interministeriel de Renseignements Administratifs)

*(01.40.01.11.01).* **Open** 9am-12.30pm, 2-5.30pm, Mon-Fri. Answers all enquiries concerning French administrative procedures, or directs you to the competent authorities.

### Préfecture de Police de Paris

*7 bd du Palais (salle sud, service étrangers), 1st (01.53.71.51.68). M° Cité.* **Open** 8.30am-4pm Mon-Fri. For information on residency and work permits for EC and other nationals. You will be directed to the appropriate service according to your nationality and status.

## Working in Paris

All EU nationals are legally allowed to work in France, but must apply for a French social security number and *carte de séjour*. Some job ads can be found at branches of the Agence National Pour l'Emploi (ANPE), the French national employment bureau. This also the place to go to sign up as a *demandeur d'emploi* (employment seeker), to be placed on file as available for work and to qualify for French unemployment benefits, should you be entitled to them. If you are coming from Britain, you can only claim French unemployment benefit if you were already signed on before you left. Non-EU nationals cannot legally work in France, unless they obtain a work permit, and are not entitled to use the ANPE network wthout valid work papers.

### Job Ads

Help-wanted ads sometimes appear in the *International Herald Tribune*, although the 'sophisticated personal companion' sort make up the bulk of them. Offers for English-speakers are sometimes listed on noticeboards at language schools and the various Anglo establishments around town, such as the American Church and Cathedral (*see below* **Religion**); most are for babysitters and language tutors. Positions as waiters and bar staff are often available at the city's many international-style watering holes: non-papered individuals may be hired under the table, but UK nationals have a better chance, being legal. The free publication *FUSAC* carries some job ads for English-speakers, mostly of the odd-job variety (*see chapter* **Media**).

If you are looking for work of a more professional kind, have your CV translated, including French equivalents for any qualifications. Most job applications require a photo and a handwritten letter; French employers are very attached to handwriting analysis when choosing candidates.

## Renting a Flat

The best flats often go by word of mouth. Although rents have fallen slightly with the recession, the rental market still strongly favours the landlord, with studio and one-bedroom flats fetching the highest prices. Flats do often change hands, particularly from May to October, but the competition for them is extremely keen. Expect to pay roughly 100F per month for every square metre (3,500F a month for a 35sq m flat, and so on); in chic neighbourhoods rents can be 50-100% more.

### Rental laws

The legal minimum period for a rental lease (*bail de location*) on an unfurnished apartment is three years; one year for a furnished flat. Both are renewable. During this period the landlord can only raise the rent by the official construction inflation index – usually around 5% per annum. At the end of the lease, the rent can be adjusted, but tenants can object before a rent board if it seems exorbitant. Tenants can be evicted for non-payment, or if the landlord wishes to sell the property or use it as his own residence. It is nearly impossible to evict non-payers between October and March, as it is illegal to throw people into the streets in winter.

Before accepting you as a tenant, agencies or landlords will probably require you to present a dossier with pay slips (*fiche de paie/bulletin de salaire*) showing three to four times the amount of the monthly rent and as a foreigner, in particular, to furnish a financial guarantee. Payments that must customarily be made when taking out a lease include the first month's rent, a security deposit (*une caution*) equal to two month's rent, and an agency fee, if applicable. It is also customary for an inspection of the premises (*état des lieux*) to be performed by a bailiff (*huissier*) at the beginning and end of the rental period to assess the flat's condition, the cost of which (around 1,000F) is shared by landlord and tenant.

Landlords sometimes ask that tenants, especially foreign ones, pay rent in cash and do without a written lease. This can get you flats not otherwise available, but the renter may have difficulty in establishing his or her rights – which, in addition to avoiding tax, is why landlords do it.

### Flat hunting

The largest lists of ads offering furnished (*meublé*) and unfurnished (*vide*) flats for rent are in Tuesdays' *Le Figaro*. Most are placed by agencies. Pricey flats offered to prosperous foreigners, and occasionally to students, are advertised in the daily *International Herald Tribune* and English-language fortnightly *FUSAC* (*see chapter* **Media**), although, again, rents tend to be higher than in the French press. *See also chapter* **Study**. Short-term flat agencies (*see chapter*

**Accommodation**) can simplify things, but are not cheap either. Local bakeries often post up notices of flats for rent direct from the owner. Non-agency listings are also available in the weekly *De Particulier à Particulier*, published on Thursdays, and via **Minitel** 3615 PAP. There's also a commercial Minitel flat rental service on 3615 LOCAT. In ads, landlords often list a visiting time; prepare to meet hordes of other flat-seekers on the staircase and take your supporting documents and cheque book with you.

### Bureau d'Informations et de Protection des Occupants (BIPO)

*6 rue Agrippa-d'Aubigné, 4th (01.42.71.31.31).*
*M° Sully-Morland.* **Open** 9am-5pm Mon-Thur; 9am-4.30pm Fri.
Run by the Mairie de Paris, the Bureau d'Informations et de Protection des Occupants provides free advice (in French) about renting or buying an apartment, housing benefits, rent legislation, tenants' rights and related matters.

### SOS Locataire

*42bis rue Sedaine, 11th (01.48.06.82.75). M° Voltaire.*
**Open** 2.30-5pm Mon, Tue, Thur, Fri.
Legal advice on tenants' rights.

## Facilities

### Electricity & Gas

Electricity in France runs on 220V. Visitors with British 240V appliances can simply change the plug or use a converter (*adaptateur*), available at most hardware shops. If you have US 110V appliances, you will need to use a transformer (*transformateur*) available at the **Fnac**, Darty chains or in the basement of the **BHV** (*see chapter* **Specialist Shops**).

Gas and electricity are supplied by the state-owned **EDF-GDF** (*Electricité de France-Gaz de France*). They are the ones to contact for queries concerning supply, bills, or in case of power failures, gas leaks and so on (*see above*, **Emergencies**). If you have an immediate problem, you'll have to phone a plumber or electrician (*see below* **Emergency Repairs**). During the day it's best to phone a local repair service, which you'll find in the *Pages Jaunes* under *Plombiers* or *Electricité*.

## Emergency Repairs

Numerous 24-hour emergency repair services deal with plumbing, electricity, heating, locks, car repairs and much more. Most charge a minimum of 150F call-out and 200F per hour's labour, plus parts; more on Sunday and at night.
**Allô Assistance Dépannage** (08.00.07.24.24).
**Numéro Un Dépannage** (01.43.31.51.51).
**SOS Dépannage** (01.47.07.99.99): double the price, but claim to be twice as reliable. 400F call out 400F/hour.

## Communications

### Postal Services

If you're simply mailing a letter or postcard, it is much quicker to buy stamps at a tobacconist (*tabac*) than at a post office. Post offices (*bureaux de poste*) are open from 8am to 7pm Monday to Friday; 9am to noon Saturday. All are listed in the phone book: under *Administration des PTT* in the *Pages Jaunes*; under *Poste* in the *Pages Blanches*. Automatic envelope-weighing machines now grace most post offices, which instruct you in English, print out a stamp and give you change.

---

# Minitel

Long before everyone went Internet crazy, France Telecom pioneered *Le Minitel*, an interactive information service available to any telephone subscriber. Unfortunately, it has never been developed to its full potential and many services are slow and expensive. Its hundreds of services give access to hotel and ticket reservations, airline and train time-table information, weather forecasts, a constantly-updated phone directory, and so on.

As well as all kinds of business information, you can find dozens of recreational lines that include 'dating' hook-ups, many of them highly raunchy and with enticing names like *Cum*. There's a particular boom in gay mini-tel lines. There are also horoscope, film credit or pop quiz connections, all of which can make astronomical inroads into your phone bill, as will any 3615, 3616 or 3617 prefixed numbers (3614 is less expensive).

### Minitel rates
**Telephone directory information** for all of France: dial 3611 on the keyboard, wait for the beep and press *Connexion*, then type in the name and city of the person or business whose number and/or address you're looking for, and press *Envoi*. Basic Minitel directory use is free for the first three minutes, then costs 36 centimes per minute. Hotels are often Minitel-equipped and most post offices offer free use of the terminals for basic telephone enquiries.
**Minitel directory in English** dial 3614 on the keyboard, press *Connexion*, then type *ED* and *Envoi*.

---

### Main post office
*52 rue du Louvre, 1st (01.40.28.20.00). M° Châtelet-Les Halles or Louvre.* **Open** 24 hours daily for *Poste Restante*, telephones, telegrams, stamps and fax.
This around-the-clock post office is the best place to get your mail sent to if you haven't got a fixed address in Paris. Mail should be addressed to you in block capitals, followed by *Poste Restante*, then the post office's address. There is a charge for each letter received.

### Late-opening post office
*71 av des Champs-Elysées, 8th (01.44.13.66.00). M° Franklin D Roosevelt.* **Open** 8am-10pm Mon-Sat; 10am-noon, 2-7pm, Sun.
There is only basic postal service after 7pm.

### Postcodes
Letters will arrive sooner if they feature the correct five-digit postcode. **Within Paris**: postcodes always begin with '75'; if your address is in the 1st *arrondissement*, the postcode is 75001; in the 15th, the code is 75015. The 16th *arrondissement* is subdivided into two sectors, 75016 and 75116. Some business addresses have a more detailed postcode, followed by a Cedex number which indicates the *arrondissement*.

### Telephones

#### Charges
Charges depend on the distance and duration of the call. Calls within Paris cost 73 centimes for three minutes, standard rate. Within Metropolitan France, calls outside a 100km (60 mile) radius are charged at the same long-distance rate regardless of distance. Calls to the UK cost 3.65F per minute peak rate; calls to the US cost 6.69F per minute peak rate.
**Reduced rates on calls within France**: from 10.30pm to 8am Monday to Friday, and from 2pm Saturday to 8am Monday. Calls are as much as 50% cheaper.
**Reduced rates to the UK and Northern Ireland**: from 9.30pm to 8am Monday to Friday; from 2pm Saturday and all day Sunday and public holidays. Cost: 3.04F per minute.
**Reduced rates to the US and Canada**: the cheapest rates (4.98F per minute) apply from 2am to noon Monday to Friday. Another cheap rate (5.72F per minute) applies from noon to 2pm and 8pm to 2am, Monday to Saturday, and also from noon to 2am Sunday and public holidays.

#### 24-Hour Telephone Services
**Engineers** if your phone is out of order, dial 13.
**News** international news (French recorded message) dial 08.36.68.10.33.
**Telegram** all languages, international 0800.33.44.11; France 36.55. 01.05.33.44.11.
**Time** dial 36.99.
**Traffic news** dial 01.48.99.33.33.
**Weather** for specific enquiries on weather around the world and throughout France, dial 08.36.70.12.34; for a recorded weather announcement for Paris and region, dial 08.36.68.02.75.

#### Phone books
Phone books are found in all post offices and in most cafés (ask if you don't see them by the phone). The White Pages (*Pages Blanches*, two volumes) lists names of people and businesses alphabetically. The *Pages Jaunes* (Yellow Pages) lists businesses and services under category headings.

## Disabled Travellers

Disabled visitors to Paris are advised to buy the specialist guide *Access in Paris*. The tourist office (*see chapter* **Essential Information**) also produces a free pamphlet, *Touristes Quand Même*, giving details of facilities for the disabled at major tourist attractions. For details of public transport facilities and companies that specialise in disabled transport, *see chapter* **Getting Around**.

### Access in Paris

An excellent English-language guide for the disabled by Gordon Couch and Ben Roberts, published by Quiller Press, London (price £7). Can be ordered from RADAR, Unit 12, City Forum, 250 City Rd, London EC1V 8AS/0171-250 3222.

### Association des Paralysés de France

*22 rue du Père-Guérain, 13th (01.44.16.83.83).*
*M° Pl d'Italie.* **Open** 9am-12.30pm, 2-6pm, Mon-Fri.
This association publishes a guide, *Où ferons-nous étape?* (Where will we stop off?), listing hotels and motels around France with facilities for the disabled (80F by mail).

## Driving in Paris

If you drive in France with your own car you will need to bring the car registration and insurance documents (an insurance green card, available from insurance companies and the AA and RAC in the UK, is no longer compulsory but is advisable). It is also advisable to carry spare lightbulbs, a first-aid kit and a red warning triangle, although, again, these items are not obligatory.

As you come into Paris you will inevitably meet the *Périphérique*, the giant ringroad around central Paris that carries all the heavy traffic in, out and around the city. Map out your route carefully or you may end up going round the *Périphérique* several times. Its intersections – which lead onto other main roads – are called *portes* (gates). Driving on the *Périphérique* is not as hair-raising as you might expect, even though it's often congested. However, morning and evening rush hours (especially Friday evenings) and the beginning and end of the peak local holiday times (July-August) are times to be avoided like the plague.

You can get traffic condition information for the Ile de France on 01.48.99.33.33. In summer, the organisation *Bison Futé* hands out brochures on regional traffic conditions at the *péages* (toll stations) on motorways, suggesting routes that are likely to be less crowded. For more on driving outside Paris, *see chapter* **Getting Started**.

There are also some points to be born in mind wherever you drive in France:
• France now uses white headlights like the rest of Europe, but if you're driving a British right-hand drive vehicle the lights must be screened or adjusted for left-hand drive.
• It is obligatory for drivers and front- and back-seat passengers to wear seat belts at all times.
• Children under ten are not allowed to travel in the front of a car, except in a special seat facing backwards.
• At intersections where no signposts indicate the right of way, the car coming from the right has priority. Many roundabouts now give priority to those on the roundabout, but if this is not indicated (by road markings or *vous n'avez pas la priorité*), priority will still be on the right. This applies to some of the most hair-raising turns in Paris – the Arc de Triomphe and place de la Concorde – where you will dis-

cover sneaky drivers try to have continual priority by zipping round on the right.
• When oncoming drivers flash their lights at you, this means that they will *not* slow down (contrary to British practice) and are warning you to keep out of the way. Friendly drivers also flash their lights to warn you when there are *gendarmes* lurking the other side of the hill.
• In Paris, try not to be put off by honking, screeching brakes and general aggression from other drivers. It's normal.
• Do not leave anything of value in your car, and do not leave bags or coats in view on the seats.
• Carry some loose change, as it's quicker to head for the exact-change line on toll bridges or *péage* motorways; however, cashiers do give change and *péages* accept credit cards.

## Breakdown Services

British organisations such as the AA or RAC do not have reciprocal arrangements with an equivalent organisation in France, so it is advisable to take out additional breakdown insurance cover. The following breakdown services offer 24-hour assistance (the smaller, the cheaper):

### Assistance Auto Parisienne

*212 rue de la Croix-Nivert, 15th (01.42.50.48.49).*
**No credit cards.**

### Aligre Dépannage

*14 rue Alsace-Lorraine, 19th (01.42.06.44.32).*
**No credit cards.**

## Parking

There are still a few free on-street parking areas left in Paris, but they're usually full when you find them. If you park illegally, you risk getting your car clamped or towed away (*see below*). In central zones, parking meters have been replaced by *Horodateurs*, pay-and-display machines. To avoid having to use large amounts of change, you can buy special cards to use in them from *tabacs*.

In the past few years, numerous underground car parks have been built in central Paris indicated on Michelin maps with a 'P' sign. Most cost 12F-15F per hour; 80F-130F for 24 hours; some offer lower night rates after 7pm.

### 24-hour parking

The following car parks, listed in order of *arrondissement*, are open 24 hours daily: **Parking Pont-Neuf** *pl Dauphine, 1st (01.46.33.97.48).* **Parking des Pyramides** *opposite 15 rue des Pyramides, 1st (01.42.60.53.21).* **Berri Washington** *5 rue de Berri, 8th (near the Champs-Elysées) (01.45.62.72.09).* **Chauchat-Drouot** *14 rue Chauchat, 9th (01.42.46.03.17).* **Paris-Gare de Lyon** *193 rue de Bercy, 12th (01.40.04.61.26).* **Tour Montparnasse** *17 rue de l'Arrivée, 15th (01.45.38.68.00).* **Place de Clichy/Montmartre** *12 rue Forest, 18th (01.43.87.64.50).*

### Parking near the Périphérique

If you've come to Paris by car, it's a good idea to park at the edge of the city and then use public transport. The car parks listed here are by main routes into Paris, near Métro stations. **Porte de St Ouen** *17 av de la Porte de St-Ouen, 17th (01.42.29.31.96).* **Open** 24 hours daily. **Rate** 20F per day. **Porte de Clignancourt** *30 av de la Porte de Clignancourt, 18th (01.42.64.03.82).* **Open** 7am-10pm Tue-Fri; 7am-11pm Sat, Sun. **Rate** 45F per 24 hours Tue-Fri; 100F per 24 hours Sat, Sun. **Porte de Bagnolet** *rue*

*Jean Jaurès, Bagnolet (01.43.63.19.99)*. **Open** 24 hours daily. **Rate** 40F per 24 hours. **Porte d'Italie** *8 av de la Porte d'Italie, 13th (01.45.89.09.77)*. **Open** 7am-8pm Mon-Sat. **Rate** 40F per 24 hours. **Porte Maillot** *pl de la Porte Maillot, 17th (01.40.68.00.11)*. **Open** 24 hours daily. **Rate** 100F per 24 hours.

## Clamps & Car Pounds

If you've had the misfortune to have your car clamped, contact the local police station. There are eight car pounds (*fourrières*) in Paris. You'll have to pay a 630F removal fee plus 30F storage charge per day; add to that a parking fine ranging from 230F to 900F (for parking in a bus lane). If your car is confiscated at night it goes first to *prefourrières* **Bercy** for southern Paris or **Europe** for the north; and will be sent to the car pound for the relevant *arrondissement* after 48 hours. For general information call 08.36.67.22.22.

**1st, 2nd, 3rd, 4th** *Parking St Eustache, Forum des Halles, pl Carrée entrance, level-4, 1st (01.42.21.44.63)*. *M° Les Halles*. **Open** 8am-8.30pm Mon-Sat.
**5th, 12th, 13th** *Bercy, 18 bd Poniatowsky, 12th (01.43.46.69.38)*. *M° Porte de Charenton*. **Open** 24 hours daily.
**6th, 7th, 14th** *33 rue du Commandant Mouchotte, 14th (01.43.20.65.24)*. *M° Montparnasse-Bienvenüe*. **Open** 8am-8pm Mon-Sat.
**8th, 9th** *Europe, 43bis bd des Batignolles, 8th (01.42.93.51.30)*. *M° Rome*. **Open** 24 hours daily.
**10th, 11th, 19th, 20th** *15 rue de la Marseillaise, 19th (01.44.52.52.10)*. *M° Porte de Pantin*. **Open** 8am-8pm Mon-Sat.
**15th/16th (south)** *51 bd Général Martial-Valin, 15th (01.4.54.20.31)*. *M° Balard*. **Open** 8am-8pm Mon-Sat.
**16th** *Parking Étoile Foch, 8 av Foch, 16th (01.45.01.80.13)*. *M° Charles de Gaulle-Étoile*. **Open** 8am-8.30pm Mon-Sat.
**17th, 18th** *8 bd Bois Leprêtre, 17th (01.53.71.33.238)*. *M° Porte de St-Ouen*. **Open** 6.30am-7.30pm Mon-Sat.

### 24-Hour Petrol Stations

**1st** *arrondissement*. 336 rue St-Honoré. **2nd** pl de la Bourse. **3rd** 42 rue Beaubourg. **5th** 36 rue des Fossés St-Bernard. **7th** 6 bd Raspail. **8th** corner of av des Champs-Elysées and av George V; pl de la Madeleine. **10th** 1 bd de la Chapelle; 2 rue Louis-Blanc; 166 rue du Fbg-St-Martin; 152 rue Lafayette; 1 bd de la Chapelle. **12th** 55 quai de la Rapée. **13th** 2 pl du Docteur Yersin. **14th** av de la Porte de Châtillon. **15th** 95 bd Lefebvre. **16th** 24 av Paul-Doumer. **17th** 6 av de la Porte de Clichy. **18th** 30 av Porte de Clignancourt. **20th** 217 bd Davout. **Périphérique** Porte de Vincennes.

## Embassies & Consulates

Before going to an embassy or consulate, phone and check opening hours. You may also need to make an appointment. Outside office hours, consulates generally have answerphones which will give an emergency contact number. There's a full list of embassies and consulates in the *Pages Jaunes* under *Ambassades et Consulats*. For general enquiries or problems with passports or visas, it is usually the consulate you need. For specialised business services provided by the US and British consulates, *see chapter* **Business**.

### Australian Embassy
*4 rue Jean-Rey, 15th (01.40.59.33.00)*. *M° Bir-Hakeim*. **Open** 9am-6pm Mon-Fri. **Visas** 9.15am-12.15pm Mon-Fri.

### British Embassy
*35 rue du Fbg-St-Honoré, 8th (01.44.51.31.00)*. *M° Concorde*. **Open** 9.30am-1pm, 2.30-6pm, Mon-Fri. **Consulate/Visas** *16 rue Anjou, 8th (emergencies 01.42.66.29.79/information 01.40.39.80.63/Visa information 01.40.39.83.01 )*. *M° Concorde or Madeleine*. **Open** 9.30am-12.30pm, 2.30-5pm, Mon-Fri.

### Canadian Embassy
*35 av Montaigne, 8th (01.44.43.29.00)*. *M° Franklin D Roosevelt*. **Open** 8.30-11am, 2-5pm, Mon-Fri. **Visas** *(01.44.43.29.16)*. **Open** 8.30-11am Mon-Fri.

### Irish Embassy
*12 av Foch, 16th*. **Consulate** *4 rue Rude, 16th (01.44.17.67.00)*. *M° Charles de Gaulle-Étoile*. **Open** For visits 9.30am-noon Mon-Fri. **By phone** 9.30am-1pm, 2.30-5.30pm, Mon-Fri.

### New Zealand Embassy
*7 ter rue Léonard-de-Vinci, 16th (01.45.00.24.11)*. *M° Victor-Hugo*. **Open** 9am-1pm, 2-5.30pm, Mon-Fri.

### South African Embassy
*59 quai d'Orsay, 7th (01.45.55.92.37)*. *M° Invalides*. **Open** 8.30am-5.15pm Mon-Fri, by appointment.

### US Embassy
*2 av Gabriel, 8th (01.43.12.22.22)*. *M° Concorde*. **Open** 9am-6pm Mon-Fri. **Consulate/Visas** *2 rue St-Florentin, 1st (01.43.12.22.22)*. *M° Concorde*. **Open** 8.45-11am Mon-Fri.

## Health

All EU nationals staying in France are entitled to take advantage of the French Social Security system, which refunds up to 70 per cent of medical expenses. To get a refund, British nationals should obtain form E111 before leaving the UK (or form E112 for those already in treatment). Nationals of non-European countries should make sure they take out insurance before leaving home. Consultations and medicine have to be paid for in full at the time of purchase, and are reimbursed, in part, on receipt of a completed *feuille*.

If you do have treatment while in France the doctor will give you a prescription and a *feuille de soins* (statement of treatment). At the pharmacy, the medication will carry *vignettes* (little stickers) which you must stick onto your *feuille de soins*. Send this, along with the prescription and form E111, to your local *Caisse Primaire d'Assurance Maladie* (listed in the phone book under *Sécurité Sociale*). Refunds can take a month or two to come through. Be sure to make photocopies of all forms and receipts, just in case.

## Help Lines & Out of Hours Calls

*See also above*, **Emergencies**.
**Nurses (SOS Infirmiers)** *(01.43.57.01.26/08.36.60.50.50)*. House calls 8pm-midnight, generally around 150F.
**SOS Dépression** *(01.45.22.44.44)*. People listen and/or give advice, and can send a counsellor or psychiatrist to your home in case of crisis.
**SOS Médecins** *(01.47.07.77.77/01.43.37.77.77)*. If you don't know of any doctors or are too ill to leave your

Late-night hub **place de la Bastille.**

bed, this service dispatches doctors for house calls. Anything will be taken on board, from emergency action to prescribing medication for a cold. A normal home visit in Paris or its suburbs costs 145F-350F before 7pm, from 310F thereafter.
**Urgences Médicales de Paris** *(01.48.28.40.04)*.
Doctors who will make house calls. Some speak English.
**Urgences Dentaires de Paris** *(01.47.07.44.44)*.
Will offer advice by phone or refer you to nearby dentists; after 10pm all are sent to the Hôpital Salpêtrière.
**SOS Dentaire** *87 bd Port-Royal, 5th (01.43.37.51.00). RER Port-Royal.*
Is open until 11.45pm for emergency dental care.
**Alcoholics Anonymous in English** *(01.46.34.59.65)*.
The 24-hour recorded message gives schedules of the AA meetings at the American Church (*see below* **Religion**) and some members' phone numbers for additional information.

## Hospitals

For a complete list of hospitals in and around Paris, consult the *Pages Blanches* under *Hôpital Assistance Publique*, or ring their headquarters on 01.40.27.30.00. All hospitals have an emergency ward open 24 hours daily. The following is a list of hospitals specialising in particular fields:
**Burns:** *Hôpital Cochin, 27 rue du Fbg-St-Jacques, 14th (01.42.34.17.40). M° St-Jacques. RER Port Royal; Hôpital St-Antoine, 184 rue du Fbg-St-Antoine, 12th (01.49.28.20.00). M° Faidherbe-Chaligny.*
**Children:** *Hôpital Necker, 149 rue de Sèvres, 15th (01.44.49.40.94). M° Duroc.*
**Children's Burns**: *Hôpital d'Enfants Armand-Trousseau, 26 av du Dr-Arnold-Nettes, 12th (01.44.73.74.75). M° Bel-Air.*
**Dog Bites:** *Institut Pasteur, 209 rue de Vaugirard, 15th (01.40.61.38.00). M° Pasteur.* **Service Anti-rabique open** 9am-noon Mon-Fri; 9-11.30am Sat.

**Drugs:** *Hôpital Ste-Anne, 1 rue Cabanais, 14th (01.45.65.80.00). M° Glacière. Hôpital Marmottan, 19 rue d'Armaille, 17th (01.45.74.00.04). M° Argentine.*
**Poisons:** *Hôpital Fernand Widal, 200 rue du Fbg St-Denis, 10th (01.40.05.45.45). M° Gare du Nord.*

### American Hospital in Paris
*63 bd Victor Hugo, 92202 Neuilly (01.46.41.25.25). M° Porte Maillot, then bus 82 to the terminus opposite the hospital.* **Open** 24 hours daily.
A private hospital. French Social Security will refund only a small percentage of treatment costs, although the hospital has an agreement with Blue Cross insurance in the US whereby hospitalisation costs (but not consultation fees) are covered for policy holders. All personnel speak English.

### Hertford British Hospital (Hôpital Franco-Britannique)
*3 rue Barbès, 92300 Levallois-Perret (01.46.39.22.22). M° Anatole-France.* **Open** 24 hours daily.
A private hospital. Most doctors are English-speaking. Linked to BUPA.

### General Clinics
**Centre Figuier** *2 rue du Figuier, 4th (01.42.78.55.53). M° St-Paul.* **Open** 9am-7pm Mon-Fri; 9-11am Sat.
**Centre Médico-Social** *3 rue Ridder, 14th (01.45.43.83.78). M° Plaisance.* **Open** noon-6.30pm Mon-Fri; 9.30am-noon Sat.
These centres are smaller and less bureaucratic than regular hospitals, and often more convenient for minor problems. They also carry out HIV tests (*dépistages*).

## Pharmacies

Pharmacies sport a green neon cross. They have a monopoly on issuing medication, and even on the sale of certain brands of deodorant, shampoo and skin-care lotion. Many other everyday items such as toothbrushes, razors and sanitary products are usually much cheaper in supermarkets.

Most pharmacies are open from 9am or 10am to 7pm or 8pm, sometimes with a break for lunch. Staff can provide basic medical services like disinfecting and bandaging wounds (for a small fee) and will indicate the nearest doctor on duty. French pharmacists are highly trained and you can sometimes avoid having to visit a doctor by describing your symptoms to them.

Paris has a rotating system of *Pharmacies de Garde* – pharmacies that open at night and on Sunday on a duty-rota basis. A closed local pharmacy will have a sign in its window indicating the nearest open pharmacy. Below we list late-opening pharmacies, in order of *arrondissement*.

### Allô Pharma
*(01.40.54.01.02)*. **Open** 24 hours daily. **Delivery** charge 60F day non-urgent; 90F day urgent; 150F night. **No credit cards.**
This service transports your prescription medication when pharmacies are closed (non-prescription exceptions can be made). Manned primarily by medical students who speak some English, they work in association with Dérhy (*see below*).

### Pharmacie des Halles
*10 bd de Sébastopol, 4th (01.42.72.03.23). M° Châtelet-Les Halles.* **Open** 9am-midnight Mon-Sat; noon-midnight Sun.

Paris' **CRS Police** *look the part.*

## Complementary Medicine

Most pharmacies also sell homeopathic medicines.

### Académie d'Homéopathie et de Médecines Douces
*2 rue d'Isly, 8th (01.43.87.60.33). Mᵒ St-Lazare.*
**Open** 9am-11.30pm, 2.30-5.30pm, Mon-Fri.

### Association Française d'Acuponcture
*3 rue de l'Arrivé, 15th (01.43.20.26.26). Mᵒ Brochart.*
**Open** 9.15-11.30am, 2.15-5.30pm, Mon, Tue, Thur, Fri;
1.30-6.30pm Wed.

### Centre d'Homéopathie de Paris
*48 av Gabriel, 8th (01.45.55.12.15). Mᵒ Franklin D Roosevelt.* **Open** 8am-6pm Mon-Thur; 9am-1pm Fri, Sat.

## AIDS, HIV & Sexually Transmitted Diseases

### AIDES
*247 rue de Belleville, 20th (01.44.52.00.00).*
*Mᵒ Télégraphe.* **Open** 9am-8pm Mon-Fri.
Volunteers providing a range of services for Aids-sufferers.

### AJCS (Association des jeunes contre le Sida)
*36 rue Geoffroy L'Asnier, 4th (01.44.78.00.00).*
*Mᵒ St-Paul.* **Open** 10am-7pm Mon-Fri; 2-7pm Sat.
An anti-Aids youth association.

### Dispensaire de la Croix Rouge
*43 rue de Valois, 1st (01.42.61.30.04). Mᵒ Palais Royal.*
A medical centre specialising in sexually related problems.
Also offers HIV tests (*dépistages*). Phone for appointment.

### SIDA Info Service
*(08.00.84.08.00).* **Open** 24 hours daily.
Confidential AIDS-information freephone in French.

## Legal Advice

Town Halls also answer legal enquiries (free service). Phone for details and times; ask for *consultations juridiques.*

### Avocat Assistance et Recours du Consommateur
*8 quai du Marché Neuf, 1st (01.43.54.32.04). Mᵒ St-Michel.*
**Open** 2-6pm Mon-Fri.
Lawyers here deal with consumer-related cases. The fee is
200F for a consultation. Call for an appointment.

### Direction Départmentale de la Concurrence, de la Consommation, et la Répression des Fraudes
*8 rue Froissart, 3rd (01.40.27.16.00). Mᵒ Sébastien-Froissart.* **Open** 9-11.30am, 2-5.30pm, Mon-Fri.
This subdivision of the Ministry of Finance deals with consumer complaints. They will investigate, put pressure on the seller to satisfy you and/or instigate litigation.

### Palais de Justice
*Galerie de Harlay, escalier S, 4 bd du Palais, 4th*
*(01.44.32.48.48). Mᵒ Cité.* **Open** 9.30am-noon Mon-Fri.
Free legal consultation. Arrive early and pick up a numbered
ticket. For phone advice, *see below* **SOS Avocats.**

### SOS Avocats
*(43.29.33.00).* **Open** 7-11.30pm Mon-Fri.
Free legal advice over the telephone.

### Dérhy/Pharmacie des Champs
*84 av des Champs-Elysées, 8th (01.45.62.02.41).*
*Mᵒ George V.* **Open** 24 hours daily.

### Matignon
*2 rue Jean Mermoz, 8th (01.43.59.86.55). Mᵒ Franklin D Roosevelt.* **Open** 8.30am-2am Mon-Sat; 10am-2am Sun.

### Altobelli
*6 bd des Capucines, 9th (01.42.65.88.29). Mᵒ Opéra.*
**Open** 8am-midnight Mon-Sat; 3pm-11pm Sun.

### Pharmacie Européenne de la Place de Clichy
*6 pl de Clichy, 9th (01.48.74.65.18). Mᵒ Place de Clichy.*
**Open** 24 hours daily.

### La Nation
*13 pl Nation, 11th (01.43.73.24.03). Mᵒ Nation.* **Open**
noon-midnight Mon; 8am-midnight Tue-Sat; 8pm-
midnight Sun.

### Pharmacie d'Italie
*61 av d'Italie, 13th (01.44.24.19.72). Mᵒ Tolbiac.*
**Open** 8am-midnight daily.

## Doctors & Dentists

A complete list of practitioners is in the *Pages Jaunes* under
*Médecins Qualifiés.* In order to get a Social Security refund,
choose a doctor or dentist registered with the state system;
look for *Médecin Conventionné* after the name. Consultations
cost around 130F with a generalist and 250F upwards with
a specialist, of which a proportion can be reimbursed.

### Centre Médical Europe
*44 rue d'Amsterdam, 9th (01.42.81.93.33/dentists*
*01.42.81.80.00). Mᵒ St-Lazare.* **Open** 8am-7pm Mon-Fri;
8am-6pm Sat.
Practitioners in all fields under one roof, charging minimal consultation fees (110F for foreigners). Appointments advisable.

### SOS Racisme

*1 rue Cail, 10th (01.42.05.44.44). M° La Chapelle.*
**Open** 3-6pm Mon-Fri.
A non profit-making association defending the rights of ethnic minorities.

## Police, Security & Lost Propery

If you are robbed or attacked you should report the incident as soon as possible. To report a crime officially, though, you will need to make a statement at the *commissariat* in the *arrondissement* in which it was committed. To find the appropriate *commissariat*, phone the *Préfecture Centrale* (01.53.71.53.71) day or night, or look in the phone book. You will be asked to make a statement, which will be typed out for you. It is unlikely that stolen goods will be recovered, but you will need the police statement for insurance purposes.

### Bureau des Objects Trouvés

*36 rue des Morillons, 15th (01.40.06.75.27).*
*M° Convention.* **Open** 8.30am-5pm Mon, Tue, Thur; 8.30am-4pm Wed, Fri.
Enquiries are not dealt with by phone, so visit in person (with ID) to fill out a form, specifying the date, time and place your item disappeared. A 20F-30F fee for returned goods.

## Religion

Churches and religious centres are listed in the phone book under *Eglises* and *Culte*. Paris has several English-speaking churches and other religious communities. The *International Herald Tribune*'s Saturday edition lists services in English.

The Liberal English-speaking Jewish community has rotating services in Paris and the western suburbs. For details, contact Kehilat Gesher, 10 rue de Pologne, 78100 St-Germain en Laye (01.39.21.97.19).

**American Cathedral** *23 av George V, 8th (01.53.23.84.00). M° George V.*
**American Church in Paris** *65 quai d'Orsay, 7th (01.40.62.05.00). M° Invalides.*
**Church of Scotland** *17 rue Bayard, 8th (01.48.78.47.94). M° Franklin D Roosevelt.*
**St George's English Church** *7 rue Auguste-Vacquerie, 16th (01.47.20.22.51). M° Charles de Gaulle-Etoile.*
**St Joseph's Roman Catholic Church** *50 av Hoche, 8th (01.42.27.28.56). M° Charles de Gaulle-Etoile.*
**St Michael's Church of England** *5 rue d'Aguesseau, 8th (01.47.42.70.88). M° Madeleine or Concorde.*

## Vets/Animals

### Dispensaire Populaire de Soins pour Animaux

*8 rue Maître-Albert, 5th (01.46.33.94.37). M° Maubert-Mutualité.* **Open** 9.30am-5.30pm Mon-Fri by appointment.
Very small fees for check-ups and castrations.

# Size conversion chart for clothes

| **Women's clothes** | | | | | | | | | |
|---|---|---|---|---|---|---|---|---|---|
| British | 8 | 10 | 12 | 14 | 16 | 18 | • | • | • |
| American | 6 | 8 | 10 | 12 | 14 | 16 | • | • | • |
| French | 36 | 38 | 40 | 42 | 44 | 46 | • | • | • |
| **Women's shoes** | | | | | | | | | |
| British | 3 | 4 | 5 | 6 | 7 | 8 | • | • | • |
| American | 5 | 6 | 7 | 8 | 9 | 10 | • | • | • |
| French | 36 | 37 | 38 | 39 | 40 | 41 | • | • | • |
| **Men's suits/overcoats** | | | | | | | | | |
| British | 38 | 40 | 42 | 44 | 46 | • | • | • | • |
| American | 38 | 40 | 42 | 44 | 46 | • | • | • | • |
| French | 48 | 50/52 | 54 | 56 | 58/60 | • | • | • | • |
| **Men's shirts** | | | | | | | | | |
| British | 14 | 14.5 | 15 | 15.5 | 16 | 16.5 | 17 | • | • |
| American | 14 | 14.5 | 15 | 15.5 | 16 | 16.5 | 17 | • | • |
| French | 35 | 36/37 | 38 | 39/40 | 41 | 42/43 | 44 | • | • |
| **Men's shoes** | | | | | | | | | |
| British | 8 | 9 | 10 | 11 | 12 | • | • | • | • |
| American | 9 | 10 | 11 | 12 | 13 | • | • | • | • |
| French | 42 | 43 | 44 | 45 | 46 | • | • | • | • |
| **Children's shoes** | | | | | | | | | |
| British | 7 | 8 | 9 | 10 | 11 | 12 | 13 | 1 | 2 |
| American | 7.5 | 8.5 | 9.5 | 10.5 | 11.5 | 12.5 | 13.5 | 1.5 | 2.5 |
| French | 24 | 25.5 | 27 | 28 | 29 | 30 | 32 | 33 | 34 |

**Children's clothes**
In all countries, size descriptions vary from make to make, but are usually based on age or height.

# Further Reading

## History, Art & Culture

**Beevor, Antony, & Cooper, Artemis:** *Paris After the Liberation*
Life in the city in the years of rationing, liberation, political instability and existentialism on the Left Bank.
**Christiansen, Rupert:** *Tales of the New Babylon*
The Paris of Napoléon III, from sleaze, prostitution and Haussmann's bulldozer to the bloody Commune.
**Cole, Robert:** *A Traveller's History of Paris*
A useful general introduction.
**Cronin, Vincent:** *Napoleon*
A fine biography of the great megalomaniac who left France wondering what-might-have-been for ever.
**Fitch, Noel Riley:** *Literary Cafés of Paris*
Who drank where and when.
**Littlewood, Ian:** *Paris: Architecture, History, Art*
A good general survey intertwining the city's history with every era of its treasures in stone, paint and glass.
**Lurie, Patty:** *Guide to Impressionist Paris*
Impressionist paintings matched to their exact Paris locations as they look today.
**Marnham, Patrick:** *Crime and the Académie Française*
Fascinating, wry accounts of the quirks and scandals of Mitterand-era Paris.
**Martin, Hervé:** *Guide to Modern Architecture in Paris*
An accessible, bilingual illustrated guide to significant buildings in Paris since 1900, arranged by area.
**Mitford, Nancy:** *The Sun King* and *Madame de Pompadour*
Mitford's biographies, although some years old, are still the best gossipy accounts of the courts of the *ancien régime*.
**Johnson, Douglas, & Johnson, Madeleine:** *Age of Illusion: Art & Politics in France 1918-1940*
Every aspect of the culture of France in an era when Paris was more than ever at the forefront of modernity.
**Rudorff, Raymond:** *Belle Epoque: Paris in the Nineties*
Glamorous *fin-de-siècle* Paris: great exhibitions, the birth of modernism and of modern cabaret
**Salvadori, Renzo:** *Architect's Guide to Paris*
Plans, illustrations and a guide to Paris's growth, of interest to the general reader as well as to architects.
**Schama, Simon:** *Citizens*
Giant but wonderfully readable account of the Revolution, in every one of its myriad aspects.
**Zeldin, Theodore:** *The French*
Idiosyncratic and enormously entertaining survey of modern France.

## French Literature

**Abaelardus, Petrus & Heloise:** *Letters*
The full details of Paris's first great drama.
**Aragon, Louis:** *Paris Peasant*
A great Surrealist view of the city.
**Balzac, Honoré de:** *Le Père Goriot*
All of Balzac's 'Human Comedy' deals with Paris, but the story of old Goriot is one of the most acute of his novels.
**Beyah, Calixthe** *Loukoum*
Controversial Cameroonian's entertaining chronicle of the daily life of African immigrants in Paris.
**Céline, Louis-Ferdinand:** *Mort à Crédit*
Remarkably vivid, largely autobiographical account of an impoverished Paris childhood.

**Pierre Daninos:** *Les Carnets de Major Thompson*
Understand why the French have such odd ideas about the English: the French as seen by a retired English major. Lots of people fell for it when published in the '50s.
**Desforges, Régine:** *The Blue Bicycle*
A vivid, easy-read drama of resistance, collaboration and sex during the German occupation. First of a trilogy.
**Hugo, Victor:** *Notre Dame de Paris* and *Les Misérables*
Quasimodo and the romantic vision of medieval Paris; in *Les Mis* and all the giant passions of the Romantic era.
**Modiano, Patrick** *Honeymoon*
Evocative story of two lives that cross in Paris.
**Maupassant, Guy de** *Bel-Ami*
Gambling and dissipation.
**Perec, Georges:** *Life, A User's Manual*
Fascinating Parisian, intellectual portrait of the inhabitants of a Haussmannian apartment building.
**Restif de la Bretonne, Nicolas:** *Les Nuits de Paris*
The sexual underworld of the Paris of Louis XV, by one of France's most famous defrocked priests.
**Queneau, Raymond:** *Zazie in the Metro*
Paris in the 1950s: bright and very *nouvelle vague*.
**Sartre, Jean-Paul:** *Roads to Freedom*
Existential angst as the German army takes over Paris.
**Simenon, Georges:** The Maigret series
All of Simenon's books featuring his laconic detective provide a great picture of Paris and its underworld.
**Vian, Boris:** *Froth on the Daydream*
Wonderfully funny Surrealist satire of Paris in the goldern era of Sartre and St-Germain.
**Zola, Emile:** *Nana, L'Assommoir* or *Le Ventre de Paris*
These are perhaps Zola's most vivid accounts of the underside of life in the Second Empire.

## The Ex-Pat Angle

**Hemingway, Ernest:** *A Moveable Feast*
Big Ern drinks his way around 1920s writers' Paris.
**Littlewood, Ian:** *Paris: A Literary Companion*
Great selection of pieces by all kinds of writers on Paris.
**Miller, Henry:** *Tropic of Cancer* and *Tropic of Capricorn*
Low-life and lust in Montparnasse.
**Nin, Anaïs:** *Henry and June*
Lust in Montparnasse with Henry Miller and his wife.
**Orwell, George:** *Down and Out in Paris and London*
Exactly what the title says.
**Rhys, Jean:** *After Mr Mackenzie*
Life as a kept woman in seedy hotels.
**Somerset Maugham, W:** *The Moon and Sixpence*
Impoverished artist in Montmartre and escape to the South Seas, inspired by the life of Gauguin.
**Stein, Gertrude:** *The Autobiography of Alice B Toklas*
Ex-pat Paris, from start to finish.
**Suskind, Patrick:** *Perfume*
Pungent murder in odorous Paris on the eve of the Revolution by German author.

## Food & Drink

**Toklas, Alice B:** *The Alice B Toklas Cookbook*
Literary and artistic life, and how to cook fish for Picasso.
**Tessa Youell & George Kimball:** *French Food & Wine*
A handy pocket glossary.

# Index

# Advertisers' Index

Please refer to the relevant pages for addresses/telephone numbers.

# Maps

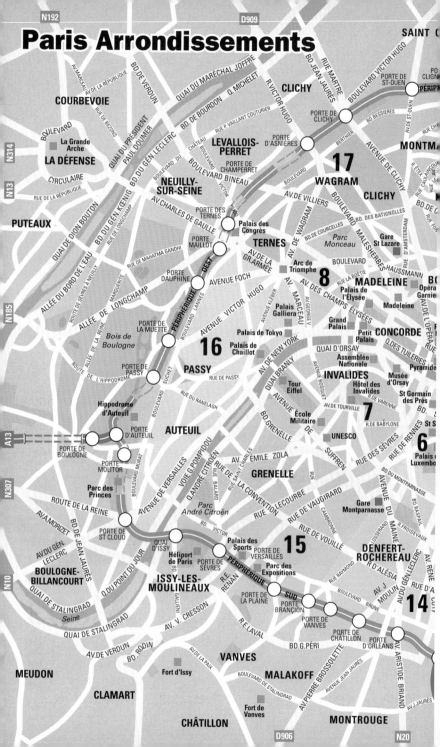

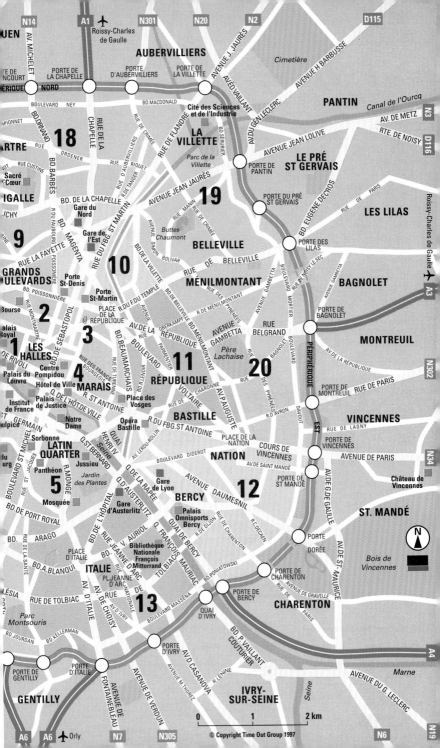

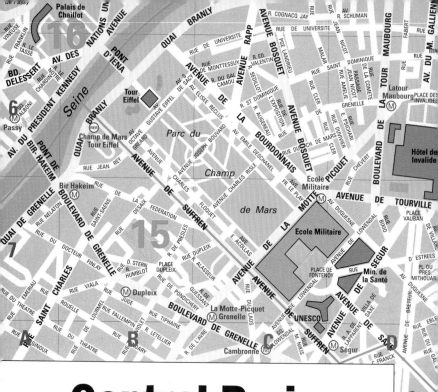

# Central Paris

## Key to maps & legend

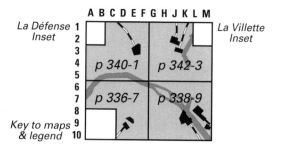

|   | A | B | C | D | E | F | G | H | J | K | L | M |
|---|---|---|---|---|---|---|---|---|---|---|---|---|
| 1 | | | | | | | | | | | | |
| 2 | | | | | | | | | | | | |
| 3 | | | | | | | | | | | | |
| 4 | | | | p 340-1 | | | | p 342-3 | | | | |
| 5 | | | | | | | | | | | | |
| 6 | | | | | | | | | | | | |
| 7 | | | | p 336-7 | | | | p 338-9 | | | | |
| 8 | | | | | | | | | | | | |
| 9 | | | | | | | | | | | | |
| 10 | | | | | | | | | | | | |

*La Défense Inset*

*La Villette Inset*

*Key to maps & legend*

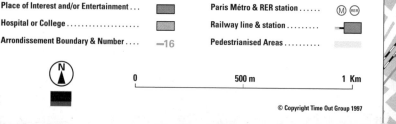

Place of Interest and/or Entertainment . . .

Hospital or College . . . . . . . . . . . . . . . . . . . .

Arrondissement Boundary & Number . . . .  —16

Paris Métro & RER station . . . . . .  Ⓜ ⓇⒺⓇ

Railway line & station . . . . . . . . .

Pedestrianised Areas . . . . . . . . . .

N

0          500 m          1 Km

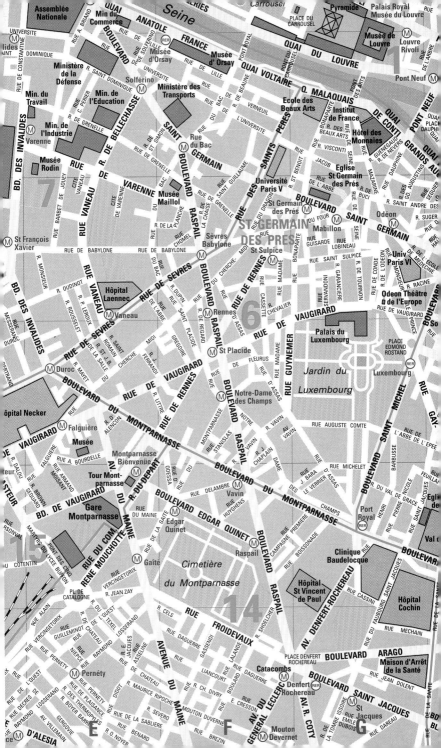

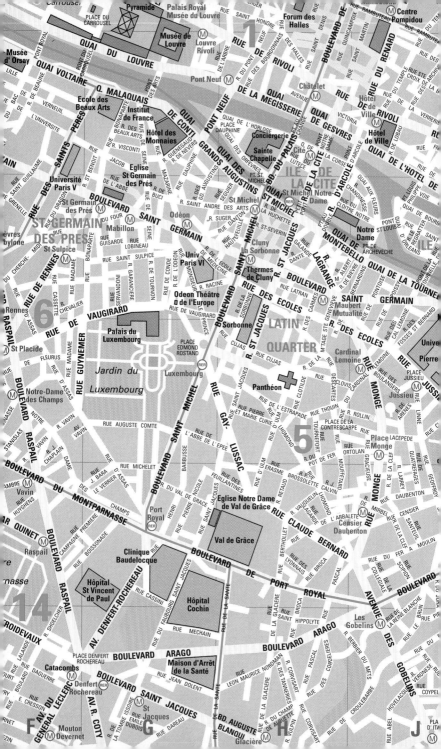

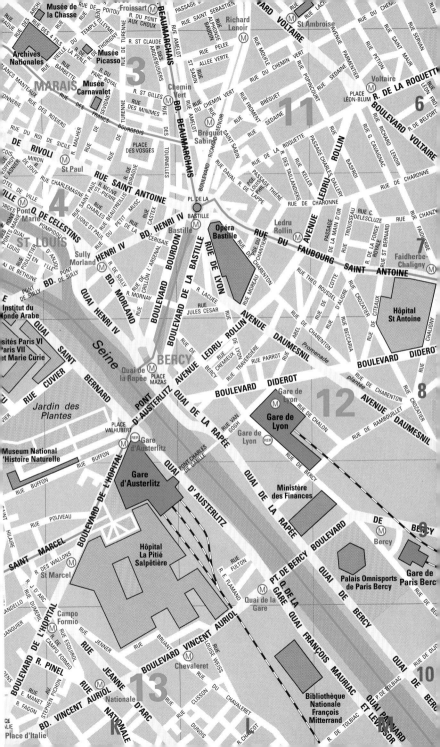

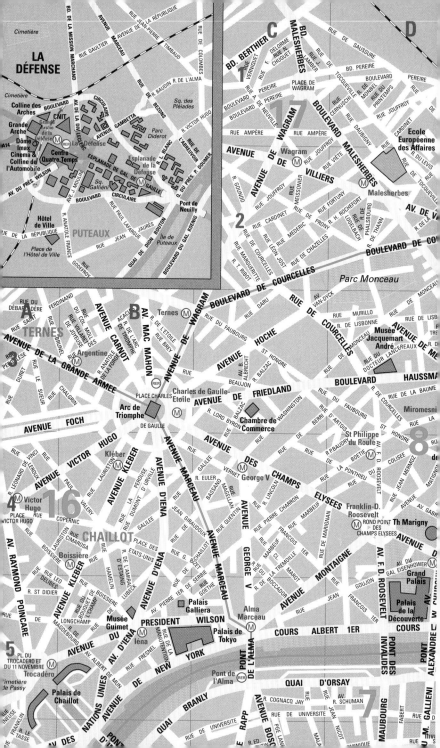

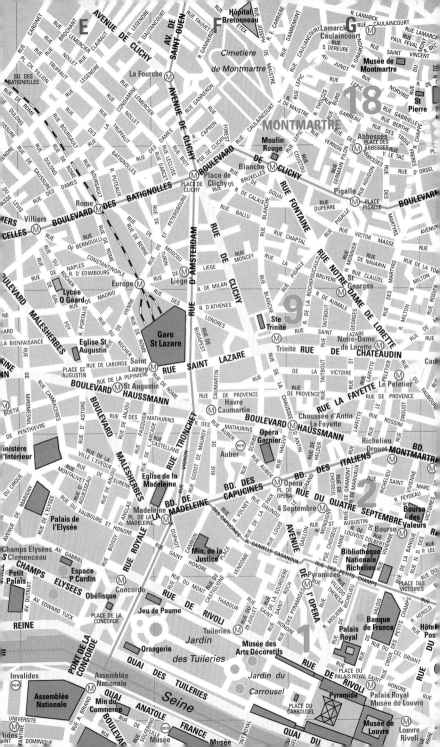

# Street Index

# RER

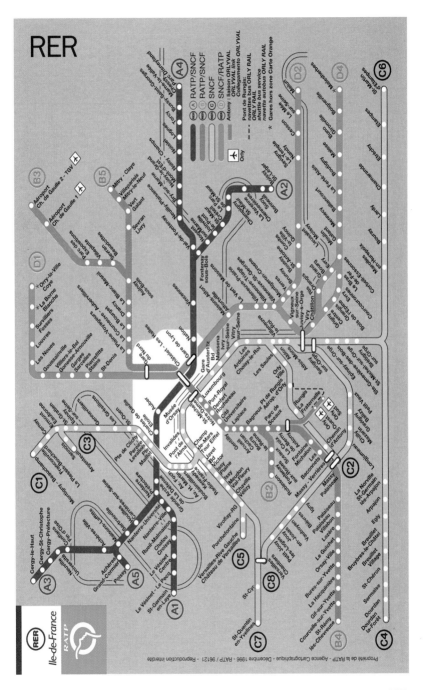

RER
Ile-de-France
RATP

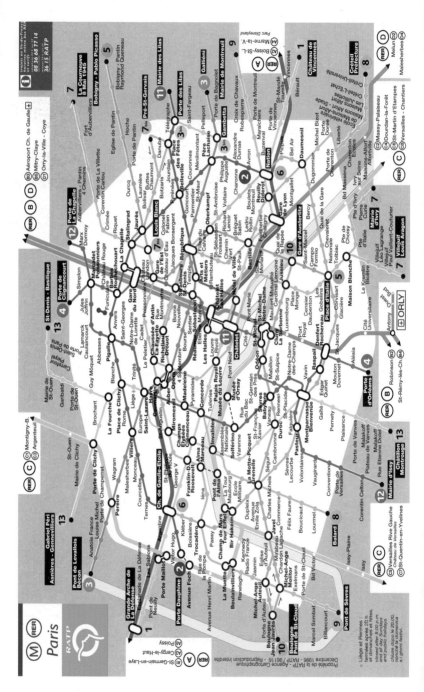